DATE DUE

Brodart Co.   Cat. # 55 137 001   Printed in USA

CCNA Cloud
CLDADM 210-455
Official Cert Guide

CHRIS JACKSON, CCIE NO. 6256

HANK PRESTON, CCIE NO. 38336

STEVE WASKO

Cisco Press

800 East 96th Street

Indianapolis, IN 46240

CCNA Cloud CLDADM 210-455 Official Cert Guide

Chris Jackson
Hank Preston
Steve Wasko

Copyright© 2017 Cisco Systems, Inc.

Published by:
Cisco Press
800 East 96th Street
Indianapolis, IN 46240 USA

Printed in the United States of America

1   16

Library of Congress Control Number: 2016952324

ISBN-13: 978-1-58714-453-0

ISBN-10: 1-58714-453-0

Warning and Disclaimer

This book is designed to provide information about the CCNA Cloud CLDADM 210-455 certification. Every effort has been made to make this book as complete and as accurate as possible, but no warranty or fitness is implied.

The information is provided on an "as is" basis. The authors, Cisco Press, and Cisco Systems, Inc. shall have neither liability nor responsibility to any person or entity with respect to any loss or damages arising from the information contained in this book or from the use of the discs or programs that may accompany it.

The opinions expressed in this book belong to the author and are not necessarily those of Cisco Systems, Inc.

Trademark Acknowledgments

All terms mentioned in this book that are known to be trademarks or service marks have been appropriately capitalized. Cisco Press or Cisco Systems, Inc., cannot attest to the accuracy of this information. Use of a term in this book should not be regarded as affecting the validity of any trademark or service mark.

Special Sales

For information about buying this title in bulk quantities, or for special sales opportunities (which may include electronic versions; custom cover designs; and content particular to your business, training goals, marketing focus, or branding interests), please contact our corporate sales department at corpsales@pearsoned.com or (800) 382-3419.

For government sales inquiries, please contact governmentsales@pearsoned.com.

For questions about sales outside the U.S., please contact intlcs@pearson.com.

Feedback Information

At Cisco Press, our goal is to create in-depth technical books of the highest quality and value. Each book is crafted with care and precision, undergoing rigorous development that involves the unique expertise of members from the professional technical community.

Readers' feedback is a natural continuation of this process. If you have any comments regarding how we could improve the quality of this book, or otherwise alter it to better suit your needs, you can contact us through email at feedback@ciscopress.com. Please make sure to include the book title and ISBN in your message.

We greatly appreciate your assistance.

Editor-in-Chief: Mark Taub

Product Line Manager: Brett Bartow

Business Operation Manager, Cisco Press: Ronald Fligge

Executive Editor: Mary Beth Ray

Managing Editor: Sandra Schroeder

Development Editor: Ellie Bru

Senior Project Editor: Tonya Simpson

Copy Editor: Bill McManus

Technical Editors: Blair Hicks, Mike Tokarz

Editorial Assistant: Vanessa Evans

Cover Designer: Chuti Prasertsith

Composition: Studio Galou

Indexer: Ken Johnson

Proofreader: Chuck Hutchinson

CISCO

Americas Headquarters
Cisco Systems, Inc.
San Jose, CA

Asia Pacific Headquarters
Cisco Systems (USA) Pte. Ltd.
Singapore

Europe Headquarters
Cisco Systems International BV
Amsterdam, The Netherlands

Cisco has more than 200 offices worldwide. Addresses, phone numbers, and fax numbers are listed on the Cisco Website at www.cisco.com/go/offices.

About the Authors

Chris Jackson, CCIE No. 6256, is a Distinguished Systems Engineer working in world-wide sales training and enablement and the author of *Network Security Auditing* (Cisco Press, 2010). Chris is focused on all aspects of Cisco data center and cloud, not only in a technology perspective but through thought leadership in helping Cisco and customers better leverage the business transformational aspects these technologies provide. He holds dual CCIEs in security and routing and switching, CISA, CISSP, ITIL v3, seven SANS certifications, and a bachelor's degree in business administration. Residing in Franklin, Tennessee, Chris enjoys tinkering with RC drones, robotics, and anything else that can be programmed to do his bidding. In addition, he is a black belt in Taekwondo and a rabid Star Wars fan, and has a ridiculous collection of Lego. His wife, Barbara, and three children, Caleb, Sydney, and Savannah, are the true joy of his life and proof that not everything has to plug into a wall outlet to be fun.

Hank Preston, CCIE No. 38336, has been with Cisco for five years, starting as a systems engineer and then moving into a data center and cloud architect–focused position working with large enterprise customers on developing their cloud strategy. Prior to Cisco, Hank spent much of his career with partners designing and implementing solutions across IT, not just networking. In fact, before deciding to focus and specialize in the networking space, Hank was a programmer and database designer, spent a good amount of time as a sysadmin managing Microsoft, VMware, and Citrix-based solutions, and has worked in many IT areas. This well-rounded experience gives him a great foundation to work from when discussing "The Cloud," as like few other technology trends, the cloud touches all areas of IT. Prior to moving into IT, Hank worked in the entertainment industry running lights and sound for musicals, stage plays, and concerts. Having never lost the love of the stage, he still spends time in community theatre productions when time allows.

Steve Wasko is a systems engineer at Pure Storage, one of the fastest-growing companies in Silicon Valley. Combining his years of experience with enterprise applications, networking, and compute gives him a unique perspective at Pure Storage. Prior to Pure Storage, Steve spent the previous 11 years at Cisco involved in application networking, storage networking, cloud, unified computing, and data center virtualization solutions. His recent work there over the past decade led to dozens of large, complex, enterprise implementations of UCS as well as multiple UCS Central deployments and private cloud implementations.

Before Cisco, Steve spent seven years at Microsoft as a senior product manager in the Windows Server division as well as time as a senior technology specialist in the Microsoft Enterprise field. Before that, Steve spent time at IBM and EDS. Past certifications include CNE, MCSE, CCNA, and ITIL. In his spare time, Steve enjoys his family, CrossFit, hunting, and technology.

About the Technical Reviewers

Blair Hicks is an Orchestration and Automation specialist with over 15 years of experience managing solutions for application service providers and global financial solutions. He has served as a technical lead for both VMware and Cisco, helping to enable large enterprise and service providers to adopt data center orchestration practices. He loves the diverse challenges that arise from designing new ways to automate core operations in cloud provisioning and consumption. When he is not in front of a computer keyboard, he enjoys motorcycling, ORVs, and bicycling. Follow his sporadic tweets @tuxdbird.

Mike Tokarz is a consulting systems engineer for data center technologies at Cisco Systems. He has been working in the data center space for 15 years, most recently focusing on cloud and automation. Mike attended Northern Illinois University, where he majored in theoretical computer science. In his free time, he runs long distance and backpacks in the mountains.

Dedications

Chris Jackson: This book is dedicated to my family, those with me and those who are not. Any success I have in life is on the shoulders of those who have shaped, supported, encouraged, and driven me to follow my passions. Special thanks to my lovely wife and wonderful children, who sacrificed and gave me the time to get things done. Wouldn't have happened without you.

Hank Preston: This book is dedicated to my always-supportive wife, Charity, and children, Natalie and Alex. You make me strive to excel in everything I do and live up to the love you give me. Taking on projects like writing this book impact us all, and you are always my biggest champions.

Steve Wasko: To the incredible woman who walks this crazy world with me and gives me the strength and motivation to succeed, I dedicate this book to Vanessa, and to my family, Thomas, Raegan, and Luke. To my wife, I wouldn't be where I am today without your love, kindness, and support. To my kids, aim high and never settle for anything but the best—you guys deserve it!

Acknowledgments

Chris Jackson: Writing a book is like having children. The first one is a crash course in understanding the definition of patience, commitment, and love. The second one only happens when you have given yourself enough time to forget how hard the first one was! If it wasn't for Hank and Steve, this book would have never been published. You guys are fantastic and it has been wonderful working with professionals of your caliber. I am honored to have been a part of your first book.

The Cisco Press crew are the best in the industry. They are patient, but know how to crack the whip when necessary. Denise Lincoln, Mary Beth Ray, and Ellie Bru were a joy to work with through this process. We will always have Vegas!

Our tech editors had their hands full for sure. Blair Hicks and Mike Tokarz gave great advice and truly cared about the final product. Feedback is a gift and you two beat us over the heads with your gifts. Thanks for all of your hard work.

To my management team, Chris Gaito and Linda Masloske, thank you so much for all of your support and encouragement over the years. This book would not have been possible without you. To my co-workers in WWSPT, Laura Tilton and David Whitten, thanks for picking up the slack while I continue to bite off more than I can chew. You are the best and I feel blessed to work with you on a daily basis.

Barbara, Caleb, Sydney, Savannah, and my neurotic cat Pip deserve a medal for putting up with me. I love you guys more than words can convey. Yes, I am finished and can come outside and play.

Hank Preston: First I must thank my co-authors, Chris Jackson and Steve Wasko. This is my first book and I am glad to have had their partnership to learn the way. Chris's experience as a published author was very helpful to get started writing. And Steve, we'd tackled so many projects together already, having our names together on this book is a great addition.

I would also like to thank the many members of the Cisco Press team that worked with us to pull the book together. We weren't an easy bunch to corral, but you all stuck with us and kept us moving forward.

Blair Hicks and Mike Tokarz, you both had the thankless job of going through our material and keeping us honest and accurate. Though I may have cursed you both at least once, your work made this book better in so many places.

I didn't start my career in IT at Cisco, but joining the company was one of the best decisions I made. I would like to thank Eric Knipp for seeing something in me worth taking a bit of a risk on. You've been the most supportive friend, mentor, and leader I've ever had the opportunity to work with.

Finally, to my family… Whether it was writing this book, preparing for a certification exam, or creating content for a class or presentation, you've all been there and understanding when I've had to spend late nights and weekends working. Charity, you are the best partner I could ask for. You are my world.

Steve Wasko: Similar to Hank's acknowledgments, I would also like to thank Hank Preston and Chris Jackson. Writing a book is a pretty awesome experience and you guys have been great to work and collaborate with. I wish you both the best success at Cisco or wherever the winds of opportunity send you.

Mike Tokarz and Blair Hicks, who did the technical editing on this book, deserve a massive amount of credit. As a former technical editor for the Cisco Press title *Application Acceleration and WAN Optimization Fundamentals*, I know it's a difficult and tireless job, and this book will be better because of your efforts. Thank you.

Also thank you to the entire Pearson Cisco Press crew for hanging with us. I know we were a challenge, but your professionalism and structure made this a great project.

Cisco is one of the greatest places I have worked in my IT career, and even though I've moved on to Pure Storage, I regard my time at Cisco as one of the highlights of my career. Cisco is like a huge family and I want to thank some of my key mentors there: Bob Hlavacek, Glenn Graber, Tim Fiedler, Kevin Williams, and Greg Gilley. We changed the face of the data center market and you guys made me reach for more than I ever thought was possible.

Most importantly, my family is my rock and where I draw my strength from. To Thomas, you've exceeded every expectation I've ever had and will do great at anything you choose. To Raegan, you have taught us the most important lessons in life and you have a beautiful future in front of you—your strength is awe inspiring. To Luke, you are everything a dad could ever ask for and the world is yours for the making! And to Vanessa, thank you for this incredible life and family. I love you all.

Contents at a Glance

Online Elements

Reader Services

Register your copy at www.ciscopress.com/title/9781587144530 for convenient access to downloads, updates, and corrections as they become available. To start the registration process, go to www.ciscopress.com/register and log in or create an account[*]. Enter the product ISBN 9781587144530 and click Submit. Once the process is complete, you will find any available bonus content under Registered Products.

*Be sure to check the box that you would like to hear from us to receive exclusive discounts on future editions of this product.

Contents

Online Elements

Icons Used in This Book

Command Syntax Conventions

The conventions used to present command syntax in this book are the same conventions used in the IOS Command Reference. The Command Reference describes these conventions as follows:

- **Boldface** indicates commands and keywords that are entered literally as shown. In actual configuration examples and output (not general command syntax), boldface indicates commands that are manually input by the user (such as a **show** command).

- *Italic* indicates arguments for which you supply actual values.

- Vertical bars (|) separate alternative, mutually exclusive elements.

- Square brackets ([ ]) indicate an optional element.

- Braces ({ }) indicate a required choice.

- Braces within brackets ([{ }]) indicate a required choice within an optional element.

Introduction

Welcome to the *CCNA Cloud CLDADM 210-455 Official Cert Guide*. The CCNA Cloud certification is designed to validate associate-level knowledge of successful deployment and operation of cloud technologies. Cloud administration represents the operational aspect of cloud, which is one of the most challenging components of realizing the promise of cloud for your business. While technology is a crucial building block, how you use it, and ultimately how you map your company's business needs, processes, and workflows to those cloud technologies, is the difference between success and failure in a cloud deployment. Utilizing various cloud product suites from Cisco, along with ruthless standardization and workflow optimization, can enable a company to achieve substantial operational efficiencies, agility, and a level of flexibility never thought possible. A CCNA Cloud Administrator can be that "guiding light" for their organization as they embark on their cloud journey.

The *CCNA Cloud CLDADM 210-455 Official Cert Guide* is a self-study guide covering all of the topics from the corresponding Cisco exam blueprint. This book delves into the many operational and administrative processes and tasks that would be required to successfully operate a Cisco cloud environment.

This book is broken up into four parts. Part I starts with foundational topics that present the key concepts and background necessary to provide context on why cloud is important to transform an organization into an agile, flexible, and operationally efficient business. Part II provides an overview of the Cisco technology and software suites relevant to the exam. Part III delves into cloud administration and operations concepts such as deploying virtual machines and application containers, managing role based access control, services catalogs, and reporting and chargeback systems. Part IV closes out the book by exploring cloud monitoring, capacity planning, and remediation methodologies.

We hope you enjoy this book and find it a useful exam preparation resource. Good luck on your test!

Goals and Methods

Obviously, the primary objective of this book is to help you pass the CCNA Cloud CLDADM 210-455 exam. However, as previously mentioned, it is also designed to facilitate your learning of foundational concepts underlying cloud computing that will carry over into your professional job experience; this book is *not* intended to be an exercise in rote memorization of terms and technologies.

With the intention of giving you a holistic view of cloud computing and a more rewarding learning experience, the order in which we present the material is designed to provide a logical progression of explanations from basic concepts to complex architectures. Notwithstanding, if you are interested in covering specific gaps in your preparation for the exam, you can also read the chapters out of the proposed sequence.

Each chapter roughly follows this structure:

- A description of the business and technological context of the explained technology, approach, or architecture
- An explanation of the challenges addressed by such technology, approach, or architecture
- A detailed analysis that immerses you in the main topic of the chapter, including its characteristics, possibilities, results, and consequences
- A thorough explanation of how this technology, approach, or architecture is applicable to real-world cloud computing environments

Who Should Read This Book?

CCNA Cloud certification candidates are the target audience for this book. However, it is also designed to offer a proper introduction to fundamental concepts and technologies for engineers, architects, developers, analysts, and students that are interested in cloud computing.

Strategies for Exam Preparation

Whether you want to read the book in sequence or pick specific chapters to cover knowledge gaps, we recommend that you include the following guidelines in your study for the CCNA Cloud CLDADM 210-455 exam each time you start a chapter:

- Answer the "Do I Know This Already?" quiz questions to assess your expertise in the chapter topic.
- Check the results in Appendix A, "Answers to the 'Do I Know This Already?' Quizzes."
- Based on your results, read the Foundation Topics sections, giving special attention to the sections corresponding to the questions you have not answered correctly.
- After the first reading, try to complete the memory tables (where applicable) and define the key terms from the chapter, and verify the results in the appendixes. If you make a mistake in a table entry or the definition of a key term, review the related section.

Remember: Discovering gaps in your preparation for the exam is as important as addressing them.

How This Book Is Organized

In times where blog posts and tweets provide disconnected pieces of information, this book intends to serve a complete learning experience, where order and consistency between chapters do matter.

For such purpose, Chapters 1 through 14 cover the following topics:

- **Chapter 1, "An Introduction to Cloud"**—The term *cloud* is used so readily in the industry that it's often difficult to nail down a solid definition. Is cloud a place? Is cloud something I swipe a credit card and purchase? Is it a managed service with a slew of four-letter acronyms? This chapter introduces the three primary cloud models, public, private, and hybrid, and also introduces you to a bit of history and the players in this space. The intent is to show you that the true value of cloud is in enabling a new paradigm for managing and consuming IT services.

- **Chapter 2, "Cloud: A New Operations Model for IT"**—Traditional IT operating models are very expensive and resource intensive. Cloud provides a way to reduce much of the operating expense, duplication of efforts, and redundancy through automation. To take advantage of automation, it's important to understand how IT organization structures fit into this new model. No longer can groups within IT work alone in their silos; cloud busts down those silos and provides a common set of tools and technologies through which standards and templates can drive new levels of efficiency and speed in deploying new applications and services.

- **Chapter 3, "The Cloud Operation Journey"**—You are buying into all of the "cloud talk"? Awesome! Now, where do you start? Not every business is ready to jump into cloud with both feet. For those that want to dip their toe in, or maybe wade in a bit, it helps to think of cloud as a journey. There are numerous things that have to be in place for a cloud operating model to be successful. This chapter provides a roadmap for the operational side of cloud and describes the many lessons learned along the way.

- **Chapter 4, "Cisco Cloud Automation/Orchestration Suites"**—Cloud orchestration and automation suites provide the framework that enables the logical abstraction of the underlying hardware and software that make up network, compute, and storage in the data center. For the Cisco CLDADM exam, UCS Director and Cisco Intelligent Automation for Cloud (CIAC) are the two platforms that are tested. This chapter will dive into both platforms and describe their architecture, components, and functionality.

- **Chapter 5, "Cisco Prime Service Catalog"**—Prime Service Catalog is a platform that provides an easy-to-use portal that enables anyone within an organization to access and request applications and services from their cloud environment. This product takes standardized application packages and serves them up in a shopping cart–like format that automates the delivery of new services and applications to a company's lines of business. What used to take weeks and hundreds of phone calls and emails can now be accomplished in minutes!

- **Chapter 6, "Cisco Cloud Infrastructure"**—The underlying physical and virtual infrastructure is the "pool of resources" controlled by a cloud automation and orchestration suite. It is important to understand how these pieces fit together and the types of services they can offer. This chapter covers Cisco Virtual Application Cloud Segmentation (VACS), Nexus 1000V, Virtual Security Gateway (VSG), Cloud Services Router (CSR), and Application Centric Infrastructure (ACI) specifically from a cloud management and orchestration perspective.

- **Chapter 7, "Managing Users and Groups"**—Role-based access control is the foundation for both security and segmentation of operational responsibilities. This chapter covers the aspects of creating multiple user types, privileges, and profiles for cloud users and administrators.

- **Chapter 8, "Virtual Machine Management"**—The care and feeding of virtual machines in a cloud environment is covered in this chapter, with emphasis on the most common tasks that a typical cloud administrator needs to know how to perform. Editing VM parameters, migrating VMs from host to host, and managing VM snapshots are all tasks described in detail in this chapter.

- **Chapter 9, "Automating Cloud Infrastructure with UCS Director"**—At the foundation of any cloud is a layer of infrastructure that needs to be managed and configured through automation. UCS Director provides an infrastructure automation platform for rapidly developing policies for deploying storage, network, compute, and virtualization resources.

- **Chapter 10, "Building a Service Catalog and User Portal with UCS Director and Prime Service Catalog"**—After you provision a service in Prime Service Catalog, you must ensure that everything works as expected. This chapter covers how to prepare and test a user portal and service catalog in PSC and UCS Director, and how your users will place orders, verify that the orders were provisioned successfully, and access the VMs and applications provisioned.

- **Chapter 11, "Deploying Virtual Application Containers"**—Application containers logically separate different tenants from each other and enable each tenant to specify their own security and application services (like load balancers and firewalls). This chapter covers the deployment of the different virtual container options within UCS Director, including the VACS product.

- **Chapter 12: "Chargeback, Billing, and Reporting"**—A chargeback system is often put in place to "pay for" IT services consumed by the company's lines of business. Implementing a cost structure and chargeback policy is a crucial mechanism to assign a value to the utilization of a shared resource. This chapter covers these aspects of cloud administration and provides an overview of the reporting system that shows cloud utilization and the billing records associated with each tenant.

- **Chapter 13, "Cloud Performance and Capacity Management"**—When do I add capacity? How healthy is my cloud environment? These are questions that cloud administrators better be able to answer! This chapter shows you how to utilize various serviceability options to get visibility into the underlying hardware and components of the cloud infrastructure. In addition, this chapter demonstrates how to use UCS Performance Manager for capacity management and bandwidth monitoring.

- **Chapter 14: "Monitoring and Maintaining the Health of Your Cloud"**—Looking at the cloud stack as a whole, this chapter shows how to leverage Prime Service Catalog and UCS Director to manage the cloud environment from the top down through custom monitoring and health dashboards.

- **Chapter 15: "Final Preparation"**—This chapter lists a series of tasks that you can use for your final preparation before taking the exam.

Certification Exam Topics and This Book

Although this certification guide covers all topics from the CCNA Cloud CLDADM 210-455 exam, it does not follow the exact order of the exam blueprint published by Cisco. Instead, the chapter sequence is purposely designed to enhance your learning through a gradual progression of concepts.

Table I-1 lists each exam topic in the blueprint along with a reference to the book chapter that covers the topic.

Table I-1   CLDADM Exam 210-455 Topics and Chapter Cross References

CLDADM 210-455 Exam Topic	Chapter(s) in Which Topic Is Covered
1.0 Cloud Infrastructure Administration and Reporting	Chapters 6, 7, 8, 11
1.1 Configure users/groups and role-based access control in the portal, including basic troubleshooting	Chapter 7
1.1.a Describe default roles	Chapter 7
1.1.b Configure new user with single role	Chapter 7
1.1.c Describe multirole user profiles	Chapter 7
1.1.d Configure a user profile	Chapter 7
1.2 Perform virtual machine operations	Chapter 8
1.2.a Configure live migrations of VMs from host to host	Chapter 8
1.2.b Edit VM	Chapter 8
1.2.c Configure VM snapshots	Chapter 8
1.2.d Describe reverting a VM to a snapshot	Chapter 8
1.3 Deploy virtual app containers	Chapters 6, 11
1.3.a Provide basic support and troubleshoot app container with firewall, networking, and load balancer	Chapters 6, 11
2.0 Chargeback and Billing Reports	Chapter 12
2.1 Describe the chargeback model	Chapter 12
2.1.a Describe chargeback features	Chapter 12
2.1.b Describe budget policy	Chapter 12
2.1.c Describe cost models	Chapter 12
2.1.d Describe adding a cost model to a tenant	Chapter 12
2.2 Generate various reports for virtual and physical accounts	Chapter 12
2.2.a Execute billing reports	Chapter 12
2.2.b Execute a system utilization reporting	Chapter 12
2.2.c Execute a snapshot report	Chapter 12

CLDADM 210-455 Exam Topic	Chapter(s) in Which Topic Is Covered
3.0 Cloud Provisioning	Chapters 6, 8, 9, 10
3.1 Describe predefined Cisco UCS Director-based services within the Cisco Prime Service Catalog	Chapters 6, 10
3.1.a Describe the configuration of service names and icons	Chapter 10
3.1.b Describe order permissions	Chapter 10
3.1.b (i) RBAC	Chapter 10
3.1.c Describe template formats	Chapters 6, 10
3.1.c (i) Storage	Chapter 10
3.1.c (ii) Compute	Chapter 10
3.1.c (iii) Network	Chapters 6, 10
3.1.c (iv) Virtualization	Chapters 6, 10
3.2 Describe provisioning verification	Chapters 8, 10
3.2.a Describe how to place an order for a service from the Cisco Primer Service Catalog as an end-user	Chapter 10
3.2.b Verify that provisioning is done correctly	Chapter 10
3.2.c Access VMs and applications that have been provisioned	Chapters 8, 10
3.3 Deploy preconfigured templates and make minor changes to the service catalog offerings that do not affect workflows or services	Chapters 6, 9
3.3.a Describe the deployment of templates: storage, compute, network, and virtualization	Chapters 6, 9
3.3.b Describe differences between the templates	Chapter 9
3.3.c Describe the need to convert between templates	Chapter 9
4.0 Cloud Systems Management and Monitoring	Chapters 4, 5, 13, 14
4.1 Identify the components of Cisco Prime Service Catalog	Chapter 5
4.1.a End-user store front	Chapter 5
4.1.b Stack designer	Chapter 5
4.1.c Heat orchestration	Chapter 5
4.2 Describe the components of Cisco UCS Director	Chapter 4
4.2.a Describe infrastructure management and monitoring	Chapter 4
4.2.b Describe orchestration	Chapter 4
4.2.c Describe the portal	Chapter 4
4.2.d Describe the Bare Metal Agent	Chapter 4

CLDADM 210-455 Exam Topic	Chapter(s) in Which Topic Is Covered
4.3 Describe Cisco UCS Performance Manager	Chapters 5, 13, 14
4.3.a Describe capacity planning	Chapters 5, 13, 14
4.3.b Describe bandwidth monitoring	Chapters 5, 13, 14
4.3.c Describe how host groups facilitate dynamic monitoring	Chapters 5, 13, 14
4.4 Describe the components of Cisco IAC	Chapter 4
4.4.a Describe Cisco Process Orchestrator	Chapter 4
4.4.b Describe Cisco Prime Service Catalog	Chapter 4
4.4.c Describe Cisco Server Provisioner	Chapter 4
4.5 Perform cloud monitoring using Cisco Prime Service Catalog, Cisco UCS Director, Cisco Prime infrastructure	Chapters 13, 14
4.5.a Describe fault monitoring	Chapters 13, 14
4.5.b Describe performance monitoring	Chapters 13, 14
4.5.c Describe monitoring of provisioning outcomes	Chapters 13, 14
4.6 Create monitoring dashboards	Chapters 13, 14
4.6.a Configure custom dashboards	Chapters 13, 14
4.6.b Configure threshold settings	Chapter 14
5.0 Cloud Remediation	Chapters 13, 14
5.1 Configure serviceability options	Chapter 13
5.1.a Configure syslog	Chapter 13
5.1.b Configure NTP	Chapter 13
5.1.c Configure DNS	Chapter 13
5.1.d Configure DHCP	Chapter 13
5.1.e Configure SMTP	Chapter 13
5.2 Interpret Logs for root cause analysis	Chapters 13, 14
5.2.a Analyze fault logs	Chapters 13, 14
5.2.b Analyze admin logs	Chapters 13, 14
5.2.c Analyze application logs	Chapters 13, 14
5.3 Configure backups	Chapters 13, 14
5.3.a Configure database backup	Chapters 13, 14
5.3.b Configure database restore	Chapters 13, 14

The CCNA Cloud CLDADM 210-455 exam may have topics that emphasize different functions or features, and some topics may be rather broad and generalized. The goal of this book is to provide the most comprehensive coverage to ensure that you are well prepared for the exam. Although some chapters might not address specific exam topics, they provide a foundation that is necessary for a clear understanding of important topics. Your short-term goal might be to pass this exam, but your long-term goal should be to become a qualified cloud professional.

It is also important to understand that this book is a "static" reference, whereas the exam topics are dynamic. Cisco can and does change the topics covered on certification exams often.

This exam guide should not be your only reference when preparing for the certification exam. You can find a wealth of information available at Cisco.com that covers each topic in great detail. If you think that you need more detailed information on a specific topic, read the Cisco documentation that focuses on that topic.

Taking the CCNA Cloud CLDADM 210-455 Exam

As with any Cisco certification exam, you should strive to be thoroughly prepared before taking the exam. There is no way to determine exactly what questions are on the exam, so the best way to prepare is to have a good working knowledge of all subjects covered on the exam. Schedule yourself for the exam and be sure to be rested and ready to focus when taking the exam.

The best place to find out about the latest available Cisco training and certifications is under the Training & Events section at Cisco.com.

Tracking Your Status

You can track your certification progress by checking http://www.cisco.com/go/certifications/login. You must create an account the first time you log in to the site.

Cisco Certifications in the Real World

Cisco is one of the most widely recognized names in the IT industry. Cisco Certified cloud specialists bring quite a bit of knowledge to the table because of their deep understanding of cloud technologies, standards, and designs. This is why the Cisco certification carries such high respect in the marketplace. Cisco certifications demonstrate to potential employers and contract holders a certain professionalism, expertise, and dedication required to complete a difficult goal. If Cisco certifications were easy to obtain, everyone would have them.

Exam Registration

The CCNA Cloud CLDADM 210-455 exam is a computer-based exam, with around 55 to 65 multiple-choice, fill-in-the-blank, list-in-order, and simulation-based questions. You can take the exam at any Pearson VUE (http://www.pearsonvue.com) testing center. According to Cisco, the exam should last about 90 minutes. Be aware that when you register for the exam, you might be instructed to allocate an amount of time to take the exam that is longer than the testing time indicated by the testing software when you begin. The additional time is for you to get settled in and to take the tutorial about the test engine.

Companion Website

Register this book to get access to the Pearson IT Certification test engine and other study materials plus additional bonus content. Check this site regularly for new and updated postings written by the authors that provide further insight into the more troublesome topics on the exam. Be sure to check the box that you would like to hear from us to receive updates and exclusive discounts on future editions of this product or related products.

To access this companion website, follow the steps below:

1. Go to http://www.pearsonITcertification.com/register and log in or create a new account.
2. Enter the ISBN: **9781587144530**.
3. Answer the challenge question as proof of purchase.
4. Click the **Access Bonus Content** link in the Registered Products section of your account page, to be taken to the page where your downloadable content is available.

Please note that many of our companion content files can be very large, especially image and video files.

If you are unable to locate the files for this title by following the preceding steps, please visit http://www.pearsonITcertification.com/about/contact_us and select the **Site Problems/Comments** option in the Select a Topic drop-down menu. Complete and submit the form with your issue described in the Comments/Issues/Feedback field and a customer service representative will assist you.

Pearson IT Certification Practice Test Engine and Questions

The companion website includes the Pearson IT Certification Practice Test engine— software that displays and grades a set of exam-realistic multiple-choice questions. Using the Pearson IT Certification Practice Test engine, you can either study by going through the questions in Study Mode, or take a simulated exam that mimics real exam conditions. You can also serve up questions in a Flash Card Mode, which will display just the question and no answers, challenging you to state the answer in your own words before checking the actual answers to verify your work.

The installation process requires two major steps: installing the software and then activating the exam. The website has a recent copy of the Pearson IT Certification Practice Test engine. The practice exam (the database of exam questions) is not on this site.

Note The cardboard case in the back of this book includes a piece of paper. The paper lists the activation code for the practice exam associated with this book. Do not lose the activation code. On the opposite side of the paper from the activation code is a unique, one-time-use coupon code for the purchase of the Premium Edition eBook and Practice Test.

Install the Software

The Pearson IT Certification Practice Test is a Windows-only desktop application. You can run it on a Mac using a Windows virtual machine, but it was built specifically for the PC platform. The minimum system requirements are as follows:

- Windows 10, Windows 8.1, or Windows 7
- Microsoft .NET Framework 4.0 Client
- Pentium-class 1-GHz processor (or equivalent)
- 512 MB RAM
- 650 MB disk space plus 50 MB for each downloaded practice exam
- Access to the Internet to register and download exam databases

The software installation process is routine as compared with other software installation processes. If you have already installed the Pearson IT Certification Practice Test software from another Pearson product, there is no need for you to reinstall the software. Simply launch the software on your desktop and proceed to activate the practice exam from this book by using the activation code included in the access code card sleeve in the back of the book.

The following steps outline the installation process:

1. Download the exam practice test engine from the companion site.

2. Respond to Windows prompts as with any typical software installation process.

The installation process will give you the option to activate your exam with the activation code supplied on the paper in the cardboard sleeve. This process requires that you establish a Pearson website login. You need this login to activate the exam, so please do register when prompted. If you already have a Pearson website login, there is no need to register again. Just use your existing login.

Activate and Download the Practice Exam

Once the exam engine is installed, you should then activate the exam associated with this book (if you did not do so during the installation process) as follows:

1. Start the Pearson IT Certification Practice Test software from the Windows Start menu or from your desktop shortcut icon.

2. To activate and download the exam associated with this book, from the My Products or Tools tab, click the **Activate Exam** button.

3. At the next screen, enter the activation key from the paper inside the cardboard sleeve in the back of the book. Then, click the **Activate** button.

4. The activation process will download the practice exam. Click **Next**, and then click **Finish**.

When the activation process completes, the My Products tab should list your new exam. If you do not see the exam, make sure that you have selected the **My Products** tab on the menu. At this point, the software and practice exam are ready to use. Simply select the exam and click the **Open Exam** button.

■ To update a particular exam you have already activated and downloaded, display the **Tools** tab and click the **Update Products** button. Updating your exams will ensure that you have the latest changes and updates to the exam data.

■ If you want to check for updates to the Pearson Cert Practice Test exam engine software, display the **Tools** tab and click the **Update Application** button. You can then ensure that you are running the latest version of the software engine.

Activating Other Exams

The exam software installation process, and the registration process, only has to happen once. Then, for each new exam, only a few steps are required. For instance, if you buy another Pearson IT Certification Cert Guide, extract the activation code from the cardboard sleeve in the back of that book; you do not even need the exam engine at this point. From there, all you have to do is start the exam engine (if not still up and running) and perform Steps 2 through 4 from the previous list.

Assessing Exam Readiness

Exam candidates never really know whether they are adequately prepared for the exam until they have completed about 30 percent of the questions. At that point, if you are not prepared, it is too late. The best way to determine your readiness is to work through the "Do I Know This Already?" quizzes at the beginning of each chapter and review the foundation topics and key topics presented in each chapter. It is best to work your way through the entire book unless you can complete each subject without having to do any research or look up any answers.

Premium Edition eBook and Practice Tests

This book also includes an exclusive offer for 70 percent off the Premium Edition eBook and Practice Tests edition of this title. Please see the coupon code included with the cardboard sleeve for information on how to purchase the Premium Edition.

CHAPTER 1

An Introduction to Cloud

You have to start somewhere, right? Defining the cloud is not as easy a task as it would appear at first glance. Depending on your point of view, that definition can vary widely. To many people the cloud is a managed service or application; to others it is a new spin on virtualization; and to some it is a brand new operational model for IT. Regardless of which camp you are in as it pertains to cloud, it is important to have a common vernacular to describe what your business is trying to accomplish with this whole cloud thing. This chapter is intended to provide a high-level overview of what a cloud is, the history of cloud, types of cloud services, and the role of software-defined networks (SDN) and applications as they pertain to a cloud operational model.

"Do I Know This Already?" Quiz

The "Do I Know This Already?" quiz allows you to assess whether you should read this entire chapter thoroughly. If you are in doubt about your answers to these questions or your own assessment of your knowledge of the topics, read the entire chapter. Table 1-1 lists the major headings in this chapter and their corresponding "Do I Know This Already?" quiz questions. You can find the answers in Appendix A, "Answers to the 'Do I Know This Already?' Quizzes."

Table 1-1   "Do I Know This Already?" Section-to-Question Mapping

Foundation Topics Section	Questions
What Is Cloud	1
NIST Definition of Cloud	2–4
SDN and Cloud	5, 6
Cloud Applications	7–10

Caution   The goal of self-assessment is to gauge your mastery of the topics in this chapter. If you do not know the answer to a question or are only partially sure of the answer, you should mark that question as wrong for purposes of the self-assessment. Giving yourself credit for an answer you correctly guess skews your self-assessment results and might provide you with a false sense of security.

1. What are two areas in which cloud impacts how a business leverages IT?

   a. Consumption of IT services

   b. Credit card use in purchasing services

   c. Operation of IT service delivery

   d. Outsourcing of IT

2. Launching the public cloud is attributed to which company?

   a. Cisco

   b. SalesForce.com

   c. Amazon

   d. Google

3. What are two attributes of cloud computing?

   a. Broad network access

   b. Free trial periods

   c. Payment by credit card

   d. Measured service

4. What does PaaS stand for?

   a. Protocol as a Service

   b. Pascal as a Service

   c. Python as a Service

   d. Platform as a Service

5. What is the name of the type of cloud that resides on both a private cloud and a public cloud provider?

   a. Hybrid cloud

   b. Community cloud

   c. Intermediate cloud

   d. Public cloud

6. SDN was developed to address which of the following? (Choose two.)

   a. Control and data plane separation

   b. Box-by-box configuration

   c. Hardware cost reduction

   d. Operational complexity

7. Name three ways in which Cisco offers SDN. (Choose three.)

   a. Overlays

   b. Agents and APIs

   c. Yang

   d. ACI

8. Which two of the following best describe a traditional application? (Choose two.)

   a. Monolithic application architecture

   b. Microservice-based architecture

   c. Client/server access model

   d. Cloud scale access model

9. What is the primary purpose of server virtualization?

   a. Increase power consumption on a single server

   b. None, because virtualization has nothing to do with servers

   c. Sharing compute resources among multiple workloads

   d. Simplifies server administration

10. Which best describes a cloud-native application?

   a. A distributed application that is built in a modular fashion such that individual components can be added or subtracted based on application load

   b. Any workload in the cloud

   c. A monolithic application that is built in a modular fashion such that individual components can be added or subtracted based on application load

   d. A myth used to sell consulting services

Foundation Topics

What Is Cloud?

The cloud has permeated almost every facet of life. It has become central to how we interact with our friends, buy things, watch TV and movies, and even run our businesses. So what is it really? Well, that is a very subjective question that has to take into account your own personal perspective. If you were to ask five people what the term "cloud" means in the context of IT, you would probably get eight different answers. Nearly half of all business meetings about cloud, when it was in its infancy, were spent determining what it is. Is it a service? Is it a product? Is it something magical that will solve all of our business problems?

The biggest problem with this line of thinking is in trying to call cloud a "thing" in the first place. Cloud really gives us a new way of operating IT, allowing it to be fast, agile, and able to align better to the goals of the business. From this perspective, cloud can help transform manual and inefficient processes into something that the business can leverage as a competitive advantage and a way to better serve its customers.

To gain a bit of perspective, it often helps to look at history to see how we got to where we are today.

History of Cloud

While the term "cloud" is relatively new to the IT world, the underlying concepts that make cloud computing possible are not. The reality is, the core tenants and concepts that support a cloud environment have been around for many years; it just took time for technology, software, and ubiquitous network access to evolve to a point where organizations could share resources, provide rapid scalability, and automate service delivery regardless of physical location. This evolution didn't happen overnight, and much of what we see today in a modern cloud architecture has its roots in technologies all the way back to the 1950s. With that in mind, let's take a quick trip down memory lane to when this whole cloud concept started.

Mainframe Computing

In the 1950s, mainframe computing was all the rage. Large businesses were investing in these warehouse-sized monsters in a big way. There was a business need to provide access to computing resources to more people within the company. These computers cost a fortune, and it was not practical or even physically possible for companies to buy a mainframe for each team. The solution to this resource dilemma was to share access to the computer through much lower cost "dumb" terminals that were "slaved" to the mainframe computer. This concept of shared access was very effective and responsible for supporting everything from manufacturing and distribution to missions to the moon.

Unfortunately, many of these mainframes were like islands onto themselves, with only the largest institutions having them linked through expensive private line connections. In the early 1960s, J.C.R. Licklider, the first director of the Information Processing Techniques

Office at the Pentagon Advanced Research Projects Agency (ARPA), imagined a day when computers would be networked together to create an "electronic commons open to all, and the main and essential medium of information interaction for governments, institutions, corporations, and individuals." Being an early SciFi nerd, Licklider called it the Intergalactic Computer Network. His role and vision at ARPA led to the development of the ARPANET, which was the precursor to our modern Internet.

John McCarthy is attributed as making one of the earliest references to the concept of computing as a utility and consumed through a "pay and use" model. In a speech delivered at MIT in 1961, he said, "If computers of the kind I have advocated become the computers of the future, then computing may someday be organized as a public utility just as the telephone system is a public utility... The computer utility could become the basis of a new and important industry." This concept of a utility model of cloud computing is the core premise of many of the cloud services we know today.

The Rise of the Virtual Machine

It should be pretty apparent that the 1950s and 1960s were important from a computing standpoint. The advent and adoption of the mainframe also led to some other notable advances that have driven cloud. In 1959, Christopher Strachey published a paper titled "Time Sharing in Large Fast Computers" that got people thinking about how better to use these massively expensive mainframes that businesses had invested in. The idea of the virtual machine grew out of this "time sharing" concept, leading to technological advances that enabled multiple users to use the same computer concurrently. To the application that the user was running, it appeared that it had full access to the computer's resources, but in reality the computer was switching between multiple applications in time slices. During the time in which the application was active, it got to use the resources it needed. When the application was idle between processes, the application was suspended in memory and a different application was executed. To manage this application juggling act, the management and allocation of time slices was conducted by a controller that operated independently of the applications the user ran. This controller abstracted the underlying hardware from the application, which is the basis for full hardware virtualization we see today in the modern virtual machine.

The virtual machine first appeared in the IBM mainframe in 1972 and was extremely popular. In the 1980s, general-purpose desktop PCs hit the scene and became the platform of choice. There were lots of early software emulators that ran on top of existing operating systems, but they were often horribly slow. Virtualization on the desktop didn't really start to become feasible until the late 1990s when Intel began offering more powerful processors. In 1997 the Disco project at Stanford published a paper detailing the creation of a virtual machine monitor for the Iris operating system on an x86 processor. Why did the researchers name their project Disco? Because they were trying to bring back the virtual machine monitor introduced in the '70s, which also happened to be the height of the disco dance craze. So, in effect, they were bringing back disco. (Who said computer geeks don't have a sense of humor?)

Three of the four researchers behind Disco boogied their way to forming a company called VMware, and in 1999 they released the 1.0 version of VMware Workstation. This gave end users the ability to run other operations systems on top of their native operating system with usable performance. While Workstation had its uses, the team had set its sights on building a server-based virtualization platform, and in 2001 VMware ESX and GSX servers were released. GSX allowed users to run virtual machines on top of an existing operating system (like Microsoft Windows or Linux), also known as a type-2 hypervisor. ESX, on the other hand, was a type-1 hypervisor that did not require a host operating system and had its own kernel (vmkernel) and file system (VMFS). The release of ESX enabled huge improvements in performance and portability and mainstreamed the use of virtual machines in the modern data center.

Virtual Private Network

In the late 1990s, virtual private networks (VPN) began to be offered by network service providers as a reduced-cost alternative to expensive dedicated connections. A company could get the same level of service for a fraction of the cost, because the service provider would be able to share network resources among multiple customers instead of having to build out massive amounts of infrastructure. From a customer's perspective, they could use a single physical connection to the service provider and logically segment it just as if they had a dedicated circuit. The use of the Internet as a connectivity mechanism to remote branch offices and other data centers became a reality. The VPN in effect provides a way to connect any service regardless of location and is often used today to connect to public cloud services so that applications can communicate directly and securely.

Application Service Providers

Application service providers first emerged in the late 1990s, riding on this new wave of network access. Instead of buying software, installing it, patching it, securing it, and maintaining it, a company could contract with an ASP, letting the ASP handle the operational burden, and simply pay the ASP for the use of the software. This became a very attractive model for businesses that didn't have the staff or desire to own the software, but still wanted to use its benefit. The term ASP has since evolved to Software as a Service (SaaS), but for practical purposes the terms mean the same thing. Salesforce.com was founded in 1999 and took this software model to the next level by building its application in a multitenant model that could scale to massive numbers of customers. Salesforce's CRM application is an example of one of the first SaaS offerings and has had a meteoric rise in popularity. Salesforce has since branched off into multiple product software offerings outside of CRM and is the largest SaaS provider in the world.

Amazon Web Services

Imagine you work for a retail business, and every year you go through four months of craziness during the holiday season. How do you keep your applications from being overwhelmed from the spike in business? You could overbuild your infrastructure to address those busy months, but you would end up using just a portion of that capacity the rest of the year. Hardly an efficient model. This problem was not a trivial one for Amazon back in 2000 as it had experienced explosive growth in its online retail business and had built up some significant infrastructure, 90 percent of which was sitting idle during nonpeak time. What did Amazon do? Chris Pinkham, an engineer in charge of global infrastructure in the early 2000s, had an idea to decentralize the infrastructure in such a way as to allow for better services for development teams. Partnering with another engineer named Benjamin Black, they authored a paper for Amazon's CEO outlining the plan to offer an "infrastructure for the world." Clearly, it was well received. In 2002 Amazon launched Amazon Web Services (AWS), which provides virtualized computing resources over the Internet, and quickly saw that there was an appetite in the market for just such a service. In 2006 Amazon launched Amazon Elastic Compute Cloud (EC2). This platform was wildly successful, and by 2008 more than 330,000 customers had signed up. Since then, AWS has continued to grow and evolve into multiple offerings used by the likes of Netflix, Adobe Systems, and Pinterest.

Cloud Computing Today

Today Amazon, Google, Microsoft, Cisco, and others all offer cloud services. Many startups are building their applications and services completely in the cloud. Why would startups choose to do this? Because cloud computing offers lower initial startup costs, faster time to market, vast scalability, and a global presence. You can also try out a new business idea without being stuck with huge amounts of infrastructure if the idea doesn't pan out. Uber, for example, has completely transformed the transportation service industry through a cloud-based application that allows anyone to easily find an Uber-approved driver willing to pick them up and take them were they want to go. Square has transformed credit card processing by allowing anyone with a smartphone and an inexpensive hardware add-on to swipe a credit card as payment. The growth of cloud services like these will continue at a steady pace, forcing businesses to rethink how they engage with their customers and operate business-critical services.

NIST Definition

To define cloud, we need a common taxonomy, and for that (and the purposes of the CLDADM exam) we will turn to the National Institute of Standards and Technology (NIST), which is a US government agency responsible for standardizing weights, measurements, and technology standards and practices. NIST Special Publication 800-145, "The NIST Definition of Cloud Computing," was written to solve the "what is cloud" dilemma. NIST defines cloud computing as such: "Cloud computing is a model for enabling ubiquitous, convenient, on-demand network access to a shared pool of configurable computing resources (e.g., networks, servers, storage, applications, and services) that can be rapidly provisioned and released with minimal management effort or service provider interaction." While 800-145 is a rather short document, it hits on all the major aspects of cloud and is testable material on the CLDADM exam. Figure 1-1 shows the NIST map that defines the core elements of a cloud.

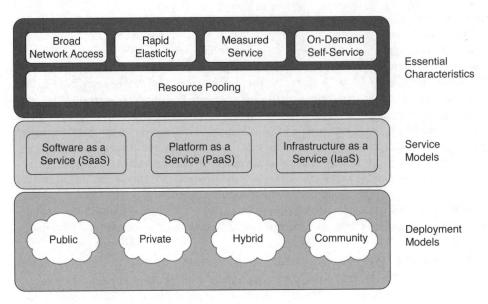

Figure 1-1 *NIST Cloud Definition*

NIST defines cloud through the following categories:

- Essential characteristics
- Service models
- Deployment models

These three categories are detailed further in the following sections.

Essential Characteristics

The essential characteristics describe the core requirements of any cloud:

- **Broad network access:** Services are available over the network and accessed via standard protocols and communications technologies on any type of client device (mobile phone, tablet, desktop, etc.).
- **Rapid elasticity:** Capacity can be automatically provisioned and decommissioned to scale the service to demand.
- **Measured service:** Cloud systems measure resource utilization (compute, storage, network) and charge for those services accordingly. Utilization can be monitored, controlled, and reported on, allowing transparency for the service provider and customer.
- **On-demand self-service:** The cloud consumer can provision compute, storage, and network services as needed, without human interaction, through automation or self-service portals.
- **Resource pooling:** A provider's infrastructure is a common pool of resources that can serve multiple customers at the same time. Customers do not interact with the underlying hardware, and their workloads can be moved within the cloud provider's environment based on demand without their knowledge or involvement.

Service Models

The three cloud computing service models presented in NIST SP 800-145 and listed next are examples of the most common cloud offerings today, with the biggest difference between each being how much control over resources the cloud customer has and how much administration the cloud customer needs to perform. Unlike the traditional IT service model (still one of the most common operating models IT departments use today), in which you are responsible for all aspects of installing, deploying, managing, and maintaining your application, the cloud service models unburden you of some or all of those responsibilities depending on which service model you choose. Figure 1-2 shows this comparison in more detail.

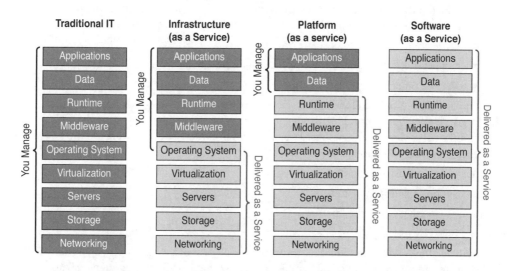

Figure 1-2 *Comparison of NIST Cloud Computing Service Models and Traditional IT Model*

- **Software as a Service (SaaS):** The service provider hosts, manages, and controls an application and offers it to the customer to use. The customer does not interact at all with the underlying infrastructure, operating systems, storage, or network. There may be some customization capabilities, but they are usually limited to application-specific configuration.

- **Platform as a Service (PaaS):** The provider supplies a software platform composed of a predefined set of application programming interfaces (API), libraries, software development kits (SDK), and/or other tools and services, that the customer can integrate with their own applications. The customer can program their application in any way they choose and customize it directly to their own workflow as long as they work within the parameters of the service provider's offering. The customer will not have any management responsibilities for the underling infrastructure.

- **Infrastructure as a Service (IaaS):** The provider offers the ability for the customer to provision compute, storage, and networking to run any combination of software and operating systems. The customer has no control over the underlying cloud platform, but they have full control over what software and services they deploy within the cloud. The customer is also responsible for the maintenance of the software they deploy and also patching and upgrading.

Deployment Models

Cloud can be deployed in a number of ways. The choice of deployment models really comes down to whether you want to own the cloud, rent the cloud, or a mixture of both. That choice is guided by a multitude of factors, such as concerns about protecting sensitive data, economics, availability, and speed, all of which need to be weighed in making the choice between deployment models.

- **Private cloud:** A private cloud is provisioned for a single organization, which may have multiple service consumers within its business units or groups. The organization may own the private cloud or lease it from another entity. The cloud infrastructure does not have to reside on the organization's premises and may be in another facility owned and operated by a third party. The following are the key characteristics of a private cloud:
  - Dedicated resources for a single organization
  - Connectivity through the Internet, fiber, or a private network
  - May be on premises or off premises

- **Public cloud:** A public cloud is provisioned for open utilization by the public at large. Anyone with a credit card can gain access to a public cloud offering. A public cloud exists solely on the premises of the cloud provider. The following are the key characteristics of a public cloud:
  - Publicly shared resources
  - Supports multiple customers
  - Connectivity over the Internet
  - Billed by usage

- **Hybrid cloud:** A hybrid cloud is composed of one or more cloud deployment models (private and public, for example) and is used to extend capabilities or augment capacity during peak demand periods (called cloud bursting), as shown in Figure 1-3. The key characteristics of a hybrid cloud are
  - The combination of public and private cloud
  - On-premises and off-premises resources
  - Orchestration between the two clouds

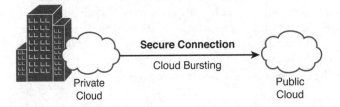

Figure 1-3 *Hybrid Cloud*

- **Community cloud:** A community cloud is unique in that it is provisioned for the sole utilization of a specific community of customers. This could be a school district, for example, or multiple government agencies. Basically, any group of entities with a common interest in policy, security, compliance, or mission can join together and implement a community cloud. The following are key characteristics:

- Collaborative cloud effort that shares infrastructure between several similar organizations with common needs
- Can be owned, managed, and operated by one or more members of the community or a third party
- May reside on or off premises

SDN and Cloud

Software-defined networking (SDN) and cloud aren't the same thing, but they definitely share a lot of the same goals: to streamline and speed up the deployment of new applications and to reduce the cost of operations. There is often confusion about what SDN is and how it applies to a cloud environment. Some IT organizations look at SDN as simply another name for network management, while others think it is all about technologies like OpenFlow or Virtual Extensible LAN (VXLAN). Still others buy in to the SDN hype and think it is going to solve all of the world's problems with the touch of a button, like some kind of magical spell. The truth is, SDN is simply another way to control and provision the network in an automated fashion.

An SDN Definition

A widely accepted definition of SDN, much like that of cloud, is a challenge to pinpoint. Part of the reason for this is that IT vendors have liberally sprinkled the term SDN into many of their product names. For example, what used to be a management application for the network is now an "SDN controller." Marketing has had a field day plastering everything with the SDN moniker. How do you discern marketing fluff from something real that your business can benefit from? It comes down to SDN's value and utility in your environment.

SDN is a software-centric approach to networking that reduces capital and operational expense of network infrastructure, by abstracting the complexity of building the network in favor of simplifying the utilization of the network. In other words, the business benefit of SDN truly revolves around reducing the many manual inefficiencies in delivering new services to the business. It's about being faster, more flexible, and better able to react to changing requirements. By software enabling the control and provisioning of network elements, you can move from slowly rolling out new services over months to being able to do it in minutes at a scale you simply could not accomplish with manual provisioning. SDN capabilities can be automated and scripted, which can greatly reduce how long it takes to deploy network services.

The Challenges SDN Solves

SDN can be used to solve three primary problems facing network administrators:

- **Box-by-box configuration:** Traditional network devices need to be configured and deployed individually. That means if you have 100 switches, you need to configure each one before it can be added into production. If you need to upgrade software on the device and it takes you 20 minutes per device, you can quickly see how much of an operational bottleneck this can be. By leveraging SDN, you turn on the device and it is then added to the pool of resources and gets its configuration from the network itself automatically.

■ **Applications and services tied to network elements:** For the most part, network devices in a traditional networking model are inexplicably intertwined with the services they offer. If you need to provide quality of service (QoS), for example, that capability is dependent on the hardware and software available to your device. This makes it difficult to make changes to network topology without a major undertaking. In an SDN environment the underlying networking hardware is treated as a common pool of resources, and the configuration and features are logically separated through the use of a controller. The SDN controller is the brain, and the hardware acts like a muscle giving you the ability to deploy network capabilities (intelligence) anywhere without being tied to a specific router or switch in your network.

■ **Operational complexity:** Let's face it, networks are complex. There are hundreds of protocols running between devices and through devices every second. All of this activity adds to operational complexity and difficulty in troubleshooting problems when they arise. SDN can help to solve this by simplifying the network topology and treating the network as a system instead of individual components. Need to make a configuration change to many devices at the same time in your network? That could be a multiweek project depending on how many devices you have. With SDN you can do it with the click of a button, which saves time, and a significant amount of headache.

SDN Is a Cloud Enabler

Why all of this talk about SDN in a Cloud CCNA exam book? Recall from the NIST definition of a cloud that rapid elasticity and resource pooling are requirements. Compute and storage are fairly easy to automate through virtualization, but without SDN the physical network provisioning and configuration management become a stumbling block to speed and agility. Virtual networking is great for providing connectivity within a hypervisor, but ultimately the network traffic will need to exit the server and cross a physical switch. Although SDN is not a hard and fast requirement for cloud, the ability SDN provides for automating physical network provisioning is essential in delivering a modern cloud environment.

Cisco offers numerous ways to deliver SDN; many of the technologies are described in this book and in the *CCNA Cloud CLDFND 210-451 Official Cert Guide*. Cisco offers the following SDN technologies that you need to be aware of:

■ **APIs:** Cisco has enabled application programming interfaces across the vast majority of the product line. These APIs can be used to customize the operation of network elements and to provide a control point for other software (such as cloud orchestration software). An API is simply a standard and documented way to programmatically control a piece of hardware or software. For example, you can write a script/application in Python, Java, Ruby, or any other programming language that supports REST APIs and parse JSON or XML output to make changes to these devices quickly. APIs are a crucial integration point and should be a requirement for any device you place in the network to support a cloud environment.

■ **Plug-ins:** Plug-ins are pieces of software that allow for integration into other systems. For example, Cisco has an OpenStack plug-in for the Nexus switch line that enables OpenStack to directly control the configuration and provisioning of these switches from within the cloud platform.

- **Agents:** An agent is a piece of software that resides on a networking device and enables integration with other technology platforms like OpenFlow, Puppet, and Chef. Agents can be used to automate network configuration and create templates you can use to standardize deployments.

- **Cisco Application Centric Infrastructure (ACI):** ACI is the most complete SDN platform in the market today. It provides a turnkey solution that delivers all of the value promised by SDN for both the physical environment and virtual environment. ACI integrates with all major hypervisor vendors and provides a common policy domain that allows them to work together seamlessly.

- **Network virtual appliance:** A network virtual appliance is a software variation of a hardware-based network element. These appliances run as virtual machines and can be firewalls, load balancers, switches, routers, and any other network function you want to add to support your applications. Cisco has a full suite of these products as well as a rich ecosystem of partners that ensure tight integration.

Ultimately, SDN concepts are becoming intertwined with cloud and represent a fairly significant component of maximizing operational efficiency. After all, isn't that what cloud is all about?

Applications and Cloud

What is IT's value to the business if you boil it down to the simplest aspect? IT is charged with supporting and maintaining applications that the business relies upon. No one builds a network first and then looks for applications to stick on it. Instead, the network is built to connect the applications to employees and customers. The application has become an essential way in which customers are acquired, retained, and engaged. The value of the application to the business and the competitive pressure for rapid development and continual enhancement have made flexibility and speed afforded by a cloud environment even more important. Unfortunately, not all applications fit easily into the cloud based on application architecture and/or backend service requirements. Understanding some of the different ways in which applications are deployed will arm you with knowledge you can use to identify which applications in your environment are good candidates for migrating to the cloud.

Traditional Applications

The traditional application stack is fairly well known. It's how the vast majority of applications have been deployed over the past 30 years. As Figure 1-4 shows, traditionally, one server is devoted to the task of running a single application. This one-to-one relationship gives the application dedicated access to all of the resources of the server it is running on. If you need more memory or processing capability, however, you must physically add new memory or a CPU, or transfer the application to a whole new server.

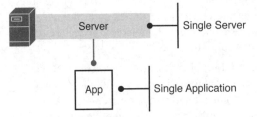

Figure 1-4   *Traditional Application Stack*

Although the traditional application stack is an effective way to isolate applications and get consistent performance characteristics, it's very inefficient. In fact, many of these traditional server deployment models result in enormous amounts of waste in regard to power and cooling of servers when they are not under load. It is not uncommon to find a server during nonpeak hours using less than 10 percent of its capacity. Not very cost effective.

Some applications work best on a dedicated server where they can utilize all of the resources available. An application that is memory, CPU, or I/O intensive or that depends on custom hardware often will not perform as well in a shared environment as it does in a dedicated server. These workloads can consume 100 percent of the resources of the server, making them poor candidates for virtualization.

Virtualized Applications

Virtualization was developed to address the problems of traditional one-to-one server deployments where the server capacity was poorly utilized. The objective of virtualization is to build one large server and then run more than one application on it. Sounds simple, right? As discussed earlier, many of the techniques from the days of the mainframe were leveraged to create an environment where the underlying server hardware could be virtualized. The hypervisor was created to handle all of the time slicing and hardware virtualization. This made it possible to run various applications and operating systems at the same time and reap the benefit of better utilization of resources. Figure 1-5 shows this concept.

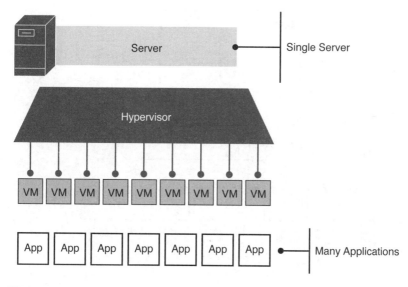

Figure 1-5   *Virtualized Application Stack*

Virtualizing hardware has other benefits too. The ability to make applications portable and not tied to a single server allows for mobility in the data center. If a server needs to be worked on, you simply move the running virtual machine to another server and never need to take the application down. You also can create common deployment packages for new virtual machines and applications, which gives administrators the ability to quickly provision a new server in a consistent and secure manner.

The virtualized application is a key aspect of cloud, but they are not synonymous. Configuring a cloud environment to automate the deployment of a physical server could be accomplished just as easily as configuring it to automate the deployment of a virtual machine. Conversely, just because you have a virtualized infrastructure doesn't mean you have a cloud, either.

Cloud-Native Applications

Cloud-native applications are the further intersection and evolution of virtualization and a cloud environment. As virtualization became more popular, application developers started to ask themselves why they needed a full operating system to run their applications on top of. All of the patching, driver, and configuration requirements don't go away just because you load a virtual machine. These requirements still need to be attended to. What if applications could be written as simpler packages that do not need a hypervisor or full-blown operating system to function? That's exactly what happened. Developers created *microservices*, which are small, stateless applications that can run on any server in the data center. These applications are lightweight and independent of each other, allowing for massive scalability and built-in resiliency. As Figure 1-6 shows, cloud-native applications run on multiple servers in parallel with each other.

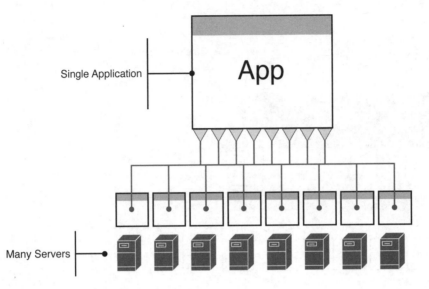

Figure 1-6 *Cloud-Native Applications*

If a server goes bad in a cloud-native application environment, no one worries, because the application is distributed across many servers in the data center. If you need more capacity, just add a new server and it is added to the server pool automatically. The application orchestration function within the cloud will deploy the application onto the new server, instantly increasing capacity. If load decreases, the cloud orchestration can shut down unused nodes automatically to save money. Large-scale cloud applications such as Facebook and Twitter all operate in this fashion, which is why they appear to have infinite capacity from the user's perspective.

CHAPTER 2

Cloud: A New Operations Model for IT

Thanks to a lot of new and exciting technology, a cloud operational model is possible within businesses of all sizes. While virtualization, automation, and software-defined networking are components that can be used in building a cloud, the most valuable aspect is not the technology itself, but how the technology can be used to streamline and accelerate the delivery of applications and services that the business can leverage to meet its goals and objectives. The point of this chapter is to discuss the operational benefits and capabilities that cloud offers and to give the context needed to better understand the types of questions you may see on the CCNA Cloud Administration exam.

"Do I Know This Already?" Quiz

The "Do I Know This Already?" quiz allows you to assess whether you should read this entire chapter thoroughly. If you are in doubt about your answers to these questions or your own assessment of your knowledge of the topics, read the entire chapter. Table 2-1 lists the major headings in this chapter and their corresponding "Do I Know This Already?" quiz questions. You can find the answers in Appendix A, "Answers to the 'Do I Know This Already?' Quizzes."

Table 2-1 "Do I Know This Already?" Section-to-Question Mapping

Foundation Topics Section	Questions
IT Operations Past, Present, and Future	1, 2
The Rise of DevOps	3–5
Service Catalog	6–8
Self-Service Portal	9, 10

Caution The goal of self-assessment is to gauge your mastery of the topics in this chapter. If you do not know the answer to a question or are only partially sure of the answer, you should mark that question as wrong for purposes of the self-assessment. Giving yourself credit for an answer you correctly guess skews your self-assessment results and might provide you with a false sense of security.

1. What challenges does a waterfall development approach have?

    a. Problems roll down hill.

    b. It is a sequential development model that doesn't handle change well.

    c. It is a parallel development model that doesn't handle change well.

    d. It has no challenges.

2. What is Agile based on?

    a. Toyota Production System

    b. ITIL

    c. SCRUM

    d. Lean manufacturing

3. What is IT's role in cloud evolving into?

    a. Irrelevance, because all workloads will move to the public cloud

    b. Broker of services

    c. Service provider

    d. Advisor to the business

4. Which of the following best describes DevOps?

    a. Development and operations working together

    b. A culture of sharing

    c. Automation and measurement

    d. All of the above

5. What is continuous integration?

    a. Software package delivery mechanism for releasing code to staging for review and inspection

    b. Relies on CI and CD to automatically release code into production

    c. Merging development code into a software versioning system for automated testing and build

    d. All of the above

6. Which of the following are principles used in developing a service catalog?

    a. Repeatability

    b. Standardization

    c. Self-service

    d. Static environment

7. Which Cisco products provide a service catalog?

    a. Prime Service Catalog

    b. Prime Infrastructure

    c. UCS Director

    d. UCS Manager

8. Which of the following items are included as part of defining a service catalog?

    a. Service description

    b. Service cost

    c. Service decommissioning

    d. BYOD

9. What is a self-service portal?

    a. Web-based central repository for ordering IT service offerings

    b. REST-based interface for interacting with a cloud platform

    c. IT ticketing system replacement

    d. Internal IT-facing view of the service catalog

10. Which of the following is a benefit of the self-service portal?

    a. Lower-cost switches

    b. Higher operational cost

    c. Loads VM faster

    d. Better operational efficiency

Foundation Topics

IT Operations, Past, Present, and Future

The pace of change in IT has always been something of a roller coaster ride. The twists, turns, and speed are part of why many people choose technology as a career field. It simply doesn't get boring. While change has been a constant factor, the volume of change seen in the last ten years has been incredible. If anything, it's just gaining momentum. Cloud has become one of the most influential shifts and is touching every part of business operations. No longer are you stuck with a single model of buy and build to add new IT resources and services. As a technologist, you now have a very wide range of consumption models that you can choose from to deliver to your end users. It's almost like being a stock broker, where you can pick the best choice based on the needs and requirements of your customer, lines of business, or business function.

The challenge for the IT admin is to manage their technology offerings in such a way that they can be efficiently consumed following the cloud principles. In-house managed IT services are no longer the only game in town, and as such they must compete with public cloud, SaaS, and other types of technology services. Your users now demand upfront guidance on the cost, capabilities, and delivery of IT services. If in-house managed offerings cannot meet those demands, customers will seek alternatives.

Choice and flexibility are great, but the burden now rests on the shoulders of the IT professional to help the end user navigate the various cloud options to deliver a solid solution that minimizes risk and maximizes return. An IT professional requires a wide view of the various ways in which you can solve business requirements with cloud solutions. To do that successfully, you need to understand the evolution of IT operations. The following sections describe that evolution.

Waterfall

Back in the 1950s, when large companies started to purchase large mainframe computers to crunch numbers, there was no existing model for how to run an IT organization. It really wasn't anything that had been done before, and for the most part computers were really understood only by an elite group of scientists. Programming the mainframe needed structure and a process. This caused a problem for businesses looking to tap into the capabilities of these new systems because there wasn't a well-known method to create business applications. So what did they do? They looked around at other industries for guidance.

The construction industry was booming in the 1950s, and early software engineers recognized that the complexity of designing and constructing a building was similar to that of creating software applications. The construction industry followed a rigid process where every step along the way was dependent on the completion of the previous step in the process. If you expect your building to not tumble over or look like an M.C. Escher drawing, you can't start construction until you have a plan and analyze the requirements of the new tenants. This thought process mapped nicely to software development. The waterfall model became one of the more popular software development lifecycle (SDLC) approaches. Figure 2-1 shows a graphical representation of waterfall development.

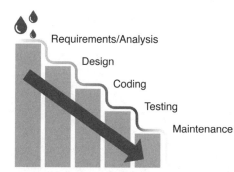

Figure 2-1   *Waterfall Approach*

Waterfall is a serial approach to software development. Each part of the process is divided into these phases:

- **Requirements/analysis:** Software features and functionality needs are cataloged and assessed to determine what the necessary capabilities of the software are.
- **Design:** The software architecture is defined and documented.
- **Coding:** Software coding begins based on the previously determined design.
- **Testing:** Completed code is tested for quality and customer acceptance.
- **Maintenance:** Bug fixes and patches are applied.

Although this approach has worked successfully over the years, it has a number of short-comings that have proven to be weaknesses in many scenarios. First, the serial nature of the waterfall approach, while easy to understand, means that the scope of a software project is fixed at the design phase. Just like in construction, making changes to the first floor of a building after you have begun on the fifth floor is extremely difficult, if not impossible, to accomplish without basically knocking the building over and starting from scratch. In essence, the waterfall approach does not handle change well at all. For example, if you finally get to the coding phase of the application development process and you learn that the feature you are building isn't needed anymore or a new way of accomplishing a design goal has been discovered, you are limited in deviating from the predetermined architecture without redoing the analysis and design. This is like being halfway finished with building a bridge over a river that becomes unnecessary and no one needs anymore. Do you just stop and tear down the bridge or keep going? Unfortunately, it is often more painful and waste-ful to start over than to keep building.

The second shortcoming of the waterfall approach is apparent when you factor in time to value. Why do we write software? To automate some business function or capability. Value is realized only when the software is in production and producing results. With the waterfall approach, value is not achieved until the end of the whole process. Although you may be 50 percent finished with the project, you have 0 percent usable code or value back to the business. Figure 2-2 shows this concept.

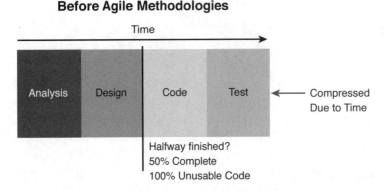

Figure 2-2 *Non-Agile Development Methods*

The third shortcoming of the waterfall approach is that quality may be compromised. As previously mentioned, time is the enemy when it comes to delivering value. If we had unlimited time, we could create perfect software every time, but we simply don't live in that world. When software developers run out of time, testing often suffers or is sacrificed in the name of getting the project out the door.

The preceding shortcomings of the waterfall approach led to demands for a new approach to creating software that would be faster, better, and more adaptive to a rapidly changing environment.

Lean

After World War II, Japan was in desperate need of rebuilding. Most of Japan's production capabilities had been destroyed, one of which was the auto industry. The necessity to rebuild the auto industry not only prompted new architectural designs for the buildings and infrastructure but also provided a spark to approach production differently. Out of this effort, the Toyota Production System (TPS) was born. Created by Taiichi Ohno, Sakichi Toyoda, Kiichiro Toyoda, and Eiji Toyoda (founders of Toyota), this management and manufacturing process has a focus on the following:

- **Elimination of waste:** If something doesn't add value to the final product, get rid of it. It's wasted work.

- **Just in time:** Don't build something until the customer is ready to buy it. Excess inventory wastes resources.

- **Continuous improvement:** Always improve your processes with lessons learned and communication.

While these approaches seem glaringly obvious, and practical, TPS was the first implementation of these principles as a management philosophy. TPS was the start of the more generalized *lean manufacturing* approach that was introduced to the Western world in 1991 through a book written by Womack, Jones, and Roos: *The Machine That Changed the World*. This book was based on the results of a five-year study conducted by MIT on the Toyota Production System and has been attributed to the development of lean concepts and processes beyond the auto industry.

You may be asking yourself, "Why spend this time talking about moldy old management books?" Because lean was the impetus for Agile software development, which has served as an instigator of change for IT operations.

Agile

Agile is an implementation of lean principles as it pertains to software development. Many of the lessons learned optimizing the manufacturing process could be directly applied to the discipline of creating software. In 2001, 17 software developers converged on the Snowbird resort in Utah to discuss new lightweight development methods. Tired of missing deadlines, endless documentation, and the inflexibility of existing software development practices, these Agile pioneers (self-named The Agile Alliance) created the *Manifesto for Agile Software Development* (aka "Agile Manifesto"), an attempt to codify the guiding principles for Agile development practices. The following 12 principles are the core of the Agile Manifesto:

- Prioritize customer satisfaction through early and continuous delivery of valuable software.

- Embrace changing requirements to help the customer achieve a competitive advantage, even late in the development cycle.

- Deliver working software frequently in as short a time frame as possible (weeks rather than months).

- The business leaders and developers must work together daily throughout the project.

- Build software projects around motivated individuals that you trust to get the job done, and give them the support and environment to make it possible.

- Effectively share information through face-to-face conversation within the development team.

- Working software is the principal measure of progress and success.

- Agile promotes sustainable development where the sponsors, developers, and users can maintain a constant pace throughout the project and don't get overwhelmed.

- Pay continuous attention to technical excellence and good design to increase agility.

- Focus on simplicity to ensure that unnecessary work is not introduced into the project.

- The best architectures, requirements, and designs emerge from self-organizing teams.

- On a regular basis the development team adjusts its behavior to become more effective.

These core tenants were the main spark of the Agile movement. Mary and Tom Poppendieck wrote *Lean Software Development: An Agile Toolkit* in 2003 based on the 12 principles of the Agile Manifesto and their many years of experience developing software. This book is still considered one of the best on the practical uses of Agile.

Developing software through Agile results in a very different output than developing via the slow, serial manner of the waterfall approach. With waterfall, you have to wait until the end to have a "finished" project that could be deployed. With Agile, you move to a model where the time frame for outputs is changed to two-week increments, or *sprints* in the Agile world. These sprints encompass the full process of analysis, design, code, and test but on a much smaller aspect of the applications. The goal is to finish a feature or capability for each sprint, resulting in a potentially shippable incremental piece of software. In this way, if from a time perceptive you are 40 percent complete with the project, you will have 100 percent usable code that can go into production. Figure 2-3 shows how this process looks on a timeline.

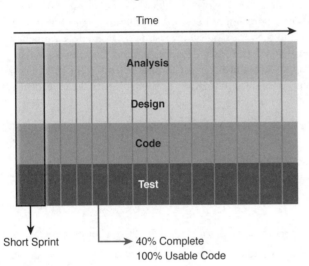

Figure 2-3 *Agile Development Practices*

By leveraging Agile, you can keep adding value immediately and be nimble at adapting to change. If you discover a new capability is needed in the software, or a feature that was planned is determined to no longer be necessary, the project can pivot quickly and make those adjustments.

Moving Faster

This is a book about cloud administration, right? Why all of the talk about application development? To be brutally honest, IT only exists to support business applications. You don't build networks and then look for applications to stick on top of them. Instead, you have applications that you need to connect together. Applications have always been important to IT, but we have begun to see a significant elevation of the application from something that ran our businesses to a vehicle for interacting with customers and transforming how businesses operate. Think of companies such as Uber or Amazon. The application is central to their business model. With Uber, you can use an application on your smartphone to immediately gain access to transportation anywhere. Not only that, but you can see in real time where your driver is, and the driver can see where you are, connecting supply and demand in a very transformational way. Amazon took a primarily brick-and-mortar business model and morphed it into an online marketplace where you can buy and sell anything imaginable. What is the common theme here? The criticality of the application. In these instances, the application *is* the businesses.

All of these applications are serving to digitize more and more traditional business functions and models. The only problem is, these new types of applications require business to move faster than they ever have before. No longer can a company wait six months to a year for a new software package to be built and delivered. They need it now, or their competitors will beat them to the punch. Applications are expected to add new features and functionality continuously, in a consistent delivery. Can you imagine rolling out new applications or updates to your company's applications many times a day? That's the new expectation. Faster wins the race.

The Future of IT Operations

Unless you are working for a startup, IT operations, for the most part, are a result of organizational history and organic growth, and as such, the way in which you do things today is often directly related to seeds that were planted long ago. What does the future of IT operations look like? While no one knows with 100 percent certainty, IT operations will definitely require a different model than the manual, slow, and inflexible ways that organizations have operated for many years. Agile is a great first step along this path, but you can't just throw out everything and start from scratch; it would simply be too disruptive to the business. To address this disconnect between innovation and keeping traditional systems and processes in place, companies have started to look at ways to implement both. Gartner, which is an IT technology research organization, took up this challenge and developed an operational model called Bimodal IT.

Bimodal IT describes two distinct modes, or speeds, that IT functions operate at. Mode 1 is focused on traditional IT operations related to business processes and applications that are crucial to the business. Mode 1 is all about maintaining stability and not introducing undue risk into the mix. Mode 2, on the other hand, is all about innovation, agility, speed, and experimentation. You can think of Mode 1 as being like a marathon runner, trained for endurance and distance. Mode 2 is more like a sprinter, able to move extremely fast at short distances. Both have their place depending upon the race being run. Figure 2-4 shows Gartner's view of Bimodal IT.

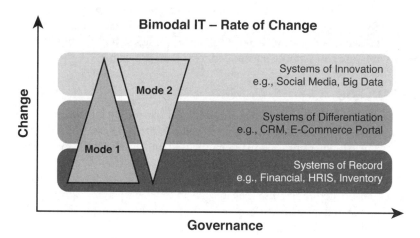

Figure 2-4   *Gartner Bimodal IT (Photo Credit Gartner, Inc.)*

One of the first things you will notice about Bimodal IT is that the two modes are really focused on handling change in core IT functional areas. Change is often looked at as the enemy of stability, and what Bimodal IT is attempting to do is to provide a better way to manage the rate of change in applications and the infrastructure, by segmenting applications that need a traditional operating model from those that need a faster, more agile model (i.e., lots of changes and modification) while minimizing unforeseen issues that could damage mission-critical systems.

The following classifications outline the types of IT applications that fall within the three application categories as identified by Gartner:

- **Systems of record:** Packaged or custom applications that support the core foundation of the business. These applications have minimal changes and mature operational processes. Examples include financial, HR, and inventory applications.

- **Systems of differentiation:** Applications that are unique to the business and represent a competitive differentiator. The applications in this class support moderate levels of change to accommodate a changing business environment. Examples include CRM and e-commerce applications.

- **Systems of innovation:** New applications built as needed to capitalize on new business needs or opportunities. Applications in this category have very high levels of change with significant experimentation used to uncover new business opportunities. Examples include social media and big data applications.

IT as a Broker of Services

In a cloud operational model, IT will need to increase its role as a broker for various services the business needs. While IT has always been in the business of contracting services for the business, the advent of cloud has increased the breadth and scope of the types of services available. Many organizations are moving to cloud as a means to outsource expensive services that they once ran internally. Email is a prime example of this trend, as many businesses either have moved or are moving to cloud-based email services. IT would "broker" and manage the service instead of all of the technology and servers. The economics are much more enticing, and resources can be diverted to activities that generate more revenue. Ultimately, IT becomes a services dealer, with a portfolio of offerings that is composed of both services offered in house and services outsourced to a cloud provider.

The Rise of DevOps

Agile has dramatically changed the landscape of software development, by introducing a more efficient and faster way of delivering software and value to the business. Much of the improvement in the development process has been focused on delivery speed. You can have as much agile development as you want, but if you can't get the software deployed in a timely manner, you can't take advantage of its capabilities. Agile software developers have embraced public cloud infrastructure because it enables them to provision their software easily and frequently. Non-cloud infrastructure, on the other hand, is not as quickly provisioned, which results in developer dissatisfaction.

Traditionally software was built and tested by the developers, and if it worked on their laptops or test systems, they gave it to IT operations to deploy. When things did not go as smoothly as planned, there was a significant amount of troubleshooting and finger point-ing that would ensue, with the developers claiming that the software worked fine in testing on their laptops, and that the infrastructure must be broken. The operations teams would lament about the buggy and poorly written software that was stressing their environment and creating all kinds of extra work. While both groups were working hard to accomplish the goals of the business and get things up and running, they were coming from very differ-ent perspectives and simply were not coordinated.

In addition, the two groups often have very different expectations and metrics for suc-cess. Developers care about writing code, working code, APIs, libraries, services, and Agile sprints. Success to them means that software works on their laptops and in testing, and that they finish their latest sprints in time. Operations, on the other hand, cares about the environment being stable, standards, templates, and, perhaps most importantly, not getting woken up at 2:00 a.m. to go fix a problem. Success to operations means that software and applications are stable, backup and restore processes work, and all systems are operating within defined thresholds. Developers want to drive innovation and create new features and capabilities in their software to meet the goals of the business. In other words, change is a constant in a developer's world, whereas operations are primarily looking to maintain stabil-ity and uptime in their environment.

If you take a calendar view of the two organizations, as shown in Figure 2-5, a major chal-lenge becomes very apparent. How can you possibly deploy new features and capabilities added every two weeks as part of an Agile sprint, when your operational maintenance win-dow is only open every six months?

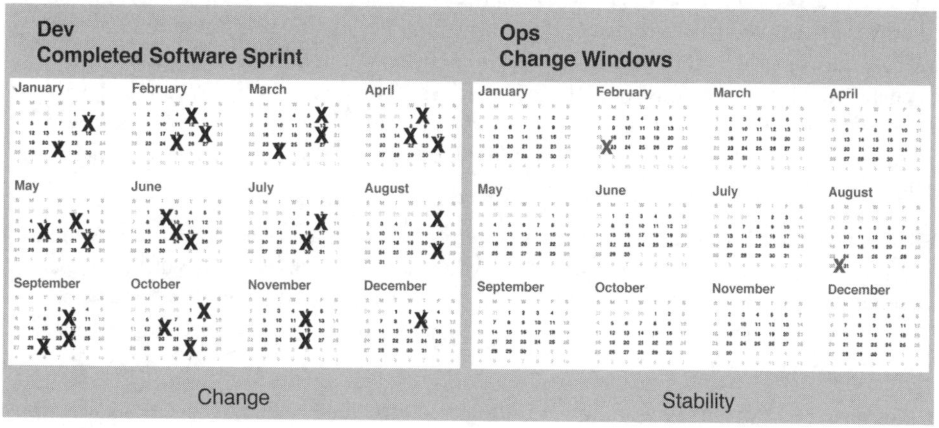

Figure 2-5 *Dev and Ops Calendar Comparison*

Traditional IT service delivery is slow, manual, and often prone to errors. The infrastruc-ture is a shared resource and, as such, one change can have a ripple effect that could break other, unrelated systems. The fragile nature of the infrastructure makes it very hard to anticipate issues that can arise. To combat this, many IT organizations create layers upon layers of approval process. While this sounds like a rational way to protect the business from downtime, the real effect is to slow down new deployments to a glacier-like pace. Figure 2-6 shows the traditional, burdensome waterfall approach to operations.

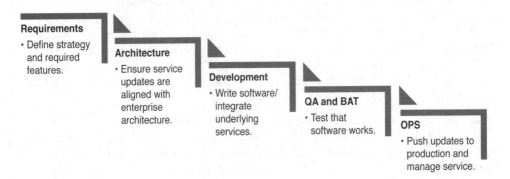

Figure 2-6 *Operational Waterfall Approach*

The rise of DevOps occurred relatively recently. In 2009, two employees at Flickr (an image-sharing site), John Allspaw and Paul Hammond, delivered their "10+ Deploys Per Day: Dev and Ops Cooperation at Flickr" presentation to a bunch of developers at the O'Reilly Velocity Conference. The point of this presentation was to make the case that the only way to build, test, and deploy software was for development and operations to be integrated together. The sheer audacity of being able to deploy new software so quickly fueled the launch of the DevOps concept. Over the years since 2009, DevOps has moved from being exposed by a small group of zealots and counterculture types to becoming a very real and quantifiable way to operate the machinery of software creation and release.

The key takeaway from Flickr's presentation was that they didn't decide to make a change to how they handled software innovation on a whim, but in direct response to constantly evolving customer demands and increased competition in the file-sharing space. They had to change their model to differentiate their business. The vast majority of companies that do software development are looking for ways to capture the efficiencies of this model to give them a competitive edge, and be better able to adapt to change from a customer and industry perspective.

What is DevOps? It is a culture of sharing where developers and operations are one unit, that rise and fall together. It is the practical applications of both lean and agile. The goal of DevOps is to be a real-time business enabler by removing wasted effort and bureaucracy from getting in the way of better addressing the needs of the customer. To this end DevOps has five guiding principles:

- **Culture:** For DevOps to work, organizational culture must change. This culture shift must occur across the whole organization, not just the Dev and Ops teams. It is by far one of the most difficult aspects to embrace, but it's the single most important factor for success. DevOps requires a culture of sharing that.

- **Automation:** While DevOps is more than just a set of software tools, automation is the most easily identifiable benefit. When you leverage automation techniques, the deployment process is greatly sped up, defects are caught and corrected earlier, and repetitive tasks no longer need human intervention.

- **Lean:** Reducing wasted efforts and streamlining the process are the goals of lean. It's a management philosophy of continuous improvement and learning.

- **Measurement:** Without measuring your results, you can never improve. Success with DevOps requires the measurement of performance, process, and people metrics as often as is feasible.

- **Sharing:** Feedback and sharing of information is the kind of culture that is needed for DevOps to flourish. Breaking down silos and creating an inclusive, shared-fate environment is the ultimate goal.

Figure 2-7 shows the core components of DevOps and how they are interrelated.

Lean Business Practices

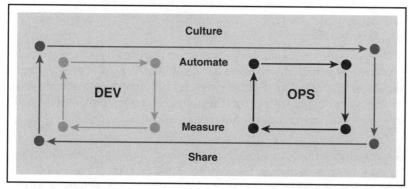

Figure 2-7   *DevOps Core Components*

Introducing DevOps into your organization breaks down into two major aspects: practices and tools.

Practices cover not only development and operations methodologies but also interactions between the two teams and their reporting structures. Often one of the first things you see new DevOps teams do is add operations engineers to the software project team. This reinforces the fact that the two are not separate but part of a value chain, with the result being a successful software release. Operations engineers will participate in project meetings, develop infrastructure configuration scripts, and support infrastructure integration with automated software testing tools.

The tools of DevOps include the various components that will be used to automate software testing and deployment. Selecting the appropriate tools is a joint effort between Dev and Ops and is essential to a functioning environment. The DevOps tool landscape is very large, with new components being added all of the time. To make selecting tools simpler, you should think of the major function of each tool and how it fits into the software development to release pipeline. The tool categories include

  IaaS: Infrastructure as a Service is the foundation for DevOps. Without a flexible and programmable underlying architecture, you would not have the dynamic pooling of resources or rapid scalability that cloud can offer. IaaS can be private, public, or a combination (hybrid). Examples include Cisco Metacloud, OpenStack, Amazon EC2 Container Service (ECS), and Amazon Web Services.

PaaS: The Platform as a Service layer is how many developers prefer to integrate their software development activities too, because it simplifies and abstracts the complexity of the underlying infrastructure so that they can focus on building their software. Network, storage, and compute resources are handled by the PaaS orchestration tools. Some example services are Kubernetes, Pivotal Cloud Foundry, Apprenda, and Cisco Mantl.

Source control: Source control (also called version control) tools provide a place for developers to store current and past versions of software code. These tools allow visibility into who is working on what parts of the software and provide change control. Some examples are GitHub, GitLab, Bitbucket, and Apache Subversion (SVN).

Image control: Image control tools provide a place to store finished software that is ready for deployment. Developers call finished software packages or components *artifacts*. An image control tool is similar to a source control system, but instead of managing software code, it manages the versioning of software builds. Some image control examples are Docker, Quay, and Artifactory.

Collaboration: DevOps collaboration tools are essential to keeping everyone in sync with the status of software builds and software feature completion. These tools often integrate with other components in the DevOps pipeline to receive and archive various activities of the software development and release process. They often include chat, file sharing, conferencing, and project management features. Some examples are Cisco Spark, Jive, Slack, and Trello.

Configuration management: Configuration management tools are responsible for transforming the deployment of infrastructure components into a descriptive language that can be automated. Often referred to as infrastructure as code, these tools provide much of the automation necessary to perform on-demand software testing in DevOps. Some examples are Puppet, Chef, Ansible, and SaltStack.

Continuous integration: Continuous integration tools are the brains behind the DevOps pipeline. They monitor source control systems and, when a change is made to source code, can kick off automated testing and building of the new software code. Through integration with configuration management tools, they can also launch the deployment of infrastructure as well. Some examples are Jenkins, Travis CI, Drone, and TeamCity.

Figure 2-8 shows how these tools would work together in a real-world environment, the steps of which are described here:

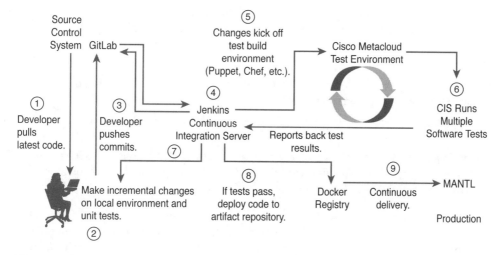

Figure 2-8   *DevOps Tool Pipeline*

Step 1.   A developer pulls the latest code from the source control system to her local laptop.

Step 2.   The developer makes changes to the code on her local laptop, and then submits the modified code back to the source control system.

Step 3.   The developer submits a code commit to the versioning control system, signaling that new code is ready to build.

Step 4.   The continuous integration server sees that there is code waiting to be built via its integration with the versioning control system and pulls down the new committed code and builds the software.

Step 5.   The continuous integration server initiates an infrastructure build to create a test environment through a configuration management tool such as Puppet or Chef.

Step 6.   The continuous integration server then runs multiple tests against the built software to ensure that it works as expected. The results of these tests are reported back to the developer and archived.

Step 7.   The continuous integration server sends the test results and whether or not the software tested successfully to the developer's collaboration tool so that everyone can see the current build status.

Step 8.   Once the software has passed testing, the continuous integration server sends the working code to the image control (artifact) repository.

Step 9.   The code is ready to be deployed to production either automatically or after further testing and approval.

There are three primary stages that are often attributed to implementing DevOps within your organization. They follow a natural progression that leads to a fully automated software coding to production deployment operational model. These stages are additive and build upon the previous one. The stages are

- **Continuous integration:** Merging of development work with the code base constantly so that automated testing can catch problems early.

- **Continuous delivery:** Software package delivery mechanism for releasing code to staging for review and inspection.

- **Continuous deployment:** Relies on the previous stages of Continuous Integration and Continuous Deployment to automatically release code into production as soon as it is ready. Constant flow of new features into production.

The purpose of going through all of this software development and Agile "stuff" is to give some context and background to the types of forces that are driving cloud adoption today. It comes down to moving faster and delivering value to the customer quicker. The primary goal is to go from a new business idea to monetization of that idea faster. Figure 2-9 shows how lean, Agile, and DevOps fit together to achieve the business expectations.

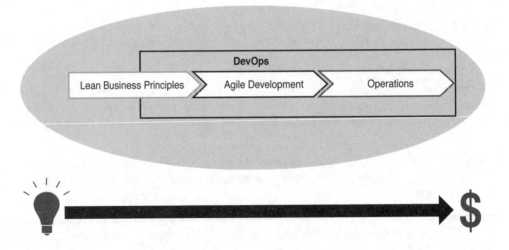

Figure 2-9 *From Idea to Money Streamlined*

The next two sections cover two very important concepts that are fundamental to understanding modern cloud operations. The service catalog and self-service portal are tightly connected but serve different functions in cloud.

Service Catalog

Imagine going to a restaurant and trying to order a meal without the help of some type of menu. You would have to guess or exhaustively interrogate restaurant staff as to what ingredients the restaurant had available, what type of equipment was in the kitchen, and the chef's experience with the type of meal you wanted. You would never know what to expect, or have any clue how long it would take. For the restaurant, there would be no way to control inventory because they would never know what the customer was going to order. The restaurant would not be able to staff appropriately or even know what to charge for a meal. The menu is not just a list of predetermined items to be offered, but is directly tied to the success or failure of the business. This example applies to IT and the difficulty business users have in requesting new services from IT without a menu of services to choose from. For a cloud environment, the service catalog is just as important. Without it, you are stuck with manual processes and no standardization, both of which result in long delivery times and unhappy customers. In effect, a service catalog is not just a nice-to-have administrative exercise, but provides a way to define essential characteristics of cloud, such as on-demand self-service and metered services. Without a service catalog of some sort, it's hard to imagine an effective cloud environment.

A service catalog is a central concept for administering a cloud environment. The various items that IT offers are "services" the business units and segments can consume. A service catalog can be defined as a curated collection of technology-enabled services an organization provides to its customers, employees, or business functions. Think of the service catalog as a tangible representation of the operational capabilities of IT. It includes information about the various offerings, costs, contact points, ordering, and request processes. A properly architected service catalog can mean the difference between an IT group that is struggling to keep up and one that is exceeding expectations. Some examples of service catalog items are

- **Communication services:** Ordering a phone for a new employee, moving a phone to a new desk, upgrades, and replacements
- **Business applications:** Standard line of business applications, middleware, platforms, etc.
- **Personal software:** Personal software applications and licensing
- **Laptops/desktops:** Personal computing hardware lifecycle management and ordering
- **Network:** Network access requests and services
- **Compute:** Compute provisioning, support, and maintenance
- **Storage:** Storage access and support
- **Mobile devices:** Mobile device network access, ordering, and support

A service catalog is crucial to cloud for a number of reasons. First, it aligns the services IT offers to the business and end users. This is one of the more valuable aspects of the service catalog, because it takes the guesswork and inconsistency out of offerings. Second, it can help optimize and streamline service delivery by defining the process and workflow needed. This will help accelerate delivery and responsiveness, which can go a long way toward ensuring happier end users. A service catalog will also help to reduce support costs by giving better visibility into the services most often requested and the true cost to deliver those services. In addition, a service catalog can help to centralize request management for "one-stop ordering" of services.

Service catalog software is used to document the service packages and automate the request management and service delivery process and life cycle. It will often integrate with various systems in your organization, such as accounting, helpdesk, and purchasing systems, to facilitate service delivery. Cisco Prime Service Catalog is an example of just such a software package (as covered in much greater depth in Chapter 5). Service catalog software will often provide the following:

- **Service description:** What the service is/offers and how it can be delivered
- **Service-level agreements:** Expectations and guarantees of expected service availability, security, and performance
- **Service cost:** How much the service costs on a recurring or one-time basis to the department or cost center
- **Compliance:** Ensure compliance with governance and standards through default configurations and preapproved services

A service catalog is built by taking business requirements and aligning them to infrastructure capabilities. End-user requirements and business needs are itemized and analyzed, with the resulting list becoming the basis for the catalog. Infrastructure capabilities, platforms, and systems will also be assessed to determine scale and capacity available. The results of these exercises will produce a detailed menu of services that can be input into the service catalog with the corresponding details. This process is by no means as simple as just described and, depending on the size of your organization, could take significant effort. The point is to look at everything IT does as a regular "offering" to the business, quantify it, create a workflow, and publish it to the catalog. As new technologies and services become available, they can simply be added to the list, providing a great way to introduce new technologies and to enforce corporate standards, governance, and budgeting.

A cloud service catalog should be built with the following guiding principles in mind:

- **Repeatable:** A service catalog item should be standardized and able to be offered to multiple customers at the same time.
- **Measurable:** Service catalog items should be quantifiable measures to ensure accurate cost accounting for the purposes of chargeback or showback.
- **Comprehensive:** The catalog should provide as wide a range of common offerings as possible so that an organization would not need to deviate to a custom build.
- **Scalable:** Services should be capable of scaling up or down easily through automation based on service utilization.
- **Flexible:** New technologies and capabilities can be added quickly to address new business requirements.

The service catalog can also provide a tangible link between what IT offers and what the business is expecting. One of the benefits of creating a service catalog is in monitoring how the organization is operating and what services are used or not used. These metrics give many insights into the supply and demand aspect of cloud delivery. Some of the key performance indicators that can be tracked are

- Services that are used the most and the least
- Successful and unsuccessful service delivery
- Number of customers requesting each service type
- Which group or individuals are using the most or fewest services
- Time to approve service requests
- Financial governance; how much is spent on each service by type

As you can see, the service catalog is a key component of offering a cloud operational model. The next section describes the end-user interface to the service catalog, the self-service portal.

Self-Service Portal

A cloud self-service portal is a web-based central repository for ordering all of the applications, systems, and infrastructure components standardized on by an organization. Just like going to their favorite online retail site, end users can browse the self-service portal to pick and choose what they want and then "check out" at the end, with the price of the items listed and terms of delivery. The mechanics of how end users' requests get delivered to them is not something they need to concern themselves with as recipients of the products or services. They get it on demand and in the amount they need. That's the benefit of cloud offered by an organization to its users. The benefit to the organization is that consistent service and ordering can be automated and delivered at a much lower cost.

A self-service portal is the end-user/line-of-business interface to the IT service catalog. Instead of having to custom build every new service, there is an easy-to-access list of common offerings that the end user can simply select from. No more waiting for manual intervention, or committee meetings to get a new application deployed; you just click a button and in a few minutes the system is up and running and waiting for you to use it. Streamlining this process through backend automation reduces an enormous amount of operational burden, which helps IT run more efficiently and results in much more satisfied customers.

A self-service portal should have the ability to handle user entitlement and role-based access control (RBAC). Not every user in the organization may have the business need or even the technical understanding to provision certain services or applications. The self-service portal software needs to be able to provide differentiated access to users to address what things they can and cannot order. In addition, RBAC features will allow for the monitoring, auditing, and management of the self-service portal system. In the case of Cisco Prime Service Catalog, all of these capabilities are built in to the application with a high degree of customization. Figure 2-10 shows the self-service cloud portal for Prime Service Catalog.

Figure 2-10 *Cisco Prime Service Catalog E-Store*

Policy-based approvals allow an organization to automate the approvals process to streamline ordering and fulfillment of new service requests. If an employee requests a new laptop, for example, there should be a process in place to request manager and/or financial analyst approval before the order is forwarded on to purchasing. These checks and balances may be done in a manual way today, but with a self-service portal it can all be automated and documented by the system.

Services have a life cycle, from initial creation to modification, updating, and ultimately decommissioning of the service when no longer needed. In addition, you can automate the approval process for service catalog items that fall below a certain cost or other threshold. All transactions are documented, so there is a complete audit trail if needed. A self-service portal can provide end-user access to self-service support and management of the full life cycle of their applications. End users can deploy, modify, and decommission their own services. Through web-based forms, the end users can handle much of these activities by themselves without having to involve IT.

IT service and applications are not free and must be accounted for. To address that need, the self-service portal can be customized with cost-accounting and demand-management capabilities. You can define how much a service costs for initial setup, ongoing resource consumption, and utilization.

One of the greatest capabilities of the self-service portal is the automation of repetitive tasks. Once a service is defined, you can leverage integrated automation functionality to initiate the service delivery itself. Everything from the creation of a virtual environment to provisioning a new user account on an internal system can be automated through the self-service portal.

The key benefits of a self-service portal are

- Reduction in manual errors in the ordering process
- Integration with orchestration software to automatically fulfill service requests
- Faster IT service delivery
- Greater agility and flexibility
- Better operational efficiency
- Lower cost

In subsequent chapters we will go into Prime Service Catalog and UCS Director self-service portal capabilities in greater detail. You will be expected to know these concepts for the CCNA Cloud Administration exam.

CHAPTER 3

The Cloud Operation Journey

Over the last few chapters we have covered what cloud is, and how it changes IT operational and consumption models that businesses have become accustomed to. Unless you are starting a brand new business, it is very difficult to flip the switch and move to a fully automated and orchestrated cloud environment. More than anything, the adoption of cloud is both a journey and a process. In this chapter we will discuss some good practices and tactics that are necessary to implement to start benefiting from cloud today.

"Do I Know This Already?" Quiz

The "Do I Know This Already?" quiz allows you to assess whether you should read this entire chapter thoroughly. If you are in doubt about your answers to these questions or your own assessment of your knowledge of the topics, read the entire chapter. Table 3-1 lists the major headings in this chapter and their corresponding "Do I Know This Already?" quiz questions. You can find the answers in Appendix A, "Answers to the 'Do I Know This Already?' Quizzes."

Table 3-1 "Do I Know This Already?" Section-to-Question Mapping

Foundation Topics Section	Questions
Embracing Cloud	1–5
Cisco Domain Ten	7–10

> **Caution** The goal of self-assessment is to gauge your mastery of the topics in this chapter. If you do not know the answer to a question or are only partially sure of the answer, you should mark that question as wrong for purposes of the self-assessment. Giving yourself credit for an answer you correctly guess skews your self-assessment results and might provide you with a false sense of security.

1. What is shadow IT?

    a. Unauthorized use of public cloud resources for corporate software development purposes

    b. IT services that have been compromised by an attacker

    c. Authorized use of public cloud resources that is charged via a credit card

    d. A public cloud offering

2. What are some of the issues with shadow IT?

    a. Higher costs

    b. Data privacy

    c. Compliance and security

    d. All of the above

3. What best describes the difference between cloud automation and orchestration?

    a. Automation is easy and orchestration is hard.

    b. Automation is focused on tasks and orchestration is focused on processes.

    c. None of the above.

    d. All of the above.

4. What is the value of standardization for cloud offerings?

    a. Consistency

    b. Lower total cost

    c. Speed

    d. All of the above

5. Which item best describes workflow from a cloud perspective?

    a. Workflow is the execution and automation of business process.

    b. Workflow must have flow charts and solid documentation to function.

    c. Workflow should be loosely coupled to process for maximum agility.

    d. None of the above.

6. The role of culture is crucial in cloud because:

    a. Culture is not an issue for cloud.

    b. A rigorous culture is necessary for success in cloud.

    c. A fun culture is important.

    d. Cloud changes how people and systems interact.

7. What is Cisco Domain Ten?

    a. The next version of Domain Nine

    b. A framework that is useful in guiding an organization in its cloud transformation

    c. A marketing plan to help business leaders understand cloud

    d. None of the above

8. At what level is virtualization addressed in Domain Ten?

    a. Domain 3

    b. Domain 5

    c. Domain 2

    d. All of the above

9. Which domains are the user portal reliant upon being in place?

    a. Domains 3 and 4

    b. Domains 1 and 5

    c. Domains 5 and 6

    d. All of the above

10. Automation and orchestration are covered in which domain?

    a. Domain 3

    b. Domain 6

    c. Domain 7

    d. None of the above

Foundation Topics

Embracing Cloud

The business climate today requires businesses to continually innovate and move faster than they ever have before. Your company has to find a way to get closer to customers, lower costs, and deliver a better service than your competitors. For many companies that means they have to reinvent themselves on a continual basis to maintain relevance. The disruption caused by new and nimbler competitors has proven to be a real threat for even the largest and most established companies. A small company with a hot new application can capture a surprising amount of market share in a very short time. This threat of digital disruption is requiring a very different way of thinking when it comes to IT and applications. Implementing a cloud operational model and technologies can allow your company to compete in a business environment that rewards speed to market. Ultimately, fast always wins the race.

It is important to recognize at the beginning that cloud is a different IT delivery model from the traditional one that many companies follow. Cloud requires a shift in thinking away from a device-centric approach to application delivery, to one that is focused on the offering of a service. Do your users care which server their application sits on? Do they know if it's in your data center or sitting in someone else's out on the Internet? The use of the service is what really matters to your business, and regardless of how the service is delivered, it must be high quality and reliable. The service can reside within your data center, where you maintain and operate it, in a public cloud provider, where you leverage their infrastructure, or as a Software as a Service (SaaS) application that you simply use. This services-centric approach is one of the reasons why more and more businesses are turning to SaaS to reduce the complexity and cost of maintaining some applications.

The SaaS consumption model can satisfy business and user needs while netting the saving from a provider's lower cost model. Consider email, for example. It is an expensive application to run, not only from a compute and storage perspective, but also in terms of the manpower needed just to keep it operating. With all of the security patching, operating system updates, database maintenance, and configuration requirements, those tasked with keeping email up and running have little time for anything else. Email is a crucial tool for business, no doubt about it, but the cost of offering this service is fairly high. By outsourcing email to a SaaS cloud provider, companies no longer have to dedicate so much time, energy, and resources to delivering the service. The business gets the service it needs, but at a lower cost. Engineers can now work on new projects that help the business serve its customers better.

Shadow IT

More and more we are seeing services that were traditionally run in house moving to a cloud provider. Lines of business have found it quicker to just contract for a service themselves and bypass traditional IT. Why? Because in many cases it is faster than waiting for a traditional IT shop to get a new application rolled out. IT is inundated with a backlog of work from just keeping existing systems up and running, often preventing IT from moving as fast as the business needs. This disconnect has caused numerous problems and tension within the business. Delays rolling out new projects that allow the business to generate more revenue have caused lines of business to go out on their own and embrace external cloud service providers. With all of the advances in self-service offerings and on-demand access to resources and capabilities, it is little wonder that businesses are struggling with "shadow IT," where internal IT is bypassed entirely. While this may seem like a quick fix, it really exacerbates the problem. Some of the major issues of shadow IT are

- **Compliance and governance:** Complying with PCI, SOX, HIPAA, and the rest of the alphabet soup of regulations that IT organizations have to ensure they are compliant with can be a real challenge in a shadow IT world. Lack of compliance can be very costly, and if you aren't in full control of your IT environment, it can be easy to run afoul of these regulations. Without the appropriate data protection controls in place, your business can be at considerable risk from shadow IT.

- **Technology and management silos:** Who manages the service? In a shadow IT situation, it becomes the responsibility of the part of the organization that signed up for the service. It's not a full-time job and often the people responsible for managing the service are not trained to do it properly. Things like single sign-on and other services also will not be available without getting IT involved, so you will have separate account access and passwords that need to be managed.

- **Application portability:** Moving your application from one cloud provider to another can be very difficult or, in some cases, impossible without rewriting parts of the application. Many cloud providers have lots of advanced features that you can use as a service within your application, but those services are only available if you are their customer. This can act as a lock that will prevent you from negotiating better rates, or finding a different provider. Lines of business may not understand this impact when building applications in the cloud on their own.

- **Data privacy:** Who can see the data, and where is it stored? This has always been a major concern for businesses considering a move to the cloud. They are still responsible for keeping information safe, but now they don't get full visibility into the data protection controls that their provider has implemented.

- **Higher cost:** Shadow IT can get expensive really fast. One of the benefits of having a centralized purchasing process is that you can leverage volume discounts and track and monitor overall usage costs. By going off on their own, each department will be a separate "customer" to the provider, resulting in serious duplication of effort and less optimization of resources.

- **Lack of consistency:** If the accounting department needs project management software, for example, they will go out and get whatever they feel meets their needs. If another group, like HR, needs the same software, they will not be privy to the fact that accounting already has an application that they could simply use. Instead, HR may pick a different platform, which may be more expensive and totally incompatible. This lack of consistency can interfere with business logic and make it harder for different groups within the same business to work together.

The Journey Starts Here

To stay relevant and help the business better achieve its goals, an IT organization is going to have to embrace a mixture of public, private, and hybrid services. Some applications will be better suited for running on premises and others will work fine in a public cloud. There will also be a need for applications that are in a private cloud and a public cloud for scaling and better geographic performance. The key is to catalog the capabilities and requirements of existing and new applications and match them to the delivery model that makes the most sense. In this way IT becomes a broker of services and can begin to embrace cloud as a business enabler, as discussed in Chapter 2, "Cloud: A New Operations Model for IT." Through this approach, IT becomes a better business partner and can be a driving force for better business results. IT has to move away from being just a cost center and become a new business-acceleration engine.

Unfortunately, there is no magic cloud bean that you can plant in your data center. Realistically, you need to expect a multiyear journey as you change how you operate IT services and implement a robust cloud infrastructure. That's not to say that your company can't benefit today from cloud capabilities; it is just not going to happen all at once. How fast your organization can transition to cloud depends on its size and appetite for change. A large enterprise with thousands of applications will take longer than a small organization to transition due to the complexity of the environment of a large business. You must consider the fact that you are in effect rewriting the rule book for how you deploy, maintain, and operate business applications. You also must consider the various departments and divisions that will need to be included to ensure that they are not unduly impacted by the move to the cloud. Regardless of the size of the organization, it is wise to start your cloud journey on small, focused areas of the business that can handle the changes that cloud will require.

In Chapter 1, "An Introduction to Cloud," you were introduced to IaaS, PaaS, and SaaS as deployment models for cloud services. There are many existing applications and services in your business for which you can find opportunities to take advantage of cloud practices and deployment models. Some good areas to look at are

- **Collaboration applications:** These applications allow for internal collaboration between employees and external collaboration with customers. There are numerous SaaS offerings as well as cloud-friendly private options like Cisco Spark.

- **Business support applications:** These apps are important to the business but often are expensive to run and require dedicated expertise. Examples include email, marketing, CRM, and sales apps.

- **Customer-facing web applications:** Dynamic scaling and availability can all be increased by moving these services to a cloud environment.

- **Branch office infrastructure services:** Telephony, Wi-Fi, and networking can all be moved to the cloud to simplify management and support. Cisco Meraki is a prime example of leveraging the cloud to reduce cost and ease administrative burden.

- **Disaster recovery services:** You certainly could build a dedicated backup site, but it often makes more sense financially to use a cloud provider to handle these services.

- **Development test environments:** This is one of the most useful areas to use cloud. Developers need access to test environments that closely resemble production, and they often need these test beds on demand. Implementing cloud can help keep them from trying to solve this need themselves (shadow IT).

- **File storage:** File storage is a necessity for every one of your users. With good Internet access, a centrally managed cloud storage solution is a very effective way to provide this service at a lower overall operational cost.

In the next section we discuss Domain Ten, a full framework for cloud adoption that Cisco has built. It is a fantastic resource for planning and developing your own journey to the cloud.

Cisco Domain Ten

Domain Ten is a framework that can be useful in planning an organization's cloud transformation. It consists of ten key elements that cover everything from the infrastructure all the way to organization and governance. The intent of the framework is to map businesses-specific desires and outcomes to the cloud capabilities IT can offer, which can be very valuable in creating a road map for planning a transition to a public, private, or hybrid cloud. The best part of Domain Ten is that it builds capabilities in a natural way, from the infrastructure components to operations and governance. By ensuring each domain is adequately cared for, you will minimize gaps that often cause cloud projects to fail. Cisco even offers a fee-based assessment service that will map your environment and give you recommendations on what you need to do next. Figure 3-1 shows a graphical representation of the Domain Ten framework.

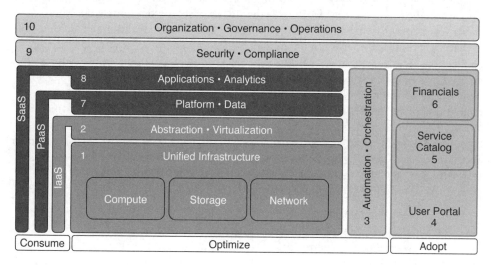

Figure 3-1 *Domain Ten*

Domain 1: Unified Infrastructure

There are two primary components of Domain 1: infrastructure, which includes the servers, network, and storage, and environment, which consist of the space, power, and cooling capabilities within the data center. The infrastructure forms the foundation for the resource layer on top of which your cloud environment will be built. The goal is to standardize on hardware components to make it simpler to add capacity and maintain the data center in as much of a plug-and-play fashion as possible. If you need more compute, simply add another server and add it to the pool of resources at the infrastructure layer. The same thing applies to both network and storage. It's just easier and often more cost effective to manage a consistent set of hardware components. While a single set of standard components may not be feasible, the goal is to minimize the number of unique components as much as possible. By doing this you are able to more easily pool like resources, which is an essential foundation for virtualization and allows for dynamic provisioning. In addition, it is important to have infrastructure that is designed from the ground up to operate as a system, which will help simplify operations, lower overall costs, make virtualization and automation less complex, and help transition legacy systems to a modern architecture.

Environmental factors dictate the amount of resource you can host within your data center. Network infrastructure takes up space, needs power, and has to be kept cool to operate adequately. You must plan out your growth strategy to take these factors into consideration. High-density computing requires less space but significantly better cooling, and your existing data center design can easily become overutilized.

Domain 2: Abstraction and Virtualization

Virtualization allows for better utilization of data center resources by enabling you to run on a single server multiple workloads that in the past would require a dedicated server for each. Most organizations have made the shift to virtualization technologies in their data centers, and it is not uncommon to see 70 to 90 percent virtualization of applications. The benefit of virtualization is that it allows a common set of resources to be used in very efficient ways. Server virtualization has driven advances in storage and network virtualization as well. Storage virtualization combines physical storage from numerous storage devices to appear as one device, with scalable capacity. Network virtualization combines available network resources into a single pool of resources that can be redeployed in real time to meet user demand. CPU, memory, network, and storage can be added or subtracted as the application needs it, either with the click of a button or automatically. The flexibility, scalability, and resource pooling afforded by virtualization are core tenets of building a cloud infrastructure.

Abstraction provides a logical representation of the physical hardware underneath. By making this separation, you remove the traditional dependencies of specific hardware such as drivers and low-level device control code. Anyone who has had to load server-specific drivers in an operating system knows how painful it is if you have to move that application to a new server (even from the same vendor). Abstraction removes those problems and allows the application and operating system to be very portable. The independence from the hardware enables an organization to be flexible and to support many different types of internal customers. Users don't care which server their application is running on in the data center. They just want it to be fast and always available.

There are many different technologies that you can choose to enable virtualization. Microsoft, VMware, KVM, and Docker containers are all viable platforms to run your virtualized environment on. Each has its own specific pros and cons. It is important to standardize as much as possible to simplify the administrative burden. A multi-hypervisor environment doesn't have to be a bad thing, but you have to plan for the differences in architecture for things like QoS, policy, security, and metrics.

Another important aspect of Domain 2 is understanding the types of virtualized workloads that are going to be required. Some applications work very well in a virtual environment, whereas others require all of the CPU and memory a server can supply and, as such, work best on a dedicated physical server. Will your organization be virtual only in your cloud offerings, or offer bare metal as an option as well? In the public cloud you often must use virtualization in a cost-effective manner. These decisions will impact the types of offerings your organization will be able to provide within the service catalog.

Figure 3-2 shows Domains 1 and 2 and their functional relationship in the Domain Ten framework.

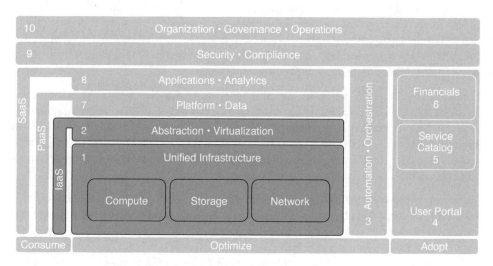

Figure 3-2   *Domains 1 and 2 of the Domain Ten Framework*

Domain 3: Automation and Orchestration

What is the difference between automation and orchestration? While they are similar concepts, their scope is ultimately where the core difference lies. *Automation* is accomplished on a task or a function without human intervention. When you open your garage door, the light comes on automatically and shuts off after a period of time. While this is a very simple example of automation, it highlights one of its most important values. It is great for repetitive and monotonous activities. If you had unlimited money, you could hire someone to flip on the light switch and then turn it off when you went in to the house. Could you even imagine how boring and wasteful that job would be? Unfortunately, there are a lot of similar activities that you must endure today within IT. From a speed perspective, a human being could never accomplish the same task as quickly as a computer. Computers are excellent at executing repetitive tasks quickly and consistently. Human beings, on the other hand, do a poor job with repetitive tasks, often introducing inconsistencies, which prevents standardization. The speed you get from automation is substantial. Automation technologies also don't have to take days off for vacations. They work around the clock, on holidays, and on weekends without getting tired, like the good robots that they are.

Orchestration is the sequential coordination and direction of automated processes. Continuing our garage light example, orchestration is a layer above automation that takes inputs from tasks and acts on the bigger picture. Using orchestration, I can detect that the garage door light automatically came on and infer that the owner of the home was coming inside. That trigger from the light could be used to kick off a workflow that lowers the temperature in the home (in summer), turns on the hallway light, and plays some music. Orchestration is the "brains" behind cloud, and is used to translate complex workflows into something actionable. It also is the mechanism used to tie business logic to technology.

Domain 3 is where IT begins the cloud journey in earnest. What starts as a desire to make managing all of the complexity of a traditional data center easier can turn into a need for automation technology that can remove as much manual work as possible. It doesn't take long to figure out that many IT processes are filled with repetitive tasks that don't add value and suck up way too much time and energy. If you are manually provisioning infrastructure today, using automation technologies will seem like magic.

In simple terms, orchestration is the logical sequencing of automated tasks. Think of a conductor of an orchestra, responsible for ensuring that a melody is created from the sound generated by each of the instruments. Orchestration applies workflow and business logic to automation technologies to produce the same effect in IT. The full life cycle of an application can be orchestrated from provisioning, patching, and decommissioning without a single human being having to touch the infrastructure underneath.

Orchestration requires customization to be truly effective. While there are many good products from Cisco to help right off of the shelf, the real power comes from mapping IT's workflow into instructions that the automation/orchestration tools can follow. This means that you have to understand and document the various processes you want to automate. It's time consuming but worth it. You simply can't have a functioning cloud environment without this step.

Figure 3-3 shows Domain 3 in the Domain Ten framework.

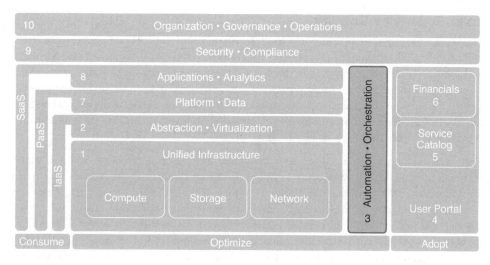

Figure 3-3 *Domain 3 of the Domain Ten Framework: Automation and Orchestration*

Domain 4: User Portal (Self-Service Portal)

The user portal is the way in which your internal customers will interact with IT in a functional cloud environment. There are typically two main components: the customer portal itself, which is a web page that allows for the ordering of IT services, and the workflow and backend systems that are responsible for delivering the requested services through automation. The user portal is the face of IT and, as such, needs to be easy to interact with and request services from. It's essential that the interface be built from the user's perspective and hide as much of the backend complexity as possible. Bob in accounting doesn't need to know what VLAN his accounting server needs to be in, for example; the system should automatically determine that as part of the service delivery.

Role-based access control is another important aspect of this domain. Who can access what services? If you are a developer, you need access to different services than those an office administrator needs access to. Is there an approval process and, if so, who needs to be part of that process? How is software licensing handled? You could easily run out of licenses without a way to automate the delivery and reclamation of unneeded applications. All of these types of questions need to be explored for the customer portal to be effective. (Domains 9 and 10, discussed later, cover security and governance in more detail and from a top-down perspective.)

Domain 4 is tightly coupled with Domains 5 and 6 because it can be thought of as a presentation of the service catalog and financial chargeback/showback models in use. The self-service portal is responsible for providing cost estimates, delivery times, and service operational status. The user simply needs to know what their requirements are so that they can select the best offering from the service catalog.

Domain 5: Service Catalog

The service catalog is a map for your cloud. It will describe all of the various services IT will offer. It is like a menu in a restaurant; whatever is in the catalog is something that the end user can order. As mentioned in the prior section, the self-service portal is where this information will be displayed, and it may also include details about the financial obligation tied to the service. The concept of the service catalog was covered in Chapter 2. Domain 5 is about the creation of an effective service catalog, in which one of the most important aspects is the standardization of IT offerings.

The service catalog needs a ruthless level of standardization to be effective. Without standardization you simply cannot offer a viable self-service cloud offering. An easy way to better understand the role of standardization is to look at the construction industry. There are two types of home builders: custom builders and spec home builders. Both will build you a house, but in very different ways. The custom builder offers the most options. If you can draw it on paper, the custom builder can potentially build it for you. You will get exactly what you want, from the type and brand of hardwood floor to the color of the bathroom toilet paper holder. It is completely customizable. It can also become very expensive really quickly. That Italian marble you want might be very difficult to attain and be at a premium price because it is not as commonly bought. The builder is going to pass that cost on to you, inflating your ultimate bill. A custom home will also take longer to build. All of the detail work requires extra time and added labor to complete. These builders don't often build a large number of homes in a year, so they need to make as much as possible on the ones they do build, which inflates the cost even further.

The spec home builder, on the other hand, has a very different business model. They typically have a limited set of floor plans, with four or five models at most, which makes building each home simpler. They also offer a specific set of customized options (colors, carpet types, tile, etc.) that are pre-priced and able to be added to the home easily. These builders are looking to minimize the variability between homes so that they can build them faster, taking advantage of consistency to drive down the cost of building. All of these factors give the spec home builder the ability to better anticipate their potential profit and build a larger number of homes.

Traditional IT processes build custom apps, whereas the cloud model looks to deliver spec apps for all the same reasons that spec home builders choose to deliver spec homes. It is less costly and faster to deliver something that you can replicate, where all of the nuances of the platform and configuration are already worked out in advance for you. If you want to move fast, you have to be ruthless in defining the standard offerings within your service catalog. If you remove as much variability as possible, the process of accounting for the true cost of the offering is dramatically simpler.

Standardized offerings are also much easier to automate. Automation can handle some variability, but the more you add, the more complex the logic becomes and the more potential that exists for failures to creep into the equation. Complexity is what you are trying to remove with cloud, not add it back in. The service catalog isn't just a one-time exercise, but rather needs to change based on new technologies and services being offered. The self-service portal represents the service catalog to the end user and should enable easy changes to service details and map back to the associated workflows necessary for delivery.

Domain 6: Financials

The financials domain is the area in which you define the mechanism and cost structure for usage-based IT chargeback and showback. This will allow your users to pay for the services and resources that they request from the user portal. Because cloud is based predominantly on a utility model, just like electricity, you are charged for the amount you use.

In cloud you pay for the CPU, storage, and bandwidth used by your applications. The hard part of creating these cost models is to define a realistic "cost" for the service. You have to factor in the cost of hardware, power and cooling, network infrastructure, and software, as well as any labor or administration costs associated with provisioning the service itself. Even if the service is fully automated, there is a cost associated with building and maintaining the service that needs to be accounted for.

Chargeback is important to pay for a service, but what about the question of whether or not a service needs to be in house or moved to the public cloud? This almost always comes down to a question of cost and risk. Is the security risk sufficiently high to justify the additional cost of hosting the service within your own data center, or is it so much cheaper in the public cloud that it is worth the risk of not having complete control over the application? To answer this, you need to have a solid understanding of the real costs of the application or service, as detailed earlier, to get an apples-to-apples comparison. You can, of course, choose a hybrid approach, in which case you should have a strategy that supports the coexistence of private and public cloud solutions. This way, a workload or application can be appropriately placed based on its technical and business requirements, and taking into account any trade-offs in flexibility, security, and costs.

Domains 1 through 6 are the foundation of a cloud environment, and are what is needed to provide Infrastructure as a Service. IT is opened up like an online retailer, enabling users to consume services as if they were buying books or toasters. A private cloud doesn't have to be the only service offered; you can augment with public cloud services and capabilities too. Figure 3-4 shows Domains 4 through 6 as the combined user portal.

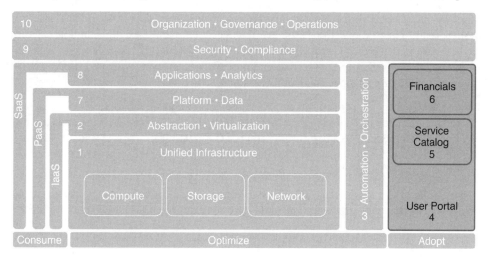

Figure 3-4   *Domains 4 Through 6: User Portal Components*

Domain 7: Platform and Data

Platform in cloud refers to the selection of software elements that sit on top of the infra-structure and run the applications themselves. There are typically three components that make up the platform domain:

- Operating systems
- Middleware
- Database

All of these components are provisioned through the user portal and built on demand. If a developer needs an operating system and a database for her new application, she can simply select it from the catalog and provision the infrastructure and software needed for it auto-matically. This capability is in essence a Platform as a Service.

The platform domain is one of the most important to create strong standards for. If IT cus-tomers can choose any OS combination, with any CPU or storage requirement they see fit, then the ability to automate simply disappears. You have to decide what you will and will not support so that you can provide consistent and replicable offerings. The benefit is the ability to move away from manual and custom provisioning into a highly automated cloud environment.

Domain 8: Applications and Analytics

Applications are what run and support the business, and it is IT's job to make sure they are available and operating as they should. An application can be a home-grown custom app, an off-the-shelf commercial app, or a SaaS app. The goal of this domain is to build an applica-tion strategy to determine the best deployment model that meets the needs of the business. All applications need to be assessed for cloud readiness. Many legacy applications are just not a good fit for a cloud environment because they were not developed to take advantage of cloud infrastructure and may need to be rewritten (modernized) or upgraded.

Many businesses are still reluctant to host the most sensitive of data in the public cloud and, as such, tend to keep applications used in HR and accounting, for example, in house. Really, any application that stores personally identifiable information (PII), doesn't have a web front end, or needs direct access to backend processing/mainframe will need special atten-tion when considering a move to a public cloud.

Beyond the security concerns of data privacy, there are a number of application characteris-tics that need to be considered before moving into a cloud environment. First and foremost, was the application built to allow for portability? Older applications were conceived and architected before virtualization was a viable option. Their inherent architectures just don't do well when virtualized.

Maybe some of the components are looking for specific pieces of hardware, like a crypto card, meaning they will continue to need dedicated hardware until they are rewritten or retired.

Where data is stored can also be a challenge for legacy applications. If your application needs data access to production systems, this could be problematic if hosted in a public provider. The application would have to either replicate the data over the Internet or pull the data directly from the production data store. Both of these can be design nightmares if not properly planned for.

Hosting the application yourself, migrating to the public cloud, or using a SaaS offering are a few of your choices. This analysis of your applications is the first step in determining the viability of migrating an app to the cloud. Figure 3-5 shows the Domain 7 (PaaS) and Domain 8 (SaaS) layers.

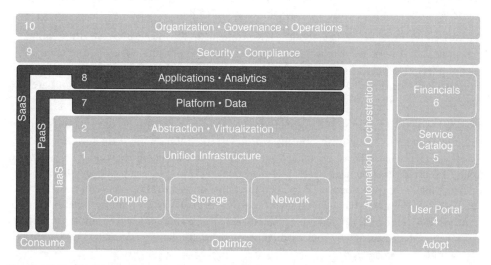

Figure 3-5   *Domains 7 and 8: PaaS and SaaS*

Domain 9: Security and Compliance

While cloud security and compliance sit in Domain 9, they apply to the entire cloud stack. Securing the provisioning process and safeguarding the various components of the cloud environment must be planned out and implemented. Every industry has specific regulations and laws that businesses need to comply with. Documenting and implementing the necessary security controls and safeguards keep data safe, and your CEO out of the newspapers.

Domain 10: Organization, Governance, and Operations

Organization, governance, and operations comprise the tenth and final domain of the Domain Ten framework. This domain details how the business will structure IT groups and departments, the safeguards and enforcement of corporate standards, and operational processes and procedures. Because you don't operate a cloud the same way you do a traditional IT environment, your staffing and skill requirements will be different. Do you train existing resources, or hire someone new? Governance issues will always pop up as you embrace cloud. Who gets access to what? What services should be put in the service catalog? Last but not least is the need for strong operational models that fit cloud. Ideally you will have significant automation within your cloud, because manual processes just don't work in a cloud model.

The role of culture and organizational structure in cloud is very important to its success. Cloud changes how applications, data center infrastructure, and devices interact with each other, but it also changes how people interact with IT as well. Automation is king and manual interaction is avoided at all costs. This is a very different environment than many people and IT organizations are used to. When you move to a cloud operational model, you just can't continue doing things like you used to. Change is hard and can be difficult for an organization to embrace. Do you rip off the bandage or pull it off slowly? That's up to the individual organization to decide. While change often is easy to implement, making it stick can be very difficult if your own people are resistant to it.

The various teams that have been built up over time in an IT organization are often in their own silos. Developers, security groups, storage administrators, and infrastructure teams are insulated from the needs of the other groups within IT. Cloud changes all of that, by breaking down many of those barriers. People have to work together because the systems are integrated.

A workflow is the execution and automation that follows a specific set of procedures and activities in order to accomplish a business process task. Think of all of the processes you follow on a daily basis. From brushing your teeth to making breakfast. More than likely you follow a routine that you have developed over time. This routine is a workflow. In IT there are many different workflows used to keep the lights on and the data center infrastructure running. When building a cloud environment, the goal is to leverage automation and orchestration as much as possible to accelerate activities and minimize the amount of effort needed. In order to automate your cloud environment, you have to document and codify your workflow processes.

A workflow is not just a combination of technical steps, but is also inclusive of the business process. Deploying a new server would include purchasing and acquiring the server, asset tagging, and depreciation accounting in addition to loading software and physically installing it. Complete workflow documentation is essential to successful cloud automation because it provides you all of the details necessary to implement the workflow in your cloud orchestration software, such as UCS Director. Workflows help you build the automation rules for your self-service user portal.

When you document a workflow, the goal is to leverage the lean techniques discussed in Chapter 2 to identify the minimum set of instructions necessary to achieve the desired outcome of the workflow. Simplification and optimization can be the benefit of this process, because they will also remove excess complexity in your automation scripts, which means less to troubleshoot.

When documenting the workflow, you start at the beginning and finish at the end result. In the middle will be all of the steps needed to move your process along to its desired result. You may also have decision questions that occur throughout the process that cause you to need to accomplish different activities. For example, say you want to document the process of mailing a letter. Your first step is to write the letter, the second step is to put it in an envelope, the third is to put a stamp on it, and the fourth is to drop it in the mailbox. Pretty simple, right? What if you don't have stamps? Step 3 could then represent a decision step where you first check if you have stamps. If yes, then you put a stamp on the envelope. If no, then you need to create another set of steps for acquiring stamps. This is the same methodology that you will use to create automation workflows within UCS Director. Figure 3-6 shows an example workflow decision tree.

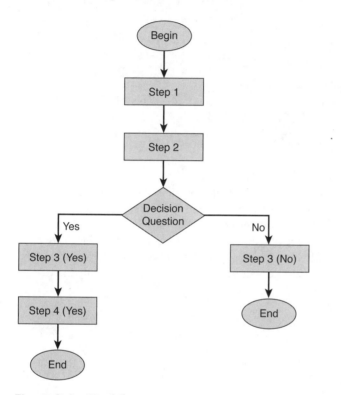

Figure 3-6   *Workflow Decision Tree*

By automating workflows, you can greatly reduce the time it takes to process the task and also reduce the potential for errors that could be introduced in a manual process. The best part of a workflow is that it provides a level of visibility and assurance that every step in the process is followed consistently every single time. From a security and compliance perspective, this is a fantastic benefit, because so many security issues occur from people just not following standard practices. With automation, you can build the level of security required into the workflow itself, making it easier to pass security audits.

Figure 3-7 shows the final two domains.

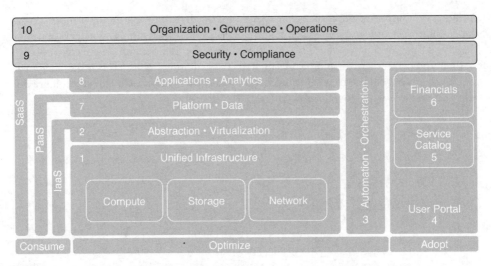

Figure 3-7   *Domains 9 and 10 of the Domain Ten Framework*

Cisco Domain Ten is a good high-level framework that can help ensure all of the right components are in place to have a successful cloud environment. Each organization will have different cloud needs, so Domain Ten should not be looked at as a one-size-fits-all solution. Maybe IaaS is all you are interested in deploying today. The most important thing is that to get there, you need all of the first six domains in place. By focusing on thinking through and developing the right foundation for the next building block, you will greatly increase your chances for success.

This chapter covers the following topics:

4.0   Cloud Systems Management and Monitoring

4.2   Describe the components of Cisco UCS Director

    4.2.a   Describe Infrastructure Management and Monitoring

    4.2.b   Describe Orchestration

    4.2.c   Describe the Portal

    4.2.d   Describe the Bare Metal Agent

4.4   Describe the components of Cisco IAC

    4.4.a   Describe Cisco Process Orchestrator

    4.4.b   Describe Cisco Prime Service Catalog

    4.4.c   Describe Cisco Server Provisioner

CHAPTER 4

Cisco Cloud Automation/ Orchestration Suites

The previous chapters have been about providing context and background to better understand the topics you will find on the CCNA Cloud Admin exam. As mentioned previously, the exam focuses very heavily on the operational aspects of the day-to-day running of a cloud environment. This chapter provides an overview of Cisco automation and orchestration suites and introduces the UCS Director platform, which you will be expected to know for the exam.

"Do I Know This Already?" Quiz

The "Do I Know This Already?" quiz allows you to assess whether you should read this entire chapter thoroughly or jump to the "Exam Preparation Tasks" section. If you are in doubt about your answers to these questions or your own assessment of your knowledge of the topics, read the entire chapter. Table 4-1 lists the major headings in this chapter and their corresponding "Do I Know This Already?" quiz questions. You can find the answers in Appendix A, "Answers to the 'Do I Know This Already?' Quizzes."

Table 4-1 "Do I Know This Already?" Section-to-Question Mapping

Foundation Topics Section	Questions
Cisco Cloud Solutions	1–2
Introducing UCS Director	3–5
Orchestration with UCS Director	6–8
UCS Director Baremetal Agent	9–10

Caution The goal of self-assessment is to gauge your mastery of the topics in this chapter. If you do not know the answer to a question or are only partially sure of the answer, you should mark that question as wrong for purposes of the self-assessment. Giving yourself credit for an answer you correctly guess skews your self-assessment results and might provide you with a false sense of security.

1. What are three components of Cisco ONE Enterprise Cloud Suite? (Choose three.)

   a. Prime Service Catalog

   b. UCS Director

   c. UCS Manager

   d. Intercloud Fabric

2. What are two Cisco OpenStack offerings? (Choose two.)

   a. Metacloud

   b. Nova

   c. UCSO

   d. Cloud Foundry

3. Which hypervisors does UCS Director support? (Choose three.)

   a. Microsoft Hyper-V

   b. VMware vSphere

   c. Red Hat KVM

   d. Xen

4. What are the two primary components of UCS Director? (Choose two.)

   a. Bare Metal Support

   b. Baremetal Agent

   c. UCS Director Virtual Machine

   d. UCS Director License

5. How many service nodes are installed for a small deployment of USCD?

   a. One

   b. Six

   c. Two

   d. None of the above

6. What is the purpose of Workflow Designer in UCS Director?

   a. Graphical interface for constructing automation workflows

   b. A workflow execution engine

   c. Integration with OpenStack

   d. None of the above

7. How is a trigger used in UCS Director?

   a. Create an abstraction layer for workflow implementation details

   b. Automation tool

   c. A workflow variable

   d. None of the above

8. Which of the following best describes a task?

    a. UCS Director workflow

    b. A technical term for automation

    c. Smallest atomic (self-contained) action

    d. None of the above

9. What protocols does the BMA use to bootstrap a server?

    a. TFTP

    b. DHCP

    c. PXE

    d. All of the above

10. How is Baremetal Agent deployed?

    a. A separate virtual machine that must be integrated with UCS Director

    b. Licensed in UCS Director and deployed as a module

    c. As part of ACI

    d. None of the above

Foundation Topics

Cisco Cloud Solutions

The CCNA Cloud Admin exam focuses heavily on testing your understanding of the core components of Cisco ONE Enterprise Cloud Suite, which are UCS Director, Prime Service Catalog, Intercloud Fabric for Business, and Virtual Application Cloud Segmentation (VACS). In addition, you are expected to know the basic components of Cisco Intelligent Automation for Cloud (CIAC). In addition to these cloud stacks, Cisco also offers solutions based on OpenStack, which is an open source cloud management suite. While you are not expected to know the OpenStack offerings for the exam, it is important that you see how these various solutions and bundles fit into the Cisco cloud portfolio.

Automated Service Delivery

As mentioned in Chapter 3, "The Cloud Operation Journey," IT is undergoing some significant changes to meet the needs of the business. The business is demanding faster and more cost-effective services. The business expects IT to be more than a cost center by becoming a competitive differentiator that enables new ways to reach customers and take advantage of new market opportunity. In short, IT needs to evolve past its traditional operation model and embrace a new way of delivering services and value back to the business.

This shift from the old IT model to the new IT model will leverage cloud in a very significant way. To this end, Cisco cloud management suites are built to facilitate this operational change. Cloud can become the change agent that allows the IT organization to evolve. Table 4-2 shows some of the differences between the two IT models.

Table 4-2   Old IT Versus New IT

Old IT	New IT
Customized services and applications	Ruthless standardization
Manual provisioning of services	Fully automated infrastructure and business services
Costly management and maintenance	Time and cost savings
Inflexible and fragile infrastructure	Agile and flexible infrastructure
Poor predictability for projects	Predictable and consistent projects
Small number of highly scalable service offerings	Smaller number of scalable service offerings

Why does it take so long for IT to deliver a new service or offering? To figure that out, you have to take a look at the service delivery process. When a new project is initiated, there is a very sequential and time-consuming chain of events that occurs. The first step is to gather the requirements and architect a solution. After the architecture is determined, the design process begins, where you map the requirements of your architecture to a technical platform. The next question is, where do you put the new hardware? Is there enough rack space, power, and cooling? Once that is sorted out, then the manual procurement of hardware, installation, configuration, and security happen. Once everything is finally up and running, then the new application and underlying hardware need to be tested. By the time all of this is finished, the application can finally be put into production. Weeks or months have passed before the business can benefit from the new application at all. Figure 4-1 shows the traditional service delivery process.

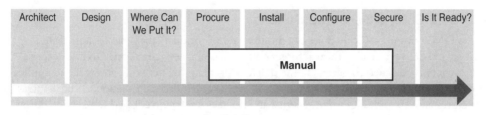

Figure 4-1 *Traditional Service Delivery Process*

To embrace this new IT model, the service delivery process needs to shift from a linear approach to one that is streamlined and automated. In this model, when a new project is initiated, a solution is architected based on the application requirements. From there the design process occurs, utilizing standard pretested software packages. Operating systems, databases, and other components are standardized on and used for new applications instead of building everything from scratch. At this point automated self-service provision is initiated, giving you the platform you need for your new application in minutes instead of weeks. In Figure 4-2 you can see how much simpler the process is to deploy a new application in an automated service delivery environment. Much of the manual process associated with determining where an application will go in the data center, the provisioning process itself, and validating that the application is up and running will all be handled by the cloud management software.

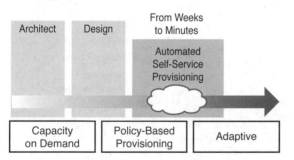

Figure 4-2 *Automatic Service Delivery Process*

Some of the key benefits of automated service delivery are

- On-demand resource access
- Standardized provisioning
- It's better able to adapt to the needs of the business
- Faster deployment times
- Integrated pretested security
- Flexibility and agility

Cisco has brought to market a number of platforms to facilitate on-demand automated service delivery. In the next section you will be introduced to the main cloud software suites that Cisco currently offers. For the exam, you will need to know Cisco ONE Enterprise Cloud Suite and Cisco Intelligent Automation for Cloud. Cisco's OpenStack solutions are mentioned as well to round out the portfolio view.

Cisco ONE Enterprise Cloud Suite

Cisco ONE Enterprise Cloud Suite is a modular set of products that enables automated on-demand delivery of IT infrastructure, applications, and services. Cisco ONE Enterprise Cloud Suite is designed to automate the delivery of compute, network, storage, and applications across both virtual and physical pools of resources. It uses automation to fulfill infrastructure requests and can ensure security and policies are followed. The self-service portal approach enables users within the organization to request their own services, freeing up resources and speeding up the delivery process of new applications. The portal includes

- A modern storefront for ordering services based on your business policies and governance requirements
- Role-based access to service catalog items, such as virtual machines, and application templates
- Full pricing and chargeback models to allow lines of business to "pay" for IT services
- Tracking and monitoring of service usage
- Prebuilt templates for enterprise applications
- A customer application stack designer

Cisco ONE Enterprise Cloud Suite consists of the following four primary components, as shown in Figure 4-3:

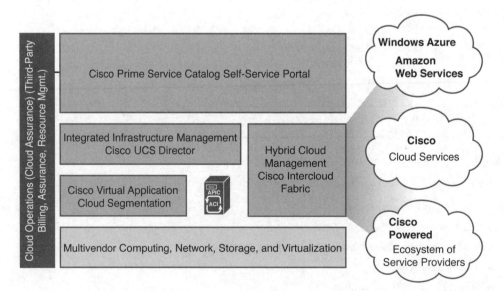

Figure 4-3 *Cisco ONE Enterprise Cloud Suite*

- **Cisco Primes Service Catalog:** End-user storefront for IT and data center services

- **UCS Director:** Converged infrastructure management (compute, storage, and network), automation and orchestration of service catalog items

- **Intercloud Fabric for Business:** Hybrid cloud management that supports virtual machines on Amazon Web Services, Microsoft Azure, and Cisco Intercloud partners

- **Virtual Application Cloud Segmentation (VACS):** Provides secure application segmentation and provisioning of virtualized security services

Cisco Intelligent Automation for Cloud

Cisco Intelligent Automation for Cloud (CIAC) is a bundled cloud solution along the same lines as Cisco ONE Enterprise Cloud Suite in that it includes a number of components that work together to deliver a comprehensive cloud management platform. The primary difference between the two solutions comes down to the level of customization and integration you are looking to achieve with your existing backend management systems. Cisco ONE Enterprise Cloud Suite is designed to work out of the box with Cisco and third-party products, but you are limited to a finite set of tested integration components. With CIAC you have functionality out of the box, but can extend it to support a much wider range of systems that you may have in your environment. CIAC is also built with multiple-cloud and multitenant capabilities. Most organization that have deployed CIAC have customized it to match their own workflows and backend systems to support complex IaaS use cases. For the purposes of the CCNA Cloud Admin exam, you will need to know the core components of CIAC at a high level, but will not be expected to know all of the nuances and details of how the various components are configured.

CIAC is a suite of products, or "software stack," that includes the following core components:

- **Cisco Prime Service Catalog:** This is the same self-service portal and IT service catalog that is bundled with Cisco ONE Enterprise Cloud Suite and serves the same function as well. Chapter 5, "Cisco Prime Service Catalog," and other parts of this book cover this component in great detail.

- **Cisco Process Orchestrator (CPO):** CPO performs the automation of IT process and end-to-end service delivery across the entire IT landscape. CPO is the brains behind CIAC and is highly extensible and customizable with over 500 extension points. It has more than 800 prebuilt workflows and offers consistency with industry best practices such as IT Information Library (ITIL). Through the use of automation packs, CPO can support practically any IT service your organization may want to offer. In addition, it includes extensive reporting and auditing capabilities.

- **Cisco Server Provisioner:** Cisco Server Provisioner is built to provide similar capabilities as the Baremetal Agent (BMA) with UCS Director in that it allows for automating the provisioning, cloning, bare-metal recovery, initial configuration, and software installation of a server through the Preboot Execution Environment (PXE) boot process. The PXE boot process is covered in more detail later in this chapter through the discussion of UCS Director's BMA. As of this writing the Cisco Server Provisioner is no longer sold by Cisco or included in the latest version of CIAC. It is mentioned here because it is still part of the CCNA Cloud Admin exam blueprint. Figure 4-4 shows an expanded functional view of CIAC.

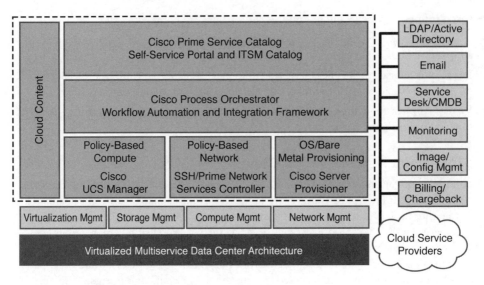

Figure 4-4 *Expanded Functional View of CIAC*

Cisco OpenStack Solutions

OpenStack is an open source software platform that can be used for cloud computing. It is not one piece of software, but numerous connected modules that operate together to control data center infrastructure. It can be managed through a web-based dashboard, through the command line, or by programming it through RESTful APIs. The OpenStack community is very active, with many large companies (Cisco included) contributing to the project regularly. The main components of OpenStack are as follows:

- **Compute (Nova):** This component is responsible for managing and automating pools of computer resources and is designed to work with many different virtualization technologies and bare-metal systems too.

- **Image service (Glance):** The image service handles the discovery, registration, and delivery services associated with disk and server images. These images can be used as templates for virtual machines or containers that can be called from a service catalog. Glance does not store the actual images themselves, but acts as a catalog for finding and retrieving them.

- **Object storage (Swift):** Swift is a scalable storage service that writes objects and files across multiple hard disks throughout the data center. Swift handles the data replication and integrity within the server clusters, allowing the addition of more capacity by simply adding a new resource to the cluster. If a hard disk fails, Swift will write that hard disk's data to another part of the cluster automatically.

- **Dashboard (Horizon):** Horizon is the graphical user interface to OpenStack for provisioning and automation of cloud resources. This interface can be customized and integrated with third-party products to add more functionality.

- **Identity service (Keystone):** Keystone is a central directory of users and provides an authentication system that maps users to the services they are allowed access to. It can also integrate with existing LDAP directory services and support various methods of authentication, from standard username and password combinations to token-based systems.

- **Networking (Neutron):** Neutron is the part of OpenStack that manages networking and IP address assignment. Neutron has a plug-in architecture that allows integration with third-party hardware and software as well. Cisco has a Neutron plug-in for the Nexus 9000 line of switches for direct integration.

- **Block storage (Cinder):** Cinder provides block storage for compute instances within OpenStack. It handles creating and attaching storage devices to servers and detaching them from servers. It supports a wide range of storage platforms.

- **Orchestration (Heat):** Heat provides orchestration capabilities to OpenStack through Heat templates. These templates allow OpenStack to launch various components of a composite cloud application together. Heat also provides programmable APIs to enable integration with third-party or custom cloud management applications.

- **Telemetry/metering (Ceilometer):** Ceilometer provides counters and monitoring capabilities for chargeback and billing systems to pull usage data from OpenStack.

Figure 4-5 shows a graphical representation of the components within OpenStack.

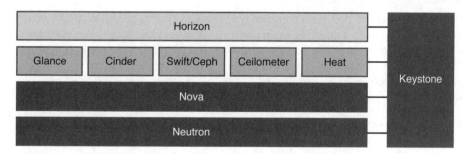

Figure 4-5 *OpenStack Components*

Cisco has two ways in which OpenStack can be implemented. For those customers who want to build their own environment from the ground up, there is the UCS Integrated Infrastructure with Red Hat OpenStack Platform. While that may be the longest solution name ever, it also gives the most flexibility for a customer that has the resources and expertise to build and deploy OpenStack on their own. This solution is a Cisco Validated design and reference architecture that can help take the guesswork out of how to build and deploy OpenStack on Cisco servers. UCS Integrated Infrastructure with Red Hat OpenStack platform benefits are

- Reduced OpenStack deployment complexity and risk
- The ability to maintain the flexibility of your own cloud environment
- Reduced cloud operating costs and accelerated return on investment through pretested and validated architecture

For those who have come to the conclusion (and rightly so) that OpenStack is a great plat-form, but they simply don't want to manage or deal with the complexity of getting it work-ing, nor the ongoing care and maintenance of the platform, Cisco Metacloud is the right choice. Metacloud gives a customer the benefit of OpenStack without the headache of run-ning it. Cisco does it for you on your own gear within your data center. When a new update comes out, the Metacloud platform is upgraded for you. Metacloud is really OpenStack as a service and offers the following core benefits:

- 24×7 cloud operations and support
- Infrastructure capacity planning
- Monitoring and error detection
- SLA guarantees
- Platform and security updates
- Cloud design and deployment support

This section gave an overview of the Cisco cloud software suites and cloud portfolio. The next section will dive deeper into the components and architecture of UCS Director, which is the primary orchestration platform that you are expected to know for the CCNA Cloud Admin exam.

Introducing UCS Director

UCS Director was built to provide a platform that enables automated on-demand delivery of IT services and infrastructure. The reality of most data centers today is that they are highly siloed environments that create an enormous amount of inefficiency between the groups and organizations that are responsible for deploying applications for the business. You will often see the following groups and their responsibilities when deploying a new application:

- **Server:** Set up servers, bare-metal provisioning, configure server, create storage re-sources, create VLAN, add VLAN to profile
- **Network:** Create VLANs, update switch configuration, create network profiles, create UCS service profiles, configure SAN zoning
- **Storage:** Create IP space (for SAN access), create vFilters, add vFilters to groups, map storage LUN, create storage policy, UCS Blade Server power on
- **Security:** Map application connectivity needs, create access control lists, deploy ACLs to network devices, validate security controls

Looking through the previous list of activities and the amount of coordination it requires, it becomes pretty obvious why a new application can take so long to roll out. The high operational cost of this model makes it very expensive and inefficient. UCS Director was created to address this issue head on by creating an automation platform that can provide end-to-end infrastructure automation and lifecycle management. All of the steps outlined previously can be mapped into an automation workflow that ensures consistency, speed, and security.

UCS Director provides the following benefits to an IT organization:

■ Delivers infrastructure resources faster

■ Discovers and maps your existing environment

■ Allows you to create workflows based on organizational policies and standard practices

■ Automates the workflow and delivers the requested capabilities to the requestor

■ Easy automation, provisioning, and management of infrastructure resources and services

■ Reduced operational complexity because of support of multivendor environments

Figure 4-6 shows UCS Director as a turnkey solution.

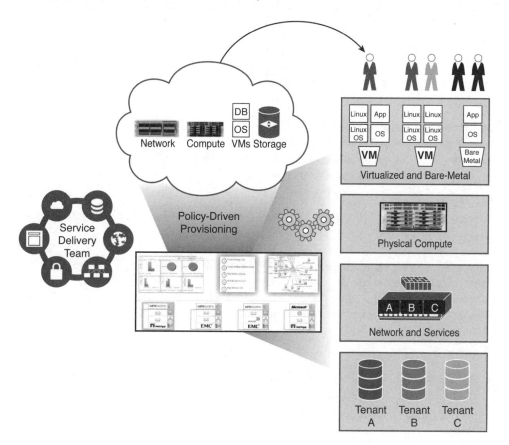

Figure 4-6 *UCS Director Turnkey Solution*

UCS Director Architecture

UCS Director is the leading automation and orchestration engine of the Cisco cloud stack. It relies on a catalog of over 2200 out-of-the-box prebuilt workflows that are designed to allow the end user to quickly search for and find common IT tasks that can then be automated and orchestrated. Figure 4-7 shows a graphical representation of UCS Director's functional architecture.

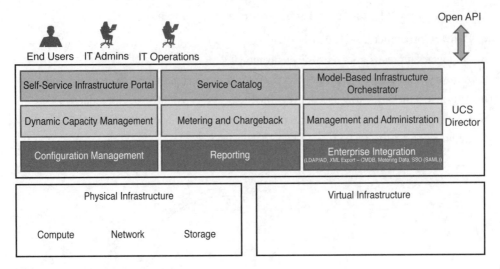

Figure 4-7 *UCS Director Functional Architecture*

UCS Director is designed to work in a multivendor and multi-hypervisor environment, providing flexibility and interoperability across a number of hardware and software components. UCS Director unifies network, compute, and storage into a single system and supports the following hypervisors:

- VMware vSphere
- Microsoft Hyper-V
- Red Hat KVM

From a physical infrastructure perspective, UCS Director has native integration with Cisco data center gear for easy deployment and automation. It also works well in a multivendor environment and includes support for many of the leading compute and storage platforms. For a complete list of supported devices, please see the Release Notes for UCS Director at Cisco.com.

There are nine core components that make up UCS Director:

- **Self-service infrastructure portal:** A built-in web-based interface geared toward internal IT, for ordering infrastructure resources from the services catalog
- **Service catalog:** List of prebuilt hardware and software items available for consumption by lines of business or end users
- **Model-based infrastructure orchestrator:** Workflow execution engine for provisioning and lifecycle management of items in the service catalog
- **Dynamic capacity management:** Trigger-based automatic actions in response to capacity and resource constraints
- **Metering and chargeback:** Full consumption and resource chargeback mechanism to ensure service costs are accounted for

- **Management and administration:** Web-based platform management and administration interface

- **Infrastructure configuration:** Automated infrastructure configuration component that enables dynamic provisioning

- **Reporting:** Full health, usage, and capacity reporting capabilities

- **Enterprise integration:** Integration into LDAP/Active Directory. XML export to other systems, change management database integration, single sign-on (SAML) support, and a robust programmable API for custom software integration.

The next section digs deeper into how UCS Director works.

How UCS Director Works

UCS Director abstracts the configuration of hardware and software into programmable tasks that are mapped together to provision compute, network, and storage. Just like the conductor of an orchestra takes the sounds made by individual instruments to create a symphony, UCS Director is the conductor for your data center. Model-based orchestration allows each subject matter expert in your organization to add their piece to the mix, creating an automation workflow that can be replicated as many times as the business needs. Once the policy is defined and added to the service catalog, it can be provisioned with the click of a button. Under the hood, UCS Director takes that workflow and executes the various parts to create the desired system automatically. Figure 4-8 shows the process used to provision a new server under UCS Director.

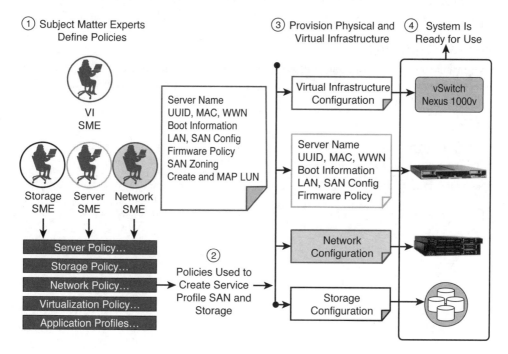

Figure 4-8 *How UCS Director Works*

When you first install UCS Director, it maps your existing infrastructure hardware and software into programmable tasks. These tasks can be pulled from over 2200 preconfigured tasks, and linked together into a powerful automation workflow through the drag-and-drop Workflow Designer. Provisioning of data center resources is then just a matter of linking those tasks and workflows together.

Key Topic

Installation Components of UCS Director

The installation and deployment of UCS Director starts with the two primary components in virtual machine format. The simplest install consists of two VMware-compatible OVF files or Microsoft-compatible VHD files that contain the virtual UCS Director appliance and the Baremetal Agent. *Baremetal* is a term used to describe a server with little to no configuration and no software installed (i.e., operating system or hypervisor). The UCS Director virtual machine can be installed as a single, self-contained instance of UCS Director with all of the core functionality in the same virtual machine. This setup can support between 2000 and 5000 virtual machines depending on the RAM and CPU resources you allocate to the virtual machine.

The Baremetal Agent (great name for a heavy metal band!) virtual machine is installed if you want to support provisioning of bare-metal servers. In other words, if you want to be able to rack up a new server and automate the provisioning of server hardware, then you will need to install this capability as well.

The BMA works by providing PXE boot capabilities to your servers through Dynamic Host Configuration Protocol (DHCP) options. The BMA will also act as a software image repository, enabling the server to load its base operating system software automatically.

Multinode Deployment

If you want to support more than 5000 virtual machines, you will need to deploy UCS Director as a multimode installation. A multimode UCS Director installation will include the following virtual machines:

■ One primary node

■ One or more service nodes (up to six)

■ One monitoring database

■ One inventory database

Figure 4-9 shows how a multinode environment topology is constructed.

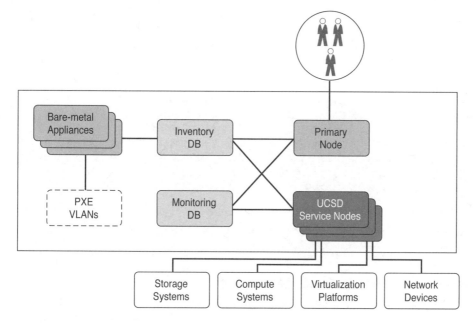

Figure 4-9 *UCS Director Multinode Topology*

All multinode deployments require one primary node, one monitoring node, and one inventory node. The difference in scale comes down to the number of service nodes attached. As always, review the official documentation for more details and any changes between releases. The multinode setup will allow you to scale UCS Director up to 50,000 VMs in the increments shown in Table 4-3.

Table 4-3 UCS Director Multinode Deployment Sizes

Deployment Size	Number of VMs Supported	Number of Service Nodes
Small	5,000 to 10,000	2
Medium	10,00 to 20,000	3
Large	20,000 to 50,000	6

UCS Director Self-Service Portal

UCS Director includes a built-in self-service portal, designed to provide an interface for more technical users to access automation workflows and service catalog items. The biggest difference between what is offered with Prime Service Catalog and the one native within UCS Director comes down to ease of use and extensibility. Prime Service Catalog can be used to provision infrastructure, software, and other business services like mobile phones. It is much simpler for a nontechnical person to navigate. You can open Prime Service Catalog up to your entire company. UCS Director's portal, on the other hand, is not really designed for the same use case. Think of it as more of an interface built for IT administrators and staff and not your general user population. Figure 4-10 shows UCS Director's self-service portal.

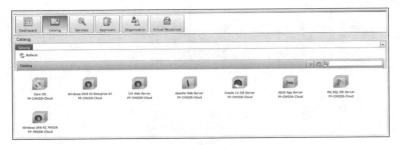

Figure 4-10 *UCS Director Self-Service Portal*

Orchestration with UCS Director

Today, many IT tasks are done manually on an ad hoc basis. For example, new business requirements are often brought to the IT team. As a member of either the storage, network, compute, or virtualization team, you then have to make a variety of decisions. See Figure 4-11. Do we have the capacity on hand today or do we need to order additional gear? What team needs to do their part first? How long will a project to meet these requirements take? What other projects am I currently working on that may impact my ability to accomplish this new project?

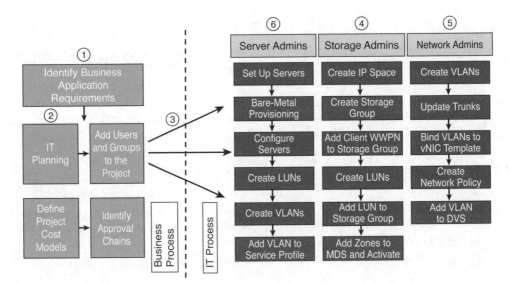

Figure 4-11 *Sample IT Workflow Without Automation*

In addition to adding new projects and capabilities, you are often faced with having to make daily small adds and changes to your existing infrastructure. Some of these tasks are trivial. Others, such as adding a VLAN across a data center campus, can be fairly daunting in nature due to the high likelihood of human error or misconfiguration. Who hasn't missed a switch configuration on a device or two during a change control window at 2:00 a.m.?

The main goal of automation and orchestration is to allow you, the administrator or architect, to accomplish common tasks quickly and easily, the same way, time after time. Think of automation and orchestration as a very similar concept to a hopefully not too distant in the future concept. How great would it be if you could travel to a remote destination simply by hopping into your autonomous vehicle, inputting a destination address, and letting your vehicle drive you safely and reliably to your destination, giving you the chance to read, surf the web, talk on the phone, or simply attend to other tasks during the driving portion of your journey? All the while, you would have complete control to step in and take over if necessary to adjust your route, respond to an unforeseen situation, etc.

IT automation and orchestration are much like the previously described scenario. You have a mountain of tasks that you face daily in your job. Some are simple, one-step tasks. Others are compound tasks that are fairly order specific and complex. With automation and orchestration, much like the autonomous vehicle, you program in the tasks you want to accomplish and the vehicle takes care of the rest. In a cloud infrastructure, UCS Director is your vehicle. You program it to automate simple or complex IT tasks. You do this in conjunction with members of your organization from the other areas of infrastructure management discipline. The end results are great. You have taken a task or set of tasks that is manual in nature, time consuming, and prone to error and you've automated them with a few mouse clicks. More importantly, if there is a problem, you have the ability to roll back these changes immediately.

So to get your mind around the power of automation and orchestration, look at the list of daily/weekly tasks or projects that you face in IT and ask, "Is this something that I could automate? If I automated it, would it save time and allow me to work on more exciting projects?" If the answer to those questions is yes, congratulations, you are well on your way to bringing the power of Cisco Cloud to your organization!

UCS Director Orchestrator

UCS Director's orchestration capabilities are one of the most powerful aspects of UCS Director. Through the Orchestrator you can automate the vast majority of data center tasks, saving you time and money operating your IT infrastructure. The Orchestrator has the following capabilities and benefits:

- Visual construction of workflows through a graphical user interface
- Automation of manual operational and maintenance tasks
- Alerting and responding to predefined conditions or workflows
- Simplification of IT management by automating complex tasks

By being able to connect automated tasks together in an Orchestration workflow, such as the provisioning of a virtual machine, you can gain significant time savings, reduced downtime and recovery, and the ability to ensure security controls are in place to meet compliance requirements.

You can automate a number of IT processes through UCS Director Orchestration:

- **Infrastructure provisioning:** Bare-metal, compute, storage, and network
- **Virtual machine automation:** Provisioning, scale up, scale down, snapshots, and consolidation of VMs
- **Service delivery approvals:** Request and approval tracking system
- **Disaster recovery:** Backups, recovery on failure

All of these things are accomplished through the Orchestrator's 2200-task built-in library, and by creating your own workflow with the Workflow GUI designer.

Workflow Designer

The Workflow Designer GUI makes it easy to construct or edit complex tasks and processes that UCS Director can automate. It allows you to drag and drop common tasks and construct your own advanced automation functions without having to be a software developer. From the start point you connect your first task, second task, and so on until you get to the end of the workflow with either a success or failure in execution. The interface can help you create some really complex workflow, with the goal of customization and mapping the technology to your individual or organizational standards. Figure 4-12 shows the drag-and-drop interface of Workflow Designer.

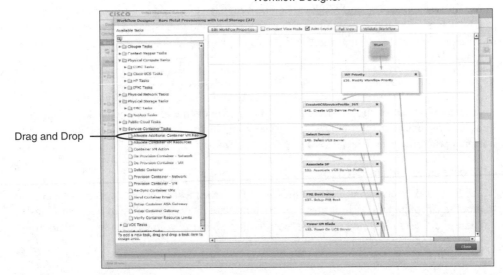

Figure 4-12 *Workflow Designer*

Building a Workflow

A task is the smallest atomic (self-contained) action or operation that can be accomplished at once, like starting a virtual machine. A workflow is an organized set of tasks that can be executed on demand or in response to a predefined trigger. Workflows can automate and orchestrate both the physical and virtual environment. The smallest functional workflow is simply two joined tasks. Tasks are executed in the logical order in which they are defined in the workflow. The output of one task can also feed the input of another task, such as the assigning of a name or IP address to a virtual machine in a workflow.

Triggers

A trigger will execute a workflow based on meeting a predefined set of conditions. A trigger can be either stateful or stateless. A *stateful trigger* records data and executes actions only when there is a change in the recorded state. A *stateless trigger* is checked based on a frequency selected at the time of creation. If a VM power status is being monitored, for example, and someone shuts down the VM, then the trigger would respond.

Triggers are extremely useful in automation. Say you want to automatically increase the amount of memory in a virtual machine if utilization reaches 80 percent. With a trigger, once you go over your threshold, a workflow can be kicked off to dynamically increase the memory and then also send you an alert that it happened. This kind of capability can help avoid problems that might require someone to get out of bed in the middle of the night because an application crashed.

Activities

Activities are a way to create an abstraction layer by being a placeholder for workflow implementation details. In this way a single activity can call multiple workflows based on a set of variables. With an activity, you can create a generic task and then associate the activity to one or more workflows. An example of this would be creating data stores on more than one type of SAN appliance. If you have a NetApp appliance and an EMC appliance, they have different workflows for creating a data store. You can use an activity as a way to associate both of those workflows together. The activity will look at input conditions to determine which workflow to follow. If it is EMC, then the EMC create data store workflow would execute, and likewise for the NetApp appliance.

Validating Workflow

Once you've built your workflow, UCS Director can execute a process that validates the workflow to ensure that it is constructed correctly, and all of the various input and output parameters each task needs are properly connected. It allows for testing to ensure that the data bindings and connections between task elements in a workflow are functioning as they should.

Many common errors can be identified quickly with the workflow validation process. The following are some of the items checked:

- Mapping mismatches
- Missing mandatory fields for tasks
- Task handler not found
- Missing admin or task inputs after task import or upgrade

Figure 4-13 points out the Validate Workflow button in the Workflow Designer GUI.

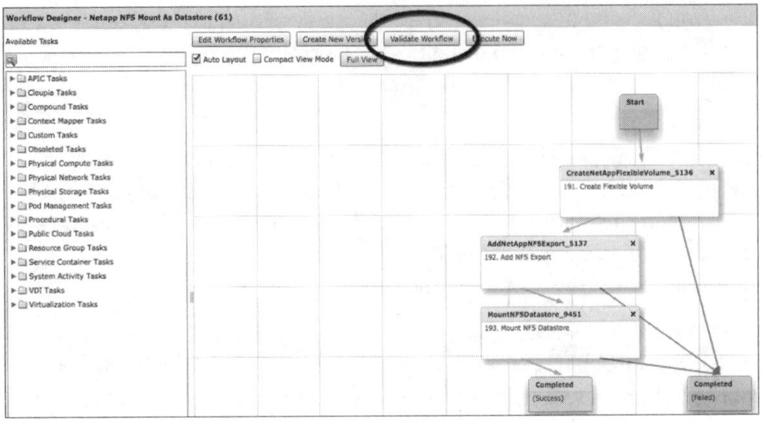

Figure 4-13 *Workflow Designer Validation*

Approvals

An approval process is often used in IT to ensure that a change that is being made to the infrastructure has the correct level of visibility by an administrator who can validate the request before submitting it. This way, errors and outages can be minimized. Within UCS Director there is a built-in approval process that prevents a workflow from being executed until approved by an administrator. You can also create Custom Approval Tasks that can allow the administrator to input values at the time of approval. For example, you could submit a request to resize the data store of a particular virtual machine, but require the administrator to input the resulting data store size. Figure 4-14 shows the approval request page.

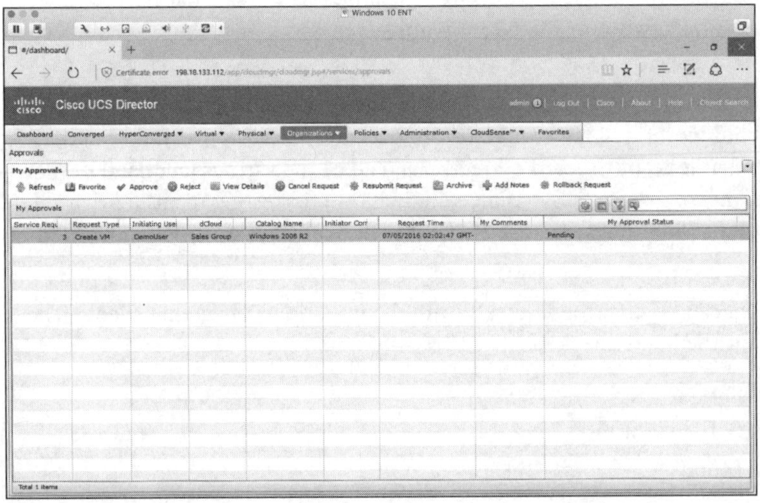

Figure 4-14 *Approval Request Page*

Rollback

Rollback is the ability to "undo" a workflow that might have been launched in error, a workflow that is not functioning as it should be, or a workflow that includes an application or infrastructure component that an administrator needs to decommission. The operating state is returned to the same as it was before the workflow was executed. All tasks in a workflow are executed in the order in which they are listed. Rollback works because each task has two scripts attached to it. One of them performs the actions of the task, and the other executes the action in reverse. All rollbacks create a new service request that is separate from the original. This way you can store state information on previous values before the workflow was executed, such as the memory size of a virtual machine. A workflow can partially succeed, with some of the tasks failing to complete, requiring you to undo the workflow. It is important to note that while you can roll back a workflow starting at any task, you cannot partially roll back a single task. Tasks are "atomic" and cannot be divided into subactions. Figure 4-15 shows a rollback request.

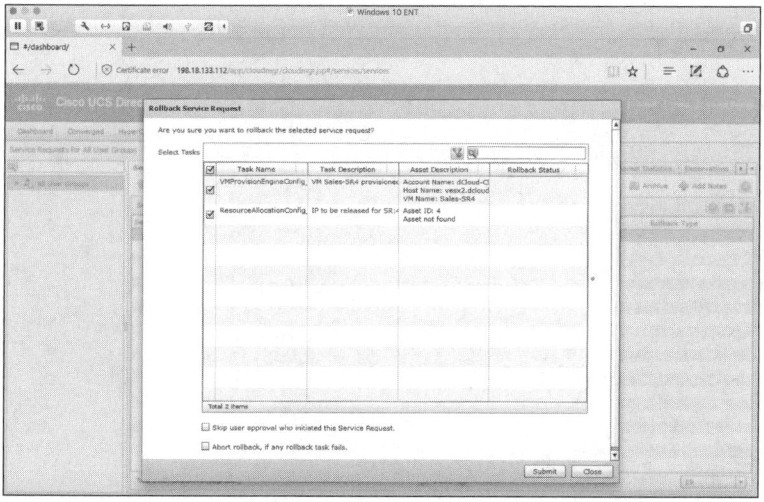

Figure 4-15 *Rollback Request*

UCS Director Baremetal Agent

The Baremetal Agent (BMA) within the UCS Director product set is a separate installed virtual appliance. When joined properly to UCS Director, the BMA allows you to build PXE installation tasks into infrastructure workflows, allowing for the installation of supported operating systems to bare-metal hosts.

The BMA virtual appliance provides the following services:

- A PXE boot service
- DHCP
- An image repository of operating systems

- HTTP (Hypertext Transfer Protocol)
- TFTP (Trivial File Transfer Protocol)

To add a previously configured Baremetal Agent to UCS Director, after it has been installed, navigate to **Administration > Physical Accounts** and click the **Baremetal Agents** tab, and then click the Add button. You will need to provide the following mandatory information in order to connect to a previously configured BMA virtual appliance:

- Account Name
- Management/PXE Address
- Login ID
- Password
- Database Address

Figure 4-16 shows the UCS Director Baremetal Agent integration form.

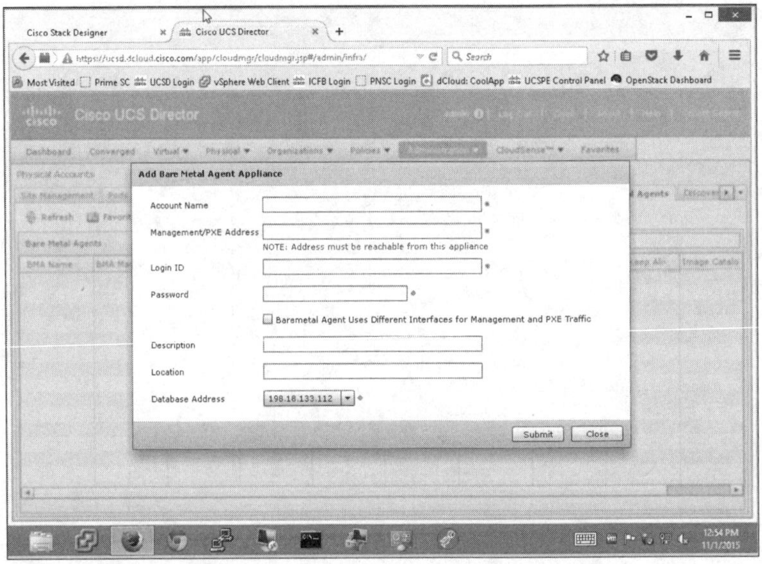

Figure 4-16   *UCS Director Baremetal Agent Integration*

Note that once all information has been provided correctly, the Reachable column for the BMA will show a status of YES, as shown in Figure 4-17. You can also click on **Service Status** in the menu bar to get a status of the connection and services running on the BMA.

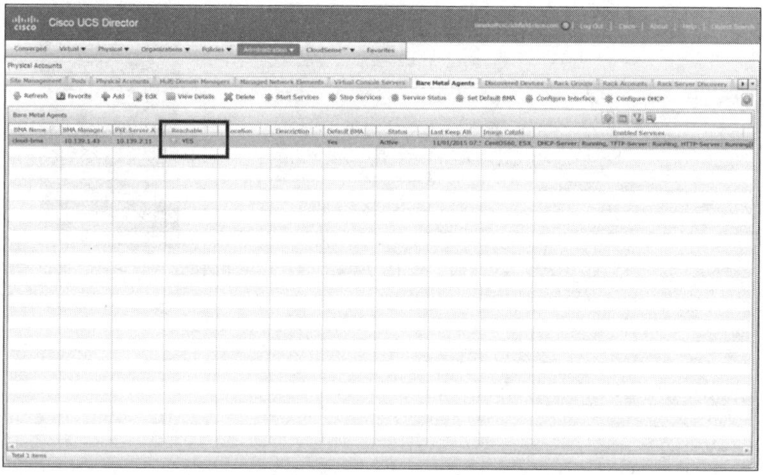

Figure 4-17 *UCS Director Baremetal Agent Reachability Status*

How BMA Works

Once installed, the Baremetal Agent will automate the deployment of new servers in the data center. Once you have it integrated into UCS Director, it will share the UCS Director console and database, meaning all of the configuration is done within the GUI of UCS Director. There are a few requirements that you should be aware of:

- The Baremetal Agent must be able to reach UCS Director over the network
- UCS Director must be able to reach the Baremetal Agent over the network
- Servers and Baremetal Agent must also be on the same network
- In versions prior to 5.2 you can have only one Baremetal Agent per UCS Director installation

Figure 4-18 shows the process of adding a new server in a data center that is running the Baremetal Agent to automate provisioning.

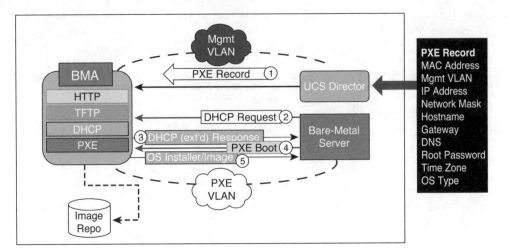

Figure 4-18 *UCS Director and BMA with New Server*

The process occurs as follows:

Step 1. UCS Director sends a PXE record to the Baremetal Agent for the new server.

Step 2. The new server is connected to the network and makes a DHCP request.

Step 3. BMA provides the IP address, DHCP options that inform the server of the TFTP location used to house the base operating system for PXE boot to function.

Step 4. PXE boot is initiated on the server.

Step 5. BMA provides the operating system image via HTTP server or redirects to an image repository to boot the server.

Exam Preparation Tasks

As mentioned in the section "How to Use This Book" in the Introduction, you have a couple of choices for exam preparation: the exercises here, Chapter 15, "Final Preparation," and the exam simulation questions on the Pearson IT Certification Practice Test.

Review All Key Topics

Review the most important topics in this chapter, noted with the Key Topics icon in the outer margin of the page. Table 4-4 lists a reference of these key topics and the page number on which each is found.

Table 4-4   Key Topics for Chapter 4

Key Topic Element	Description	Page Number
Section	Cisco Intelligent Automation for Cloud	69
Paragraph	UCS Director architecture	73
Section	Installation Components of UCS Director	76
Section	Orchestration with UCS Director	78
Paragraph	UCS Director Orchestrator	79
Paragraph	How BMA Works	85

Define Key Terms

Define the following key terms from this chapter and check your answers in the glossary:

UCS Director, virtual data center (vDC), vDC categories, workflow, service request, Rollback, Prime Service Catalog, service catalog, Stack Designer, UCS Director, Workflow Designer, application containers, Baremetal Agent (BMA), Custom Approval Task, chargeback

This chapter covers the following topics:

4.0 Cloud Systems Management and Monitoring

4.1 Identify the components of Cisco Prime Service Catalog

4.1.a End user store front

4.1.b Stack Designer

4.1.c Heat Orchestration

CHAPTER 5

Cisco Prime Service Catalog

This chapter provides an introduction to Cisco Prime Service Catalog, a platform that incorporates an easy-to-use portal with a shopping cart checkout process that is similar to the process used by popular online retailers. The portal enables anyone within your company to request applications and services from your cloud infrastructure. Prime Service Catalog automates the delivery of these applications and services quickly, and removes the burden of coordinating the various complex interactions within IT that would take hundreds of phone calls and emails and take weeks or months to get your application deployed.

"Do I Know This Already?" Quiz

The "Do I Know This Already?" quiz allows you to assess whether you should read this entire chapter thoroughly or jump to the "Exam Preparation Tasks" section. If you are in doubt about your answers to these questions or your own assessment of your knowledge of the topics, read the entire chapter. Table 5-1 lists the major headings in this chapter and their corresponding "Do I Know This Already?" quiz questions. You can find the answers in Appendix A, "Answers to the 'Do I Know This Already?' Quizzes."

Table 5-1 "Do I Know This Already?" Section-to-Question Mapping

Foundation Topics Section	Questions
Introducing Prime Service Catalog	1
Prime Service Catalog Concepts and Components	2–4
End-User Storefront	5, 6
Stack Designer	7, 8
Heat Orchestration	9, 10

Caution The goal of self-assessment is to gauge your mastery of the topics in this chapter. If you do not know the answer to a question or are only partially sure of the answer, you should mark that question as wrong for purposes of the self-assessment. Giving yourself credit for an answer you correctly guess skews your self-assessment results and might provide you with a false sense of security.

1. What is the role of Prime Service Catalog in delivering cloud services?

    a. Orchestration engine

    b. Part of UCS Director

    c. Help desk software

    d. Web-based front end that provides self-service provisioning of IT services

2. What is Stack Designer used for?

    a. Nexus 9000 switch management software

    b. Design of orderable application software and infrastructure stack templates

    c. Nothing in the Cisco Enterprise Cloud Suite

    d. Billing module in Prime Service Catalog

3. What protocol does RabbitMQ use to communicate?

    a. REST

    b. AMQP

    c. TCP port 2342

    d. BOCCE

4. Where in Prime Service Catalog can you change email notification templates?

    a. You can't

    b. SendMail

    c. Service Designer

    d. Portal Designer

5. How can you find services in the end-user storefront of Prime Service Catalog?

    a. Search for keywords

    b. Browse the catalog

    c. Click Service Items on the main page

    d. All of the above

6. Where can you see a list of service items that you have provisioned under your account?

    a. Stuff

    b. Completed orders

    c. My Stuff

    d. None of the above

7. How do you change the graphical image of the application template in the service catalog?

   a. Edit the application template and input a new URL with the image you want displayed

   b. Upload a new image to the end-user storefront

   c. Use the camera in your laptop to take a picture and then import it via email

   d. All of the above

8. What functions can you perform in Service Designer?

   a. Create authorization flows

   b. Order cellular service

   c. Drag and drop application components together

   d. Create bundled offerings

9. When you click Build Service within Stack Designer, what template is generated?

   a. Heat

   b. CFN

   c. Service Catalog Template

   d. Cloud Pivot

10. Which open source project uses Heat?

   a. OpenDaylight

   b. Apache ZooKeeper

   c. OpenStack

   d. Snort

Foundation Topics

Introducing Prime Service Catalog

IT service requests can come from anywhere within a business, and to deal with the various activities generated, most IT organizations have some form of help desk to triage and manage those requests. The bottleneck this generates slows down service delivery and often frustrates the end user, who has no idea of the complexity their request may involve. Prime Service Catalog was built to address this aspect of IT service delivery, through the automation of the request process and the ultimate provisioning of services, reducing inefficiencies and human intervention.

Prime Service Catalog accomplishes the goal of automating service delivery by allowing the user to self-provision common service offerings. When a user needs an IT service, or to make changes to a service already in production, they can log in to Prime Service Catalog and request the new service or change directly from the service catalog. As mentioned in previous chapters, the service catalog is really just a prepared menu of offerings or templates. By exposing this menu to the user, the whole process of provisioning services is greatly streamlined. Prime Service Catalog's self-service portal provides the following:

- **Easy-to-use interface:** The interface is simple and familiar, not unlike that of your favorite online retailer.

- **Comparison of standard options:** You can view multiple offerings side by side to determine which best meets your requirements.

- **Rich interactive web forms:** The user can choose from fully HTML5-based ordering forms that enable the creation of simple but sophisticated offerings. You can prepopulate values or ask for direct input from the user.

- **Policy control and governance:** IT policy and governance are built in to the system to ensure that security and resource allocation is managed in real time.

- **Ordering and approvals:** The ordering system includes cost and billing mechanisms as well as a built-in order approval workflow if needed for costly resources.

- **Online status updates:** A built-in status system can provide real-time updates on the provisioning status of your application or service.

Figure 5-1 shows Prime Service Catalog's role in managing IT service requests.

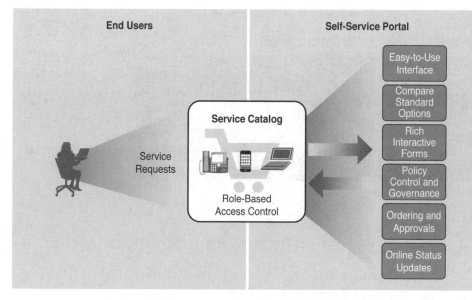

Figure 5-1 *Prime Service Catalog and Managing IT Service Requests*

Managing Requests for IT Services

Prime Service Catalog is the main portal for end-user interaction. The Service Catalog module is based on HTML5 and provides users with a shopping cart experience very similar to that of many mobile app stores or e-commerce sites. Its main function is to enable IT as a service (ITaaS), which is a term used to describe an operational model that is focused on providing IT services to the business in a user-friendly, simplified, and standardized manner. Although ITaaS is not an official NIST cloud service model, it is an effective way for business to reduce costs and increase IT customer satisfaction. The main Service Catalog module included with Prime Service Catalog provides

- A home page that can be customized using custom style sheets either for the entire site or by different organizations, each of which may brand their IT experience in the catalog

- Individual Showcase sections of the home page that can be defined by setting up service categories using concepts such as hierarchy, service name, or service description

- Options to search for a service or browse through categories on the screen

- A Manage My Stuff tool to help IT consumers manage subscriptions or orders

- A Notification icon that lists all open orders and open authorizations for the user

- A shopping cart where you can see ordered items and check out, similar to many popular e-commerce sites

- A Home button to return to the home page at any time

Figure 5-2 shows the home page view of Prime Service Catalog.

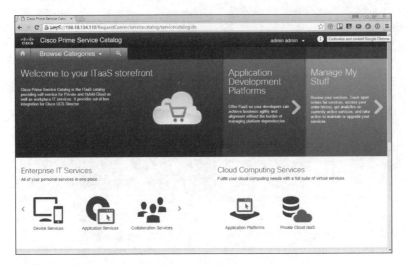

Figure 5-2   *Prime Service Catalog Home Page*

Again, the main goal of Prime Service Catalog is to provide a self-service portal into the IT service catalog for full lifecycle management of IT services that allows the users in your organization to order those services with a pleasant "consumer of IT" shopping experience. Prime Service Catalog offers very advanced functionality, such as employee onboarding (processes such as ordering business cards, as a business process portal to order new employee laptops, and much more), but for the purposes of this book, we will focus on the use case of Prime Service Catalog as a tool for ordering Infrastructure as a Service (IaaS) and Platform as a Service (PaaS).

In addition to the portal, Prime Service Catalog also includes the following:

■ **Service Designer:** Used to build a category-structured list of orderable service items that can consist of physical hardware, virtual services, account setup, or any other class of service that IT offers

■ **Stack Designer:** Used to build application stack templates that can consist of physical or virtual infrastructure and software

■ **Portal Designer:** Used to create and modify the layout of the web portal for organizational customization

On-Demand Service Delivery

The main interface for Prime Service Catalog is both intuitive and simple to understand at a glance. The end user can browse through the various categories and select the types of services they are looking for. Looking through the catalog, you can see the service offered, a description of the service itself, and even a user rating system. Figure 5-3 shows the catalog view.

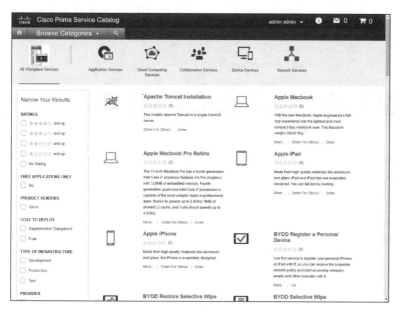

Figure 5-3   *Prime Service Catalog Service Offering View*

When you click an offering, you are presented with a detailed description of the service itself and any details you may need to know about what you should expect from the service. There can be videos, tutorials, and links to other web resources that the user may find valuable. In addition, you can find other user "reviews" of the service, including their comments and lessons learned. Figure 5-4 shows the bring your own device (BYOD) service description.

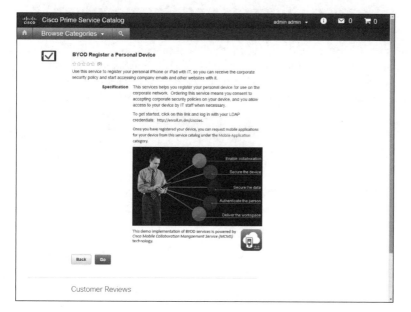

Figure 5-4   *BYOD Service Description*

Under the My Stuff section of the main interface, you can see all of the services that are currently provisioned for your account. This view will show the service status, when it was provisioned, and other information about the service itself. You can also make changes to your services from here. Figure 5-5 shows the My Stuff view.

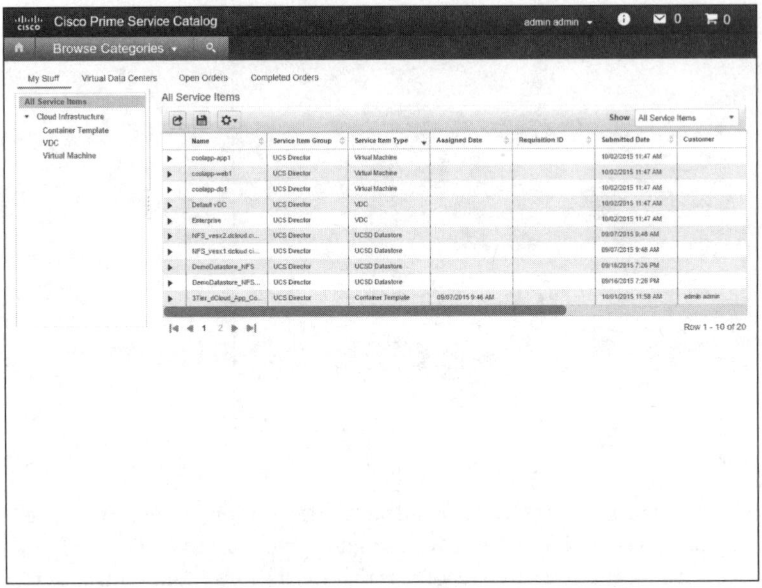

Figure 5-5   *My Stuff View*

Prime Service Catalog Concepts and Components

Prime Service Catalog (PSC) is a user interface for businesses that want to deliver IT services in an automated manner. By using standard services that are displayed as a catalog of items a user can choose from, it can become the front-end "face" of IT. Prime Service Catalog consists of a number of core components that allow it to automate and orchestrate the complex process of service provisioning and delivery. The following is an overview of the parts that make up PSC.

End-User Storefront

The end-user storefront is the primary interface for interacting with the system. It is built on an HTML5 graphical user interface that will run in any browser without the need for plug-ins. The end-user storefront is shown in Figure 5-6.

Figure 5-6 *End-User Storefront*

Stack Designer

Stack Designer allows you to develop standardized application offerings and publish them to the Prime Service Catalog portal. The Stack Designer uses the concepts of templates and services. Using Stack Designer, an application stack template can be constructed and published as an orderable service. Templates are created by adding application components, such as web servers and databases, into infrastructure logical containers through a graphical interface that makes it easy to visualize how the application components interact. Stack Designer also ships with many predefined templates. Services are the end result of publishing a container in the service catalog as a service that can be ordered, used, and consumed by a Prime Service Catalog end user. A service can be an application such as Microsoft SharePoint or a J2EE middleware server.

Stack Designer makes it easy to create application templates and publish them as a service in the service catalog. Stack Designer not only lets you visualize the logic connectivity of the application but also allows you to drag and drop application components into the application stack. Figure 5-7 shows the infrastructure view of Stack Designer.

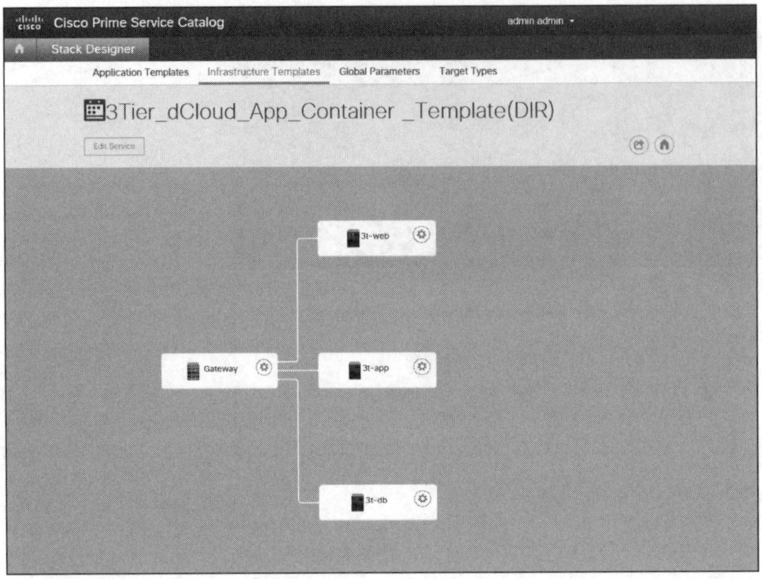

Figure 5-7   *Stack Designer Infrastructure View*

Portal Designer

The Portal Designer lets you design and manage the pages and portal content displayed as part of Prime Service Catalog to the end user. It allows an administrator granular role-based access control of service content by user or group. Portal Designer can help create a highly customized user interface that affords control over the appearance and functionality of Prime Service Catalog. To access Portal Designer from the Prime Service Catalog home page, choose **admin > Switch To > Portal Designer** from the menu, as shown in Figure 5-8.

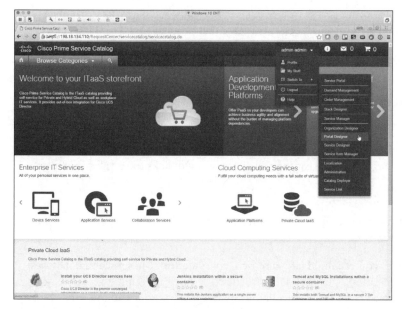

Figure 5-8   *Accessing Portal Designer*

Figure 5-9 shows the main page for Portal Designer, which gives you access to all of the customization capabilities for how Prime Service Catalog's user portal looks and operates.

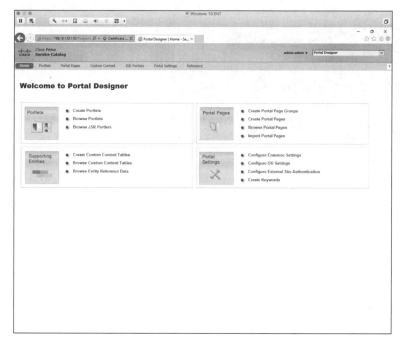

Figure 5-9   *Portal Designer*

The front-end portal exposes access to services, service items, standards, and offerings through *portlets*, which are small pieces of software that provide access to the technical underpinnings of a service. You can replace these portlets with your own custom code, enabling you to build your own interface. Portlets can be built in JavaScript/HTML, ad hoc lists, or third-party compliant portlets.

With Portal Designer you can do the following:

■ Create portlets from external or third-party sources

■ Create portlets to highlight common services

■ Create portlets to show users what they already own, with links to services related to those items

■ Show announcements, video, or other types of media

■ Leverage RBAC to create a flexible user interface that is at once simple for casual users and advanced for power users

With Portal Designer you can build a feature-rich, consumer-of-IT interface that matches how your own organization operates and is structured. While PSC is intuitive and easy to use out of the box, the ability to create a unique experience for your end users may be a requirement for your organization. Cisco uses Prime Service Catalog internally (called eStore) and has customized its look and operation. Figure 5-10 shows Cisco's implementation of Prime Service Catalog.

Figure 5-10 *Cisco's Internal eStore*

Note   Portal Designer is a separately licensed addition to PSC, and is beyond the scope of what you need to know to pass the CCNA Cloud Admin exam.

Service Designer

Service Designer is the module in Prime Service Catalog where you can configure and design service packages for end-user consumption from the service catalog. Service Designer allows you to do the following:

■ Create categories and keywords that end users may use to search for a particular service

■ Design the look and behavior of service forms, the interactive web page, determining which service requisitions are ordered and tracked in Prime Service Catalog

■ Construct request or service fulfillment plans

■ Configure authorization flows for service delivery

■ Configure service ordering permissions

■ Link email templates with processes that require email notifications

The Service Designer module is shown in Figure 5-11. The various tabs on the left side of the web interface are used to construct or modify a service, as described here:

■ **Services:** Create and modify service groups and their service definitions, including the delivery plan and presentation of the service. It also includes any active form components that are used in the service form. You can configure service order permissions, configure authorization flows for service delivery approval, and link email templates with processes that need email notification.

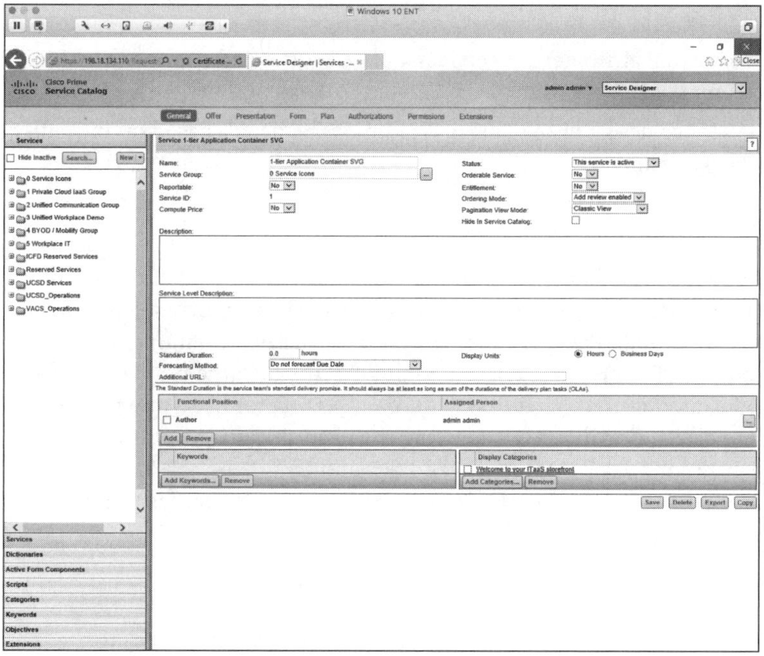

Figure 5-11   *Service Designer Interface*

- **Dictionaries:** Create and modify the dictionaries that specify the data fields required in a service. Dictionaries, a basic building block of a service form, include a group of data elements (fields) that allow users and service performers to enter and view data required to fulfill the service request.

- **Active Form Components:** Create and modify reusable form components, which specify both the service's look (via the configuration of previously defined dictionaries) and feel (via the definition of rules that can dynamically adjust both the form's appearance and behavior). The appearance and behavior of a service form is determined by how the dictionaries and their component fields are configured as part of the active form components that are used in the service definition. Active form components provide the potential for reusability across service forms. With careful and thoughtful design, a designer may create an active form component from a commonly used dictionary, or set of dictionaries, and configure it only once. Then this form component can be included in as many services as necessary, with no additional configuration.

- **Scripts:** Write JavaScript functions to supplement the rules defined in active form components and maintain JavaScript libraries.

- **Categories:** Specify how services and service categories are displayed in the Service Catalog module. Customers may use categories to search for a particular service.

- **Keywords:** Define and manage the keywords used in the service catalog search engine. Customers may use keywords to search for a particular service.

- **Objectives:** Define and manage the measurable service delivery objectives defined in the Service Definition Offer tab.

- **Extensions:** Define custom attributes for services and categories and manage the presentation of categories on the landing page of the Service Catalog module.

- **History:** Track the service design change history and view the details based on the entity type or filter by the username.

UCS Director

UCS Director plays a crucial role in provisioning services through Prime Service Catalog, and is used for infrastructure provisioning and management. The supported components that can be orchestrated through PSC are Standard Catalog, Service Container Catalog, Fenced Container Template, Cisco VACS, and Cisco APIC (the brains of Cisco Application Centric Infrastructure). In addition, all of UCS Director users and groups are mapped to Prime Service Catalog directly, removing the need to manage multiple user accounts. If the organization uses LDAP, however, PSC (and UCS Director) will use those accounts instead. Chapter 4, "Cisco Cloud Automation/Orchestration Suites," discusses UCS Director in more detail.

RabbitMQ

RabbitMQ is an open source application message broker that allows applications to exchange information in an asynchronous manner. Modern distributed applications must be able to exchange data reliably and flexibly, especially in a work environment where automation and orchestration can dynamically add and remove components of an application on-the-fly as scaling needs change. RabbitMQ handles the communication of those types of applications using an open standard called Advanced Message Queuing Protocol (AMQP). RabbitMQ is included in PSC to enable open interaction with other systems and orchestrators that speak AMQP.

Puppet

Puppet is an open source configuration management tool that enables a standard method for delivering and managing software and the underlying hardware. Configuration management is different from just writing a script that performs some task or another. Configuration management is a process that systematically handles changes to a system while maintaining the integrity of the system as a whole. Puppet uses a modeling language that describes the desired state and then uses automation to add software or change configuration of the infrastructure to achieve that state. The concept of infrastructure as code is derived from this process where the modeling language (or code) configures the infrastructure dynamically at run time from a pool of resources.

Puppet uses an easy-to-read modeling language built on Ruby (a programming language) that allows you to deploy and provision software and hardware as needed. Puppet operates in a client/server model with the Puppet master as the server and the Puppet agent as the client. Puppet is model driven and very popular among organizations leveraging DevOps practices. Prime Services Catalog does not bundle a full Puppet implementation, but it does include a Puppet master to communicate with a Puppet environment if it is used to automate application or infrastructure deployment within IT. Cisco has a number of infrastructure platforms, such as the Nexus 9000 Series, that have a Puppet agent built in. Puppet is just one more way to interoperate with existing systems.

Intercloud Fabric for Business

Prime Service Catalog has built-in support for the Cisco hybrid cloud solution Intercloud Fabric for Business. Intercloud Fabric enables you to offer services that extend from your private cloud environment into the public cloud. Intercloud Fabric handles the provisioning and deployment of your application automatically just like any other service catalog item, allowing for consistent security and policy implementation regardless of where the actual workload resides.

Navigating the End-User Storefront

As mentioned previously in this chapter, the end-user storefront is the main interface that your users will see when ordering a service from IT. It is essential that you are comfortable with the process of ordering a service and verifying its successful delivery as part of your preparation for the CCNA Cloud Admin exam.

In this section you will see how to navigate the Prime Service Catalog interface, order a service from within it, and validate that your service is up and running.

Logging In

Key Topic

Step 1.   At the Cisco Prime Service Catalog login page, shown in Figure 5-12, enter your username and password and click **Log In**.

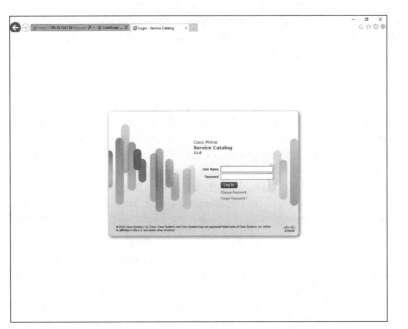

Figure 5-12 *Login Screen*

> **Step 2.** Your home page will be displayed. You will see in the upper left of the page the home button (looks like a small house) and a Browse Categories drop-down link to browse categories of service catalog items, as shown in Figure 5-13. If they are configured, you can also see commonly ordered services with a direct link at the bottom of the page.

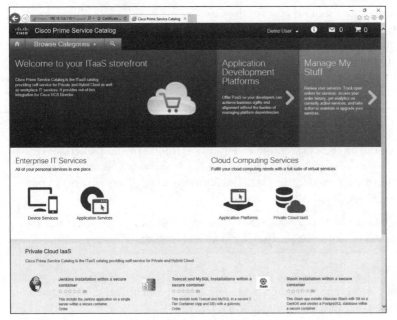

Figure 5-13 *Prime Service Catalog Home Page*

Locating Services

Before you can order a service, you must locate the service you want to order. In Prime Service Catalog the various services and offerings are grouped into categories. You can locate a particular service either by browsing through the categories or searching for keywords.

Browsing for Services

Step 1.   On the home page, click the **Browse Categories** button and select a category name or its icon from the drop-down list. Prime Service Catalog displays the subcategories and services in that category, as shown in Figure 5-14 for Cloud Computing Services. In addition, you can click Browse All to get a complete list of all catalog items.

Figure 5-14   *Browse Categories*

Step 2.   If there are additional subcategories within a category, continue to click through each subcategory until you locate the service you want. In Figure 5-15 you can see the two subcategories Application Platforms and Private Cloud IaaS, with Application Platforms selected.

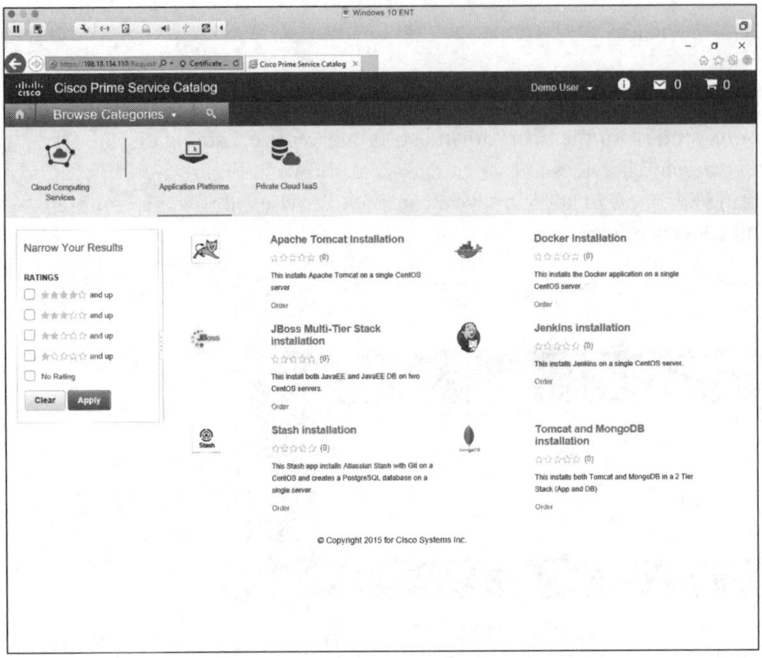

Figure 5-15   *Category List*

Step 3.   Once you have found the service you are looking for, do either of the following:

Click the name of the service to view a complete description of the service, cost structure, and any other pertinent information.

OR

Click **Order** to fill in the order form and order the service.

Searching for Services

Step 1.   On the Prime Service Catalog home page, click the **Search** icon to open the search box (see Figure 5-16), enter a word or phrase in the search box, and then press **Enter**. Service Catalog displays an alphabetical list of services that match your search criteria, as shown in Figure 5-17.

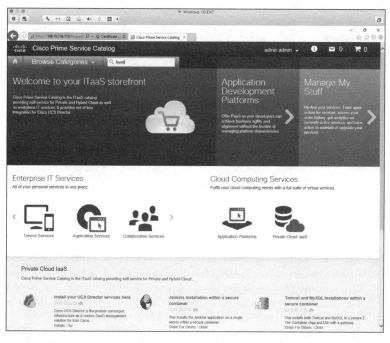

Figure 5-16   *Search Field*

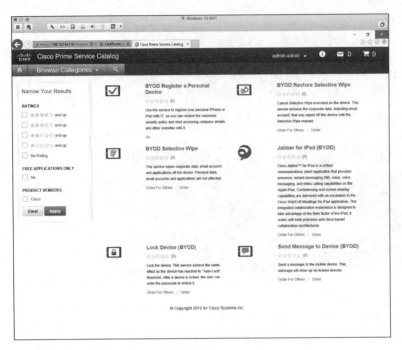

Figure 5-17   *Search Results*

You can also perform a wildcard search by using the options shown in Table 5-2. Search parameters are not case sensitive.

Table 5-2   Wildcard Search Methods

Wildcard (*) Search Criteria	Search Results
Enter the * symbol alone	All services in the system. You must enter the wildcard alone to see all possible selections. (The full list of options does not necessarily appear by default.)
Enter * before the service name or * after the service name (with no spaces; for example, *service or service*)	All services with something either in front of the service name or after the service name that match the search entry.
Enter * before and after the service name (with no spaces; for example, *service*)	All services that have something in front of the service name and after the service name that match the search entry.

Step 2.   Once you have found the service you are looking for, do either of the following:

Click the name of the service to view a complete description of the service, cost structure, and any other pertinent information.

OR

Click **Order** to fill in the order form and order the service.

Service Overview

When you click the name of a service in the search results, the service overview that appears describes the service and provides summary information about pricing and service delivery, as shown in Figure 5-18.

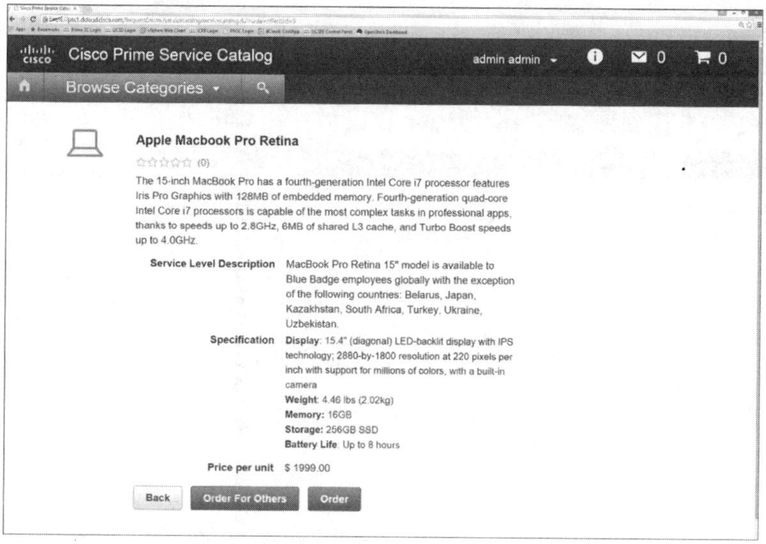

Figure 5-18 *Service Description*

The service description can include some or all of the following information as seen in Table 5-3.

Table 5-3 Service Overview

Service Item	Description
Standard Duration	Amount of time, usually in business days, in which IT has committed to delivering the service, after any required authorizations have been approved
Service Level Description	Description of the service
Price	Price, if any, for this service, which is used for showback/chargeback purposes
Price Type	Type of pricing, such as Fixed pricing or Time & Materials, for this service
Price Description	Brief description or explanation of the pricing for the service

Ordering a Service

Once you have located the service you want to order, understand how much it will cost you, and are ready to initiate the order, your next step is to complete the order form itself. Once you click the Order button for the service, you will be presented with an interactive form that you will need to fill out.

Step 1.   Click **Order** and complete the order form (see Figure 5-19).

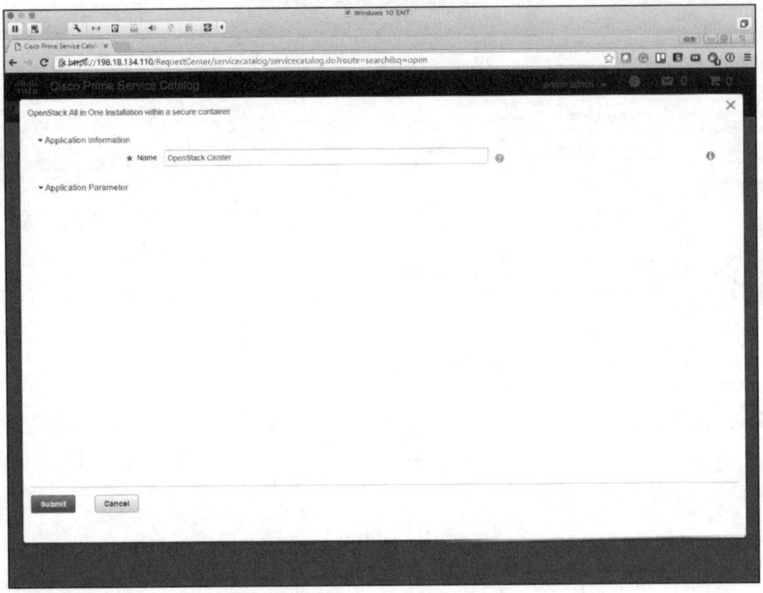

Figure 5-19   *Order Form*

Mandatory fields on the order form are indicated by a red asterisk (*) and require you to fill them out before continuing. The information that you input on the order form is used by reviewers, authorizers, and service performers during the services delivery process. Whenever possible, Service Catalog will prefill information about you from your LDAP or local PSC profile.

Step 2.   Once you complete the order form, click **Submit**. You will then see your order on the My Cart page, as shown in Figure 5-20.

Some of the items you can order immediately. With others you can add multiple items to the shopping cart and order them all together.

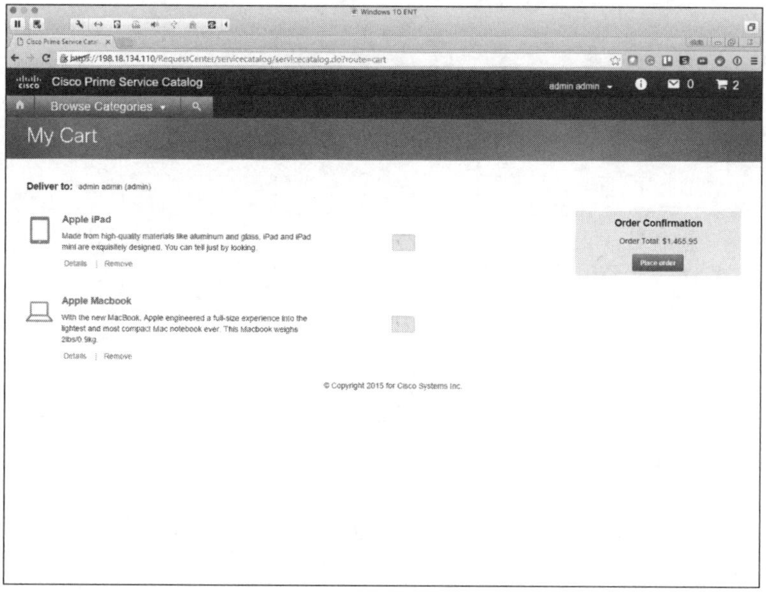

Figure 5-20   *My Cart*

Step 3.   Click **Place Order** on the My Cart page to order the service and finish the ordering process.

Viewing Order Status Details

The requisition status page displays details about the status of a single request, along with all the services in the request. You can create and view comments, as well as attach and view documents.

To view order status details:

Step 1.   Go to **Service Catalog > Manage My Stuff > Open Orders**; example results are shown in Figure 5-21.

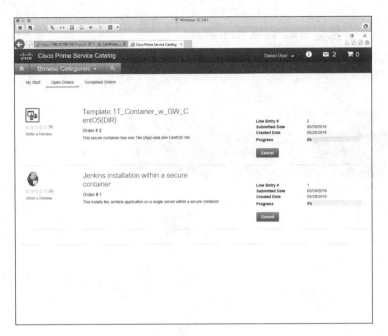

Figure 5-21 *Open Orders*

Step 2.   Click the requisition number to view the order details shown in Figure 5-22.
As shown in the box on the right, three different views are available: Summary,
Comments & History, and Attachments.

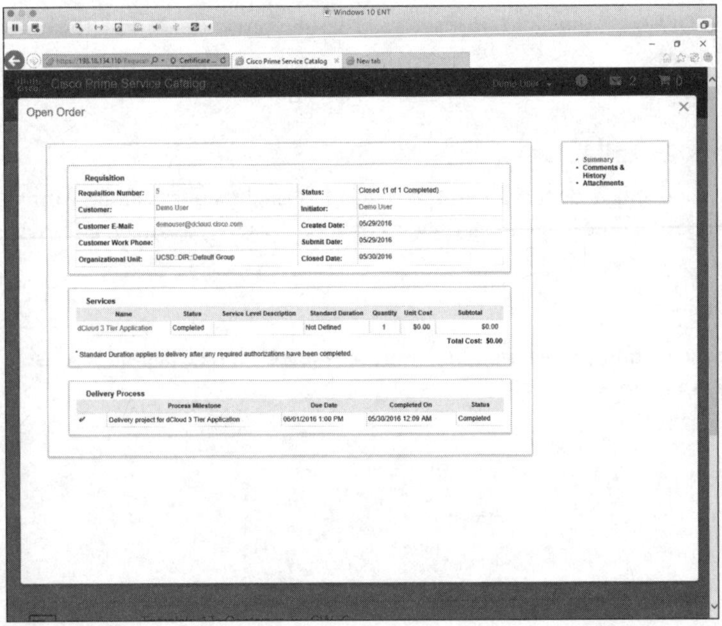

Figure 5-22 *Summary View*

The Summary view of the requisition displays the following sections:

- **Requisition:** Provides customer and initiator information, overall status of the requisition, and create/submit dates.

- **Services:** Lists the name of each service in the requisition, along with its current status, standard duration, and cost information. Click the service name to view the completed order form.

- **Delivery Process:** Lists the milestones (the major tasks of reviewers, approvers, and service performers) in the service delivery process, along with the due date for each milestone and its current status. The possible Status column values are

  - **TBD:** The due date will be determined when any required authorizations have been completed.

  - **Approximate:** The due date forecast has been approximated based on the calendar of the task's default delivery team.

  - **Estimated:** The due date forecast estimate has been based on the duration of scheduled tasks when the order is submitted.

  - **Completed:** A task in a service delivery plan has been successfully completed.

The Comments & History view displays the comments of reviewers, authorizers, and performers who work on the service request. It also displays a history of actions, such as automated email and task completions, that are logged by the system. To add a comment, enter it in the Add Comments field and then click **Add**. Your comment will be visible to all users who can view the requisition.

The Attachments view enables you to view and attach documents associated with the requisition. To associate a document to the requisition, click **Browse**, locate and choose the file you wish to attach to the requisition, and click **Add**.

Stack Designer

Stack Designer allows you to create application templates that include the application and infrastructure components as one complete unit. You can dynamically assemble application components and infrastructure in a graphical interface that can then be reused. Once the stack is defined, it can then be published to the catalog and provisioned by end users.

Stack Designer Templates

When you launch Stack Designer, you are presented with predefined application templates that you can use as is, or clone and modify. If you want to create a new application, you can do that as well by clicking Add New Template. Figure 5-23 shows the Stack Designer Application Templates page.

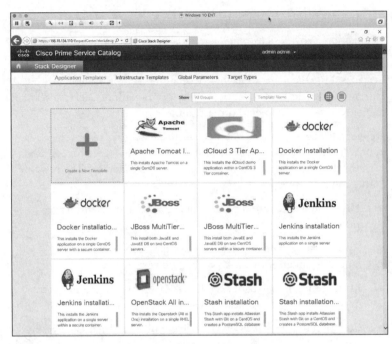

Figure 5-23   *Stack Designer Application Templates*

In addition to Application Templates, Stack Designer has tabs for Infrastructure Templates, Global Parameters, and Target Types.

Infrastructure templates are imported from UCS Director and, if installed, Cisco Virtual Application Cloud Segmentation (VACS) and Intercloud Fabric for Business. The types of services available from UCS Director are container templates, container catalogs, and standard catalog virtual machines. These infrastructure templates include networking configuration, virtual machine images, and topology. From VACS, Prime Service Catalog imports the following templates: Cloud Services Router virtual machine, Virtual Security Gateway virtual machine, and application virtual machines. Figure 5-24 shows the Infrastructure Templates tab.

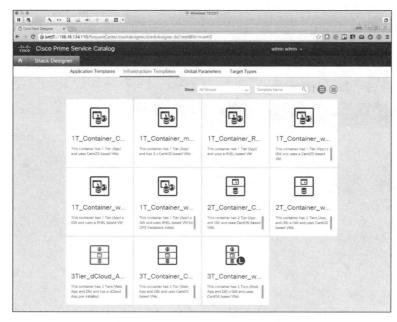

Figure 5-24   *Stack Designer Infrastructure Templates*

The Global Parameters tab, shown in Figure 5-25, stores commonly used configuration parameters needed for application provisioning. These can be added here or as part of the application stack building process.

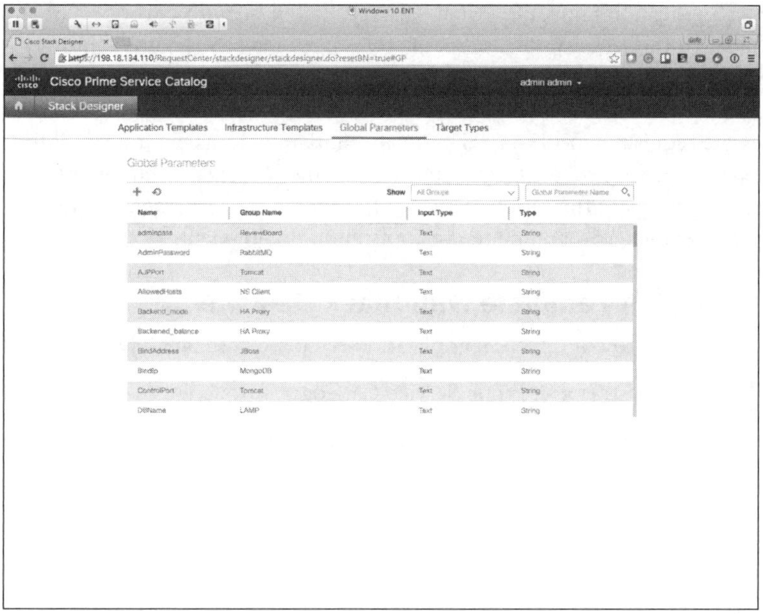

Figure 5-25   *Stack Designer Global Parameters*

Target types are integration points that the application stack can be built against. The default target type for Enterprise Cloud Suite is UCS Director. Figure 5-26 shows the Target Types tab.

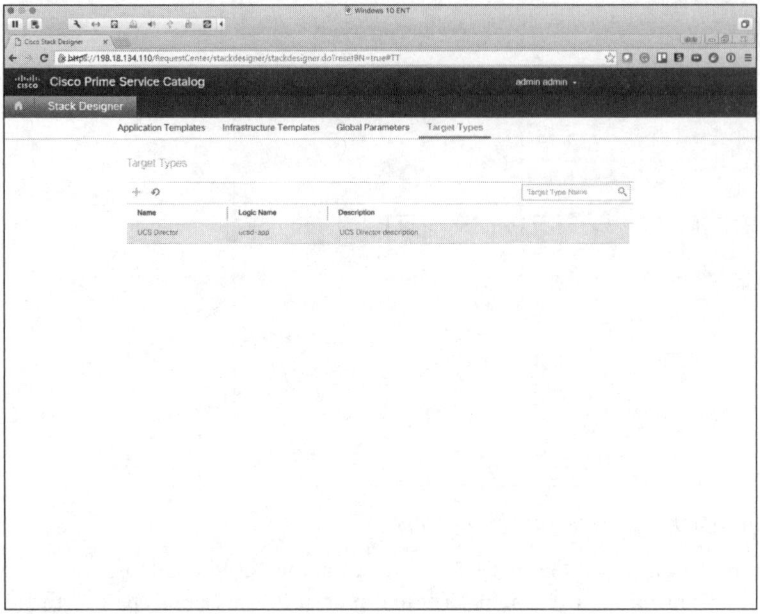

Figure 5-26   *Stack Designer Target Types*

When a user orders an application template, Prime Service Catalog begins the process of managing the fulfillment of the request. PSC starts off by processing any required approval steps. Once the request is approved for execution, PSC determines if any UCS Director–managed infrastructure provisioning must take place. If so, PSC makes a remote call to UCS Director and initiates the requisite workflow. PSC can also initiate external actions via internal scripts, integration with Cisco Process Orchestrator, and other external components. As PSC moves into the application configuration element of the request, it leverages its internal Puppet service and Heat templates to complete the application deployment.

Configuring an Application Template with Stack Designer

The following steps detail how to configure an application template with Stack Designer.

Key Topic

Step 1.   Log in as an administrator in Prime Service Catalog.

Step 2.   Choose **admin > Switch To > Stack Designer** (see Figure 5-27).

Step 3.   In Stack Designer, click **Create a New Template** (see Figure 5-28).

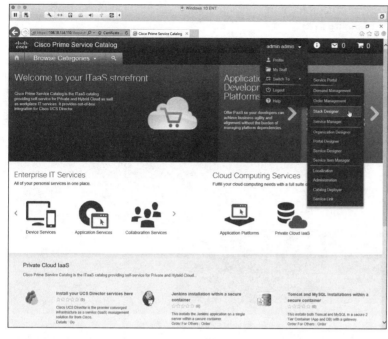

Figure 5-27 *Switching to Stack Designer Module*

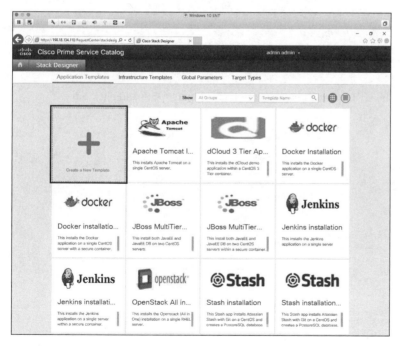

Figure 5-28 *Creating a New Template*

Step 4. Enter basic information about your application, as shown in the Catapp example in Figure 5-29.

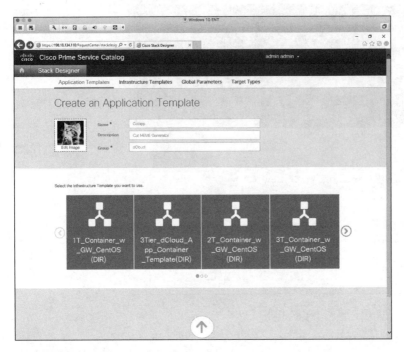

Figure 5-29 *Application Information*

Step 5. Click **Add Image** to select an image that will be displayed in the service catalog.

Step 6. Enter the URL for the image location (see Figure 5-30) and click **Save**.

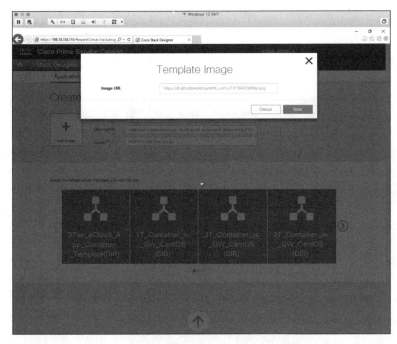

Figure 5-30 *Enter URL for Image*

Step 7.   Select an infrastructure template. Figure 5-31 shows the result of selecting the template for a two-tier application.

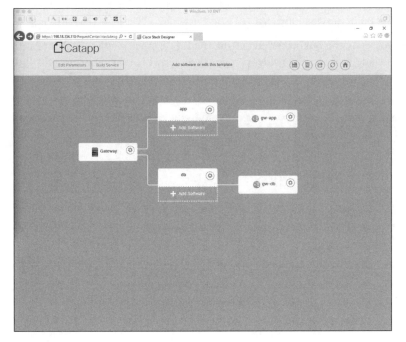

Figure 5-31 *Infrastructure Template Selected*

Step 8. Add software components and input required service parameters, similar to the example shown in Figure 5-32.

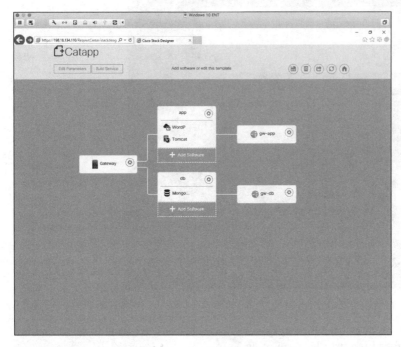

Figure 5-32 *Adding Software Components*

Step 9. Click the **Build Service** button.

Step 10. After you click the Build Service button, the Edit Service window will appear. Click Include to select the folder categories under which the new service will appear when searching or browsing through the catalog (see Figure 5-33).

Step 11. Click the Permissions tab of the Edit Service window, and then click the Add Permission drop-down arrow to select who in the organization can see the new template (see Figure 5-34).

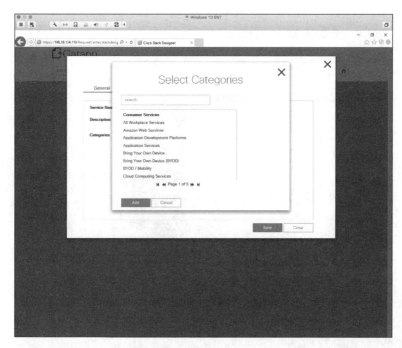

Figure 5-33 *Select Categories Dialog Box*

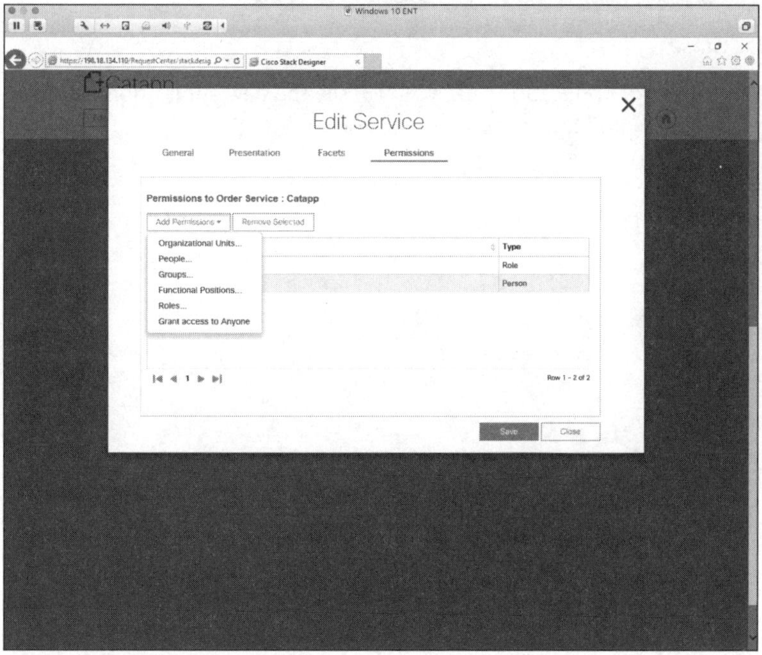

Figure 5-34 *Selecting Permissions*

Step 12.   You will be notified when the service has been saved successfully, as shown in Figure 5-35. Click **Save** and then **Close**.

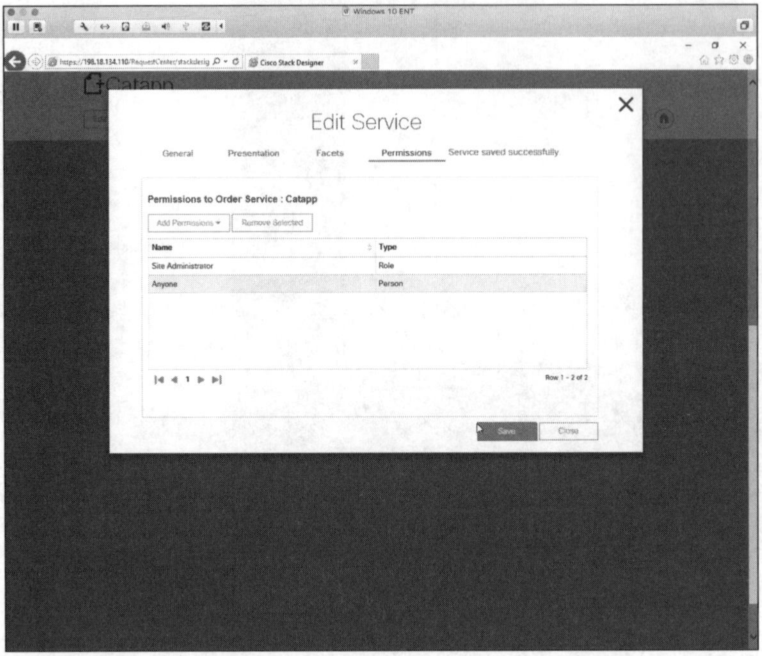

Figure 5-35   *Save and Close*

Step 13.   Return to the list of applications and you will see the new application listed, as shown for Catapp in Figure 5-36.

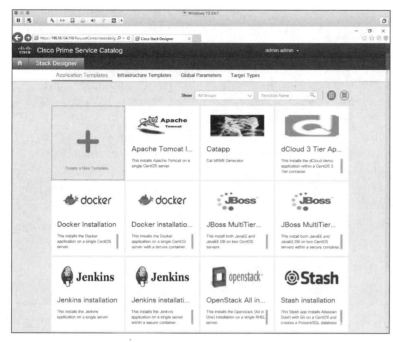

Figure 5-36 *New App Template*

Heat Orchestration

Prime Service Catalog utilizes Heat orchestration as its embedded orchestration service along with OpenStack Keystone and RabbitMQ server. Heat is an OpenStack project whose main goal is to allow administrators to describe complex cloud-based applications in a logical modeling language text file. These text files, referred to as templates, then get interpreted by the Heat engine for execution. This service allows you to orchestrate a large number of components as a single unit. Keystone handles identity management, while RabbitMQ is responsible for passing service requests from Prime Service Catalog to the orchestrator for provisioning via the AMQP protocol.

Heat is exclusively used in Prime Service Catalog to orchestrate application model templates that are built with Stack Designer. These templates can be constructed in the Heat Orchestration Template (or HOT) format and allow for interoperability because Heat is a nonproprietary open source technology. HOT is often written in YAML (Yet Another Markup Language) and is easy to read. These templates have become a common way to provide Heat resource plug-ins that allow Heat to orchestrate UCS Director and Puppet.

The goal of Heat is to create a stack that represents a collection of virtual machines and their configurations, including networks, security groups, and other parameters. A Heat Template file is made up of four sections:

- **Resources:** This has the details of the stack you are building and includes the objects that will be created and/or modified when Heat orchestration executes. Resources can be virtual machines, data store volumes, security groups, IP addresses, or any other object within UCS Director.

- **Properties:** Properties are the variables within your template and can either be hard coded (i.e., a specific virtual machine image) or can be placeholders that the user is prompted to input.

- **Parameters:** Parameters are the actual property values that must be passed when executing the Heat template.

- **Output:** Output includes the return values sent to the user or Prime Service Catalog upon execution of the template.

Example 5-1 shows a HOT file example written in YAML.

Example 5-1   *Output of a HOT File Example Written in YAML*

```
{
  "heat_template_version" : "2013-05-23",
  "parameters" : {
    "CreateServiceName" : {
      "type" : "string",
      "description" : "Create Service name"
    },
  },
  "resources" : {
    "container" : {
      "type" : "Cisco::ServiceCatalog::Service",
      "properties" : {
        "createservice" : {
          "Ref" : "CreateServiceName"
        },
        "deleteservice" : {
          "Ref" : "DeleteServiceName"
        },
        "customerloginname" : {
          "Ref" : "CustomerName"
        },
        "sections" : {
          "UCSD_ContainerInformation" : {
            "Name" : {
              "Ref" : "ContainerName"
```

Exam Preparation Tasks

As mentioned in the section "How to Use This Book" in the Introduction, you have a couple of choices for exam preparation: the exercises here, Chapter 15, "Final Preparation," and the exam simulation questions on the Pearson IT Certification Practice Test.

Review All Key Topics

Review the most important topics in this chapter, noted with the Key Topics icon in the outer margin of the page. Table 5-4 lists a reference of these key topics and the page number on which each is found.

Key Topic

Table 5-4   Key Topics for Chapter 5

Key Topic Element	Description	Page Number
Section	Identify the components of Prime Service Catalog	96
Steps	Understand the end-user storefront and how to order a service	103
Table 5-2	Wildcard search methods	108
Steps	Process for ordering a service	110
Paragraph	Understand Stack Designer	114
Steps	Configure an application template with Stack Designer	116
Paragraph	Understand Heat orchestration	123

Define Key Terms

Define the following key terms from this chapter and check your answers in the glossary:

Prime Service Catalog, service catalog, lifecycle management, BYOD, templates, Portal Designer, Service Designer, Stack Designer, AMQP, RabbitMQ, Heat orchestration, OpenStack, Keystone, YAML

This chapter covers the following topics:

1.0 Cloud Infrastructure Administration and Reporting

1.3   Deploy virtual app containers

1.3.a   Provide basic support and troubleshoot app container with firewall, networking, and load balancer

3.0 Cloud Provisioning

3.1   Describe predefined Cisco UCS Director-based services with the Cisco Prime Service Catalog

3.1.c   Describe template formats

Task 3.1.c(iii): Network

Task 3.1.c(iv): Virtualization

3.3   Deploy preconfigured templates and make minor changes to the service catalog offerings that do not affect workflows or services

3.3.a   Describe the deployment of templates: storage, compute, network, and virtualization

CHAPTER 6

Cisco Cloud Infrastructure

As you have seen in previous chapters, a cloud infrastructure is composed of a variety of components, from physical switches, storage arrays, and compute node to many virtual appliances. Each of these has a key function in the operation and administration of a cloud infrastructure, and this chapter looks at both the virtual and physical components necessary to build a cloud infrastructure suited for automation and orchestration.

This chapter starts with an overview of the main Cisco and third-party products that can be connected into a Cisco Powered cloud for automation and orchestration. The main virtual and physical components that make up an on-premises cloud infrastructure will be reviewed. The major sections provide an overview of the physical and virtual switches, the virtual appliances, the compute components, storage, and Cisco Intercloud Fabric. We'll then summarize how these components can be joined together to work in a Cisco Powered cloud.

"Do I Know This Already?" Quiz

The "Do I Know This Already?" quiz allows you to assess whether you should read this entire chapter thoroughly or jump to the "Exam Preparation Tasks" section. If you are in doubt about your answers to these questions or your own assessment of your knowledge of the topics, read the entire chapter. Table 6-1 lists the major headings in this chapter and their corresponding "Do I Know This Already?" quiz questions. You can find the answers in Appendix A, "Answers to the 'Do I Know This Already?' Quizzes."

Table 6-1 "Do I Know This Already?" Section-to-Question Mapping

Foundation Topics Section	Questions
Physical Switching	1–3
Virtual Switching	4–6
Virtual Application Cloud Segmentation (VACS)	7–9
Intercloud Fabric	10

Caution The goal of self-assessment is to gauge your mastery of the topics in this chapter. If you do not know the answer to a question or are only partially sure of the answer, you should mark that question as wrong for purposes of the self-assessment. Giving yourself credit for an answer you correctly guess skews your self-assessment results and might provide you with a false sense of security.

1. You can connect using SSH into which of the following switches to manage them? (Choose all that apply.)

   a. Nexus 1000V Series

   b. Nexus 2000 Series

   c. Nexus 5000 Series

   d. Nexus 7000 Series

   e. Nexus 9000 Series

   f. All of the above

2. FEX stands for:

   a. Fabric Enhanced Extension

   b. Fabric Ethernet Extension

   c. Fabric Extender

   d. Fiber Extender

3. The Nexus 9000 line of switches supports which of the following GE port speeds?

   a. 1/10

   b. 1/10/100

   c. 10/100

   d. 1/10/25/40/50/100

   e. 10/50/100

4. What are the main components of the Nexus 1000V? (Choose all that apply.)

   a. Virtual Ethernet Module

   b. Logical Ethernet Module

   c. Logical Supervisor Module

   d. Virtual Supervisor Module

   e. Application Policy Connector

5. AVS stands for:

   a. Application Velocity System

   b. Application Virtual System

   c. Application Virtualized System

   d. Application Virtual Switch

6. For an ACI-enabled network, which would be the best product to use to deliver virtual switching services?

   a. VMware NSX

   b. Nexus 1000V

   c. VMware DVS

   d. Application Virtual Switch

7. Which of the following are not benefits of VACS? (Choose all that apply.)

   a. Easy installation within UCS Director

   b. Port-based firewall

   c. Zone-based firewall

   d. Hardware-based load balancing

   e. All the above are benefits of VACs

8. Choose all the valid VACS container types.

   a. 2 Tier

   b. n Tier

   c. 3 Tier Internal

   d. 3 Tier External

9. Which of the following can be a VACS container gateway of choice? (Choose all that apply.)

   a. The built-in virtual gateway, the CSR 1000V

   b. A physical gateway such as one from Palo Alto Networks

   c. A logical gateway within the application tier of an *n*-tier software application

   d. Another virtual gateway such as the ASAv, vGW, or vPAN

   e. None of the above

10. What level(s) of encryption is supported by Intercloud secure network extension? (Choose all that apply.)

   a. AES 128 bit

   b. AES 256 bit

   c. AES 512 bit

   d. AES 1024 bit

   e. None of the above

6

Foundation Topics

How Automation and Orchestration Relates to Infrastructure

The underlying physical and virtual infrastructure within your private on-premises data center is the "pool of resources" that you can control by a cloud automation and orchestration suite. It is important to understand how automation and orchestration relates to infrastructure (whether physical or virtual) and how all the pieces fit together to help you deliver the types of services required by your organization. This chapter discusses products and technologies such as the Cisco Nexus Series Switches, Application Centric Infrastructure (ACI), Virtual Application Cloud Segmentation (VACS), Nexus 1000V, Virtual Security Gateway (VSG), Cloud Services Router (CSR), and more.

Today, many IT tasks are done manually on an ad hoc basis. For example, new business requirements are often brought to the IT team. As a member of either the storage, network, compute, or virtualization team, you then have to make a variety of decisions. See Figure 6-1. Do we have the capacity on hand today or do we need to order additional gear? What team needs to do their part first? How long will a project to meet these requirements take? What other projects am I currently working on that may impact my ability to accomplish this new project?

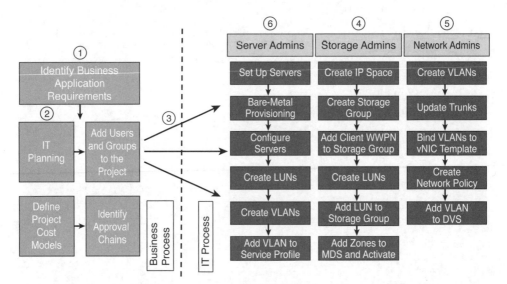

Figure 6-1 *Sample IT Workflow Without Automation*

In addition to adding new projects and capabilities, you are often faced with having to make daily small adds and changes to your existing infrastructure. Some of these tasks are trivial. Others, such as adding a VLAN across a data center campus, can be fairly daunting in nature due to the high likelihood of human error or misconfiguration. Who hasn't missed a switch configuration on a device or two during a change control at 2:00 a.m.?

The main goal of automation and orchestration is to allow you, the administrator or architect, to accomplish common tasks quickly and easily, the same way, time after time. Think of automation and orchestration as a very similar concept to a hopefully not too distant in the future concept. How great would it be if you could travel to a remote destination simply by hopping into your autonomous vehicle, inputting a destination address, and letting your vehicle drive you safely and reliably to your destination, giving you the chance to read, surf the web, talk on the phone, or simply attend to other tasks during the driving portion of your journey? All the while, you would have complete control to step in and take over if necessary to adjust your route, respond to an unforeseen situation, etc.

IT automation and orchestration are much like the previously described scenario. You have a mountain of tasks that you face daily in your job. Some are simple, one-step tasks. Others are compound tasks that are fairly order specific and complex. With automation and orchestration, much like the autonomous vehicle, you program in the tasks you want to accomplish and the vehicle takes care of the rest. In a cloud infrastructure, UCS Director is your vehicle. You program it to automate simple or complex IT tasks. You do this in conjunction with members of your organization from the other areas of infrastructure management discipline. The end results are great. You have taken a task or set of tasks that is manual in nature, time consuming, and prone to error and you've automated it with a few mouse clicks. More importantly, if there is a problem, you have the ability to roll back these changes immediately.

So to get your mind around the power of automation and orchestration, look at the list of daily/weekly tasks or projects that you face in IT and ask, "Is this something that I could automate? If I automated it, would it save time and allow me to work on more exciting projects?" If the answer to those questions is yes, congratulations, you are well on your way to bringing the wonderful benefits of a Cisco Powered cloud architecture to your organization!

Physical Switching

Founded in 1984, Cisco has a rich history in LAN switching. From the groundbreaking Catalyst series of switches that put Cisco on the map as an enterprise switching contender to the new Nexus and ACI products, Cisco's expertise and history in switching have made it one of the most widely deployed switching products in most organizations today. For the purposes of this book, we will focus on the Nexus product line and Application Centric Infrastructure as products and concepts.

Nexus Series Switches

Starting with the Cisco Catalyst Series Switches as its current offering, Cisco set out to create its next generation of enterprise-class switches for the data center. Building on many of the concepts and the architecture of the extremely popular MDS (Multilayer Director Switch) Fibre Channel switch, Cisco introduced the Nexus Series Switches in 2008 with the introduction of the Nexus 7000. Since that time, Cisco has continued to round out the portfolio of offerings, covering a gamut of Ethernet connectivity options from 10 Mbps to 100 Gbps. Architecturally speaking, the Nexus product line runs Cisco NX-OS (Nexus Operating System), which was derived from SAN-OS, which powered Cisco's Fibre Channel

Series Switches previously. Whereas Ethernet products historically had moved megabits of traffic, the Cisco MDS had a proven track record of moving megabytes of Fibre Channel payloads through many organizations. The entire switch lineup can be seen in Figure 6-2.

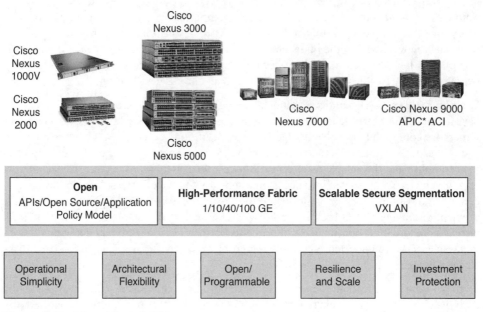

Figure 6-2   *Nexus Switch Lineup*

Let's take a look at the Cisco current switching portfolio.

The Nexus 2000 Series Fabric Extenders

Marking a significant departure from previous products, the Cisco Nexus Fabric Extenders (FEX) don't operate as a switch per se, but rather as a remote linecard to a parent switch.

Prior to Fabric Extenders, management functions were typically all located within the confines of a single chassis. For example, switches were either large (modular) or small (fixed), but configuration happened on just that switch. In many designs, large switches were located in the middle of a data center row or in the end of a data center row and used to aggregate connections from multiple smaller switches. Configurations had to be applied to both the large switch and the smaller switches. See Figure 6-3.

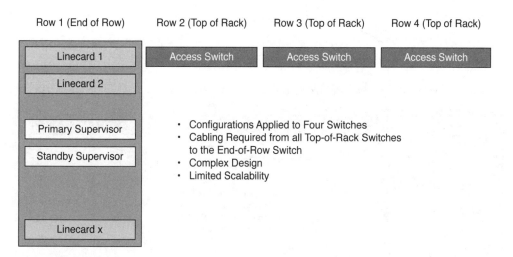

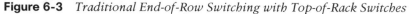

Figure 6-3 *Traditional End-of-Row Switching with Top-of-Rack Switches*

This led to multiple challenges:

■ Increase in cabling between switch rows

■ Increased requirements for firmware management

■ Increased port and switch management

■ Less scalability

With the advent of the Nexus 2000 Fabric Extender, the Nexus 2000 device acts like a remote linecard to a central Nexus switch. All configuration for all ports gets applied to the single central switch. Also, multiple FEXs are supported per central Nexus switch. This leads to multiple benefits:

■ Decrease in cabling between switches in rows

■ Decreased number of firmware management points (because FEX firmware is managed from the parent switch it is connected to)

■ Decreased port and switch management (one device as opposed to many devices)

■ More scalability and density

A Fabric Extender gets managed from its parent switch. This makes management much simpler, as shown in Figure 6-4.

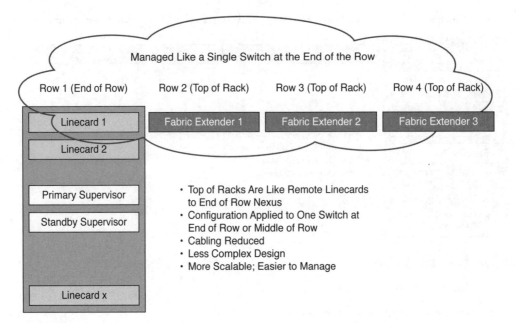

Figure 6-4 *Nexus Fabric Extender Design*

As of the writing of this book, Cisco has the following FEX models available (see Figure 6-5):

- **100/1000 BASE-T:** Nexus 2224TP, Nexus 2248TP (48 ports), and Nexus 2248TP-E (48 ports with extended buffers)
- **10GBASE-T Fabric Extender:** Nexus 2232TQ, 2348TQ, 2348TQ-E, 2232TM-E, and 2232TM
- **10G SFP+ Fabric Extender:** Nexus 2348UPQ, 2248PQ, and 2232PP

Figure 6-5 *Nexus 2000 Fabric Extenders*

Fabric Extenders can be mixed and matched in different types to create the connections and port densities required. Be sure to check with the configuration limits of each parent switch to ensure you don't try to connect to many Fabric Extenders in a topology.

Cisco Nexus 3000 Series Switches

The Cisco Nexus 3000 Series Switches are designed for top-of-rack 1/10/25/40/50/100-GE connectivity with extremely low latencies and densities ranging from 24 to 128 ports. In addition, the Nexus 3000 Series supports Virtual Extensible LAN (VXLAN) for mobility and tenant isolation as well as accessibility via common scripting tools such as Python (see Figure 6-6).

Figure 6-6   *Cisco Nexus 3000 Series Switches*

Cisco Nexus 4000 Series Switches

Purpose built for the IBM BladeCenter chassis, the Nexus 4000 is a high-speed 10-GE switch that supports both 1/10-GE uplinks (see Figure 6-7).

Figure 6-7   *Cisco Nexus 4000 Series Switch*

Cisco Nexus 5000 Series Switches

Designed for low oversubscription of 1/10/40/100-GE top-of-rack access deployments or as a consolidation point for multiple Nexus 2000 Series Fabric Extenders, the Nexus 5000 Series of switches supports up to 128 fixed ports. However, with support for 24 to 48 total Fabric Extenders connected to the parent Nexus 5000 (depending on Nexus 5000 model), the total number of ports managed under a single Nexus 5000 can be extremely dense (see Figure 6-8).

Figure 6-8   *Nexus 5000 Series Switches plus Fabric Extenders*

In addition, the Nexus 5000 line supports both Fibre Channel over Ethernet (FCoE) and Fibre Channel (FC) in 1/2/4/8/16-Gbps speeds (support and speed vary per switch model). As of the time of this writing, Cisco had six Nexus 5000 switches available: Nexus 5672UP, 5672UP-16G, 56128P, 5624Q, 5648Q, and 5696Q.

Cisco Nexus 6000 Series Switches

The Nexus 6000 lineup is designed for access- and space-constrained aggregation deployments, offering up to 384 ports of 10 GE or 96 ports of 40 GE and up to 160 unified ports supporting FCoE. It also supports Fabric Extenders. The chipset has been optimized and tuned for faster 10-GE and 40-GE traffic as opposed to Gigabit network flows (see Figure 6-9).

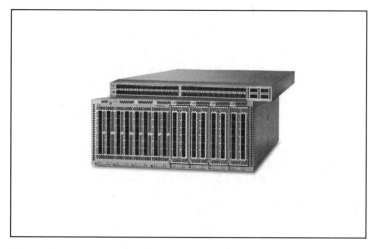

Figure 6-9 *Nexus 6000 Series Switch*

Cisco Nexus 7000 Series Switches

The Nexus 7000 switch was the first Nexus switch released in the product family in 2008. Ideal uses include data center access, aggregation, and core deployments. With the advent of virtual device contexts (VDC), the Nexus was the first switch in its class to allow switch virtualization and separation of services, allowing the collapsing (in many networks) of the access and aggregation layers, resulting in less complex, extremely scalable fabrics. With support for in-service software upgrades (ISSU), Fabric Extenders, and speed options from 1/20/40/100 GE, the Nexus 7000 is designed as a true enterprise-class workhorse for the most demanding networks (see Figure 6-10).

Figure 6-10 *Nexus 7000 Series Switch*

Cisco Nexus 9000 Series Switches

The Nexus 9000 Series Switch marks the next exciting evolution in the Cisco Nexus switching products. The Nexus 9000 can operate in two modes. For compatibility with existing networks, the switch can run in NX-OS standalone mode. This allows the Nexus 9000 to be introduced into existing fabrics in place of other platforms, such as the Nexus 5000 or Nexus 7000. However, for those with an eye on the next level of programmability and centralization of management in an enterprise network, the Nexus 9000 line can also be put into ACI mode, which will be described in detail in the next section on ACI. Offering speeds of 1/10/25/40/50/100 GE and a deep set of switch- and fabric-level software-defined programmable features, the Nexus 9000 line is helping Cisco usher in the area of software-defined networking (SDN). See Figure 6-11.

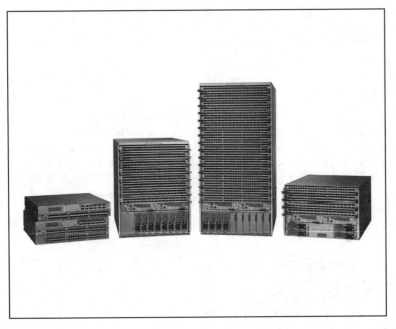

Figure 6-11   *Nexus 9000 Series Switch*

Cisco Cloud Programmability of Nexus Switches

Now the great news. Everything that you can accomplish as a network administrator using the command-line interface (CLI) or with scripts can also be accomplished in a Cisco Powered cloud deployment. Tasks that are time consuming, mundane, and prone to error can now be automated and orchestrated within UCS Director and executed predictably, repeatedly, and easily with UCS Director automation and orchestration tasks and workflows. Take just one simple scenario: adding a new VLAN to a large enterprise data center fabric. Imagine that your fabric has 60 switches. If you're a network administrator, you know the tension and tedious nature of such a change as you ready a window (usually in the middle of the night on a weekend) to perform this operation over and over on each switch in the entire fabric. If you miss one, traffic can be dropped and problems can arise. With UCS Director, you could create an automation task that predictably and repeatedly rolls out a new VLAN across all switches in the data center campus, with literally just a few clicks. Unlike a network administrator relying on caffeine and pizza during a 2 a.m. change window, UCS Director will apply this to all the switches without missing a single switch. And if there is a problem? One-button rollback on some or all of the fabric is a core feature of UCS Director.

Introduction to Application Centric Infrastructure

As mentioned previously in this chapter, Cisco recognizes that as fabrics become larger and as layers of virtualization via hypervisors (in compute) and virtualized network services (in the fabric) add more functionality, the previous method of configuring on a device-by-device basis is no longer feasible. If we recap the progression of administration, the Catalyst line of products required administrators to touch every single platform. The Nexus line, with Fabric Extenders, consolidated management onto fewer devices, while technologies such as VDCs allowed further consolidation still. However, as fabrics continue to grow in size and complexity, a better way is needed to program both virtual and physical network resources. Enter Application Centric Infrastructure (ACI). ACI allows the rapid deployment of applications onto networks with scale, security, and full visibility, whether those networks are physical or virtual (see Figure 6-12).

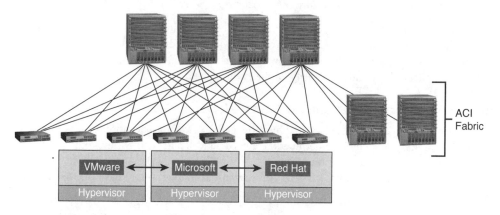

Figure 6-12 *Application Centric Infrastructure*

The concept behind ACI is simple yet powerful. Using a set of redundant Application Policy Infrastructure Controllers (APICs), you can define and apply network policy in a single location to literally hundreds or thousands of devices all across your network. Once defined at the APIC level, that policy can easily be deployed across a variety of physical (bare-metal) network ports as well as ports within a variety of hypervisors such as VMware ESX, Microsoft Hyper-V, and Red Hat KVM (see Figure 6-13).

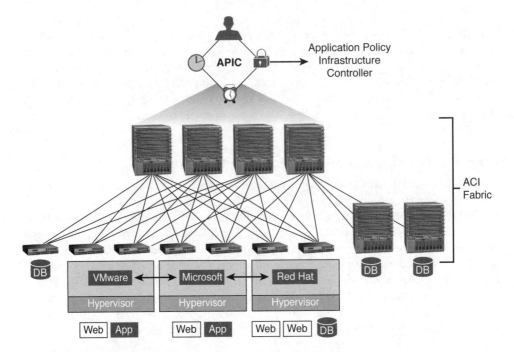

Figure 6-13 *Cisco Application Policy Infrastructure Controller*

These policies are defined as high-level application connectivity/security needs, but instead of tightly coupling them with a large network the way you previously did on a per physical or virtual port basis, these policies can now be abstracted from the complicated details of a large network topology and then easily applied where needed.

Application Network Profiles and How They Work

At the top level, ACI is an object model built on a concept of one or more tenants. Tenants in the ACI model can include something like a particular department within your organization, a business unit, an application group, etc. A service provider hosting multiple customers may have dozens of tenants, whereas your organization may simply have one tenant, the name of your company.

Underneath the concept of the tenant in ACI there exists a context. A context can be thought of as a set of rules for separate IP spaces or virtual routing and forwarding instances. A context is simply a further way to segment and separate forwarding requirements within a tenant. A tenant can also, hierarchically, have multiple contexts.

Within the context you will find a series of objects that define actual applications on the network called endpoints (EPs) and endpoint groups (EPGs) as well as the policies that define the relationships between the EPs and EPGs. These policies are not only access control lists (ACL), but also inbound and outbound filters, quality of service (QoS) settings, marking rules, redirection rules, and other settings that define specific L4–L7 interactions between the EPGs (see Figure 6-14).

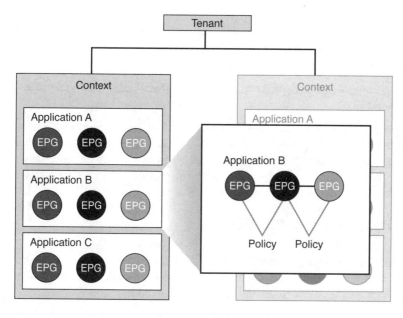

Figure 6-14 *ACI Logical Object Model*

Now that we have a frame of reference for how objects are referenced within an ACI environment, we can look at how application network profiles (ANP) work. An ANP can be used to define permissible (or denied) interactions between EPGs. For example, if we imagine a three-tier application of Web, App, and Database, each tier would exist as an EPG and potentially contain endpoints. We will discuss a theoretical application that has five web servers, two app servers, and one database server (see Figure 6-15):

- Web EPG, consisting of five web EPs
- Application EPG, consisting of two app EPs
- Database EPG, consisting of one database EPs

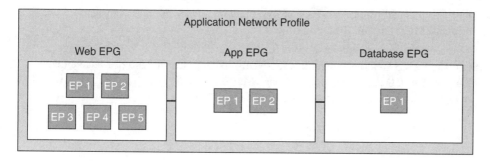

Figure 6-15 *Three-Tier Application Network Profile*

Once you have an idea of how you need the application tiers to interact, you would create the EPGs per tier, then create the policies to define connectivity between EPGs (such as log, mark, redirect, permit, deny, copy, etc.), and then create the connection between the EPGs. These connections between EPGs are known as *contracts*.

The ANP therefore is composed of a contract or contracts between multiple EPGs containing one or more EPs per EPG.

As your organization transitions from traditional NX-OS and CLI-based administration to an ACI-based network, UCS Director once again can provide a tremendous amount of value to you as many of the ACI- and APIC-related functions that you would perform on a daily basis are available within UCS Director as tasks that can be chained together into workflows to help create self-service capabilities for an ACI-enabled network.

Infrastructure Automation and UCS Director

Once the main components of a Cisco Powered cloud (Prime Service Catalog and UCS Director) have been implemented, they need to connect to various components in your data center to do automation and orchestration (see Figure 6-16). Some of the devices that can be attached to UCS Director for automation and orchestration include:

- Physical Ethernet switches such as those in the Cisco Nexus family and Catalyst family as well as various third-party switches

- Virtual Ethernet switches such as the Cisco Nexus 1000V or Application Virtual Switch (AVS), as well as various third-party virtual switches, including the VMware Distributed Virtual Switch (DVS)

- Nexus 9000 APIC, which enables the UCS Director administrator to issue automation and orchestration commands against a Nexus 9000 Application Programmable Interrupt Controller

- Other Ethernet network physical and virtual appliances such as Cisco VACS, Cisco CSR 1000V, ASA 1000V, and third-party physical and virtual networking appliances such as an F5 BIG-IP load balancer

- Fibre Channel switches including Cisco MDS and Brocade Fibre Channel switches

- Fibre Channel and IP-based storage arrays, including many popular arrays from Pure Storage, EMC, NetApp, IBM, and others

- Compute platforms including support for Cisco UCS Central, Cisco UCS Manager, Standalone UCS C-Series rackmount servers (utilizing Cisco Integrated Management Controller, or CIMC), as well as third-party servers such as those from HP, Dell, and IBM through standards like IP Management Interface (IPMI)

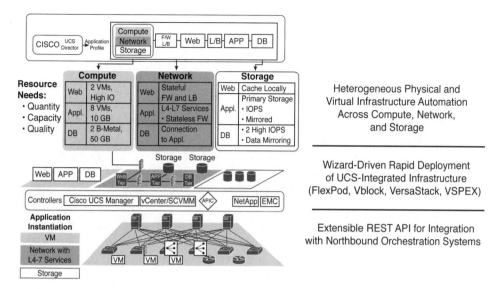

Figure 6-16 *Infrastructure Automation with UCS Director*

Virtual Switching

According to Moore's law, processor transistor capacity approximately doubles on average every two years. This hypothesis was first posited in 1965 by Gordon Moore, one of Intel's cofounders. To date, it has largely held true. In the mid-to-late 1990s, realizing that most bare-metal operating systems and applications were consuming only a fraction of available CPU and memory capacity, vendors started to introduce hypervisors in the server space to help more efficiently use the excess memory and CPU capacity that had been created as processors continued to become faster, denser, and more capable over time.

Before servers were virtualized, life was much simpler for network and server administrators. One (physical) server usually ran one application and consumed one (physical) network port. With the advent of the hypervisor, IT administrators also entered a new chapter in their careers, where multiple servers and applications, each with potentially different connectivity requirements, started to intermingle on a single physical host with a hypervisor installed, such as VMware ESX. With these changing requirements, the days of having a single host with a single application connected to a single switch port were gone. IT simply needed more flexibility. This brings us to the advent of the virtual switch.

Virtual Switching Overview

In the simplest terms, a virtual switch acts much like a physical switch, only it's made in software as opposed to being a physical/tangible switch that you could pick up and hold with your hands. A virtual switch is software that sits within a hypervisor on a physical host to provide VM-to-VM communication within that single host and also VM communication with other endpoints (such as a user running a query from their desktop against a database running on a virtual server) elsewhere on the network. In addition, virtual switches rely on the generic capabilities of the x86 processor and consume some CPU and memory overhead from that processor (that is therefore not available to the rest of the compute functions in the cluster). By contrast, physical switches, such as the Cisco Nexus 9000, use purpose-built ASICs in the hardware that are designed specifically for high-speed switching and packet processing.

As virtualization continued to grow in popularity, the industry started moving beyond the capabilities of a single virtual switch on a single physical host. As multiple physical hosts were joined together into more powerful clusters, the concept of having a single virtual switch tied to a single virtual host was no longer practical because every time a new hypervisor-based host was added to the network, another virtual switch had to be configured.

This led to the advent of the distributed virtual switch (DVS). A DVS sits within the hypervisor of multiple physical hosts, providing distributed networking services between multiple hosts in a cluster. As clusters have grown in size from 2 hosts to now up to 32 or more hosts, having a DVS is no longer a luxury; it is a necessity.

Cisco has two offerings in the DVS category: Nexus 1000V and the Application Virtual Switch. Let's take a quick look at each.

Nexus 1000V

The Cisco Nexus 1000V was created with the main Nexus product family during the advent of the Nexus 2000/5000/7000 product line and is geared mainly for traditional Nexus networking environments. It works very much like a virtual version of a Nexus 5000 or Nexus 7000 (with Nexus 2000 Fabric Extenders) architecture.

In the physical switching world, the main Nexus 5000 device acts as the management and configuration plane for building the switch configuration and services. Ports on a Nexus 2000–connected FEX receive their port configuration from the Nexus 5000.

A Nexus 1000V architecture (see Figure 6-17) typically has three main components:

- A Virtual Supervisor Module (VSM)
- A Virtual Ethernet Module (VEM)
- Integration with a virtual management console such as VMware Virtual Center or Microsoft SCVMM

In this model, you log in (usually via SSH/CLI) to the VSM and create a port configuration(s) for a virtual machine (called a virtual Ethernet, or vEthernet, interface). Those configurations then get pushed out from the VSM to VEMs that should receive that configuration.

The Nexus 1000V is fully integrated with UCS Director and comes with many prebuilt tasks required for administering and managing the Nexus 1000V within automation tasks.

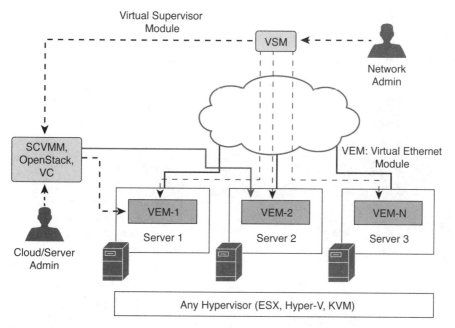

Figure 6-17 *Nexus 1000V Architecture*

AVS Architecture and Components

With the advent of the Cisco Nexus 9000 Series Switches, the Application Policy Infrastructure Controller (APIC), and the Application Centric Infrastructure (ACI), you no longer have to go to separate physical and virtual devices to apply network policy and configuration. In a Nexus 9000 environment in ACI mode, configuration happens one time at the APIC level and that configuration can then be applied to physical network ports as well as to virtual network ports using the Application Virtual Switch (AVS).

Similar in concept, the use case for AVS differs from Nexus 1000V as highlighted in Table 6-2.

Table 6-2 Comparison of Nexus 1000V and the Application Virtual Switch

	Nexus 1000V Virtual Switch	Application Virtual Switch
Target Network Fabric	Traditional Nexus 2000–7000 or 9000 running in standalone or non-ACI mode as well as Dynamic Fabric Automation	Application Centric Infrastructure (ACI)
Single Point of Management	To each Virtual Supervisor Module (VSM) needing configuration	Application Policy Infrastructure Controller (APIC) for both physical and virtual networking
Hypervisor Support	vSphere, Hyper-V, KVM/Xen	vSphere, Hyper-V, KVM/Xen

So while materially similar, the AVS is targeted for ACI-enabled networks, whereas the Nexus 1000V is the right tool of choice for non-ACI-enabled networks.

Architecturally, AVS has two major components (see Figure 6-18):

■ The AVS-DVS (Distributed Virtual Switch) on vCenter

■ An AVS kernel module on each ESXi host that is ACI enabled

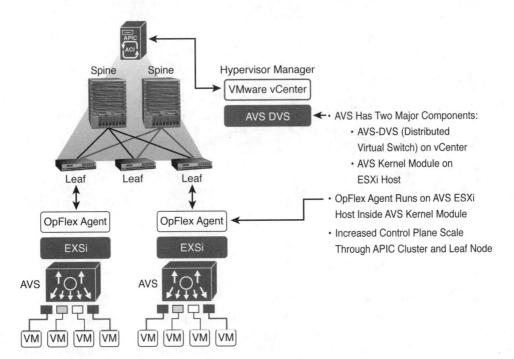

Figure 6-18 *AVS Architecture and Components*

Virtual Application Cloud Segmentation (VACS)

The entire purpose of building a Cisco Powered cloud is so that you can quickly provision complete Infrastructure as a Service (IaaS) and Platform as a Service (PaaS) offerings for your internal users. In the previous section, we saw how ACI using the AVS with Nexus 9000 and APIC can offer rich L4–L7 network services for virtual machines.

In situations where ACI may not yet be deployed but the need still exists for rich networking services to be deployed alongside virtual machines, Cisco Virtual Application Cloud Segmentation (VACS) can be a great fit (see Figure 6-19). VACS offers the following:

■ Easy installation within UCS Director for automated provisioning and orchestration

■ Load balancing

■ Routing (using the Cisco CSR 1000V)

■ Edge firewall capability (using Cisco CSR 1000V)

■ Zone-based firewall (using Cisco Virtual Security Gateway)

■ Virtual fabric (using Cisco Nexus 1000V)

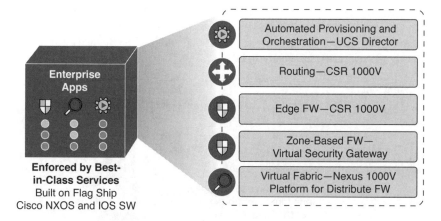

Figure 6-19 *Virtual Application Cloud Segmentation*

With deep integration into UCS Director, this allows secure segmentation and rapid deployment of applications in virtual data centers by helping to consolidate physical assets onto a single infrastructure that can then be virtualized to provide deep security and network services. In addition, VACS brings all the products previously mentioned into a single unified license, making it easy to deploy, license, and manage all the components included within VACS.

When you are allocating L4–L7 network services physically for virtual machines, service times typically increase as complexity increases and many points of management have to be configured in a solution. For example, if a particular virtualized server and application are using network load-balancing services as well as firewall services that are physical, you would be required to not only procure, rack, stack, and configure those physical devices, but also create configurations for your virtual services on each independent device (see Figure 6-20).

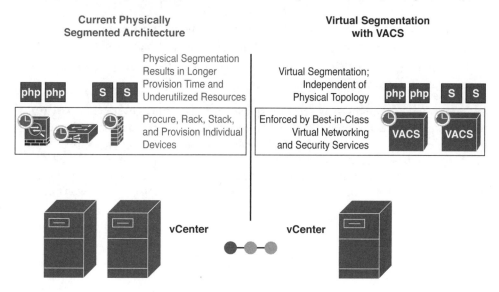

Figure 6-20 *Secure Segmentation on Shared Infrastructure*

Alternatively, leveraging virtual segmentation with VACS allows single-click installation within the Cisco Powered cloud framework (within UCS Director) and allows you to focus on one place to go to set up best-in-class virtual networking and security services. This is accomplished easily with wizards (see Figure 6-21).

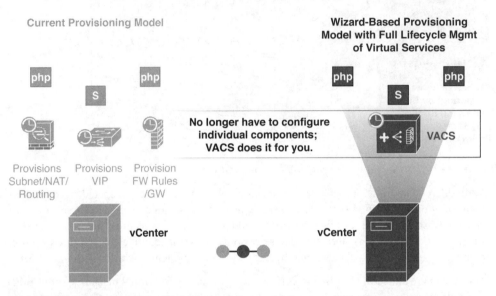

Figure 6-21 *Simplified Virtual Networking and Security on Shared Infrastructure*

VACS Containers

Within VACS, there is a concept known as a container. Containers are defined by the following:

- Virtual network and security services templates for application workloads
- Topology configurations designed for logical secure isolation and compliance
- Exposed through the UCS Director GUI to allow rapid and consistent provisioning of secure applications and rich L4–L7 services

Containers can be thought of as situation-specific templates that govern connectivity, security, and services in a multitiered virtualized application environment. Again, using our previous example of a three-tier application consisting of a web tier, an application tier, and a database tier, let's look at two different types of VACS containers, the VACS 3-tier internal container template and the 3-tier external container template (see Figure 6-22). A third example would be a VACS custom container template, which won't be covered here.

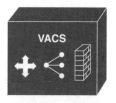

3 Tier: Internal Container   3 Tier: External Container   Custom Container

Figure 6-22 *Types of VACS Logical Container Templates*

VACS 3-Tier Internal Container Template

Let's assume the business has a requirement for you to deploy a three-tier application internally. They want to ensure that only authorized users, authenticated from the web tier, can access this application. If you were to build this manually, it would require (at a minimum):

- Deploying virtual web servers and configuring the application layers of the VMs

- Deploying virtual application servers and configuring the application layers of those VMs

- Deploying virtual database servers and configuring the application layers of those VMs

- Deploying a physical firewall and configuration application connectivity policies between the web tier, app tier, and database tier of the preceding three virtual systems

- Determining the best way to route traffic securely through each application tier into the firewall and applying the appropriate firewall rules to each step of the application

- Inserting load-balancing services in front of the web tier to provide proper load balancing

This would be quite a bit of configuration, just to get that one instance of the three-tier application up. Whenever another application owner came along with the same request, you would find yourself completing the same steps yet again (and again as more application requirements came to you from the business side of your organization).

Using one of the defined VACS 3-tier internal container templates, you could simply click the container template and create a new container for the application. All the proper rules for firewalling, load balancing, and routing would be predefined within the 3-tier internal container template via policy (see Figure 6-23).

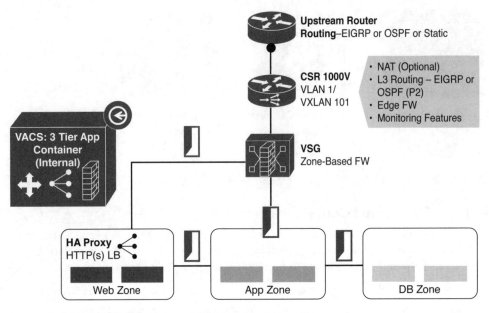

Figure 6-23 *VACS Containers: 3-Tier Internal*

As you can see, given that security requirements are not quite as tight for this internal application, connectivity from the Virtual Security Gateway (VSG) zone-based firewall flows toward the web zone's load balancer and, from there, to the app zone and DB zone. Now you have a template that you can predictably and repeatedly invoke whenever a new three-tier application requirement comes your way.

VACS 3-Tier External Container Template

If the application requires greater security and increased firewall use for security or compliance purposes, the 3-Tier External Container Template, shown in Figure 6-24, provides additional security because the firewall is in the communication path between all layers of the three-tier application.

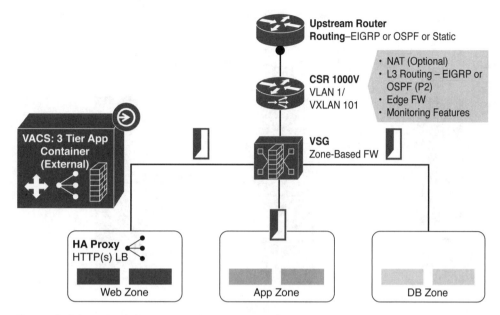

Figure 6-24   *VACS Containers: 3-Tier External*

As previously mentioned, it is also very straightforward to create custom VACS Container Templates for one-tier, two-tier, three-tier, or n-tier applications and define communication, security, load balancing, and other requirements between the different zones in the VACS custom container template. Saving this template will then give you a quick way to consistently and predictably deploy similar application services should the need arise in the future.

Building a VACS Container with Gateway of Choice

Often, existing standards in the environment may dictate using an existing technology as the default gateway for a VACS container. Within VACS, there is an option and the flexibility to combine both VACS services with standard deployed services in the environment.

For example, as shown in Figure 6-25, VACS can use

- The built-in virtual gateway, the CSR 1000V

- A physical gateway, such as one from Palo Alto Networks or Checkpoint, or a Cisco ASA

- Another virtual gateway, such as the Cisco Adaptive Security Virtual Appliance (ASAv), Juniper Virtual Gateway (vGW), or Virtual Palo Alto Networks (vPAN)

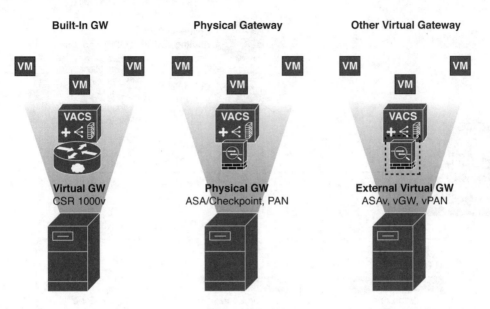

Figure 6-25   *Building VACS Container with Gateway of Choice*

When you're deploying VACS and choosing the gateway of choice, it's important to know how to operationalize this choice. You will need the gateway IP and you will get it installed as part of the VACS report after you spin up a VACS container from a template. You can use this information to program in any device (physical or virtual) of your choice as mentioned in the previous list.

Intercloud Fabric

As we've looked at the core components of a Cisco Powered cloud, we've focused a lot of discussion on the components that exist on premises. However, many IT workloads are also taking advantage of public cloud offerings such as Microsoft Azure, Amazon Web Services, or other Cisco Powered cloud ecosystem providers (see Figure 6-26).

Therefore, any good cloud solution should not only address multiple clouds (on premises and public as well as hybrid), but also different capabilities for configuration of an on-premises or public cloud infrastructure across a wide variety of public cloud services. Such is the role of Intercloud Fabric.

As with any strategy, the decision on where to host IT infrastructure (on premises or in the public cloud) boils down to a variety of factors. Some of them may be regulatory (such as needs around data sovereignty), or economic (workloads that are highly elastic or only needed during a short period of time each month/quarter/year). Figure 6-27 shows some of the criteria that go into choosing where to host a particular workload in a hybrid cloud deployment.

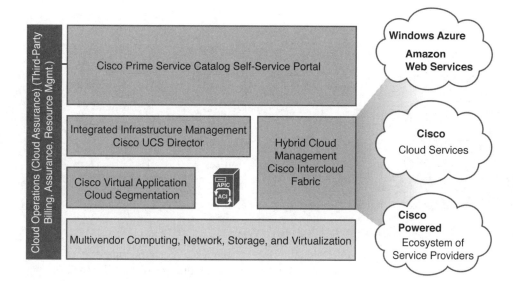

Figure 6-26 *Cisco ONE Enterprise Cloud Suite*

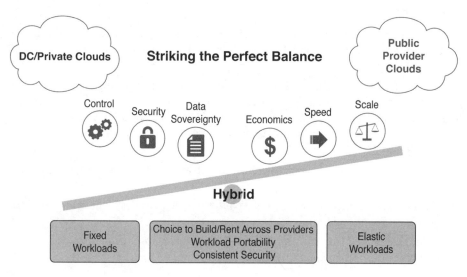

Figure 6-27 *Why Hybrid?*

Why Hybrid

Intercloud Fabric uses a similar architecture to that of distributed virtual switches such as the Nexus 1000V, as discussed earlier in the chapter. In a modular switch such as a Nexus 7000, the supervisors and linecards all exist in one modular chassis (unless using "distributed linecards" such as a Fabric Extender). In Intercloud Fabric, you interact with the on-premises component of the virtual "supervisor" while linecards are distributed throughout various public cloud services (see Figure 6-28).

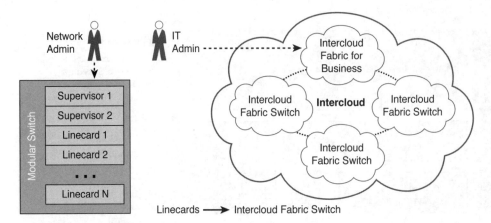

Linecards ——→ Intercloud Fabric Switch

Figure 6-28   *Intercloud Fabric Analogy of a Switch*

This gives you the ability to address public cloud resources in much the same way operationally as you do your internal private cloud resources. Hybrid really provides the best of both worlds. Host-critical or latency-sensitive applications and virtual machines on premises "burst or flex" less important (or seasonal) workloads out into the public cloud. This provides many benefits:

- Layer 2 IP addressing used within your organization can be securely extended into various public cloud spaces, allowing VMs to use similar IP addresses as they would use internally.

- It enables integration with Prime Service Catalog to allow IT to become the broker for public cloud services. Today your IT team may be largely unaware of the extent and use of public cloud services. With Intercloud Fabric, you become aware of public cloud projects and can quickly and securely offer these services to your internal consumers of IT.

- Security and policy can be set within the organization and applied/enforced into public cloud services.

- Virtual machine portability and the ability to move virtual machines from on premises to public cloud providers and back.

- Automation, including complete VM lifecycle management, automated operations, and an open API for easy programmatic access.

Let's look at how this is accomplished.

How It Works

Architecturally, Intercloud Fabric has two different products that are used to address both the on-premises and public portions of the cloud.

Intercloud Fabric for Business

Intercloud Fabric for Business is the enterprise portion of the solution that you install on premises. It allows you to transparently extend your internal VLANs and Layer 2 segments securely from within your private cloud infrastructure out to public cloud services while keeping the same level of security and policy across both the private and public environments. It is composed of two different components:

- Cisco Intercloud Fabric Director
- Cisco Intercloud Fabric Secure Extender

Cisco Intercloud Fabric Director is used to provide workload management in your hybrid cloud environment by allowing you to not only create, manage, and extend network services between private and public clouds, but also offer policy and a self-service IT portal that makes it easy for you to define and provide services (such as virtual machines and the secure network policies associated with them) to your end users. This allows you to publish catalogs to your internal end users that will rapidly allow them to request, for instance, different virtual machine types in different public cloud providers.

Intercloud Fabric for Providers

This is the portion of the architecture that exists in provider cloud environments and provides the "receiving end" of the end-to-end components that stretch from your private on-premises cloud out into a public cloud provider. Getting into more detail on Intercloud Fabric for Providers is beyond the scope of this book, but you can easily research it in greater detail on Cisco.com.

Secure Network Extender

To extend portions of your private, on-premises cloud infrastructure out into a public cloud provider, you use the Intercloud Fabric Secure Extender. This provides an AES 256-bit encrypted tunnel between your data center and the public cloud, securely extending VLANs and Layer 2 spaces out into the public provider cloud. This allows policy, security, and connectivity to be defined within the DC/private cloud infrastructure (as endpoints) while being enforced on any virtual machines created in the public cloud through Intercloud Fabric Director (see Figure 6-29).

6

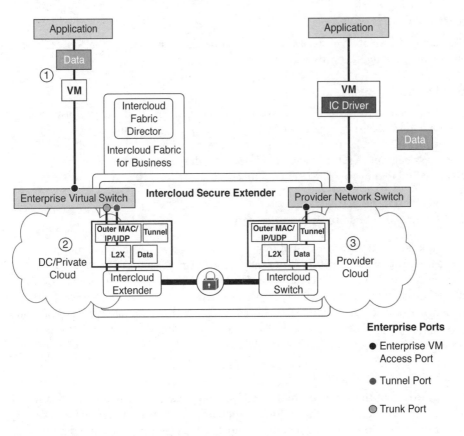

Figure 6-29 *Secure Network Extension*

Secure Network Extension to the Public Cloud

Once you have secure tunnels connected between your private data center cloud and certain public cloud providers, you will realize many benefits. Having a secure network extension to the public cloud with Intercloud Fabric can help with the following challenges in your organization:

■ **Shadow IT:** In many cases you don't have visibility into public cloud resources being used by your organization.

■ **Compliance:** Your job of securing access to different resources gets obfuscated once workloads move from your purview/control on premises to public cloud infrastructures.

■ **Different IP/VLAN/Layer 2 address ranges:** If, for example, an application is rapidly prototyped externally in a public cloud space, how would you easily bring it back on premises to move it from dev/test into production?

Intercloud Fabric solves these and many other challenges you face in interacting with public cloud services. For example, Intercloud Fabric provides these solutions (see Figure 6-30):

- Secure Layer 2 network extension from on premises to dozens of public cloud providers

- Automated workload mobility to and from public cloud providers

- The ability for you to manage both on-premises and public cloud resources through a single management console

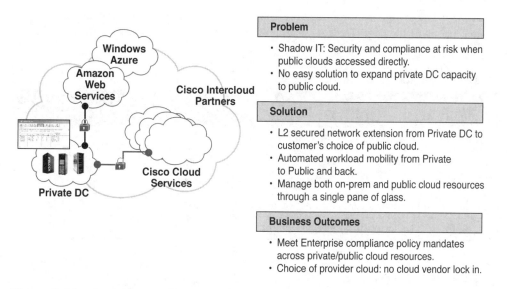

Figure 6-30 *Secure Network Extension to Public Cloud*

In the end, this helps you meet enterprise compliance more easily because secure networking and policy get extended into a myriad of public cloud offerings. Additionally, this gives you and your organization freedom of public cloud provider choice and prevents cloud provider vendor lock-in.

Exam Preparation Tasks

As mentioned in the section "How to Use This Book" in the Introduction, you have a couple of choices for exam preparation: the exercises here, Chapter 15, "Final Preparation," and the exam simulation questions on the Pearson IT Certification Practice Test.

Review All Key Topics

Review the most important topics in this chapter, noted with the Key Topics icon in the outer margin of the page. Table 6-3 lists a reference of these key topics and the page number on which each is found.

Table 6-3   Key Topics for Chapter 6

Key Topic Element	Description	Page Number
Section	Cisco Nexus 9000 Series Switches	138
Paragraph	Explanation of ACI	140
Paragraph	Explanation of application network profiles (ANPs)	141
Paragraph	Infrastructure Automation and UCS Director	142
Paragraph	Description of virtual switching	143

Define Key Terms

Define the following key terms from this chapter and check your answers in the glossary:

Application Policy Infrastructure Controller (APIC), Application Centric Infrastructure (ACI), Catalyst, Nexus, Fibre Channel over Ethernet (FCoE), Multilayer Director Switch (MDS), Fabric Extender (FEX), virtual device context (VDC), in-service software upgrade (ISSU), ACI tenant, ACI endpoint group (EPG), ACI contract, Virtual Supervisor Module (VSM), Virtual Ethernet Module (VEM), Application Virtual Switch (AVS), Virtual Application Cloud Segmentation (VACS), software-defined networking (SDN), Nexus 1000V (N1KV), Virtual Security Gateway (VSG), Cisco Adaptive Security Virtual Appliance (ASAv), Juniper Virtual Gateway (vGW), Virtual Palo Alto Networks appliance (vPAN)

This chapter covers the following topics:

1.0   Cloud Infrastructure Administration and Reporting

1.1   Configure users/groups and role-based access control in the portal, including basic troubleshooting

1.1.a   Describe default roles

1.1.b   Configure new user with single role

1.1.c   Describe multirole user profiles

1.1.d   Configure a user profile

CHAPTER 7

Managing Users and Groups

In all systems, it is important to ensure that users as well as administrators within the organization have proper access to the private cloud. Ensuring that your organization's end users are able to perform the necessary functions when interacting with Cisco ONE Enterprise Cloud and that various administrators have the proper rights to perform their duties is paramount to a successful private cloud project.

"Do I Know This Already?" Quiz

The "Do I Know This Already?" quiz allows you to assess whether you should read this entire chapter thoroughly or jump to the "Exam Preparation Tasks" section. If you are in doubt about your answers to these questions or your own assessment of your knowledge of the topics, read the entire chapter. Table 7-1 lists the major headings in this chapter and their corresponding "Do I Know This Already?" quiz questions. You can find the answers in Appendix A, "Answers to the 'Do I Know This Already?' Quizzes."

Table 7-1 "Do I Know This Already?" Section-to-Question Mapping

Foundation Topics Section	Questions
Overview of Users and Groups	1–5
Default Roles in UCS Director	6–8
Configuring a New User with a Single Role	9, 10

Caution The goal of self-assessment is to gauge your mastery of the topics in this chapter. If you do not know the answer to a question or are only partially sure of the answer, you should mark that question as wrong for purposes of the self-assessment. Giving yourself credit for an answer you correctly guess skews your self-assessment results and might provide you with a false sense of security.

1. To set up directory services integration in Prime Service Catalog, you should:

    a. From the main portal, click **Browse Categories** and select **User Administration**.

    b. From the main portal, click the **Search** icon and search for **directory integration**.

    c. From the main portal, click your username and choose **Switch To > Service Manager**.

    d. From the main portal, click your username and choose **Switch To > Administration**.

2. Prime Service Catalog integrates with which of the following directory services? (Choose all that apply.)

    a. OpenLDAP Server

    b. NetIQ eDirectory

    c. Sun ONE Directory

    d. Microsoft Active Directory

    e. IBM Tivoli Directory Server

    f. Only a and d above

    g. Only c and e above

3. Prime Service Catalog can connect to various directory services using which of the following protocols or methods? (Choose all that apply.)

    a. Netbind

    b. MS-RPC

    c. LDAP

    d. NetBEUI

    e. None of the above

4. Configuring UCS Director with local users and local groups can be considered a best practice. Select the best answer regarding this statement.

    a. True.

    b. False; only configuring UCS Director with local users is a best practice.

    c. False; only configuring UCS Director with local groups is a best practice.

    d. False; neither configuring UCS Director with local users nor configuring UCS Director with local groups is a best practice.

5. UCS Director integrates with which of the following directory services? (Choose all that apply.)

    a. OpenLDAP Server

    b. NetIQ eDirectory

    c. Sun ONE Directory

    d. Microsoft Active Directory

    e. IBM Tivoli Directory Server

    f. Only a and d above

    g. Only c and e above

6. UCS Director ships with _____ default roles.

    a. 10

    b. 11

    c. 12

    d. 15

    e. 20

7. Which role in UCS Director has the highest-level permissions?

    a. IS Admin

    b. MSP Admin

    c. All Policy Admin

    d. Group Admin

    e. System Admin

8. Custom roles created within UCS Director can be which of the following types? (Choose two.)

    a. Operator

    b. Policy Administrator

    c. End User

    d. Admin

    e. Supervisor

9. True or False. Users can belong to more than one role.

    a. True

    b. False

10. Which of the following statements is correct?

    a. Custom roles can be embedded within default system roles.

    b. Custom roles cannot be embedded within default system roles.

    c. Custom roles can be embedded within default system roles only if the custom role has less restrictive permissions than the default system role.

    d. Custom roles can be embedded within default system roles only if the custom role has more restrictive permissions than the default system role.

Foundation Topics

Overview of Users and Groups

With the ability to integrate into directory services such as Microsoft Active Directory for user and group authentication and authorization, both Prime Service Catalog and UCS Director give you a flexible framework for ensuring both end users and administrators of your private cloud have proper access. This section looks at the process for each in turn.

Prime Service Catalog

Prime Service Catalog offers rich integration with a variety of directory services such as Microsoft Active Directory, Sun ONE Directory, and IBM Tivoli Directory Server. This allows you to tie into existing enterprise directories for the purpose of user and group mapping.

To do this, you first have to switch from the default portal view of Prime Service Catalog to the Administrator's view. Perform the following:

Step 1.   Log in as an administrator and, in the upper-right corner of the Prime Service Catalog screen, choose **username > Switch To > Administration** as shown in Figure 7-1.

Figure 7-1   *Prime Service Catalog Main Menu Screen*

Step 2. On the Home screen of the Administration view, click the first box in the upper left titled **Link to Directories** (see Figure 7-2).

Figure 7-2 *Prime Service Catalog Administration Home Screen*

Step 3. On the Directories screen for creating a new directory connection from Prime Service Catalog, click the **Add** button on the Datasources page, as shown in Figure 7-3.

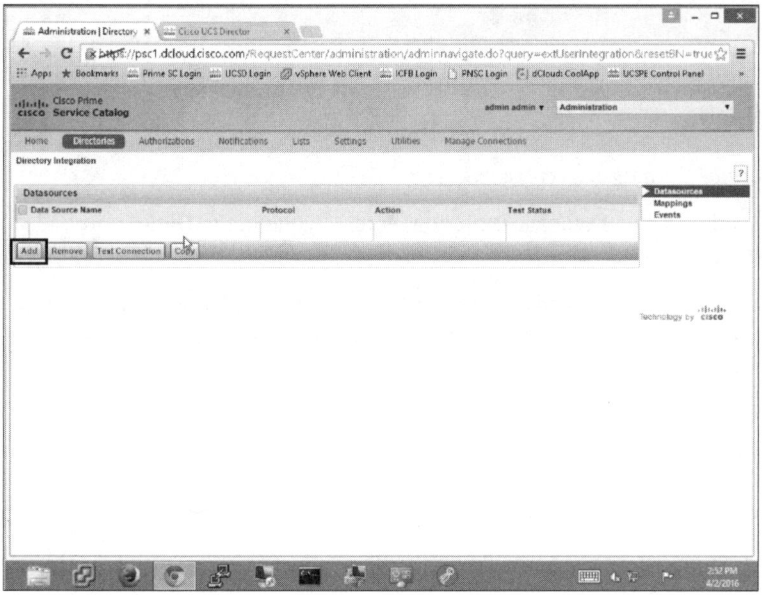

Figure 7-3 *Prime Service Catalog Add Directories Option*

Step 4. The screen expands to display the Datasource Configuration form, which includes the following sections (see Figure 7-4):

- Add or Edit a Datasource

- Select protocol and server product

- Connection Information

- Security Certificate Information

- Referral Datasource

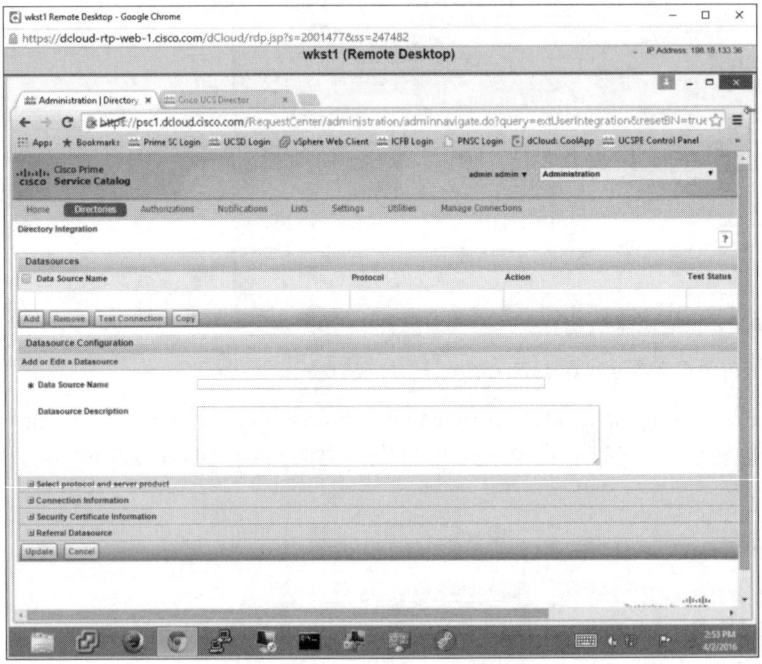

Figure 7-4 *Prime Service Catalog Directories Screen*

In the Add or Edit a Datasource section, enter a name in the **Data Source Name** field.

Step 5. Expand the **Select Protocol and Server Product** section. Notice that the only protocol available is LDAP, but for Server Product, you have the following choices (see Figure 7-5):

- Sun One Directory

- MS Active Directory

- IBM Tivoli Directory Server

Step 6. Choose the server product you intend to use.

Step 7. Expand the **Connection Information** section, as shown in Figure 7-6.

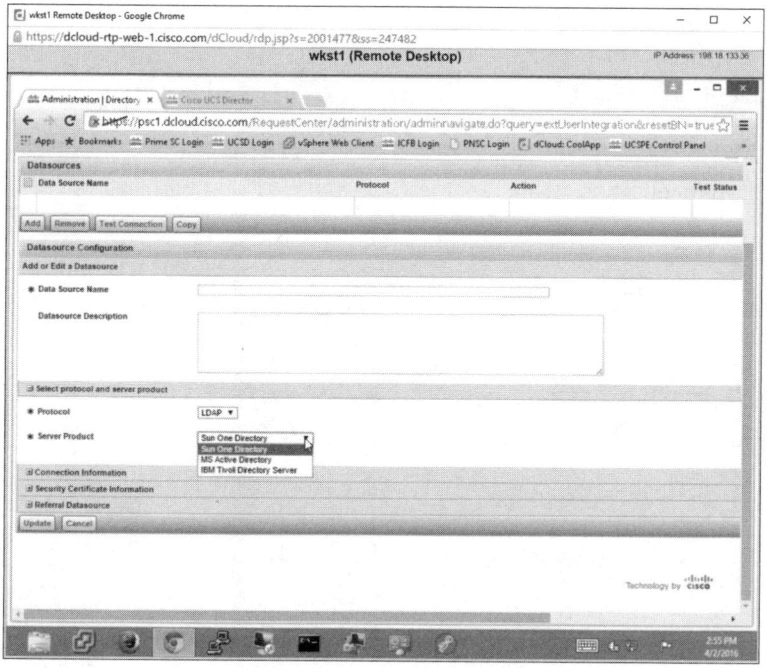

Figure 7-5 *Prime Service Catalog Directory Options*

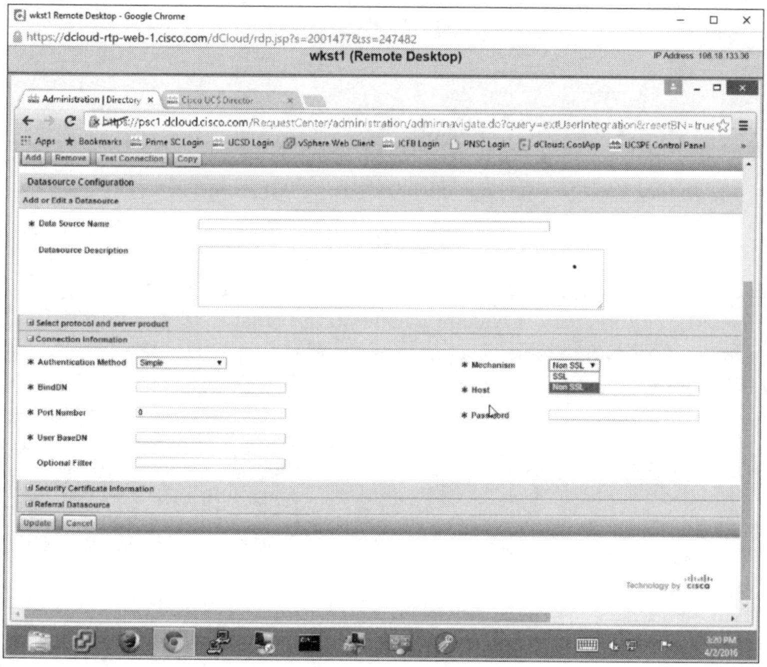

7

Figure 7-6 *Prime Service Catalog Connection Information Settings*

Step 8.   Open the Authentication Method drop-down list and choose one of the following options (see Figure 7-7):

- Simple

- Anonymous

- SASL Authentication

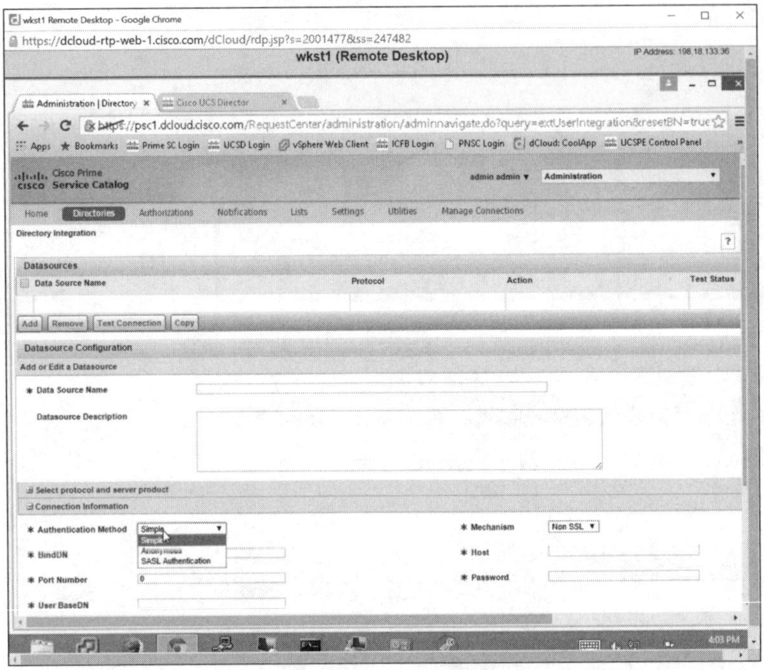

Figure 7-7   *Choosing the Prime Service Catalog Authentication Mechanism*

Step 9.   For the Mechanism field, choose **SSL** or **Non SSL**.

Step 10.   For the directory service you chose in Step 6, enter the bind DN in the BindDN field, the directory service hostname in the Host field, the port number in the Port Number field, a password, and the user base DN in the User BaseDN field.

> **Note**   *Bind DN* refers to the user in the LDAP server who is permitted to search the LDAP directory within the defined search base. *Base DN* refers to the location in LDAP where a server will start its search for users.

Step 11.   Expand the **Security Certificate Information** section and click **Add Certificate**, as shown in Figure 7-8. Input the requested information for the certificate.

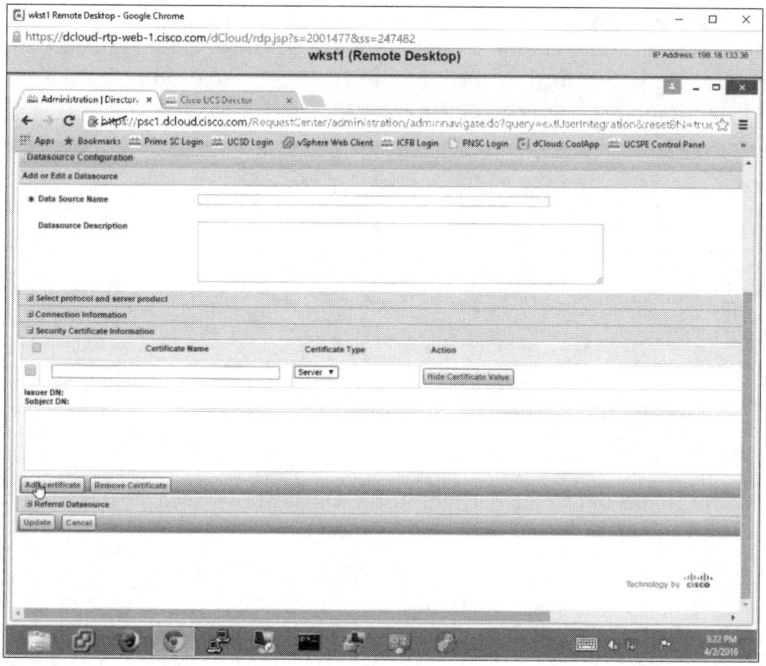

Figure 7-8 *Prime Service Catalog Security Certificate Information Settings*

Step 12. Expand the **Referral Datasource** section and click the **Add Referral** button
(see Figure 7-9.) Enter names in the Data Source Name and Mapping Name
fields.

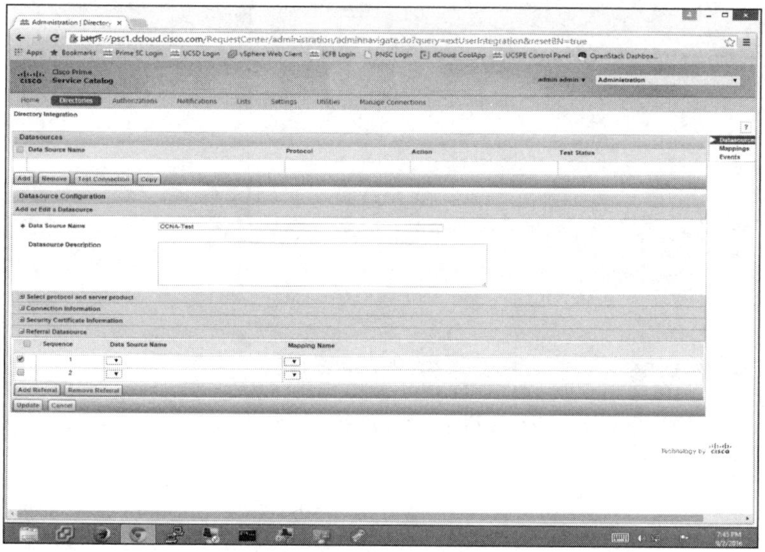

Figure 7-9 *Prime Service Catalog Add Referral Button*

Step 13. Click the **Update** button at the bottom of this form. At the top of the Directories screen, you will now see an option to test the directory connection you just created. Select the data source name you just created, and click the **Test Connection** button shown in Figure 7-10.

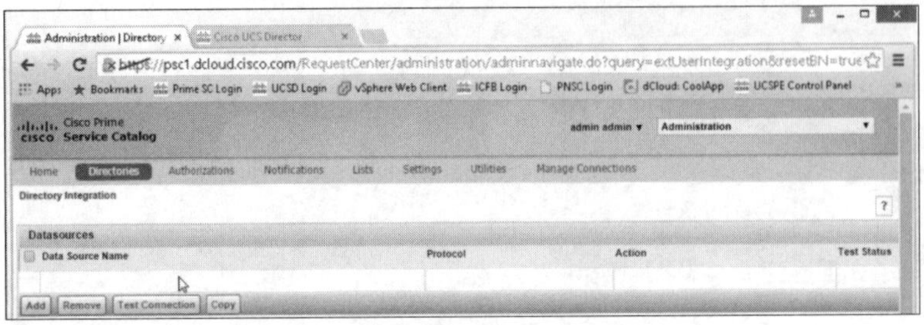

Figure 7-10 *Testing the Directory Connection*

Step 14. Click the **Mappings** tab to the far right of the Directories screen, as shown in Figure 7-11, to open the Mapping Configuration page.

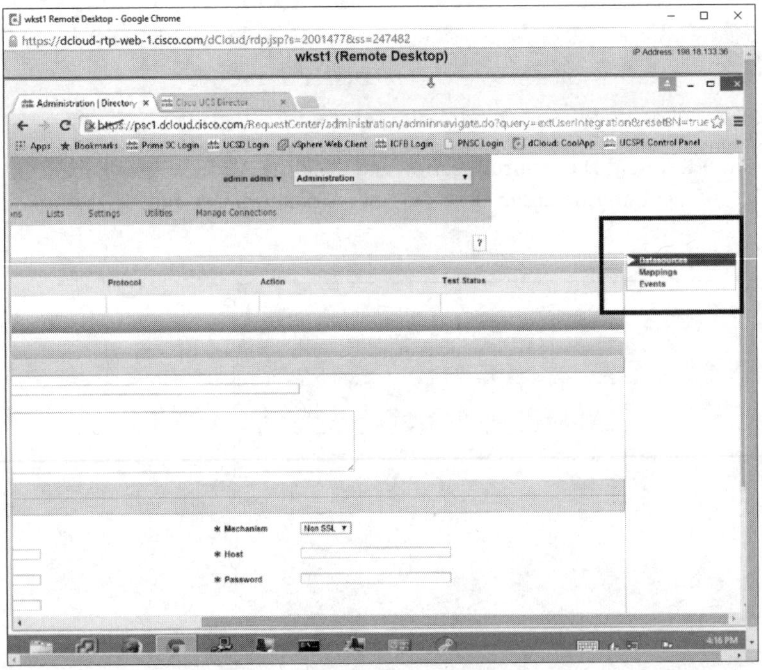

Figure 7-11 *Switching from the Datasources Page to the Mapping Configuration Page*

Step 15. In the Add or Edit a Mapping Name section, shown in Figure 7-12, enter a name in the Mapping Name field.

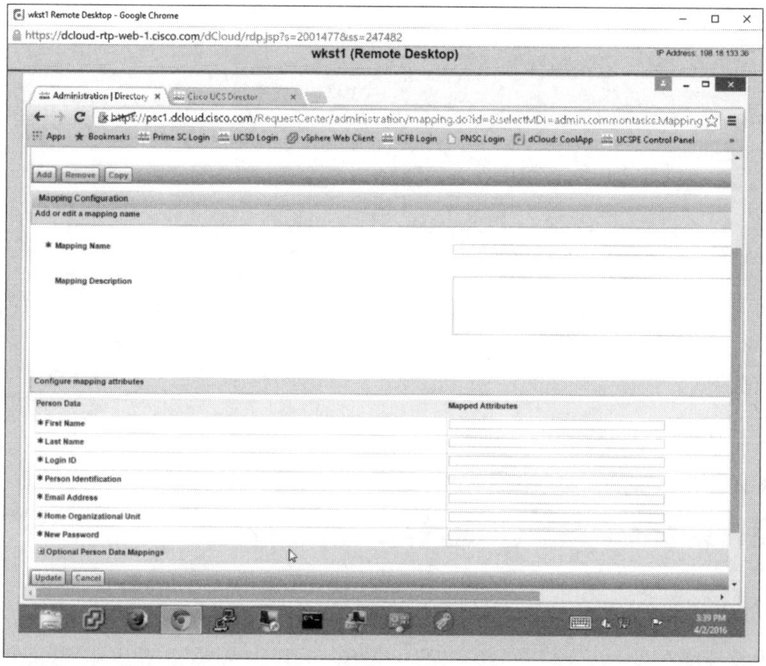

Figure 7-12 *Prime Service Catalog Mapping Configuration Page*

Step 16. Expand the **Configure Mapping Attributes** section and fill out all of the required fields, also shown in Figure 7-12, and then click on the **Update** button. This will create an LDAP mapping for a particular user.

Step 17. Repeat this process as necessary to create additional mapping names in Prime Service Catalog.

Step 18. Back to the far right of the Directories screen, as referenced previously in Figure 7-11, click the **Events** tab. On the Events page, you can enable or disable the directory connection for the following actions, as shown in Figure 7-13:

- Login

- Person Lookup for Order on Behalf

- Person Lookup for Service Form

- Person Lookup for Authorization Delegate

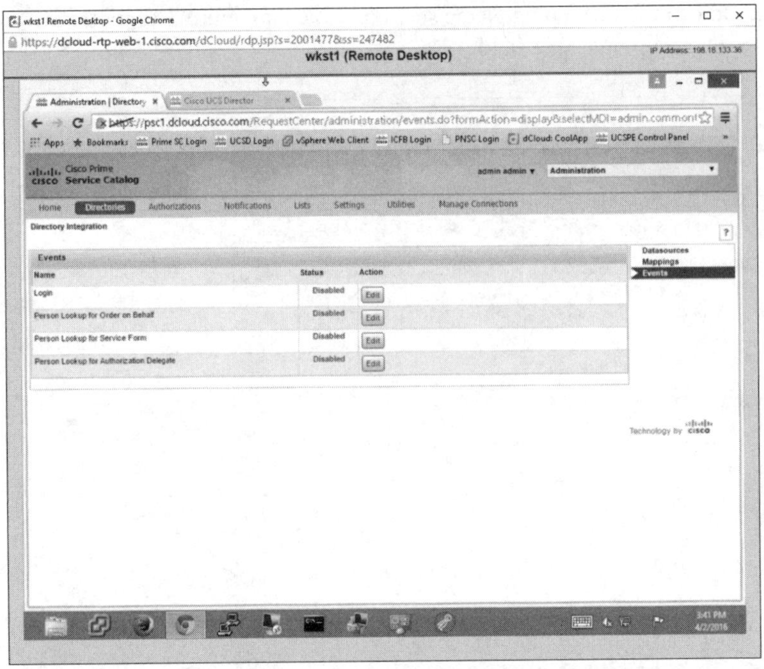

Figure 7-13 *Prime Service Catalog Events Page*

As you have seen, it is very easy to tie Prime Service Catalog into existing directory sources within your organization to create custom authentication and authorizations for your organization's users.

Managing Connections Between Prime Service Catalog

Now that you have completed the Link to Directories activity, you are ready to look at how to link Prime Service Catalog to other products such as UCS Director. On the Home screen of the Administration view, notice the Manage Connections option as shown in Figure 7-14. Choosing this option will allow you to connect Prime Service Catalog to UCS Director. Details on how to manage this connection can be found in Chapter 7, "Managing Users and Groups."

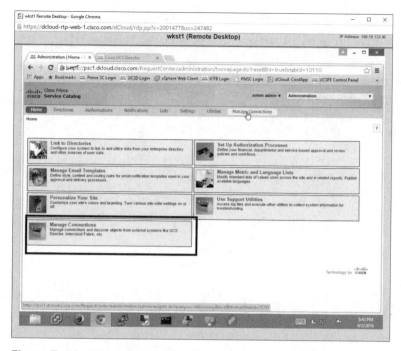

Figure 7-14 *Prime Service Catalog Manage Connections Option*

Now let's look at how we can create users and groups and connect to external directories in UCS Director.

UCS Director

Similar to Prime Service Catalog, UCS Director offers rich integration with directory services. This allows you to leverage an existing enterprise directory, such as Microsoft Active Directory, when tying your organization's user population into UCS Director. Local users and groups are also supported in the case where you do not wish to leverage an enterprise directory service with UCS Director.

We'll first look at how to create local users and groups within UCS Director, and then explore how to tie UCS Director into directory services. For purposes of demonstration, the configuration examples assume Microsoft Active Directory is the directory service being utilized for directory integration.

Local Users in UCS Director

If your organization doesn't require external directory services, users can be created directly within the UCS Director virtual appliance and will reside locally within the virtual appliance. This is less than ideal because passwords for cloud users have to be maintained separately from their enterprise directory credentials. It is highly recommended that when you integrate UCS Director into your organization you take advantage of LDAP integration. For those of you who wish to forge ahead with UCS Director for one reason or another, this section covers local user creation.

After logging in to UCS Director as an administrator, perform the following steps:

Step 1. Choose **Administration > Users and Groups**, as shown in Figure 7-15.

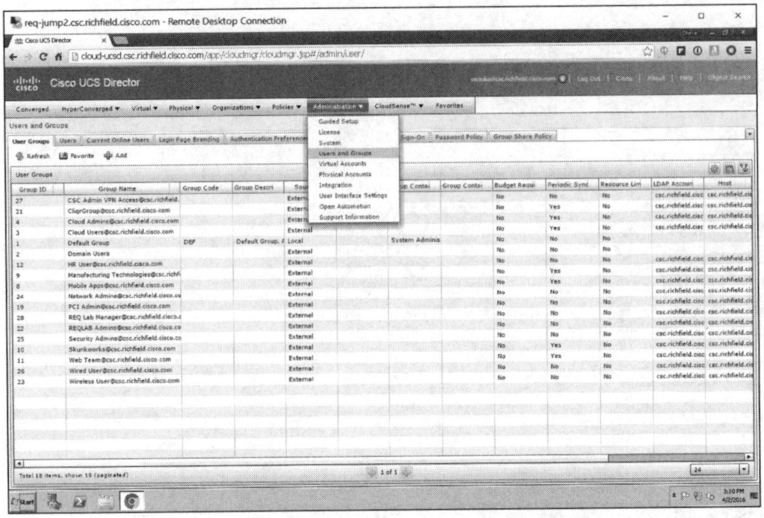

Figure 7-15 *UCS Director Administration Options Menu*

Step 2. On the Users and Groups screen, click the **Users** tab; then click **Add** as shown in Figure 7-16.

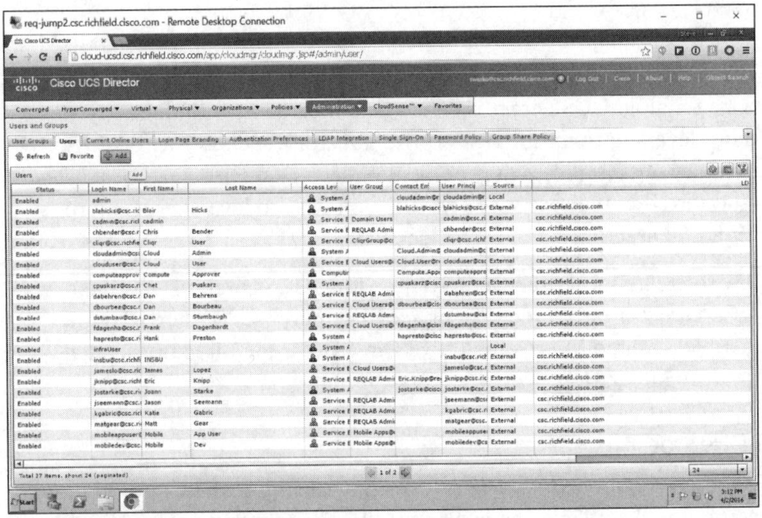

Figure 7-16 *Adding Users in UCS Director*

Step 3.   In the Add User dialog box, click the **User Role** drop-down list box and choose a user role, as shown in Figure 7-17. (User roles are covered in more detail later in the chapter in the section "Default Roles in UCS Director.") Next, do the following:

- Select a login name (follow the recommendations for special characters).

- Select and confirm the user's password.

- Enter the user's email address in the User Contact Email field.

- Optionally, fill out the remaining fields on the form shown in Figure 7-17.

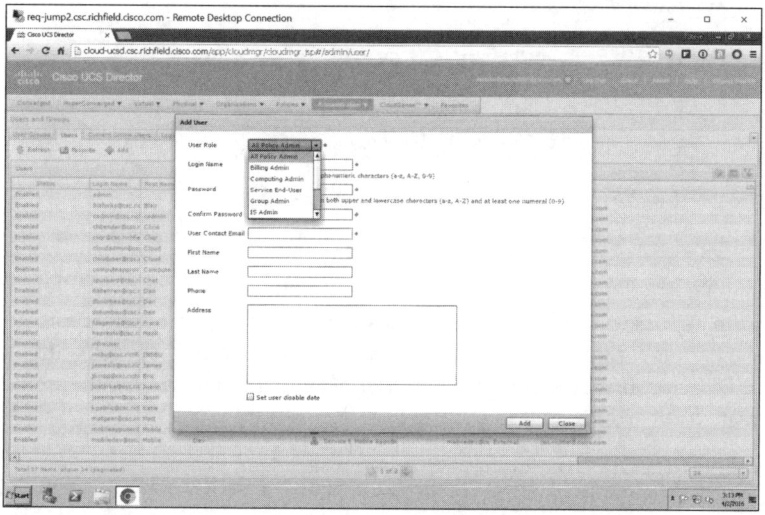

Figure 7-17   *UCS Director Add User Dialog Box*

Step 4.   Click **Add** to add the user and return to the main Users tab. Notice in the example shown in Figure 7-18 that the local user CCNA has been created and that the Source column identifies CCNA as Local (created locally within UCS Director as opposed to being imported from Active Directory or another directory service).

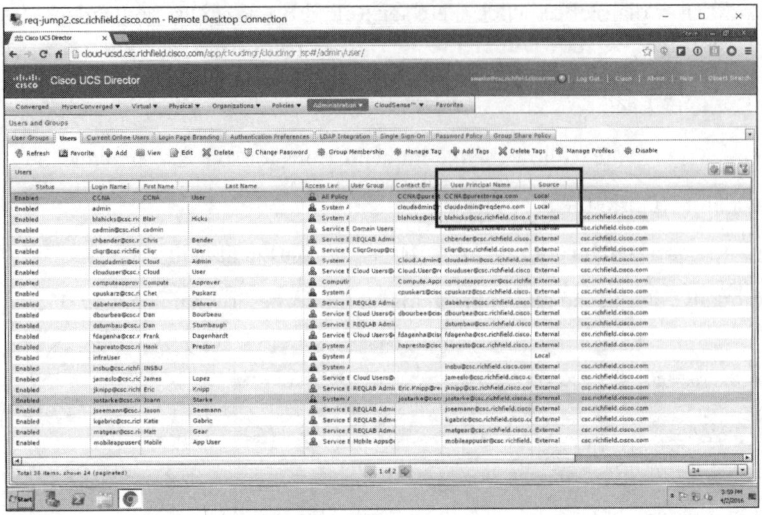

Figure 7-18   *UCS Director User Principal Name and Source Columns*

Local Groups in UCS Director

Key Topic

Just as local users can be created within UCS Director, local groups can also be created. Again, the same caution applies to using local groups as applies to using local users. Best practices are to leverage your enterprise Active Directory (or other directory service) infrastructure within UCS Director. If that is impractical or not needed, though, follow the steps presented next to create local groups.

Step 1.   From within UCS Director, log in as an administrator and choose **Administration > Users and Groups** (refer to Figure 7-15).

Step 2.   On the User Groups tab, click the **Add** button as shown in Figure 7-19.

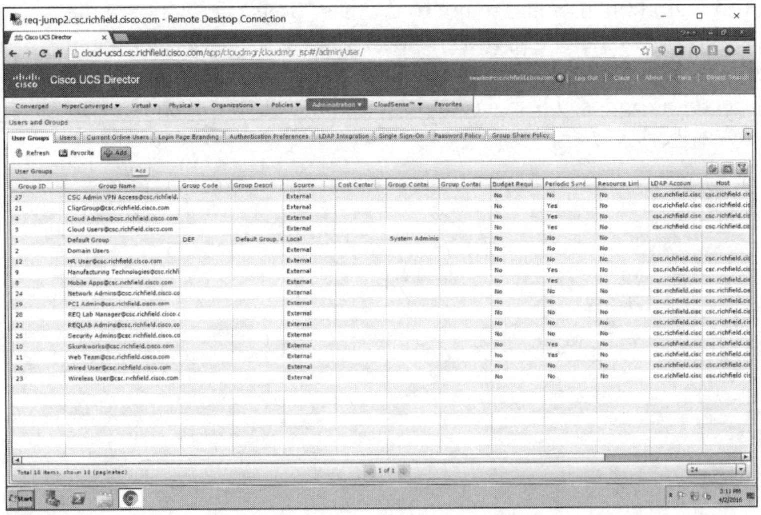

Figure 7-19   *Adding User Groups in UCS Director Administration*

Step 3.   In the Edit Group dialog box, shown in Figure 7-20, choose a name for the group and enter a contact email. All other fields are optional. The contact email is used for system-generated messages that result as actions are taken by members of the group, such as an approval email going to a particular group.

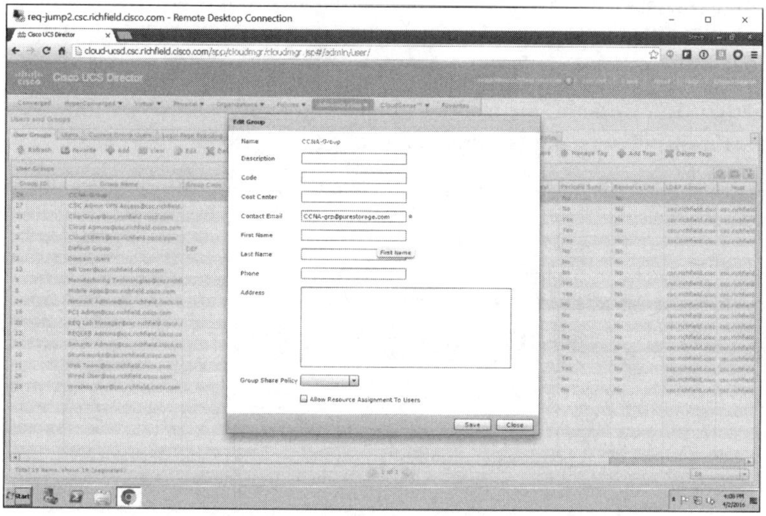

Figure 7-20   *UCS Director Edit Group Dialog Box*

Step 4.   Click **Save**; then notice that the group has been created as a local group as opposed to an external group (being imported from Active Directory or another directory service). See Figure 7-21. Click **Save**.

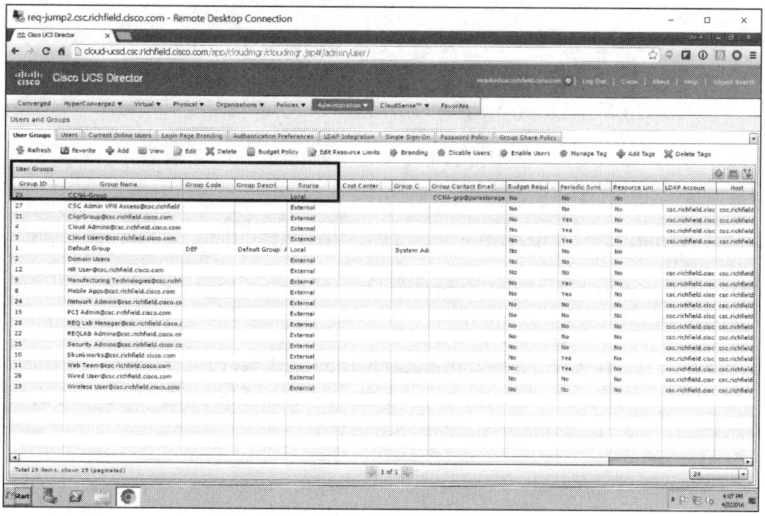

Figure 7-21   *Successfully Created Local Group*

LDAP Integration for UCS Director

As mentioned previously, LDAP directory integration with UCS Director is the preferred deployment mechanism in that it simplifies the administrative steps required to manage user and admin access to UCS Director by quickly and easily allowing you to add existing Active Directory (or other directory service) user accounts into groups. This streamlines the management and administrative functions required for you, the private cloud owner. To set up LDAP integration, follow these steps:

Step 1. From within UCS Director, log in as an administrator and choose **Administration > Users and Groups** (refer to Figure 7-15).

Step 2. Navigate to the **LDAP Integration** tab and click the **Add** button, as shown in Figure 7-22.

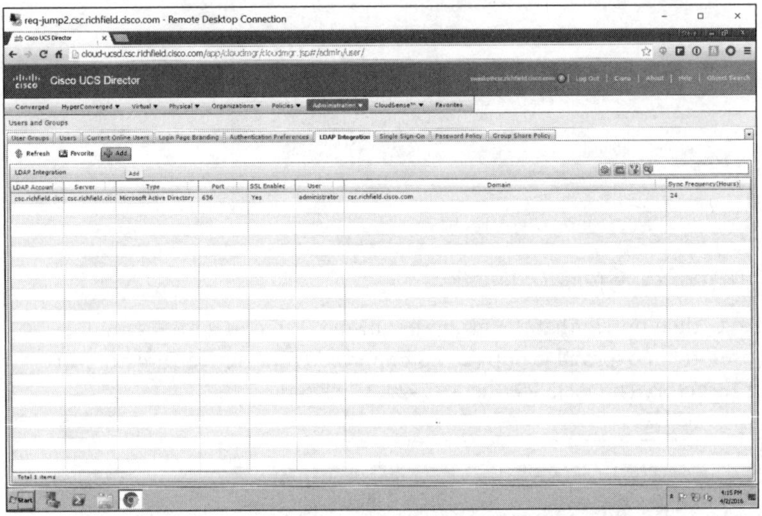

Figure 7-22 *UCS Director Add LDAP Integration Option*

Step 3. Fill out the following fields on the LDAP Configuration page of the LDAP Server Configuration wizard (see Figure 7-23):

■ **Account Name:** The name you want to call this particular connection.

■ **Server Type:** Choose Microsoft Active Directory or OpenLDAP, as appropriate to your environment.

■ **Server:** Enter the fully qualified domain name (FQDN) or IP address of the directory server you want to create a connection to. Check the **Enable SSL** check box if a secure connection is required.

■ **Port:** Enter the port used for the connection. The default port number for a non-SSL-enabled LDAP connection is 389.

■ **Domain Name:** Enter the domain name of your organization.

■ **Username and Password:** Enter the combination for the connection that will be used to connect to the directory server.

■ **Synchronization Frequency:** Set the interval at which the UCS Director virtual appliance will poll the directory server for changed/updated user/ group information. Setting this to 1 hour will ensure that changes made (user or group adds) will synchronize quickly with UCS Director. Note that users or groups in UCS Director are imported if they do not exist. If they do exist, UCS Director will ignore them and the "changes" will never take place.

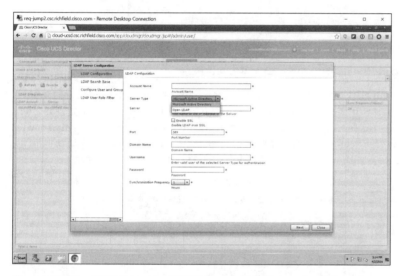

Figure 7-23 *UCS Director LDAP Server Configuration Wizard*

Step 4.   Click **Next.** On the LDAP Search Base page, shown in Figure 7-24, click the **Select** button to select the LDAP search base to the OU (organizational unit) where you want to look for UCS Director users and groups. Note the message stating that "The page may take a while to load depending on the number of OUs in the Domain." It isn't uncommon for this operation to take many seconds to a few minutes in very large directory services implementations.

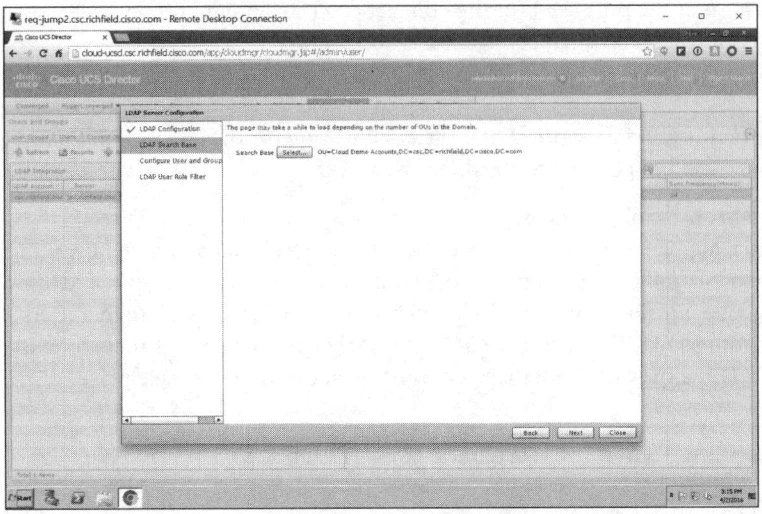

Figure 7-24 *UCS Director LDAP Search Base Wizard Page*

Step 5. After you click the Select button, you can filter or query for keyboards in the upper right of the Select dialog box. In the example shown in Figure 7-25, the search is for the keyword Demo to limit the number of objects shown in the Search Base selection screen to only those containing the word "Demo." Click **Select** to return to the LDAP Search Base page, and then click **Next**.

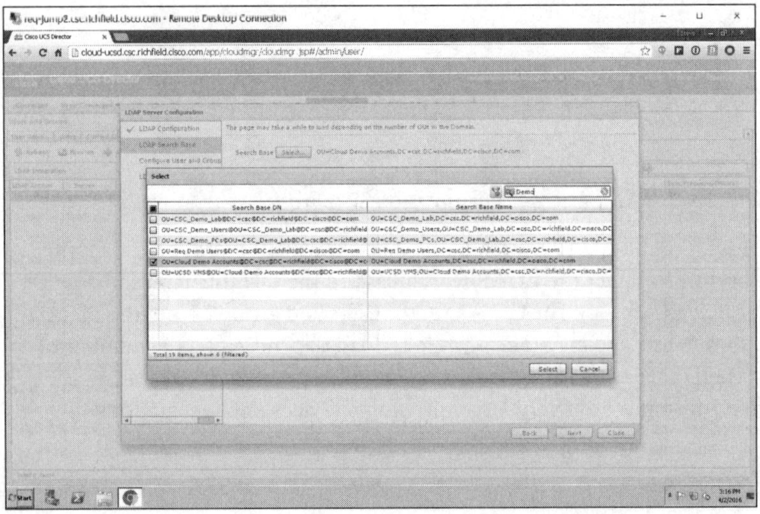

Figure 7-25 *UCS Director Searching and Selecting a Base DN*

Step 6.   On the Configure User and Group Filters page, shown in Figure 7-26, the default, setting cn (container name) with an Operator value of equals, will suffice in mapping users and groups in the previous OU to UCS Director. Note that at least one of the Group/User filters must be configured. The purpose of these filters differs. The User filter will limit users imported from the base OU selected in Step 5 and show only those that match the User filter. The same rules apply for the Group filter. The Group filter will limit groups imported from the base OU selected in Step 5 to only those that match the Group filter.

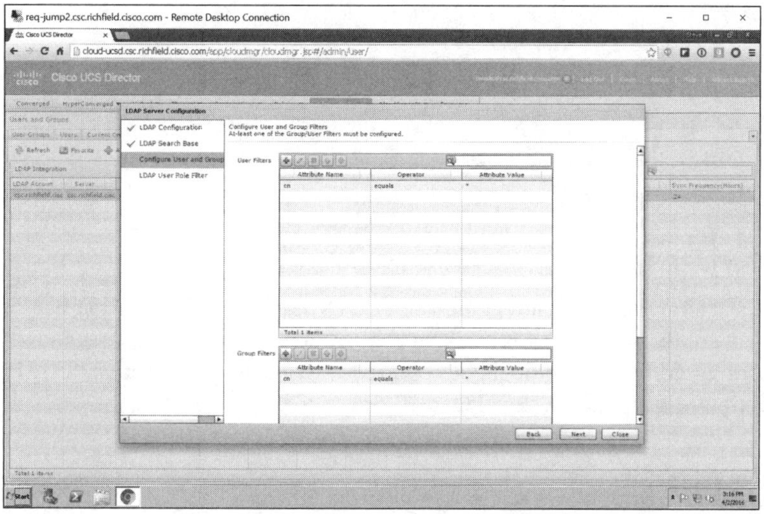

Figure 7-26   *UCS Director LDAP Configure User and Group Filters Wizard Page*

Step 7.   Click **Next**. On the LDAP User Role Filter page, set user role filters for any groups you want to map from within your directory service to UCS Director. In the example shown in Figure 7-27, Cloud Admins in the directory service maps to the Admin (User) user role in UCS Director, while Cloud Users in the directory service maps to the Regular (User) user role in UCS Director. Note that by default, imported users are created as Service End Users. However, by specifying a user role filter, users matching that filter will be created with the specified user role, such as System Admin, Compute Admin, and so on.

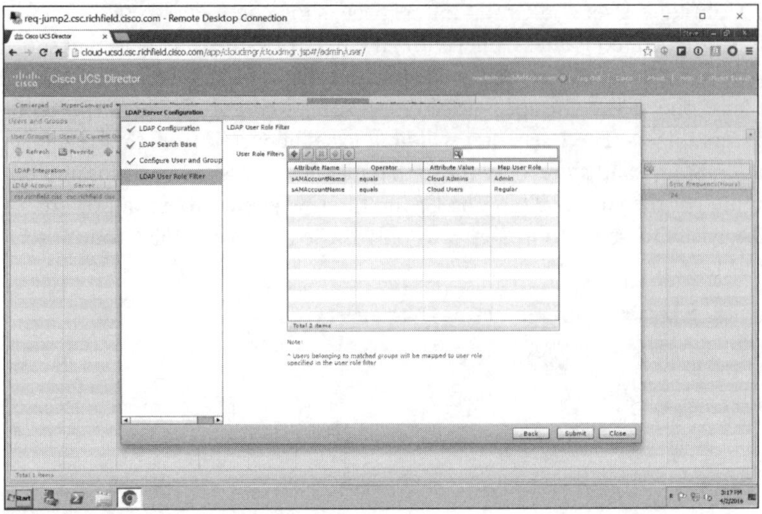

Figure 7-27 *UCS Director LDAP User Role Filter Wizard Page*

Step 8. Finally, back on the LDAP Integration screen, click the **Test Connection** button to ensure that everything is working properly (see Figure 7-28). Assuming all is configured properly, you'll be presented with a dialog box stating "LDAP Connection test successful." See Figure 7-29.

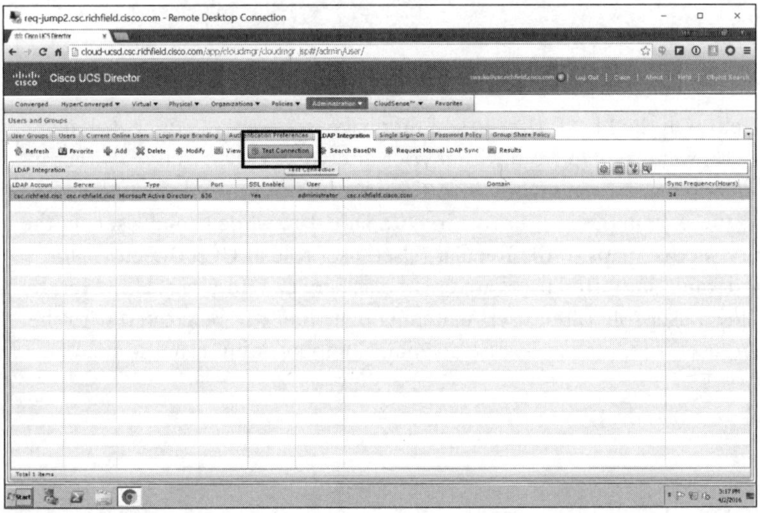

Figure 7-28 *UCS Director LDAP Integration Test Connection Button*

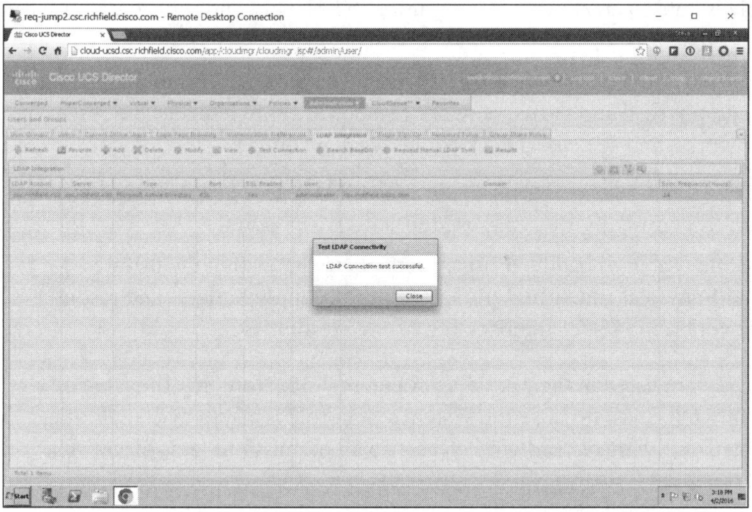

Figure 7-29   *UCS Director Test LDAP Connectivity Dialog Box*

Next, we'll discuss the purpose of roles in UCS Director. All users of UCS Director, whether created locally or being imported externally from a properly configured directory service, will be assigned a role.

Default Roles in UCS Director

Roles in UCS Director provide a very flexible framework for assigning rights and permissions to end users and administrators within the private cloud infrastructure. This flexibility allows you as the administrator to ensure that users have the permissions they need but are kept away from areas to which they shouldn't have access. Note that a user can only be part of one role.

By default, UCS Director comes preconfigured with one system default role (system admin) and ten custom roles. The roles are listed here, along with a brief description of the permissions enabled for each role:

- **System Admin:** Role has admin/superuser permissions to do all tasks within UCS Director
- **All Policy Admin:** Role is able to administer most policies within UCS Director
- **Billing Admin:** Role designed for doing chargeback, budgeting, accounting, and resource limit reporting
- **Computing Admin:** Role designed for working with physical and virtual servers and compute policy
- **Group Admin:** An end user with the privilege of adding users to a group or groups
- **IS Admin:** Role is able to assign VMs to vDCs, create new vDCs, create new catalogs, create/modify Deployment Policy and SLA Policy, and perform orchestration

- **MSP Admin:** Role is able to create virtual computing, VM labels, and service group service requests
- **Network Admin:** Role is able to handle most aspects of networking within the private cloud as well as add physical and virtual network resources, apply budgets and resource accounting to networks, and see chargeback for network resources
- **Operator:** Role can create VM labels and assign VMs to vDCs
- **Service End User:** Role can only view and use the self-service portal
- **Storage Admin:** Role is able to handle most aspects of storage within the private cloud as well as add physical and virtual storage resources, apply budgets and resource accounting to networks, and see chargeback for storage resources

The permissions by role are listed in their entirety in Figure 7-30. Note that the table in Figure 7-30 shows only ten roles, because the system admin role is a system default role that cannot be disabled and that has read/write access to all permissions and roles within UCS Director.

User Roles and Permissions
The following tables shows a list of permissions that are mapped to each admin user type:

Permission	All Policy Admin	Billing Admin	Computing Admin	Group Admin	IS Admin	MSP Admin	Network Admin	Operator	Service End User	Storage Admin
Virtual Computing	Read		Read	Read/Write	Read	Write	Read	Read	Read/Write	Read
VM Label	Write		Write	Write	Write	Write	Write	Write	Write	Write
Assign VM to vDC	Write				Write			Write		
Virtual Storage	Read		Read		Read		Read	Read		Read
Virtual Network	Read		Read		Read		Read	Read		Read
Physical Computing	Read/Write		Read/Write		Read		Read	Read	Read	Read
Physical Storage	Read/Write		Read	Read/Write	Read		Read	Read	Read	Read/Write
Physical Network	Read/Write		Read		Read		Read/Write	Read/Write		Read
Group Service Request	Read/Write	Read	Read	Read/Write	Read	Read/Write	Read	Read/Write	Read/Write	Read
Approver Service Request	Read/Write		Read/Write	Read/Write	Read/Write	Read/Write	Read/Write	Read	Read/Write	Read/Write
Budgeting	Read	Read/Write	Read		Read	Read/Write	Read	Read		Read
Resource Accounting	Read	Read	Read	Read	Read	Read	Read	Read	Read	Read
Chargeback	Read	Read	Read	Read	Read	Read	Read	Read	Read	Read
System Admin	Read		Read		Read		Read	Read		Read
Users and Groups	Read		Read		Read		Read	Read		Read
Virtual Accounts	Read		Read		Read		Read	Read		Read
Catalogs	Read		Read	Read	Read	Read	Read	Read	Read	Read
vDC	Read		Read	Read	Read/Write	Read	Read	Read	Read	Read
Computing Policy	Read/Write		Read/Write		Read		Read	Read		Read
Storage Policy	Read/Write		Read		Read		Read	Read		Read/Write
Network Policy	Read/Write		Read		Read		Read/Write	Read		Read
Deployment Policy	Write		Read		Read/Write		Read	Read		Read
SLA Policy	Write		Read		Read/Write		Read	Read		Read
Service Delivery	Read/Write		Read		Read/Write		Read	Read		Read
Resource Limit Report	Read	Read	Read	Read	Read	Read	Read	Read	Read	Read
Group Users	Read		Read	Read/Write	Read	Read/Write	Read	Read		Read
Cloudsense Reports	Read	Read/Write	Read	Read/Write	Read		Read	Read	Read	Read
Cloudsense Assessment Reports	Read	Read/Write	Read				Read			Read
Orchestration	Read/Write		Read/Write		Read/Write		Read/Write			Read/Write
Discovery	Read	Read	Read		Write		Read/Write			Read/Write
MSP	Write	Read/Write	Read/Write		Write	Read/Write	Read/Write			Read/Write
Open Automation Modules										
CS Shared Reports				Read/Write		Read			Read	
CS Shared Assessments				Read/Write						
Remote VM Access										
Mobile Access Settings										
End User Chargeback				Read		Read			Read	
Write Resource Accounting		Write								
Write Chargeback	Write	Write								
UCSD Cluster										
Resource Groups			Read/Write		Read/Write		Read/Write			Read/Write
Tag Library			Read/Write		Read/Write		Read/Write			Read/Write

Figure 7-30 *Table of UCS Director User Roles and Permissions*

In addition to the system-generated roles within UCS Director, there exists support for a maximum of 48 total system roles (including default roles). This will allow you as the administrator of the private cloud solution to create custom roles with custom Read/Write permissions for scenarios that aren't addressed by the 10 default roles included.

To create a custom role, use the following steps:

Step 1.   Log in with administrator credentials, choose **Administration > System**; then navigate to the **User Roles** tab, as shown in Figure 7-31.

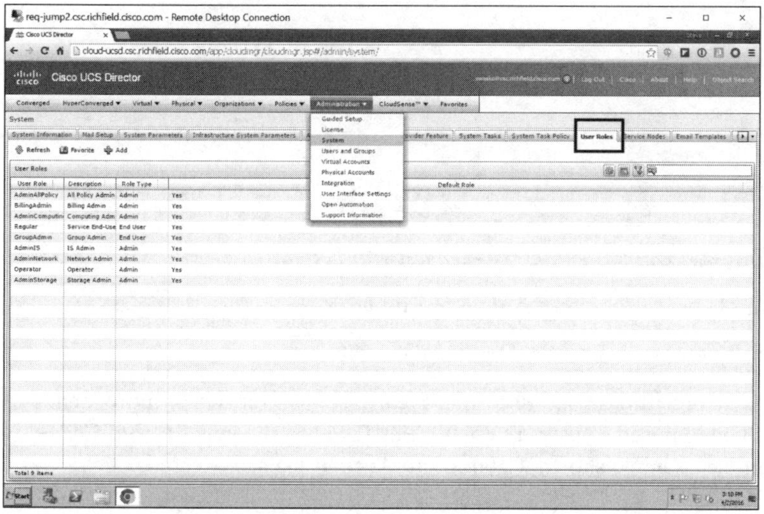

Figure 7-31   *UCS Director User Roles Tab*

Step 2.   The User Roles tab lists the default system roles that have been created within UCS Director. Notice that the fourth column is labeled Default Role and, because this is a new installation, all of the roles show Yes, indicating that they're system default roles.

Step 3.   To add a custom role, click the **Add** button.

Step 4.   On the User Role page of the Add User Role wizard, shown in Figure 7-32, give the role a name. In the example shown, we are creating a user role named Custom-CCNA-Role.

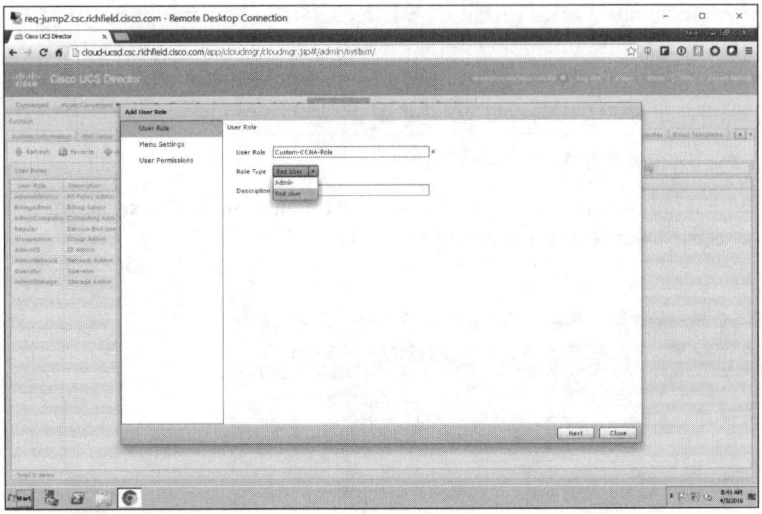

Figure 7-32 *UCS Director Add User Role Wizard User Role Page*

Step 5.   For Role Type, select either **Admin** or **End User**.

Step 6.   Optionally give the role a description. Click **Next**.

Step 7.   On the Menu Settings page, shown in Figure 7-33, select one or more menus that will be exposed to users that will be assigned to the new Custom-CCNA-Role. In the example shown, Catalog and Accounting are selected. Click **Next**.

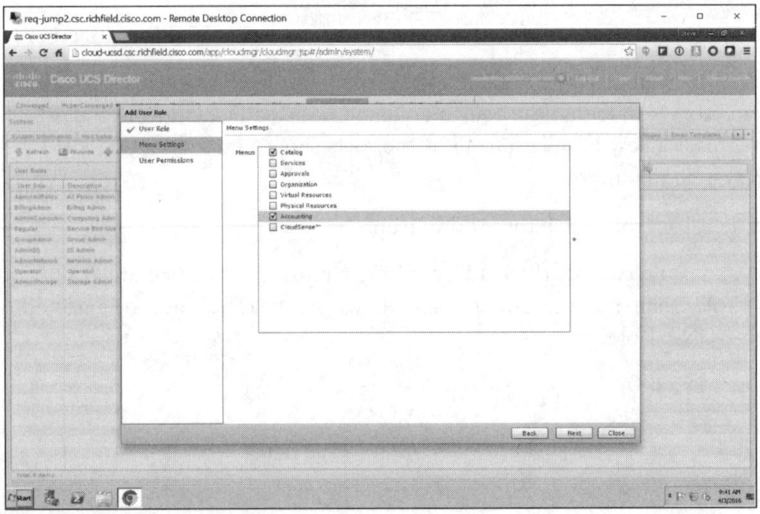

Figure 7-33 *UCS Director Add User Role Menu Settings*

Step 8. On the User Permissions page, shown in Figure 7-34, select the following permissions that will be exposed to users that will be assigned to the new Custom-CCNA-Role:

- Read – Virtual Computing

- Read – Resource Accounting

- Read – Catalogs

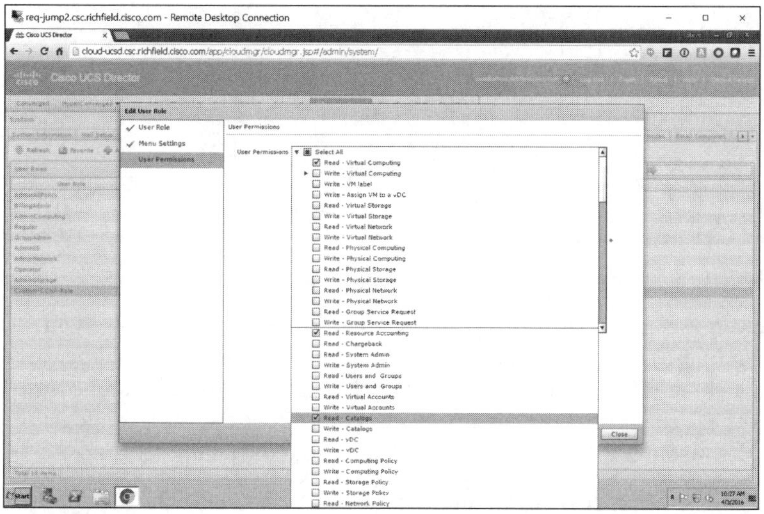

Figure 7-34 *UCS Director Add User Role Wizard User Permissions Page*

Step 9. Click **Submit**. After you acknowledge the role creation and are returned to the User Roles tab of the Administration System screen, shown in Figure 7-35, note that the new role created appears at the bottom of the User Role column and that the Default Role column shows a value of No (indicating that this is a custom role and not one of the system default roles).

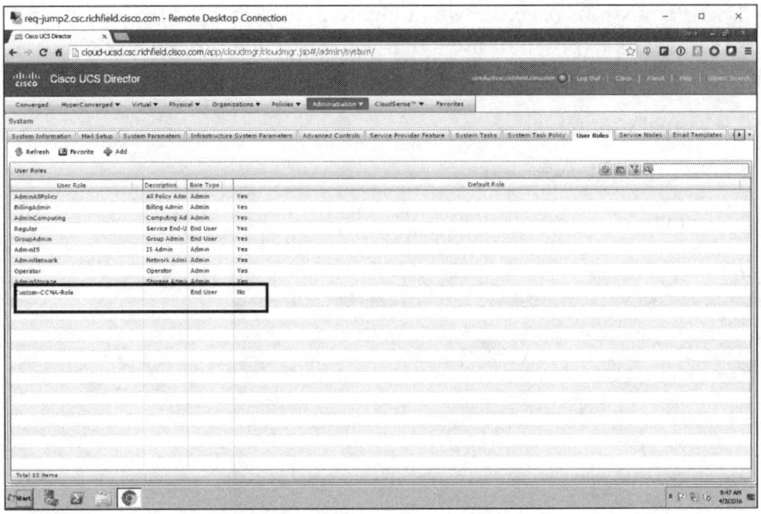

Figure 7-35   *UCS Director Custom-CCNA-Role User Role*

This section introduced you to the UCS Director system default roles and showed you how to create custom roles. This gives you great flexibility in designing roles and permissions for your private cloud infrastructure that can match nearly any use case and ensure that the proper users have the proper permissions required to browse service catalogs, order resources, create resources, report on resources utilized, consume resources, etc.

The next section describes the process of creating a new user and assigning that user to the custom role that was created in this section.

Configuring a New User with a Single Role

Key Topic

Roles cannot be embedded within other roles. For example, you aren't allowed to create a custom role and embed that role within a default system role. That shouldn't pose a problem, however, because you can create multiple custom roles, up to 48 total (as mentioned previously in this chapter), which gives you tremendous flexibility to design roles with just the right level of access for users and administrators within your organization. Additionally, within the default system roles, you can modify both the menu settings presented and the user permissions granted. Please note however that a best practice is to clone a default system role and then make changes to the copy, as opposed to modifying the default system roles.

The previous section showed how to create a new custom role called Custom-CCNA-Role. Now, let's create a new user, CCNA User, and assign it to this role. You will then log in to that role and see how the permissions applied in the previous section affect the end user's visibility and actions they can perform in the service catalog.

Step 1. Starting out from the main login screen while signed in as an administrator within UCS Director, choose **Administration > Users and Groups** (see Figure 7-36).

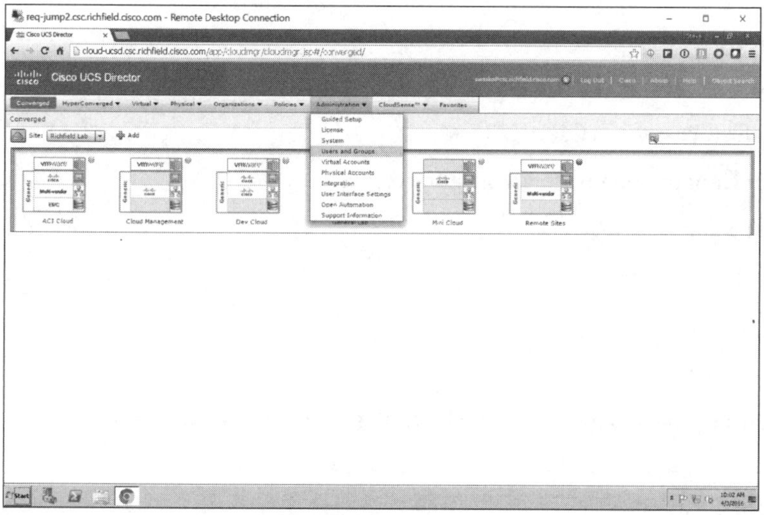

Figure 7-36 *UCS Director Admin, Users and Groups Menu*

Step 2. Navigate to the **Users** tab and click the **Add** button, as shown in Figure 7-37.

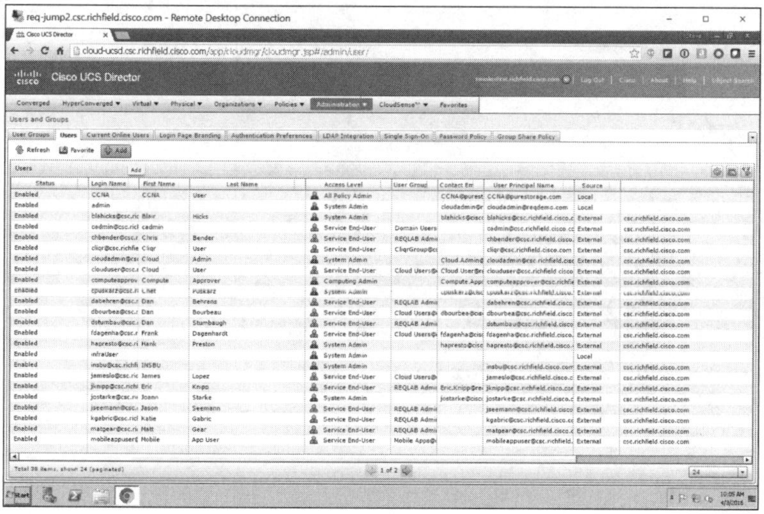

Figure 7-37 *UCS Director Add Users Button*

Step 3.   Complete the Add User dialog box as listed here and shown in Figure 7-38:

■ **User Role:** Custom-CCNA-Role

■ **User Group:** Default Group

■ **Login Name:** CCNA

■ **Password:** C1sc0123

■ **Confirm Password:** C1sc0123

■ **User Contact Email:** user@purestorage.com

■ **First Name:** CCNA

■ **Last Name:** User

■ **Phone:** Optional

■ **Address:** Optional

■ **Set user disable date:** Check the box and set a date 24 hours from now

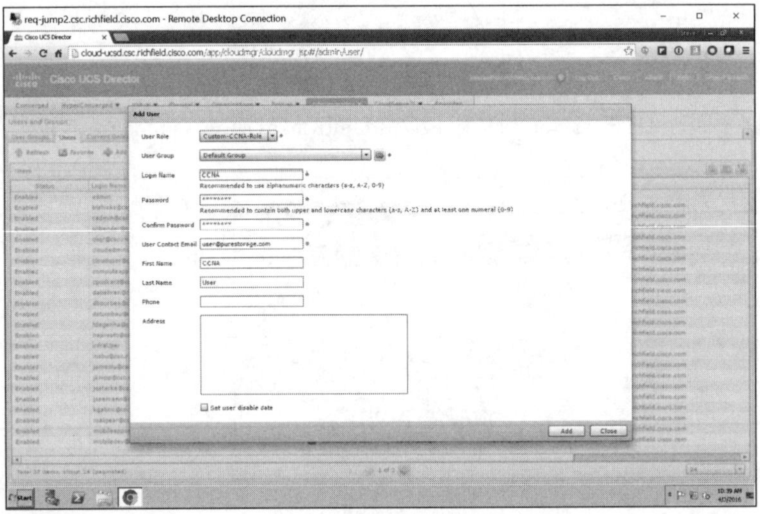

Figure 7-38   *UCS Director Add User Dialog Box*

Step 4.   Click **Add**. As shown in Figure 7-39, the user now appears at the top of the Users list, the Access Level column shows Custom-CCNA-Role (the role created in the previous section), and the Source column shows Local.

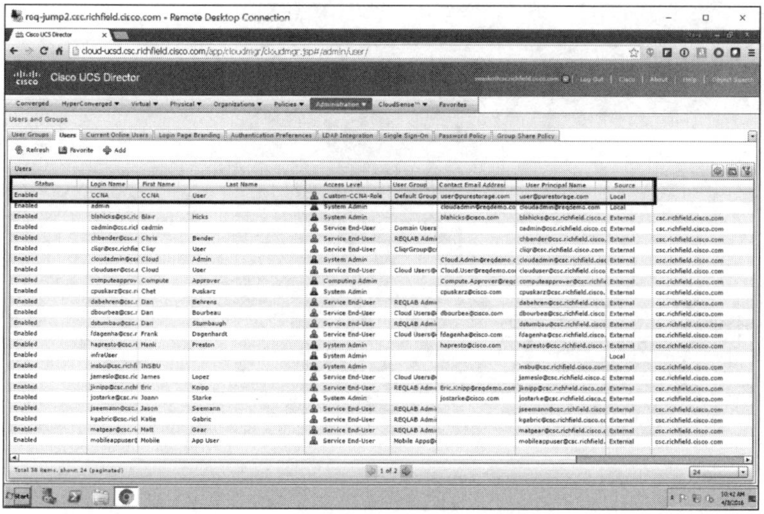

Figure 7-39   *UCS Director Custom CCNA User*

Step 5.   Log out of UCS Director by clicking **Log Out** at the top of the window, as shown in Figure 7-40.

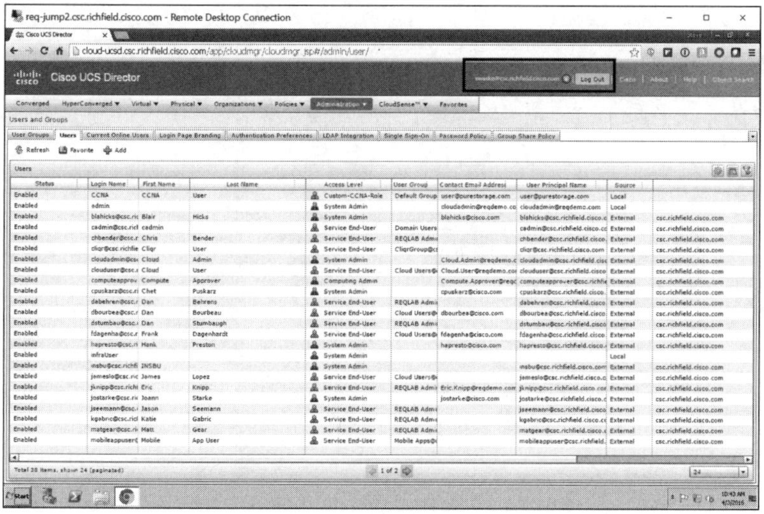

Figure 7-40   *Logging Out of UCS Director*

Step 6.   Log in as user **CCNA** with a password of **C1sc0123** (see Figure 7-41).

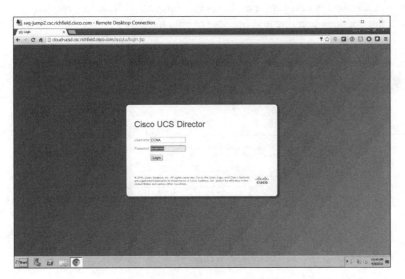

Figure 7-41   *Logging In to UCS Director as Custom User*

Step 7.   As shown in Figure 7-42, your newly created CCNA user with the custom role of Custom-CCNA-Role can see two top-level menu options: Catalog and Accounting. Recall from the previous section that we created a very restricted user role with just the ability to see virtual machine resources and with read-only permissions to Catalogs and Accounting information.

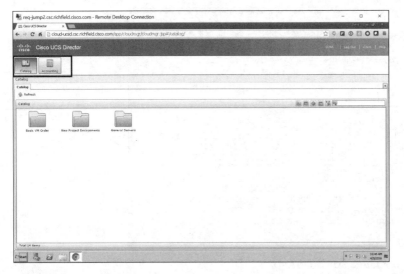

Figure 7-42   *UCS Director CCNA User Service Catalog View*

Step 8.   Explore what rights (very few!) your newly created user with this custom role has; then click **Log Out** to log out of user CCNA.

Custom roles are a great tool to use when the default system roles provided with UCS Director don't quite grant the proper level of access desired to achieve a particular end result. As many organizations have different approval, reporting, and consumption levels internally, custom roles give you as the private cloud administrator a very powerful set of capabilities to ensure proper access under a wide variety of organizational scenarios.

7

Exam Preparation Tasks

As mentioned in the section "How to Use This Book" in the Introduction, you have a couple of choices for exam preparation: the exercises here, Chapter 15, "Final Preparation," and the exam simulation questions on the Pearson IT Certification Practice Test.

Review All Key Topics

Review the most important topics in this chapter, noted with the Key Topics icon in the outer margin of the page. Table 7-2 lists a reference of these key topics and the page number on which each is found.

Key Topic

Table 7-2   Key Topics for Chapter 7

Key Topic Element	Description	Page Number
Section	Understand local users in UCS Director	173
Section	Understand local groups in UCS Director	176
Section	Understand default roles in UCS Director	183
Section	Configure a new user with a single role	188

Define Key Terms

Define the following key terms from this chapter and check your answers in the glossary:

UCS Director, virtual data center (vDC), Lightweight Directory Access Protocol (LDAP), user role, user groups, fully qualified domain name (FQDN), LDAP search base, base DN, bind DN

This chapter covers the following topics:

CHAPTER 8

Virtual Machine Management

As of the writing of this book, many organizations are well on their way to virtualizing workloads within their environments. In the experience of the authors working with many organizations, nearly all of our customers tell us they are over 75 percent virtualized in their x86 compute workloads.

Many organizations have a guiding principle of "virtualization first" whereby new business requirements and projects that are brought to IT are immediately assumed to be candidates for virtualization unless a very compelling business case (performance, throughput, criticality, scale, etc.) can be made for that application to reside on bare metal. By approaching workloads and projects in this way, many organizations have come to rely on x86 server virtualization as one of the core tenants of provisioning new compute workloads in their data centers and remote locations.

The Cisco ONE Enterprise Cloud Suite stack offers a comprehensive set of products and tools to help you handle the challenges of managing virtualization as a service within your organization. This chapter provides an overview of virtualization and why automating it is important. It describes the idea of a service catalog as being paramount to the end-user experience when ordering and consuming virtual assets. It discusses both the end-user and administrator experiences available within Cisco ONE Enterprise Cloud Suite.

"Do I Know This Already?" Quiz

The "Do I Know This Already?" quiz allows you to assess whether you should read this entire chapter thoroughly or jump to the "Exam Preparation Tasks" section. If you are in doubt about your answers to these questions or your own assessment of your knowledge of the topics, read the entire chapter. Table 8-1 lists the major headings in this chapter and their corresponding "Do I Know This Already?" quiz questions. You can find the answers in Appendix A, "Answers to the 'Do I Know This Already?' Quizzes."

Table 8-1 "Do I Know This Already?" Section-to-Question Mapping

Foundation Topics Section	Questions
Understanding VM Virtualization in Cisco ONE Enterprise Cloud Suite	1, 2
Overview of End-User VM Operations in UCS Director	3–5
Understanding Common Administrative Workflows on VMs in UCS Director	6, 7
Prime Service Catalog VM Integration	8–10

> **CAUTION**   The goal of self-assessment is to gauge your mastery of the topics in this chapter. If you do not know the answer to a question or are only partially sure of the answer, you should mark that question as wrong for purposes of the self-assessment. Giving yourself credit for an answer you correctly guess skews your self-assessment results and might provide you with a false sense of security.

1. UCS Director can provide automation and orchestration of which of the following? (Choose all that apply.)

   a. VMware ESXi

   b. Citrix XenServer

   c. Red Hat KVM

   d. A Nexus switch

   e. StorageTek tape libraries

   f. AmigaOS

2. Which of the following statements correctly describes Cisco Intercloud Fabric?

   a. Allows an organization to securely connect two private clouds together

   b. Securely connects two companies together so they can pass traffic in a secure, encrypted fashion

   c. Creates a secure, encrypted connection between your on-premises data center and one of many public cloud offerings and helps your IT organization to become the "organizational broker" to the consumption of virtual machines in public cloud offerings

   d. Securely connects two public clouds together so an organization can easily migrate machines from one public cloud offering directly to another public cloud offering

3. Which of the following is an important goal of the Cisco ONE Enterprise Cloud Suite?

   a. Give you as an architect or administrator a flexible set of tools to offer an e-commerce/shopping-cart like experience to your internal IT users

   b. Give you a central location to do asset reporting and trouble ticketing

   c. Give you as an architect or administrator the ability to automate the installation of desktops within your organization

   d. Give you the ability to centralize and control access to consumer-based cloud services from within your network for all of your end users

4. True or False. UCS Director provides a default way for end users to select and mount an ISO image as a CD/DVD drive into a virtual machine that they own.

   a. True

   b. False

5. Which of the following tasks could be performed as an advanced or custom VM operation within UCS Director? (Choose all that apply.)

   a. Run a PowerShell script

   b. Run a Python script

   c. Query for custom VM performance statistics

   d. Order pizza

   e. Provision mainframe LPAR services

6. Which of the following hypervisors has the most administrative workflows available out of the box within UCS Director?

   a. Microsoft Hyper-V

   b. Red Hat KVM

   c. VMware ESXi

   d. Dec Alpha

7. Which of the following are common administrative workflows on Hyper-V VMs in UCS Director? (Choose all that apply.)

   a. Add VM disk

   b. Add VM NIC

   c. Create VM snapshot

   d. Delete VM disk

   e. Delete VM NIC

8. True or False. UCS Director is a full-fledged, end-user-friendly service catalog.

   a. True

   b. False

9. UCS Director provides which of the following? (Choose all that apply.)

   a. An IT-focused experience that is tightly coupled with technical IT task automation

   b. An end-user-focused experience that is highly polished and focuses on end-user usability

   c. A way to provision virtual machines in popular public cloud services such as AWS and Azure

   d. A, B, and C

   e. None of the above

10. In Prime Service Catalog, "My Stuff" refers to:

   a. A list of all IT assets assigned to you, such as your laptop, monitor, any personal printers, etc.

   b. A location for you to store all of your documents centrally within the organization

   c. A list of all the backups made for any systems you manage

   d. A list of assets that have been provisioned within Prime Service Catalog, such as VMs

8

Foundation Topics

Understanding VM Virtualization in Cisco ONE Enterprise Cloud Suite

While the need for bare-metal applications still exists, virtualization is here to stay. Furthermore, many organizations are now adopting a "dual hypervisor" strategy to hedge their bets and ensure that there is no sort of longer-term vendor lock-in concerns. Add to that the fact that most organizations are also leveraging compute in public cloud offerings such as Amazon Web Services (AWS) and Microsoft Azure, as well as in other public cloud providers such as Cisco Powered clouds and other third-party offerings, and the landscape of solutions to support in the data center with regard to virtualization becomes fairly vast.

While virtualization does increase asset utilization by carving up a single physical system into a system that can run multiple virtual workloads, it also adds complexity to IT operations (see Figure 8-1).

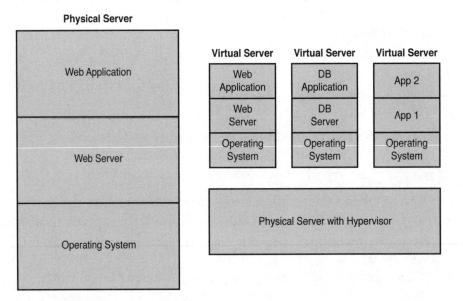

Figure 8-1 *Physical Server Versus Physical Server with a Hypervisor*

With this added complexity comes added work for IT to operate and maintain the virtual environment. Add in a second hypervisor and the need to keep track of public cloud options for your internal IT customers, and the workload can get busy very quickly.

Luckily, automating and orchestrating multiple virtual environments are cornerstone capabilities of the Cisco ONE Enterprise Cloud Suite of products. Two products in particular that help are

- **UCS Director:** Assists in the automating and orchestration tasks of virtual machines running on VMware ESXi, Microsoft Hyper-V, Red Hat KVM, and Citrix Xen. With the ability to create common workflows and to easily add provisioning of VMs from these environments to the UCS Director Service Catalog, you have a very agile toolset for automating many of the daily functions required of IT when it comes to virtual machine provisioning.

- **Intercloud Fabric:** Assists your IT department in understanding what workloads are being provisioned into public cloud solutions such as Cisco Powered cloud providers, Amazon AWS, and Microsoft Azure. Intercloud Fabric creates a secure, encrypted connection between your on-premises data center and one of many public cloud offerings and helps your IT organization to help become the "organizational broker" to the consumption of virtual machines in public cloud offerings. This gives you additional visibility and control that allows IT to understand the consumption and usage patterns of public cloud usage in the organization while still providing the governance, security, and control of those virtualized workloads.

Both UCS Director and Intercloud Fabric maintain separate service catalogs that show, for example, a list of VMs that can be created on premises (with UCS Director) and a list of VMs that could be created in the public cloud (with Intercloud Fabric). Figures 8-2 and 8-3 show these two catalogs. Note that these figures depict a new installation where folders have been created but no virtual machines have been added to the catalog for the user to order (see Figure 8-3).

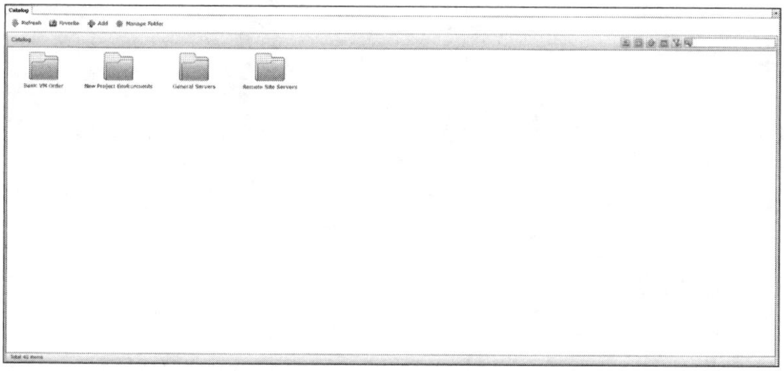

Figure 8-2 *UCS Director Folder of Servers Available*

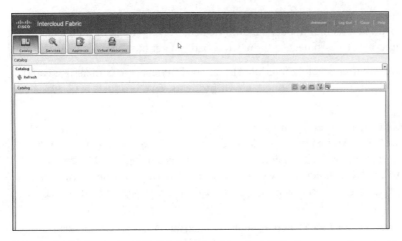

Figure 8-3 *Intercloud Fabric Service Catalog Offerings*

With the goal of simplification of the environment and creating a single self-service portal for viewing and accessing VMs both within UCS Director and via Intercloud Fabric, both products can be connected to Cisco Prime Service Catalog (PSC) to give a unified experience to your end users to see their VMs (regardless of whether they're in the private cloud or public cloud), take common actions on those VMs, and potentially (if given permissions) perform cold migration of those VMs from on premises to off premises or vice versa (see Figure 8-4).

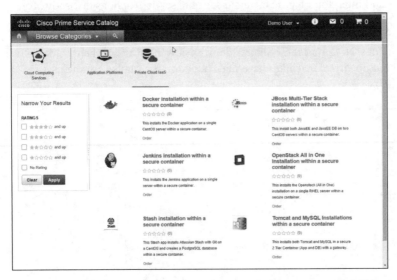

Figure 8-4 *Prime Service Catalog Showing On-Premises and Off-Premises VM Offerings*

This gives you the flexibility of offering both on-premises and off-premises virtualized workloads from a single catalog, which will streamline workload provisioning, lower overall organizational costs, and give IT visibility into public cloud usage within the organization.

Overview of End-User VM Operations in UCS Director

An important goal of Cisco ONE Enterprise Cloud is to give you as an architect or administrator a flexible set of tools to offer more of an e-commerce/shopping-cart like experience to your internal IT users, giving IT the tools to efficiently provision and manage workloads across any cloud. Today's manual IT processes of provisioning infrastructure and applications for users are cumbersome, lengthy, and often prone to error. As the responsibilities increase for many IT administrators, just keeping things running becomes a greater and greater challenge. By moving to automation and orchestration with a self-service catalog for your internal users, you are moving IT into the Industrial Revolution factory-line processes of the IT World. Ensuring that your users have a flexible and consistent experience in this new world is the ultimate goal. If your users aren't happy with how easy it is to consume IT processes and Infrastructure as a Service (IaaS) internally, they'll simply circumvent the IT department and go straight to public cloud offerings, reducing your organizational effectiveness and making management question just what sort of value IT is providing for the organization.

UCS Director will enable your end to perform many functions that would normally require IT intervention, such as

- Browsing for and ordering virtual machines (from many hypervisors, as previously discussed)

- Selecting options for VMs ordered, such as number of virtual CPUs (vCPUs), RAM amount, and volume size

- Common VM functions such as powering on or off a virtual machine, performing a snapshot on a virtual machine, adding additional virtual NICs (vNICs) to the VM, and much, much more

Let's look at some of the operations you need to perform as an administrator to connect hypervisors into UCS Director. Then we'll look at actions that your end users will be able to perform within UCS Director. Note this assumes that pods have already been created in UCS Director and that you'll be adding these accounts to existing pods.

Adding a Virtual Hypervisor to UCS Director

Before you can begin modifying actions an end user can take on their virtual machines, you first have to connect hypervisor accounts to UCS Director in the pod of your choice. To do this, select the pod you want to add the hypervisor account to; then choose **Administration > Virtual Accounts**, as shown in Figure 8-5.

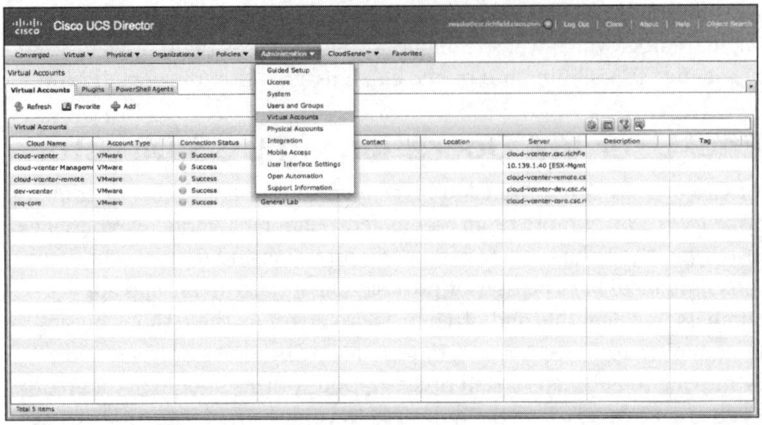

Figure 8-5 *Accessing the UCS Director Administration Virtual Accounts Tab*

On the Virtual Accounts tab, click the **Add** button to open the Add Cloud dialog box. Choose a cloud type from the **Cloud Type** drop-down menu, as shown in Figure 8-6. For purposes of this example, we'll select a Hyper-V account to add.

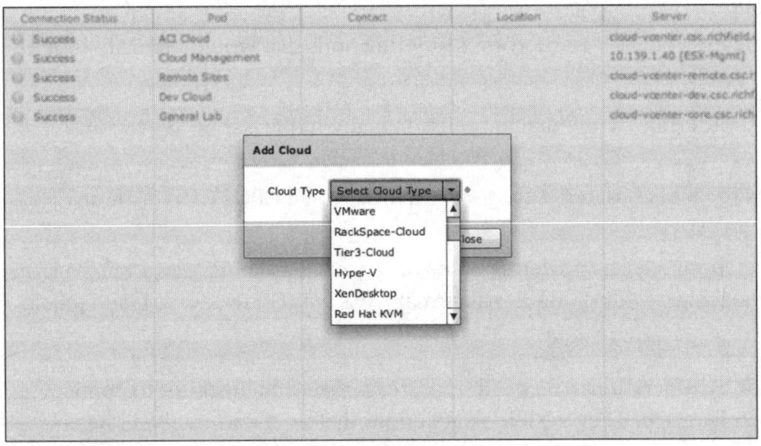

Figure 8-6 *UCS Director Add Cloud Dialog Box*

Once the Hyper-V account has been selected, fill in the following details in the resulting Add Cloud dialog pane:

■ **Cloud Type:** Hyper-V should be selected.

■ **Cloud Name:** A friendly name for the cloud.

■ **PowerShell Agent:** For Hyper-V, this is the link to a system running the UCS Director PowerShell Agent (PSA). This is a system that UCS Director can point to that will run PowerShell commands. The PowerShell Agent will be discussed in additional detail in the following section.

- **Server Address:** The IP address or fully qualified domain name of the hypervisor you are looking to add to UCS Director.

- **Server User ID:** Administrator ID to connect UCS Director to the hypervisor to allow it to control actions of that hypervisor through API calls.

- **Server Password:** The password on the hypervisor for the ID in the previous field.

- **Domain:** The NTLM/AD domain the server resides in.

- **Pod:** The Pod you are adding this hypervisor account to.

- **Optional information:** Description, Contact Email, Location, Service Provider.

Installing PowerShell Agent

As an administrator, being able to leverage Microsoft PowerShell commandlets from within UCS Director opens up immense possibilities to extend automation and orchestration to many Windows systems, services, and applications. Once this is done, you have the ability to add PowerShell scripts at will to your automation and orchestration workflows. As an example, it is common to call a PowerShell script toward the end of VM provisioning to automatically add a record to Active Directory DNS with the hostname of the new virtual machine that was just created into DNS. The following steps explain how to set up PowerShell access from within UCS Director.

The whole reason a PowerShell agent is needed within UCS Director is because the UCS Director appliance is based on CentOS and not Windows and, as such, cannot directly execute PowerShell commands as there was no native PowerShell interpreter available on CentOS/Linux at the time this functionality was included in UCS Director.

Step 1.   Navigate to **Administration > Virtual Accounts**.

Step 2.   Click the **PowerShell Agents** tab, which is shown in Figure 8-7.

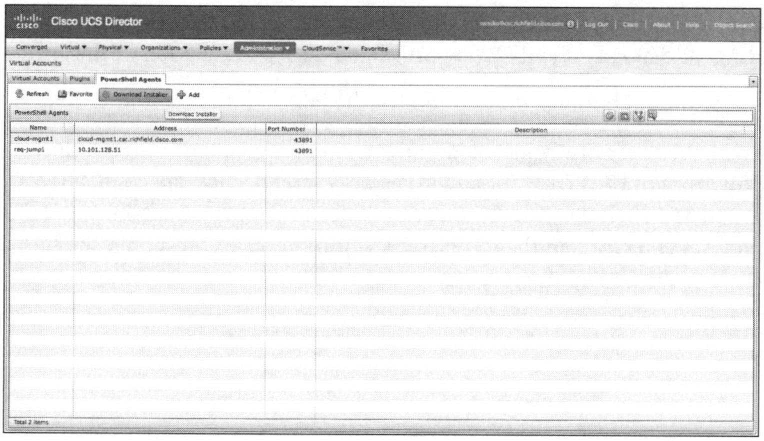

Figure 8-7   *UCS Director PowerShell Agents Tab*

Step 3.   Click the **Download Installer** button, which opens the Download Agent Installer dialog box shown in Figure 8-8.

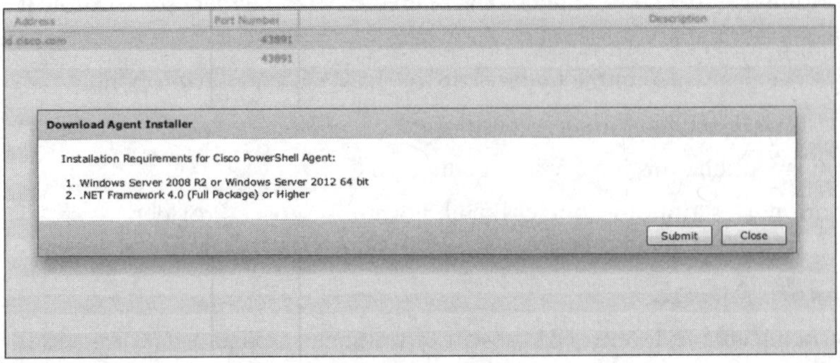

Address	Port Number		Description
d.cisco.com	43891		
	43891		

Download Agent Installer

Installation Requirements for Cisco PowerShell Agent:

1. Windows Server 2008 R2 or Windows Server 2012 64 bit
2. .NET Framework 4.0 (Full Package) or Higher

[Submit]   [Close]

Figure 8-8   *UCS Director Download Agent Installer Dialog Box*

Step 4.   Click **Submit** to install that file on a remote system that meets the requirements defined in the UCS Director PSA documentation.

Step 5.   After the installation is complete, return to UCS Director and click the **Add** button. Fill in the following details of the Add Agent dialog box, as shown in Figure 8-9:

- **Agent Name:** A system-friendly name for the PSA connection. You can have multiple PSA connections.

- **Agent Address:** The IP address or fully qualified domain name of the PSA server installed on the remote server that you previously installed.

- **Agent Access Port:** The UDP port used to communicate between UCS Director and the PSA running on the remote server.

- **Access Key:** A unique value that must be entered in both the UCS Director Add Agent dialog box and in the PSA screen during installation of the agent.

- **Description:** An optional description for the PSA.

Step 6.   After you have successfully installed the PowerShell Agent and entered the access key both in UCS Director and in the PSA screen, click the connection you created and click the **Test Connection** button to verify communication between UCS Director and the PSA server. Upon success, you should see the dialog box shown in Figure 8-10.

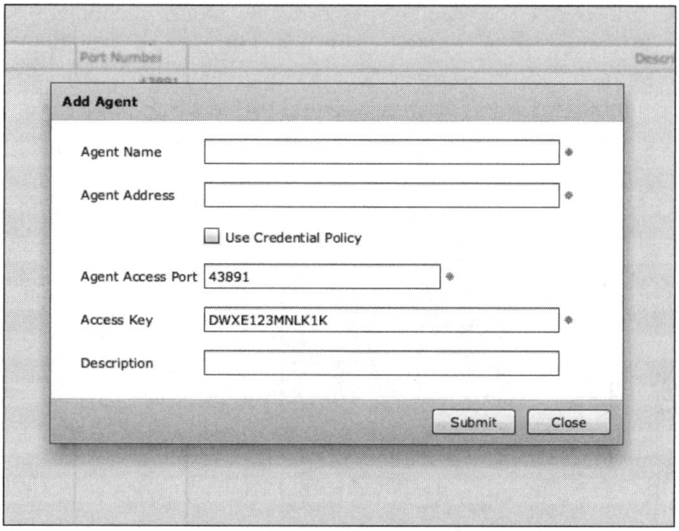

Figure 8-9   *UCS Director Add Agent Dialog Box*

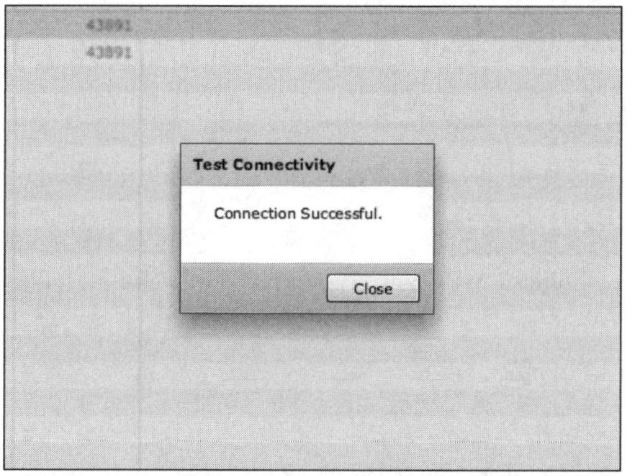

Figure 8-10   *UCS Director PSA Installation Test Connectivity Dialog Box*

Once you've added one or more virtual accounts to UCS Director in their respective pods, you can explore what can be exposed to end users via VM actions.

Standard VM Operations

As the administrator of Cisco ONE Enterprise Cloud Suite, you have the ability to expose certain tasks to end users. Normally, many of these tasks may require administrative interruption to accomplish. By creating an End User Self-Service Policy, you can tailor the actions end users can take on VMs that they create. Note that policies are applied to a virtual data center (vDC), not to a pod. vDCs are covered in Chapter 4, "Cisco Cloud Automation/Orchestration Suites."

The ability to create multiple End User Self-Service Policies gives you a lot of flexibility. For example, you can create different policies for different vDCs of infrastructure within a UCS site. Let's say that, for example, your main site where you're using UCS Director has both a Development pod and a Production pod of infrastructure. Let's develop policies for each pod that give the rights shown in Figure 8-11.

UCS Director
Development
Pod

Development End User Self-Service Policy
End User Actions Power On Power Off Suspend, Standby, Reset Reboot, Shut Down Resize VM Snapshot Management Delete VM Configure VM Networking Mount ISO to VM Clone VM Actions

UCS Director
Production
Pod

Production End User Self-Service Policy
End User Actions Power On, Off, Reboot, Shut Down Mount ISO to VM

Figure 8-11 *UCS Director Custom VM Example Between Development and Production*

To begin, let's create a policy for our Development pod:

Step 1.   In UCS Director, navigate to **Policies > Virtual/Hypervisor Policies > Service Delivery**.

Step 2.   Click **End User Self-Service Policy**.

Step 3.   Click **Add**.

Step 4.   For the Development pod, check all the items listed, as shown in Figure 8-12. You will be checking all available options to give users in the Development pod access to do all actions on VMs, including

- **VM Power Management:** Power ON, Power OFF, Suspend, Standby, Reset, Reboot, Shutdown Guest

- **VM Resizing:** Resize VM

- **VM Snapshot Management:** Create Snapshot, Revert Snapshot, Mark Golden Snapshot, Delete Snapshot, Delete All Snapshots

- **VM Deletion Management:** Delete VM

- **VM Disk Management:** Create VM Disk, VM Disk Resize, Delete VM Disk

- **VM Network Management:** Add vNICs, Delete vNICs, VM Resync

- **VM Lease Expiry:** Configure Lease Time

- **VM Console Management:** Launch VM Client, Configure VNC, Test VNC, Enable/Disable VMRC Console

- **VM Clone and Template Management:** Clone, Clone VM as Image, Convert VM as Image, Move VM to VDC, and Assign VMs to VDC

- **VM ISO Management:** Mount ISO Image as CD/DVD Drive

Step 5.   After you have checked all of these options, click **Submit**.

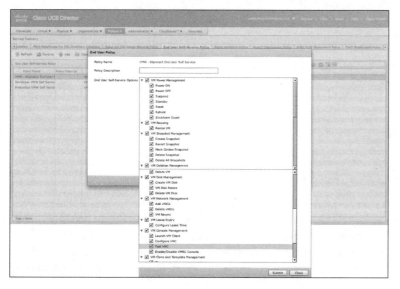

Figure 8-12 *UCS Director Development End-User Policy*

The resulting policy will enable all users in the Development pod to perform all available standard actions on VMs that they create in that environment. Note that this assumes that a single vDC applies to the Development pod, but that isn't necessarily always the case.

Many organizations have much more stringent rights and access policies for what can be done in production. So let's create a new policy for our Production pod.

To create the policy for the Production pod:

Step 1.   Within UCS Director, navigate to **Policies > Virtual/Hypervisor Policies > Service Delivery**.

Step 2.   Click **End User Self-Service Policy**.

Step 3.   Click **Add**.

Step 4.   For the Production pod, check the items as shown in Figure 8-13. You will be checking the following selections to give users in the Production pod access to do a much more limited set of actions on VMs:

- **VM Power Management:** Power ON, Power OFF, Reboot, Shutdown Guest

- **VM ISO Management:** Mount ISO Image as CD/DVD Drive

Step 5.   After you have checked all of these options, click **Submit**.

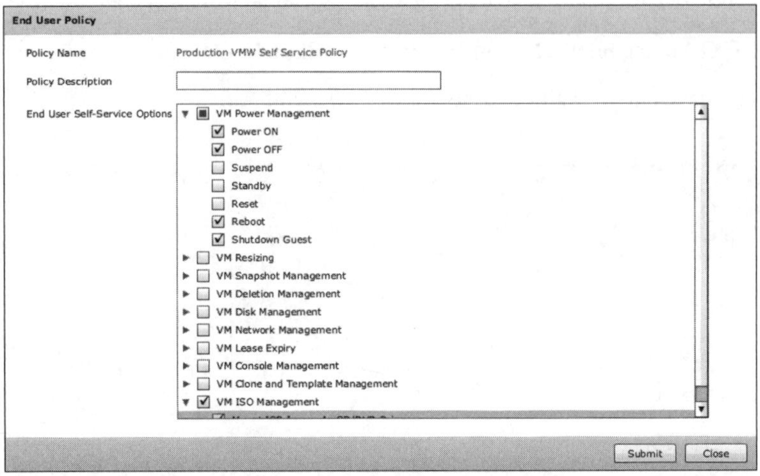

Figure 8-13 *Edit End User Policy Tab*

As you can see, End User Self-Service Policies give you the flexibility to give the necessary access to end users based on the environments in which they are operating their virtual machines. You can put the proper, granular controls in place to limit users' abilities to perform actions that may be undesirable in production environments while giving them complete abilities to do things in a development or test environment and offering tremendous amounts of flexibility.

But what if your end users require even more advanced options for their virtual machines? Good news! UCS Director offers even more capabilities by enabling you to create custom VM operations that can be attached to a user's virtual machines, giving them even more flexibility.

Advanced or Custom VM Operations

Beyond the actions discussed in the previous section, you may desire to give your users the ability to perform even greater actions on virtual machines. UCS Director enables you to set custom or advanced virtual machine options for end users. This can dramatically extend the use cases that can be solved in your organization with UCS Director. Custom VM Action Policies can be used to execute a custom workflow against a provisioned VM. What task that actual workflow executes is highly variable. The following are a couple of use cases that come to mind:

- Give Windows virtual machine users the ability to register their newly created VMs with Microsoft System Center Configuration Manager (SCCM) so that those VMs can be remediated post provisioning to include any relevant operating system patches or applications that have been advertised to different SCCM collections. A representative use case of where this could be helpful would be to give the end user the ability to create a generic Windows Server virtual machine and then, after creation, give them custom icons that offer the ability to add the VM to the Web, Application, or Database SCCM collection so that Internet Information Services (IIS), .NET, or SQL Server gets installed to that VM.

- Give Linux virtual machine users the ability to register their newly created VMs with different Puppet classes so that those VMs can be remediated post provisioning to include any relevant operating system patches or applications that have been assigned to different Puppet classes. An example of this would be to give the end user the ability to create a generic Linux virtual machine and then, after creation, give them custom icons that offer the ability to add that VM to a Web, Application, or Database Puppet class so that Apache, Java, or MySQL gets installed to that VM.

In both of these examples, custom VM operations enable your end users to move beyond an Infrastructure as a Service model (a bare, generic VM) into more of a Platform as a Service model (a VM with a complete app stack installed on it). This *dramatically* increases the use cases for UCS Director as a tool in your IT automation framework and provides VM customization capabilities to end users while allowing for complete automation, orchestration, and self-service capabilities to end users of both VMs and the applications within those VMs.

Some other examples that come to mind of custom actions that may be applicable to your end users include

- Registering a VM via PowerShell to an Active Directory domain.

- Giving end users a button to click in the UCS Director catalog for their VM to redirect them to your organization's internal change management database system (CMDB) to open a ticket on potential issues they may be experiencing with that VM or applications within the VM.

- Providing a custom policy button to allow the end user to request archives of the VM (in a test/development environment) in a situation where you are not utilizing lease durations within UCS Director on VMs. This would allow your users to request archives of the VM to a lower tier of storage or to an offline storage option so that it could be preserved for a duration of time for either development purposes, future access purposes, or government and regulatory purposes (for cases where nonactive VMs may need to be preserved for a period of time in case future access is required).

These are just some examples of how custom VM operations can be added within UCS Director to drastically extend the functionality and usefulness of available actions for end users in a self-service fashion, allowing them to perform the actions automatically without taking up valuable time and resources of your IT staff. Next, let's discuss how to set custom virtual machine policies.

Custom VM Action Policies

Within UCS Director, we have looked at how straightforward it is to create policy to allow a wide variety of functions that end users can take on virtual machines they've ordered through UCS Director's catalog, actions such as powering on or off the VM, creating snapshots, changing attributes of the VM such as resizing it or adding a vNIC, etc.

Creating custom VM policies gives you an easy way to enable users to add additional, custom capabilities to their VMs and their UCS Director user dashboard.

At a high level, this is accomplished in four parts:

1. Create a custom workflow action.
2. Test and execute the custom workflow.
3. Assign that custom workflow action to a custom user VM policy.
4. Assign the custom user VM policy to a vDC.

Create a Custom Workflow Action

You first create a custom workflow action in UCS Director that executes the custom policy action you desire. After that workflow has been created, it can then be accessed via a User VM Action Policy that you create. Let's look at an example where you can create a very simple workflow that runs a shell command on a Linux system.

Step 1. Within UCS Director, choose **Policies > Orchestration**. The Orchestration window opens with the Workflows tab displayed.

Step 2. On the Workflows tab, click the **Add Workflow** button (see Figure 8-14). Note that Figure 8-14 shows the Edit Workflow properties because the example included here was created previously; therefore, the option to Add is not available, only Edit. The first time you create a workflow, you will see Add Workflow displayed.

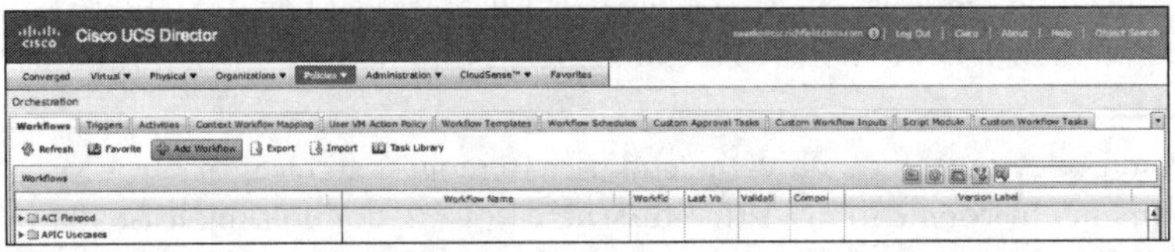

Figure 8-14 *Accessing the Add Workflow Button in UCS Director Policies*

Step 3. On the Workflow Details page, give the workflow a name. In this example, use **Show free disk space**.

Step 4. Give the workflow an optional description.

Step 5.   Select where the workflow can run. In this case, set Workflow Context to **Selected VM**. When Selected VM is the context, the shell command is permitted to run within the particular VM that will be selected by the end user. Note that when Selected VM is chosen, this allows a whole bunch of predefined variables to be exposed about the VM, which we will use later when we create the workflow for this example. A complete list of these workflows is shown in Figure 8-15.

Key Topic

For workflows that are executed in the context of a VM, these additional variables can be used in a macro:

Name	Description
${VM_NAME}	The name of the VM.
${VM_IPADDRESS}	The IP address of the VM.
${VM_STATE}	The state of the VM (ON or OFF).
${VM_STATE_DETAILS}	The state of the VM, power-on or power-off.
${VM_PARENT}	The ESX server or host node that is hosting the VM.
${VM_CLOUD}	The name of the cloud used for VM provisioning.
${VM_HOSTNAME}	The hostname of the VM
${VM_GROUP_NAME}	The name of the group to which the VM belongs.
${VM_GROUP_NAME}	The group ID to which the VM belongs.
${VM_CATALOG_ID}	The catalog ID used for VM.
${VM_ID}	The VM ID of the chosen VM.
${VM_SR_ID}	The VM service request ID.
${VM_COMMENTS}	The comments specified by the requesting user.
${VM_VDC_NAME}	The name of the vDC.
${VM_VDC_ID}	The vDC ID.
${VM_TYPE}	The type of the VM.
${VM_SCHED_TERM}	The scheduled termination time for the VM.

Figure 8-15   *Table of Defined Variables for Selected VM*

8

Step 6.   In the Save Options section, use the **Select Folder** field to choose a folder in which to save the workflow. Folders give you a way to conveniently organize workflows within UCS Director in a way that makes the most sense for your organization. Some larger organizations will have a very large folder structure for categorizing workflows within UCS Director, while others may find it simpler to put everything in a single folder. It is better to create folders from the start, though, for organizational purposes (see Figure 8-16). Note that Figure 8-16 shows the Edit Workflow properties because the example included here was created previously; therefore, the option to Add is not available, only Edit. The first time you create a workflow, you will see Add Workflow displayed.

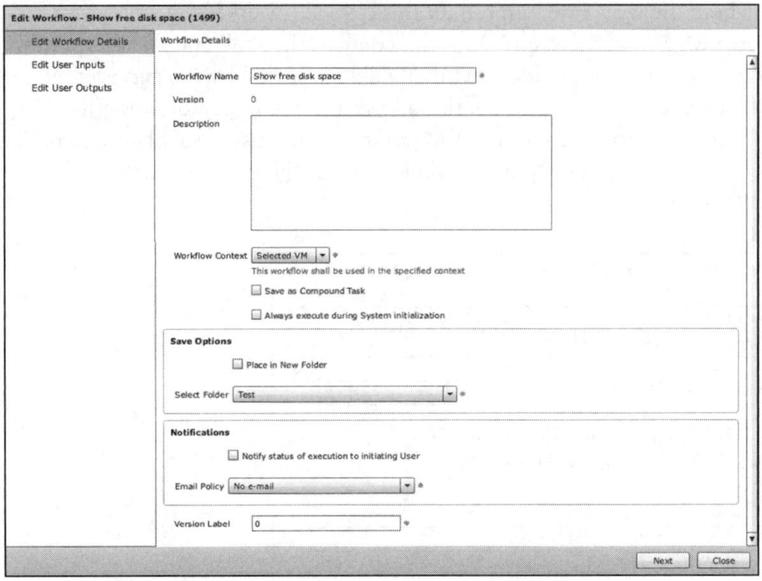

Figure 8-16   *UCS Director Add Workflow Dialog Box*

Step 7.   In the Notifications section, select an email policy for the workflow. In this case, as you won't require any email notifications for this example, leave Email Policy set to **No e-mail**.

Step 8.   Click **Next**.

Step 9.   On the Edit User Inputs screen, click the green plus sign to add an input label. Create three total input labels, as listed next and shown in Figure 8-17. Pay particular attention to the Type for each label.

   a.   Input Label of **Email address** with a Type of **email_address_list**

   b.   Input Label of **Username** with a Type of **gen_text_input**

   c.   Input Label of **Password** with a Type of **password**

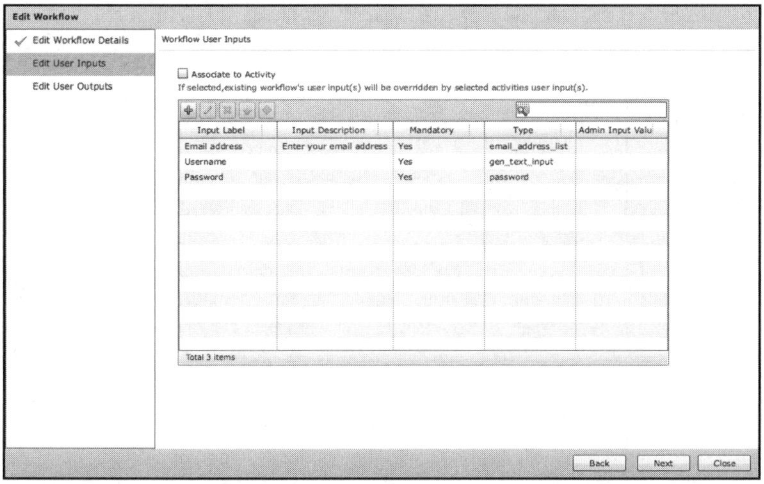

Figure 8-17 *Completed Workflow User Inputs Screen*

Step 10. Click **Next** to move to the final screen, Edit User Outputs. No outputs need to be specified, so click **Submit**.

Step 11. The workflow now appears under the folder named Test, as shown in Figure 8-18.

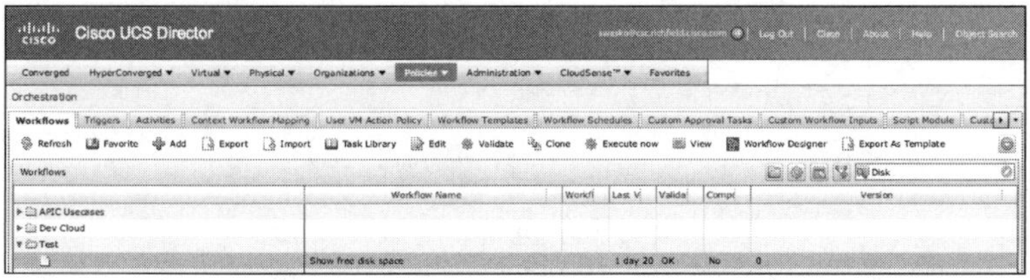

Figure 8-18 *Workflow Titled "Show free disk space"*

Step 12. Double-click the workflow name to launch the Workflow Designer application within UCS Director. For the purposes of this example, we will be creating a workflow that has two steps:

    a. Execute a VIX script to show free disk space

    b. Email the results to the end user

Step 13. Using the upper-left search pane of the Workflow Designer, search for **VIX** (see Figure 8-19).

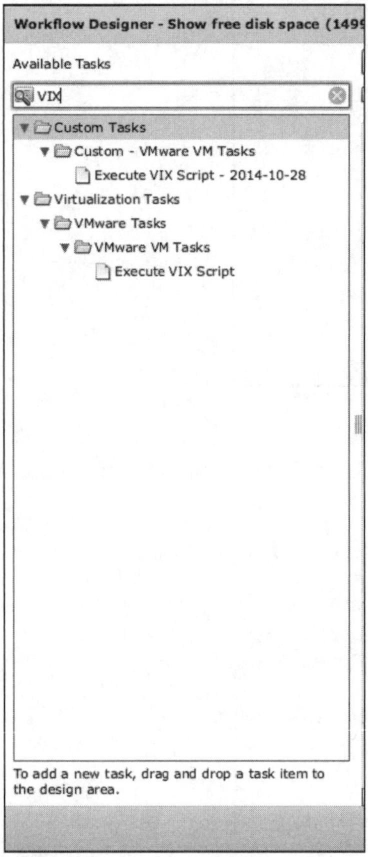

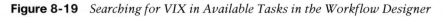

Workflow Designer - Show free disk space (1499

Available Tasks

🔍 VIX ⊗

▼ 🗁 Custom Tasks
   ▼ 🗁 Custom - VMware VM Tasks
       📄 Execute VIX Script - 2014-10-28
▼ 🗁 Virtualization Tasks
   ▼ 🗁 VMware Tasks
      ▼ 🗁 VMware VM Tasks
         📄 Execute VIX Script

To add a new task, drag and drop a task item to the design area.

Figure 8-19 *Searching for VIX in Available Tasks in the Workflow Designer*

Step 14. From the search results, drag and drop the **Execute VIX Script** action onto the Workflow task pane. The Add Task wizard opens with the Task Information page displayed. Give the task a name such as **Show free disk space**, as shown in Figure 8-20.

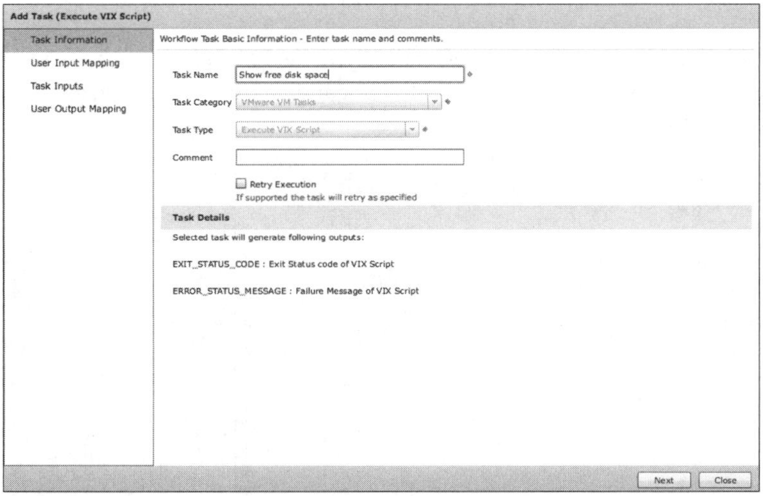

Figure 8-20   *Providing Task Information for the VIX Script*

Step 15.   Click **Next**.

Step 16.   On the User Input Mapping page, make the following configurations, as shown in Figure 8-21:

■ Under Select VM (Mandatory), check the **Map to User Input** check box and set the User Input field to **VM Selected (Context).**

■ Under Login, check the **Map to User Input** check box and set the User Input field to **Username.**

■ Under Password, check the **Map to User Input** check box and set the User Input field to **Password.**

Note that no additional information needs to be provided on this page.

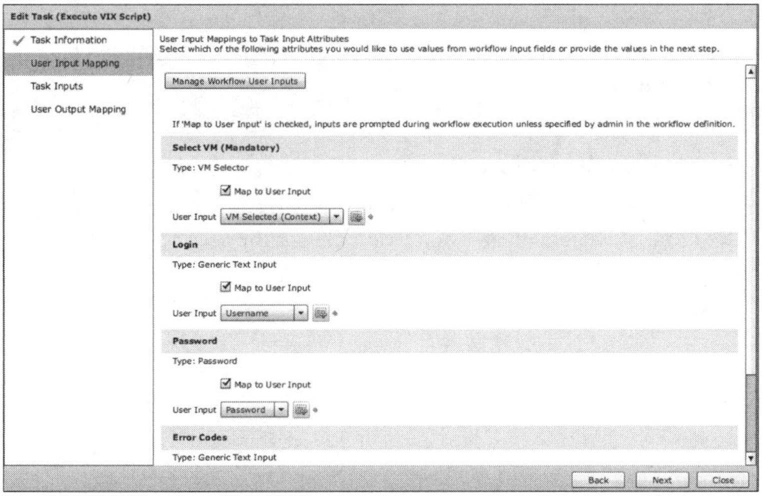

Figure 8-21   *User Input Mapping Selections*

Step 17. Click **Next**.

Step 18. On the Task Inputs page, set the Credential Type field to **Login**. In the Script pane, enter the simple Linux command to look at disk free space, **df-h**, as shown in Figure 8-22.

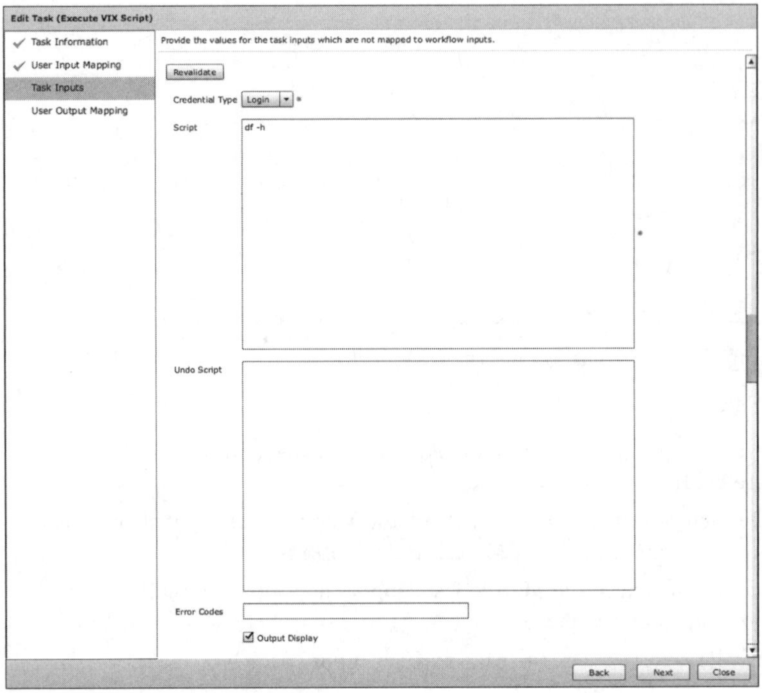

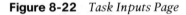

Figure 8-22 *Task Inputs Page*

Step 19. Click **Next**.

Step 20. No changes are required on the User Output Mapping page, so simply click **Submit** to save the workflow.

Test and Execute the Custom Workflow

Step 1. You should now test the workflow and monitor the results of running this single VIX script, as we'll need an output variable for the second task that we create a bit later.

Step 2.   Before testing the workflow, drag your cursor over the bottom edge of the "Show free disk space" task in the Workflow Designer. Note that as you move your cursor from left to right, you will see the ability to define where the workflow should go on success or failure. Click the **On Success** option to display what is shown in Figure 8-23. Select the drop-down menu option **Completed (Success)** and notice that a green arrow now connects the task to the green Completed (Success) box, as shown in Figure 8-24.

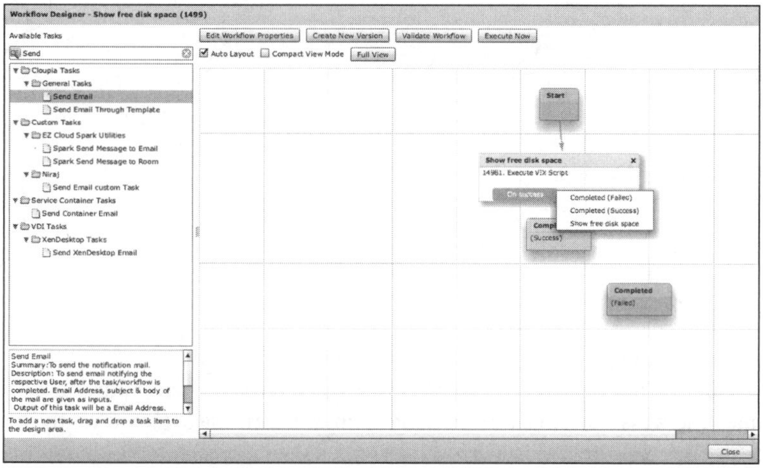

Figure 8-23   *On Success Workflow Option*

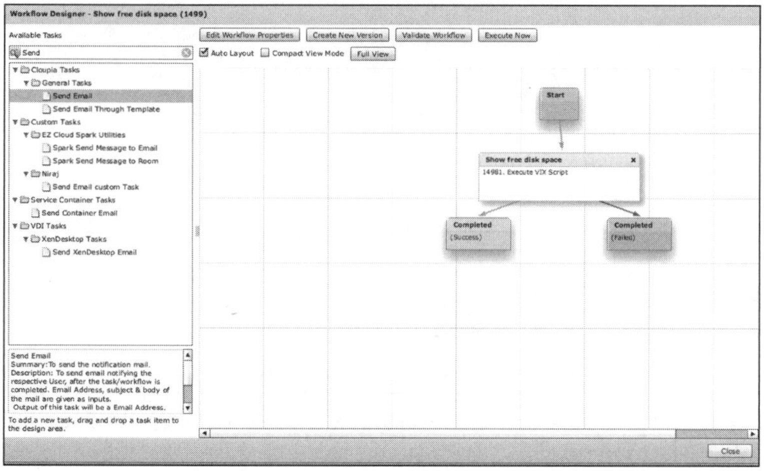

Figure 8-24   *Showing Task Linked to Completed*

Step 3.   Complete Step 2 for the **On Failure** option, clicking the **Completed (Failed)** menu option for the task to connect it with a red arrow to the red Completed (Failed) box.

Step 4. Click the **Execute Now** button (see Figure 8-25).

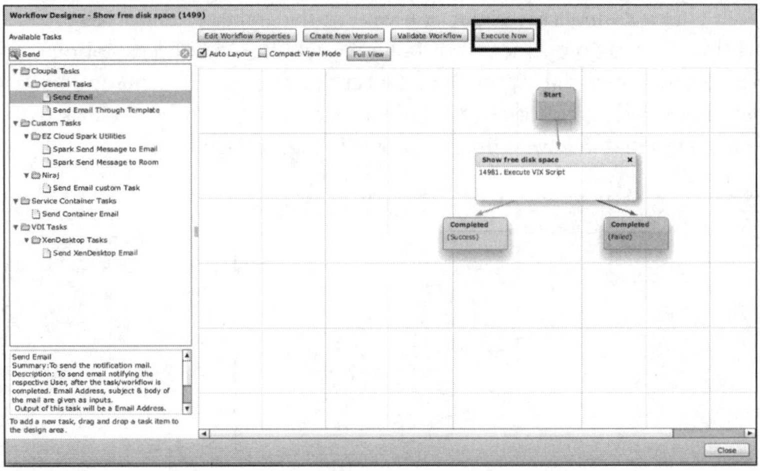

Figure 8-25 *Execute Now Button*

Step 5. In the Executing Workflow: Show free disk space dialog box, shown in Figure 8-26, select a target VM (**y4040** for this example), email address, username, and password (used to run this command on the selected Linux VM); then click **Submit**.

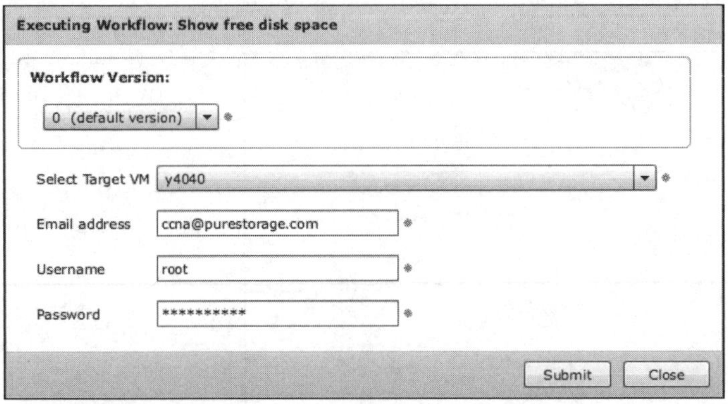

Figure 8-26 *Executing Workflow: Show Free Disk Space Dialog Box*

Step 6. In the Service Request Submit Status dialog box (see Figure 8-27), click the **Show Detail Status** button.

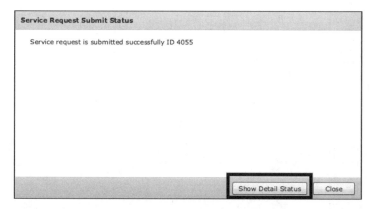

Figure 8-27 *Show Detail Status for Service Request*

Step 7.   Click the **Log** tab and, toward the bottom, search for the words ERROR_
STATUS_MESSAGE (see Figure 8-28). Write down this variable *exactly* as it
appears, including capital letters and underscores, for use in the second step of
our workflow. Once noted, click **Close** to return to the Workflow Designer.

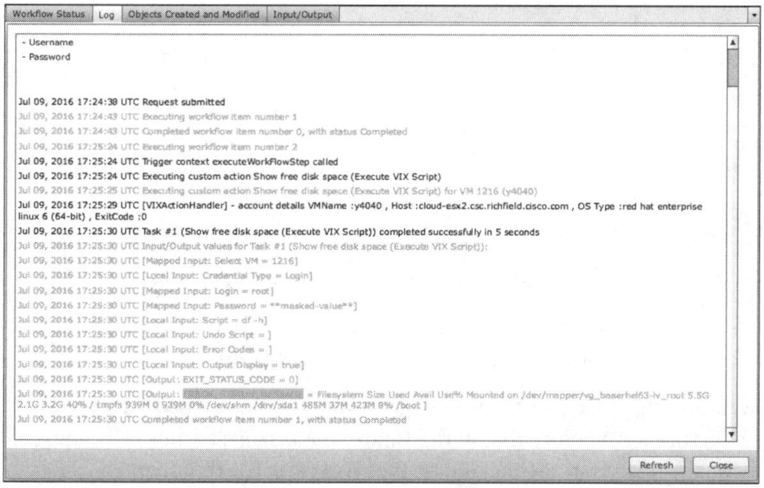

Figure 8-28 *Log Tab of Workflow Status*

Step 8.   Using the upper-left search pane of the Workflow Designer application, search
for either **send** or **email**. You are searching for an action to send an email, so
experiment with different searches to become more familiar with different
tasks in UCS Director (see Figure 8-29).

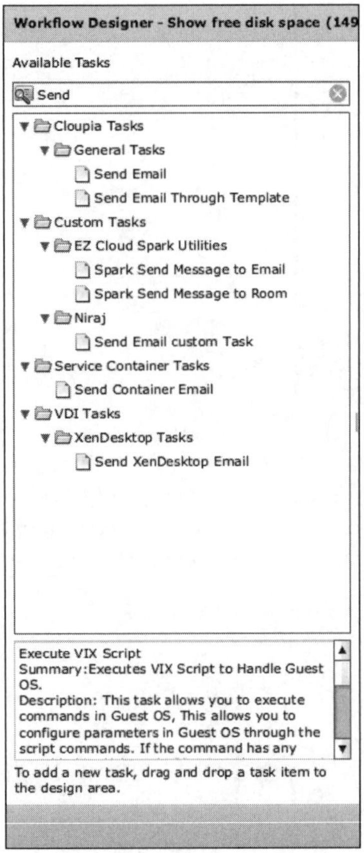

Figure 8-29   *Searching for email in Available Tasks in the Workflow Designer*

Step 9.   From the search results, drag the **Send Email** task onto the workflow pane. The Edit Task wizard will automatically open for editing the task.

Step 10.   If you want, on the Task Information page, give the task a name and a comment (see Figure 8-30). Note that in the figure, the task isn't editable because it was previously created in the making of the workflow for this chapter.

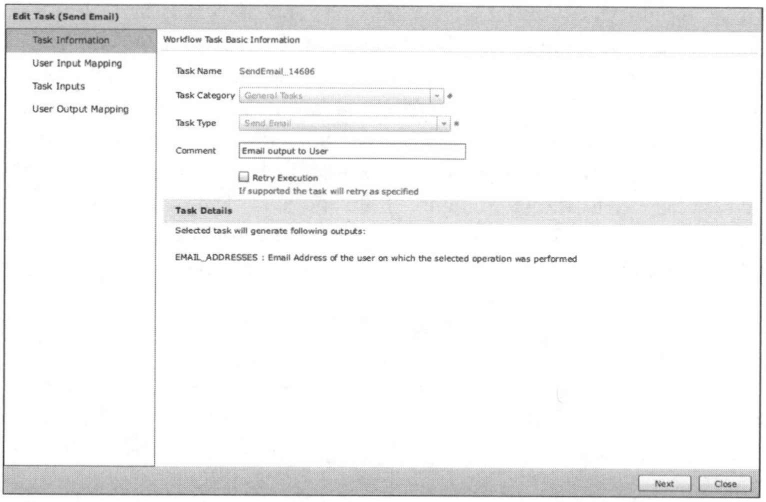

Figure 8-30 *Task Information Page for Send Email Task*

Step 11. Click **Next**.

Step 12. On the User Input Mapping page, under the section titled E-mail Addresses (Mandatory), check the **Map to User Input** check box and set the User Input field to **Email address** (see Figure 8-31).

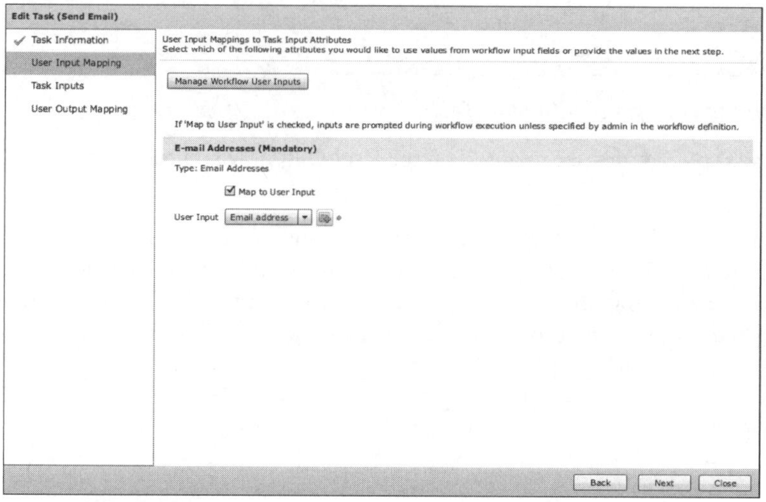

Figure 8-31 *User Input Mapping Page for Send Email Task*

Step 13. Click **Next**.

Step 14. On the Task Inputs page, you set up a subject line and body message. Notice in the Body field shown in Figure 8-32 the use of the ERROR_STATUS_MESSAGE variable that you wrote down in Step 27 from Figure 8-28. Enter an appropriate subject and body, ensuring that you copy the variable information **${Show free disk space.ERROR_STATUS_MESSAGE}** exactly as shown in Figure 8-32. Note that Figure 8-32 shows the Add Task Wizard as opposed to the Edit Task Wizard as shown in Figures 8-30 and 8-31. The dialog box will always show Add Task if a new task is being created or Edit Task if an existing task is being modified.

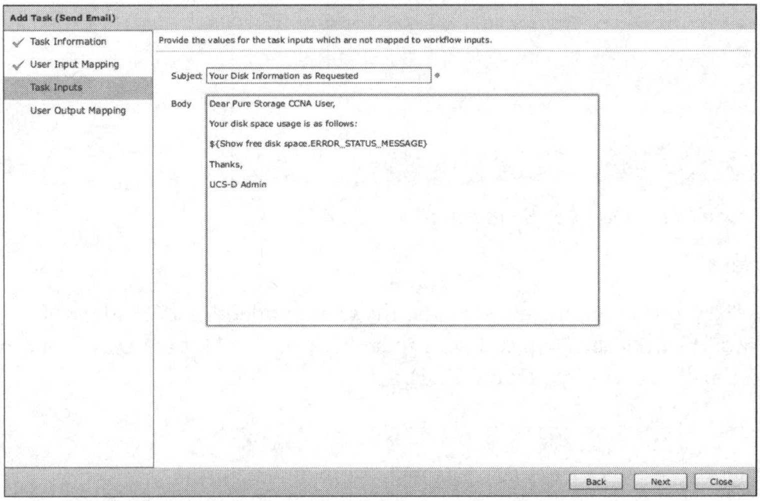

Figure 8-32 *Task Inputs Page for Send Email Task*

Step 15. Click **Next**. No entries are required on the User Output Mapping page, so click **Submit**.

Step 16. Back in the Workflow Designer, we now want to modify where our On Success and On Failure options for the "Show free disk space" command point. The new hierarchy of order should flow from Start > Task 1 > Task 2 > Completed. Modify the arrows so that your task flow looks like that shown in Figure 8-33.

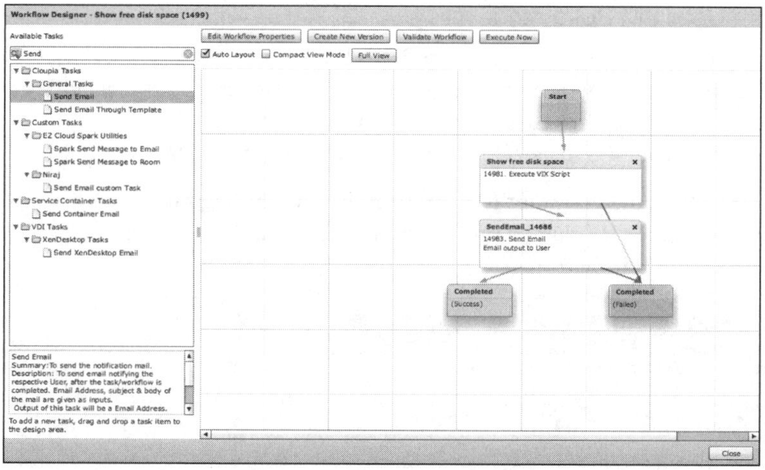

Figure 8-33 *Completed "Show free disk space" Workflow*

Step 17. Click **Execute Now** to run the workflow. As previously done in Step 5, select the target VM, username, and password for that VM, as well as the email address where the output should be sent. Click **Submit**. Optionally, feel free to then click the **Show Detail Status** dialog box and monitor the Log tab for progress on the workflow. Or simply wait for the email to arrive in your inbox with the requested information.

Step 18. Check your email inbox for the address you entered in Step 17. If all worked well, you should find an email similar to the one shown in Figure 8-34.

cloud-ucsd@reqdemo.com
To: Steve Wasko
Your Disk Information as Requested

Dear CCNA User,

Your disk space usage is as follows:

Filesystem Size Used Avail Use% Mounted on /dev/mapper/vg_baserhel63-lv_root 5.5G 2.1G 3.2G 40% / tmpfs 939M 0 939M 0% /dev/shm /dev/sda1 485M 37M 423M 8% /boot

Thanks,

UCS-D Admin

Figure 8-34 *Email from UCS Director Showing Disk Usage for VM y4040*

Assign the Custom User VM Policy to a vDC

Step 1.   Now that the workflow has been created and has run successfully, we must make it available to one or more vDC(s) within UCS Director, and then add the custom action to end-user virtual machines in that particular vDC. To do this, navigate to **Policies > Virtual/Hypervisor Policies > Virtual Data Centers**.

Step 2.   Select the vDC name you want to map the policy to. In the example shown in Figure 8-35, the vDC named prd-ImportantACMEApp-y4027 has been selected. Click the **Edit** button.

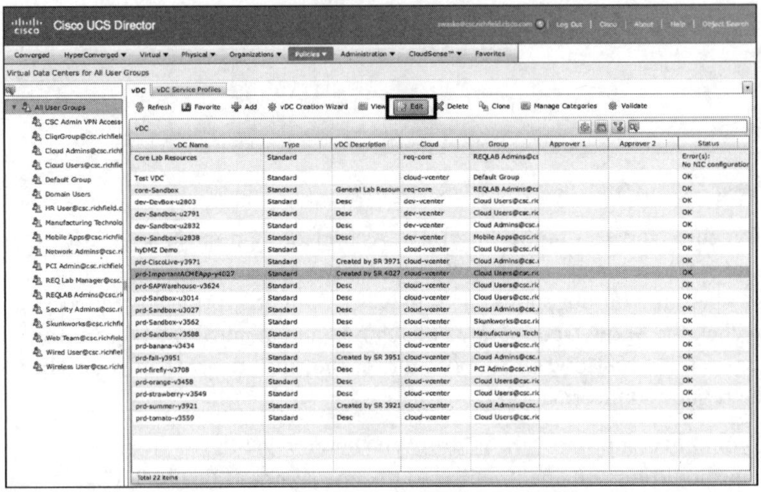

Figure 8-35   *List of Virtual Data Centers for All User Groups*

Step 3.   In the Edit vDC dialog box, scroll down to the Policies section and look for the User Action Policy drop-down list box. From the drop-down list, choose **Disk Free**, as shown in Figure 8-36, and then click **Save**.

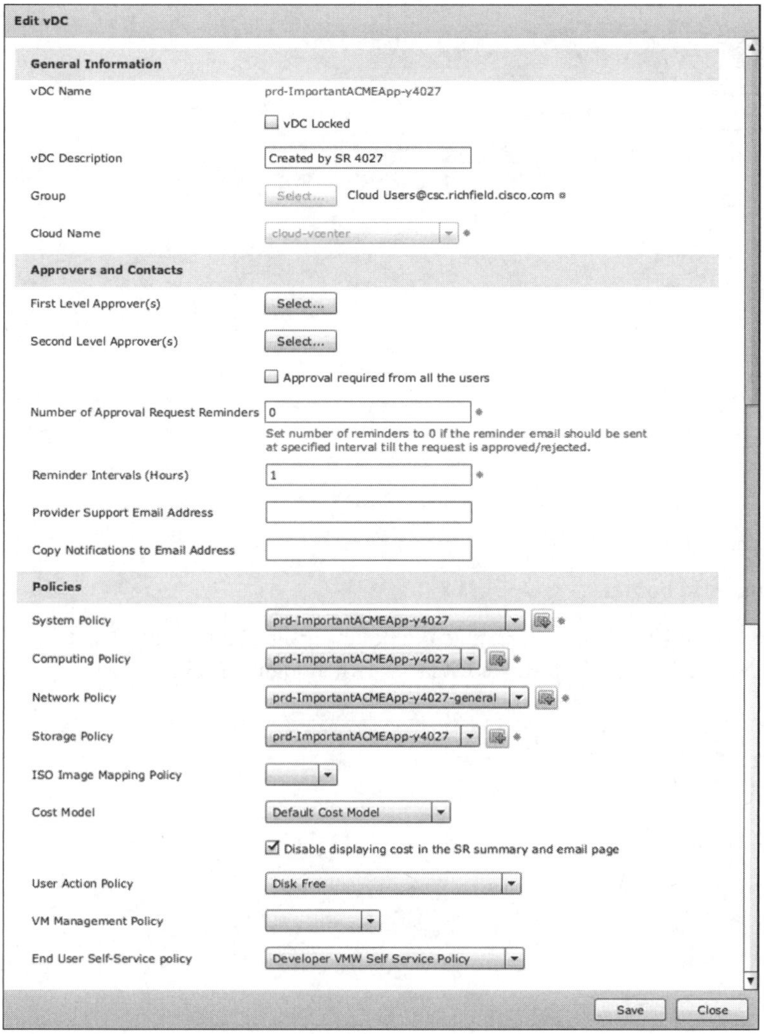

Figure 8-36   *Edit vDC Dialog Box*

Assign the Custom Workflow Action to a Custom User VM Policy

Step 1. Now that the policy has been assigned to a vDC, let's add the Custom User VM Policy to VMs in that vDC. Navigate to **Policies > Orchestration** and then click the **User VM Action Policy** tab, as shown in Figure 8-37.

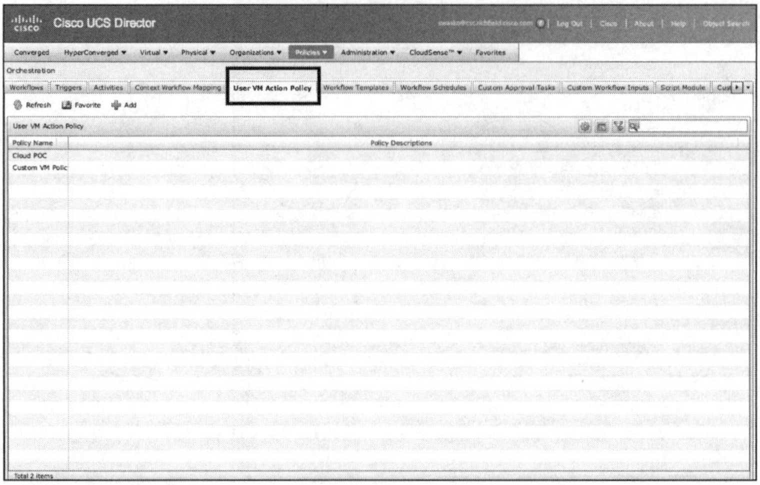

Figure 8-37 *User VM Action Policy Tab*

Step 2. Click the **Add** button.

Step 3. On the Create New Policy page, give the policy a name and choose **1** in the Select No. of Actions drop-down list (as shown in Figure 8-38).

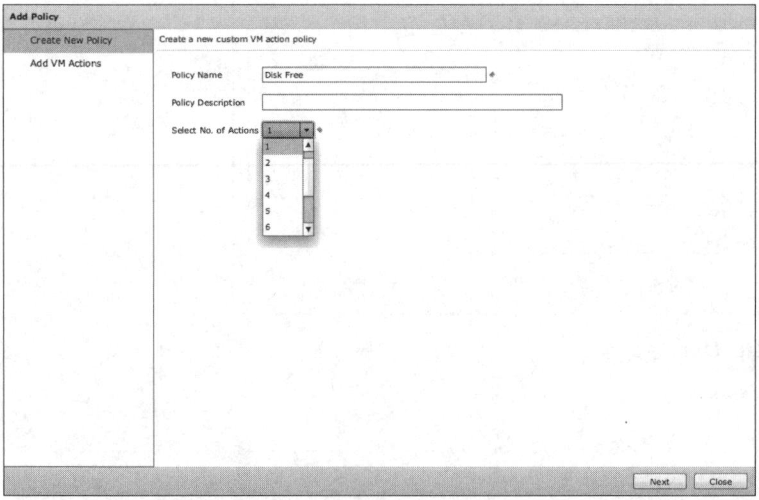

Figure 8-38 *Create New Policy Page*

Step 4. Click **Next**.

Step 5.   On the Add VM Actions page, give the button a label in the Action Label field, select the workflow to perform when the button is clicked (**1499 Show free disk space** in this example), and then select the Authorized User Types by clicking on the **Select** button next to Authorized User Types and then choosing Service End-User, as shown in Figure 8-39.

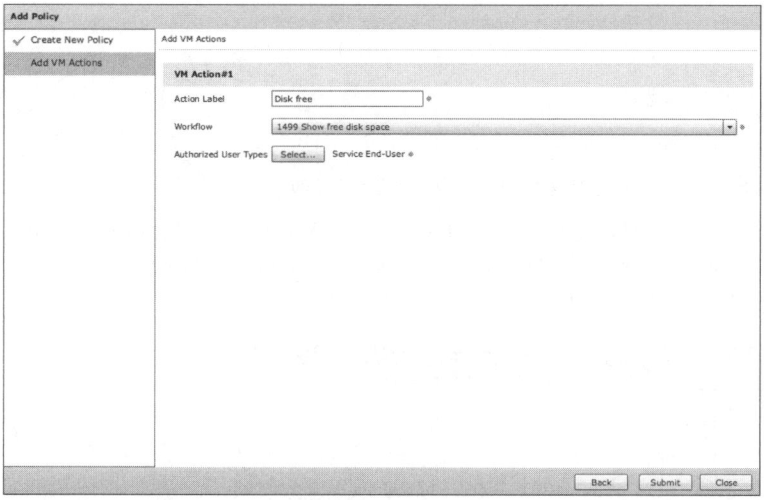

Figure 8-39   *Add VM Actions Page*

Step 6.   Click **Submit**.

The final steps are to log out of UCS Director as an admin, and log in to UCS Director as an end user that has permissions to the vDC we just mapped this custom User VM Action Policy to.

Step 7.   In the upper-right corner of UCS Director, next to your username, click **Log Out**, as shown in Figure 8-40.

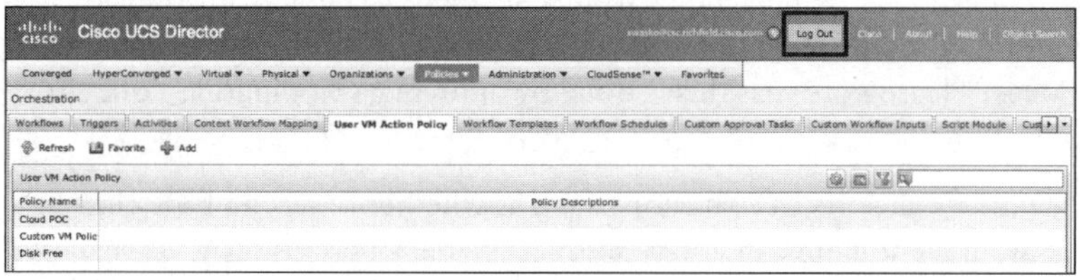

Figure 8-40   *Logging Out of UCS Director*

Step 8. Log in to UCS Director as an end user. At the top, you will see the Virtual Resources menu option, as shown in Figure 8-41. Click that icon.

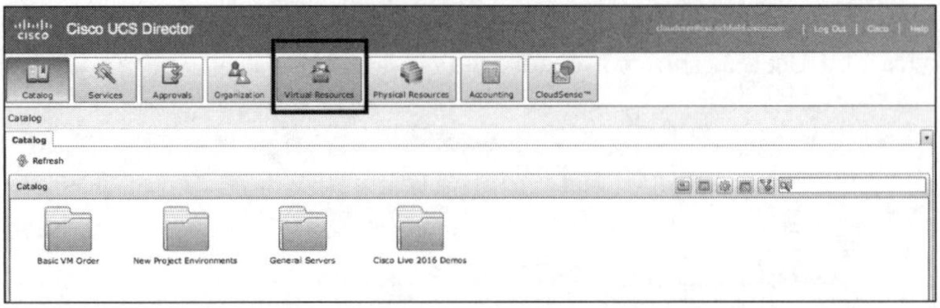

Figure 8-41 *Virtual Resources Icon in End-User Service Catalog*

Step 9. Navigate to the **VMs** tab and select the previous VM you used for testing (for the example, VM Name **y4040**). Notice that the menu now has a "Disk free*" menu option, as shown in Figure 8-42.

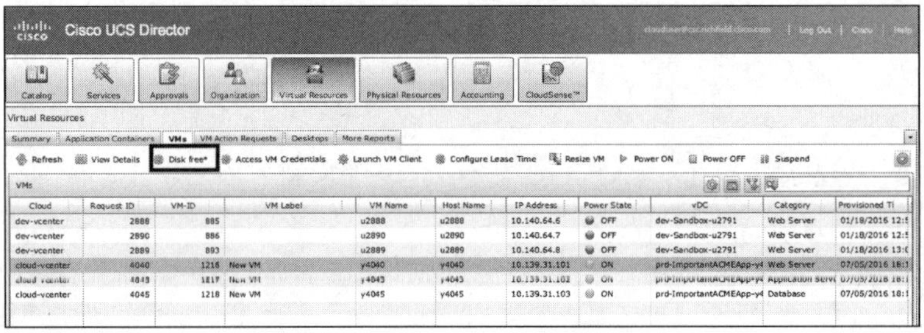

Figure 8-42 *Disk free Menu Option*

Step 10. Log out of UCS Director as the end user.

Setting VM Options for End-User Selection

When your users are requesting virtual machines from a Standard Catalog or Advanced Catalog, you have the ability to create conditions that can be enforced for the users by creating a Computing Policy. Please note that this is done by applying a Computing Policy to vDCs that you choose.

The Computing Policy drives all sorts of behaviors, such as whether or not an ESX cluster in a pod of infrastructure has enough vCPU or memory available to provision VMs successfully. In addition, you can set default options for permitted values of vCPUs and memory for end users.

As the UCS Director administrator, the Computing Policy allows you to focus on delivering varying tiers of service to virtual computing. As an example, you can choose older ESX clusters with less memory or CPU resources for a development vDC while choosing a new ESX cluster with more CPU/memory for a production vDC.

To create a Computing Policy, follow these steps:

Step 1.   Within UCS Director, select **Policies > Virtual/Hypervisor Policies > Computing**.

Step 2.   Navigate to the hypervisor of your choice. In this example, select the **VMware Computing Policy** tab.

Step 3.   Click the **Add** button to open the Add Computing Policy dialog box, shown in Figure 8-43.

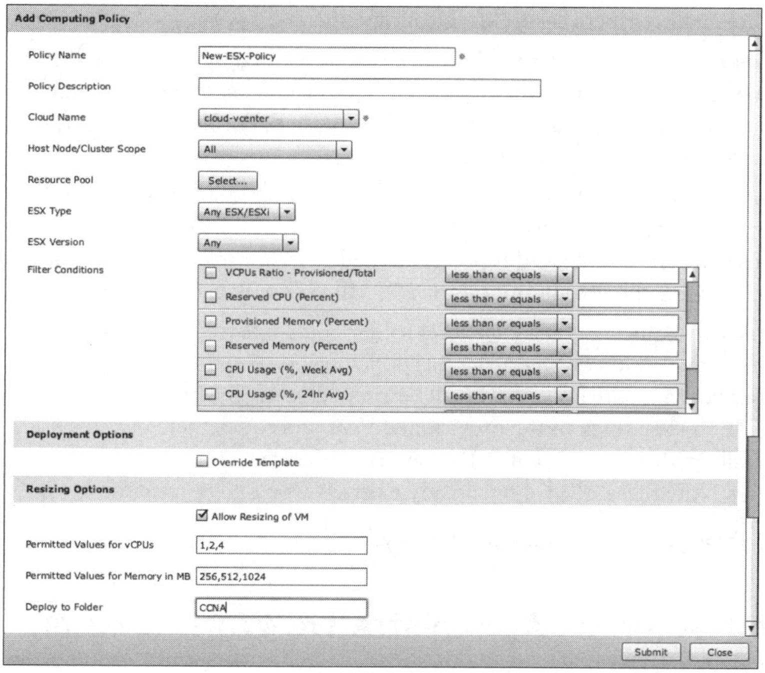

Figure 8-43   *Adding a Computing Policy*

Step 4.   Give the Computing Policy a name and, optionally, a description. In this example the policy is named **New-ESX-Policy**.

Step 5.   In the **Cloud Name** drop-down list box, select the cloud you would like to provision this policy for. In this example, **cloud-vcenter** is selected.

Step 6.   If you want the Computing Policy to operate within the constraints of an ESX resource pool, click **Select** to the right of Resource Pool and choose a resource pool.

Step 7.   Keep ESX Type set to **Any ESX/ESXi**.

Step 8.   Keep ESX Version set to **Any**.

Step 9.   The Filter Conditions scrollable pane gives you a myriad of options. For brevity purposes, they won't be listed here, but refer to Figure 8-43 to see a partial list of options. You can set parameters such as guests per host, VCPUs Ratio, Provisioned Memory, etc. If any of these conditions aren't met when an end user requests resources in the vDC where this Computing Policy is applied, the provisioning process may not complete successfully due to a lack of available resources. This gives you the ability to ensure clusters don't get over-provisioned as part of the end-user service catalog ordering process.

Step 10.   Scroll down to the Resizing Options section, check the **Allow Resizing of VM** check box, and compete the fields as follows:

- **Permitted Values for vCPUs:** Enter a string (separated by commas) of valid vCPU options that will be presented to the end user when they go to provision a virtual machine with this policy applied. For this example, 1, 2, and 4 vCPUs have been allowed.

- **Permitted Values for Memory in MB:** Enter a numeric string (separated by commas) of permitted memory amounts to be allowed when provisioning a virtual machine that has this policy applied to it. For this example, we are only allowing the default options of 256 MB, 512 MB, and 1024 MB.

- **Deploy to Folder:** Enter a name of a folder you'd like to create in Virtual Center where VMs created from this policy will reside. If the specified folder does not already exist, it will be created by UCS Director. This is helpful to keep track of the provisioned VMs and to see them organized logically within VirtualCenter. For this example, we have created a **CCNA** folder. Note that if the folder already exists, it won't be re-created.

Step 11.   Click **Submit** to add the Computing Policy.

Understanding Common Administrative Workflows on VMs in UCS Director

UCS Director comes with a default set of administrative workflows that can be leveraged out of the box in your task of automating and orchestrating virtual machine actions within your private cloud infrastructure. This section is certainly not an exhaustive list of workflows but will cover some of the more common ones. You are encouraged to review many more of these within UCS Director in preparation for working with the product in your organization and for the purposes of studying for your CCNA certification.

Step 1.   In UCS Director, navigate to **Policies > Orchestration**.

Step 2.   Go to the **Default** folder and expand the **Default\VMware** folder.

Step 3.   Select any workflow. For illustration purposes, select the **VMware Clone VM As Image** workflow.

Step 4.   Double-click the selected workflow and you will see the Workflow Designer screen shown in Figure 8-44. Notice that the Workflow Designer screen has two main sections. On the left is a list of available tasks. On the right is a "canvas" similar to that found in many popular diagramming applications that allows you to simply drag and drop workflow tasks from the library on the left onto the canvas.

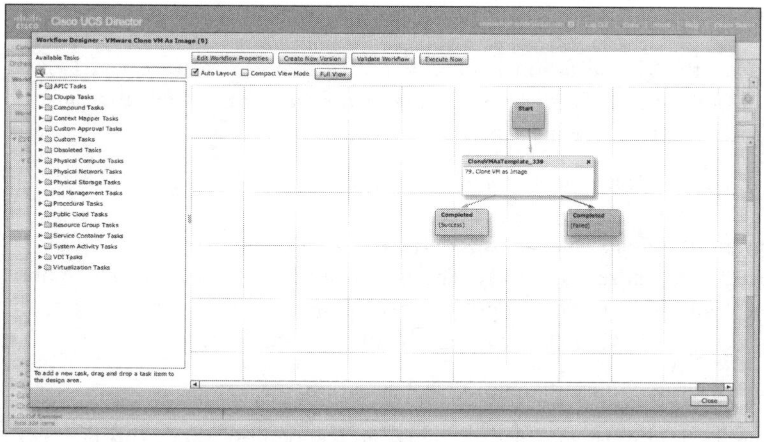

Figure 8-44   *VMware Clone VM As Image Task*

Under Available Tasks on the left of the Workflow Designer, there are two ways to find tasks to use. As you first start to work with UCS Director, it may be helpful to drill down into the various folders and subfolders to find tasks that you are interested in. As you gain more experience with the product and can start to recall task names that are frequently used, you can use the search/query field to quickly and easily search and filter based on items you are interested in.

Step 5.   To explore some of the common actions available to virtual hypervisors, expand the **Virtualization Tasks** folder, expand the **HyperV Tasks** folder, and then expand the **HyperV VM Tasks** subfolder, as shown in Figure 8-45.

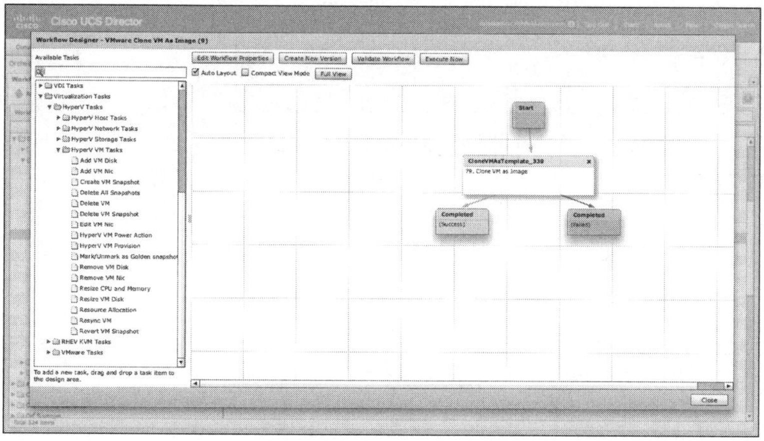

Figure 8-45   *HyperV VM Tasks Folder Options*

Step 6.   Note the common tasks available to you. You could drag and drop these items into the Workflow Designer canvas to link them with other available tasks to create more complex, multistep workflows. But for the purposes of this exercise, we won't be making any changes to the VMware Clone VM As Image workflow; we are simply observing available workflows.

Step 7.   Navigate to the **Virtualization Tasks > VMware Tasks > VMware VM Tasks** folder. Note some of the many options available that you can perform on a VMware ESX virtual machine.

Step 8.   Once you are done reviewing some of these actions, click **Close**.

To see a dynamic inventory of all available tasks defined in a particular instance of UCS Director, you can export the entire task library. This is a great reference to save offline out of UCS Director. This will allow you (if you print to PDF as an example) to have a list of all the standard tasks that ship with UCS Director for easy offline reference.

Step 1.   In UCS Director, choose **Policies > Orchestration**.

Step 2.   Click the **Task Library** icon, as highlighted in Figure 8-46. When the dialog box appears, click the **Regenerate Document** check box and then click **Submit**.

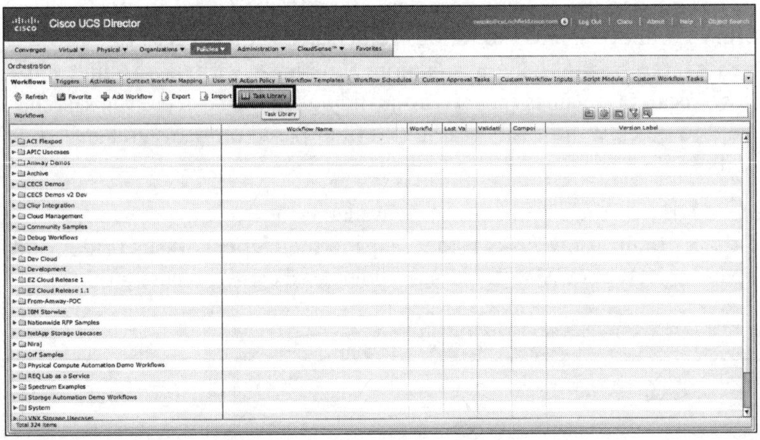

Figure 8-46   *Exporting the UCS Director Task Library*

Step 3. The resulting document can then be printed to PDF and used to reference all orchestration tasks within UCS Director (see Figure 8-47). Clicking any task will take you to a detailed summary, description, and table of inputs and outputs. Figure 8-48 shows an example of the output of the task titled VMware Host Tasks: Create Host Profile.

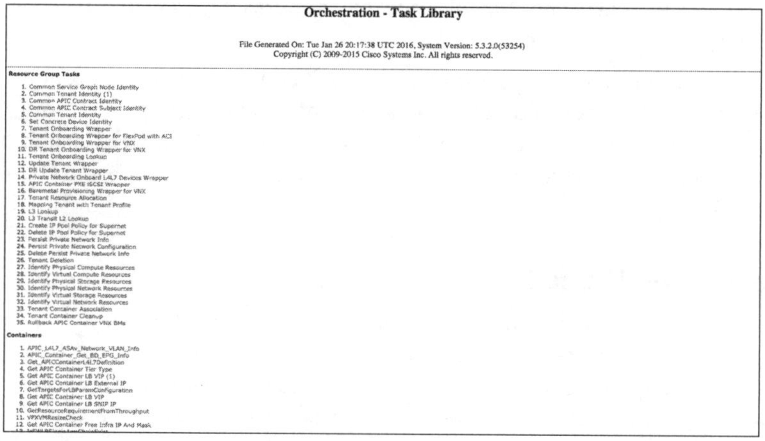

Orchestration - Task Library

File Generated On: Tue Jan 26 20:17:38 UTC 2016, System Version: 5.3.2.0(53254)
Copyright (C) 2009-2015 Cisco Systems Inc. All rights reserved.

Resource Group Tasks

1. Common Service Graph Node Identity
2. Common Tenant Identity (1)
3. Common APIC Contract Identity
4. Common APIC Contract Subject Identity
5. Common Tenant Identity
6. Set Concrete Device Identity
7. Tenant Onboarding Wrapper
8. Tenant Onboarding Wrapper for FlexPod with ACI
9. Tenant Onboarding Wrapper for VNX
10. DR Tenant Onboarding Wrapper for VNX
11. Tenant Onboarding Lookup
12. Update Tenant Wrapper
13. DR Update Tenant Wrapper
14. Private Network Onboard L4L7 Devices Wrapper
15. APIC Container PXE ISCSI Wrapper
16. Baremetal Provisioning Wrapper for VNX
17. Tenant Resource Allocation
18. Mapping Tenant with Tenant Profile
19. L3 Lookup
20. L3 Transit L2 Lookup
21. Create IP Pool Policy for Supernet
22. Delete IP Pool Policy for Supernet
23. Persist Private Network Info
24. Persist Private Network Configuration
25. Delete Persist Private Network Info
26. Tenant Deletion
27. Identify Physical Compute Resources
28. Identify Virtual Compute Resources
29. Identify Physical Storage Resources
30. Identify Physical Network Resources
31. Identify Virtual Storage Resources
32. Identify Virtual Network Resources
33. Tenant Container Association
34. Tenant Container Cleanup
35. Rollback APIC Container VNX BMs

Containers

1. APIC_L4L7_ASAv_Network_VLAN_Info
2. APIC_Container_Get_BD_EPG_Info
3. Get_APICContainerL4L7Definition
4. Get APIC Container Tier Type
5. Get APIC Container LB VIP (1)
6. Get APIC Container LB External IP
7. GetTargetsForLBParamConfiguration
8. Get APIC Container LB VIP
9. Get APIC Container LB SNIP IP
10. GetResourceRequirementFromThroughput
11. VPXVMResizeCheck
12. Get APIC Container Free Infra IP And Mask

Figure 8-47 *UCS Director Orchestration Task Library*

Key Topic

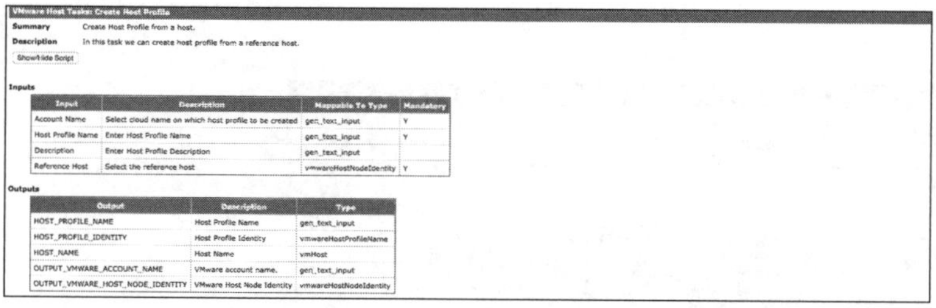

VMware Host Tasks: Create Host Profile

Summary Create Host Profile from a host.

Description In this task we can create host profile from a reference host.

Show/Hide Script

Inputs

Input	Description	Mappable To Type	Mandatory
Account Name	Select cloud name on which host profile to be created	gen_text_input	Y
Host Profile Name	Enter Host Profile Name	gen_text_input	Y
Description	Enter Host Profile Description	gen_text_input	
Reference Host	Select the reference host	vmwareHostNodeIdentity	Y

Outputs

Output	Description	Type
HOST_PROFILE_NAME	Host Profile Name	gen_text_input
HOST_PROFILE_IDENTITY	Host Profile Identity	vmwareHostProfileName
HOST_NAME	Host Name	vmHost
OUTPUT_VMWARE_ACCOUNT_NAME	VMware account name.	gen_text_input
OUTPUT_VMWARE_HOST_NODE_IDENTITY	VMware Host Node Identity	vmwareHostNodeIdentity

Figure 8-48 *Detailed UCS Director Task Inputs and Outputs*

As you can see, UCS Director allows you great flexibility with the thousands of out-of-the-box tasks. Combined with the ability to also import tasks easily into the task library from places like Cisco's UCS Director community forums or peers of yours, you can see how UCS Director provides you, the cloud administrator, with a great deal of flexibility to handle a wide range of operational tasks within your organization.

Prime Service Catalog VM Integration

The last section of this chapter focuses on how to bring the virtual machine end-user experience into Prime Service Catalog. If we think about the two different audiences each tool in the Cisco ONE Enterprise Cloud Suite serves, it can be broken down along these lines:

- **UCS Director:** A "quick and dirty" service catalog that you and your IT department can use for ordering infrastructure, ordering VMs, and automating common IT tasks (such as an Advanced Catalog entry in UCS Director to "Add a New VLAN" to the data center) quickly and easily. UCS Director provides an IT-focused experience and is tightly coupled with technical IT task automation. However, if the organizational requirements are minimal, UCS Director's service catalogs can be exposed directly to your end users for them to order infrastructure items quickly and easily. UCS Director lacks the polish, fit, and finish of Prime Service Catalog but may be good enough for your organization to compete with public cloud IaaS and PaaS offerings your internal IT users may be contemplating using or already consuming.

■ **Prime Service Catalog:** Prime Service Catalog offers a much better "fit and finish" and is much more end-user friendly for both ordering catalog items and interacting with provisioned VMs. Whereas UCS Director is an-IT focused experience, Prime Service Catalog focuses more on the end-user experience and centers on business logic more than technical IT task automation.

Linking UCS Director and Prime Service Catalog

The first step is to ensure that UCS Director is communicating properly with Prime Service Catalog. Cisco offers very easy out-of-the-box integration of these two products. The primary setup for this configuration takes place within Prime Service Catalog. Assuming connectivity has already been established, to verify connectivity, take the following steps:

Step 1. Within Prime Service Catalog while logged in as an administrator, click your name in the upper-right corner and then choose **Switch To > Administration** (see Figure 8-49).

Figure 8-49 *Accessing Administration View to Begin Prime Service Catalog and UCS Director Integration*

Step 2. Once in the Administration screen, click **Manage Connections** in the upper menu bar as shown in Figure 8-50.

Figure 8-50 *Click Manage Connections on the Home Page*

Step 3. On the Manage Connection screen, you'll see connections for UCS Director, Intercloud Fabric for Business, and Puppet. Click **UCS Director**, and then click **Connections** immediately below it. Click the **Edit** icon, denoted by a pencil (see Figure 8-51).

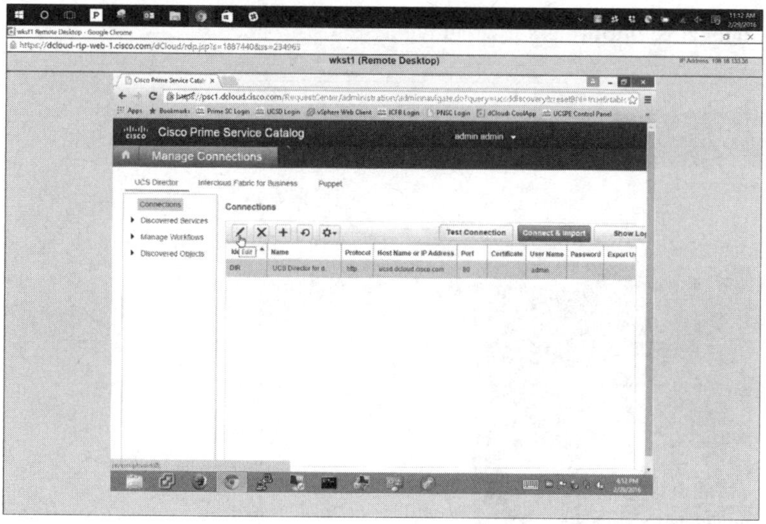

Figure 8-51 *UCS Director Connection Properties*

Step 4. Information and options for the connection are displayed across several columns: Identifier, Name, Protocol, Host Name or IP Address, Port, Certificate, User Name, Password, Export User, and Enable Background Sync (see Figure 8-52). Ensure that Export User is not checked and Enable Background is checked. Also ensure this username and password have the appropriate permissions to perform this action. Click **Save**.

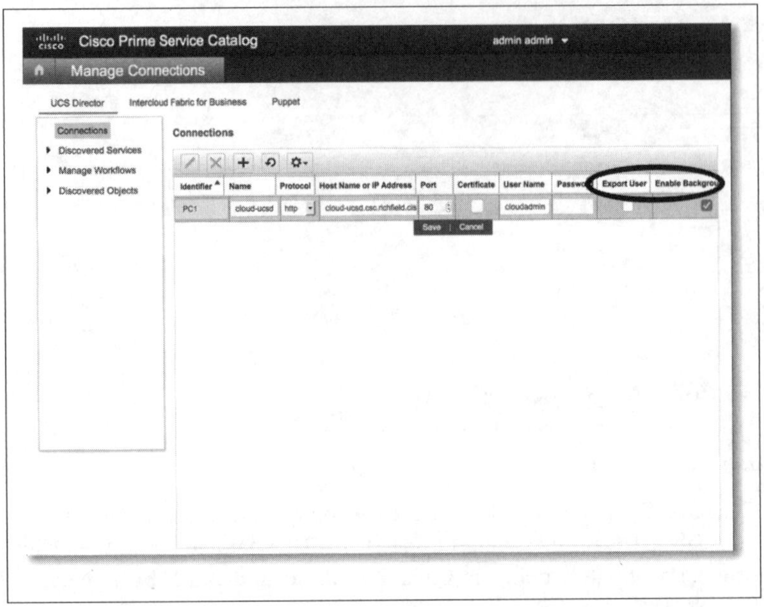

Figure 8-52   *Enabling Background Sync for the Connection*

> **Step 5.**   Click **Connect & Import** as shown in Figure 8-53.

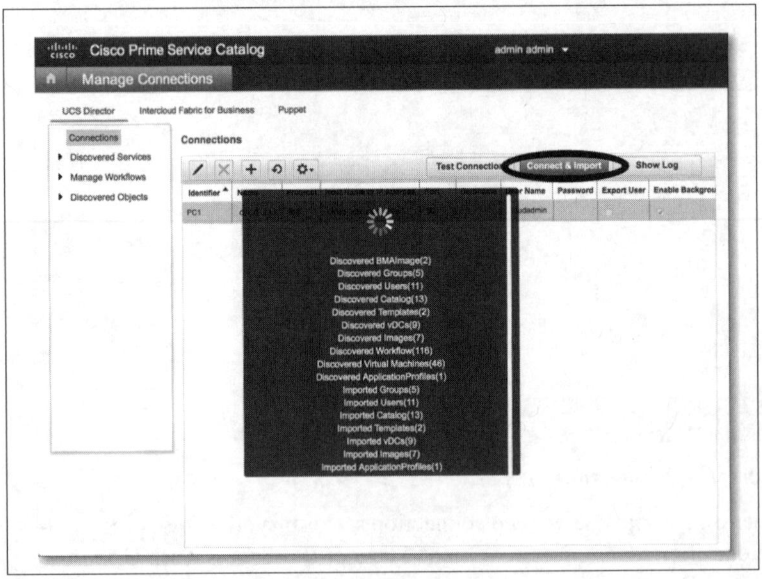

Figure 8-53   *Prime Service Catalog and UCS Director Integration: Connect & Import*

Step 6.   Once this completes successfully, expand the **Discovered Objects** list at the left and click a category, such as **Workflows**, and note the objects that have been imported from UCS Director (see Figure 8-54).

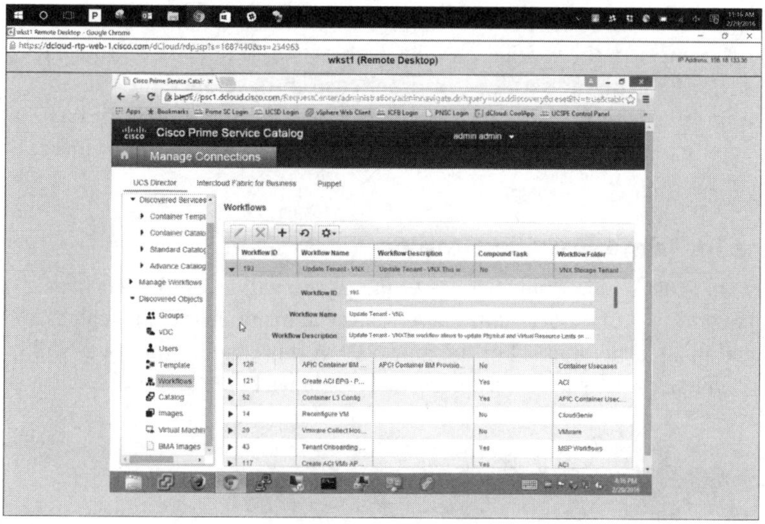

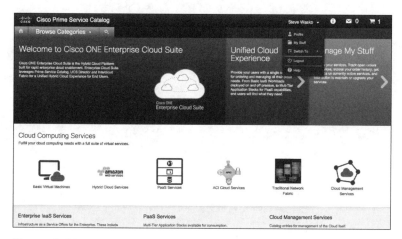

Figure 8-54   *Imported Workflows for Prime Service Catalog and UCS Director Integration*

Exploring "My Stuff"

To explore the My Stuff features, first log out as administrator and log in as an end user. Then, from the Prime Service Catalog home/welcome screen, click your username in the upper-right corner (see Figure 8-55) and click the **My Stuff** menu selection to see all of your Prime Service Catalog items. In addition, the default view of Prime Service Catalog has, as one of the main HTML5 panes, a Manage My Stuff pane, shown on the right in Figure 8-55 (partially obscured by the menu).

Figure 8-55   *Prime Service Catalog My Stuff Menu Item*

Keep in mind that if you are supporting an existing implementation of Prime Service Catalog, you may see additional items in your My Stuff view, such as mobile applications, equipment that you have ordered, etc. Remember, the power and flexibility of Prime Service Catalog extends well beyond IaaS and PaaS scenarios (though those are the focus of discussion in most of this book) and gives you the power and flexibility of placing physical items and services in the service catalog, such as the ability to order business cards, provision desktop IP telephony services, or order custom-developed, in-house applications for your mobile device. These are just some of the many examples of business processes that can be put into Prime Service Catalog's self-service portal for internal end-user consumption.

Taking VM Actions in Prime Service Catalog

As you navigate into My Stuff within Prime Service Catalog, you will see in the left pane a list of all items belonging to your user account. These items can include virtual machines, applications, vDCs, and many other items. For the purposes of this chapter, the focus will be on virtual machines. Figure 8-56 shows a list of virtual machines belonging to the currently logged-in user.

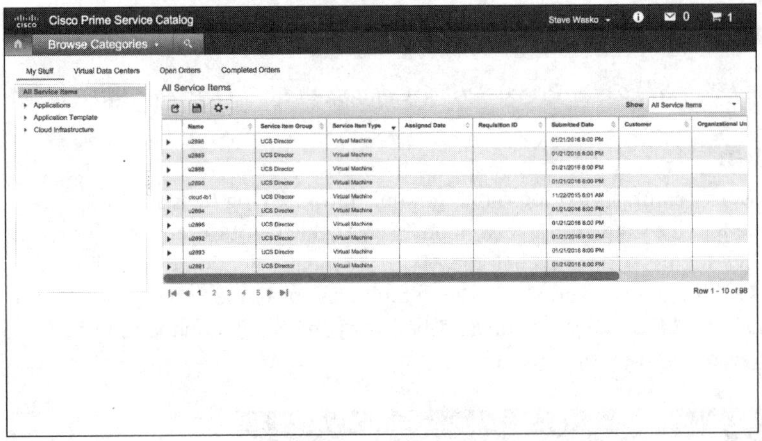

Figure 8-56   *List of Virtual Machines*

Clicking a virtual machine pops up a menu that allows you to take actions on that virtual machine. By default, as shown in Figure 8-57, you can perform some basic virtual machine functions such as

- Power off VM
- Reboot VM
- Shutdown VM Guest

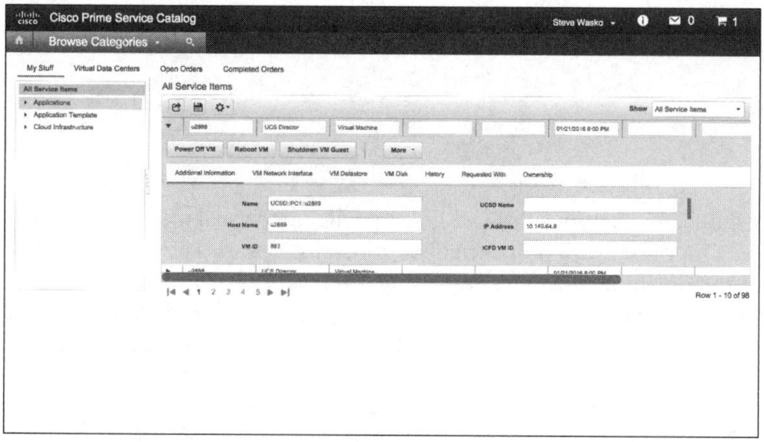

Figure 8-57   *Virtual Machine Actions*

Additionally, you can click the **More** button, as seen in Figure 8-58, to open a menu of additional virtual machine actions that you can perform on the VM.

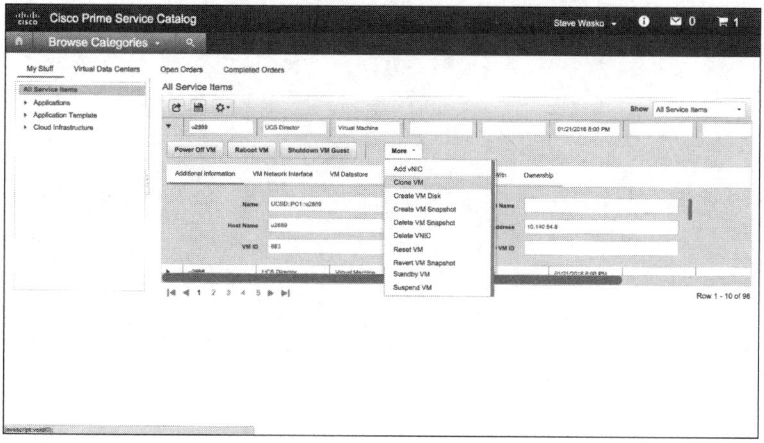

Figure 8-58   *Default List of Virtual Machine Actions*

The list of available virtual machine actions under the More button include

- Add vNIC
- Clone VM
- Create VM Disk
- Create VM Snapshot
- Delete VM Snapshot
- Delete VNIC
- Reset VM
- Revert VM Snapshot
- Standby VM
- Suspend VM

By default, there are quite a few options that can be performed on virtual machines within Prime Service Catalog. Of course, with proper rights and permissions, this list of available actions can be pared down significantly. For instance, it may be good to provide very simple functionality to production virtual machines, such as Reboot VM and Shutdown VM Guest, while allowing development or test virtual machines to have more options available to them.

Exam Preparation Tasks

As mentioned in the section "How to Use This Book" in the Introduction, you have a couple of choices for exam preparation: the exercises here, Chapter 15, "Final Preparation," and the exam simulation questions on the Pearson IT Certification Practice Test.

Review All Key Topics

Review the most important topics in this chapter, noted with the Key Topics icon in the outer margin of the page. Table 8-2 lists a reference of these key topics and the page number on which each is found.

Key Topic

Table 8-2   Key Topics for Chapter 8

Key Topic Element	Description	Page Number
Section	Installing PowerShell Agent	205
Section	Create a Custom Workflow Action	212
Figure 8-15	Table of defined variables for selected VM	213
Concept	UCS Workflow Designer	233
Figure 8-48	Detailed UCS Director task inputs and outputs	235
Section	Linking UCS Director and Prime Service Catalog	236
List	Virtual machine actions	242

Define Key Terms

Define the following key terms from this chapter and check your answers in the glossary:

Intercloud Fabric, self-service portal, service catalog, Prime Service Catalog (PSC), PowerShell, Cisco PowerShell Agent (PSA), guest, Microsoft System Center Configuration Manager (SCCM), Puppet, change management database (CMDB), virtual data center (vDC), orchestration, automation task, workflow, Amazon Web Services (AWS), Microsoft Azure, Infrastructure as a Service (IaaS), Platform as a Service (PaaS)

8

This chapter covers the following exam topics:

3.0 Cloud Provisioning

3.3 Deploy preconfigured templates and make minor changes to the service catalog offerings that do not affect workflows or services

3.3.a Describe the deployment of templates: storage, compute, network, and virtualization

3.3.b Describe differences between the templates

3.3.c Describe the need to convert between templates

CHAPTER 9

Automating Cloud Infrastructure with UCS Director

There are many reasons to decide to implement a private cloud for your enterprise. The main reason should be to better enable your users to consume and manage infrastructure resources (compute, storage, network, etc.) by providing them the capability to discover services, order services, and manage their own consumption with little to no manual interaction with the IT team. Before you can provide users with this capability, you need to develop the services that will be made available. To do this, you need a comprehensive understanding of how to deliver the infrastructure that will back these services. Policies describing the consumption of compute, network, and storage resources need to be developed. And, automation workflows to deploy the standard configurations need to be built and tested.

Cisco UCS Director provides a platform for infrastructure management and automation designed for IT infrastructure teams to work together to easily build policies for standard infrastructure offerings. The virtual data centers and workflows you will build in UCS Director provide the foundation for users to begin ordering and managing their own resources within the cloud.

"Do I Know This Already?" Quiz

The "Do I Know This Already?" quiz allows you to assess whether you should read this entire chapter thoroughly or jump to the "Exam Preparation Tasks" section. If you are in doubt about your answers to these questions or your own assessment of your knowledge of the topics, read the entire chapter. Table 9-1 lists the major headings in this chapter and their corresponding "Do I Know This Already?" quiz questions. You can find the answers in Appendix A, "Answers to the 'Do I Know This Already?' Quizzes."

Table 9-1 "Do I Know This Already?" Section-to-Question Mapping

Foundation Topics Section	Questions
UCS Director Policies, Pools, and Virtual Data Centers	1–5
UCS Director Orchestration	6–8
UCS Director Service Requests	9, 10

CAUTION The goal of self-assessment is to gauge your mastery of the topics in this chapter. If you do not know the answer to a question or are only partially sure of the answer, you should mark that question as wrong for purposes of the self-assessment. Giving yourself credit for an answer you correctly guess skews your self-assessment results and might provide you with a false sense of security.

1. How many groups will be assigned ownership of a virtual data center?

    a. One group

    b. One or more groups

    c. No groups, because virtual data centers are assigned to users

    d. All groups share the same virtual data center assignments

2. Within what construct within UCS Director will you configure the policies that determine how a new virtual machine will be deployed into a cloud?

    a. Virtual private cloud (vPC)

    b. Virtual pod (vPod)

    c. Virtual data center (vDC)

    d. Virtual tenant (vTenant)

3. Which policy determines how elements such as hostname, domain membership, DNS settings, and time zone are configured?

    a. Service Delivery Policy

    b. Computing Policy

    c. Guest Customization Policy

    d. System Policy

4. Which of the following can be configured within UCS Director as part of the integrated IP address management capabilities?

    a. Static IP pools

    b. VLAN pools

    c. IP subnet pools

    d. All of the above

    e. None of the above

5. When creating a new service profile through UCS Director, which physical infrastructure policies and templates must be configured within UCS Director itself? (Choose three.)

    a. vNIC template

    b. UCS Network Policy

    c. UCS Storage Policy

    d. UCS Bios Policy

    e. UCS Boot Policy

6. What does the Workflow Property "Mark as Compound Task" indicate?

    a. That this workflow is made up of child workflows

    b. That this workflow will be leveraged in other workflows

    c. That this workflow leverages external libraries and features

    d. That this workflow will target a specific virtual machine

7. How do you add a new task to a workflow?

   a. Right-click in the Workflow Designer design area and choose New

   b. Drag from the Available Tasks list

   c. Double-click a task in the Available Tasks list

   d. Any of the above

8. With what type of task can you ask an external user to provide an input value during workflow execution?

   a. User Approval Task

   b. Get Input Task

   c. Custom Approval Task

   d. Query User Task

9. Which tab(s) of a service request can an end user view? (Choose all that apply.)

   a. Status

   b. Log

   c. Objects Created/Modified

   d. Inputs/Outputs

10. True or False. In order to use the Rollback capability of UCS Director, you must first build a workflow that acts as an Undo for the action you wish to roll back.

   a. True

   b. False

9

Foundation Topics

UCS Director Policies, Pools, and Virtual Data Centers

To dynamically deliver infrastructure resources to users, your team of cloud architects and engineers must configure policies and workflows that reflect the intended standards for your enterprise. Several decisions must be made during provisioning, such as

- What hypervisor host and data store to instantiate new VMs on
- If and how to provide network access for new VMs
- How many virtual network adapters a new bare-metal server should have
- What VLAN and subnet to use when creating a new network segment

You will create policies, pools, and virtual data centers to provide UCS Director with the information needed to answer these and other questions during provisioning processes.

Virtual Data Center and Policies

Key Topic

The virtual data center (vDC) is the logical representation of the private cloud that your end users will be deploying new virtual machines into. An individual vDC can be assigned only to a single group, but a single group can have one or many vDCs available for their use.

You will need to determine the right number and purpose for building vDCs for your enterprise, as there are many possible strategies for using the vDC construct in a cloud. For example, an enterprise may choose to implement a very small number of vDCs based on a very coarse segmentation, such as a Production vDC, Development vDC, and Test vDC. In this case all virtual machines, no matter the application, would be deployed together and subject to the same set of policies. This model has the advantage of being simpler to initially set up, but you may find that it makes reporting on application usage and implementing flexible deployment polices more challenging. At the other end of the spectrum, you would deploy a vDC per application and environment. In this case you may have three or more vDCs per application (e.g., Production, Development, and Test). This method has the benefit of providing very granular controls and visibility over the deployed resources, but will result in a much larger number of vDCs within the environment. Whichever method you initially deploy your cloud with, you can always adjust the model as your needs evolve.

Each vDC will be made up of several policies that determine how new virtual machines will be deployed, managed, and billed back to the users and groups. Figure 9-1 provides a graphical representation of a vDC and the most important policies you will need to create.

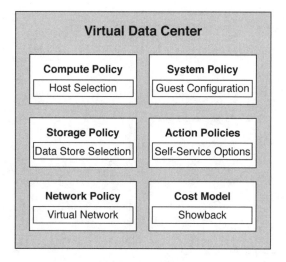

Figure 9-1   *Virtual Data Center*

Configuration of the vDC and policies is done in the Edit vDC window, accessed via the administrator portal by choosing **Policies > Virtual/Hypervisor Policies > Virtual Data Centers**, as shown in Figure 9-2. Each of the policies is leveraged by UCS Director when provisioning new virtual machines to the underlying hypervisor platform being leveraged. Therefore, you'll find that there are tabs for each of the supported cloud types. The differences between the VMware System Policy and the HyperV System Policy, as an example, are minor, and once you understand the overall usage of each policy type, it is fairly easy to leverage a different cloud type. In our discussions of the policies, we will be assuming VMware vCenter as the cloud type.

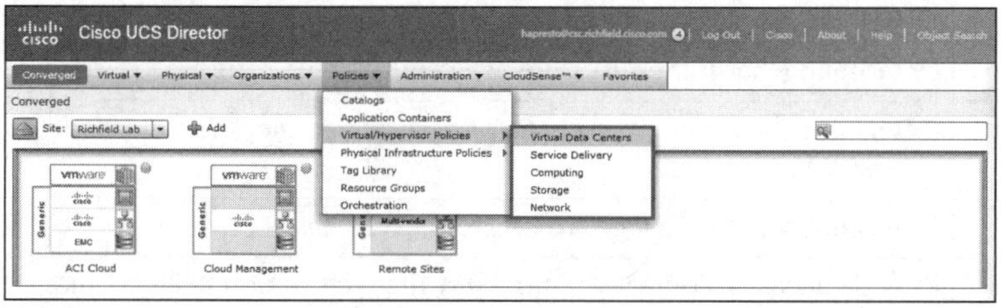

Figure 9-2   *Administrator Portal Virtual Data Centers Menu Option*

Figure 9-3 shows vDC properties where the different policies are applied. As indicated by the red asterisk, the System, Computing, Network, and Storage Policies are mandatory for vDC creation. Policies for Cost Model and User Action are optional. Table 9-2 provides a simple breakdown of each virtual data center policy and its purpose.

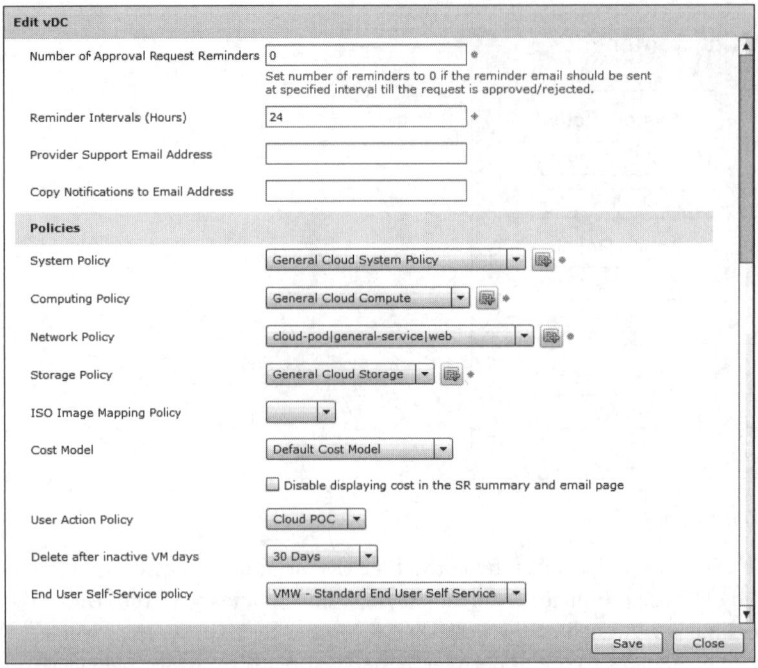

Edit vDC

Number of Approval Request Reminders [0]

Set number of reminders to 0 if the reminder email should be sent at specified interval till the request is approved/rejected.

Reminder Intervals (Hours) [24]

Provider Support Email Address [ ]

Copy Notifications to Email Address [ ]

Policies

System Policy [General Cloud System Policy ▼]

Computing Policy [General Cloud Compute ▼]

Network Policy [cloud-pod|general-service|web ▼]

Storage Policy [General Cloud Storage ▼]

ISO Image Mapping Policy [▼]

Cost Model [Default Cost Model ▼]

☐ Disable displaying cost in the SR summary and email page

User Action Policy [Cloud POC ▼]

Delete after inactive VM days [30 Days ▼]

End User Self-Service policy [VMW - Standard End User Self Service ▼]

[Save] [Close]

Figure 9-3 *Virtual Data Center Properties*

Key Topic

Table 9-2 vDC Policies

vDC Policy	Purpose
System Policy	Configure guest operating system details like hostname, DNS, and time zone
Computing Policy	Determine what hypervisor host system to deploy the VM onto
Network Policy	Determine the number and type of network connectivity needed for the VM
Storage Policy	Determine what data store to create the VM disks on
End User Self-Service Policy	Provide access to out-of-the-box VM lifecycle action tasks to end users
User Action Policy	Provide custom VM actions to end users by linking to workflows
Cost Model	Assign value to different metrics such as number of vCPUs as part of a chargeback model

System Policy

You will find the System Policy under **Policies > Virtual/Hypervisor Policies > Service Delivery** along with other polices such as Cost Model, OS Licenses (Windows OS Product Keys), and other VM-level policies. The System Policy itself determines how the guest operating system will be configured during the customization phase of creation. As shown in Figure 9-4, the main policy elements are about VM and hostname format, time zone, and DNS settings. If you configure the policy for both Windows and Linux VMs, you'll need to configure several Windows-specific elements for licensing and domain settings. Configuring a Windows Product ID/Key in the System Policy is optional, as it is more likely to attach the Product Key information to the Standard Catalogs to support multiple guest OS types within a single vDC.

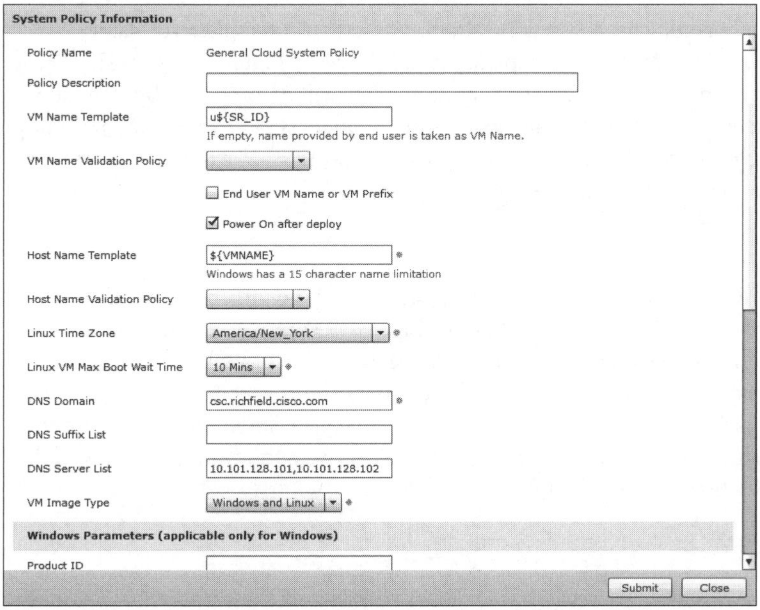

Figure 9-4   *VMware System Policy*

As you can see in Figure 9-4, UCS Director supports using variables within policies. Within UCS Director, variables are indicated and accessed through a **${Variable Name}** syntax. For example, **${GROUP_NAME}** would be replaced with the name of the group for which a resource is being provisioned, and **${USER_NAME}** would represent the requesting user's username. These variable references are often used when creating VM name and hostname templates as part of the System Policy. Table 9-3 lists and describes the available variables for use in creating hostnames and VM names.

Table 9-3   VM Template and Hostname Variables

Name	Description
${CLOUD_NAME}	The name of the cloud used for VM provisioning.
${GROUP_NAME}	The name of the group to which the VM belongs.
${CATALOG_NAME}	The name of the catalog item used for VM provisioning.
${USER}	The requesting user ID.
${SR_ID}	The service request ID.
${COMMENTS}	The comments specified by the requesting user.

Name	Description
${COST_CENTER}	The cost center that is associated with a group or customer organization. This is specified during group or customer organization creation.
${APPCODE}	The application code that is specified during catalog creation.

Administrators can mix static characters with variables to create a template for name creation. For example, the VM Name Template setting shown in Figure 9-4 is u${SR_ID}. This will create a name in which the service request number will be preceded by a single lowercase "u" character. This type of name will ensure uniqueness for new virtual machines. Administrators can choose to allow end users to provide a prefix that would be inserted before the template configured in the policy.

Computing Policy

You use the VMware Computing Policy to give UCS Director the information it needs to select a vSphere host or cluster to deploy a new VM to. UCS Director will start by considering all available hosts or clusters that you indicate are available, and then filter down the selections by excluding any host that doesn't meet the conditions specified in the policy. Figure 9-5 shows some of the common filter options, which you can use to enforce your organization's standards for guest-to-host ratio, CPU/RAM oversubscription policies, and required available capacity on a single host.

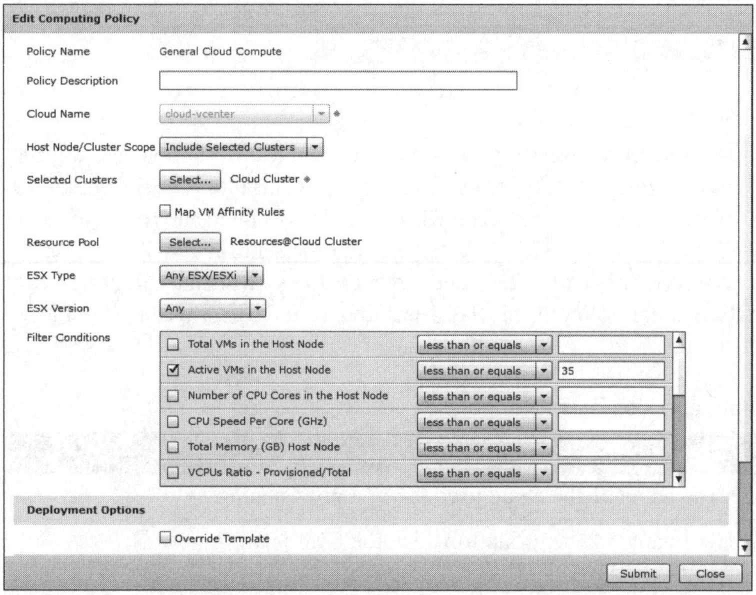

Figure 9-5   *VMware Computing Policy*

The default behavior for UCS Director when deploying a new VM is to maintain the underlying image/template settings for CPU and RAM. You can opt to give your users the ability to resize a VM at provision time by clicking the Resizing Options button near the bottom and providing a comma-separated list of options. The Override Template configuration in the policy would be a universal administrative override for all new VMs being deployed with this policy.

Network Policy

You configure network connectivity for virtual machines with the Network Policy. UCS Director supports single or multiple network connections per VM. And each can be configured for static or DHCP-assigned IP addresses. On occasions where you'd like to provide your end users some flexibility in network configuration when provisioning, you can even add choices regarding optional network adapters and the port groups being assigned.

Figure 9-6 shows the main page of the VMware Network Policy. This page lists the number of VM networks (or virtual network adapters) this policy will configure. Clicking the Add button or Edit button above the table opens the dialog box shown in Figure 9-7 where you configure the settings for an individual network adapter. Each network entry has one or more port groups listed. Any single vNIC can be assigned only a single port group at a point in time. When multiple options exist, you can allow end users to choose their desired port group if you wish; otherwise, UCS Director will select the first one available (typically due to available IP addresses). Click the Add or Edit button in the Port Groups table to open the Edit Entry dialog box, shown in Figure 9-8, where the port-group and IP assignment configuration is completed. Configuring IPv6 connectivity is an optional setting in the policy.

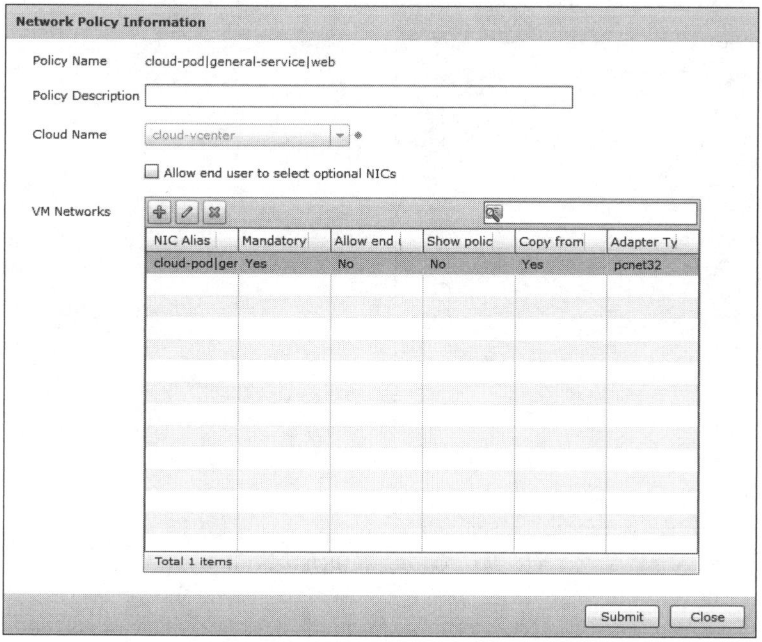

Figure 9-6 *VMware Network Policy*

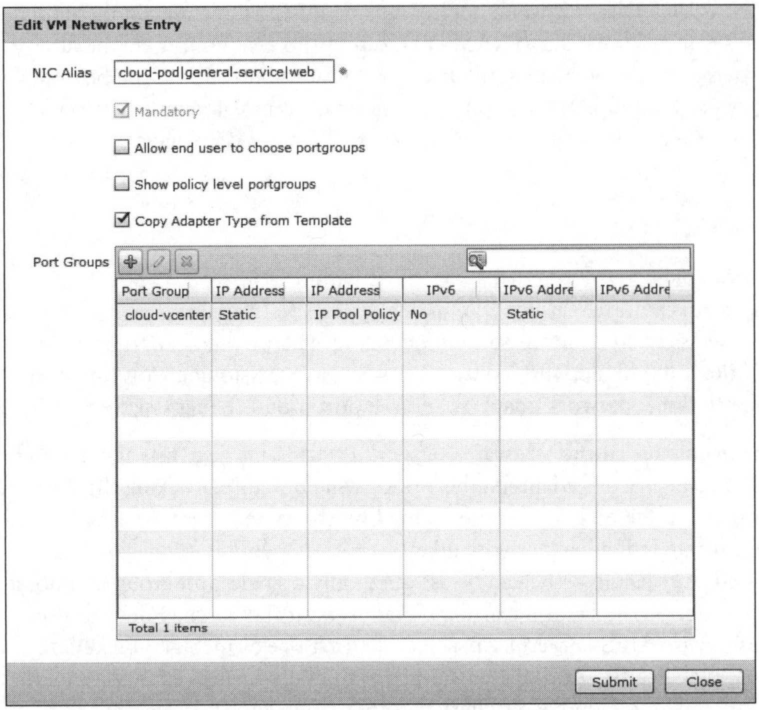

Edit VM Networks Entry

NIC Alias   cloud-pod|general-service|web ✳

    ☑ Mandatory

    ☐ Allow end user to choose portgroups

    ☐ Show policy level portgroups

    ☑ Copy Adapter Type from Template

Port Groups

Port Group	IP Address	IP Address	IPv6	IPv6 Addre	IPv6 Addre
cloud-vcenter	Static	IP Pool Policy	No	Static	

Total 1 items

Submit   Close

Figure 9-7 *VMware Network Policy: vNIC Configuration*

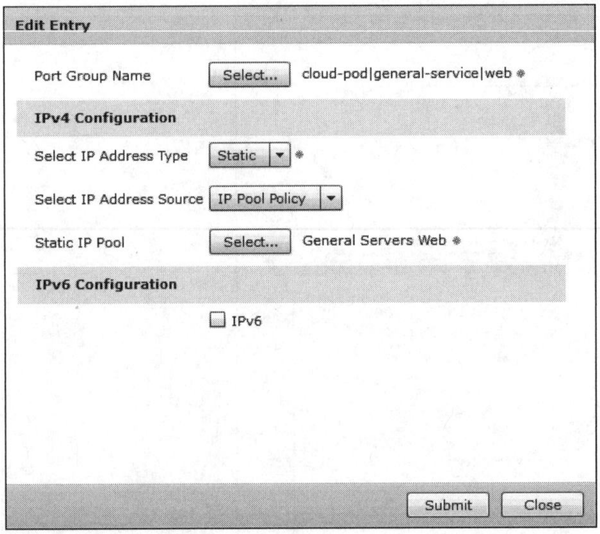

Edit Entry

Port Group Name   [Select...]   cloud-pod|general-service|web ✳

IPv4 Configuration

Select IP Address Type   [Static ▼] ✳

Select IP Address Source   [IP Pool Policy ▼]

Static IP Pool   [Select...]   General Servers Web ✳

IPv6 Configuration

    ☐ IPv6

Submit   Close

Figure 9-8 *VMware Network Policy: vNIC Port Group Configuration*

Storage Policy

Your configuration of the VMware Storage Policy will determine what data store the VM's disks will be stored on. Configured and applied very similarly to the Computing Policy, you will first indicate what possible data stores should be considered, and then what conditions would exclude an individual option. This enables you to ensure a single data store doesn't get overprovisioned. Figure 9-9 shows the configuration window, including the key elements of data store selection and filters. Also similar to the Computing Policy, you can override the template disk sizes or allow your end users to resize at provisioning.

Be aware that when creating a new Storage Policy, all storage options (Local, NFS, and SAN) are selected by default. Be sure to specify which are appropriate for your cloud. A common mistake made by administrators is to leave Use Local Storage selected, in which case UCS Director will attempt to provision new VMs to local data stores.

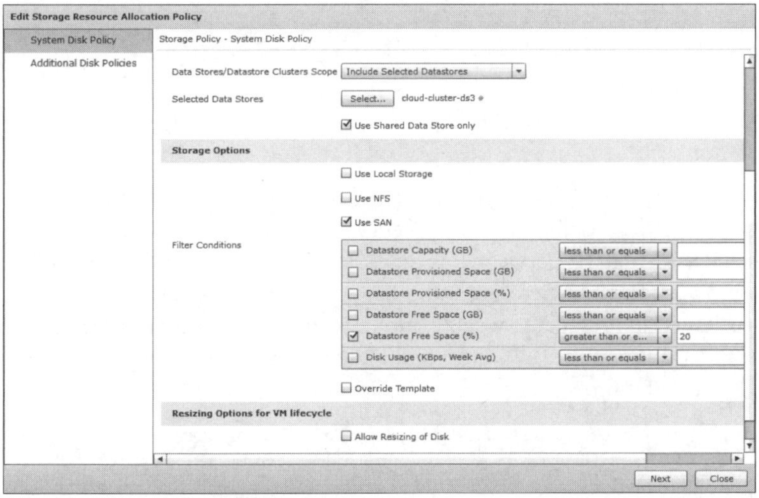

Figure 9-9   *VMware Storage Policy*

If your environment has different tiers of data stores for uses like databases, swap, or general data, you can indicate this type of configuration need in the Additional Disk Policies configuration of the Storage Policy, as shown in Figure 9-10.

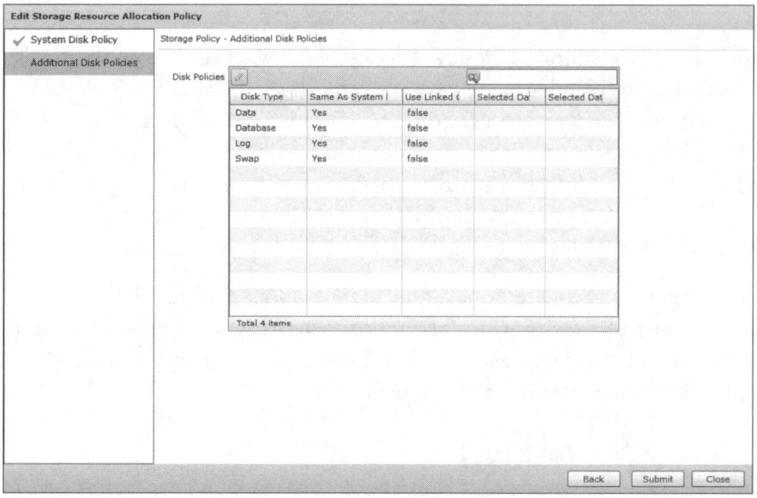

Figure 9-10 *VMware Storage Policy: Additional Disk Policies*

Cost Model

Applying a Cost Model to a virtual data center is an optional configuration for enterprises moving into a showback or chargeback model. To access the Cost Model configuration settings, choose **Policies > Virtual/Hypervisor Policies > Service Delivery > Cost Model**. UCS Director supports a very flexible metering and billing policy through the Cost Model policy. Charges can be issued hourly, daily, weekly, monthly, or yearly, and metrics for CPU, memory, network, and storage are all supported. Figure 9-11 shows an example section of a Cost Model configuration.

> **NOTE** Chapter 12, "Chargeback, Billing, and Reporting," provides a complete discussion on chargeback and billing options.

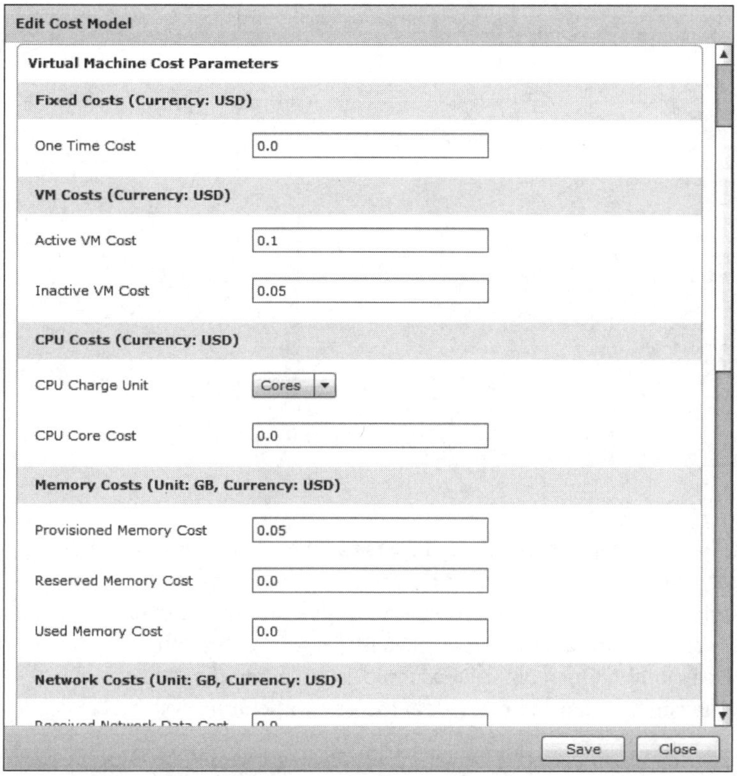

Edit Cost Model

Virtual Machine Cost Parameters

Fixed Costs (Currency: USD)

One Time Cost   `0.0`

VM Costs (Currency: USD)

Active VM Cost   `0.1`

Inactive VM Cost   `0.05`

CPU Costs (Currency: USD)

CPU Charge Unit   Cores ▼

CPU Core Cost   `0.0`

Memory Costs (Unit: GB, Currency: USD)

Provisioned Memory Cost   `0.05`

Reserved Memory Cost   `0.0`

Used Memory Cost   `0.0`

Network Costs (Unit: GB, Currency: USD)

Received Network Data Cost   `0.0`

Save   Close

Figure 9-11   *Cost Model*

Action Policies

In most cases, you will want to enable your users not only to provision new virtual machines, but also to self-manage the life cycle of those VMs. End-user productivity and satisfaction will not be much improved if end users need to open a ticket with IT every time they want to power on/off or snapshot their VM as they are managing or developing an application. There are two optional policies configurable within a vDC to enable users to take actions on their own VMs.

The End User Self-Service Policy is located at **Policies > Virtual/Hypervisor Policies > Service Delivery > End User Self-Service Policy**, and is the policy you will start with to offer end-user control of VMs. Shown in Figure 9-12, this policy provides you the options to enable which of the out-of-the-box actions supported by UCS Director the end user will have access to. There are greater than 30 possible actions you can enable covering basic power management, snapshot management, and VM resizing.

9

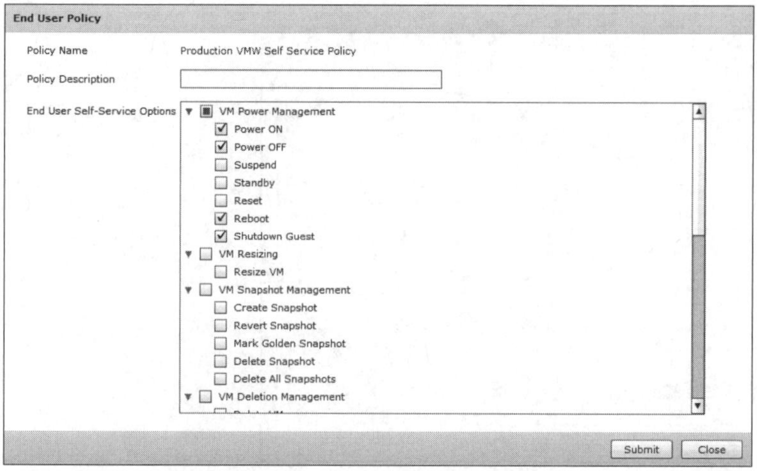

Figure 9-12 *End User Self-Service Policy*

You will likely eventually find a need to enable end users to take some action on a VM that is not an out-of-the-box capability for UCS Director, or perhaps you may simply want to change or extend the behavior of an out-of-the-box task. In this case, you can build a workflow with a VM context for the new action and leverage the User Action Policy to give users access to the new capability. One common example is extending the Add VM Disk action to include mounting and formatting the disk in the guest operating system.

The User Action Policy is configured via the **Policies > Orchestration** menu four tabs down from Workflows. Figure 9-13 shows a sample policy with some example Actions that could be built.

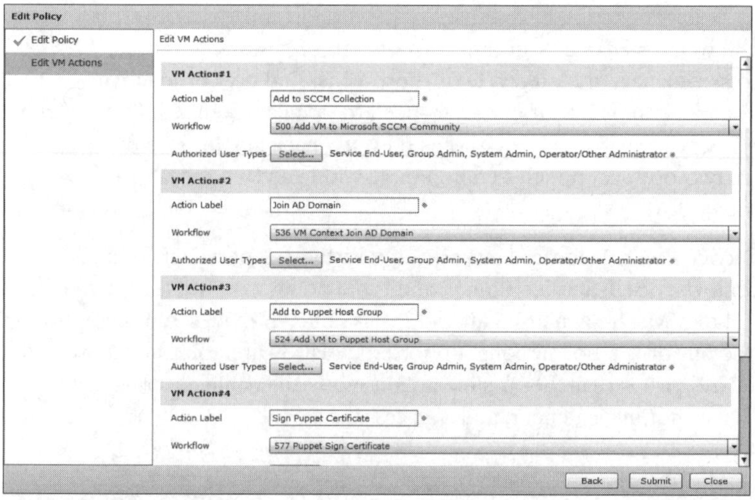

Figure 9-13 *User Action Policy*

vDC Categories

When you create a new vDC, part of the process is creating new policies, or selecting existing ones for each of the mandatory and optional types needed. This provides UCS Director the information needed to automatically deploy new VMs into the vDC based on the policy and governance needed by your organization. However, you will quickly realize that not all VMs deployed into a vDC have the same requirements for compute, network, and storage. Web and database servers have vastly different storage performance requirements. Some application servers may need a higher-performing CPU than a general server.

Virtual data center categories can help solve the problem of differentiating policies within a vDC. In the "Standard Catalog" section in Chapter 10, "Building a Service Catalog and User Portal with UCS Director and Prime Service Catalog," you learn that when creating a Standard Catalog, one parameter you configure is the category of the catalog. The category selected corresponds to one of the available categories of a vDC.

After creating a new vDC, you can select it in the **Policies > Virtual/Hypervisor Policies > Virtual Data Centers** menu and click **Manage Categories** from the action menu. Figure 9-14 shows a sample view of this interface, where you can see each of the categories listed with columns for each of the configured policies. Any policy setting configured here will override the default policy as configured on the vDC itself. In the figure you can see that the Network Policy has been adjusted to reflect web, app, and data port groups for the related categories.

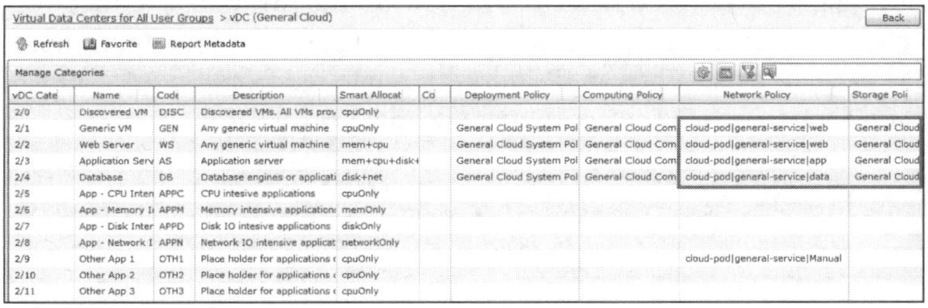

Figure 9-14   *Virtual Data Center Categories*

IP, Subnet, and VLAN Network Pools

Part of automating infrastructure delivery includes consuming resources from the cloud. Within network automation, the three most common resources that will need to be consumed are IP addresses, subnets, and VLANs. Every enterprise network team will have some process for allocating and indicating use of these resources. Many organizations are still leveraging spreadsheets for manual tracking, while others have implemented enterprise IP address management (IPAM) tools.

Whatever method your organization is using, UCS Director supports a lite-IPAM capability that will enable it to automatically allocate and record the consumption of resources as they are provisioned to new virtual machines or during a workflow execution. You configure these pools and policies from **Policies > Virtual/Hypervisor Policies > Network**. Figure 9-15 shows the Static IP Pool Policy as well as the tabs for IP Subnet Pool Policy, VLAN Pool Policy, and VXLAN Pool Policy.

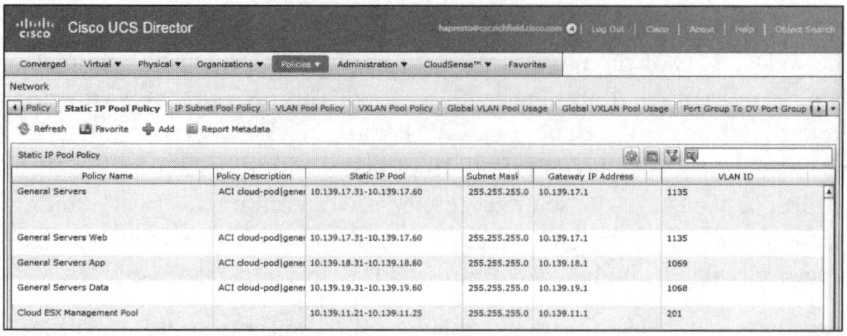

Figure 9-15 *UCS Director IPAM Options*

Static IP Pool Policy

The Static IP Pool Policy is a critical component of most vDC Network Policies because few data centers leverage DHCP for assigning IP addresses to servers. However, a single static IP pool can be used across many Network Policies as well as for any instance where an IP address from a given range is required. For example, if you build a workflow to build and provision a new bare-metal server, its IP address could come from the same pool used for VM IPs in a vDC Network Policy.

You add or edit a policy with an interface similar to Figure 9-16. A policy requires a name and optional description and one or more pools or ranges of IP addresses. If you configure more than one pool in a single policy, UCS Director will exhaust the first pool and then move to subsequent pools. Though a pool entry can include a VLAN ID, it is more for notation than an actionable piece of data. When an IP address is requested from a pool, a VLAN ID is not a consideration for determining an appropriate IP address.

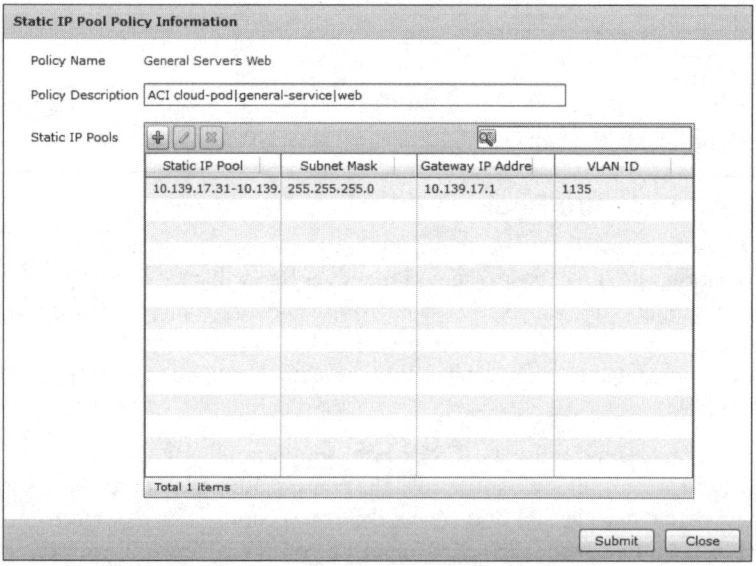

Figure 9-16 *Static IP Pool Policy Configuration*

Once a policy is created, you can double-click its name to bring up a table similar to the one shown in Figure 9-17, where each of the used IP addresses is noted along with details regarding which VM or service request has it reserved. The reservation can be cleared by rolling back the service request, or manually by the administrator.

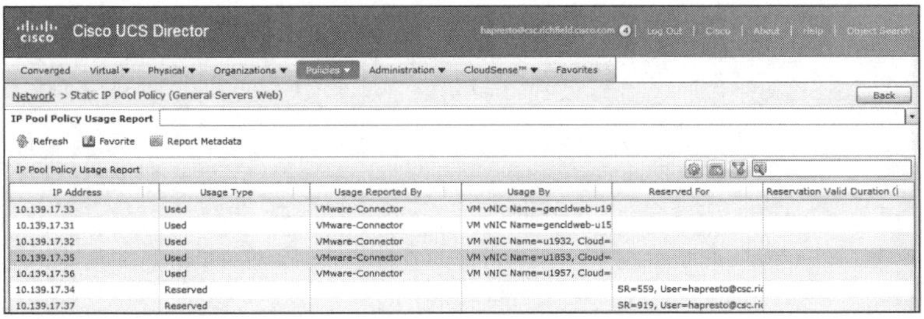

Figure 9-17 *Static IP Pool Policy Consumption*

IP Subnet Pool Policy

An IP Subnet Pool Policy is very handy when constructing automation jobs that will be building a new network segment that will require IP space to be assigned and configured. Some examples where you would do this include adding a new VLAN to a traditional network, creating a new bridge-domain subnet in an ACI-based network, or creating a level of segmentation with a firewall device.

You will only need a few pieces of information to create a new IP Subnet Pool Policy. In addition to the policy name and description, you'll need to provide a network supernet address and mask, and indicate the number of subnets required. Finally, you indicate whether the gateway address should be the first or last available address in the subnet. This is helpful because the workflow task to generate a new subnet from a pool will provide several outputs to make using the new subnet easier, one of which is the gateway IP address. You can see an example of the interface in Figure 9-18.

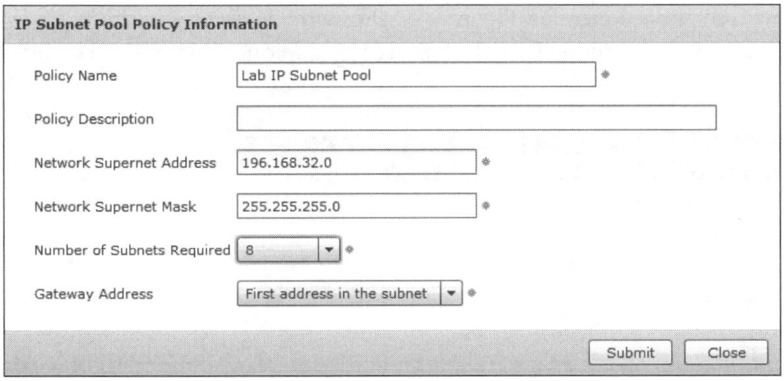

Figure 9-18 *IP Subnet Pool Policy Configuration*

VLAN Pool Policy

You will leverage a VLAN Pool Policy to generate a new VLAN ID often along with using the IP Subnet Pool Policy to add new network segments. The VLAN Pool Policy is very simple, only requiring the range of VLAN IDs to use (see Figure 9-19).

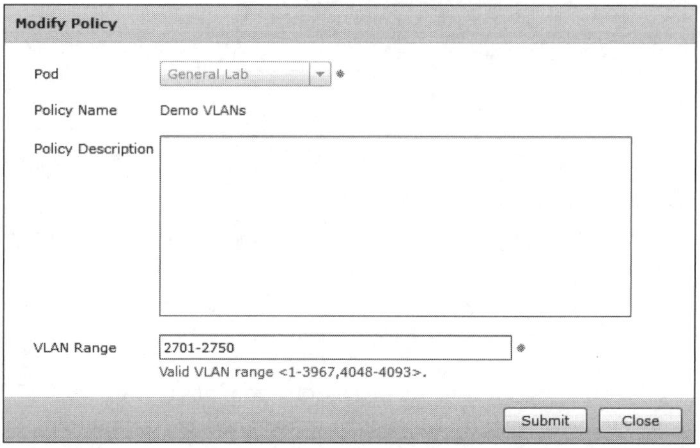

Modify Policy

Pod	General Lab ▼ ✱
Policy Name	Demo VLANs
Policy Description	
VLAN Range	2701-2750 ✱
	Valid VLAN range <1-3967,4048-4093>.

Submit   Close

Figure 9-19 *VLAN Pool Policy Configuration*

Physical Infrastructure Policies

Your data center is made up of more than just virtual resources. Even if your application workloads are 100 percent virtualized, you still must have physical servers acting as hypervisors, storage arrays to provide disk space to store all the VMs, and a network for everything to communicate over. Because you will always have to work with both physical and virtual resources, UCS Director provides methods to configure these physical resources as well.

You will find that UCS Director offers many methods of configuring infrastructure as you become more familiar, but for this book we will be discussing what is available for assisting with provisioning new UCS service profiles. Figure 9-20 shows the location of both UCS Manager and UCS Central Policies, along with Rack Server (standalone Cisco C-Series) and NetApp Policies.

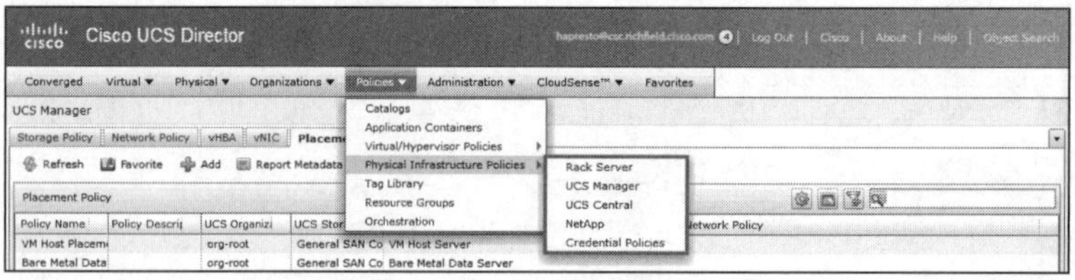

Figure 9-20 *Physical Infrastructure Policies*

UCS Policies

UCS Manager and UCS Central Policies will be used when you are looking to build a new service profile template or a new service profile without using a service profile template. In these circumstances you will require UCS policies for storage and network configuration when creating a new service profile.

The UCS Manager (or UCS Central) Network Policy simply indicates the number and type of virtual NICs (vNIC) to configure in a new template. Figure 9-21 shows a sample UCS Manager Network Policy. In the UCS Network Policy, you specify UCS Director vNIC templates for the vNIC1 and vNIC2 templates displayed in the figure. It is typical to link the UCS Director vNIC template to an underlying UCS Manager or Central template.

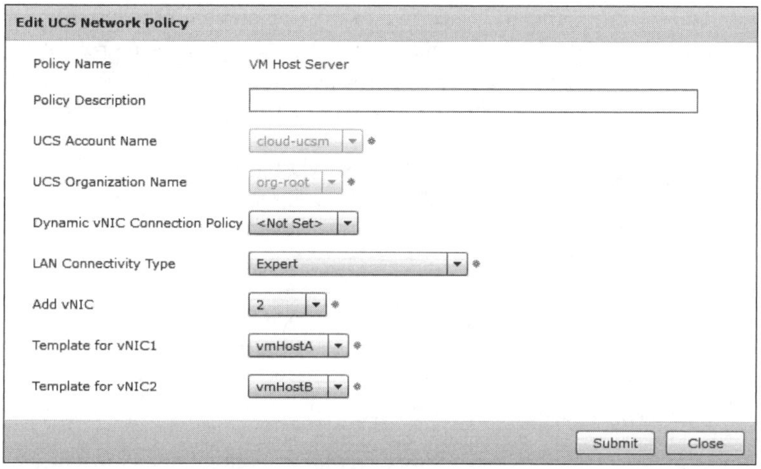

Figure 9-21   *UCS Network Policy*

The UCS Manager Storage Policy does the same thing for virtual host bus adapters (vHBA) as the UCS Manager Network Policy does for vNICs. Figure 9-22 provides a sample.

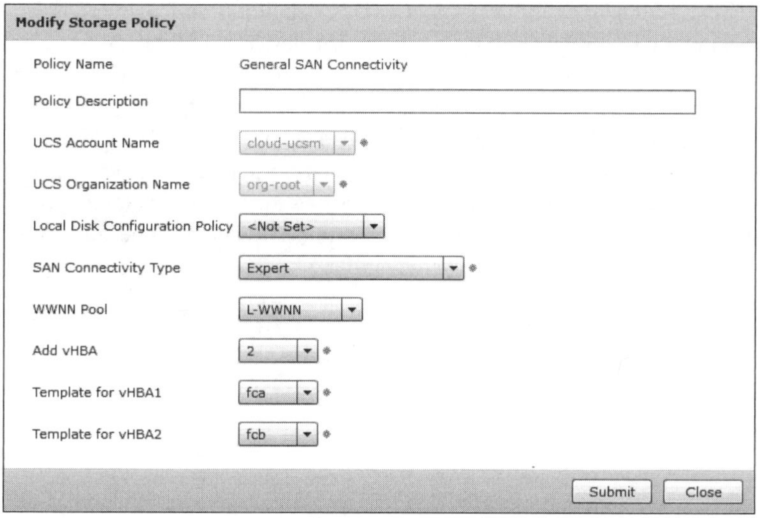

Figure 9-22   *UCS Storage Policy*

Regarding UCS Manager and UCS Central policies, templates and profiles, UCS Director will allow the creation of policies using local (from UCS Manager) or global (from UCS Central) templates; however, you should avoid mixing them when you create a service profile or template in UCS Director. Either use only local or use only global objects underlying your policies.

Once you have created the necessary policies, you can create a new service profile or template within UCS Director that leverages them. Most often you will create a service profile or template as part of a workflow, but you can also create one on demand by navigating to **Physical > Compute** and locating your UCS Account in the tree menu on the left. On the **Organizations** tab, double-click the UCS Organization that your new service profile or template will be created within, and then switch to the Profile or Templates tab. Figure 9-23 shows UCS Director navigated to the Service Profile Templates page.

Figure 9-23   *UCS Account Service Profile Templates View*

Click the **Add** button to open the Create Service Profile Template dialog box, shown in Figure 9-24, where you can create a new service profile template within your UCS environment. The Storage and Network Policies are used within this dialog box to create the desired connectivity options.

Within the dialog box to create the new service profile template is a Template Type field with options for Updating Template or Initial Template. This is an important characteristic of the service profile template to understand. New service profiles created from an Initial Template will match the template's settings at the time of creation, but if the template were to be updated in the future, any service profiles already created would not be affected. With an Updating Template, changes to the template will also change all service profiles created and bound to the service profile template. There are circumstances where you may want to leverage both of these template types within your organization. For example, your critical production database servers may be created based on Initial Templates because any updates or changes to that server must be well planned and explicitly addressed per server. However, your virtualization host servers would be created based on Updating Templates to make sure that each host in your cluster has consistent settings when changes happen, such as new VLANs being added to vNICs.

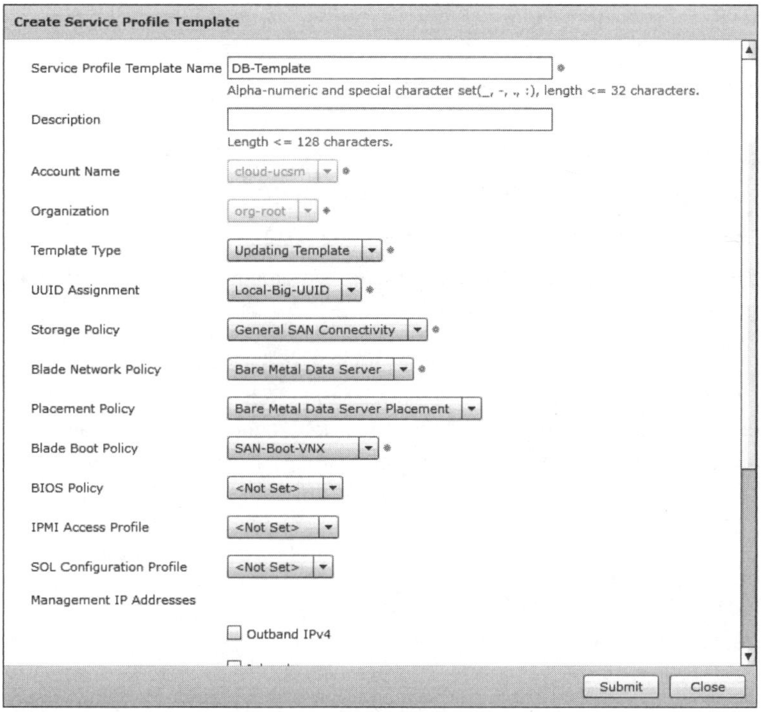

Figure 9-24   *Adding UCS Service Profile*

UCS Director Orchestration

You will really start adding value to your enterprise when you begin automating the day-to-day infrastructure delivery tasks that typically require significant planning and manual processes to complete. Enterprise IT organizations receive tasks from end users, such as "provision five new bare-metal servers for a new database cluster," and tasks more targeted at IT operational activities, such as "add capacity to the virtualization farm." In both of these cases, providing a method to provision through automation in a matter of minutes transforms the way enterprises look at IT's delivery capabilities.

Workflows

There is really no end to the possibilities for what you could do with UCS Director workflows, but you will find the types of tasks it is well suited for involve infrastructure provisioning and configuration tasks across the tiers of virtualization, compute, network, and storage. Here is a short list of some use cases you may consider ideal candidates for automation with UCS Director:

- Deploy one or more virtual machines
- Deploy new bare-metal servers for running applications on a Windows or Linux OS (including full configuration of physical compute, storage, and network requirements)

- Expand the cloud capacity of an existing virtualization solution, by adding either new compute hosts or shared storage

- Add a new network segment to the data center across physical, virtual, and compute networking domains

- Add new data drives to a virtual machine, including mounting and formatting

- Perform snapshot maintenance and purging across all VMs in the cloud

- Create or update a help desk ticket in an external ticketing system

- Construct a standard three-tier application environment including network segmentation, security policy, and load-balancing rules

Locate the Orchestration capabilities of UCS Director under **Policies > Orchestration**. Figure 9-25 shows the menu location and the initial view of the Orchestration module. You will find there are several tabs and sections of the Orchestration engine. As you become more advanced, you will learn to leverage many of the capabilities available within this interface; however, for now we will focus on the first tab, Workflows, where you build and edit workflows.

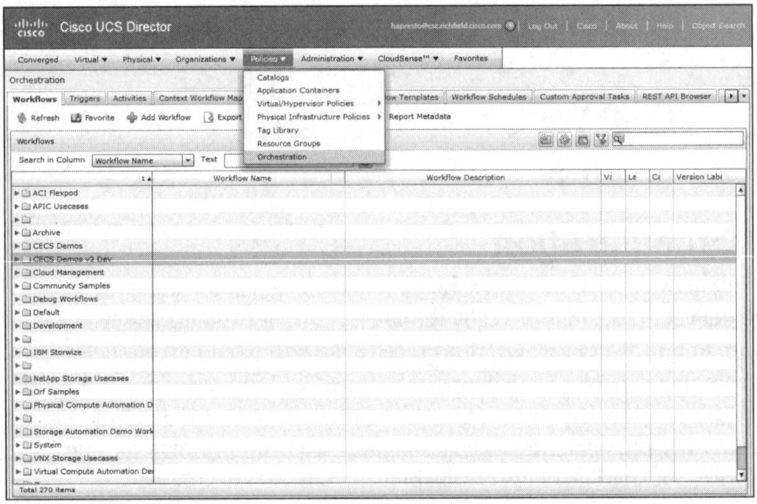

![UCS Director Orchestration interface screenshot]

Figure 9-25 *UCS Director Orchestration Menu Location and Interface*

Workflow Properties

Every workflow has a set of properties along with the actual automation logic. The first thing you will see after clicking **Add** to create a new workflow is the Add Workflow screen. Or you can click **Edit Workflow** on an existing workflow to view or make changes. As shown in Figure 9-26, the first page of the Edit Workflow window, Edit Workflow Details, includes the Workflow Name, which cannot be changed after initial creation, a Description field, and several other important workflow characteristics.

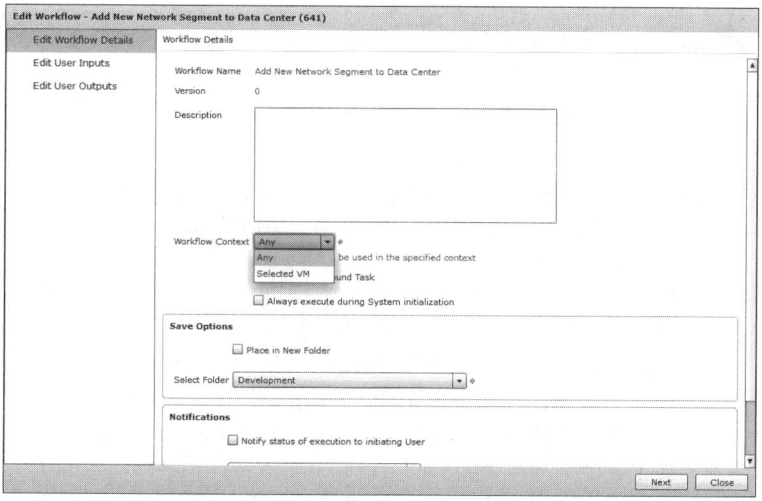

Figure 9-26 *Workflow Properties – Edit Workflow Details*

The Workflow Context field has two possible options, Any or Selected VM. Most general-purpose workflows will have a context of Any, but if you are building a workflow that is specifically intended to operate on a single VM, you can use Selected VM as the context. One advantage of setting up your workflow this way is that you will immediately have access to several inputs for tasks for details about the VM, such as its name and IP address. Table 9-4 provides a list of the additional variables available when working in a VM context. Second, this is the type of workflow you will want to use if you are building something intended to become part of a User Action Policy, as discussed earlier in this chapter.

Table 9-4 Workflow VM Context Variables

Name	Description
${VM_NAME}	The name of the VM.
${VM_IPADDRESS}	The IP address of the VM.
${VM_STATE}	The state of the VM (ON or OFF).
${VM_STATE_DETAILS}	The state of the VM, power-on or power-off.
${VM_PARENT}	The ESX server or host node that is hosting the VM.
${VM_CLOUD}	The name of the cloud used for VM provisioning.
${VM_HOSTNAME}	The hostname of the VM.
${VM_GROUP_NAME}	The name of the group to which the VM belongs.
${VM_GROUP_ID}	The group ID to which the VM belongs.
${VM_CATALOG_ID}	The catalog ID used for VM.
${VM_ID}	The VM ID of the chosen VM.
${VM_SR_ID}	The VM service request ID.

Name	Description
${VM_COMMENTS}	The comments specified by the requesting user.
${VM_VDC_NAME}	The name of the vDC.

Another important property to be familiar with is the ability to save the workflow as a compound task. This means that once the new workflow is created, it will show up in the Task Library (discussed in the next section, "Workflow Designer") as a reusable task. This allows for you to build reusable automation structures and use them within other workflows, providing for modular development. Then when you update the underlying compound workflow, all other workflows leveraging it will immediately benefit from the changes.

On the second page of the Edit Workflow window, Edit User Inputs, you indicate the number and types of user inputs that will be gathered, as shown in Figure 9-27. These user inputs are a collection of variables that can be leveraged during workflow execution. Some of these variables will come from the end users when they either directly execute a workflow or order an Advanced Catalog backed by your workflow. Others can be administratively defined by the user building the workflow. Common user inputs include names or descriptions for servers or networks, IP address details, username and passwords for systems, detail selections such as the operating system or application tier needed for a new server, and so on. The workflow shown in Figure 9-27 will add a new network segment to the data center. The end user provides the VLAN name to use for the new network, but other inputs you might expect, such as VLAN ID or IP subnet, will be dynamically determined from configured pools as described earlier in the chapter.

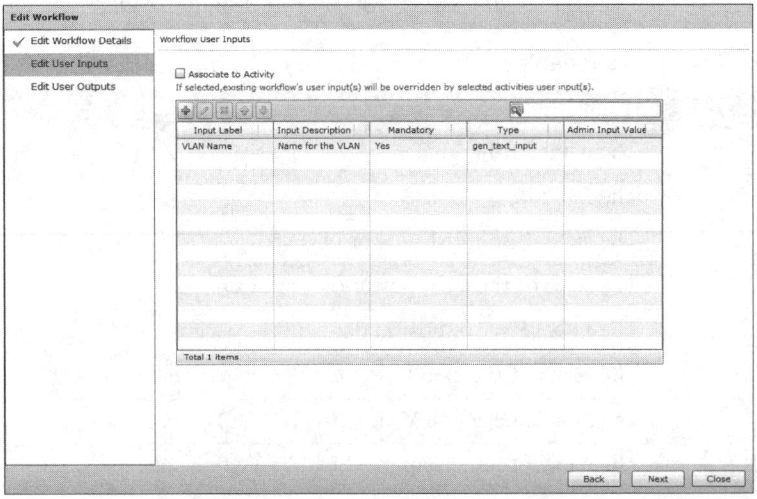

Figure 9-27 *Workflow Properties – Edit User Inputs*

One important aspect of user inputs, and of all inputs and outputs in workflows, is that UCS Director has a strongly typed model for variables. Each input will be assigned one of many types, and when you later go to use that input within a workflow task, the type of the user input must match the type that the task is expecting. The one exception to this rule is the Generic Text Input (gen_text_input) option. In most cases, any workflow task input will accept a Generic Text Input; however, it is recommended to use this sparingly. Leveraging a type of IP address or VLAN ID for an input has the added benefit that UCS Director will make sure the value provided by the user fits the type of input expected. This means that a user would not be able to enter a value of 555.555.555.555 for an IP address. Figure 9-28 shows a sample of some of the input types available within UCS Director.

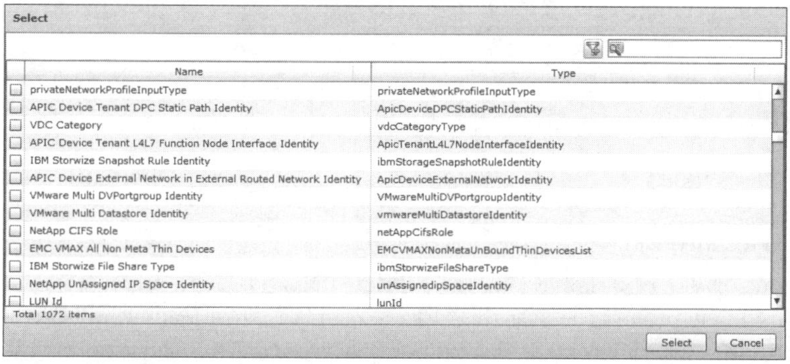

Name	Type
privateNetworkProfileInputType	privateNetworkProfileInputType
APIC Device Tenant DPC Static Path Identity	ApicDeviceDPCStaticPathIdentity
VDC Category	vdcCategoryType
APIC Device Tenant L4L7 Function Node Interface Identity	ApicTenantL4L7NodeInterfaceIdentity
IBM Storwize Snapshot Rule Identity	ibmStorageSnapshotRuleIdentity
APIC Device External Network in External Routed Network Identity	ApicDeviceExternalNetworkIdentity
VMware Multi DVPortgroup Identity	VMwareMultiDVPortgroupIdentity
VMware Multi Datastore Identity	vmwareMultiDatastoreIdentity
NetApp CIFS Role	netAppCifsRole
EMC VMAX All Non Meta Thin Devices	EMCVMAXNonMetaUnBoundThinDevicesList
IBM Storwize File Share Type	ibmStorwizeFileShareType
NetApp UnAssigned IP Space Identity	unAssignedipSpaceIdentity
LUN Id	lunId

Total 1072 items

Figure 9-28 *Input Types*

The final page of the Edit Workflow window is Edit User Outputs. Workflow outputs are used in compound tasks to pass information up to the parent workflow. Though all task outputs from the child task can be made available, often it is a subset of these outputs that will be of interest in the parent workflow. By mapping the relevant values to workflow outputs, it is much simpler to build complex workflows.

Workflow Designer

The Workflow Designer is where you build the actual automation structure for the workflow. You can access it by double-clicking the workflow name or by clicking the **Workflow Designer** button on the toolbar. Figure 9-29 shows an example of what you will see. The main section of the interface is the workspace where you drag and connect individual tasks, double-click a task to configure the task inputs to leverage a user input, output from a previous task, or administratively define the input within the task. On the left side is the Task Library, where you will find all of the available tasks organized into folders. UCS Director 5.3 ships with over 1600 tasks out of the box, and while the folder organization helps, you will often find it faster to locate a needed task by using the search box above the list. At the top of the window are buttons that allow you to edit the workflow properties, create a new version of a workflow, validate the workflow (ensure all tasks are connected and have all mandatory inputs configured), and execute the workflow.

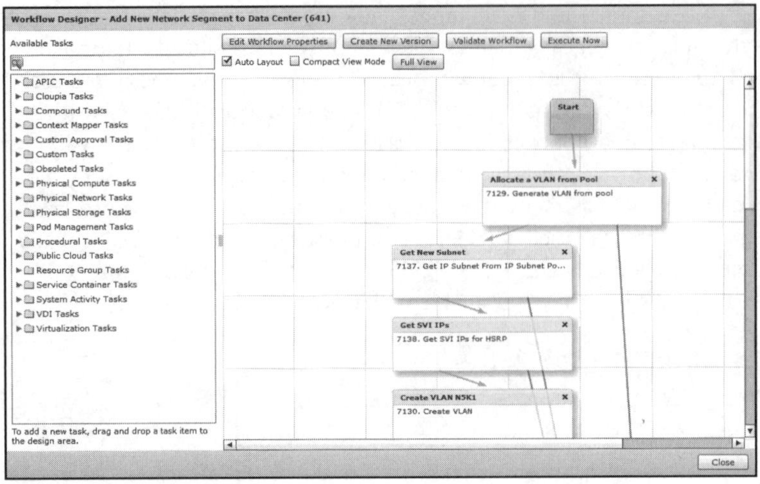

Figure 9-29 *Workflow Designer*

Workflow Creation Walkthrough

Let's walk through the creation of a simple sample workflow that adds a new VLAN to a Cisco Nexus switch. We will prompt the user for a VLAN name at execution, but will determine the VLAN ID by selecting one from a VLAN Pool Policy within UCS Director.

To begin, we need to create a new workflow using the procedure discussed in the previous "Workflow Properties" section. Figure 9-30 shows the Add Workflow Details page filled in for our new workflow, and Figure 9-31 shows the Add User Inputs page configured to prompt the user for a VLAN name.

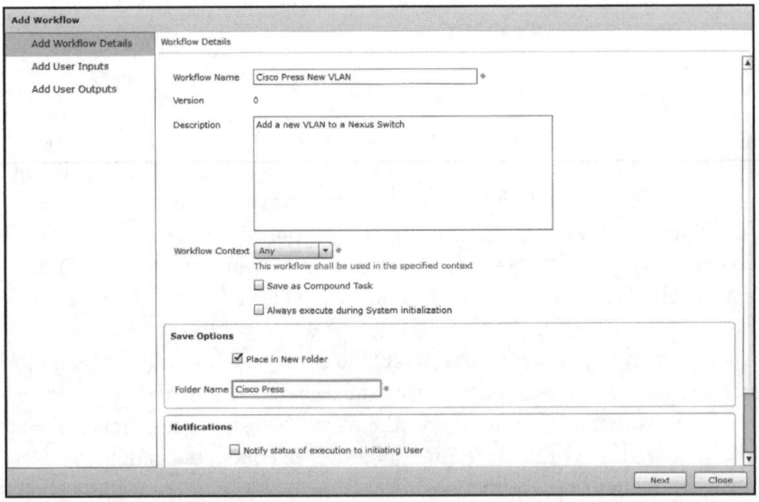

Figure 9-30 *New VLAN Workflow Details*

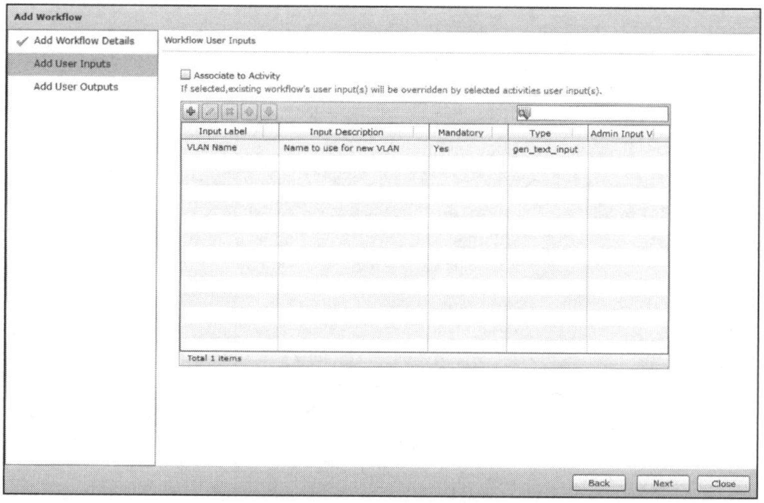

Figure 9-31 *New VLAN Workflow User Inputs*

Next, open the Workflow Designer to begin creating our new workflow. Two pieces of information are required to add a VLAN to a switch: the name and ID. The user will provide the name, but we need to generate the ID within the workflow. UCS Director provides tasks to generate available resources from pools and policies, and as shown in Figure 9-32, we leverage a task called **Generate VLAN from pool**. After dragging this task into the Workflow Designer pallet, we provide a descriptive name and comment for our task and click **Next** to continue.

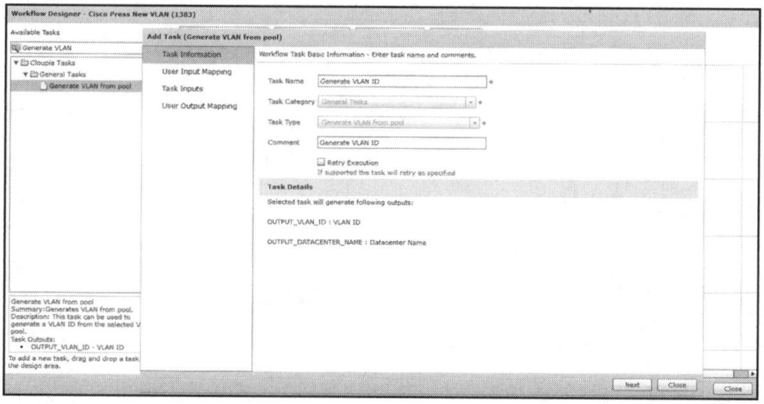

Figure 9-32 *Generate VLAN from Pool Task Information*

For this task we are not mapping any user inputs into the task, so skip the User Input Mapping page by clicking **Next** and move to the Task Inputs page. Here, as shown in Figure 9-33, we define the VLAN Pool Policy from which a new VLAN ID will be generated. Click **Next** and **Submit** on the Use Output Mapping page to save the task.

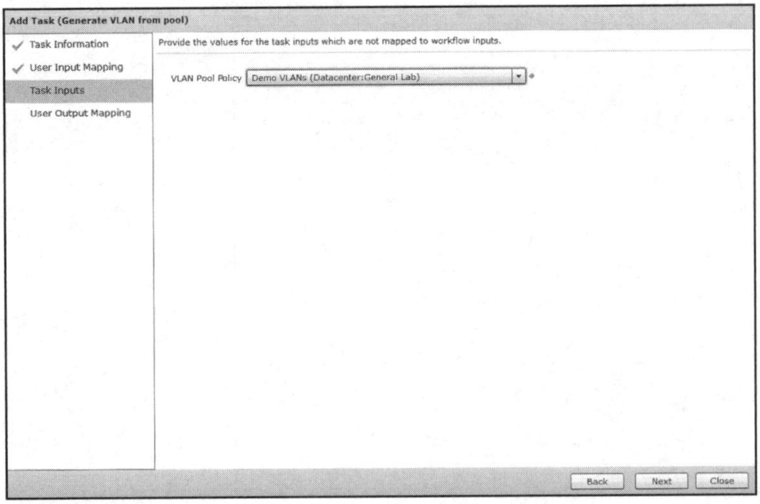

Figure 9-33   *Generate VLAN from Pool Task Inputs*

Figure 9-34 shows this first task complete and added to the design, automatically connected to Start and Completed blocks. Also shown on the left in the figure are the many possible tasks to create a new VLAN. Drag the **Create VLAN** task from the Cisco Network Tasks group onto the Workflow Designer for our next step.

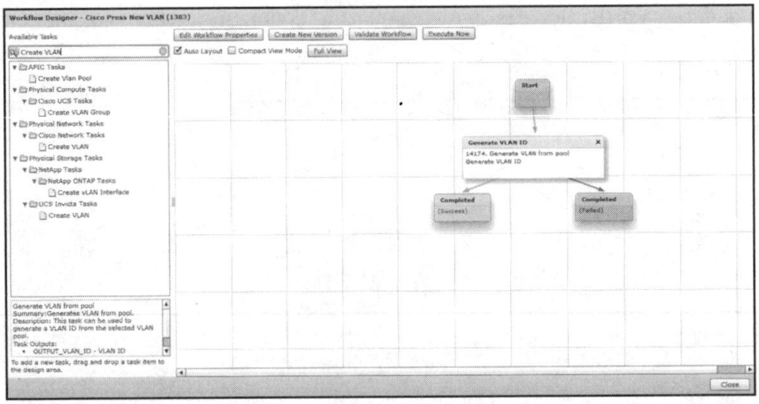

Figure 9-34   *Updated Workflow Designer with Task Added*

The first step after dragging any new task into the Designer is to provide it a name and comment. For this task, we use "Create VLAN on Switch 1" for both the name and comment. After you click **Next**, Figure 9-35 shows the User Input Mapping page of the task, where we checked the Map to User Input check boxes for VLAN ID and VLAN Name. This allows us to select either a workflow input, such as VLAN Name, or a previous task output, such as Generate VLAN ID.OUTPUT_VLAN_ID, to use as the task inputs. The latter example shows the notation used to reference task outputs within UCS Director with a TASK_NAME.OUTPUT_NAME structure.

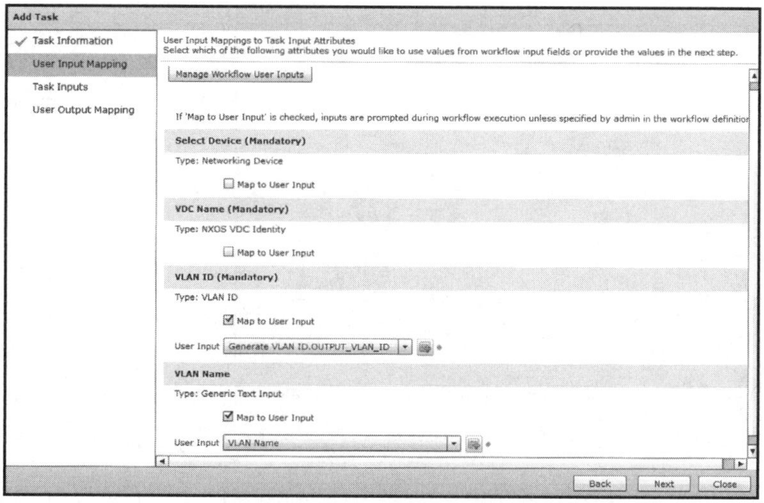

Figure 9-35 *Create VLAN User Input Mapping*

Not all of the task inputs are mapped to user inputs. After clicking **Next**, in Figure 9-36 we are identifying which switch we will be adding this VLAN to. Click **Next** and **Submit** on the Use Output Mapping page to save the task.

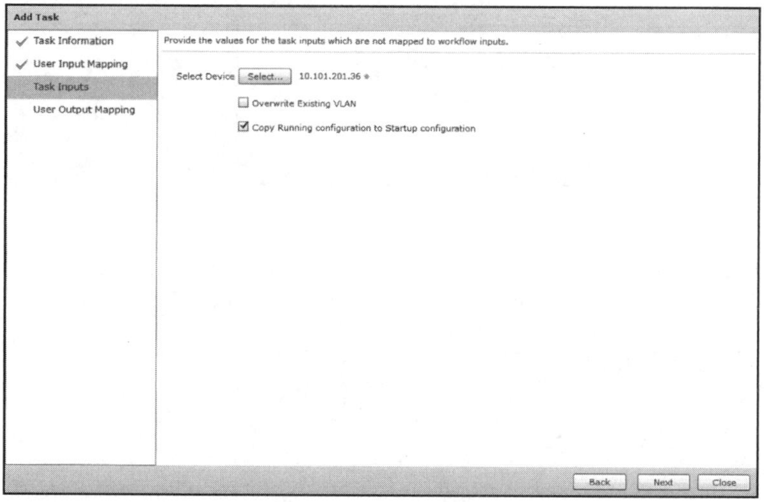

Figure 9-36 *Create VLAN Task Inputs*

After finishing the configuration of the task inputs, we still need to place the new task into the workflow processing structure. Only the first task added to a workflow is automatically added, and in Figure 9-37 we are indicating that a successful completion of the first task will lead to our new task. Figure 9-38 shows the Workflow Designer with both tasks completely configured.

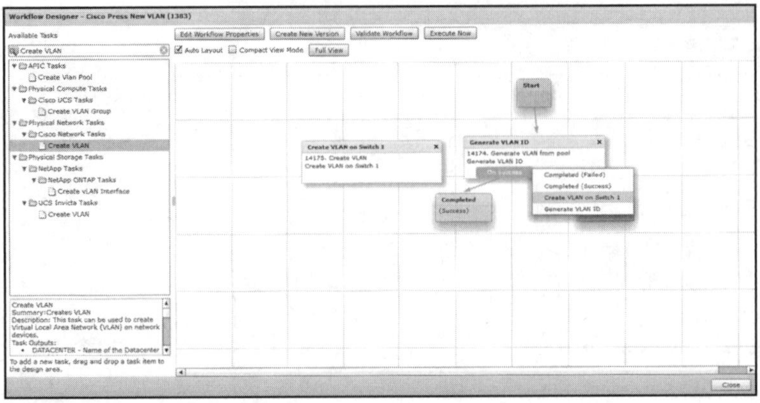

Figure 9-37 *Connecting Tasks Together*

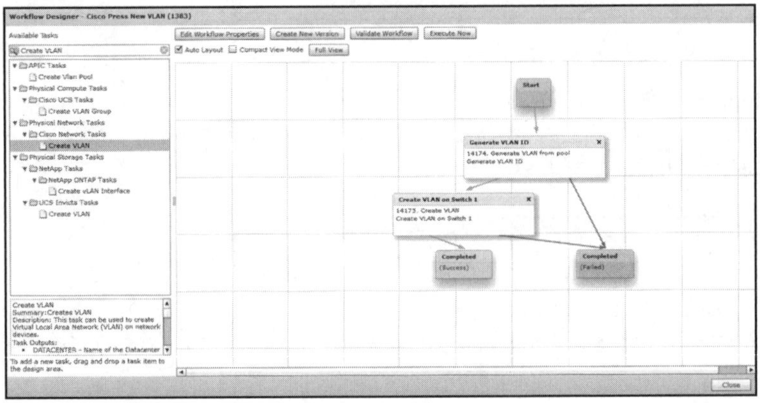

Figure 9-38 *Completed Workflow Designer*

The final step in our walkthrough is shown in Figure 9-39, where we have validated our new workflow and executed it. As expected, we are prompted to provide a new VLAN name to continue.

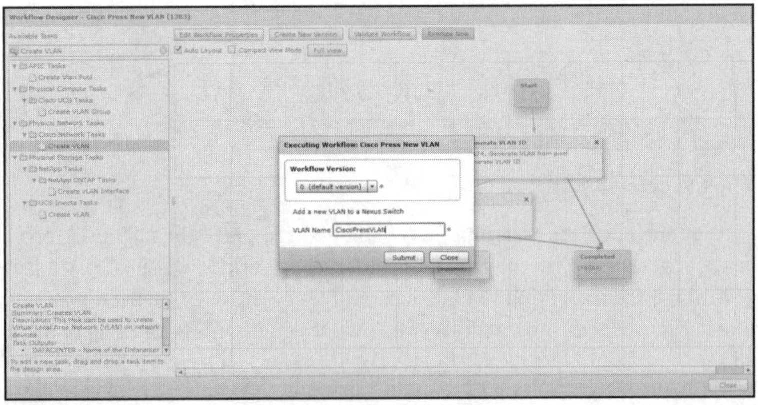

Figure 9-39 *Workflow Execution with User Input Dialog Box*

Extending Orchestration

With practice, you will be able to build workflows that are very powerful, spanning across your infrastructure using only the available tasks shipped with UCS Director out of the box. However, there will come a time when you look for a task to accomplish some configuration or customization and it is not available natively. When confronted with this challenge, there are several options for extending the automation capabilities beyond the initial installation.

Following are descriptions of the most common methods for extending Orchestration within UCS Director. Advanced discussion of these methods is beyond the scope of this book, and leveraging them is not part of the exam topics. Review the *Cisco UCS Director Orchestration Guide* and Programming Cookbooks available in the Programming Guides on Cisco.com for UCS Director.

Cloupia Script

One of the first tools you will likely use is the Execute Cloupia Script task that is within the native library. This task provides you with a text input box where you can enter raw Cloupia Script to be executed during a workflow, enabling you to write the code needed to fill a need in your workflow. Cloupia Script is a slightly customized version of JavaScript that combines the JavaScript language with included libraries to access runtime details from UCS Director itself. Within a Cloupia Script you'll have access to a context object that relates to the running instance of your workflow. This object provides details such as the requesting user, the service request details, user inputs, and task outputs.

Most Cloupia Scripts that you will write will be very simple functions. A common example would be manipulating a user input to meet some organizational standard. Figure 9-40 shows one such example where a user-provided name is appended with the service request number to ensure uniqueness and document the source of the new service profile.

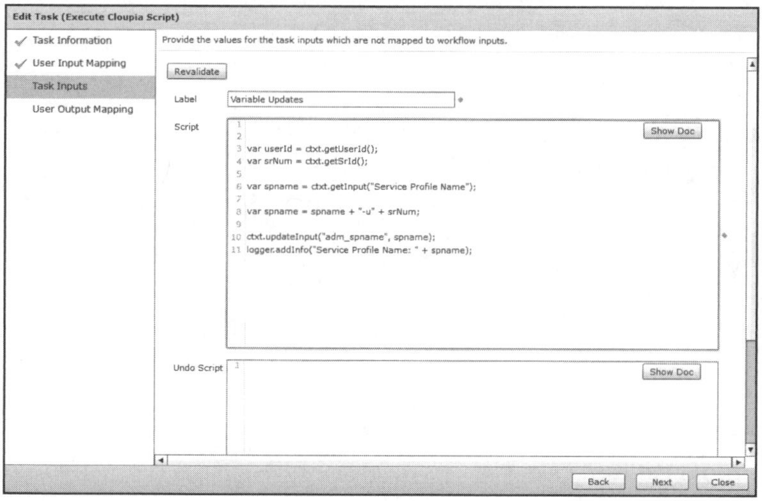

Figure 9-40   *Cloupia Script Example*

Custom Tasks

If you find that you are continually using the same Cloupia Script within several workflows, or have a need for something more complicated, the next option you have is to create a Custom Task. Custom Tasks are also written in Cloupia Script but are built to be much more reusable and portable between workflows. You will create task inputs and outputs, have an option to control the behavior of the task input interface to take action based on certain input values affecting others, and build your code using the same JavaScript-style construction from Cloupia Script. Once created, the Custom Task will show up in the Task Library under the Custom Tasks folder, and further organized as you indicated when creating the task.

Custom Approval Task

Many organizations find that though the goal may be full automation of infrastructure requests, many start with a need to insert approval steps into a workflow. You will find included tasks for single and multiuser approval capabilities that will pause a workflow while waiting for the designated users to indicate their approval for the request. This can be very helpful. However, what about a case where the approver needs to provide some input back to the workflow to complete execution? For example, consider an example where a new server is being provisioned, and the network operations team needs to identify the proper VLAN to place the server onto. For cases like these, you will build a custom approval task to use in your workflows.

You can create Custom Approval Tasks in the Orchestration interface several tabs to the right of the Workflow list. Each Custom Approval Task can be used in multiple workflows. Once created, the new task will show up in the Task Library along with all the others in a folder called Custom Approvals. Figure 9-41 shows an example Custom Approval Task where the approver will be asked to provide the vCPU and vRAM size information for a new VM.

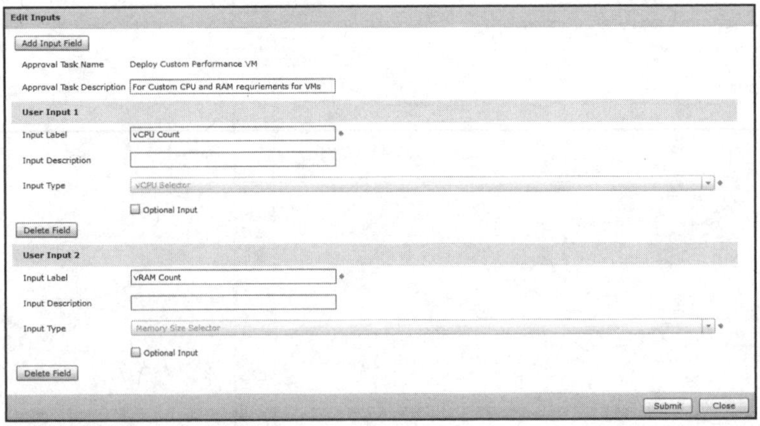

Figure 9-41 *Custom Approval Task Example*

Custom Workflow Input

You learned about the strongly typed nature of inputs within UCS Director in the "Workflow Designer" section of this chapter. There are hundreds of input types out of the box covering everything from general details like IP address and VLAN ID to infrastructure-specific types like a UCS service profile. However, you may find that you want to have your user provide input but offer a limited selection of choices. A typical example would be choosing one option from a set of appropriate entries in a drop-down list (referred to as an LOV, or list of values). You will use the Custom Workflow Input to build a new input type to use in your workflows. When you create the Custom Workflow Input, it will be based on a native type, and useable wherever that native type is supported. Figure 9-42 shows an example Custom Workflow Input called OS Choices that is based on a Generic Text Input and provides the user with a list of available operating systems supported in our environment. You can then use this input from the end user within the workflow as part of a branching logic to differentiate some aspect of the configuration based on the operating system in question.

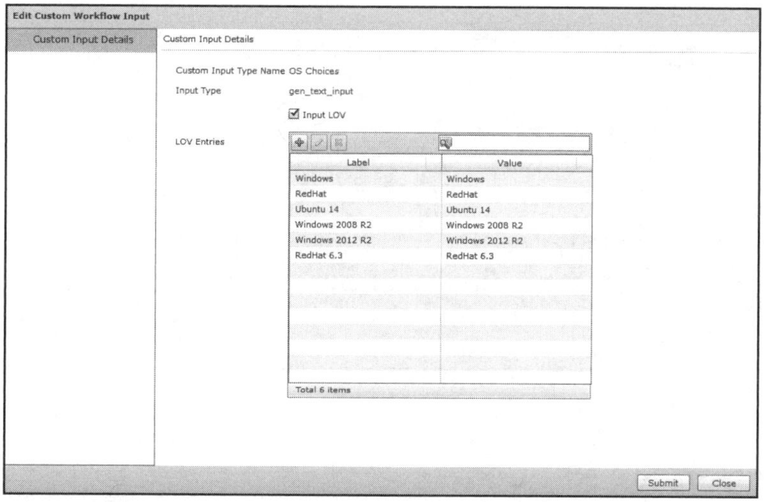

Figure 9-42   *Custom Workflow Input*

Cisco Community

You are not alone when creating workflows and automation use cases with UCS Director, and you needn't always start from an empty workflow. There is a Cisco Development Community where Cisco customers, partners, and employees share examples of work being done with all Cisco products, including UCS Director. At the time of the writing of this book, there are over 300 example workflows posted to the community that you can search and download to import into your system to use as inspiration or starting points for your own workflows, and more are being added weekly. In addition to sample workflows, there are many Custom Tasks that have been built to extend the native features of UCS Director to solve problems and fill gaps that others have found. When confronted with something that you may need, before building it yourself, take a look at the community to see if someone has already built a working task.

Also, you can often find third-party integrations posted in the community. At the time of writing, integrations to the Infoblox IPAM solution and Nimble Storage Array are two examples shared on the community.

You can find the home page for Cisco Communities at http://communities.cisco.com. The sample UCS Director workflows are located by navigating to **Data Center Community > Unified Computing System (UCS) > UCS Integrations > UCS Director Workflows**. See Figure 9-43 for a glimpse into the community.

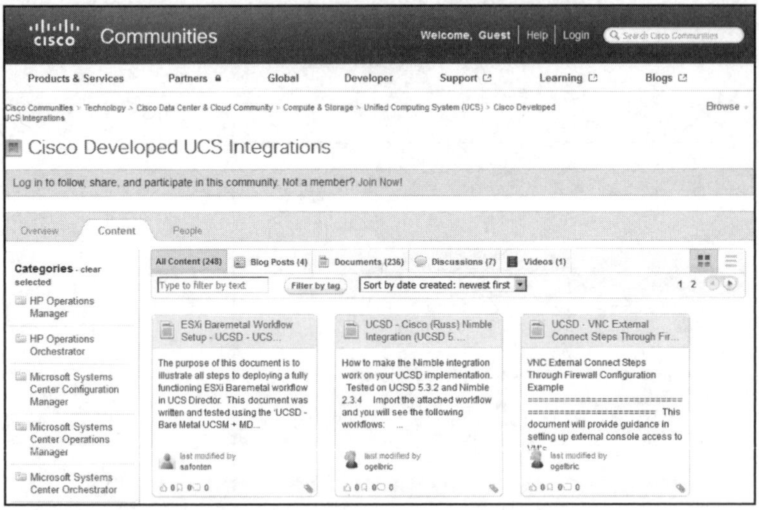

Figure 9-43 *Cisco Community*

UCS Director Service Requests

Any activity that would execute a workflow will generate a service request within UCS Director. This includes ordering any of the UCS Director Catalog types (even Standard Catalogs execute a workflow), or manually executing a workflow through the Designer or the Orchestration interface. Even rolling back a service request creates a new service request. The *service request* is a record of a single automation activity, and stores all the details about who initiated the request, the status and time for each step in the workflow, detailed logging throughout, and all infrastructure manipulations made during its execution.

Service requests are available to be viewed and leveraged in both the administrator portal and the end-user portal, but the type of details available differ. An end user will only have visibility to the service requests initiated by themselves or other members of their group. Figure 9-44 shows the Services page of the end-user portal. The user sees only three requests that were initiated. Compare this to the page available in the administrator portal at **Organizations > Service Requests** shown in Figure 9-45. The administrator sees the three requests executed by clouduser as well as those executed by user cloudadmin. Also notice that administrators have access to the archived service requests. Though end users can archive one of their service requests, they can't view or unarchive the archived requests.

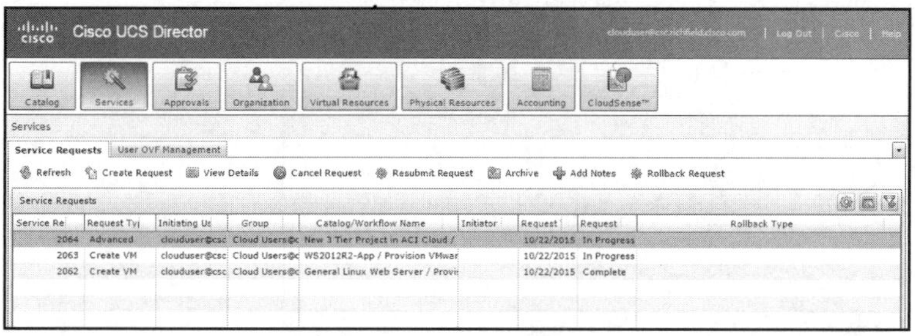

Figure 9-44   *End-User Services Page*

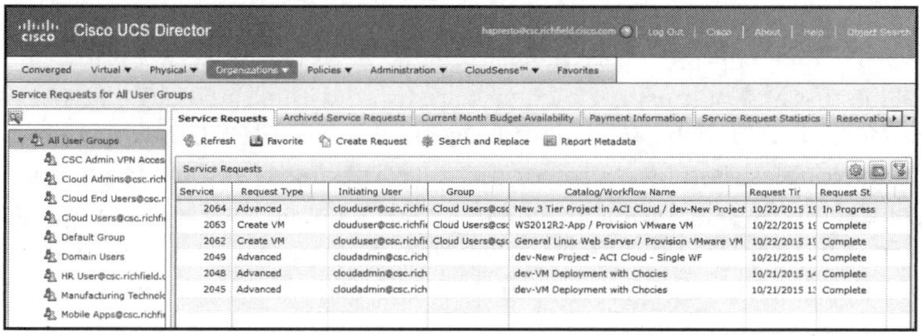

Figure 9-45   *Administrator Service Requests Page*

When an end user opens a service request to see more information, he will see the service request Status information, as shown in Figure 9-46. The Status page provides details on the request such as its Request ID, current status, the group and user who own the request, as well as a listing of each step or task in the underlying workflow indicating which steps have completed successfully (displayed in green with a time stamp) and which are currently in progress (displayed in blue), and, if applicable, which steps may have had errors (displayed in red or orange). The Status page is very helpful for end users to understand their request, but lacks the details available to an administrator in other tabs.

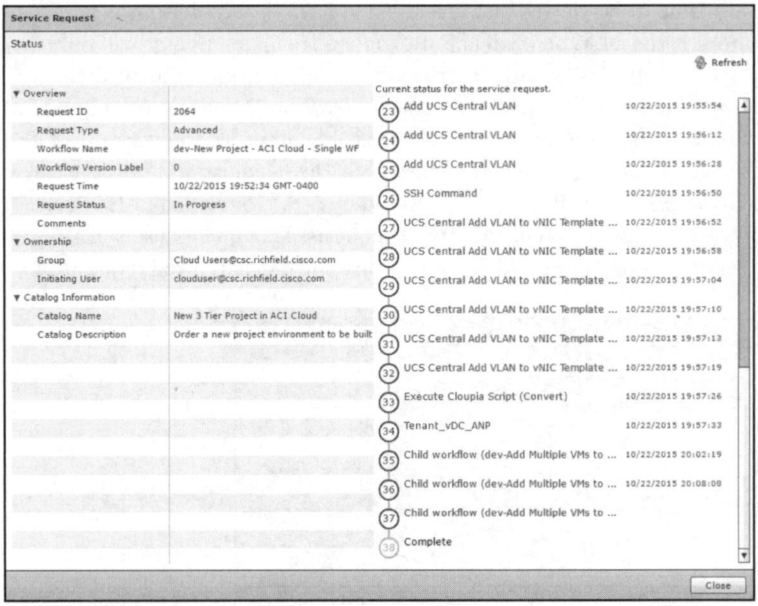

Figure 9-46   *End-User Service Request Status*

When you open a request as an administrator, the most helpful details are available on the Log tab, shown in Figure 9-47. You will find a very detailed rundown of the entire workflow and each included task. All inputs and outputs for each task are listed within the log to make it very easy to follow the progress as values change and new objects are created. When you are building a new workflow and troubleshooting a behavior that isn't working as you intended, your best tool for debugging and fixing the problem will be the Log view of your service requests. Within the Log view, different colors indicate different types of messages. Informational messages are shown in black, debug messages in gray, errors in red, and warnings in orange.

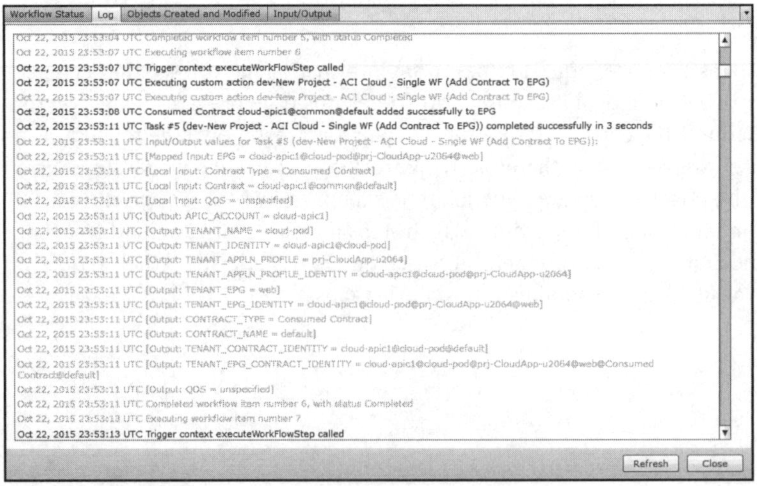

Figure 9-47   *Administrator View Service Request Log*

As an administrator, you will also have access to two other tabs providing details about the service request. First is the Objects Created and Modified tab, which shows some of the change-tracking capabilities of UCS Director. This view will list all VMs created, IP addresses reserved, VLANs created, LUNs created, and interfaces manipulated during the execution of the service request. An example of this view is shown in Figure 9-48. This information is useful as part of managing change, but even more important is how UCS Director can use this when rolling back or undoing a service request. The last tab is the Input/Output tab, where you will find a list of each task in the workflow and a breakdown of the different inputs and outputs involved. These details are also helpful during debugging workflows, or simply determining details such as what was the LUN ID of the new storage device that was created.

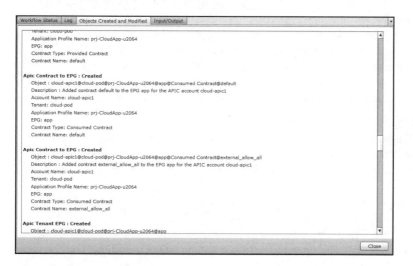

Figure 9-48 *Administrator View Service Request Objects Created*

Service Request Actions

A service request is not a read-only object in UCS Director. You can take several actions on a service request depending on its current status. The actions are available for both administrators and end users through their portal interfaces in the toolbar, as shown in Figure 9-49. You can cancel a service request that is still in progress, stopping execution at the current task. You can resubmit a request if it was canceled or failed during initial execution. This is helpful when the reason for a failure can be solved and you want to just pick up the automation from where it left off. A common example of this would be the exhaustion of an IP pool. Once additional IPs are made available, you can resubmit the request and continue from where it initially failed. Archiving a service request moves it from the main list of requests that is available to end users, and into the Archive. Once a service request is in the Archive, only administrators can view it or take action on it. Administrators do have the ability to return an archived request to the main list.

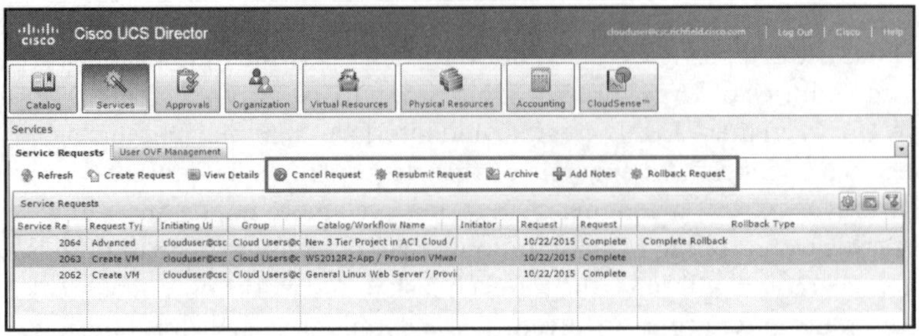

Figure 9-49   *Service Request Actions*

The most powerful of service request actions is the ability to roll back the request. A unique value provided with the automation engine of UCS Director is the integrated ability to roll back any automation workflow. UCS Director is model based, not script based. This means that a task from the library that takes an action, such as creating a new VLAN, can be undone without needing a separate task that would delete the VLAN. All tasks included in UCS Director include the capability to be rolled back, and it is best practice to consider rollback for any custom tasks or scripts you may create.

You won't need to build separate workflows to reclaim or delete resources; that logic is included when you build the initial workflow. This capability combined with the details stored in Objects Created and Modified view (previously shown in Figure 9-48) enable UCS Director to immediately and consistently roll back service requests that are executed. When you choose to roll back a service request, a new Undo service request is created. If you were not the originator of the service request being rolled back, an approval request will be sent to the original requester. UCS Director administrators have the ability to bypass this approval step. A sample Undo service request is shown in Figure 9-50. Notice that the Undo Workflow is mostly a reverse mirror of the tasks taken in the initial workflow.

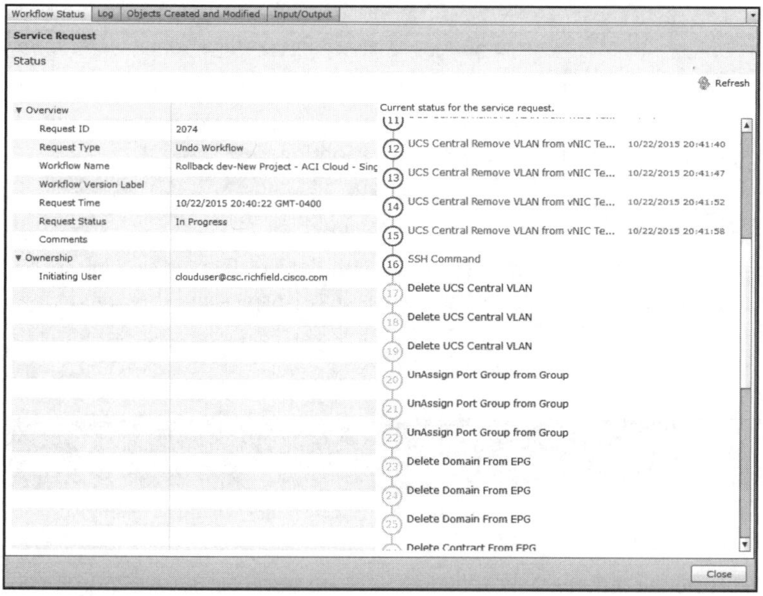

Figure 9-50   *Undo Workflow Service Request*

Reservations

Another tab in the **Organizations > Service Requests** menu worth noting is the Reservations tab. This tab, shown in Figure 9-51, provides a single view of all consumable resources that have been assigned from policies and pools to different users and groups as part of service requests. Common examples of reservations include IP address and VLANs. This view is useful for checking the status of different reservations, but can also be used to manually clear a reservation in a case where the object may have been deleted outside of UCS Director so that the reservation wasn't automatically cleared as part of a rollback.

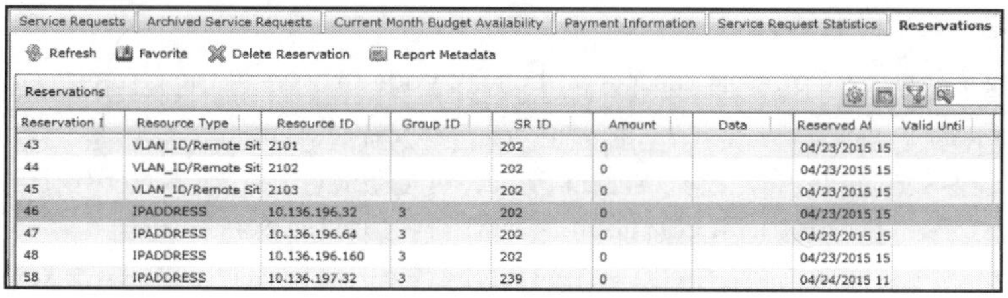

Figure 9-51   *UCS Director Reservations List*

Exam Preparation Tasks

As mentioned in the section "How to Use This Book" in the Introduction, you have a couple of choices for exam preparation: the exercises here, Chapter 15, "Final Preparation," and the exam simulation questions on the Pearson IT Certification Practice Test.

Review All Key Topics

Review the most important topics in this chapter, noted with the Key Topics icon in the outer margin of the page. Table 9-5 lists a reference of these key topics and the page number on which each is found.

Key Topic

Table 9-5   Key Topics for Chapter 9

Key Topic Element	Description	Page Number
Section	Understand the vDC construct and related policies within UCS Director.	248
Table 9-2	Describe the different vDC Policies and their purpose.	250
Paragraph	Understand UCS templates, differences between template types, and how to create templates within UCS Director.	264
Section	Describe the key workflow properties and how they impact the automation and orchestration.	266
Paragraph	Describe the information available to users about the status and history of service requests within UCS Director.	279
Paragraph	Describe the importance of the Rollback function for service requests.	282

Define Key Terms

Define the following key terms from this chapter and check your answers in the glossary:

virtual data center (vDC), System Policy, Computing Policy, Network Policy, Storage Policy, End User Self-Service Policy, User Action Policy, vDC categories, UCS Network Policy, UCS Storage Policy, workflow, compound workflow, Cloupia Script, service request, Rollback

This chapter covers the following exam topics:

3.0 Cloud Provisioning

3.1 Describe predefined Cisco UCS Director-based services within the Cisco Prime Service Catalog

  3.1.b Describe order permissions

  3.1.c Describe template formats

3.2 Describe provisioning verification

  3.2.a Describe how to place an order for a service from the Cisco Prime Service Catalog as an end-user

  3.2.b Verify that provisioning is done correctly

  3.2.c Access VMs and applications that have been provisioned

Building a Service Catalog and User Portal with UCS Director and Prime Service Catalog

In Chapter 9, "Automating Cloud Infrastructure with UCS Director," you learned about creating the policies and automation workflows that will be used to deploy into the cloud the compute, storage, and network resources required by your users. The first half of this chapter reviews how you present these capabilities to your users, leveraging user portals and service catalogs. The second half explains how end users will locate and order services, monitor the provisioning of their requests, and manage the life cycle of their resources.

"Do I Know This Already?" Quiz

The "Do I Know This Already?" quiz allows you to assess whether you should read this entire chapter thoroughly or jump to the "Exam Preparation Tasks" section. If you are in doubt about your answers to these questions or your own assessment of your knowledge of the topics, read the entire chapter. Table 10-1 lists the major headings in this chapter and their corresponding "Do I Know This Already?" quiz questions. You can find the answers in Appendix A, "Answers to the 'Do I Know This Already?' Quizzes."

Table 10-1 "Do I Know This Already?" Section-to-Question Mapping

Foundation Topics Section	Questions
UCS Director Catalogs	1
Prime Service Catalog Fundamentals	2
Connecting and Importing to Prime Service Catalog	3
Customizing Auto-Created Services	4
Ordering a Service with Prime Service Catalog	5, 6
Checking and Monitoring Status of an Order	7, 8
Accessing and Managing New Resources	9, 10

CAUTION The goal of self-assessment is to gauge your mastery of the topics in this chapter. If you do not know the answer to a question or are only partially sure of the answer, you should mark that question as wrong for purposes of the self-assessment. Giving yourself credit for an answer you correctly guess skews your self-assessment results and might provide you with a false sense of security.

1. What catalog type from UCS Director is used to enable end users to order a single basic virtual machine based on a VM image or ISO?

   a. Advanced Catalog

   b. Standard Catalog

   c. VM Catalog

   d. Service Container Catalog

2. Within Prime Service Catalog, the Showcase refers to what?

   a. Administrative Utilization Dashboard

   b. Front page of the Service Catalog

   c. Listing of all ordered services by the user

   d. Listing of the newest services

3. What type of UCS Director user account is needed when connecting to Prime Service Catalog?

   a. Compute Admin

   b. Service End User

   c. System Admin

   d. Any of the above

4. What types of UCS Director objects become Prime Service Catalog services when they are imported in?

   a. Images

   b. Catalogs

   c. Workflows

   d. vDCs

   e. Application profiles

5. Which element of the front page, or Showcase, of Prime Service Catalog provides users quick links to manage the resources they have provisioned and view open and completed orders?

   a. Manage My Stuff panel

   b. Notifications

   c. Shopping Cart

   d. Browse Categories

6. What detail must a user provide when ordering a new virtual machine through a Standard Catalog–based service?

   a. VM name

   b. vCPU count

   c. vDC

   d. vRAM

7. How can a user find the status of ongoing orders within Prime Service Catalog? (Choose two.)

   a. Look in the Shopping Cart

   b. Check the Notifications menu

   c. Within their account settings

   d. Use the Open Orders link on the Showcase

8. Within Prime Service Catalog, where can you find the UCS Director service request number for an order?

   a. Notifications menu

   b. Order Summary page

   c. Order Details Comments and History

   d. You cannot find the service request number within Prime Service Catalog

9. Which actions can end users take on their virtual machines from Prime Service Catalog? (Choose all that apply.)

   a. Power on/off

   b. Add or remove a virtual network adapter

   c. Create a snapshot

   d. Delete a snapshot

   e. Clone a virtual machine

10. How can you identify a virtual machine that is deployed to a public cloud provider through Intercloud Fabric in Prime Service Catalog? (Choose two.)

   a. Select the Cloud VMs Service Item type

   b. Check the VM details for the cloud type

   c. Look for the cloud icon in the VM list

   d. Through the Intercloud Fabric submenu in My Stuff

10

Foundation Topics

UCS Director Catalogs

Before users can order a service, you must create a catalog offer within UCS Director for the service. Catalog offers include everything from the most basic ordering of a new VM, to a sophisticated infrastructure offering that provisions physical storage, network, and compute resources all at once. Figure 10-1 shows a selection of catalog offers within the administrator portal from UCS Director. These catalogs provide the template for services that will be created in Prime Service Catalog.

Figure 10-1 *UCS Director Catalogs*

It is expected that you will have different catalogs for different groups of users at your enterprise. For example, your infrastructure engineering and operations users will need catalogs for Expanding Cloud Capacity, Adding New Network Segment, and Decommissioning a vSphere Host. However, your application development team would have no need for those catalogs, but will need catalogs for Deploy New Web/App/Data Server, Build New Application Environment, and Snapshot Application Environment. When you create the catalogs for these different capabilities, you indicate which groups will have the ability to see and order the catalogs.

Depending on the type of offer you are creating, you will use one of four types of catalogs within UCS Director:

■ Standard Catalog

■ Advanced Catalog

■ Service Container Catalog

■ VDI Catalog

Standard Catalog

The most basic type of service you'll want to provide to your end users is the ability to order new virtual machines. In today's data center, the virtual machine is nearly omnipresent and has taken over as the primary mechanism for deploying traditional client/server applications and workloads. Whether the end goal is to install all or part of a commercial software package, act as a shared database environment for multiple applications, or even provide the compute infrastructure on which a custom-developed application will be built, a project often starts with creating new virtual machines.

The Standard Catalog offering within UCS Director provides a very simple mechanism to enable users to select and order virtual machines based on the policies and templates you have configured as the administrator. When you create a Standard Catalog, you identify a source image (or ISO) from which to build the new virtual machine as well as other details that provide UCS Director with all the needed information to provision the new VM into one of the user's available virtual data centers (vDCs and their policies are covered later in this chapter).

Key Topic

The possible source images come from the virtual account (also referred to as a cloud within UCS Director) the Standard Catalog is being built for. UCS Director supports private clouds based on VMware vCenter, Microsoft System Center Virtual Machine Manager (SCVMM) for HyperV, and Red Hat Kernel-based Virtual Machine (KVM). Each of these clouds has its own templates or images for virtual machine catalogs. These templates differ based on the underlying hypervisor format being used, and a template from one cloud can't be used on another cloud without being converted to that cloud's format.

New catalogs can be created from the administrator portal at **Policies > Catalogs**. As shown in Figure 10-2, action buttons are available to add a new catalog or clone an existing one. When you click **Add**, you are presented with the Add Catalog dialog box shown in Figure 10-2, in which you can use the Catalog Type drop-down list to select Standard from among the options available and click **Submit**.

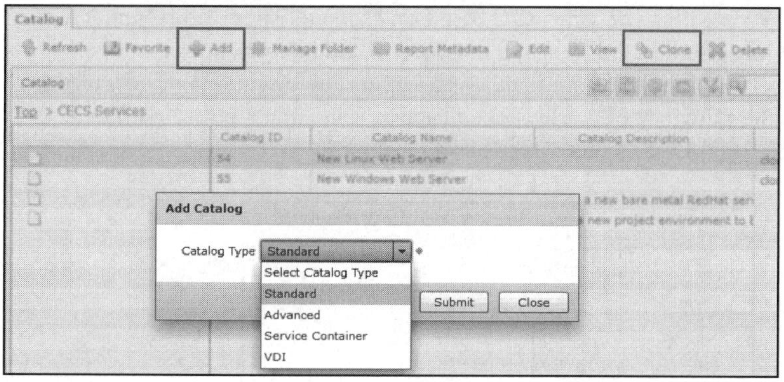

Figure 10-2 *New Catalog Creation*

The Basic Information page (see Figure 10-3) is the first part of adding a new Standard Catalog. This is where you give the new Standard Catalog a name, description, and icon that will determine how it will be presented to end users within the UCS Director end-user portal or through API calls. You also determine which groups of users (or all) will have the ability to see and order this catalog. If you have multiple virtual accounts added to your UCS Director installation (that is, vCenter and/or Microsoft SCVMM), select the corresponding cloud name from the Cloud Name drop-down list. Then click the Image field's **Select** button to identify the desired source image for the new VM. Alternatively, you can indicate that the VM will be provisioned using an ISO image from an available policy. Not shown in Figure 10-3 but available by scrolling down within the window, you can provide a Windows License Pool for Windows-based Standard Catalogs, as well as a folder to store this new catalog within.

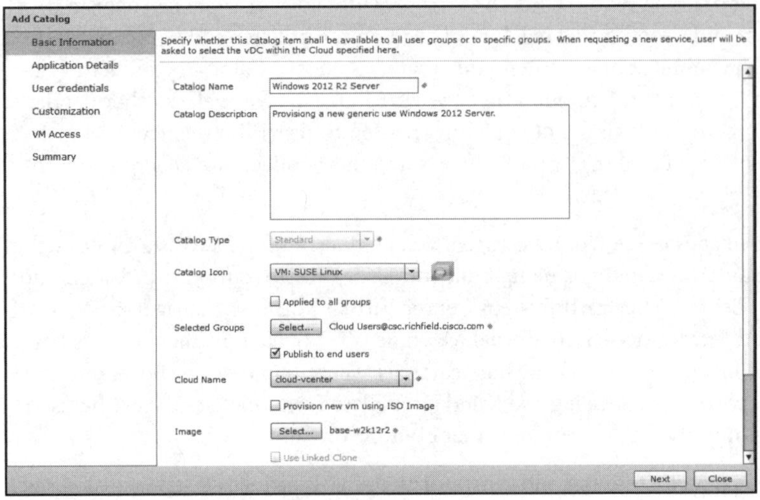

Figure 10-3 *Standard Catalog Basic Information*

Click **Next** to move to the Application Details page of the Add Standard Catalog Wizard, shown in Figure 10-4. Most of the options available here are primarily used for reporting or metering. However, Category is a powerful option to enable administrators to apply different vDC policies to VMs within the same vDC based on characteristics of different VMs. For example, a VM that will be used to host a database would likely benefit from being placed on a higher-performing data store than a web server. Full discussion of how to differentiate based on the Category of a provisioned catalog is included in the "UCS Director Policies, Pools, and Virtual Data Centers" section of Chapter 9.

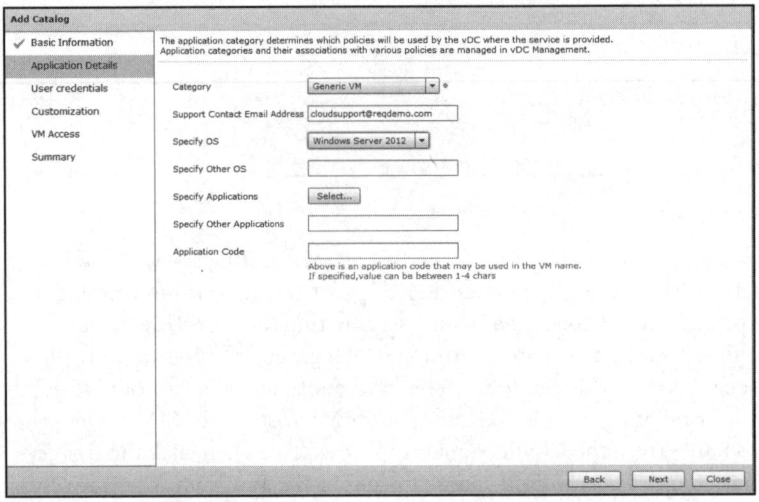

Figure 10-4 *Standard Catalog Application Details*

After you click **Next** on the Application Details page, the third page, shown in Figure 10-5, gives you options for sharing login credentials with users. You will find three options available: Do not share, Share after password reset, and Share template credentials. Typically, you would use the first option only when the end user would have another means for logging in to the new machine through a sign-on service such as Lightweight Directory Access Protocol (LDAP). When this isn't the case, you can either directly share the credentials as configured in the template, or have UCS Director generate a random password when deploying and customizing the new VM and pass this on to the user. When shared, the password will be available from the UCS Director end-user portal through a VM action **Access VM Credentials.**

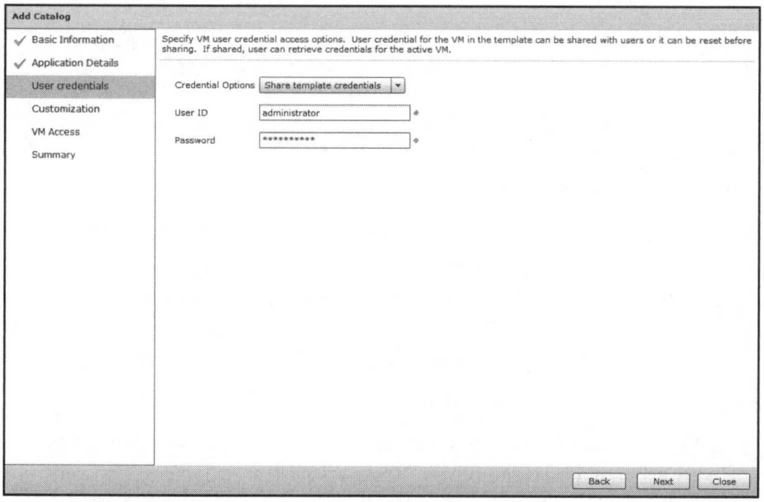

Figure 10-5   *Standard Catalog User Credentials*

On the Customization page, shown in Figure 10-6, you are given options for further customization of the new VM. Enabling Automatic Guest Customization indicates that you would like UCS Director to leverage the Guest Customization features of the hypervisor to take actions such as applying a hostname, setting the IP address for the virtual machine, and generating a new SID for a Microsoft Windows VM. Unless you plan to address these needs through a separate automated process, it is recommended to select this option. By enabling Post Provisioning Custom Actions, you can select a workflow from the Orchestration engine within UCS Director to run after the virtual machine is provisioned. When selecting a workflow, you will want to select a workflow configured to run in a VM context. Virtual Storage Catalog is an optional policy that can adjust the storage policy as defined in the vDC configuration. Checking this box will enable a drop-down list box where a previously defined Virtual Storage Catalog Policy is selected. This policy provides the user with options to specify which of the available storage policies to use for this virtual machine deployment.

10

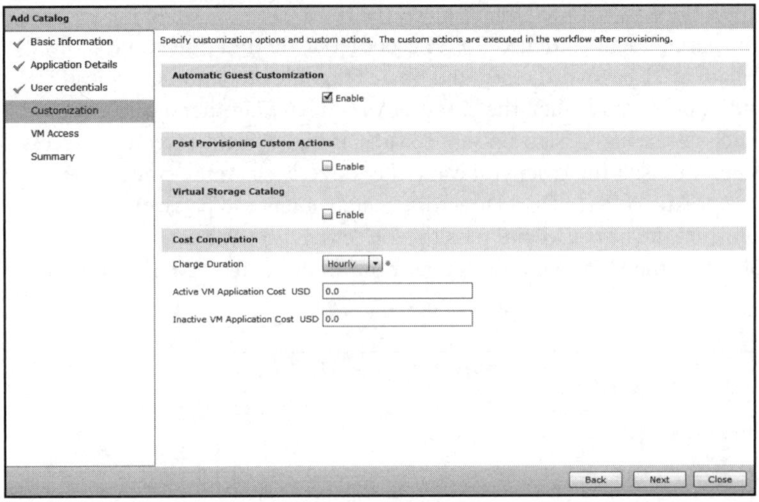

Figure 10-6 *Standard Catalog Customization*

Many enterprises are looking to begin moving to a chargeback or showback model for IT resources. UCS Director provides a very robust method for building Cost Models around resource utilization, as covered in Chapter 12, "Chargeback, Billing, and Reporting." The Cost Computation option on the Customization page is a much less granular option that can be used as a simple method of attaching value to resources before building a more robust model as discussed in Chapter 12.

The second to last page, VM Access (see Figure 10-7), enables you to indicate what type of access UCS Director should provide to the newly created VM for end users. Options include providing a cross-launch link to a web page, creating a custom Remote Desktop Protocol file that can be downloaded to open an RDP session to a Windows Server, or cross-launching to the VM Remote Console service provided by vSphere hosts.

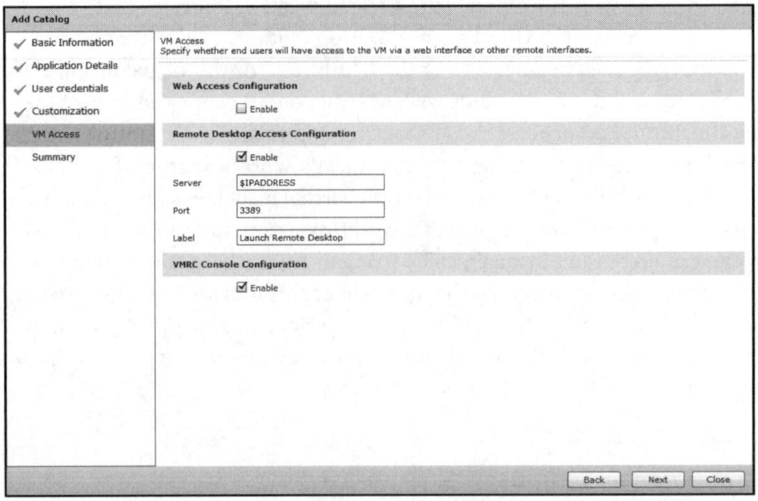

Figure 10-7 *Standard Catalog VM Access*

The final page is Summary, shown in Figure 10-8, which shows all settings you configured during the wizard. It is provided as a final review before creating the new Standard Catalog.

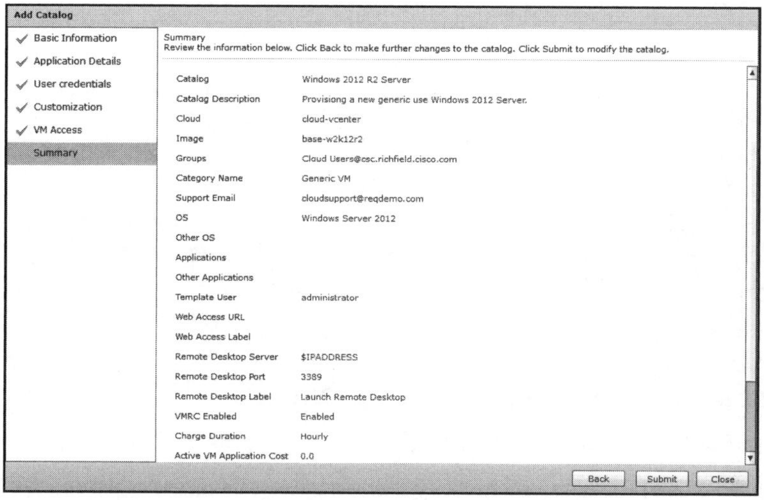

Figure 10-8 *Standard Catalog Summary*

Advanced Catalog

Somewhat counterintuitive, the Advanced Catalog is the simpler catalog to create compared to Standard, but it is much more powerful. Its simplicity comes from the fact that you will have already done all the hard work when creating the workflow that will be used as the foundation for the Advanced Catalog. A Standard Catalog is used to create a single new VM within the constructs of a vDC and with the limited set of options available in the Standard Catalog offering discussed in the previous section. When requirements deviate from what is supported with a Standard Catalog, an Advanced Catalog can enable end users to order nearly any infrastructure service as long as you, or your team of cloud architects and engineers, have built the required workflow to take the action.

In Chapter 9, you learned how to use the Orchestration engine of UCS Director to build workflows for different use cases. Let's assume you have built a workflow that would provision a new bare-metal server, and you wish to make this an orderable catalog.

Starting the same way you did to create the Standard Catalog, click **Add** in the **Policies > Catalogs** interface within the administrator portal, but this time select **Advanced** from the drop-down menu (shown earlier in Figure 10-2). Figure 10-9 shows the Basic Information page of the Advanced Catalog Wizard. Provide the new catalog a name, description, and icon for display in the end-user portal service catalog. Also indicate the group(s) who should have access to this catalog. In Figure 10-9 we have indicated that all groups will be allowed to see and order this service.

10

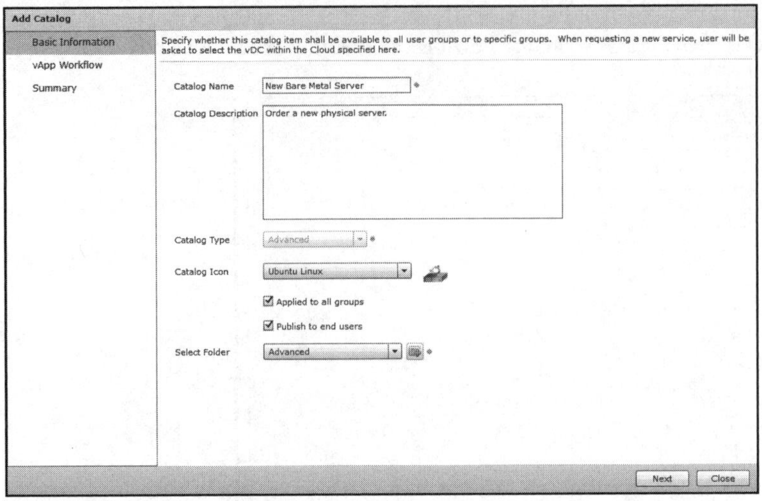

Figure 10-9 *Advanced Catalog Basic Information*

The second page of the wizard is where you identify the workflow to execute when the user orders this new Advanced Catalog. As you can see in Figure 10-10, there is nothing to indicate other than the workflow to leverage. Elements such as user inputs, approvals, and so on are all embedded in the workflow itself and will be discussed later in this chapter.

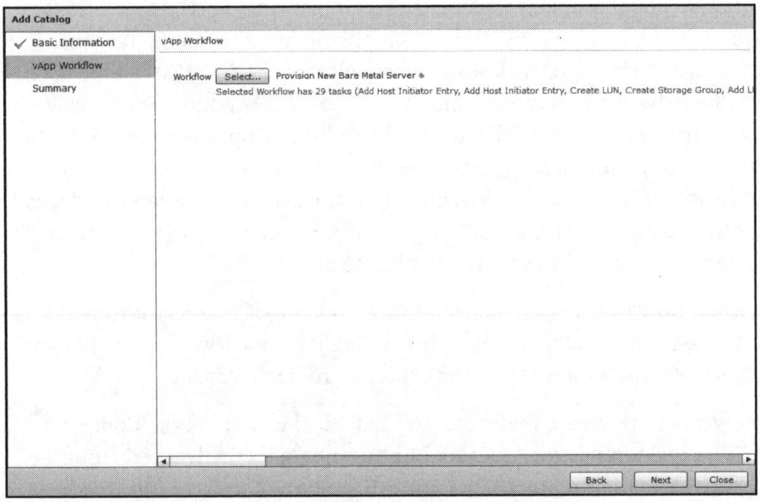

Figure 10-10 *Advanced Catalog vApp Workflow*

The final Summary page displays the details you configured on the previous pages as a final review.

Service Container Catalog

UCS Director has a construct called an *application container* that provides a mechanism for multiple virtual and physical resources to be combined together and managed as a single offering. An example would be a three-tier network structure (web, app, data) with embedded security and load-balancer policies exposing the compute resources within the network structure outside of the container in a controlled fashion. The application container can be powered on, off, or deleted as a single entity. Chapter 11, "Deploying Virtual Application Containers," provides a thorough discussion of the variety of application container types supported by UCS Director, and how to build container templates. The Service Container Catalog type is how an end user can be given the ability to order a designed application container.

Click **Add** in the **Policies > Catalogs** interface and select **Service Container** from the drop-down menu (refer to Figure 10-2) to access the Basic Information page of the new Service Container Catalog, shown in Figure 10-11. The familiar interface for name, description, and groups is presented along with a drop-down list box to select the service container template that will be used for provisioning.

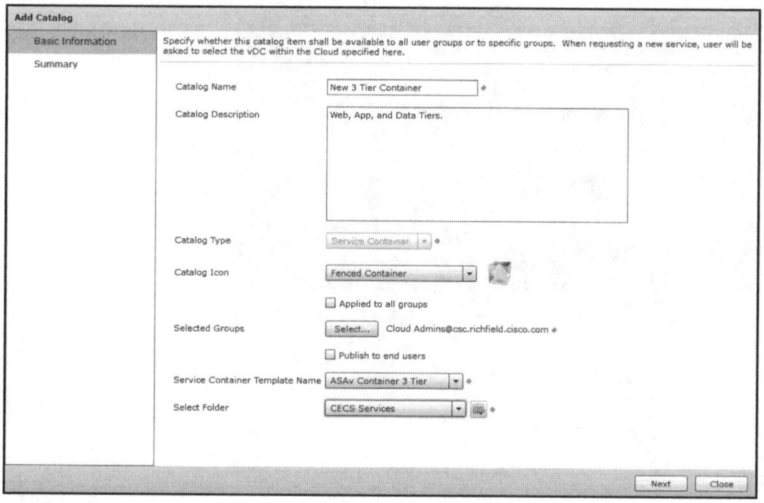

Figure 10-11 *Service Container Basic Information*

The final Summary page displays the details you configured on the previous page as a final review.

VDI Catalog

The VDI Catalog type can be used to provide end users the ability to order a virtual desktop from a managed Citrix VDI environment. This capability of UCS Director is out of scope for this book and the Introducing CCNA Cloud Administration (CLDADM) exam.

Prime Service Catalog Fundamentals

Within UCS Director you will create and test workflows, and make them orderable to end users by creating Advanced Catalog offers. You will provide the ability to order and deploy new VMs with Standard Catalogs. You will build the policies and vDCs for your end users to deploy their resources into. Once you have completed these steps, you are ready to assemble the user portal and service catalog and start having end users order and manage their resources. This is when you begin working with Prime Service Catalog.

The Showcase

The front page of Prime Service Catalog that is seen by everyone at first login is called the Showcase. The Showcase is your opportunity to welcome your users to their IT as a Service portal, educate them about new features, and provide them easy access to the most helpful or common services available in the catalog. You can see a sample front page and Showcase in Figure 10-12. The Showcase is divided into eight customizable sections that you can manipulate by linking the section to a category (described in the next section). The sample in Figure 10-12 is using only six of the possible sections, with the Bottom-Left, Bottom-Center, and Bottom-Right sections providing Enterprise IaaS Services, PaaS Services, and Cloud Management Services, respectively. The large Welcome to Cisco ONE Enterprise Cloud Suite is in the Top-Left position, with Top-Center being filled by Unified Cloud Experience. The final section customized is the Browse Categories menu that is shown but not expanded in the figure.

Figure 10-12 *Prime Service Catalog Showcase*

You will customize and choose the categories for each section of the Showcase in the Service Designer module of Prime Service Catalog. The Showcase is configurable within the Extensions menu. You can see in Figure 10-13 where the Middle-Left and Middle-Right components are currently empty. When an element is left empty by design, or a logged-in user doesn't have access to view the services within a category, Prime Service Catalog will adjust the remaining components to fill the page in an optimal way, and hide any indication something may be missing.

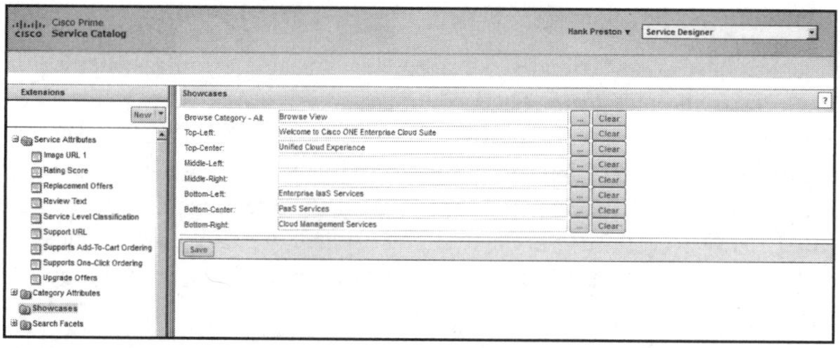

Figure 10-13 *Prime Service Catalog Showcase Configuration*

Categories

Categories are the main organizational component of Prime Service Catalog. As discussed in the prior section, the front page of the portal is built by displaying categories in configurable page elements. Categories are also used within the actual service catalog to group and display services to end users. A single individual service can be within many different categories, grouped together in whatever makes sense for an organization.

You will create many categories for your enterprise from the Service Designer module and in the Categories menu. As shown on the General page in Figure 10-14, you give each category a name and a description. You will want to make sure both are user friendly and read how you want your end users to see them, as each is displayed exactly as entered when used within the portal. Switching to the Presentation page while editing a category, you have the opportunity to link an image to the category for when it is displayed to the end user. The image can be even more valuable than the name in relating to the user the purpose of the category. You can manage the services and subcategories while editing a category, or when editing the individual services.

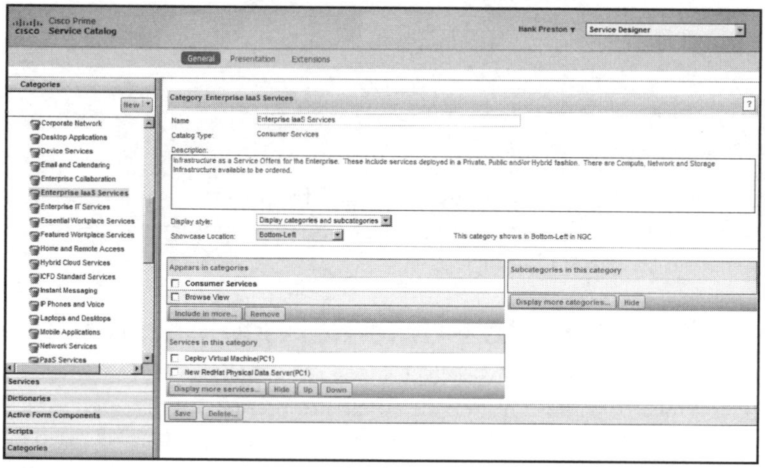

Figure 10-14 *Prime Service Catalog Category Edit View*

Services

You want your end users to have a user-friendly portal to view and request infrastructure services, and that is the primary goal of Prime Service Catalog. As part of Cisco ONE Enterprise Cloud Suite, Prime Service Catalog makes it very easy to build and customize services based on catalog offers from UCS Director and Intercloud Fabric for Business. More on that integration is covered later in the chapter in the section "Connecting and Importing to Prime Service Catalog." However, Prime Service Catalog services are very powerful and customizable objects that can meet the need of delivering any type of cloud, technology, or even nontechnology services your organization may offer users.

All services available within the catalog are located in the Service Designer module of Prime Service Catalog. Figure 10-15 shows a sample service for New Employee On Board that ships as part of example content with Prime Service Catalog. The different pages of the service offer you the ability to provide the name and description, link image files, manipulate the user input form, and build the logic needed to deliver the service, including any needed approvals or integrations with external systems.

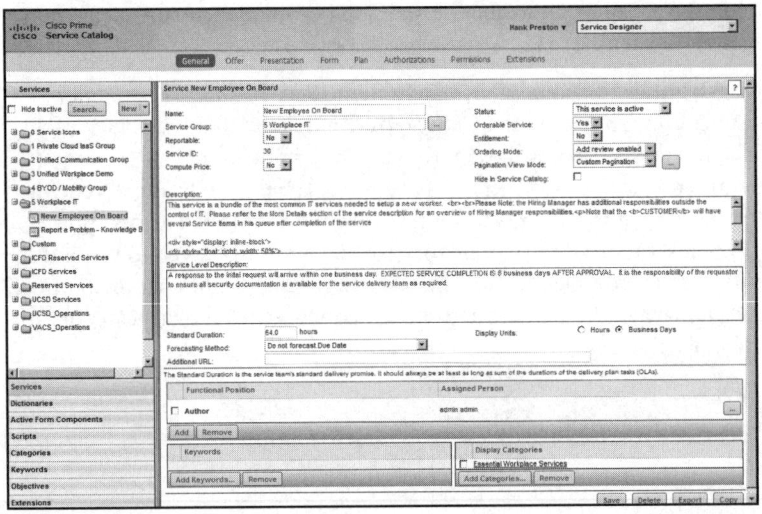

Figure 10-15   *Example Prime Service Catalog Service*

Designing and building services like New Employee On Board from scratch is out of scope for the CLDADM exam and this book; however, understanding the importance of services and what is included is good background knowledge.

Connecting and Importing to Prime Service Catalog

With a basic understanding of the key Prime Service Catalog components, you can now move to integrating UCS Director with Prime Service Catalog to present your created catalogs to end users. Prime Service Catalog and UCS Director are both components of Cisco ONE Enterprise Cloud Suite; you will find it straightforward to connect the tools together and begin customizing the auto-created services for end-user consumption.

Log in to Prime Service Catalog as Site Administrator and navigate to **Administration > Manage Connections** to see the interface shown in Figure 10-16. From this interface you can integrate UCS Director, Intercloud Fabric for Business, and Puppet with Prime Service Catalog. Clicking the button with the plus symbol will let you add a new UCS Director connection. Provide the connection information for the UCS Director instance, making sure to provide credentials for an account in UCS Director with System Admin access level. The Identifier field is a three-character alphanumeric code used within Prime Service Catalog to distinguish different external cloud connections. The Name field will be a user-friendly name used for this UCS Director connection. The Export User setting determines how users and groups will be shared between the two applications. If you will be using locally created accounts within the programs, leave the box unchecked and Prime Service Catalog will import users from UCS Director and create accounts within Prime Service Catalog. If you are integrating with an external directory such as Microsoft Active Directory, then check this box. You will almost always want to check Enable Background Sync to ensure Prime Service Catalog and UCS Director regularly communicate the state of services and resources.

NOTE   The integration of Puppet with Prime Service Catalog is out of scope for this book and exam.

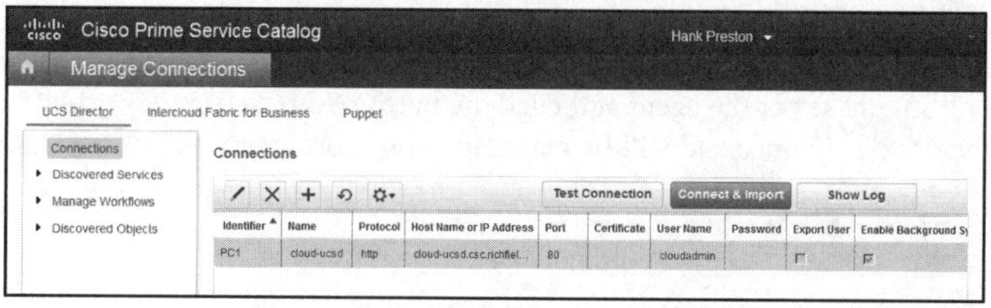

Figure 10-16   *Prime Service Catalog Manage Connections Menu*

Once you have added a new connection, click **Connect & Import** to make the initial connection and import catalogs, workflows, containers, VMs, vDCs, users, and groups all to Prime Service Catalog. The import can take some time depending on the number of objects within UCS Director being imported and processed. Once complete, you can expand the Discovered Objects menu on the left side of the Manage Connections window to view the different elements that have been discovered and imported into Prime Service Catalog. Figure 10-17 shows the discovered catalogs. You can similarly investigate each of the other object types listed.

10

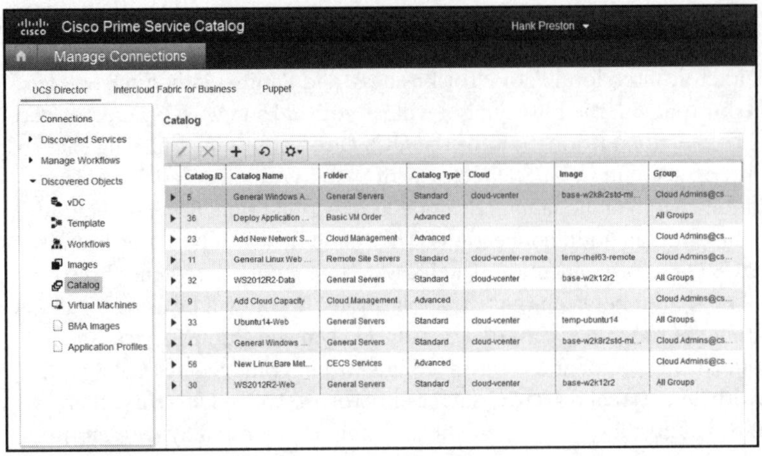

Figure 10-17 *Discovered Catalogs*

Once you have set up your first connection to a UCS Director or Intercloud Fabric for Business system, you will need to enable two settings within Prime Service Catalog to complete the integration. The first setting is found at **Administration > Settings**. It is an On/Off setting called UCSD Scheduler and must be set to On after at least one connection is set up. Shown in Figure 10-18, the simplest way to find it is to use the Find function in your browser and search for **UCSD**. The second setting is to start the Control Agent UCSDAgent. You will find this setting within the **Service Link** module of Prime Service Catalog, as shown in Figure 10-19. Simply select the agent and click the button **Start Selected**. Both of these steps need to be done only once and will be maintained on subsequent system restarts.

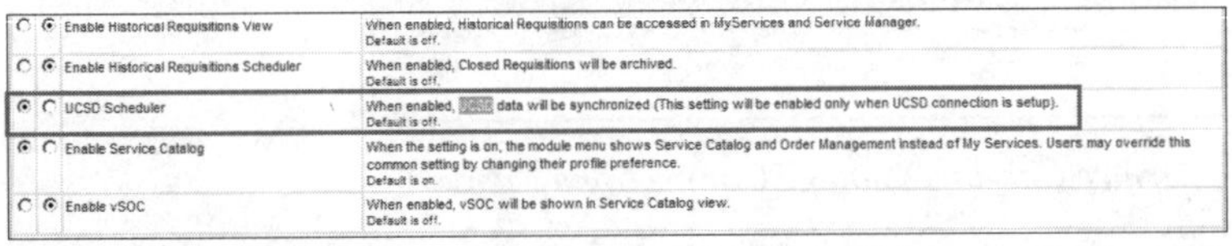

Figure 10-18 *UCSD Schedule Setting*

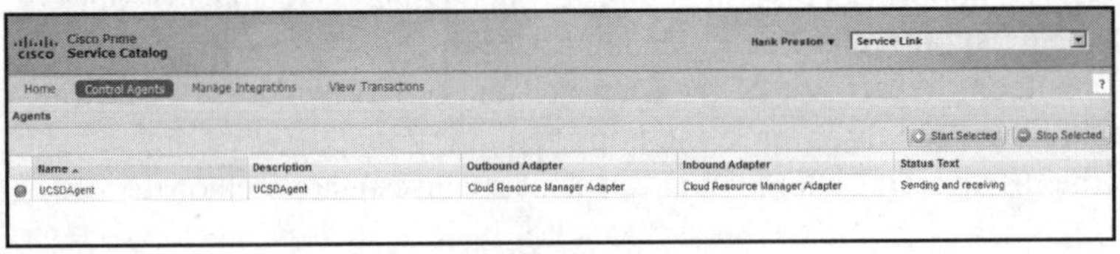

Figure 10-19 *Control Agent UCSDAgent*

Customizing Auto-Created Services

You have now imported all the catalogs from UCS Director into Prime Service Catalog and created base services that are available to be viewed and ordered by end users. However, the auto-created services are not very descriptive or in a state that you would expect in an ITaaS eStore targeting end users. Figure 10-20 shows an example of a service for a Standard Catalog to order a new Windows 2012 R2 Web Server. As you can see, there is no display icon or description, and even the name isn't very user friendly.

> **WS2012R2-Web(PC1)**
>
> ☆☆☆☆☆ (0)
>
> Order For Others | Order

Figure 10-20 *Sample Auto-Created Service*

Fortunately, you can easily update the service to make it display better within the catalog. To do so, navigate to **Administration > Manage Connections** to open the interface where you did the initial import (refer to Figure 10-16). Under **Discovered Services**, you can see all the different services that were created from the imported catalogs. Figure 10-21 shows the one for the Windows 2012 R2 Web Server from the previous example. However, here it has been customized with a better name and description. Also, it has been added to the Enterprise IaaS Services Category, which if you recall is displayed on the front page of the user portal through the Showcase configuration. You will also want to add a graphic to your services, which you can do from the Presentation tab. You can use one of the image files included with Prime Service Catalog or upload one of your own.

> **Windows 2012 R2 Web Server**
>
> ☆☆☆☆☆ (0)
>
> Order a new virtual server staged with Windows 2012 R2 and placed into the Web Zone of the indicated Virtual Data Center.
>
> Order For Others | Order

Figure 10-21 *Basic Service Customization*

Prime Service Catalog has a robust role-based access control (RBAC) system to determine who can order and even see services. When the initial service was created at import, the permissions were configured to match how the underlying catalog was configured within UCS Director. However, if you need to make changes, you can do that from the Permissions tab in the interface. Figure 10-22 shows an example of this interface; notice the way the permissions are coded with the platform type and identifier included in the name.

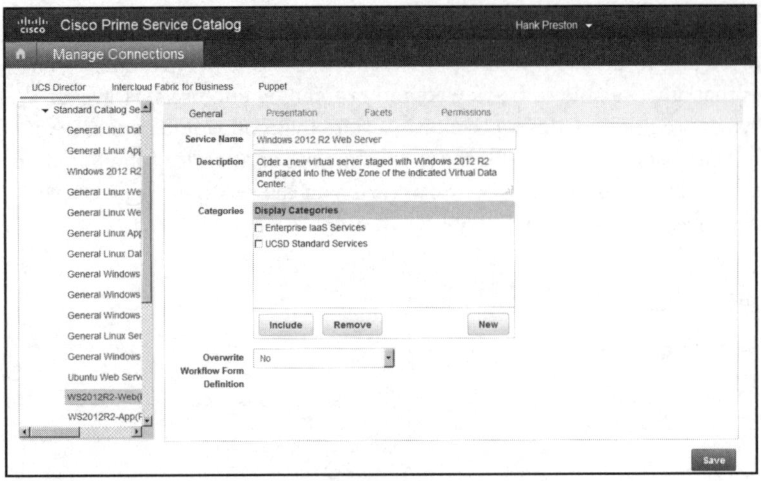

Figure 10-22   *Service Permission Customization*

With the service customized, you can see in Figure 10-23 the new view that users will be presented in the catalog. If you need to do more advanced customizations, such as add approval steps, integrate with external systems, or customize the data displayed on the form, you can do that from the Service Designer module, but that is out of scope for the CLDADM exam and this book.

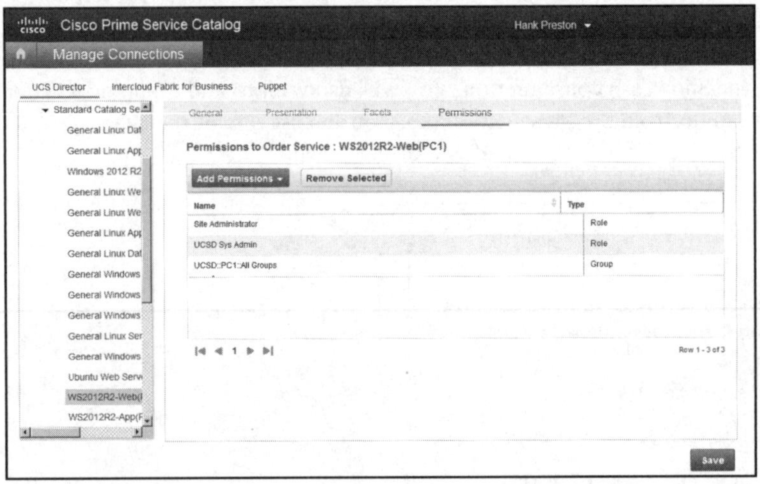

Figure 10-23   *Sample Customized Service*

Ordering a Service with Prime Service Catalog

Within Cisco ONE Enterprise Cloud Suite, Prime Service Catalog is the primary user portal and service catalog where end users will find, order, and manage their cloud resources. Prime Service Catalog is intended to be user friendly and intuitive to learn and use for most end users. It leverages concepts similar to those found ubiquitously on commercial online shopping sites, such as the Shopping Cart.

Finding Services and Their Details

A goal of a cloud administrator should be to make it very easy for users to locate their desired services. You do this by prominently displaying the most common and newest services on the Showcase (the front page), organizing services into clear categories, and building services to be easily found through the search capabilities of Prime Service Catalog.

In Chapter 9 you learned the basics of building and managing the Showcase, and now we'll take a look at how an end user would experience it to locate services. Figure 10-24 shows the Showcase with some areas marked with letter annotations for references. Each of these areas represents a key way users interact with the portal. Table 10-2 provides details on each annotated area of the Showcase and how the end user would use it.

Figure 10-24 *End-User Showcase Walkthrough*

Table 10-2 End-User Showcase Walkthrough Details

Annotation	Details
a	The Browse Categories menu is where users will find the full list of categories of services available within Prime Service Catalog. The expectation is that you as the administrator will provide the quick access and shortcuts to services on the Showcase itself, but the full list will be available through the menu.
b	The Search button will open a text box where users can try to locate a service by a keyword or description. Users will likely leverage the search tool when they know exactly what they are looking for rather than browse through categories.

Annotation	Details
c	The Notifications menu provides users information about any approvals or orders in an ongoing state. From this menu, users can quickly jump to the relevant portal pages for more details.
d	Clicking the Shopping Cart icon will expand it to show the user any items currently waiting to be ordered.
e	Clicking the Manage My Stuff panel will slide it over and provide access to links for My Stuff (an interactive list of the user's resources such as VMs and application templates), Open Orders, and Completed Orders.
f	In the Mid sections of the Showcase, users will find a scrollable list of categories. Clicking one of the categories will navigate to a full listing of services within it. When the IT as a Service eStore becomes large enough, you will find that this is a great way to prominently display the most popular categories.
g	The Bottom sections of the Showcase provide quick access to individual services from the catalog. You might want to leverage these sections for new services, or ones that are particularly popular in your organization.

Often users will come to the portal knowing exactly what service they are in need of. In this case, the Search feature typically is the fastest method for users to order the service and continue. All service names and descriptions will be scanned for search terms entered in the form and displayed back to the user. In Figure 10-25, the user has searched for the term "Ubuntu 14" and is being presented with three matching services.

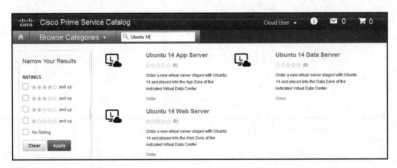

Figure 10-25   *Searching for Services*

When a user clicks a category itself to look through available services, whether this is through the Browse Categories menu or through an item displayed in the Mid section of the Showcase, Prime Service Catalog will provide the user with a display of all available services within the category for browsing and selection. An example view of the category Basic Virtual Machines is shown in Figure 10-26 along with the details for the Ubuntu 14 Web Server that are available to the user by clicking "More…" in the description. This example shows how users are provided an Order button for quick and easy access to place orders for services while browsing.

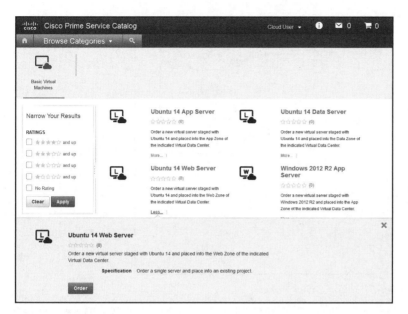

Figure 10-26 *Category and Service Details View Example*

Placing an Order

When a user finds the service that they are looking for, they can then place an order for it. This is done by filling out the order form within Prime Service Catalog and providing the details needed for this particular service. In Figure 10-27 an order form is shown that will provide the user with a new virtual machine. This order form is included with Prime Service Catalog and is used for all Standard Catalog offers imported from UCS Director. End users will have to select one of their available vDCs and provide any customization details required for the service. Upon completing the order form, the user simply clicks Submit to place the order for the new VM.

Within Cisco ONE Enterprise Cloud Suite, Prime Service Catalog provides a single portal and catalog for ordering both private cloud and public cloud resources in a consistent fashion. Orders placed for private cloud VMs would be routed to UCS Director, while orders placed for public cloud VMs would be routed to Intercloud Fabric for Business.

10

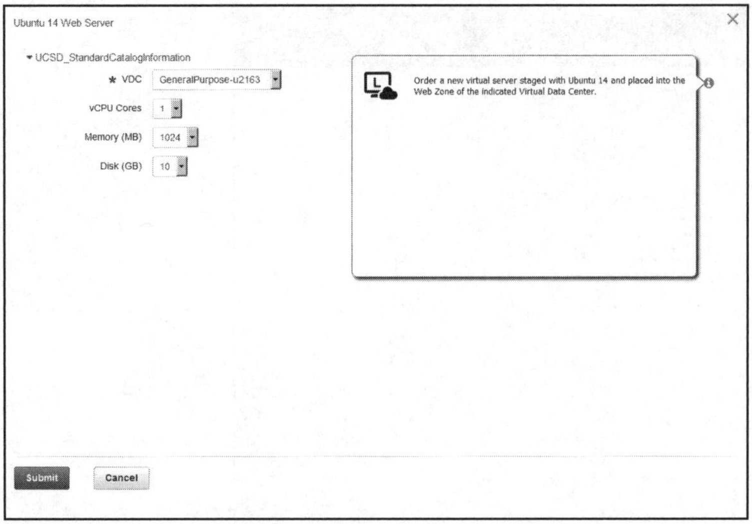

Figure 10-27   *Standard Catalog Order Form*

You have the option as the administrator of Prime Service Catalog to configure each service for immediate ordering, such as the virtual machine service in the previous example, or leverage the Shopping Cart feature. Figure 10-28 shows another example order form for a service. In this case, the end user has the option to Add to Cart rather than Submit. When using the Shopping Cart feature, a user can submit a single order within Prime Service Catalog and have it include multiple individual services. Upon adding a service to the cart, the user will be taken to their cart, shown in Figure 10-29, where they can review the service or services it currently contains. The contents of the Shopping Cart are always available through the Shopping Cart button in the upper-right corner of the portal, also shown in Figure 10-29. When the user is ready to check out, they click the Place Order button within the cart to submit the order for all the services they've collected.

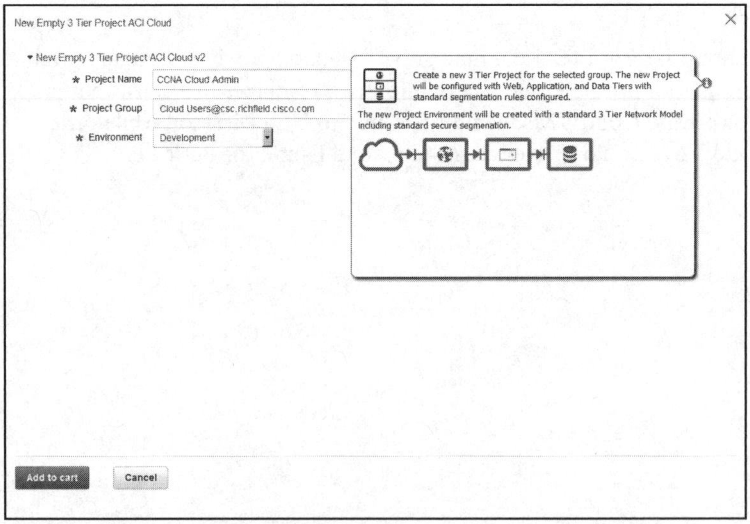

Figure 10-28   *Service Order Form with Add to Cart Option*

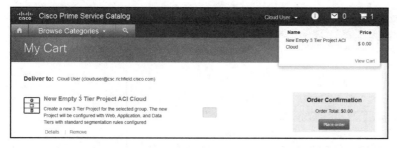

Figure 10-29 *Shopping Cart View*

Checking and Monitoring Status of an Order

After placing an order, an end user might want to check the status of their order and monitor any problems that arise during order fulfillment. End users can use Prime Service Catalog to view orders that are currently open as well as those that have completed. Should a problem occur, an administrator can leverage the Service Request logs within UCS Director to find more details about the order, identify any errors encountered, and, ideally, resolve and continue the order completion.

Key Topic

End-User Order Management in Prime Service Catalog

Immediately after submitting an order within Prime Service Catalog, you will see a notification indicator in the upper-right corner of the portal. By clicking the envelope icon, you'll be shown a display similar to Figure 10-30 where the new order is listed in the Open Orders tab. Click **More** to access details about the order.

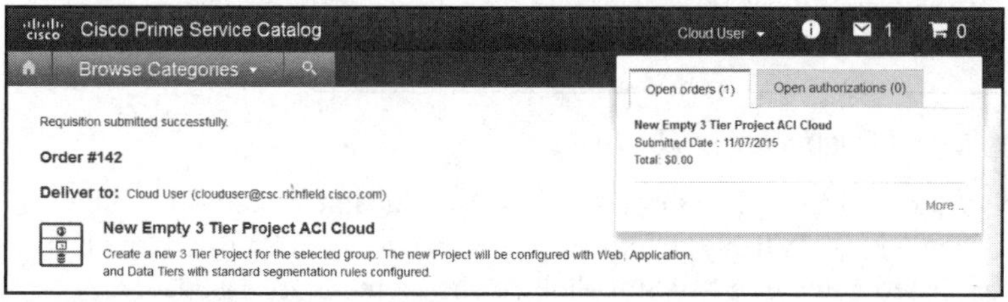

Figure 10-30 *Order Notification Within Prime Service Catalog*

You will now be taken to the Open Orders list within the portal, as shown in Figure 10-31. The basic list view shows the order number and a basic progress indicator. By clicking the **Order#** link, you will see details on the order. Within the Comments & History section, shown in Figure 10-32, you can view the status of the underlying service request from UCS Director that was created for this order. Once an order completes, you can find a list of all previous orders in the Completed Orders view.

10

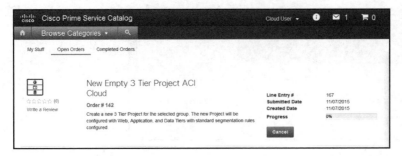

Figure 10-31 *Open Order List*

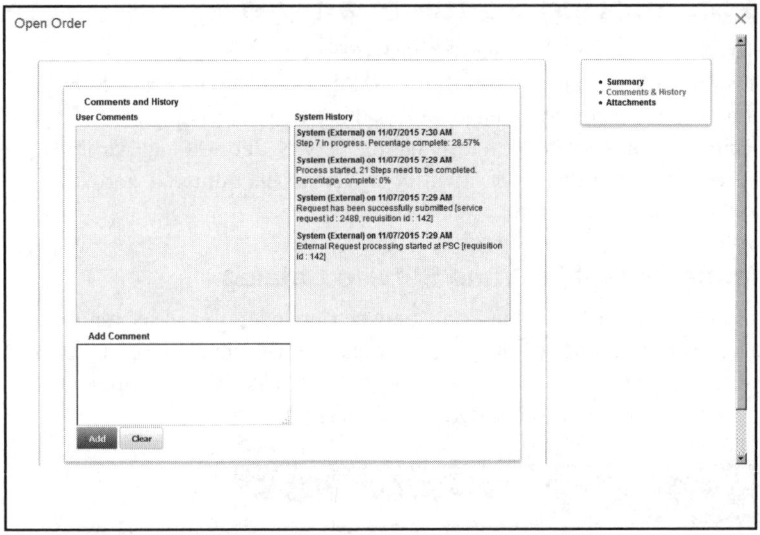

Figure 10-32 *Order Details Comments & History*

Access to the Open Orders and Complete Orders lists is also available directly from the Prime Service Catalog main page. When you expand the Manage My Stuff panel, the links for the order pages are listed below the My Stuff link, as shown in Figure 10-33.

Figure 10-33 *Manage My Stuff Panel*

Administrator Service Request Management in UCS Director

Look back at Figure 10-32 and notice the second entry from the bottom of the list reads "Request has been successfully submitted [service request id: 2489, requisition id: 142]." This indicates the exact service request number within UCS Director that is fulfilling this order. By switching to UCS Director, you can find that exact service request and look at the details of the technical automation fulfilling the order. Figure 10-34 shows the Workflow Status tab of this order, which includes each of the tasks that have been completed. As discussed in the Chapter 9 section "UCS Director Service Requests," you can leverage the other tabs in the view to get detailed information about the processing of the order and any objects created or changed. If a service request fails for some reason, you can leverage these details to resolve the problem and resubmit the request.

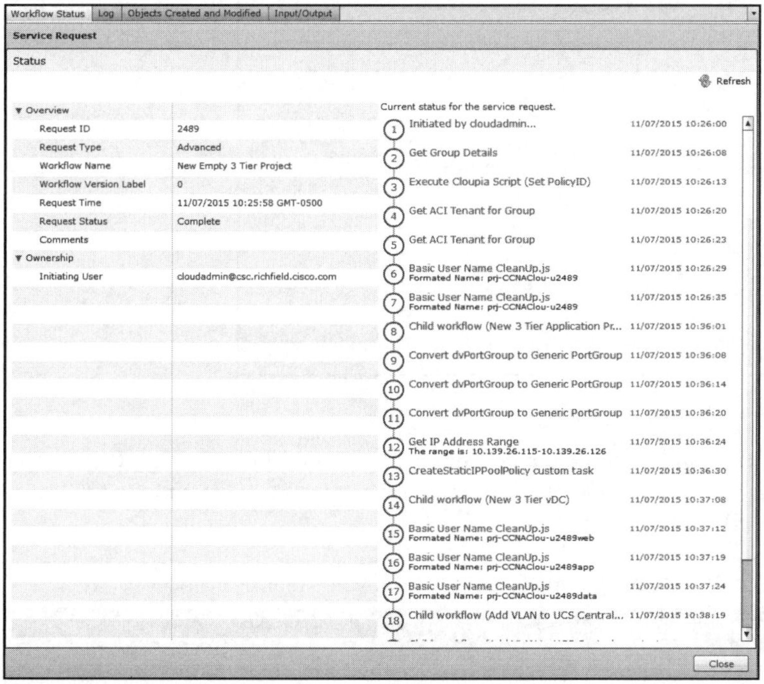

Figure 10-34   *UCS Director Service Request View*

Accessing and Managing New Resources

Enabling your end users to place orders for new virtual machines and other services on demand is a great start, but to truly move into self-service and cloud, you must provide the ability for self-management of those resources as well. User satisfaction won't improve much if they still need to open help-desk tickets or find someone from infrastructure services every time they need to power on or off their resources, resize them, or take snapshots of VMs. Within Cisco ONE Enterprise Cloud Suite, users are provided with methods for self-management in both Prime Service Catalog and UCS Director, so no matter which components of the suite you have deployed, you can enable your end users to manage their own services.

Managing "My Stuff" Within Prime Service Catalog

Prime Service Catalog enables end users to manage their service items (that is, the individual objects that have been ordered by users or assigned to them, including VMs, vDCs, and applications) from within the My Stuff interface of the portal. Figure 10-35 shows the My Stuff screen and the different categories of service items this user has available listed in the left panel. The most common service items users will look to manage are their VMs.

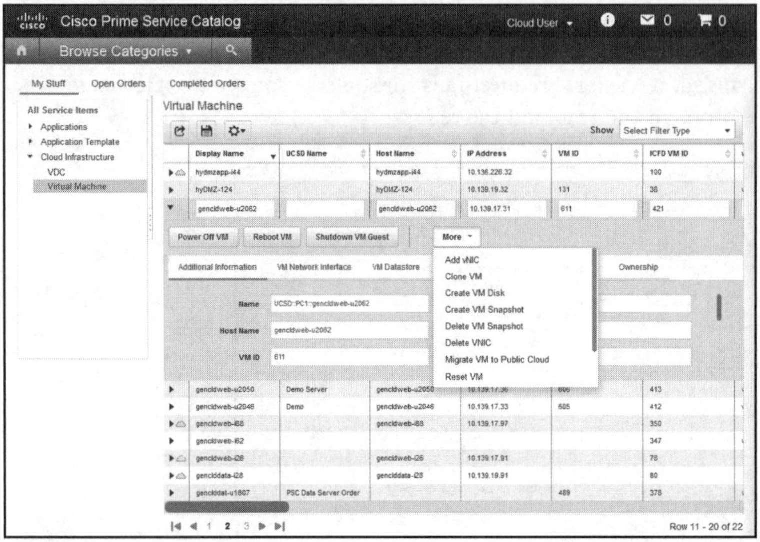

Figure 10-35 *My Stuff Screen*

Prime Service Catalog provides out-of-the-box support for many common lifecycle management tasks for virtual machines, some of which are shown in Figure 10-35 and the full list of which is detailed in Table 10-3.

Key Topic

Table 10-3 Prime Service Catalog Supported VM Lifecycle Actions

Virtual Machine Action	Description
Power On/Off VM	Change the power state of a virtual machine. Note that Power Off is different from Shutdown VM Guest.
Reboot VM*	Tell the guest operating system to reboot.
Shutdown VM Guest*	Tell the guest operating system to shut down.
Add vNIC	Add a new virtual network adapter to a VM. User will need to provide details on port-group assignment and IP information.
Clone VM	Create a copy of the VM and place into a designated vDC.
Create VM Disk	Create a new virtual hard drive and add it to the VM. Does not perform any OS provisioning.

Virtual Machine Action	Description
Create VM Snapshot	Create a new snapshot of the current state of a VM.
Delete VM Snapshot	Delete an individual snapshot of a VM.
Delete VNIC	Remove an individual virtual network adapter from a VM.
Migrate VM to Public Cloud**	Move the VM to an available vDC in a public cloud and maintain the current configuration of the VM.
Reset VM	Execute a power cycle task on the VM. This is different from Shutdown VM Guest.
Revert VM Snapshot	Restore a VM to a previously taken snapshot state.
Standby VM	Place the VM into a hypervisor-level pause state.
Suspend VM*	Execute an OS-level suspend task.

* Requires that the VM have the proper VM management tools for the hypervisor installed.
** Only available when Intercloud Fabric is integrated into Prime Service Catalog.

In addition to taking action on a virtual machine, you will also find details about the virtual machine's configuration within the My Stuff interface. Details such as hostname, IP address, category, guest OS, and much more are all available in the table views listed with each VM entry. Because Prime Service Catalog provides management of both private cloud and public cloud resources, within the table users will have a mixture of both types of resources. The best indicator of private or public status of a VM is the small cloud icon listed next to some of the VMs in Figure 10-35. Those VMs with this icon are public cloud VMs being managed by Intercloud Fabric for Business. Those lacking are private cloud VMs managed by UCS Director. For the public cloud VMs, details about the public cloud provider in use are available as VM details within the table.

Using the UCS Director End-User Portal

In most cases, you will want to deploy Prime Service Catalog as the end-user portal and catalog within your cloud architecture. However, in cases where you are in an early phase of the deployment of the cloud and Prime Service Catalog hasn't been implemented yet, or your requirements don't need the features and capabilities it brings, UCS Director includes a simplified end-user portal that can be leveraged for ordering and managing resources within the private cloud.

UCS Director users configured with an access level of Service End-User will be presented the end-user portal upon logging in to UCS Director. Figure 10-36 shows the Catalog view an end user will see upon logging in to the portal. As an end user, you are able to order any of the Standard, Advanced, or other catalog types your group has access to from within the portal. In the discussion of service requests in Chapter 9, you saw how end users can track the status of any service requests that have been submitted by their group, as well as execute a rollback of one.

10

Figure 10-36 *UCS Director End-User Portal Catalog*

You can also view and manage your VMs from within the UCS Director end-user portal. Navigate to the **Virtual Resources > VMs** page to view a list of all virtual machines contained in the different vDCs owned by your group. By selecting an individual VM, you will see a list of different actions available to you, as displayed in Figure 10-37. Which actions are displayed is determined by the End User Self-Service and User Action Policies configured on the vDC. There are a few options available in UCS Director that are not currently supported out of the box with Prime Service Catalog. Some of these are the ability to mount an ISO image to a VM, access VM credentials and launch a VM client (i.e., RDP, Web, or VMRC access), and move a VM to a different vDC.

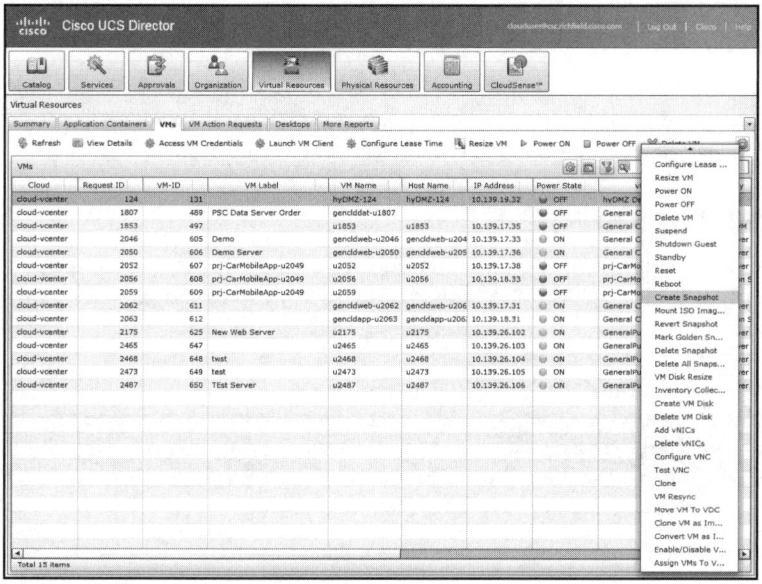

Figure 10-37 *UCS Director End-User Portal VM Management*

Exam Preparation Tasks

As mentioned in the section "How to Use This Book" in the Introduction, you have a couple of choices for exam preparation: the exercises here, Chapter 15, "Final Preparation," and the exam simulation questions on the Pearson IT Certification Practice Test.

Review All Key Topics

Review the most important topics in this chapter, noted with the Key Topics icon in the outer margin of the page. Table 10-4 lists a reference of these key topics and the page number on which each is found.

Key Topic

Table 10-4   Key Topics for Chapter 10

Key Topic Element	Description	Page Number
Section	Describe the purpose and types of UCS Director Catalogs.	290
Paragraph	Understand the differences between cloud templates.	291
Section	Describe the Prime Service Catalog component "The Showcase" and methods for customization.	298
Section	Understand the process for connecting and importing to Prime Service Catalog.	300
Section	Describe methods for customizing auto-created services in Prime Service Catalog.	303
Section	Describe how users find services and their details.	305
Section	Describe how to place an order within Prime Service Catalog.	307
Section	Explain end-user order management in Prime Service Catalog.	309
Table 10-3	Understand the different VM actions available to users within Prime Service Catalog.	312

Complete Tables and Lists from Memory

Print a copy of Appendix B, "Memory Tables" (found online), or at least the section for this chapter, and complete the tables and lists from memory. Appendix C, "Memory Tables Answer Key," also online, includes completed tables and lists to check your work.

Define Key Terms

Define the following key terms from this chapter and check your answers in the glossary:

Standard Catalog, Advanced Catalog, Showcase, Notifications menu, My Stuff, service item

This chapter covers the following exam topics:

1.0   Cloud Infrastructure Administration and Reporting

1.3   Deploy virtual app containers

1.3.a   Provide basic support and troubleshoot app container with firewall, networking, and load balancer

CHAPTER 11

Deploying Virtual Application Containers

The term *container* has become very popular in IT and application development in recent years. In most cases today, container refers to an alternative method of constructing and running software in a lightweight, highly portable, and fast-to-instantiate virtualization technology as an alternative to virtual machines. Linux has had LXC, a method for creating and managing containers, for years. However, it wasn't until Docker containers became available that the term and its use became so widespread.

Within UCS Director, an *application container* is something very different from these containers. Application containers have been available within UCS Director for many years, long before the term became so strongly associated with the containers from Docker and other companies. A UCS Director application container is an object designed to offer end users the ability to rapidly deploy and manage a group of virtual machines organized into one or more network segments, or tiers, as a single entity.

At a network layer, the application container is inherently a secure and isolated environment where the policies designed and offered in the template determine how virtual machines within the container communicate with each other, what traffic is allowed to leave the container, and what services from the container virtual machines are exposed to external users and systems. Some application container types offer network services such as load balancing, stateful firewall, and application inspection capabilities to the container virtual machines.

"Do I Know This Already?" Quiz

The "Do I Know This Already?" quiz allows you to assess whether you should read this entire chapter thoroughly or jump to the "Exam Preparation Tasks" section. If you are in doubt about your answers to these questions or your own assessment of your knowledge of the topics, read the entire chapter. Table 11-1 lists the major headings in this chapter and their corresponding "Do I Know This Already?" quiz questions. You can find the answers in Appendix A, "Answers to the 'Do I Know This Already?' Quizzes."

Table 11-1 "Do I Know This Already?" Section-to-Question Mapping

Foundation Topics Section	Questions
Understanding UCS Director Application Containers	1, 7
Types of Application Containers	2–4
Container Template Setup	5, 8, 9
Managing Deployed Containers	6
Creating Container Catalogs	10

1. An application container within UCS Director refers to which of the following?

    a. An alternative method for deploying software within a lighter-weight virtualization technology than traditional virtual machines

    b. A logical construct composed of one or more network tiers containing virtual or physical compute resources in a private and secured network environment that can be ordered, managed, and deleted as a single entity

    c. A snapshot of a configured virtual machine enabling end users to roll back to previous application states

    d. A logical construct representing a software application that can be deployed onto a selected virtual machine

2. Select all of the options that represent application container types supported in UCS Director.

    a. Docker container

    b. Fenced virtual container

    c. Virtual Security Gateway (VSG)

    d. APIC container

    e. Fabric container

    f. LXC container

    g. VACS container

3. Which technologies can provide firewall services into and within the different application containers available in UCS Director? (Choose all that apply.)

    a. Linux Gateway

    b. Virtual Security Gateway (VSG)

    c. ASA

    d. ASAv

4. Virtual Application Cloud Segmentation (VACS) containers make use of which of the following Cisco technologies? (Choose three.)

    a. Cloud Services Router (CSR)

    b. ASAv

    c. Virtual Security Gateway (VSG)

    d. Nexus 1000v

    e. Application Policy Infrastructure Controller

5. Before creating application containers, which of the following Virtual/Hypervisor Policies must be configured? (Choose three.)

    a. Computing Policy

    b. Storage Policy

    c. End User Self-Service Policy

    d. System Policy

6. True or False. Virtual machines can be added after an application container is deployed.

    a. True

    b. False

7. What will happen when you power off an application container?

    a. You will be presented an interface where you will indicate which container virtual machines to power off.

    b. All deployed virtual machines will be powered off and deleted. Network service appliances will remain powered on.

    c. All deployed virtual machines and network service appliances will be powered off but maintain all configuration and be able to be powered on again.

    d. You cannot power off an application container.

8. Which Gateway Types are options in a fenced virtual container Tiered Application Gateway Policy? (Choose two.)

    a. CSR

    b. ASA/ASAv

    c. Nexus Switch

    d. Linux

9. What are the three available container types within VACS?

    a. VACS – Custom Container

    b. VACS – Flexible Container

    c. VACS – 3 Tier (Internal)

    d. VACS – 3 Tier (Private)

    e. VACS – 3 Tier (External)

    f. VACS – 3 Tier (Public)

10. What catalog type is used when publishing a VACS container template to the service catalog?

    a. VACS container

    b. Application container

    c. Service container

    d. Advanced

11

Foundation Topics

Understanding UCS Director Application Containers

Before we explore the different types of application containers within UCS Director, let us look at their general structure and common aspects.

Every application container is instantiated from a template, and the template is simply an infrastructure model that describes the network, security, services, and compute resources that will be delivered through automation when a new application container is ordered.

The example three-tier application container represented in Figure 11-1 shows one of the most common and basic types of containers you might find offered through UCS Director. This container is composed of separate network segments for web, application, and data servers. Most containers also include a network device to provide routing and security enforcement for traffic to and from the servers in the individual tiers. This container is designed to offer a fairly typical security policy where servers in the web tier can communicate with the app tier, but not with the data tier. Only app tier servers can communicate with the data tier servers. External users are allowed to access only the web servers. Though this example leverages the ubiquitous three-tier model of an application, UCS Director application containers can be built to support one or more tier models.

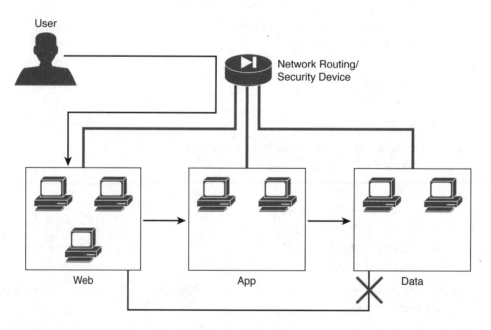

Figure 11-1   *Example Three-Tier Application Container*

In the example load-balanced application container shown in Figure 11-2, you will find a simple one-tier container where a load-balancing service is offered for the virtual machines deployed to the web tier. This makes it easy for users who are building or managing a web application to scale out the service with included management of the load-balancing configuration.

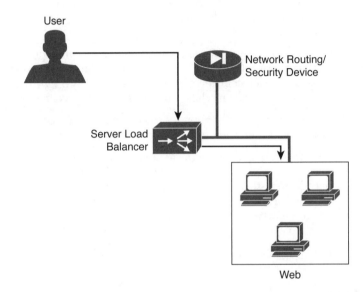

Figure 11-2 *Example Load-Balanced Application Container*

After a new application container is ordered, users manage the container as a single object within UCS Director. Actions such as Power On or Off, Clone, or Delete can be executed on a deployed container. When one of these actions is executed, UCS Director will act on all virtual machines and resources within the container. For example, when you power off a container with three web servers, two application servers, a data server, and a virtual router, all seven of the virtual machines will be shut down. If the template for the container allows for it, you can also add or remove virtual machines from a deployed container. Double-clicking a deployed application container enables you to see and interact with individual elements within the container based on the User Action Policies configured within the template.

Types of Application Containers

Several types of application containers are supported within UCS Director. The main differentiation between the types relates to how the container networking is created, and the virtual and/or physical infrastructure used to create it. Table 11-2 lists the different application container types and the key characteristics of each. Following the table, the two most common types of containers will be explored in more depth.

Key Topic

Table 11-2   UCS Director Application Container Types

Container Type	Description
Fenced virtual container	The original and most common type of application container. Doesn't require any specific network architecture to use.
Virtual Security Gateway (VSG)	Leverages the Cisco Virtual Security Gateway zone-based firewall solution to provide enhanced security for container virtual machines.
APIC container	Tightly integrated with a Cisco Application Centric Infrastructure network deployment, leverages tenant and application profiles for creating application containers. Supports bare-metal workloads as well as VMware virtual machine workloads within the container.
Fabric container	An application container option for customers with a Cisco Dynamic Fabric Automation (DFA) network deployment.
VACS container	Virtual Application Cloud Segmentation* (VACS) is a licensable feature set for UCS Director for customers looking for an advanced application container structure designed specifically for highly flexible and easy-to-deploy virtual network designs using Cisco virtual network technologies for routing, switching, and security.

* VACS was previously known as Virtual Application Container Services.

Fenced Virtual Container

Fenced virtual containers can be used in any VMware-based deployment with UCS Director. The biggest advantage of this container type is that it does not require any particular network hardware, software, or topology. The virtual network for a fenced virtual container can be provided by a standard VMware vSwitch, a VMware Distributed vSwitch, or a Cisco Nexus 1000v.

An application container requires a gateway to allow the deployed virtual machines to communicate with each other and outside of the container. The gateway provides inter-VLAN routing, security enforcement, and IP network address translation (NAT) capabilities. Fenced virtual containers support two different types of gateway devices, a Linux VM or a Cisco ASA. UCS Director can leverage any available Linux VM template as the gateway by taking advantage of the IP forwarding and embedded firewall feature (IPTables) within all Linux distributions. And for deployments, where an enterprise-class stateful firewall with application inspection option is required, the Cisco ASA or ASAv can be used (requires licensing of the ASAv).

Templates for a fenced virtual container without a gateway can be built. In these templates, you will need to address the networking design and deployment to enable communication to and from the container virtual machines outside of the template and default workflows used to build the application container. One way to accomplish this would be to build a custom workflow based on the out-of-the-box example that provides the networking needs of your environment.

Fenced virtual containers can optionally be deployed with a load-balancing policy to leverage an F5 BIG-IP application delivery controller as part of the container template. When included in a template, UCS Director will create and manage virtual server and server pool objects within the BIG-IP device automatically, but as of UCS Director 5.4, the VLAN and NAT settings within the gateway and BIG-IP device itself must be configured manually or through more customized infrastructure automation workflows. Providing automated configuration of these features as part of the fenced virtual container automation will be addressed in a future release of UCS Director.

In a fenced virtual container, the gateway device provides the security enforcement based on the policies configured in the template. This means that enforcement is done at network boundaries between container tiers, or between the container and devices outside the container. Communication within each tier is completely open and allowed. The VSG and VACS container options provide capabilities for more enhanced security by leveraging the Virtual Security Gateway and Nexus 1000v from Cisco to further segment the east-west communication within and between tiers. The security term *microsegmentation* has been coined to refer to a security style leveraging security between and within traditional security zones.

VACS Container

Virtual Application Cloud Segmentation (VACS) is an optional feature license for UCS Director available for customers looking to simplify the consumption of the robust virtual networking capabilities provided by Cisco to VMware and Hyper-V environments (VACS support for HyperV is roadmapped for CY2016). The VACS solution within UCS Director provides the following benefits to customers:

- Offers single per-hypervisor host license for required virtual network components
- Simplifies the installation and upgrade of the Nexus 1000v Virtual Switch, Virtual Security Gateway (VSG), Cloud Services Router (CSR), and Prime Network Services Controller
- Enables end users to deploy application containers backed by Cisco switching, routing, and security services
- Ensures consistent cloud tenant segmentation

VACS containers are built using proven and best-of-breed technologies. Figure 11-3 illustrates a VACS deployment and a sample application container. UCS Director provides the underlying infrastructure management and automation solution for the application container deployment. The installation of VACS into UCS Director adds the content (workflows and tasks) needed to install, upgrade, and manage the virtual network components as well as deploy and manage the application containers themselves. A first step of the installation involves deploying the Nexus 1000v Virtual Supervisor Module (VSM) into the virtualization platform in use. This installation is fully automated and doesn't require any manual configuration on the part of the cloud administrator. Prime Network Services Controller will also be automatically deployed, and it will be used to construct and deploy the network policies each time a new container is ordered. Depending on the template configuration, each application container will include a CSR, VSG, and server load balancer as required. These instances are dedicated to the container, and their life cycle will be managed as part of the container itself.

11

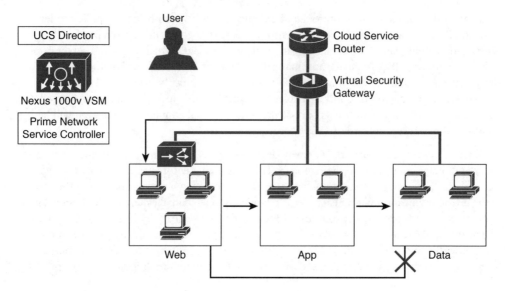

Figure 11-3   *VACS Deployment and Sample Container*

When comparing and evaluating using VACS over the fenced virtual container option within UCS Director, you should consider the following:

■ With VACS deployed, you will be able to leverage the Nexus 1000v for managing application container virtual networks as well as noncontainer-related virtual networks. This will provide you with the full Cisco switching feature set available with the Nexus 1000v Advanced License.

■ Each VACS container leverages a CSR to provide a stateful external firewall including Layer 7 application inspection of common applications including HTTP, HTTPS, FTP, DNS, ICMP, SQLnet, MSSQL, and LDAP.

■ The VSG provides east-west traffic protection, enabling you to build security policies much more granular than the network boundary–based security available with Fenced Virtual Containers.

■ By leveraging the CSR as the container gateway, your containers have available the full enterprise routing capabilities available, including dynamic routing, quality of service (QoS), VPN, and monitoring services such as NetFlow.

■ For deployments where you are looking to avoid leveraging private container networks and NATing at the gateway, VACS offers more flexible options for IP subnet, routing, and NAT.

■ Server Load Balancing (SLB) is also offered as an optional feature for each VACS container and requires no external hardware or software licenses. SLB within VACS is built on the open source HAProxy load balancer widely available and used in many enterprises and cloud applications. With VACS, you can offer this service to a container tier without any manual configuration of HAProxy itself.

Container Template Setup

Having explored the details of fenced virtual and VACS application container types, we will now walk through how to build templates and deploy each type of container. Before creating your first application container template, you need to address the prerequisites for each container type, which are covered first.

Fenced Virtual Containers

UCS Director deploys fenced virtual containers into a VMware vCenter–based cloud or virtual account, so be sure to add this account before beginning the container template process. Your container templates will also need to have access to virtual machine images (that is, VM templates) for the different VMs that will be provisioned into the new containers. This includes an image for a Linux Gateway VM if your containers will be leveraging one for the network boundary of the container. If you will be using an ASAv as the gateway, you will need to upload the ASAv OVA file to UCS Director before beginning to create the Container Policies. You can upload the OVA file by navigating to **Administration > Integration > User OVF Management**. The remaining portion of this walkthrough will leverage a Linux VM as the gateway, as this is the most common deployment method.

Once you have the VMware Cloud connected and ready, you can create the needed Virtual/Hypervisor Policies that will be used during application container provisioning to properly place and configure new virtual machines deployed. Fenced virtual containers use these policies in a very similar way as virtual data centers (vDCs), covered in Chapter 9, "Automating Cloud Infrastructure with UCS Director." Figure 11-4 provides a summary of the policies you will need to configure as well as their purpose. You will need to create VMware Computing and VMware Storage Policies to indicate on which vSphere hosts or clusters, and which data stores or data store clusters, to deploy the new virtual machines. A VMware Network Policy is used for the configuration of the gateway's outside interface. The inside interfaces and all virtual machine interfaces will be configured based on the container tiers described within the template. A VMware System Policy is used to configure DNS and time zone information on virtual machines. The container virtual machine naming convention will reflect the container name itself rather than what is configured in the System Policy. A Cost Model is optional in a fenced virtual container template configuration, but can be helpful when an enterprise is looking to implement a showback/chargeback policy as part of the private cloud deployment. Also, the End User Self-Service Policy is optional, but in most cases you will want to enable your users to have some level of administration over the container and its virtual machines.

11

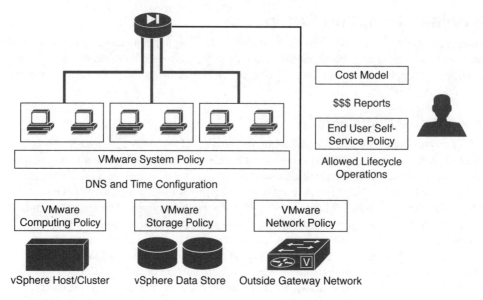

Figure 11-4 *Fenced Virtual Container Virtual/Hypervisor Policies*

When a new fenced virtual container is ordered based on one of the configured templates, UCS Director executes a workflow to do the automation to build the container network and deploy the needed virtual machines. UCS Director ships with sample workflows for deploying the container, and in most cases only very minor modifications are needed. It is recommended that you clone the provided out-of-the-box workflows, make the needed changes for your environment, and use the cloned workflow in your container templates.

Navigate to **Policies > Orchestration > Workflows** just as you would when building or managing any other automation workflow. As shown in Figure 11-5, you will find two sample workflows for Fenced Containers in the folder **Default > Containers**. The work-flow "Fenced Container Setup" is used for Linux Gateway–based templates, and "Fenced Container Setup – ASA Gateway" is used for Cisco ASA–based templates. Clone the workflow based on your needs (the screenshots and remaining walkthrough are for a Linux Gateway container) and give it a descriptive name.

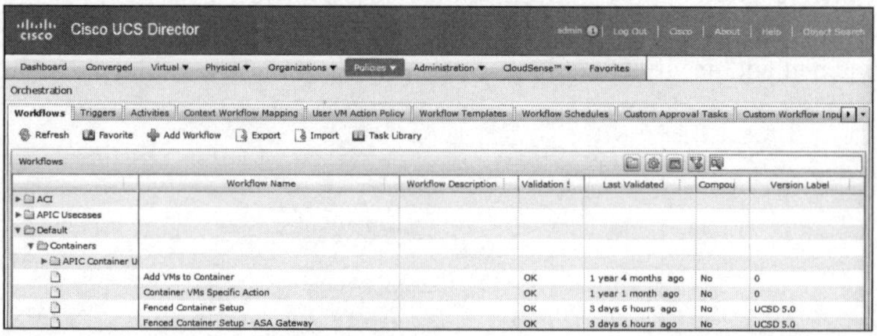

Figure 11-5 *Fenced Container Workflows*

Open the Workflow Designer for your newly cloned workflow to make the needed changes. The first task in the workflow should be Allocate Container VM Resources; double-click it to open and edit its task inputs, as shown in Figure 11-6. Choose the appropriate Virtual Network Type for your VMware deployment and enter the name of the vSwitch or DVSwitch. In our example we are using a Nexus 1000v DVSwitch named VSM. You must submit the changes to the task by clicking **Next** and **Submit**, not simply close it after making the change. With the changes to the task submitted, close the workflow designer.

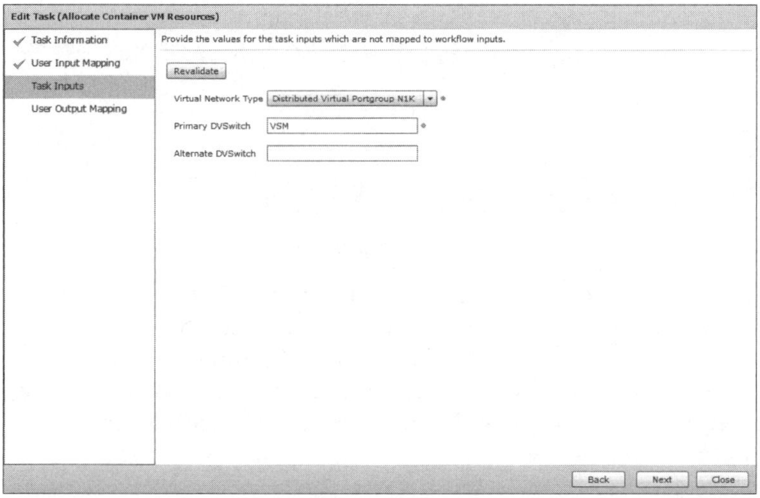

Figure 11-6   *Fenced Container Workflow Virtual Switch Configuration*

You have now completed all the preparation steps needed, and can begin creating the fenced virtual container policies and templates. Navigate to **Policies > Application Containers** for the remaining setup steps. Your goal is to create an application container template from which you can provision new application containers; however, the template requires available policies to properly provision the network elements. First navigate to the Tiered Application Gateway Policies tab and click **Add Policy**. On the first page, Policy Specification, shown in Figure 11-7, provide a Policy Name, optional Policy Description, Gateway Type (Linux, ASA, or ASAv), and Select Virtual Account for your VMware Cloud. Figure 11-7, and some later figures, shows the edit view of a policy rather than the creation view, the only difference between them being that you can't edit a policy name. Click **Next** to move forward.

11

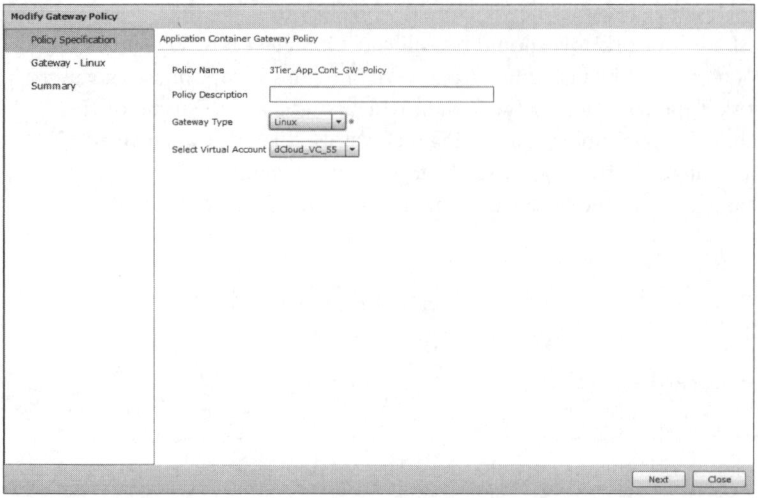

Figure 11-7 *Application Container Gateway Policy Specification*

On the second page, shown in Figure 11-8 for Gateway – Linux, you provide the details for the Linux Gateway that will be created for each new container. Select the VM image that will be used as the basis for each gateway and provide virtual hardware specifications. Provide the root credentials for the template and indicate if you want the credentials shared with end users. Click **Next** and move to the final page where you can click **Submit** after reviewing a summary of the policy you've configured.

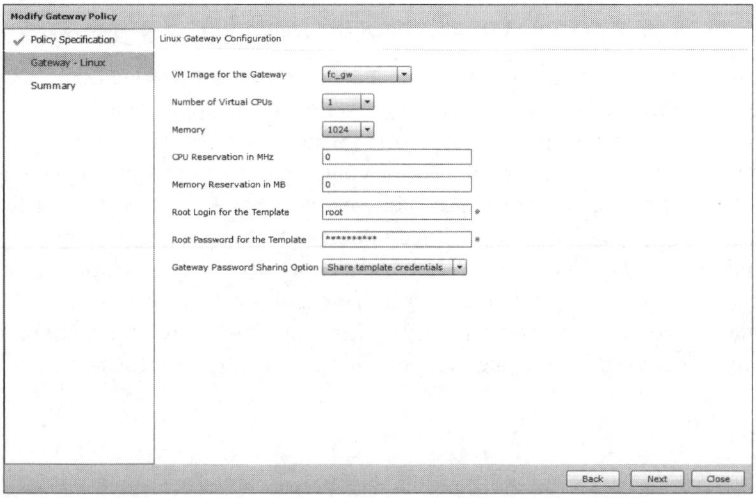

Figure 11-8 *Application Container Linux Gateway Policy*

Now navigate to the Virtual Infrastructure Policies tab and click **Add Policy**. The Virtual Infrastructure Policy will be used in the fenced virtual container template creation in the next step, and it refers to the gateway and, if being used, F5 Load Balancer policy. On the first page of the policy wizard, shown in Figure 11-9, you determine the container type being configured and the virtual account that will be used. Click **Next** and on the second page, shown in Figure 11-10, check the **Gateway Required** box (if it isn't already checked) and select the policy you configured in the previous step. Click **Next** twice to skip the F5 Load Balancer Information page, and then **Submit** the new Virtual Infrastructure Policy.

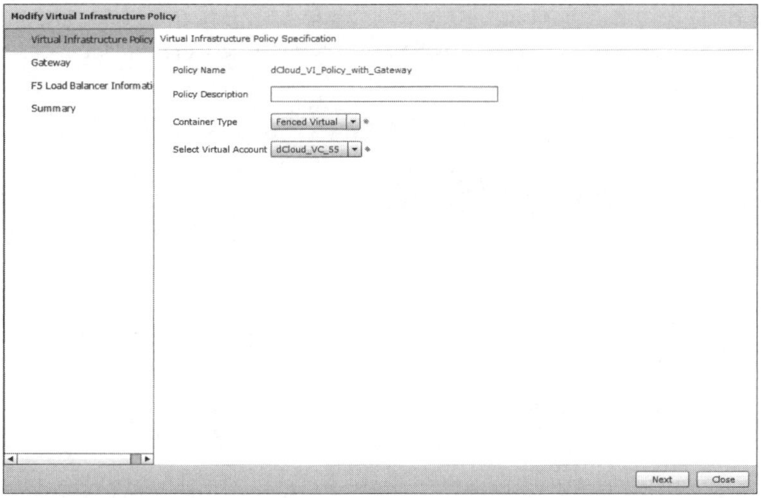

Figure 11-9   *Virtual Infrastructure Policy Specification*

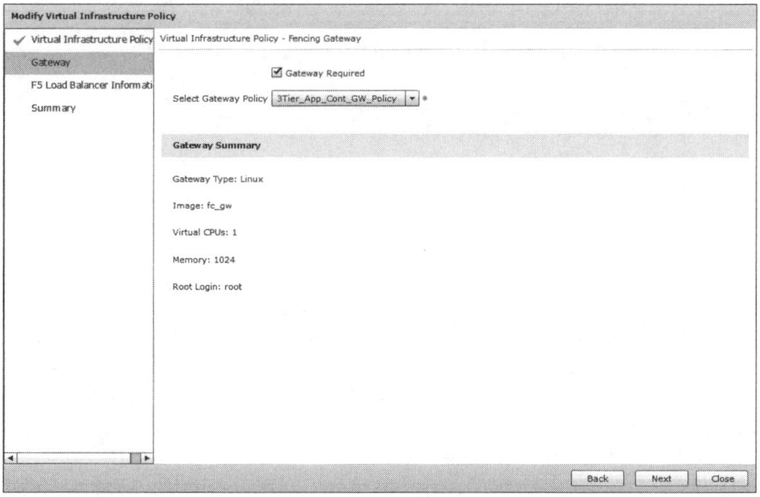

Figure 11-10   *Virtual Infrastructure Policy Gateway*

You are now ready to move to the **Application Container Templates** tab and create a fenced virtual template. Click the **Add Template** button to open the wizard. On the first page, provide a template name and optional description and click **Next**. On the second page, select the Virtual Infrastructure Policy you created in the previous step and click **Next**. You will now be on the third page of the wizard, shown in Figure 11-11, where networks are configured. Use the table displayed to add the number of tiers you desire your fenced virtual container to have. Keep in mind that in a fenced virtual container, the internal networks are private to the container and not exposed to the rest of the data center network. All traffic in and out of the container will run through IP NAT translation by the gateway. This means that all application containers deployed from a given template will leverage the same private IP network space. Figure 11-12 shows an example configuration for a web tier of a container that is accessed by the add or edit buttons (plus and pencil, respectively) in Figure 11-11. Click **Next** when finished configuring the networks.

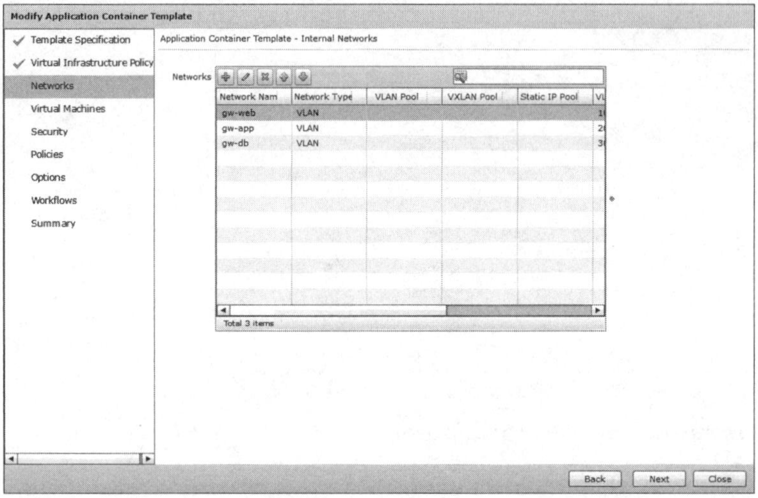

Figure 11-11 *Fenced Virtual Container Template Network Configuration*

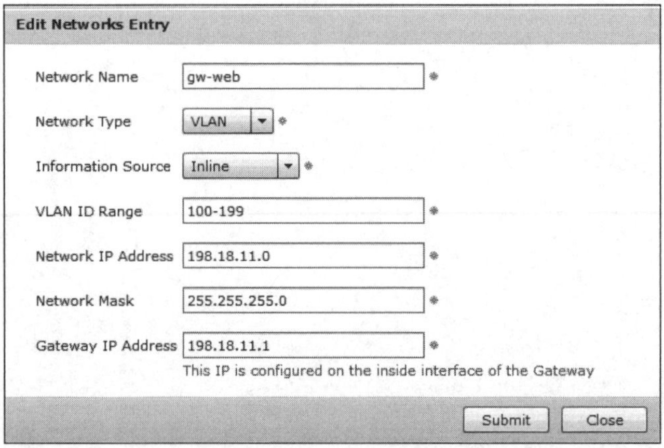

Figure 11-12 *Fenced Virtual Container Template Web Tier Configuration*

Moving on to the fourth page of the wizard, Virtual Machines, shown in Figure 11-13, you determine the number and type of virtual machines that will be available in each tier of the container. Even if you do not wish to initially deploy virtual machines as a container is built—that is, you'll allow users to add virtual machines after deploying the container—you must still add virtual machine entries for each tier of the container. As can be seen in Figure 11-13, you indicate both the maximum and initial quantities of VMs to be deployed. Simply indicate 0 as the initial quantity if you do not want to preprovision virtual machines in new containers, and then choose the template. Click **Next** to continue.

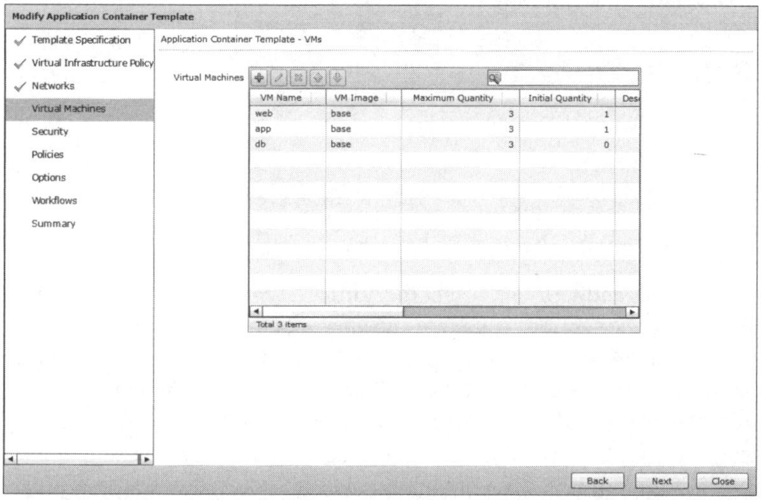

Figure 11-13 *Fenced Virtual Container Template Virtual Machine Configuration*

On the Security page, displayed in Figure 11-14, you configure the port mappings and outbound ACLs that will govern the traffic allowed in and out of the container. Because a fenced virtual container is designed to have a completely private internal network, you need to explicitly map any ports for services you wish container virtual machines to provide externally. The Remote IP Address fields are determined by the configurations you selected when configuring the networks and VMs for the container template. Also, by default no traffic will be allowed from the virtual machines out of the container. This includes standard services like DNS, LDAP, HTTP, etc. If you want container VMs to be able to access these types of services, be sure to provide the needed ACLs in the Security configuration. The configurations made here will be enforced on the gateway using platform capabilities. In our example, the Linux Gateway will leverage IPTables to apply these policies. Click **Next** to continue.

11

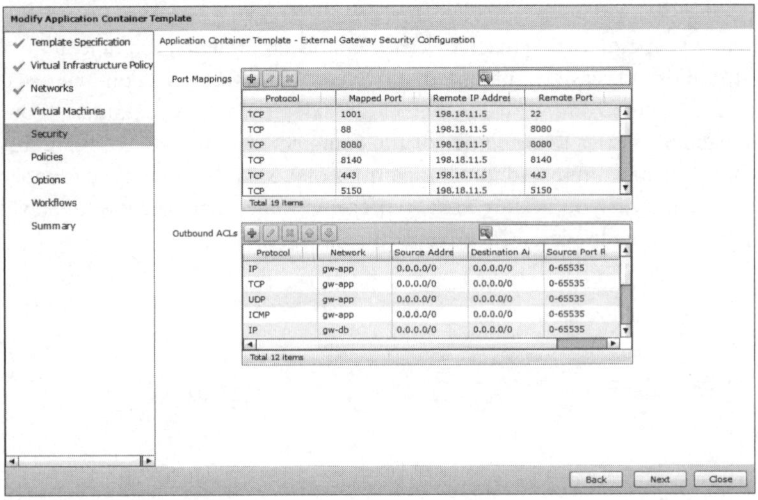

Figure 11-14 *Fenced Virtual Container Template Security Configuration*

On the next two pages, Policies and Options, select the Virtual/Hypervisor Policies that you configured in preparation. On the Options page you can also indicate whether to allow end users to delete their own containers, as well as leverage VNC-based console access to container VMs. On the second-to-last page of the wizard, Workflows, search for and select the customized workflow that you created where your virtual switching network was indicated. And then finally submit the template creation after reviewing the Summary.

Having completed the template creation wizard, you can now select your template and click **Create Container** to build your first fenced virtual container. As shown in Figure 11-15, you simply need to provide a container name, optional label, and group to own the new container. The container name must be less than 8 characters long to be valid because the container name is used as part of the virtual machine name, and Microsoft Windows restricts hostnames to 15 characters. Container names longer than 8 characters would have the potential to create invalid Windows hostnames. The creation of a container creates a service request for the workflow execution. Figure 11-16 shows a sample service request Status for a completed container creation.

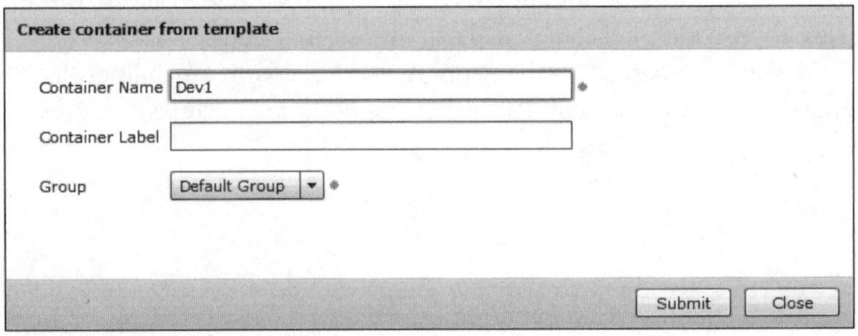

Figure 11-15 *Create Container*

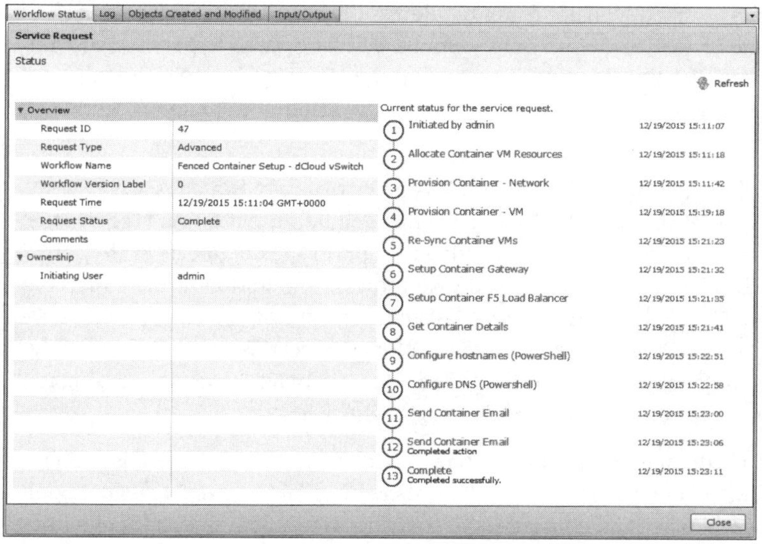

Figure 11-16   *Create Container Service Request Status*

Details on managing and working with a container will be covered in a later part of this chapter, but in Figure 11-17 you can see the newly deployed fenced virtual container in the Application Containers tab.

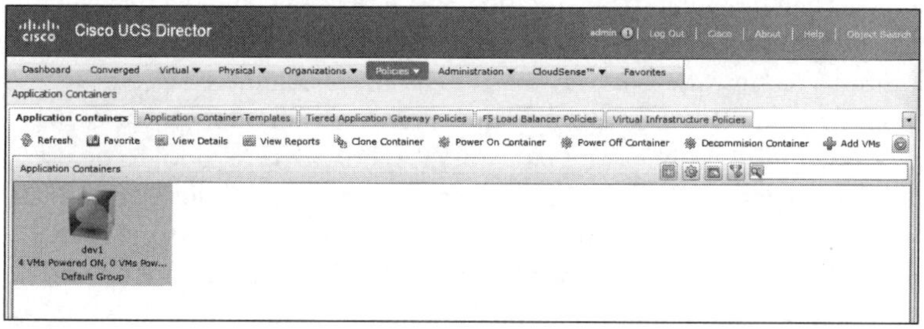

Figure 11-17   *Deployed Fenced Virtual Container*

VACS Containers

Before you can begin building VACS containers with UCS Director, you must install and license the VACS feature. The initial installation of VACS is out of scope for the CLDADM exam and this book, but you can find a detailed walkthrough of the installation and setup on Cisco.com. At the time of this writing, the latest guide is *Cisco Virtual Application Cloud Segmentation Services Installation and Upgrade Guide, Release 5.4STV3.0*, which you can easily find through an Internet search of the title. You can also find video walk-throughs of the installation and configuration by going to Cisco.com and conducting a search for **Virtual Application Cloud Segmentation Install and Upgrade Guides**.

Once you have VACS installed, you are ready to address the prerequisites for creating templates. At the time of writing, VACS only supports VMware-based hypervisor environments, so you will need to have the virtual account for the vCenter Cloud successfully added to UCS Director as well as virtual machine images available for deploying workloads into the new containers.

You can create templates that will use either VLANs or Virtual Extensible LANs (VXLAN) for network segmentation. Using VXLANs is recommended because it doesn't require the underlying physical network to have VLANs added to support the containers as they are built and changed. UCS Director could be used to automate the addition of the VLANs to physical switches and UCS Fabric Interconnects as a custom extension to the VACS workflows. However, by using VXLANs for the segmentation, this need is avoided completely. You will need to ensure a minimum Jumbo MTU size of 1600 bytes is available throughout the physical network to support the overhead of the VXLAN header.

As with fenced virtual container preparation, you need to create Virtual/Hypervisor Policies for VMware Computing, Storage, and System before creating VACS templates. These policies are used to properly place and configure the container virtual machines at deployment. No Network Policies are required for VACS templates.

Key Topic

You will need to create IP subnet pools, static IP pools, and VXLAN or VLAN pools before creating templates. Refer to the section "Network Resource Pools" in Chapter 9 for details on how to configure each of them. Each VACS container will deploy virtual network appliances for routing, security, and services, and these appliances will need management IP addresses. These addresses will be pulled from a static IP pool that you will identify when building a template. A second static IP pool is needed for the virtual router uplink interface. Both of these IP pools need to have the Gateway and VLAN fields completed as part of the configuration. Next, create an IP subnet pool from which the inside subnets for each container will be provisioned. And lastly, create either a VLAN or VXLAN pool to be used to identify each network segment for deployed containers. Be sure to provide large enough pools to meet the potential needs of your VACS usage. Having multiple network resource pools configured and used is supported, but any one template can reference only one of each type at any given time.

Key Topic

After you complete all these prerequisite steps, navigate to **Solution > VACS Container** to create the templates. Click **Add Template** to open the template wizard shown in Figure 11-18. On the first page, Template Specification, provide a name and optional description for the template, as well as identify the type of container you will be deploying. VACS provides three types from which to choose. The first two, VACS – 3 Tier (Internal) and VACS – 3 Tier (External), are very similar with only one difference. Each builds the typical three-tier network structure with a web, app, and data zone. Each also preconfigures security rules to enable the web tier (or zone) to communication with the app tier, enable the app tier to communicate with the data tier, and prevent the web tier from communicating with the data tier, as was represented in Figure 11-1. The difference between the two types is that the Internal version of the template allows communication from outside the container to reach only resources in the web tier, while the External version allows external communication to all three tiers. The last type of container is the VACS – Custom Container. This type enables the designer to control all aspects of the container template. This includes the number and names of the tiers and full control over the security policy applied.

A very useful feature of VACS is that a container can be initially created as one of the 3 Tier models, and then converted to a Custom Container for fine tuning and modification. This can make it easy to quickly get started offering VACS containers to your users, and then adjust as your end-user requirements become more understood. We will initially walk through the creation of a 3 Tier External template and then use this technique to investigate the other options available.

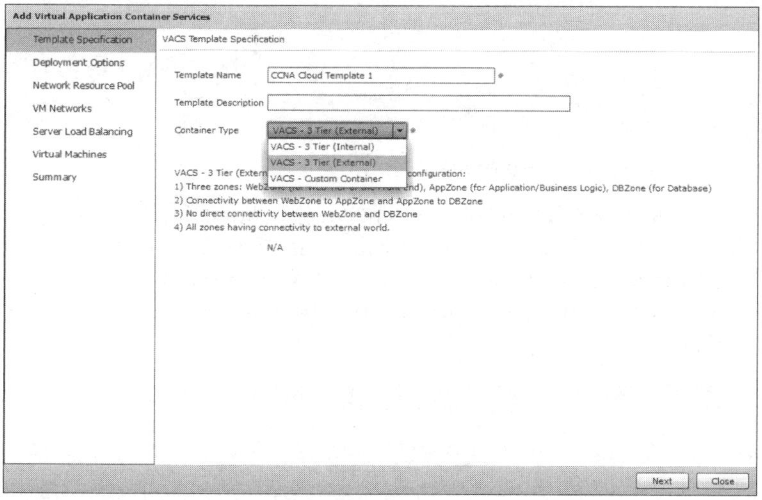

Figure 11-18 *VACS Template Wizard Template Specification*

On the second page, Deployment Options, shown in Figure 11-19, you configure the details of the size and configuration of the basic container features. First indicate whether you will deploy a Small, Medium, or Large template. Clicking the Select button will bring up an interface where you can see the RAM and CPU sizing for the different options that will affect the effective network throughput available to your container virtual machines. Select the proper virtual account, Nexus 1000v, and policies to be used. You can also check or uncheck the Server Load Balancing check box to indicate whether you want to provide SLB to one of the three tiers of the container. We will look at this feature more when we convert to a Custom Container.

11

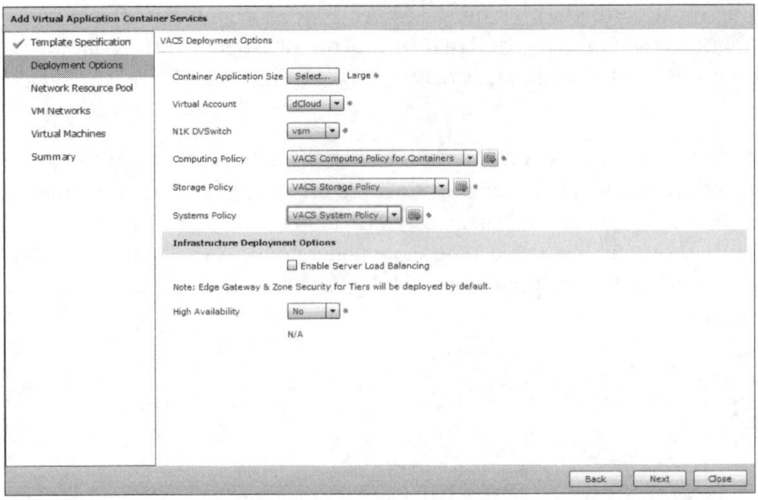

Figure 11-19 *VACS Template Wizard Deployment Options*

Network resource pool configuration is done on the third page, shown in Figure 11-20. Here you reference the management and uplink pools you set up previously. The option for Router IP Type indicates whether the container will leverage NAT from inside to outside (the Private type) or use EIGRP or Static routing to advertise the inside networks outside the container (the Public type).

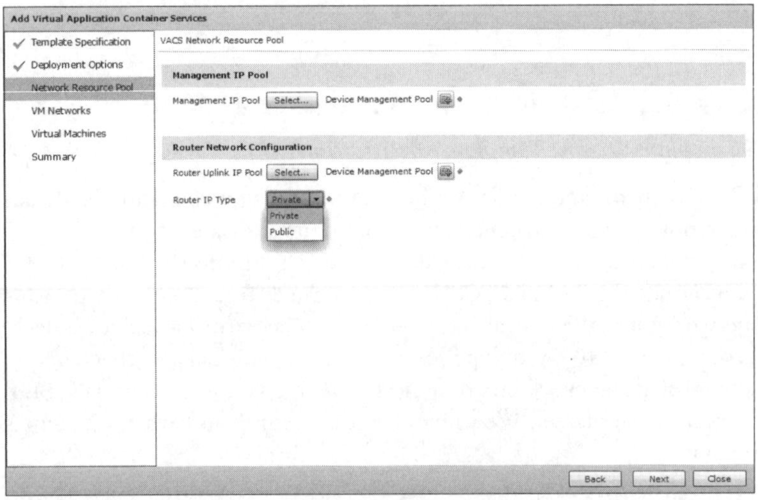

Figure 11-20 *VACS Template Wizard Network Resource Pool*

On the next page, VM Networks, you provide the details for the inside VM networks to be configured in the container. Because tier segmentation is provided by the Virtual Security Gateway based on VM attributes, the 3 Tier Container types only leverage a single virtual machine network. This is very helpful to conserve IP subnets and addresses. In Figure 11-21 you can see how a single lan0 network is configured using the VXLAN and subnet pools configured earlier.

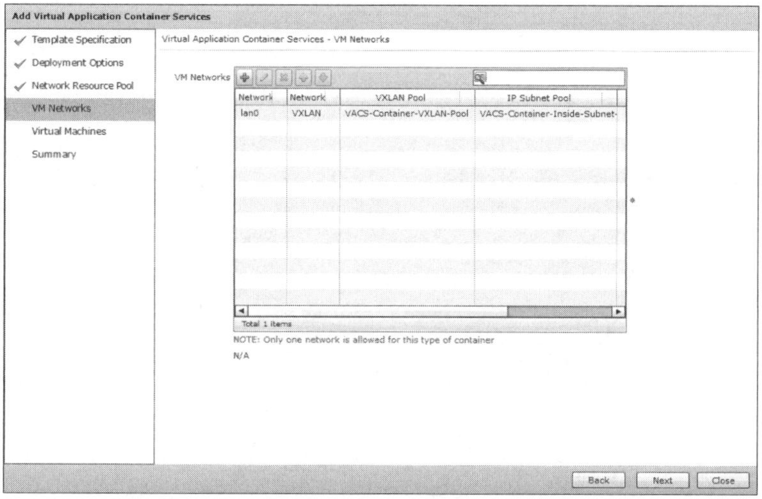

Figure 11-21 *VACS Template Wizard VM Networks*

The final configuration page, Virtual Machines, enables you to configure the details for virtual machines to be added to the container. In Figure 11-22 you can see that a VM entry for each tier has been configured. Add your virtual machines, review the summary on the final page, and click **Submit** to save your new template.

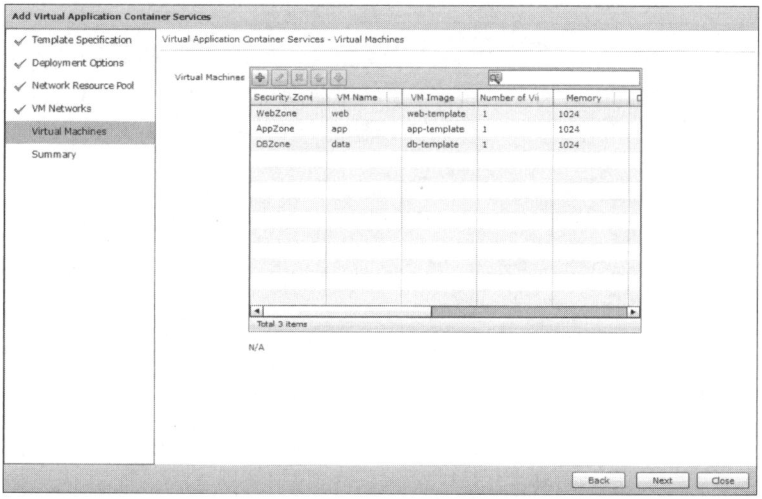

Figure 11-22 *VACS Template Wizard Virtual Machines*

Now that your new template is created, let's convert it to a Custom Template and take a look at the details of the network and security configuration that VACS abstracts and builds based on the default settings for a 3 Tier Container. Select your template and click **Edit Template** to reopen it. As shown in Figure 11-23, when you convert the type to a Custom Container, several new pages in the wizard become available.

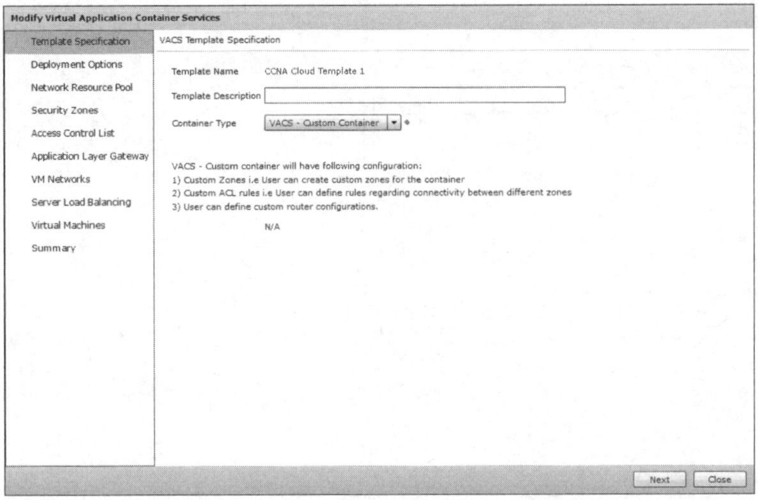

Figure 11-23 *VACS Template Wizard Custom Container Menu*

Click **Next** several times to advance the wizard to the Security Zones page. You could add, edit, or delete zones using buttons in the table, and here in Figure 11-24 we are looking at the Edit Zone Entry interface of the WebZone. You can see by default virtual machines will be placed into proper security zones based on whether web, app, or data appears in the VM Name.

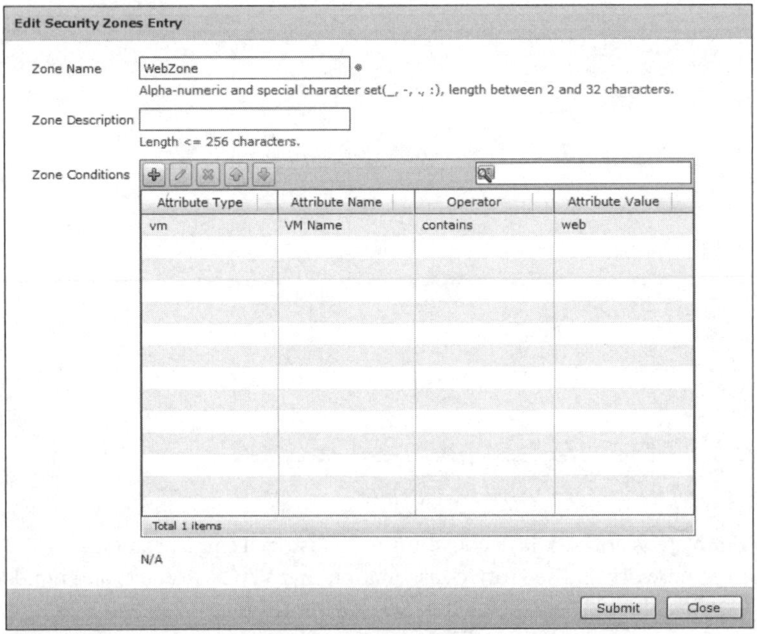

Figure 11-24 *VACS Template Wizard Security Zones*

Click **Next** to move to the Access Control List page, where, as shown in Figure 11-25, you can see the default security rules based on the 3 Tier External container type. From this interface you can add, delete, or adjust the rules to meet your security policy requirements.

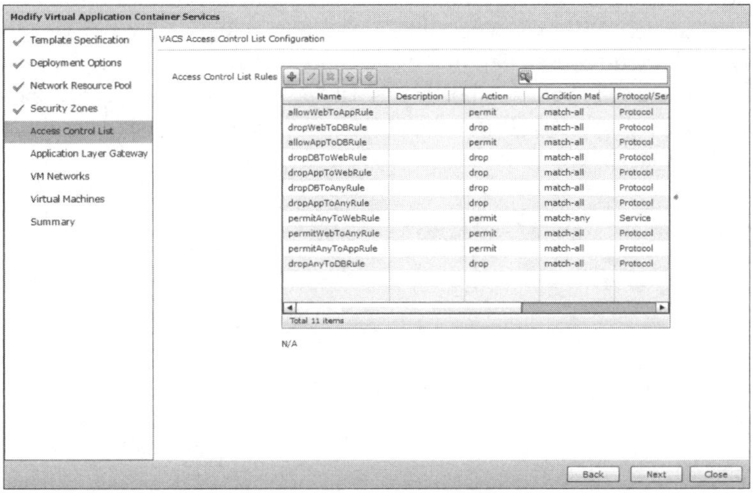

Figure 11-25   *VACS Template Wizard Access Control List*

Click **Next** to move to the last of the new pages available, Application Layer Gateway, shown in Figure 11-26. The page allows you to customize which application layer gateway (ALG) inspections are enabled on the CSR for traffic entering and leaving the container. These inspections look at traffic matching the typical protocols and ports for the enabled applications and make sure that the traffic aligns to the RFC specifications for the protocol. The goal of the inspections is to prevent unauthorized traffic from entering or leaving a container on an open port. In Figure 11-26 you can see the default inspections that are turned on with the 3 Tier Container models, as well as the additional optional protocols you can choose to enable.

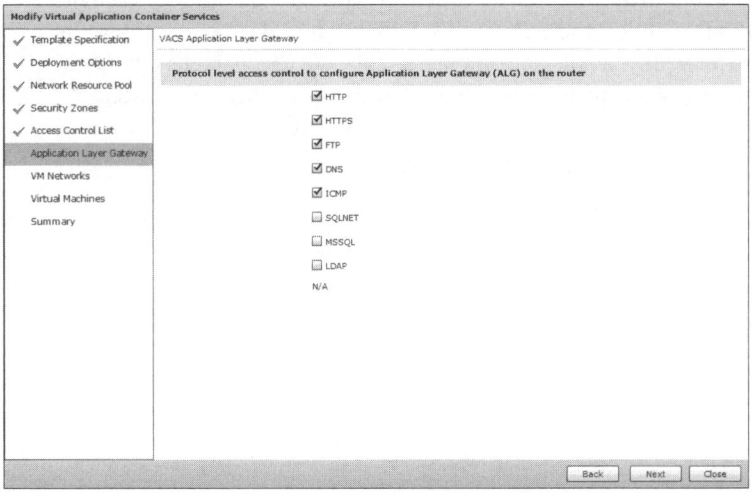

Figure 11-26   *VACS Template Wizard Application Layer Gateway*

Up to this point we have simply looked at the configuration that was applied based on our initial choice of a 3 Tier External Container. Go back to the Deployment Options page and check the box to enable Server Load Balancing. This adds an additional page to the wizard for Server Load Balancing, shown in Figure 11-27. By enabling the feature, VACS will deploy an additional service virtual machine to the container running HAProxy to load balance the virtual machines in the chosen tier. In the current release of VACS, only a single tier can be load balanced in a given container; however, enabling other options is being considered for future releases. Keep the defaults for the SLB feature and click **Submit** to submit your changes to save the container.

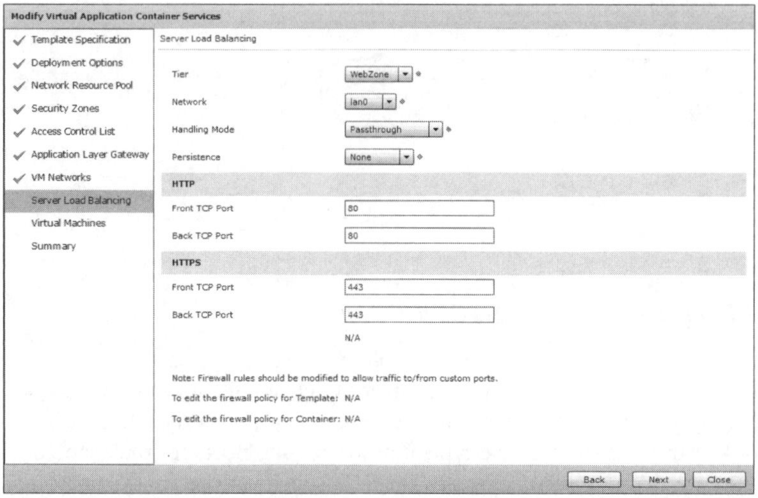

Figure 11-27   *VACS Template Wizard Server Load Balancing*

Now that your template is finished, select your container and click the **Create Container** button located on the VACS Container interface. Provide a container name and an optional label, and indicate the group that will own the container, just like you did with the fenced virtual container. The container creation creates a service request like the one shown in Figure 11-28. Once deployed, you will find and manage the VACS containers in the same Policies > Application Containers menu where fenced virtual containers are located.

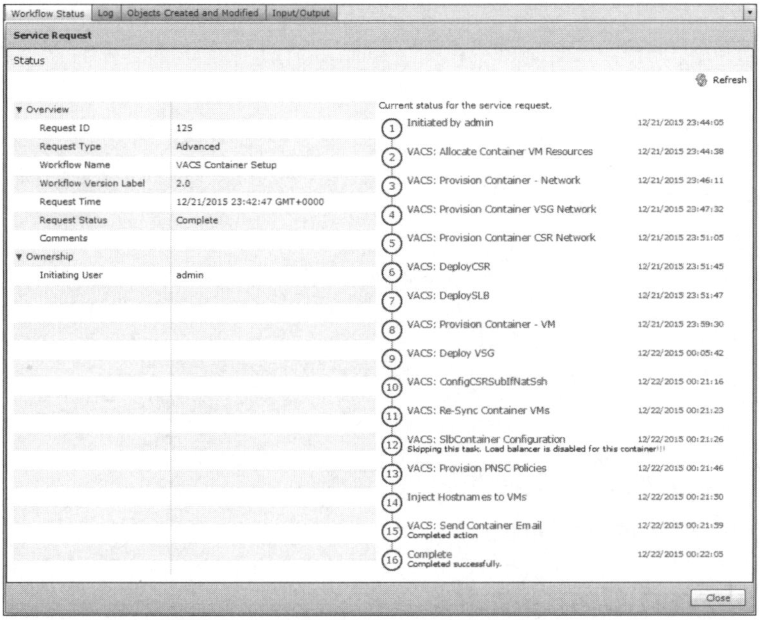

Figure 11-28 *VACS Container Service Request*

Creating Container Catalogs

No matter the type of application container, you create the catalog offers the same way. Recall from Chapter 9 that you must create catalog offers for any service that end users will be enabled to order and manage. As an administrator, you have the ability to create a new container simply by clicking the template. End users, on the other hand, do not have access to the templates; they have access only to the service catalog available. Navigate to **Policies > Catalogs** and click **Add** to create a new catalog. Choose the Service Container type from the drop-down list. Figure 11-29 shows the completed form for the new catalog that will allow end users to order and deploy a new container based on our template.

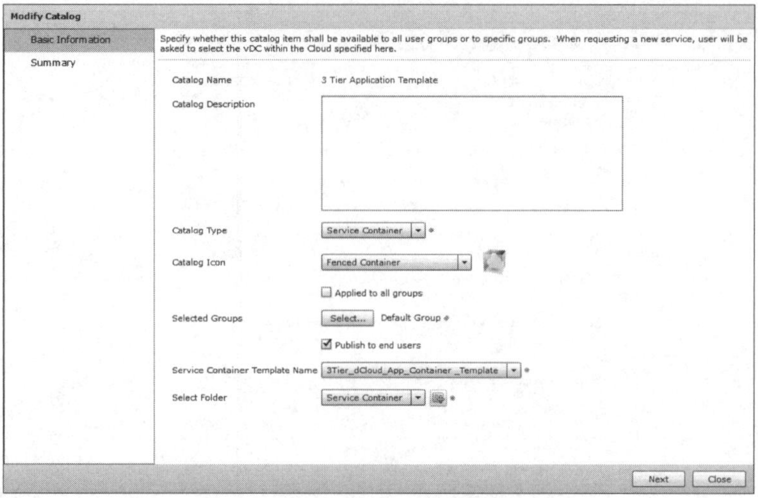

Figure 11-29 *New Service Container Catalog*

Managing Deployed Containers

Deploying a container is a great first step, but you will also want to manage the life cycle of the container and work with the VMs contained within it. Several actions are available to end users, depending on the type of container. Figure 11-30 shows the actions available for a fenced virtual container and Figure 11-31 for a VACS container. Some of the key differences and things to note about the available actions are listed here:

- Fenced virtual containers can be cloned to create a new container based on a copy of the running container.

- VACS containers support configuring ERSPAN sessions to capture traffic from the container networks and send it to a network analysis system.

- VACS containers support changing the Firewall Policy on a deployed container through the portal.

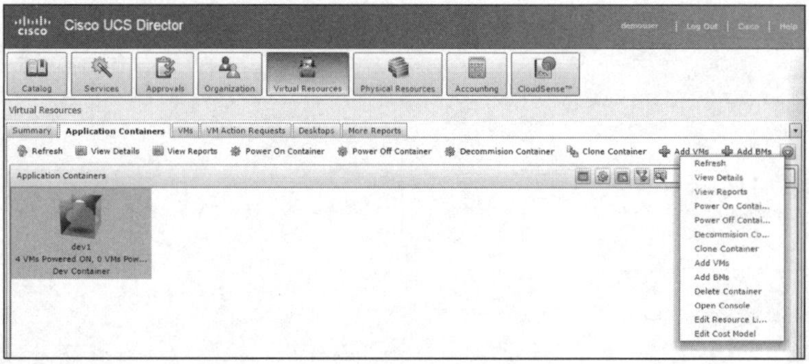

Figure 11-30 *Fenced Virtual Container Actions*

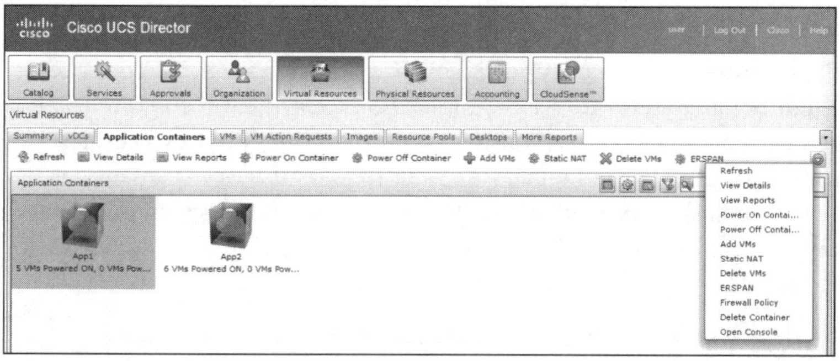

Figure 11-31 *VACS Container Actions*

Although there is an option in the Fenced Container menu to Add BMs (bare-metal servers), enabling this feature for a fenced virtual container is complex and rarely used. For containers supporting bare-metal servers, the best option will be the newest container type, APIC containers, briefly discussed in the next section.

All container types also provide end users with several report options from which they can obtain details about the container and the resources in the container. These details include the IP address, usernames and passwords, and hardware details for each virtual machine. Figure 11-32 shows an example report for a fenced virtual container. Users can find these reports by clicking the application container and selecting **View Reports**. The Detailed Report with Credentials is shown in the figure.

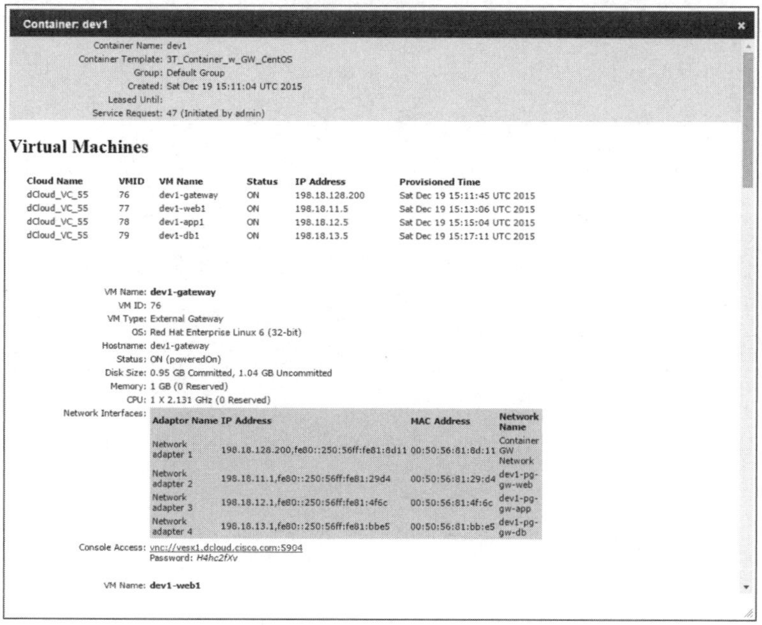

Figure 11-32 *Container Report*

APIC Containers

The newest types of application container supported in UCS Director are APIC containers. These containers are tightly integrated with Cisco Application Centric Infrastructure (ACI) and the policy-defined networking approach configured through the Application Policy Infrastructure Controller (APIC). APIC containers are built to extend the tenancy model from ACI into UCS Director and allow users to create container networks spanning virtual and physical resources, manage storage configurations for tenants, and provide robust security and services with firewall and load balancers.

The configuration and deployment of APIC containers are beyond the scope for the CLDADM exam and this book. For details, refer to the "Implementing Cisco Application Policy Infrastructure Controller Support" chapter of the *Cisco UCS Director Application Container Guide* available on Cisco.com.

Exam Preparation Tasks

As mentioned in the section "How to Use This Book" in the Introduction, you have a couple of choices for exam preparation: the exercises here, Chapter 15, "Final Preparation," and the exam simulation questions on the Pearson IT Certification Practice Test.

Review All Key Topics

Review the most important topics in this chapter, noted with the Key Topics icon in the outer margin of the page. Table 11-3 lists a reference of these key topics and the page number on which each is found.

Table 11-3   Key Topics for Chapter 11

Key Topic Element	Description	Page Number
Table 11-2	List the different application container types supported by UCS Director.	324
List	Describe the benefits the VACS feature provides to customers.	325
Paragraph	Understand the network impact of using application containers and how to control traffic entering and leaving a container with policy.	333
Paragraph	Explain the network resource pools required by VACS templates and the purpose of each one.	336
Paragraph	Describe the three types of VACS containers available for template creation and the differences between each.	336
Paragraph	Describe the application inspection feature of VACS containers and its value to customers.	341

Complete Tables and Lists from Memory

Print a copy of Appendix B, "Memory Tables" (found online), or at least the section for this chapter, and complete the tables and lists from memory. Appendix C, "Memory Tables Answer Key," also online, includes completed tables and lists to check your work.

Define Key Terms

Define the following key terms from this chapter and check your answers in the glossary:

application container, container gateway, container template

11

This chapter covers the following exam topics:

2.0   Chargeback and Billing Reports

2.1   Describe the chargeback model

2.1.a   Describe chargeback features

2.1.b   Describe budget policy

2.1.c   Describe cost models

2.1.d   Describe adding a cost model to a tenant

2.2   Generate various reports for virtual and physical accounts

2.2.a   Execute billing reports

2.2.b   Execute system utilization reporting

2.2.c   Execute a snapshot report

CHAPTER 12

Chargeback, Billing, and Reporting

This chapter discusses two tightly related components of cloud administration: reporting and chargeback. Having a solid understanding of how well any IT system is operating has been a key part of system and network administration for years, and because of the self-service and automated nature of a cloud, having that understanding is even more important. Details about the current status of the cloud infrastructure, trending information about usage, and historical data are all critical to building and maintaining a private cloud. Robust reporting capabilities are important not only for cloud administrators, but also for the end users and consumers of the cloud as part of the self-service ordering and management of cloud resources.

A key element in distinguishing a cloud model from other networking models is the way in which cloud services are consumed and paid for. Along with providing end users the ability to provision and manage their resources through a self-service portal, generally cloud computing involves having users pay for the resources they are using as an operating expense (OpEx for short). Depending on the cloud provider, users may be charged a one-time fee for ordering a resource; fees based on how long and how many resources they have active; fees based on performance characteristics such as CPU, RAM, and disk; or fees based on some combination of these and other metrics. *Chargeback* and the related concept of *showback* refer to the capability of a cloud platform to track metrics, assign them a dollar value, and generate billing reports for individual customers or groups. If an organization uses the billing reports for informational purposes but does not actually implement any financial transfers based on the reports, it is using a showback model. If the organization's governance model changes such that users and groups begin paying for the usage of cloud services, it has moved to a chargeback model.

"Do I Know This Already?" Quiz

The "Do I Know This Already?" quiz allows you to assess whether you should read this entire chapter thoroughly or jump to the "Exam Preparation Tasks" section. If you are in doubt about your answers to these questions or your own assessment of your knowledge of the topics, read the entire chapter. Table 12-1 lists the major headings in this chapter and their corresponding "Do I Know This Already?" quiz questions. You can find the answers in Appendix A, "Answers to the 'Do I Know This Already?' Quizzes."

Table 12-1   "Do I Know This Already?" Section-to-Question Mapping

Foundation Topics Section	Questions
Cloud Infrastructure Reports	1, 2, 4
Physical Infrastructure	3
Virtual Infrastructure	5, 6
CloudSense Analytics	7
UCS Director Chargeback	8
Cost Models	9
Budget Policy	10

CAUTION   The goal of self-assessment is to gauge your mastery of the topics in this chapter. If you do not know the answer to a question or are only partially sure of the answer, you should mark that question as wrong for purposes of the self-assessment. Giving yourself credit for an answer you correctly guess skews your self-assessment results and might provide you with a false sense of security.

1. Data from an infrastructure report in UCS Director can be exported in which formats? (Choose three.)

   a. PDF

   b. Comma-separated values (CSV)

   c. Microsoft Excel (XLS)

   d. Extensible Markup Language (XML)

2. Which action within an infrastructure report typically opens a new report drilling down into more details about a particular object in a table?

   a. Open

   b. View Details

   c. Expand

   d. Explore

3. Under which administrative menu option would you find details on UCS Manager accounts added to UCS Director?

   a. Administration > Compute Accounts

   b. Infrastructure > Physical > Compute

   c. Physical > Compute

   d. Site > Pod > Compute

4. What types of objects can be assigned to a user or a group in UCS Director? (Choose all that apply.)

   a. Virtual machines

   b. UCS service profile

   c. VLAN

   d. LUN

   e. Volume

5. Where would you find a report showing the number of virtual machines within a cloud account over the last month?

   a. Within a Trending Report under More Reports

   b. As part of a Historical Usage report for a virtual data center

   c. Within a Summary dashboard

   d. This information is not available within UCS Director

6. A Map Report for a cloud account in UCS Director displays which of the following?

   a. A graphical topology representation indicating the relationship between VMs, hosts, clusters, and vCenter

   b. A color-coded heat map showing relative usage of different components within the cloud

   c. Integration with Google Maps to highlight where a selected piece of infrastructure is located

   d. A graphical representation of the physical compute cluster, highlighting which physical server is hosting workloads

7. CloudSense Analytics provide administrators with which capabilities not available in other report options in UCS Director? (Choose three.)

   a. Combine information from multiple infrastructure reports into a single view

   b. Snapshot and save details about the cloud infrastructure at a particular point in time

   c. Construct custom executive reports from data throughout the cloud that can be emailed to users

   d. Provide forecast and what-if analysis across the cloud infrastructure

8. True or False. Chargeback refers to an IT governance policy where metrics and costs of IT resource consumption are tracked per user or group, and bills for that usage are paid to reimburse corporate IT for supporting applications.

   a. True

   b. False

12

9. Within a UCS Director Cost Model, which of the following metrics can be used to calculate costs? (Choose all that apply.)

   a. One-time fixed cost

   b. CPU cores

   c. Memory consumed

   d. Network bandwidth used

10. What steps are needed to implement and enforce budgets for a group? (Choose three.)

    a. Create and apply a Cost Model to vDCs

    b. Enable Budget Watch per group

    c. Create monthly budget entries per group

    d. Create approval policies and designated approvers for groups

Foundation Topics

UCS Director Reporting

Within UCS Director there are two broad types of reports available. We have referred to and looked at examples of the first type of report many times within this book already. These cloud infrastructure reports encompass all of the different tables and data available within the UCS Director administrator and end-user portals. Each time you have investigated a table of virtual machines, service requests, or VLANs, you were working with a cloud infrastructure report. The second type of reports are CloudSense Analytics, and they provide visibility into the utilization and performance across the infrastructure supporting the private cloud. These reports are leveraged to help answer questions related to utilization, trending, and forecasting. The examples in this chapter show how to access and view the reports through the UCS Director web interface; however, all of the information is also available through the REST API.

Cloud Infrastructure Reports

Cloud infrastructure reports are ubiquitous within UCS Director, and account for nearly all the screens and views both administrators and end users navigate within their interfaces. These reports show a snapshot of the current status of the infrastructure in question based on the most recent inventory polling data. This means there is always the potential for the data being shown to be slightly out of date for details that have recently changed or updated. In cases where you know a change has happened in the infrastructure outside of UCS Director, you can manually run an inventory task through the **Administrator > System > System Tasks** page. Search for **Inventory** and you'll see a list of each of the inventory tasks and their details, and be able to kick off an immediate run of the task.

A typical cloud infrastructure report, along with annotations for the common attributes found on all reports, is shown in Figure 12-1. This is the UCS Servers report for a UCS Manager account within UCS Director where the details of the physical servers (not service profiles, but the actual servers) are displayed in a tabular format. No matter what report you are viewing, all will have the following commonalities:

- The table can be sorted by any column by clicking the column name and then the up/down arrow to indicate sort direction.
- Two methods for searching or filtering the data are available:
  - Entering text in the search box in the title bar for the table will limit the view to only rows that contain the text in any column.
  - Clicking the **Advanced Filter** button displays the Search in Column dialog box, where you can provide more granular search criteria.

12

- The default view of the report may or may not show all available columns. Click the **Customize Table Columns** button, represented by a gear icon, to display or hide individual data columns.

- The data for the report can be exported from UCS Director for independent view and manipulation. Supported formats are PDF, comma-separated values (CSV), and Microsoft Excel (XLS). Note that the entire report will be exported, including all hidden columns and rows.

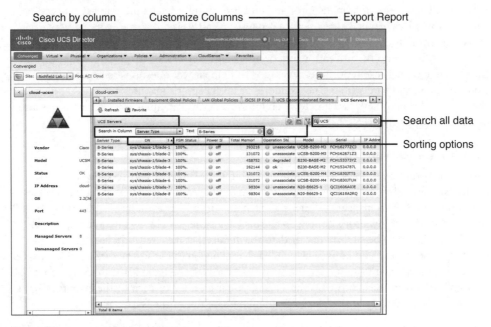

Figure 12-1 *Typical Cloud Infrastructure Report*

Another important characteristic common to many cloud infrastructure reports is the capability to take action or drill deeper into the infrastructure being displayed. Figure 12-2 shows the same UCS Server report, but this time it has been filtered down to a single blade that has been selected. Once an item in the table is selected, UCS Director shows contextual actions available for the infrastructure being investigated. As shown in the figure, you can take several actions on an individual blade, including Power On or Off and Associate or Disassociate.

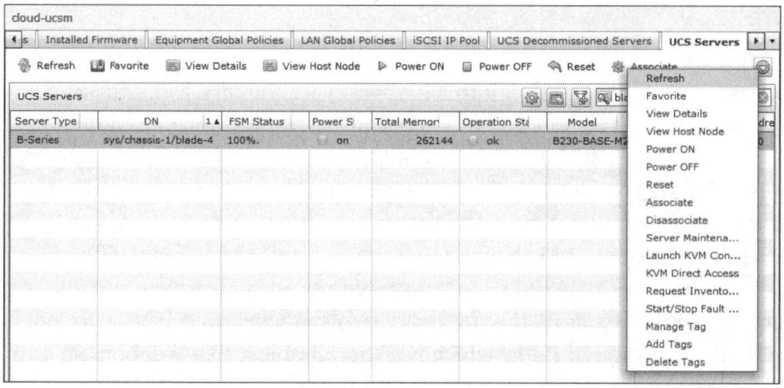

Figure 12-2 *Contextual Actions in Cloud Infrastructure Reports*

Take note of the option to view details of the blade, an action that is typically also available by double-clicking an item in a table. This action is what will drill deeper into the infrastructure in question. Figure 12-3 shows some of the details available for an individual blade within UCS Director, in particular the type of interface cards installed in the blade. You can see in the figure that once again we can click View Details to see details of the VIC itself, and in Figure 12-4 the logical network interface cards (NIC) that have been created on the Cisco VIC are displayed. It is important to remember when working with cloud infrastructure reports that there is often more information available than what is originally displayed. Get into the habit of looking for links and buttons to view details.

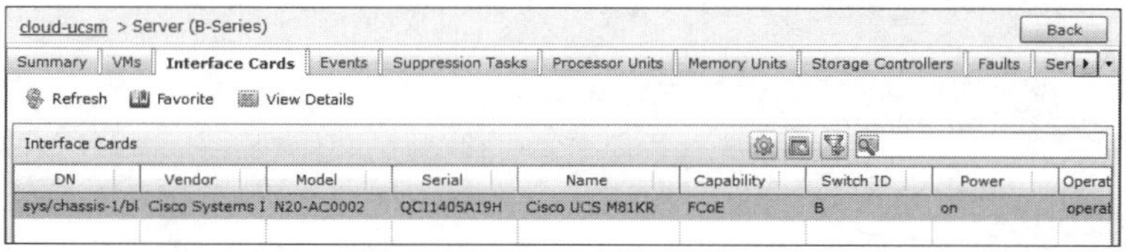

Figure 12-3 *UCS Blade Details*

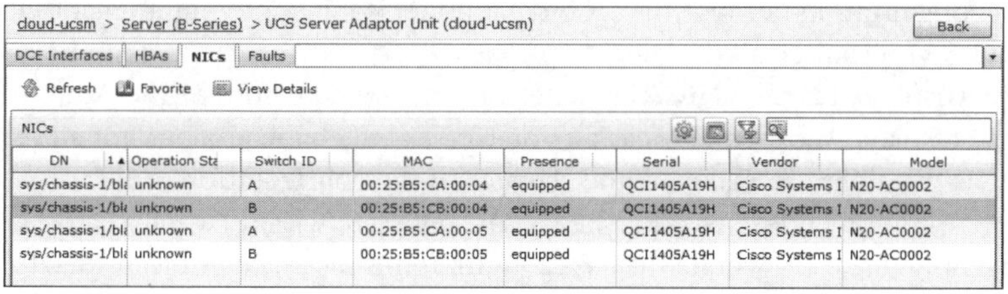

Figure 12-4 *Network Interface Card Details*

Now that you have an understanding of how to work with cloud infrastructure reports, let's explore some of the most useful reports that you will leverage within UCS Director when managing both physical and virtual infrastructure.

Physical Infrastructure

Within the Physical interface menu, you will find options for Compute, Storage, and Network. Each option will enable you to drill into and investigate the physical infrastructure making up your deployment. You can see the **Physical > Compute** view in Figure 12-5 with a UCS account selected. The first thing to note about the interface is that the organization in the left panel is based on the Site > Pod > Account hierarchical structure used within UCS Director. For example, the deployment used in the figure has two sites, Richfield Lab and Southfield Lab. Within the Richfield Lab site, there are six pods, ACI Cloud, Cloud Management, Dev Cloud, General Lab, Mini Cloud, and Remote Sites; however, not all pods contain compute accounts. Also note that there are two top-level objects that are not sites themselves. The first is Unassigned Pods, which is a special object that will contain any pods that are not specifically assigned to a site object. And the second is Multi-Domain Managers, where you will find accounts like UCS Central that can potentially span across multiple pods and sites.

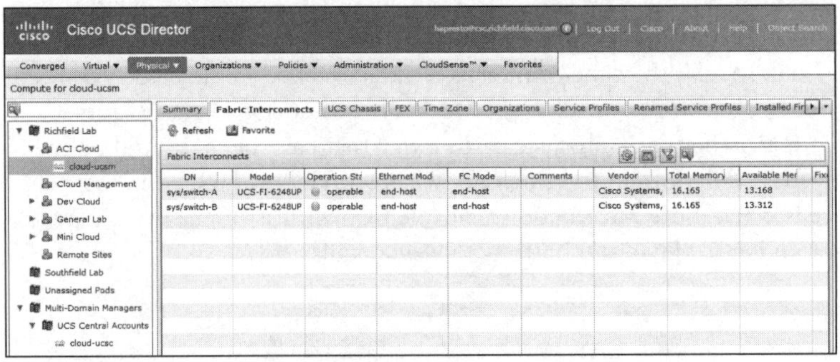

Figure 12-5   *Physical > Compute View*

UCS Compute Reports

When working with Cisco UCS accounts, you will find many of the interesting reports and interfaces available within an organization. Service profile templates, policies, and pools all exist within a specific organization because the UCS data model is inherently multitenant in structure. In Figure 12-6 you can see all the report options for a specific organization, the root org in the figure. Displayed is the vNIC Templates report, and take note of the Add button available in the display. Another key feature you can leverage in many, but not all, infrastructure reports is the ability to make ad hoc changes to the configuration of infrastructure elements. Here, if you choose to add a new vNIC template within UCS Director, the dialog box shown in Figure 12-7 will be displayed. Within this interface you can specify all the details related to the new template, and upon clicking Submit, it will immediately be configured within the UCS Manager account.

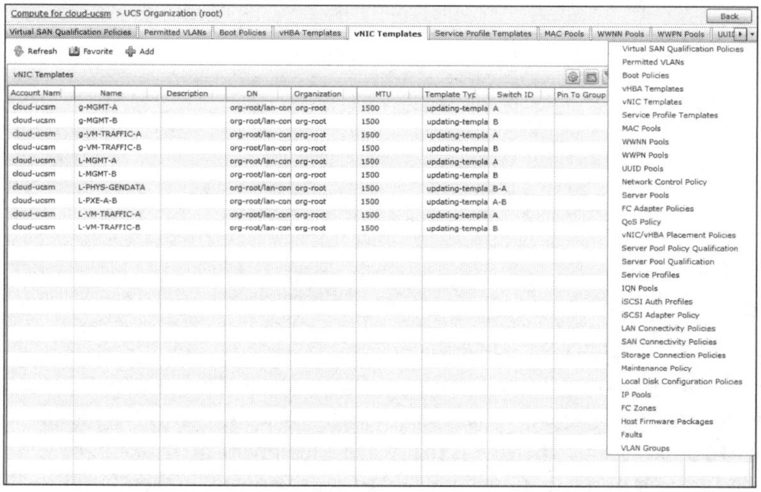

Figure 12-6 *UCS Organization vNIC Templates and Reports*

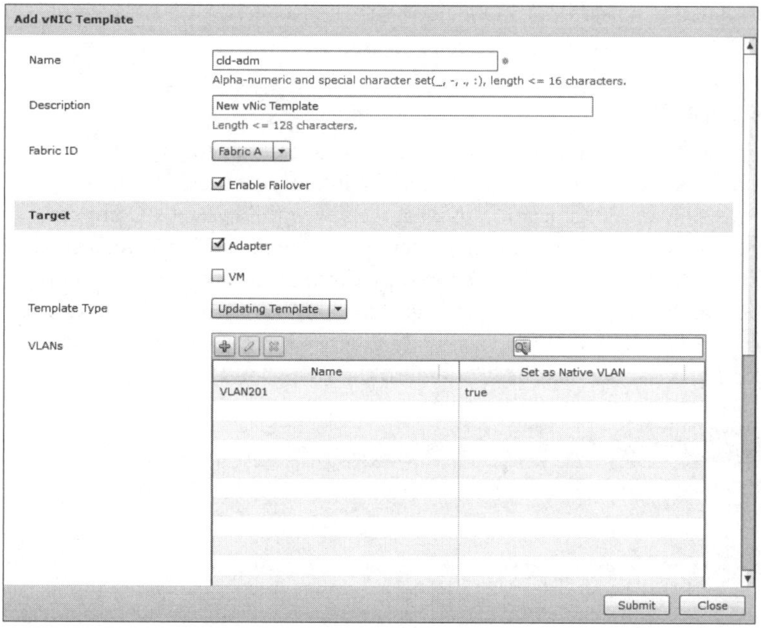

Figure 12-7 *Add New vNIC Template Dialog Box*

Service profiles are probably the most important object within UCS Manager, and UCS Director makes it very easy to view, manage, and add new service profiles using the Infrastructure Reports. In Figure 12-8 we have moved to the Service Profiles tab under the same root organization view. Here you can see the four service profiles currently created within the system, along with many important details, including association state and assigned server.

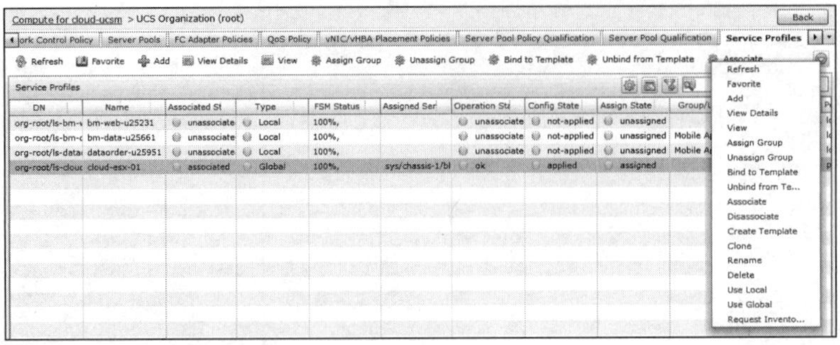

Figure 12-8 *Service Profiles Report*

Take special note of the Group/User field in the display. Many objects within UCS Director can be assigned to a specific user or group. When an object like a service profile is assigned to a group, there are two main results. The first is that when a member of the group, or the user, logs in to the end-user portal, they will be able to see the object in their interface under physical resources and take any supported actions on the object. The second is that all chargeback reports and billing calculations will start including that object. Some of the objects that can be assigned to a user or group include virtual machines, UCS service profiles, VLANs, and LUNs.

Physical Network Reports

Now let's move to **Physical > Network** and investigate some of the valuable reports features for administrating that part of the infrastructure. The initial view presented here, shown in Figure 12-9, is similar in organization to what we saw with Physical > Compute in Figure 12-5. Figure 12-9 also highlights an important characteristic of UCS Director: its multivendor capabilities. UCS Director supports not only Cisco infrastructure in compute, network, and storage, but also many other vendors used in enterprises (to see the hardware compatibility list for UCS Director, visit Cisco.com). In Figure 12-9 you can see that an F5 BIG-IP Virtual Edition Load Balancer has been added to the ACI Cloud pod.

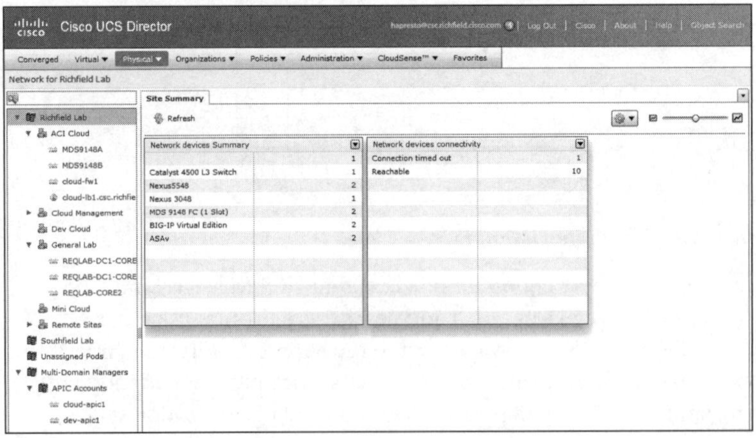

Figure 12-9 *Physical > Network View*

Within UCS Director, physical network objects include both Ethernet and Fibre Channel switches, security devices, load balancers, and SDN controllers such as the Cisco Application Policy Infrastructure Controller (APIC). In Figure 12-10 you can see the VLANs report for a Cisco Nexus 5000 Series Switch. Though it would be more common to leverage the infrastructure automation capabilities to build a workflow to add a new VLAN to all switches in your data center, you can very easily view and add or remove VLANs within the cloud infrastructure report view of UCS Director.

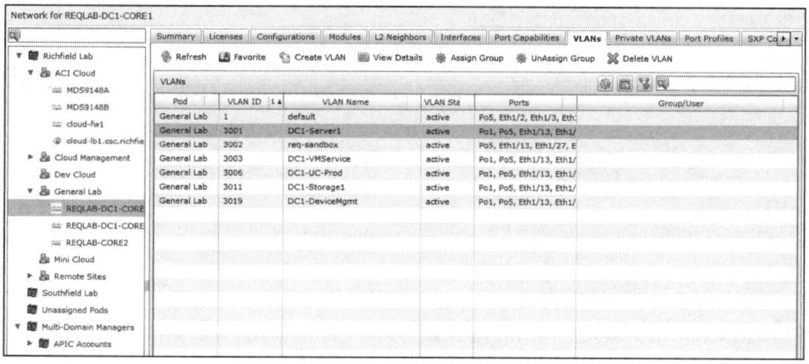

Figure 12-10   *Cisco Nexus VLANs Report*

Figure 12-11 shows the Interfaces report on the same physical switch. This view makes it very easy to see the current state of all the interfaces on an individual switch, as well as make live configuration changes. Some of the useful actions available in the interfaces context include

- Create and manage port channel interfaces
- Enable/disable ports (that is, no shutdown/shutdown)
- Configure and update VLAN trunk interfaces

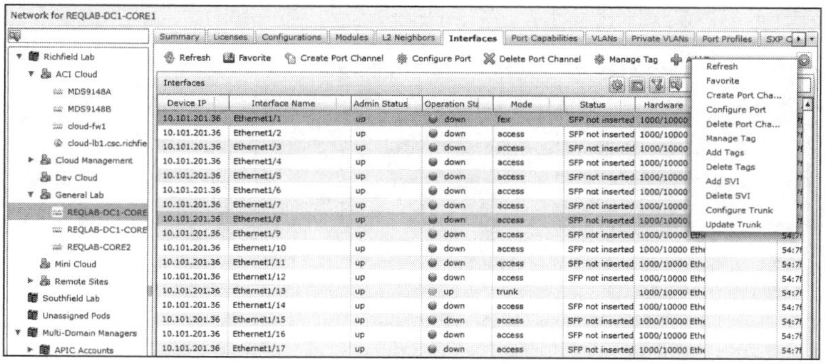

Figure 12-11   *Cisco Nexus Interfaces Report*

The last report we'll look at with this Nexus switch is the L2 Neighbors report shown in Figure 12-12. A common operations task for network administration is to identify connected devices to an individual switch. This report displays details from Cisco Discovery Protocol (CDP) and Link Layer Discovery Protocol (LLDP) tables on the switch. And in cases where you need to locate a device that may not run one of these protocols, a MAC Address Table report is also available.

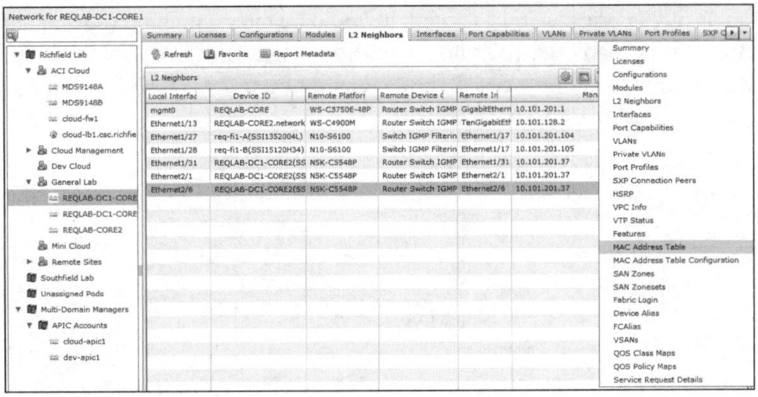

Figure 12-12 *Cisco Nexus L2 Neighbors Report*

When working with Fibre Channel switches, including both Cisco MDS/Nexus and Brocade switches, UCS Director includes reports for viewing and managing SAN zones, zonesets, and device aliases just as easily as managing VLANs and trunks.

Network Service Devices

Moving to network service devices, let's take a look at what UCS Director provides for an F5 BIG-IP device. UCS Director will never fully replace or replicate the features available in an underlying element manager for any supported device, and that is true for both Cisco and third-party devices. With this in mind, UCS Director's support for the BIG-IP appliances is targeted at enabling basic levels of self-service for private cloud use cases where load-balancing features are desired. Figure 12-13 shows the Virtual Servers report, including a Create button to create new virtual servers. UCS Director also supports the ability to modify or delete a selected virtual server.

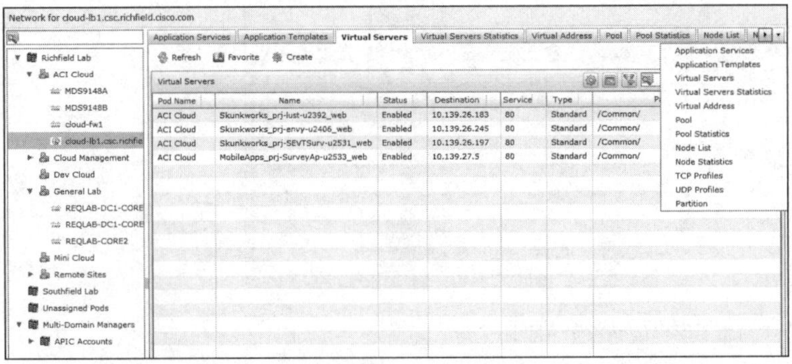

Figure 12-13 *BIG-IP Virtual Servers Report*

A virtual server requires a pool of real servers that are actually providing the service being load balanced. In Figure 12-14 you can see the Pool Members report available by double-clicking, or by clicking **View Details**, an individual pool from the Pool report. UCS Director also provides the ability to add and remove entries from a pool, along with displaying the current details.

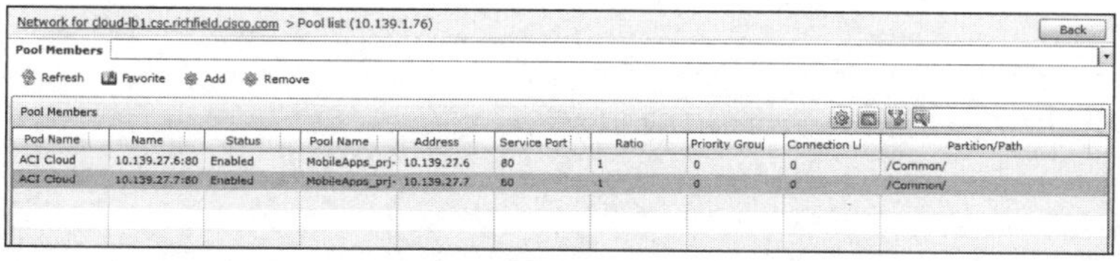

Figure 12-14 *BIG-IP Pool Members Report*

Cisco Application Centric Infrastructure

Application Centric Infrastructure (ACI) is the Cisco software-defined networking (SDN) platform for the data center and enables network configuration and management to be done through a policy definition, rather than via explicit per-device configuration. A data center network fabric built with ACI may include anywhere from four to hundreds of individual physical switches, but the entire network is managed as a single object through the APIC. This makes ACI an excellent network for building an enterprise cloud, or simply for data center automation.

Although ACI's use of policy and objects to define and describe network configurations is beyond the scope of this book and the CLDADM exam, we will highlight some key cloud infrastructure reports available within UCS Director. Similar to the use of organizations within Cisco UCS Manager, APIC is built to be a multitenant network fabric, and the most important reports and policy elements are found within a Tenant object. Figure 12-15 shows the Tenant details for a tenant called CloudAdmins in this fabric. You can see in the figure the large number of reports available at the Tenant level, with the Application Profile report visible. The Application Profile (also called Application Network Profile, or ANP) is the main object within ACI that describes an individual network construct. If you click **View Details** on an individual ANP, you will be able to investigate the endpoint groups (EPG) that make up the tiers of the Application Profile, as can be seen in Figure 12-16.

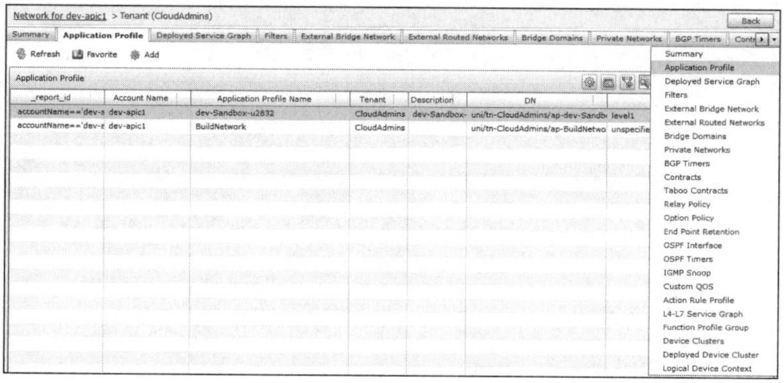

Figure 12-15 *Cisco APIC Tenant Details Report*

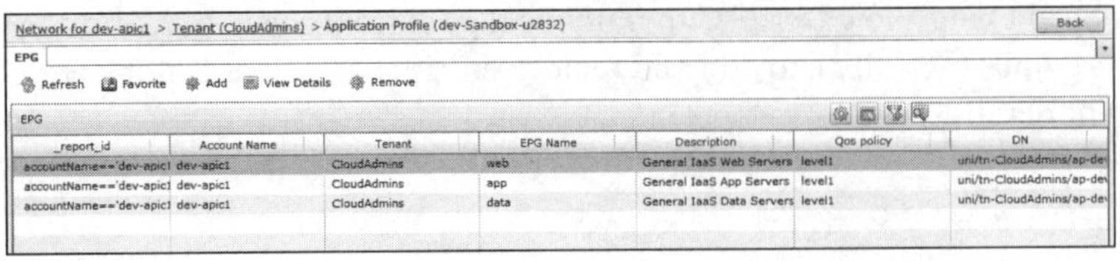

Figure 12-16   *Cisco APIC Application Profile Details Report*

Physical Storage

Out of the box, UCS Director supports storage arrays from several vendors, including EMC, NetApp, and IBM. In Figure 12-17 you can see details for an EMC VNX 5500 that is being managed by UCS Director. As with the compute and network components, reports are available for many of the different elements of the storage configuration, including the disks, volumes, and file systems providing the storage resources being consumed by servers and applications.

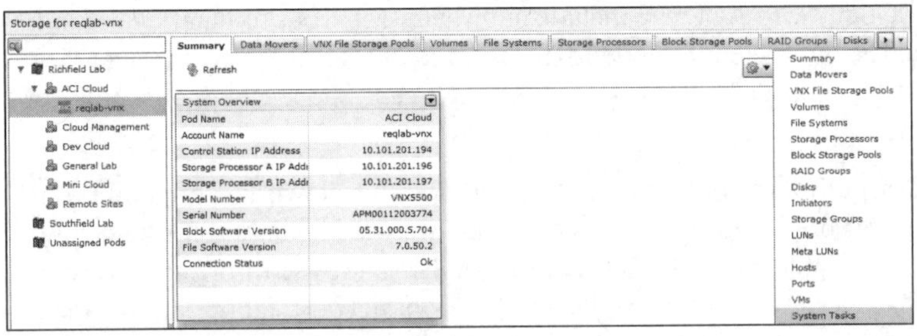

Figure 12-17   *EMC VNX Summary and Reports*

Similarly to how you can add and manage elements such as VLANs and service profiles from within UCS Director, you can use UCS Director to manage LUNs inside of a storage account, as shown in Figure 12-18.

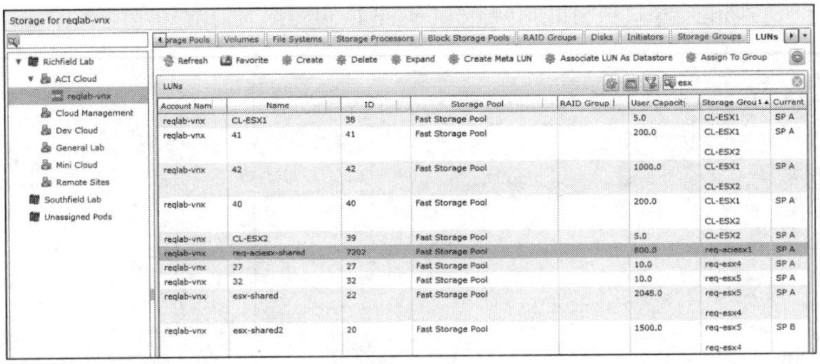

Figure 12-18   *EMC VNX LUNs Report*

In addition to the storage vendors supported natively by UCS Director, other vendors are using the available Software Development Kit (SDK) for UCS Director to provide installable plug-ins to manage other third-party storage. Hitachi, Pure Storage, and Nimble all have built and made plug-ins available.

Virtual Infrastructure

Cloud infrastructure reports for virtual infrastructure are organized and leveraged just like their physical infrastructure counterparts. Located under the Virtual interface menu are options for Compute, Storage, and Network that lead to the details for the different virtual accounts, or cloud accounts, added to UCS Director. Although the specific reports available depend on the hypervisor platform in use, many, but not all, of the following examples from VMware vCenter–based clouds apply to Microsoft Hyper-V and Red Hat KVM clouds as well.

You will most likely find the most valuable and useful reports under **Virtual > Compute**. Under this menu, details related to the clusters, host nodes, virtual machines, templates, and much more are all available, as shown in Figure 12-19. When looking at the cloud account at the top level, the individual tabs for items such as VMs (displayed in the figure) will include all objects in the cloud. Often you will find that you are interested in a subset of details pertaining to a specific vDC, cluster, or host. Though you could use the Advanced Filter options in the report to find the data you are looking for, you will likely find it easier to drill into a cluster or host and view the VMs report from within that context first.

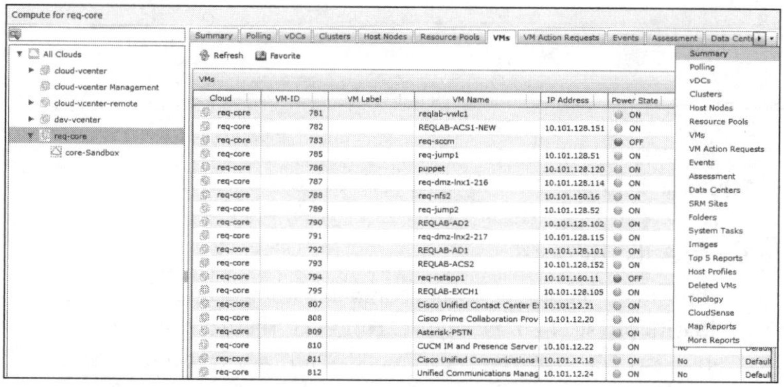

Figure 12-19 *Virtual > Compute VMs Report*

In Figure 12-20, you will find another VMs report, but this time it is based on drilling first into a cluster, and then into a host node of that cluster. You will find it important to be able to quickly narrow down the large scope of physical and virtual objects to what is relevant at a given point in time, and this technique will make it much easier to do so. Also notice in Figure 12-20 how these reports are actionable as well as informative. By selecting VMs from the list, you have access to a large number of lifecycle actions through UCS Director's administrator and end-user portals.

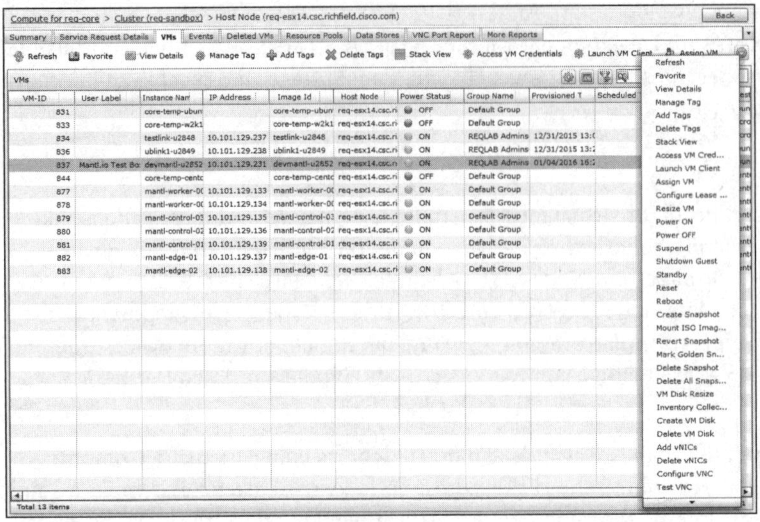

Figure 12-20 *Host Node VMs Report*

And to show the depth of details available within UCS Director, Figure 12-21 shows the result of double-clicking one of the VMs in the previous report to investigate further. Tabs such as vNICs (shown in the figure), Disks, VM Snapshots, Service Request Details, and more are all available to view more details.

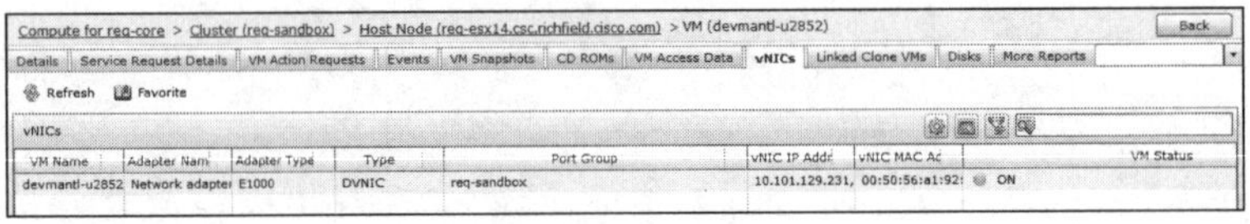

Figure 12-21 *Virtual Machine Details vNICs Report*

Virtual Infrastructure–Specific Reports

Numerous very useful reports are available for virtual compute, storage, and network that mirror the reports available with physical infrastructure. However, there are also some reports and options available only for the virtual accounts that are worth spending time looking at.

First, there are the Top 5 Reports, available from the tab of the same name when looking at a cloud account in the Virtual > Compute menu. Figure 12-22 shows an example of the Top 5 Report named VMs With Most CPU Usage. There are Top 5 Reports available that look at characteristics at the VM, group, host, and vDC levels that will allow you to find the largest consumers of cloud CPU, memory, and disk resources. The Top 5 Reports for groups and vDCs with the most VMs are also great for finding the biggest overall consumers of the cloud.

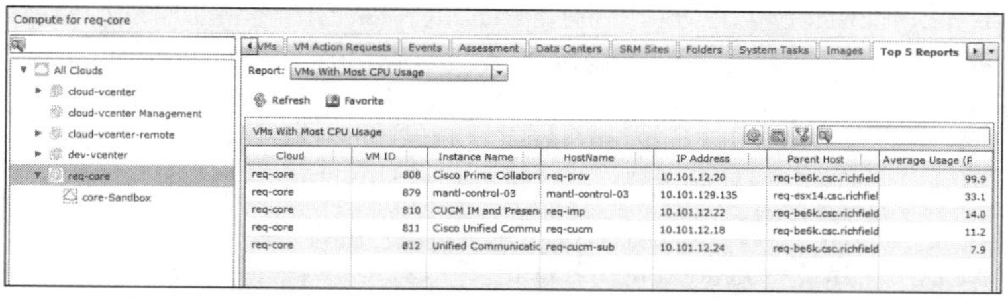

Figure 12-22 *Top 5 Report—VMs With Most CPU Usage*

The second type of unique report worth looking at is the Stack View available for individual virtual machines. The Stack View takes advantage of UCS Director's unique look across the data center infrastructure stack, and combines details from the virtual machine, hypervisor, and physical infrastructure into a single view that indicates all the resources across the data center that are involved in delivery of an individual virtual machine. You can access the Stack View as a toolbar action after you've selected a virtual machine, as shown in Figure 12-23. The report will open within the UCS Director window, also seen in Figure 12-23. Starting at the top with the VM's operating system and then moving down through the layers, Stack View describes the hard disks and network adapters used by the VM, which hypervisor hosts, data stores, port groups, and virtual switches are being leveraged, and then finally the physical compute blade, LUN and Storage Process, and physical switch involved. This unique look at a virtual machine's resources can be very powerful when identifying potential causes for problems, or scope of impact during a failure.

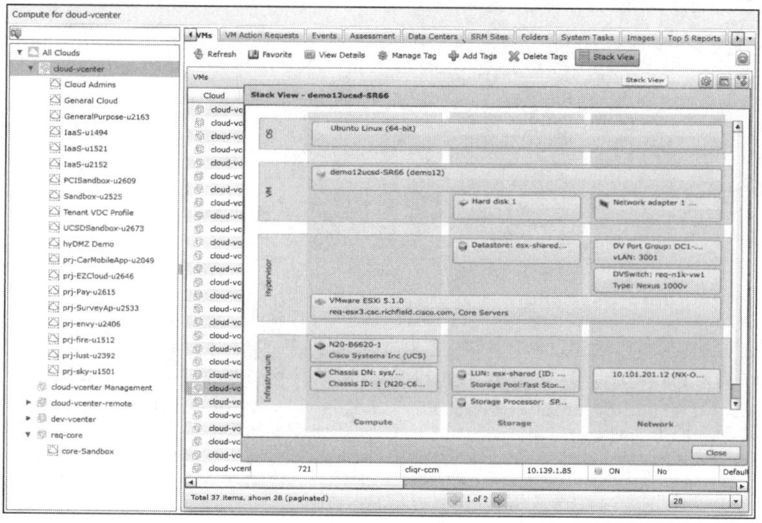

Figure 12-23 *Virtual Machine Stack View*

12

Another collection of reports that can be very helpful to a UCS Director administrator are the Map Reports. Like Top 5 Reports, Map Reports are available at the Virtual > Compute cloud account level. Map Reports present a color-coded view of the utilization of the physical cloud resources, including hosts, CPU, memory, and storage. Figure 12-24 shows a sample Map Report called CPU Utilization Map, which depicts the CPU utilization across a cloud account. In this single view, each hypervisor host is represented by a box in the image. The relative size of the box indicates the overall CPU capacity for the host in relation to the other hosts. This makes it very easy to see the hosts with the largest and smallest overall CPU horsepower. Within a host, each virtual machine active is represented by a box, where the size relates to the number of vCPUs configured and the color represents how utilized they are. The colors range from green to red, with red indicating a VM with fully utilized vCPU resources. In Figure 12-24, the host represented by the box in the lower-right corner has a VM (Cisco Prime Collaboration) in the middle with a very highly utilized CPU (displayed in red).

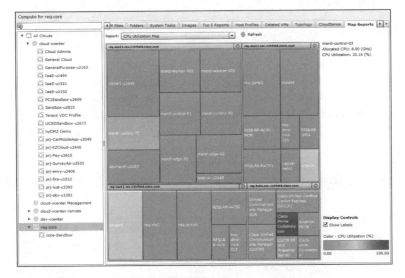

Figure 12-24   *CPU Utilization Map Report*

Figure 12-25 shows the Storage Usage Map Report. In this report, each data store is represented as a box one time, no matter how many hosts the data store may reside on. In this image, there is once again a single element (datastore1) that is very highly utilized, and it has been selected in the view so that its details are shown in the upper-right corner.

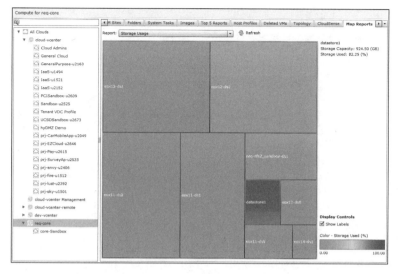

Figure 12-25 *Storage Usage Map Report*

The five Map Reports available in the Report drop-down list are

- CPU Utilization Map
- Memory Utilization Map
- VM Density
- Inactive VMs
- Storage Usage

The last of the unique reports available in the Virtual > Compute interface to cover are found on the More Reports tab with a cloud account selected. You will find a More Reports tab when looking at several other types of virtual and physical infrastructure; however, the variety of reports is unique to virtual compute accounts.

Three types of reports are available in More Reports:

- **Tabular Reports:** Provide details such as licensing, end of support, compatibility, and general status information across the cloud.
- **Instant Reports:** Provide graphical representations of the performance of the cloud; these reports are covered in more detail in Chapter 14.
- **Trending Reports:** Provide some visibility into the historical performance and changes to the environment over time. There are Trending Reports that look at VM numbers and changes, CPU and memory utilization, snapshot file sizes, and host nodes. You can view the data over configurable time ranges up to a month back. Figure 12-26 shows an example Trending Report for the Number of VMs over the Last Month. The slider bars below the graph enable you to drill in and adjust the view of the report to narrow the scope to look at spikes and valleys in the trend.

12

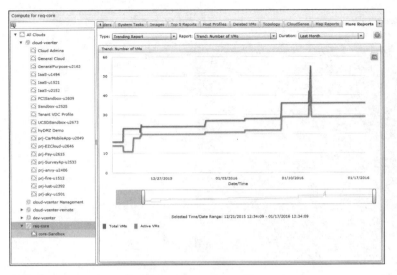

Figure 12-26   *Trending Report Number of VMs*

CloudSense Analytics

The cloud infrastructure reports available within UCS Director are very powerful and informative, but they do not provide all the reporting functionality needed for cloud administration. One limitation is that they are always very limited in scope, as they target a single element of the cloud. For example, you can get a report of all virtual machines assigned to a group or a report of all service profiles assigned to a group, but there is no infrastructure report that will show you both in a single report. Second, with the exception of the trending information available for cloud accounts, all the infrastructure reports show the current state of the cloud infrastructure when you pull up the report. Outside of exporting the data from UCS Director, there is no way to capture historical information using infrastructure reports.

Key Topic

CloudSense Analytics provide another mechanism for reporting within UCS Director that can help fill the gaps in capabilities of basic cloud infrastructure reports. A CloudSense report combines data available from different UCS Director infrastructure reports into a single view, and allows reports to be generated and saved to store a snapshot of the state of the cloud at any point in time. For example, the Group Infrastructure Inventory Report provides the administrator a single report for an individual group identifying all the servers, service profiles, storage volumes, virtual machines, and port groups assigned to that group across all the sites and pods managed by UCS Director.

The primary method to access the CloudSense reports is from the **CloudSense > Reports** menu, as shown in Figure 12-27. However, you will find a CloudSense tab available when looking at some virtual and physical accounts in other areas of UCS Director. Also under the CloudSense menu are two other options, Assessments and Report Builder. Report Builder is just what its name implies, a method to construct your own CloudSense templates from different reports available within UCS Director. Under Assessments you can generate the Virtual Infrastructure Assessment report that provides feedback on several checks that UCS

Director performs on the health of the underlying infrastructure to gauge its capability to support a private cloud with VMware vCenter. These checks include verifying clock synchronization between vCenter, UCS Director, and vSphere hosts, VMware Tools presence in templates, and compliance to hardware compatibility lists for the physical servers in use.

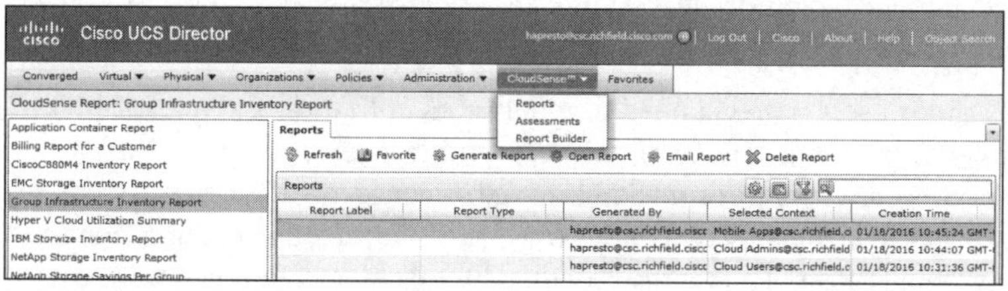

Figure 12-27 *CloudSense Reports*

The CloudSense reports available out of the box with UCS Director (as of version 5.3) include

- Application Container Report
- Billing Report for a Customer
- Cisco C880M4 Inventory Report
- EMC Storage Inventory Report
- Group Infrastructure Inventory Report
- HyperV Cloud Utilization Summary
- IBM Storwize Inventory Report
- NetApp Storage Inventory Report
- NetApp Storage Savings Per Group
- NetApp Storage Savings Report
- Network Impact Assessment Report
- Organization Usage of Virtual Computing Infrastructure
- PNSC Account Summary Report
- Physical Infrastructure Inventory Report for a Group
- Service Request Statistics
- Service Request Statistics Per Group
- Storage Dedupe Status Report
- Storage Inventory Report for a Group
- Thin Provisioned Space Report
- UCS Data Center Inventory Report
- VM Activity Report By Group
- VM Performance Summary
- VMware Cloud Utilization Summary
- VMware Host Performance Summary
- Virtual Infrastructure and Assets Report

Once a report is generated, it is saved within UCS Director and available to be accessed at any point in the future until it is deleted. Reports can be viewed or emailed in either HTML or PDF format. CloudSense reports can be generated manually by the administrator or automatically based on a schedule.

Now that you have an understanding of what CloudSense reports are, let's take a look at some sample reports available.

As your cloud grows and is used, you will need to monitor its utilization and track its consumption and available resources such as CPU, memory, and storage space. The VMware Cloud Utilization report is very useful for tracking this information on a per cloud account basis. Select the report in the menu and generate it for one of your cloud accounts. Figures 12-28 and 12-29 show some of the data that is provided by this report. In this report, overall capacity, provisioned capacity, reserved capacity, and used capacity are all indicated in easy-to-read graphs.

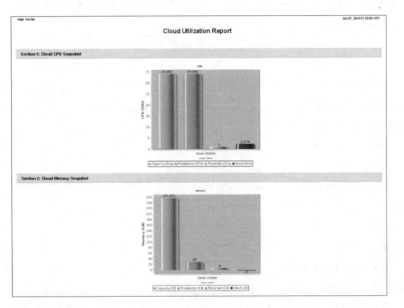

Figure 12-28 *VMware Cloud Utilization Report: CPU and Memory*

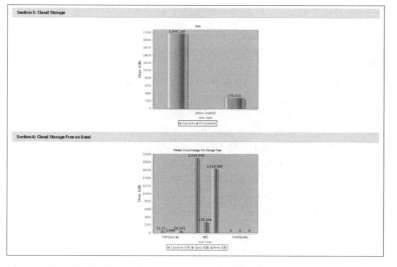

Figure 12-29 *VMware Cloud Utilization Report: Storage*

A second useful report is VM Activity Report By Group, which can highlight the groups that have deployed the most VMs to your cloud, including details on active/inactive VMs, CPU utilization, and memory utilization. Figure 12-30 is an example of this report showing the distribution of the consumption among several groups in our cloud. The entries for Default Group indicate virtual machines discovered by UCS Director but currently not assigned to any particular group.

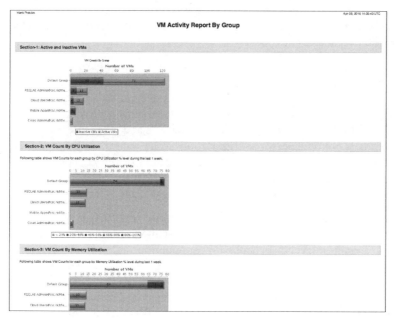

Figure 12-30 *VM Activity Report By Group*

The last CloudSense report that we will look at is Billing Report for a Customer, which is best discussed as part of the "UCS Director Chargeback" section coming up next.

UCS Director Chargeback

A major goal of most enterprise IT executives as part of a cloud initiative is to implement some form of chargeback to the business. The traditional method for budgeting and paying for hardware, software, maintenance, and manpower to design, build, and maintain data centers and IT systems has focused on IT as a cost center or as a simple cost of business. When an enterprise's governance is modeled in this way, a project to implement or upgrade a major system may include some incremental budget for the IT needs at inception; however, ongoing maintenance and support of the infrastructure are often the responsibility of enterprise IT going forward. This results in a constant pressure on IT staff to learn how to do more and more with less budget and resources, and this is not seen as a viable long-term strategy in most organizations.

Many organizations are using private cloud projects as a catalyst for changing this traditional model, enabling them to begin to replicate the operating expense model of IT that is the standard for public cloud providers. In this model, application owners, lines of business, or developers pay for their consumption of IT resources based on some agreed-upon metric and rate scale. This has benefits for both the consumers of the private cloud and the enterprise IT staff who is building and managing it.

For the consumers of cloud services, their initial investment is much lower than in a traditional project. Many projects today have unclear potential for success or impact on the business, and the typical model of large initial investment before a project proves its worth has pushed these projects to services such as public cloud. With a private cloud modeled for operating expenses like a public cloud, the line of business can align its spend with the value the project is offering through its lifetime.

With a private cloud, enterprise IT no longer is burdened with the cost of never-ending support and maintenance of applications and services that are deployed to their data centers. There is a monetary incentive for lines of business to diligently age out and move to end-of-life status systems that are no longer providing value, rather than maintain them indefinitely. Enterprise IT can also begin to move away from being seen as a cost center pulling money from an enterprise's bottom line. Most organizations won't want to see enterprise IT become a profit center, unless their business involves delivery of IT services to consumers. However, building a balanced IT budget where their expenses are offset by the paid consumption of services from the lines of business is a very reasonable and achievable goal.

To effectively implement chargeback or showback, an organization must tackle two challenges. First, there is a need for a technology platform that can monitor and track consumption of IT resources at a granular level that aligns with consumption, and then output this data as consumable reports. The metrics tracked will vary by organization, but common ones include the number of virtual machines and physical servers in use, CPU and memory consumption from the compute resources, data storage consumed, and network traffic generated. The granularity of billing will also be a major factor to determine. Hourly, daily, weekly, and monthly intervals for basing charges are all possible options for private clouds, while many public clouds track based on hourly usage.

Second, and significantly more difficult for most organizations, is determining what to actually charge for the consumption of resources in the cloud. The operation of a private cloud requires significant resources for design, engineering, and operations that are difficult, if not impossible, to directly bill to end users; however, they must be accounted for. Also, there are power, cooling, and facility charges that need to be addressed as part of the rate schedule. This means that even for organizations that have a good idea of what the compute, network, and storage costs are for a data center, work must be done to attach the less concrete costs into the rate schedule for the elements that can be easily tracked and metriced. Lastly, just because you could track and charge based on kilobyte of data transferred, megabyte of storage consumed, and gigahertz of process power utilized, that doesn't mean that there is a benefit to the organization to track at that level.

Although very important in developing a chargeback strategy for an enterprise, discussing how an organization might answer the second of these challenges is outside the scope of the CLDADM exam and this book. You will learn in the following sections about the capabilities in Cisco UCS Director to build models and rate schedules for implementing a chargeback policy, how to ensure the policy is enforced by the platform, and options for generating bills and reports per group or tenant consuming resources.

Cost Models

Once your organization has determined which metrics to track, over what duration to bill, and how much to charge, the next step is to implement and enforce that Cost Model in your cloud. Cisco UCS Director offers you a very flexible method for building differentiated Cost Models based on a number of factors.

In Chapter 9, "Automating Cloud Infrastructure with UCS Director," you learned about the virtual data center (vDC) and its related policies in UCS Director that govern details for how end users can order resources, as well as how they are deployed to the physical and virtual infrastructure. One of the optional configurable parameters of the vDC that Chapter 9 discussed is the Cost Model policy. Like other policies in UCS Director, a Cost Model is a reusable policy element that you configure and then apply to the vDCs to which it should apply. This means that in your deployment, you could have different Cost Models for different groups, or even for different vDCs for a single group. This is actually very typical and expected in a cloud deployment, as performance characteristics, service-level agreements (SLA), or response times could differ across groups and vDCs, justifying higher or lower costs.

Key Topic

Navigate to **Policies > Virtual/Hypervisor Policies > Service Delivery** to find the Cost Models tab. An initial installation of UCS Director will have a Default Cost Model with each possible metric set to zero dollars. Click the **Add** button to create a new Cost Model, as seen in Figure 12-31. The first decision and configuration you will need to make after providing a name and optional description for the policy is the Charge Duration, or how often UCS Director will take an average of consumption and record the charge to the database. Options include Hourly, Daily, Weekly, Monthly, and Yearly. This will have a significant impact on the chargeback policies for your organization. On one hand, the longer the charge duration, the less often and less data UCS Director will need to track while monitoring usage. Fewer bills would need to be generated, and IT might

12

have an easier time determining costs per metrics. However, there is a downside to using a longer charge duration. End users could end up paying exaggerated bills for resources that were used for a very short time. Consider a developer who regularly creates and deletes virtual machines several times a day, each lasting only a few hours. With a charge duration of daily, each virtual machine would result in a full day's charge, despite being in use for only a fraction of the day. This would be exaggerated for weekly or monthly durations. On the other hand, for a private cloud deployment, it might not make sense to track and bill based on hourly usage in the same way a public cloud provider might.

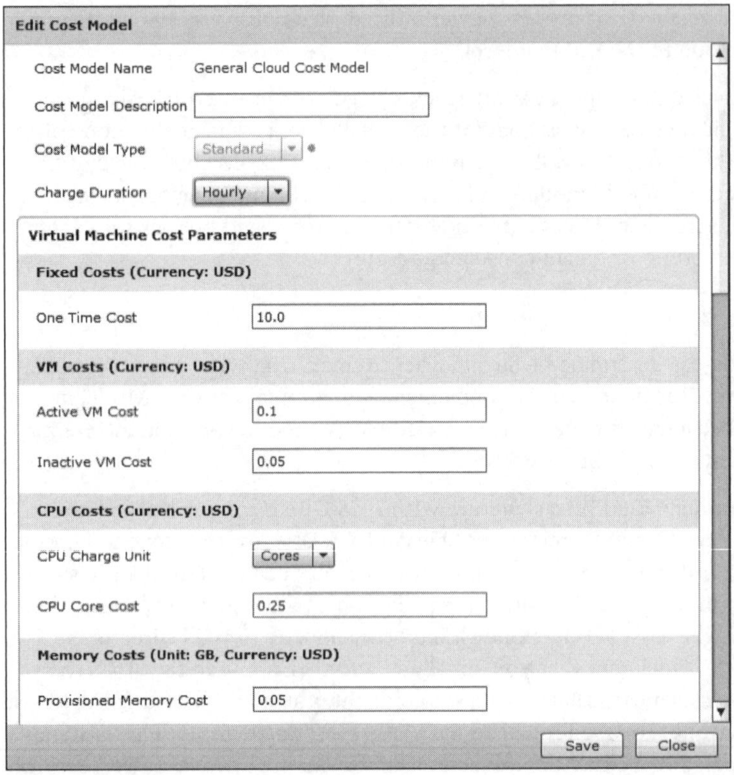

Figure 12-31 *New Cost Model*

With the Charge Duration configured, you will then begin setting the actual dollar (or whatever local currency is in use) costs for the identified metrics. A UCS Director Cost Model is used to charge for both virtual and physical servers, and it provides both coarse and granular options for calculating costs. On the coarse end of the spectrum, you can assign a one-time, initial cost for ordering a new server, as well as options for tracking active or inactive (that is, powered on or off) virtual machines with different rates. More granular options are available for tracking CPU, memory, and storage consumption by virtual and physical servers. Virtual servers have an additional metric of network bandwidth consumption, while physical servers can assign costs based on full- or half-width blades. Figures 12-32 and 12-33 (along with Figure 12-31) show the full Cost Model interface.

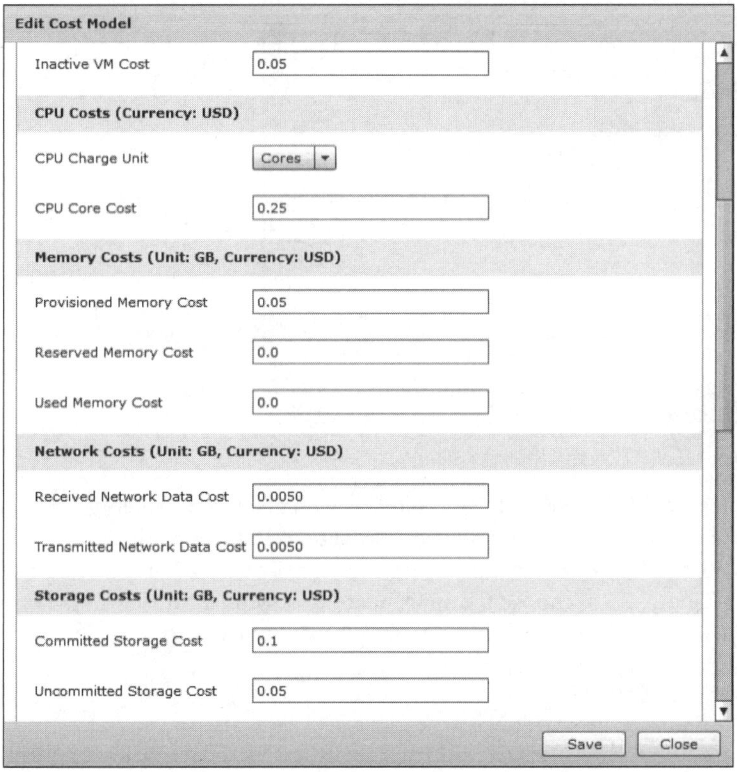

Figure 12-32 *New Cost Model Virtual Server Metrics*

12

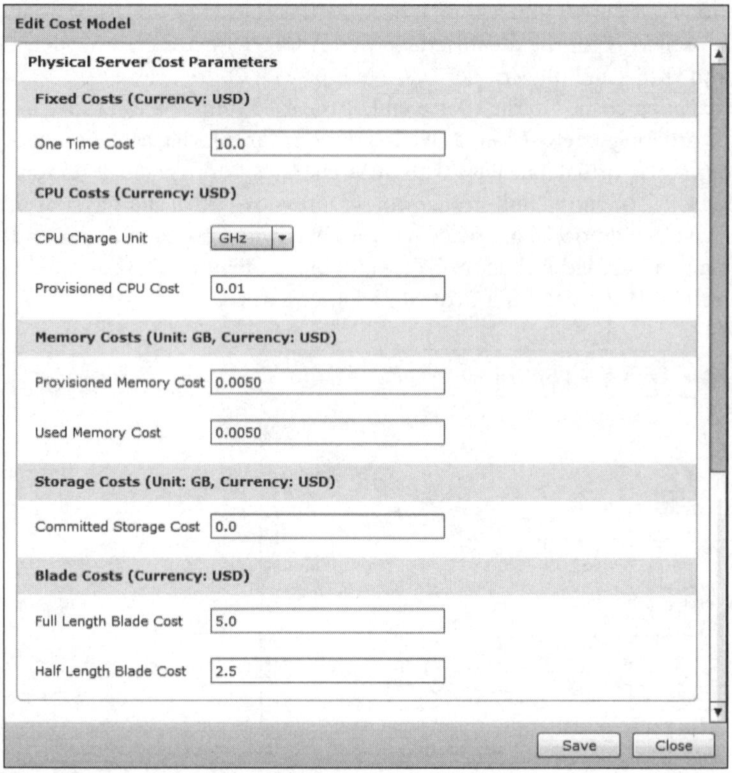

Figure 12-33 *New Cost Model Physical Server Metrics*

Once the Cost Model (or Cost Models) has been created, it won't have any effect until it is applied to vDCs. As when applying other policies, navigate to **Policies > Virtual/ Hypervisor Policies > Virtual Data Centers** and either edit an existing vDC or create a new one. Then, as shown in Figure 12-34, choose the appropriate Cost Model for the vDC. You can also indicate by checking the box whether you wish for cost estimates to be included in Service Request Summary tabs and email templates.

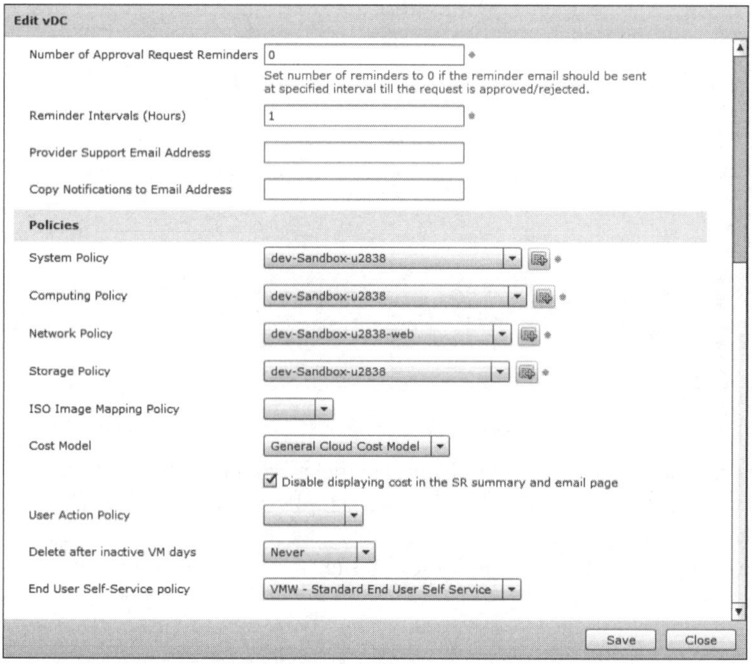

Figure 12-34 *Applying Cost Model to vDC*

The decision to implement Cost Models is not an all or nothing one. In a given deployment, you could have some vDCs with no Cost Model, others with a very basic and coarse Cost Model, and others with complex and granular Cost Models all for a single group. This capability enables organizations to implement very flexible options as they begin to roll out chargeback solutions.

Chargeback Reports

Configuring and applying a Cost Model is just the beginning of the chargeback deployment. You must also have a way to investigate the metrics that are being tracked, and generate bills for customers, whether they are actually being paid or just used for informational purposes. The majority of the information you will want to see as an administrator is found under the **Organizations > Chargeback** menu. From this interface you can investigate chargeback details at the entire deployment level (All User Groups), at the group level, or at an individual vDC level. At each level you'll find Current and Previous Month Summaries as well as several reports containing different levels of detail, ranging from month-by-month totals, down to individual metrics per virtual machine.

Figure 12-35 shows the Chargeback tab from an individual group. The number of columns displayed has been reduced to highlight several of the cost columns; however, by default the report includes the individual metrics used to generate the costs as well. In this report, notice how it provides details per virtual machine, per monthly billing cycle, the associated costs per metric (such as Active and Inactive status), and the total cost. This type of report can be very helpful for a group to identify which of their resources are resulting in the highest bills, and why.

12

Chargeback for REQLAB Admins@csc.richfield.cisco.com

| Chargeback | Current Month Summary | Previous Month Summary | Resource Accounting | Resource Accounting Details | CloudSense | More Rep ▶ ▼ |

▼ 🔒 All User Groups
  ▶ 🔒 CliqrGroup@csc.richfiel
  ▶ 🔒 Cloud Admins@csc.rich
  ▶ 🔒 Cloud Users@csc.richfield.c
  ▶ 🔒 Default Group
    🔒 Domain Users
    🔒 HR User@csc.richfield.c
    🔒 Manufacturing Technolc
  ▶ 🔒 Mobile Apps@csc.richfit
  ▶ 🔒 PCI Admin@csc.richfiel
  ▶ 🔒 REQLAB Admins@csc.r
  ▶ 🔒 Skunkworks@csc.richfi
  ▶ 🔒 Web Team@csc.richfiel

🔄 Refresh   📑 Favorite   💲 Get Quote   📋 Report Metadata

Chargeback

Instance Nam	Month	Committed C	Active VM Co	Inactive VM	Allocated Me	Storage Cost	Total Cost
test2-u2820	December, 2015	4.4	0.00	0.00	0.00	0.0	0.00
wintest-u2834	December, 2015	8.4	0.00	0.00	0.00	0.0	0.00
dev1-u2829	December, 2015	877.5	0.00	0.00	0.00	0.0	0.00
testlink-u2848	December, 2015	55.3	0.00	0.00	0.00	0.0	0.00
ublink1-u2849	December, 2015	36.1	0.00	0.00	0.00	0.0	0.00
testlink-u2848	January, 2016	4,426.6	0.00	0.00	0.00	0.0	0.00
ublink1-u2849	January, 2016	3,033.6	0.00	0.00	0.00	0.0	0.00
devmanti-u2852	January, 2016	3,271.0	0.00	0.00	0.00	0.0	0.00
reqlab-vwlc1	January, 2016	86.1	3.30	0.00	3.30	20.9	35.82
REQLAB-ACS1-R	January, 2016	850.7	3.30	0.00	6.60	874.3	900.70
req-accm	January, 2016	2,579.6	0.00	1.65	26.40	650.4	744.49
req-jump1	January, 2016	9,024.8	3.30	0.00	13.20	1,658.6	1,108.14
req-dmz-lnx1-21	January, 2016	1,285.0	3.30	0.00	3.30	133.6	148.54
req-nfs2	January, 2016	36,940.9	3.30	0.00	52.80	5,345.2	5,434.31
req-jump2	January, 2016	2,275.3	3.30	0.00	13.20	391.2	440.79
REQLAB-AD2	January, 2016	520.7	3.30	0.00	6.60	131.7	149.93
req-dmz-lnx2-21	January, 2016	1,285.3	3.30	0.00	3.30	133.7	148.58
REQLAB-AD1	January, 2016	5,666.0	3.30	0.00	3.30	820.2	835.09
REQLAB-ACS2	January, 2016	1,095.2	3.30	0.00	6.60	886.5	912.92
req-netapp1	January, 2016	133.9	0.00	1.65	1.65	21.8	33.42
REQLAB-EXCH1	January, 2016	2,224.2	3.30	0.00	6.60	315.9	342.37

Figure 12-35 *Chargeback Report for a Group*

The Chargeback reports also include some very helpful Summary dashboards to get a glimpse at the current and previous months' data. In Figure 12-36 an example Current Month Summary page is shown, providing a very quick one-page view to understand the overall status for the group's current month utilization. A similar dashboard is available showing the Previous Month Summary.

Chargeback for Mobile Apps@csc.richfield.cisco.com

| Chargeback | Current Month Summary | Previous Month Summary | Resource Accounting | Resource Accounting Details | CloudSense | More Re ▶ ▼ |

▼ 🔒 All User Groups
  ▶ 🔒 CliqrGroup@csc.richfiel
  ▶ 🔒 Cloud Admins@csc.rich
  ▶ 🔒 Cloud Users@csc.richfield.c
  ▶ 🔒 Default Group
    🔒 Domain Users
    🔒 HR User@csc.richfield.c
    🔒 Manufacturing Technolc
  ▶ 🔒 Mobile Apps@csc.richfit
  ▶ 🔒 PCI Admin@csc.richfiel
  ▶ 🔒 REQLAB Admins@csc.r
  ▶ 🔒 Skunkworks@csc.richfi
  ▶ 🔒 Web Team@csc.richfiel

🔄 Refresh   Duration for Trending Last Week ▼

Current Month Cost Summary   Current Month Top 5 Applications   Overview
                                                                  Month   January 2016
                                                                  Total Monthly Cost (US   721.2

VM/Physical Server Costs   CPU Costs   Memory Costs
Total VM/Physical Ser   79.2   Total CPU Costs (USD   192.0   Total Memory Costs (L   9.6
One Time Costs (USD   60.0   CPU Cost (Cores)USD   192.0   Allocated Memory Cos   9.6
Active VMs (USD   19.2   Allocated CPU Costs (0.0   Reserved Memory Cor   0.0
Inactive VM Costs (US   0.0   Reserved CPU Costs (0.0   Used Memory Costs (l   0.0
Active VM Hours   192.0   Used CPU Costs (USD   0.0   Allocated Memory MB-   1,108.0
Inactive VM Hours   0.0   Allocated CPU GHz-Ho   9,649.5   Reserved Memory GB   0.0
Full Blade Costs (USD   0.0   Reserved CPU GHz Ho   0.0   Used Memory GB-Hou   18.7
Half Blade Costs (USD   0.0   Used CPU GHz Hours   2.3
Fixed Costs (USD)   0.0

Storage Costs   Network Costs   VM/Physical Server Monthly Cost Summa
Total Storage Costs (L   440.4   Total Network Costs (I   0.0   Total VM/Physical Ser   440.4
Max Committed Stora   11,593.5   Received Network Dat   0.0   Server Costs (USD)   0.0
Max Uncommitted Sto   34,137.6   Transmitted Network E   0.0   Storage Costs (USD)   440.4
                                        Received Network Dat   0.0
                                        Transmitted Network E   0.2

Figure 12-36 *Current Month Summary*

Key Topic

The last report to look at here is the CloudSense report mentioned in a previous section. The Customer Billing Report is intended to be generated monthly per group or tenant in the cloud and provides a breakdown of the charges accrued through the month by the group. Figure 12-37 shows a pie chart view of the costs across categories, and in Figure 12-38 the tables of raw data are visible for deeper analysis by the customers.

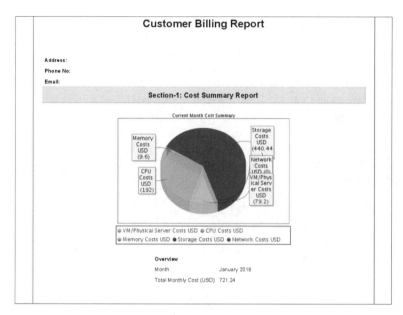

Figure 12-37 *CloudSense Billing Report – Pie Chart*

VM Costs

Total VM/Physical Server Costs (USD)	79.2
One Time Costs (USD)	60.0
Active VM Costs (USD)	19.2
Inactive VM Costs (USD)	0.0
Active VM Hours	192.0
Inactive VM Hours	0.0
Full Blade Costs (USD)	0.0
Half Blade Costs (USD)	0.0
Fixed Costs (USD)	0.0

CPU Costs

Total CPU Costs (USD)	192.0
CPU Cost (Cores)USD	192.0
Allocated CPU Costs (USD)	0.0
Reserved CPU Costs (USD)	0.0
Used CPU Costs (USD)	0.0
Allocated CPU GHz-Hours	9649.52
Reserved CPU GHz Hours	0.0
Used CPU GHz Hours	2.38

Memory Costs

Total Memory Costs (USD)	9.6
Allocated Memory Costs (USD)	9.6
Reserved Memory Costs (USD)	0.0
Used Memory Costs (USD)	0.0
Allocated Memory MB-Hours	1108.0
Reserved Memory GB-Hours	0.0
Used Memory GB-Hours	18.72

Storage Costs

Total Storage Costs (USD)	440.44
Committed Storage GB-Hours	11593.52
Uncommitted Storage GB-Hours	34137.64

Figure 12-38 *CloudSense Billing Report – Data*

Budget Policy

Having configured and deployed Cost Models and viewed the consumption reports, the next challenge you will likely be assigned is to provide some mechanism to limit active cloud consumption by a group based on some predefined budget. UCS Director provides a mechanism for individual groups to be assigned a monthly budget to be tracked in real time when new virtual resources are being ordered.

Before enabling the Budget Watch feature for a group, it is important to first establish the group's monthly budget; otherwise, the group might find itself unable to order new resources due to lack of budget. Navigate to **Organizations > Summary** to view and enter new budget entries. A single budget entry is composed of three main values: the group the entry applies to, the month and year for the budget line, and the dollar (or local currency) amount allocated for the group and month. Click the **Add** button make a new entry and display the form shown in Figure 12-39. Provide an entry name (which will be suffixed with the month and year), the group and dollar amount, and the time frame for the new entry. UCS Director allows you to easily configure repeated budget entries by allowing you to indicate a repeat count. Click **Add**, and the indicated group now has a budget to be tracked against for the months indicated.

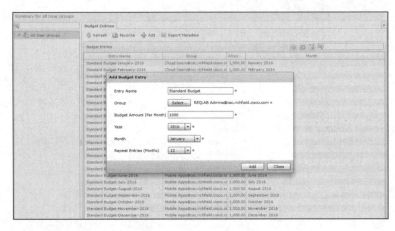

Figure 12-39   *Add Budget Entry Form*

With the budget entries for your group or groups (once again, UCS Director allows budgets to be configured and enforced per group and not globally), you need to enable the Budget Watch feature on the group itself. This is done from the User Groups configuration tab located under **Administration > Users and Groups**. Select the group that will now be under Budget Watch and click the **Budget Policy** button to open the interface shown in Figure 12-40. Then check the **Enable Budget Watch** check box and indicate whether the group should be allowed to go over budget. If the Allow Over Budget feature isn't enabled, a group will be prevented from ordering new resources once UCS Director's chargeback calculations indicate the group is out of resources for the month.

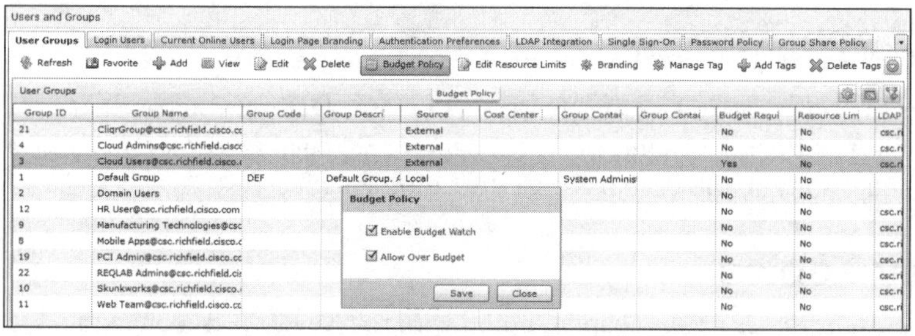

Figure 12-40 *Enable Budget Watch for a Group*

Exporting Metering Data for External Integration

Although the chargeback and reporting capabilities in UCS Director are very flexible and powerful, UCS Director is not an accounting and finance system. Most enterprises truly looking to implement a chargeback strategy will want to have an integration to their corporate accounts payable system where actual bills and records of payment can be addressed as part of typical day-to-day IT management. Rather than build direct integrations into any number of potential finance systems customers may use, UCS Director provides a mechanism to export the metering and tracking data that can be ingested by the accounting system. Navigate to **Administration > Integration** and then to the **Metering Data Export Setup** tab and you will find a screen similar to the one shown in Figure 12-41. Here you can indicate whether to export to a CSV or Extensible Markup Language (XML) data format, an FTP server destination, and the rate at which to export data. With this setup, your accounting team can monitor this destination and import the data to be fed through the proper rules and policies before generating bills, or simply initiating internal budget transfers from the groups consuming cloud services to enterprise IT.

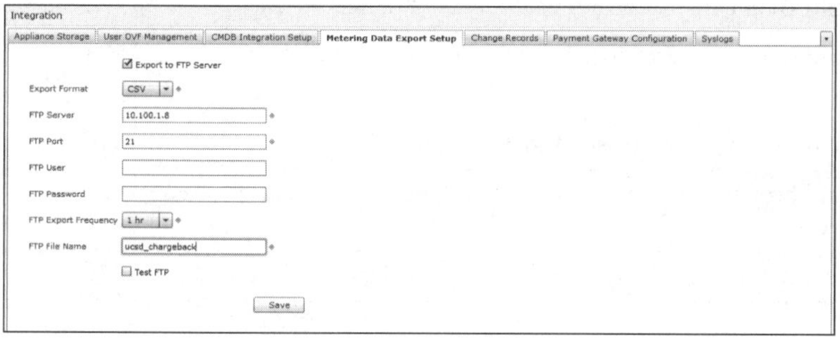

Figure 12-41 *Metering Data Export Setup*

12

Exam Preparation Tasks

As mentioned in the section "How to Use This Book" in the Introduction, you have a couple of choices for exam preparation: the exercises here, Chapter 15, "Final Preparation," and the exam simulation questions on the Pearson IT Certification Practice Test.

Review All Key Topics

Review the most important topics in this chapter, noted with the Key Topics icon in the outer margin of the page. Table 12-2 lists a reference of these key topics and the page number on which each is found.

Key Topic

Table 12-2 Key Topics for Chapter 12

Key Topic Element	Description	Page Number
Paragraph	Understand how to navigate the levels of infrastructure reports by double-clicking or using the View Details action.	355
Paragraph	Understand how to assign an object to a group and what the impact is for management and reporting.	358
Paragraph	Explain the potential lifecycle actions for a virtual machine available within UCS Director.	363
Paragraph	Understand the key differences between a CloudSense and standard infrastructure report.	368
Paragraph	Understand how to use the different utilization reports to track consumption of cloud resources.	370
Section	Understand UCS Director chargeback.	372
Paragraph	Understand how to create Cost Models within UCS Director.	373
Paragraph	Understand how to apply Cost Models to a vDC.	376
Paragraph	Understand how to generate a Customer Billing Report and what data is included.	378
Section	Know the steps to apply Budget Policies to a group.	379

Define Key Terms

Define the following key terms from this chapter and check your answers in the glossary:

chargeback, showback, Stack View, Map Report, Trending Report, CloudSense Analytics, Cost Model, Budget Watch

This chapter covers the following topics:

4.0   Cloud Systems Management and Monitoring

4.3   Describe Cisco UCS Performance Manager

4.3.a   Describe capacity planning

4.3.b   Describe bandwidth monitoring

4.3.c   Describe how host groups facilitate dynamic monitoring

4.5   Perform cloud monitoring using Cisco Prime Service Catalog, Cisco UCS Director, Cisco Prime infrastructure

4.5.a   Describe fault monitoring

4.5.b   Describe performance monitoring

4.5.c   Describe monitoring of provisioning outcomes

4.6   Create monitoring dashboards

4.6.a   Configure custom dashboards

4.6.b   Configure threshold settings

5.0   Cloud Remediation

5.1   Configure serviceability options

5.1.a   Configure syslog

5.1.b   Configure NTP

5.1.c   Configure DNS

5.1.d   Configure DHCP

5.1.e   Configure SMTP

5.2   Interpret Logs for root cause analysis

5.2.a   Analyze fault logs

5.2.b   Analyze admin logs

5.2.c   Analyze application logs

5.3   Configure backups

5.3.a   Configure database backup

5.3.b   Configure database restore

CHAPTER 13

Cloud Performance and Capacity Management

As an administrator, one of the main challenges you face when your organization is deploying infrastructure for internal use is how to plan for capacity, which includes determining what assets are available and how much they're utilized. The challenge is compounded with integrated infrastructures because you're required to look across storage, network, compute, and virtualization stacks to try and get a sense of how much capacity and performance is available within an integrated infrastructure solution. UCS Manager, UCS Central, UCS Director, and UCS Performance Manager all include key capabilities that can help you understand not only how much infrastructure has been consumed, but also when you hit particular thresholds and may require expansion of the cloud stack to accommodate new workloads. This chapter looks at the options in each of these UCS products to show how you can benefit from greater visibility into your cloud stack infrastructure. The chapter ends with a quick look at how to configure many of the serviceability options of the Cisco ONE Enterprise Cloud Suite.

"Do I Know This Already?" Quiz

The "Do I Know This Already?" quiz allows you to assess whether you should read this entire chapter thoroughly or jump to the "Exam Preparation Tasks" section. If you are in doubt about your answers to these questions or your own assessment of your knowledge of the topics, read the entire chapter. Table 13-1 lists the major headings in this chapter and their corresponding "Do I Know This Already?" quiz questions. You can find the answers in Appendix A, "Answers to the 'Do I Know This Already?' Quizzes."

Table 13-1 "Do I Know This Already?" Section-to-Question Mapping

Foundation Topics Section	Questions
Performance Management in UCS Manager	1, 2
Performance/Capacity Management in UCS Central	3, 4
Capacity Management in UCS Director	5–7
Performance Management in UCS Performance Manager	8–10
Configuring Serviceability Options	11–13

Caution The goal of self-assessment is to gauge your mastery of the topics in this chapter. If you do not know the answer to a question or are only partially sure of the answer, you should mark that question as wrong for purposes of the self-assessment. Giving yourself credit for an answer you correctly guess skews your self-assessment results and might provide you with a false sense of security.

1. What tabs in UCS Manager would you most likely frequent to look at performance information for your UCS systems? (Choose all that apply.)

   a. Equipment tab

   b. Servers tab

   c. LAN tab

   d. SAN tab

   e. VM tab

   f. Admin tab

2. Where would an administrator monitor Ethernet port channel bandwidth usage within UCS Manager?

   a. Equipment tab

   b. Servers tab

   c. LAN tab

   d. SAN tab

   e. VM tab

   f. Admin tab

3. Does UCS Central allow the administrator to easily see how many blades are associated to service profiles versus how many blades are free?

   a. Yes, within the Domains > Equipment tab.

   b. Yes, within the Statistics > Standard Reports view.

   c. Yes, within the Servers section under Servers.

   d. No, UCS Central does not provide this information.

4. UCS Central allows you to view statistics, out of the box, for which of the following using Standard Reports? (Choose all that apply.)

   a. Average Power

   b. Peak Power

   c. Peak Fan Speed

   d. Peak Temperature

   e. Receive Traffic (Rx) for Fibre Channel

   f. Transmit Traffic (Tx) for Fibre Channel

5. Within UCS Director, when looking at dashboard statistics for the Virtual > Compute view, which of the following statistics are viewable by default? (Choose all that apply.)

   a. VMs active vs. inactive

   b. VM clones

   c. VM performance statistics

   d. Memory usage (total vs. consumed, per cloud)

   e. CPU usage (total vs. consumed, per cloud)

6. CloudSense Reporting in a component of:

   a. UCS Manager

   b. UCS Central

   c. UCS Director

   d. UCS Performance Manager

7. Report Builder allows you to view reports in which formats? (Choose all that apply.)

   a. Historical

   b. Snapshot

   c. Tabular

   d. Linear

   e. Orthogonal

8. UCS Performance Manager can show performance information for which of the following? (Choose all that apply.)

   a. VMware ESXi as a hypervisor

   b. Hewlett-Packard HP C7000 Blades

   c. Cisco Unified Computing System

   d. IBM Storwize storage arrays

   e. EMC storage arrays

   f. NetApp storage arrays

9. UCS Performance Manager Topology view can show which of the following? (Choose all that apply.)

   a. UCS domains

   b. Storage arrays

   c. Nexus fabrics

   d. MDS fabrics

   e. Brocade fabrics

10. What feature in UCS Performance Manager allows you to group together multiple virtual machines and/or physical hosts into a logical container and assess performance and fault impacts within the boundaries of that container?

   a. UCS Performance Manager Application Containers

   b. UCS Performance Manager Fenced Applications

   c. UCS Performance Manager Containers

   d. UCS Performance Manager Application Groups

11. What would a severity level of Warning indicate in a syslog message?

   a. Immediate action needed

   b. Non-urgent failure

   c. An error will occur if no action is taken

   d. Normal operating behavior

13

12. True or False. An NTP server of stratum 15 would be preferred over a stratum 0 server.

   a.   True

   b.   False

13. Which details are provided to clients by the Baremetal Agent in a DHCP message? (Choose all that apply.)

   a.   IP address

   b.   Subnet mask

   c.   PXE filename

   d.   TFTP server

Foundation Topics

Performance Management in UCS Manager

As the most basic element of your cloud stack, availability of compute is an important aspect to consider. The majority of organizations employ virtualization technology via hypervisors on their compute layer, which means compute is often one of the first elements to run out of capacity within an integrated infrastructure. This section focuses on the key capabilities present in UCS Manager to assess performance and capacity. The section will look at both monitoring of hosts and the networking infrastructure within UCS Manager, such as the Ethernet, Fibre Channel, or Fiber Channel over Ethernet (FCoE) bandwidth used.

Monitoring Hosts/Blades

Understanding host utilization is one of the most important aspects of assessing cloud performance. UCS Manager has a variety of built-in views that can help you gauge performance at the host level.

Monitoring Bandwidth

In UCS, it is important to be able to identify how much bandwidth an individual blade is using. The best way to view this information is to take the approach provided in the following steps. As a refresher, in UCS, only blades with an active service profile associated with them are powered on and able to run an operating system. Without the service profile association, a blade or compute node in UCS is simply sheet metal and silicon, waiting to be programmed.

Also, within UCS Manager, the user interface is divided into two panes, the navigation pane on the left and the action pane on the right, as shown in Figure 13-1.

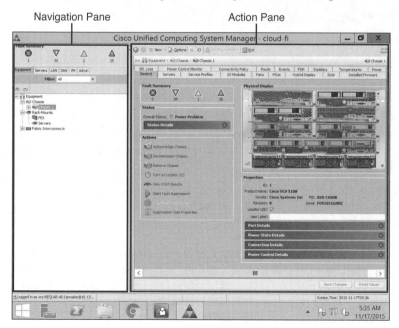

Figure 13-1 *Navigating in UCS Manager*

13

Step 1.   In UCS Manager, navigate to the **Servers** tab. Click **Service Profiles**, and then navigate to a service profile. Note the name of the service profile you are looking for.

Step 2.   On the service profile's General tab, you will see Associated Server or Blade on this pane, as seen in Figure 13-2. Note that, depending on firmware version and what object you are looking at in UCS Manager, you might see "associated server" or "associated blade."

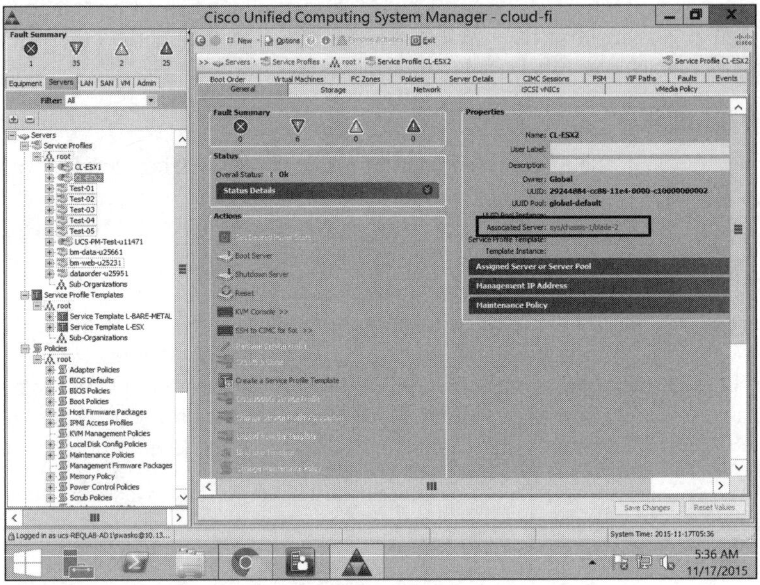

Figure 13-2   *Service Profile General Tab*

Step 3.   With the associated server or blade selected in Step 2 in mind, click the **Equipment** tab of the navigation pane and navigate to the adapter you wish to inspect, such as Adapter 1, by expanding **Chassis > Chassis** *N* **> Servers > Server** *N* **> Adapters > Adapter** *N*.

Step 4.   Click the (**+**) icon next to the subset of interfaces you want to see, such as host bus adapters (HBAs). Click the interface you want to view statistics for, such as HBA 1.

Step 5.   In the action pane on the right, click the **Statistics** tab (see Figure 13-3). This shows you information about traffic performance for each virtual adapter on the UCS blade's service profile.

From this view, you're able to determine performance of the individual adapters in the system. You can also click the **Chart** tab to see various options to chart performance over time. Note that a very limited amount of data is collected here and that this view within UCS Manager isn't meant to be a historical graph of this data. UCS Performance Manager is a better tool for longer-term performance trending over time.

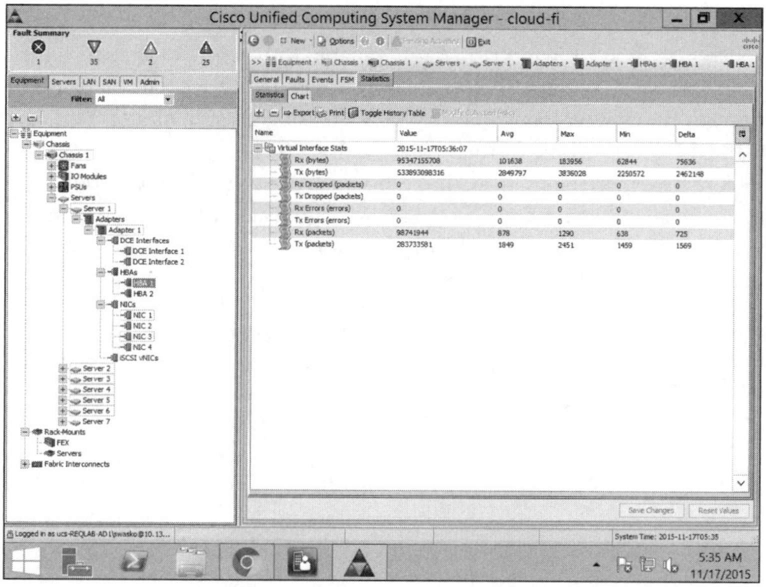

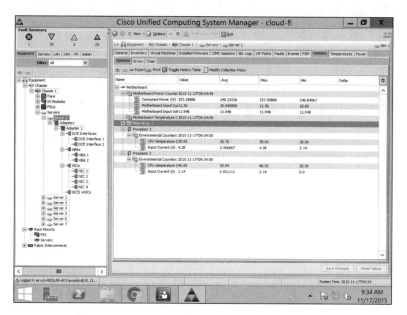

Figure 13-3 *UCS Manager HBA 1 Traffic Statistics*

Monitoring CPU/Memory

Within UCS Manager, you can monitor environmental attributes only (not usage) of a system's motherboard, CPU sockets, and memory DIMMs. Figure 13-4 shows a detailed view of navigating to Equipment > Chassis, Chassis 1 > Servers > Server 1 and clicking the Statistics tab in the action pane.

Figure 13-4 *UCS Manager Motherboard, Memory, and Processor Environmental Details*

Monitoring Other Components

There is also deep bandwidth monitoring information available for each UCS chassis' IO Module (IOM). In systems where there is a potential for throughput contention (for example, a chassis that has heavy workloads but may only be using one uplink cable on each IOM, delivering 2 × 10 GbE, or 20 Gbps, of total bandwidth to a chassis). It is important, in situations where you may be experiencing slow throughput (VMs seeing SCSI timeouts or aborts as an example), to inspect the counters on the IO Module backplane ports that are connected to the particular blade in question. Figure 13-5 shows some of the counters available for capacity planning and monitoring purposes.

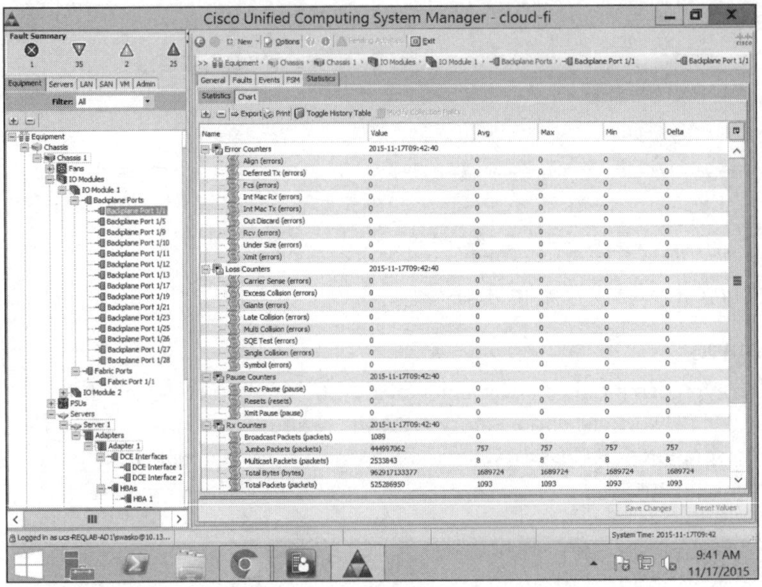

Figure 13-5 *IOM Counters for Backplane Ports*

Monitoring Infrastructure

Assessing performance on an individual blade level is important in situations where performance of a particular host or VM running on a host needs to be monitored. Equally important is the ability to ascertain the performance on the entire UCS system from a bandwidth utilization perspective. This is important to ensure that there is adequate Ethernet or Fibre Channel egress bandwidth available from the UCS Fabric Interconnects northbound, as well as to ensure the system isn't oversubscribed.

As a quick refresher, UCS Fabric Interconnects aggregate bandwidth, management, and configuration for up to 20 chassis and 160 blades (or a combination of a total of 160 blades and UCS C-Series rackmount systems that are UCS Manager integrated). A pair of Fabric Interconnects and all connected chassis and rackmount systems are known as a UCS domain. In some cases when I/O gets very heavy in the environment, the need may arise to add additional bandwidth so monitoring domainwide system bandwidth (at the Fabric Interconnect level) is very important for the overall balance and performance in the system.

Monitoring Ethernet Bandwidth

Most UCS implementations utilize Ethernet port channels for northbound Ethernet traffic leaving or entering the UCS Fabric Interconnect. UCS Manager enables you to monitor bandwidth at the individual port level as well as at the port-channel level.

To gain insight into how much bandwidth is being utilized on a per Ethernet uplink port basis, let's first determine the interface role. Within UCS Manager, navigate to **Equipment > Fabric Interconnects > Fabric Interconnect (A or B) > Fixed Module > Ethernet Ports**. From here, as shown in Figure 13-6, you can determine which ports are network ports and which are chassis-facing ports. (Note that if you have an expansion module or modules in your Fabric Interconnect, you may have to navigate to that particular module to check traffic.) In Figure 13-6, Ports 1 and 2 are network uplink modules.

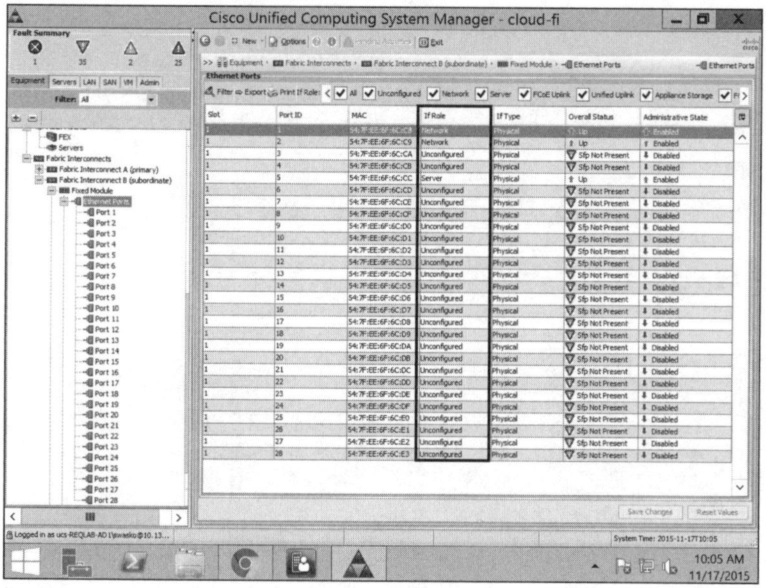

Figure 13-6 *Determining Interface (If) Role in UCS Manager*

13

Once the interface role has been determined, clicking the interface name in the navigation pane and choosing the Statistics tab in the action pane will show you all statistics for that interface, as shown in Figure 13-7.

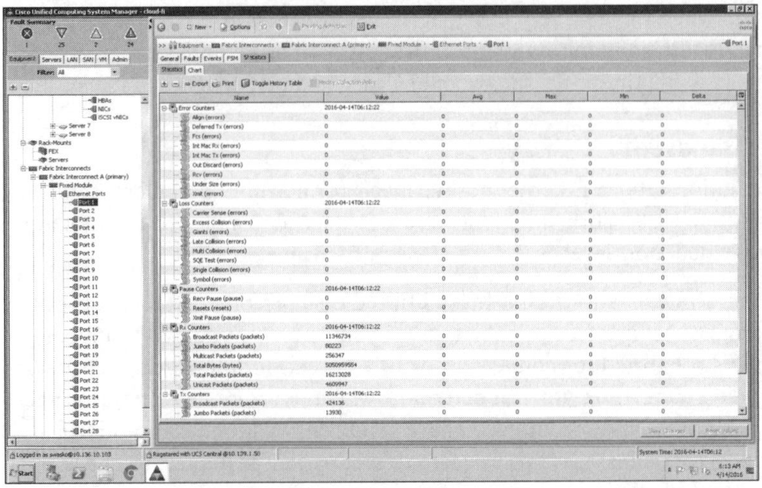

Figure 13-7   *Ethernet Uplink Single Port Statistics*

Next, assuming the interfaces are in a port channel, navigate to the UCS Manager **LAN** tab in the navigation pane, and then drill down into **LAN > LAN Cloud > Fabric A (or B) > Port Channels > Port Channel (***name***)**. In Figure 13-8, Port-Channel 1 is named aci1. Selecting Port-Channel 1 and clicking Statistics in the action pane will show all statistics for Port-Channel 1.

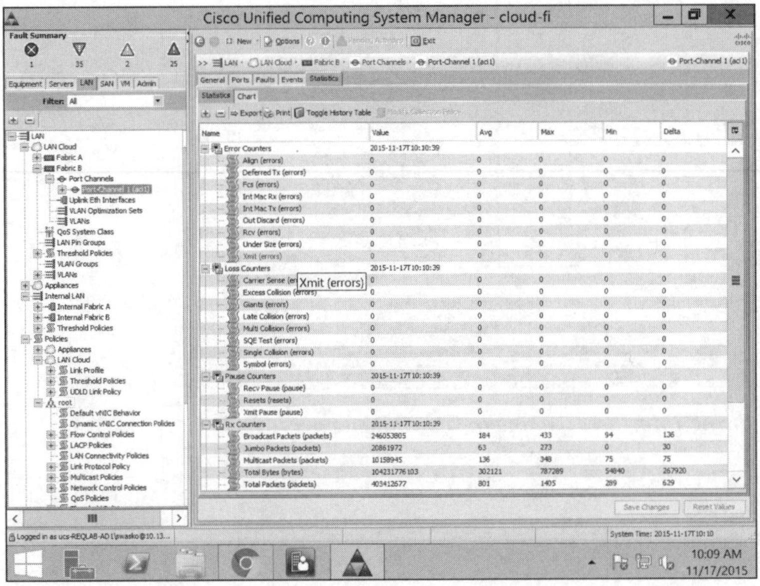

Figure 13-8   *Port-Channel 1 Statistics*

Monitoring Fibre Channel Bandwidth

Similar to the previous section where we looked at Ethernet statistics and interface information, we can do the same for Fibre Channel interfaces in UCS Manager. Also, assuming the cloud environment is utilizing Cisco MDS Fibre Channel (FC) switches or Nexus switches supporting Fibre Channel as the next hop, FC port channeling is also supported. There is not support for FC port channeling in non-UCS Fibre Channel implementations.

To see individual interface statistics, navigate to **Equipment > Fabric Interconnects > Fabric Interconnect (A or B) > Fixed Module > FC Ports**. Select the correct FC Port number and click the **Statistics** tab in the action pane (see Figure 13-9). Note that if you have an expansion module or modules in your fabric interconnect, you may have to navigate to that particular module to check interface traffic.

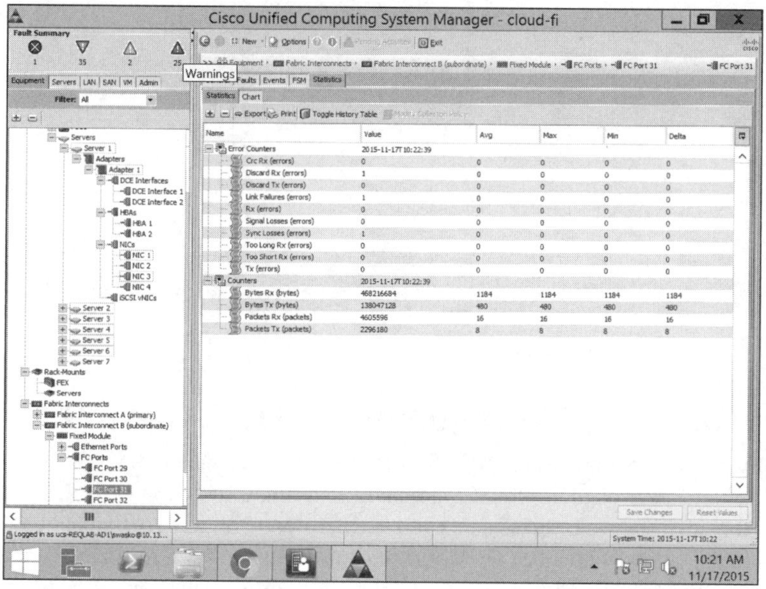

Figure 13-9   *Fibre Channel Single Port Statistics*

In addition, as discussed, with Cisco Fibre Channel products such as an MDS switch north of the UCS Fabric Interconnect, FC port channels can also be utilized. To view statistics for an FC port channel, in the navigation pane, navigate to **SAN > SAN Cloud > FC Port Channels**, click the name of the FC Port Channel, and then click the **Statistics** tab in the action pane. See Figure 13-10.

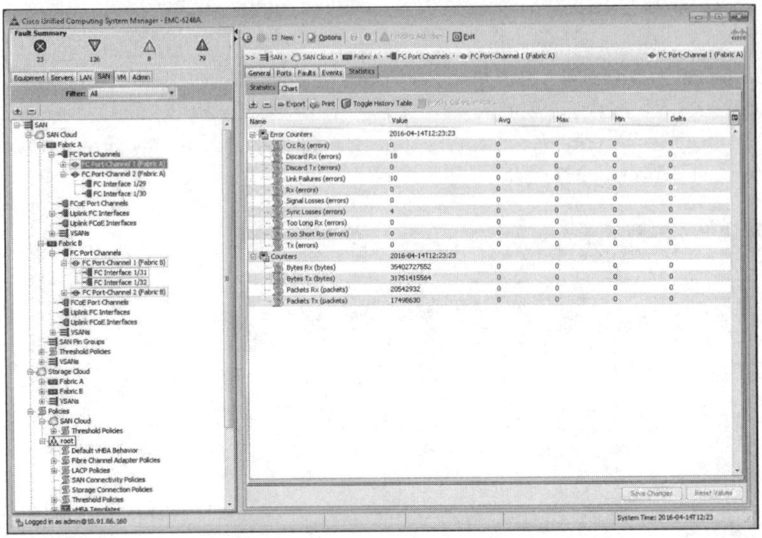

Figure 13-10   *Fibre Channel Port Channel Statistics*

Performance/Capacity Management in UCS Central

Some larger cloud environments may utilize UCS Central for UCS management. UCS Central is a centralized manager of multiple UCS domains. In a single UCS domain, UCS Manager resides on a pair of Fabric Interconnects and is where you connect to administer the system. Once you get into a handful of UCS domains (or dozens or hundreds), managing each domain by visiting the Fabric Interconnects only gives you 160:1 management scale (as each domain can grow to around 160 UCS rackmounts or blades total). As shown in Figure 13-11, UCS Central is a virtual appliance that allows you to manage up to 10,000 total endpoints, scaling to dozens or hundreds of separate UCS domains.

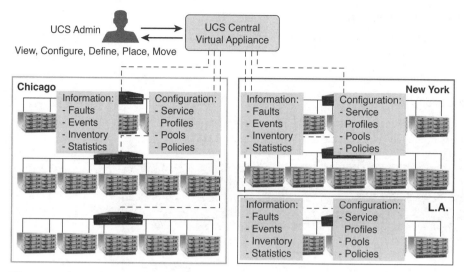

Figure 13-11 *UCS Central High-Level Logical View*

Seeing Available Host Capacity

The interface of UCS Central, much like that of UCS Manager (discussed in the previous section), has a navigation pane on the left and an action pane on the right. When you first log in to UCS Central, your default view will be of the Domains tab with the Equipment subtab in the navigation pane showing UCS Domains (see Figure 13-12). In the action pane, you will see an overview of all the UCS domains in your environment. This overview will show you how many hosts are currently used (in all domains registered with UCS Central) and how many are free. This can be very helpful in determining cloud capacity used and remaining.

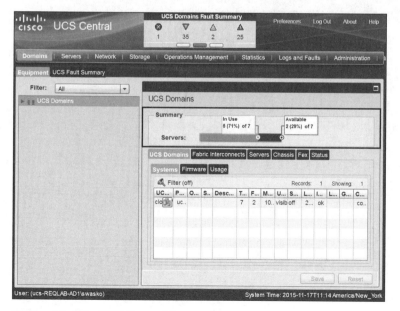

Figure 13-12 *UCS Central Servers In Use Versus Available*

Statistics and Reporting

UCS Central provides some ability to report on bandwidth utilization (Ethernet) at the UCS domain level to see which ports are the busiest. In addition, there are other standard reports that ship out of the box.

Standard Reports

In UCS Central, click **Statistics** in the menu bar to see Standard Reports and Custom Reports in the navigation pane, as shown in Figure 13-13.

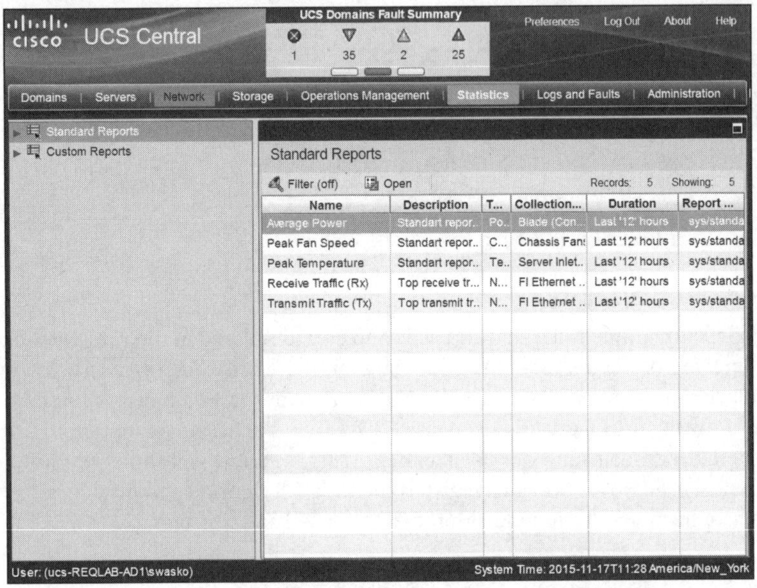

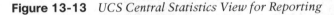

Figure 13-13   *UCS Central Statistics View for Reporting*

Within the Standard Reports, you will see the following:

- Average Power
- Peak Fan Speed
- Peak Temperature
- Receive Traffic (Rx)
- Transmit Traffic (Tx)

To view the type of information available in these Standard Reports, click **Receive Traffic (Rx)**, and then click the **Open** icon as highlighted in Figure 13-14.

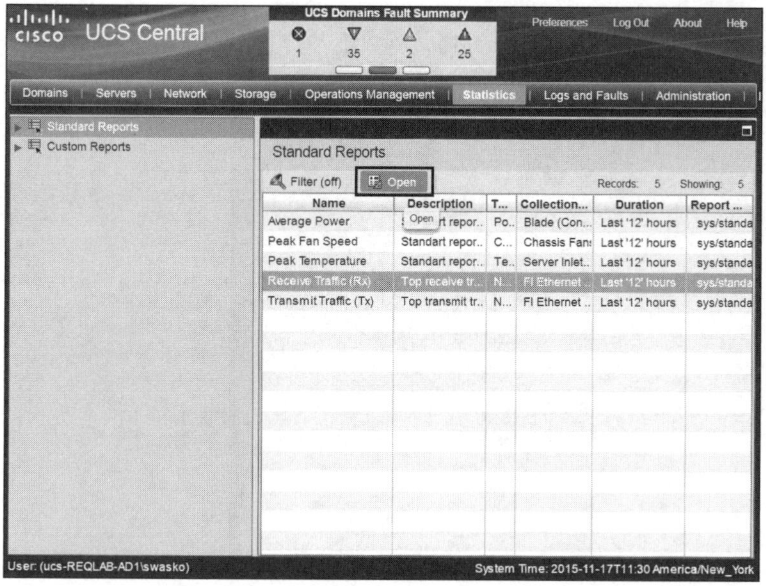

Figure 13-14 *UCS Central Opening a Standard Report*

Once the Receive Traffic (Rx) report is open, click the **Run Report > To Load Data** icon, as shown in Figure 13-15.

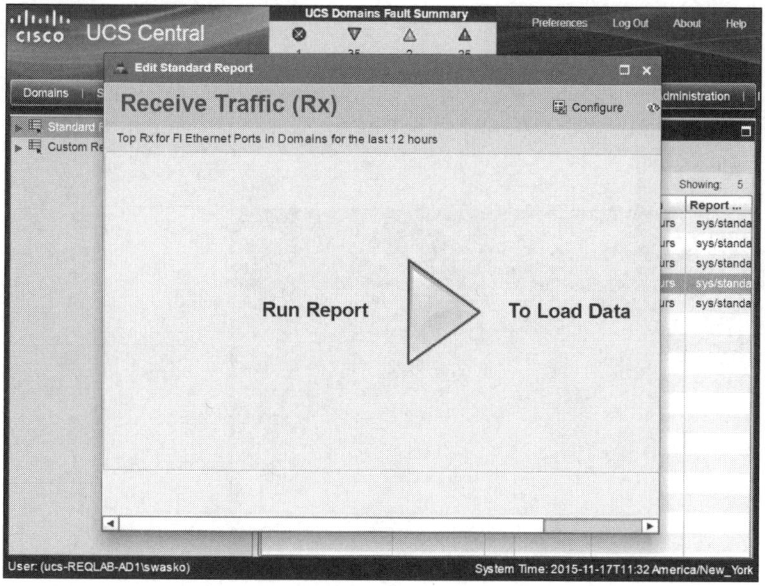

Figure 13-15 *UCS Central Run Report Screen*

Running the report will show you total bandwidth (Rx) used in the last 12 hours for each UCS domain. Figure 13-16 shows that UCS domain cloud-fi has used 1.88 TB of Ethernet Rx traffic.

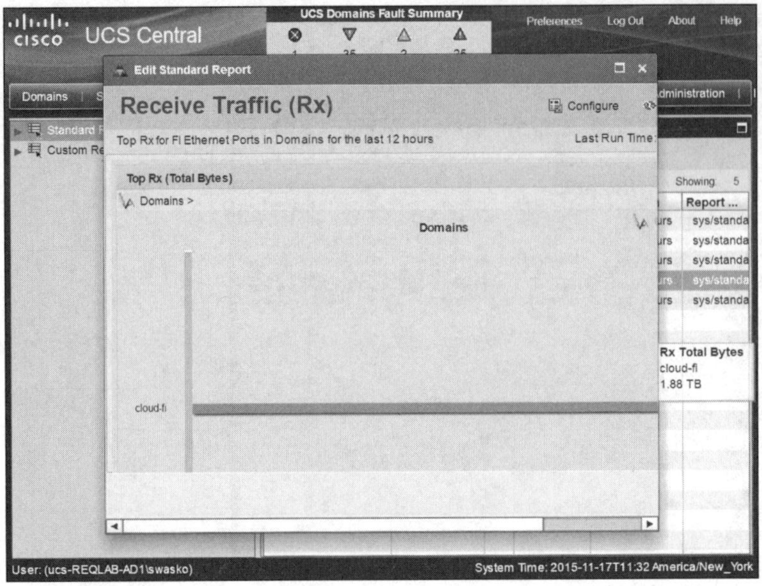

Figure 13-16   *UCS Central Receive Traffic (Rx) Report*

Custom Reports

Custom Reports within UCS Central can provide a wealth of valuable information to you as you look to understand traffic patterns in and out of your UCS-based cloud infrastructure.

Step 1.   Starting from the top-level **Statistics** menu, expand **Custom Reports** in the navigation pane, as shown in Figure 13-17. Note that you have the ability to create different groups of reports by clicking the Create Group button in the upper-right corner.

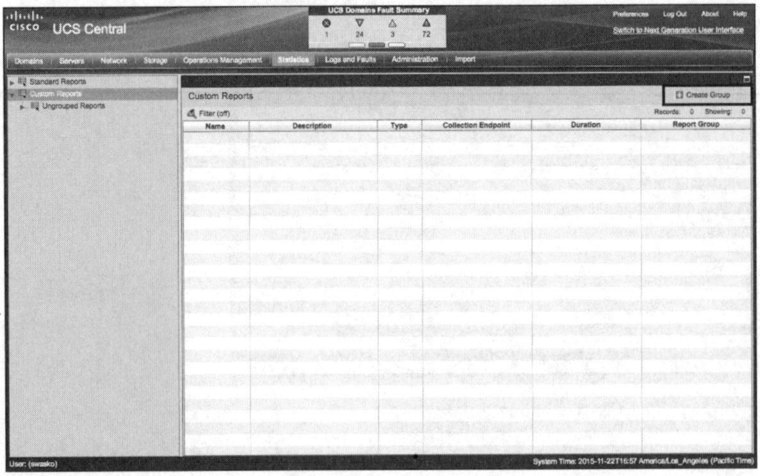

Figure 13-17   *Opening Custom Reports in UCS Central*

Step 2.   Click **Create Group** and create a new group called **New-Custom-Group**, as shown in Figure 13-18. Click **OK**.

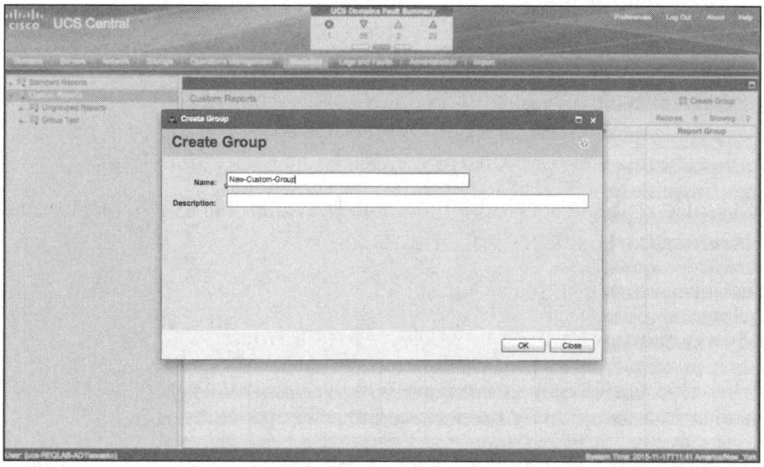

Figure 13-18   *New Custom Group in UCS Central Custom Reports*

Step 3.   Navigate to the newly created group and click the **Create Report** icon, as shown in Figure 13-19.

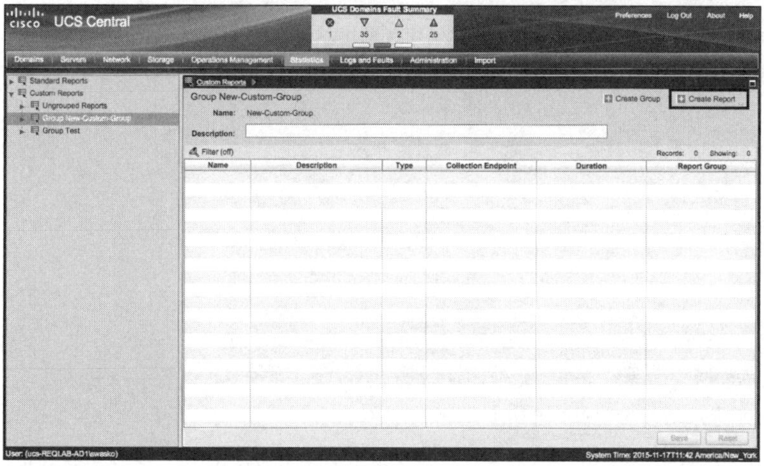

Figure 13-19   *Create Custom Report in UCS Central*

In the Create Report dialog box that opens, you can create information from a variety of sources by choosing among the options available in the **Report Type** drop-down list, including

- Cooling
- Network
- Power
- Temperature

For the purposes of cloud capacity monitoring, let's look deeper at the Network report type.

Step 1. In the Create Report dialog box, shown in Figure 13-20, give the report a name of **New-Net-Report**.

Step 2. In the Report Type drop-down list box, select **Network**.

Step 3. In the Properties section, the Default View setting gives you the option to select either a Table view or a Chart view. Select the **Chart** radio button.

Step 4. For the Display setting, check both the **Total Transmit (Tx) Traffic (Delta)** and **Total Receive (Rx) Traffic (Delta)** check boxes.

Step 5. In the For drop-down list, select **NICs**.

Step 6. In the **Duration** drop-down list box, select **Last 48 Hours**.

Step 7. For the Context option, click **Select Context** and navigate to a UCS domain or domains that you would like to report on and select those domains.

Step 8. Your report settings should look similar to those shown in Figure 13-20. Click **Save**.

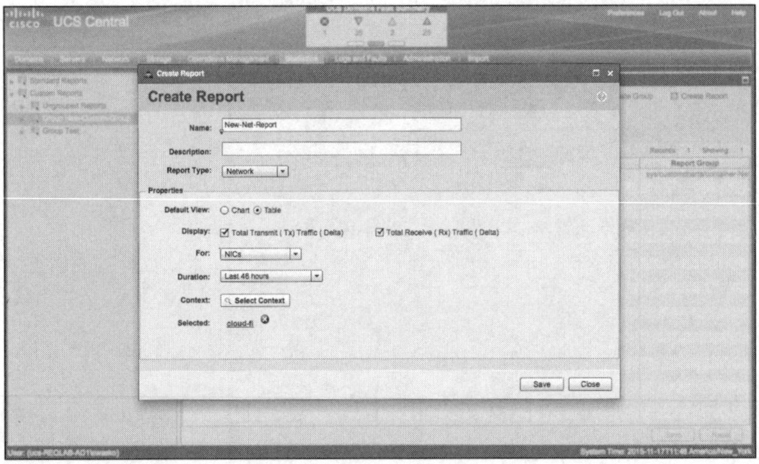

Figure 13-20 *Custom Report Properties in UCS Central*

Step 9. Once your New-Net-Report has been saved for New-Custom-Group, select it in the action pane and click the **Open** icon, as shown in Figure 13-21.

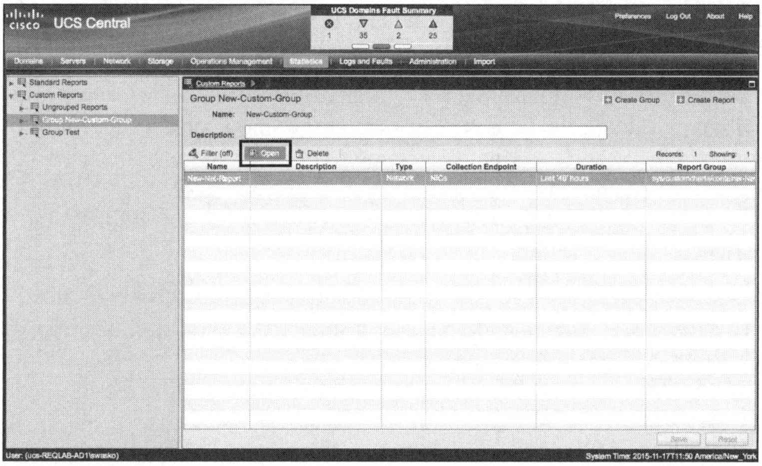

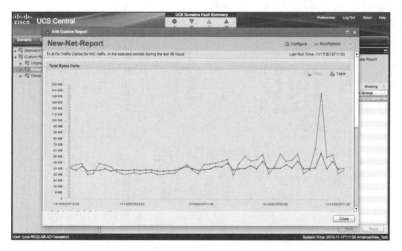

Figure 13-21   *Opening New-Net-Report in UCS Central*

> **Step 10.**   With the report opened, click the **Run Report > To Load Data** icon. Your
> report outlook should look similar to Figure 13-22.

Figure 13-22   *New-Net-Report Output in UCS Central*

> Notice in the upper-right corner of the chart that you can toggle between
> Chart view and Table view for this data. Also notice that when you are
> working with this report, hovering over the values in the chart will show you
> their absolute values, which can be helpful for monitoring bandwidth trends
> over time.

13

Capacity Management in UCS Director

As discussed earlier in this chapter, UCS Manager and UCS Central are good at showing real-time and historical performance monitoring for a variety of statistics. UCS Central also includes some capabilities for doing capacity management at the very coarse level of how many blades are consumed in a cloud offering. When you want to get more granular on capacity management, UCS Director has a lot of great information available.

Dashboard Statistics

When you first log in to UCS Director as an admin, you'll see the converged view of Sites and Pods. Navigate to **Virtual > Compute** and you'll see a variety of useful statistics regarding your cloud usage. See the example shown in Figure 13-23.

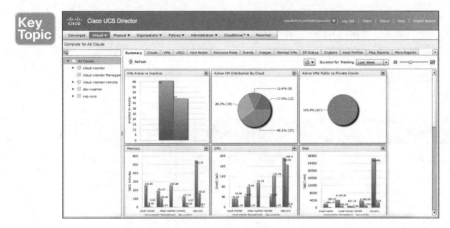

Figure 13-23   *UCS Director All Clouds Dashboard View*

The Summary tab in the action page shows statistics that include

- Total number of clouds registered to UCS Director
- Total memory footprint of all compute nodes in these clouds
- Storage statistics including total combined capacity as well as free GB and free space as a percentage

Additionally, you can navigate to **Physical > Compute** in UCS Director to see compute statistics regarding the total number of UCS servers that are associated versus those that are unassociated, and the total number of servers and total number of chassis in the cloud.

CloudSense Reporting

As discussed previously, CloudSense reports within UCS Director give you a lot of powerful information and reporting capabilities. Within CloudSense, there are three different reporting areas, as shown in Figure 13-24:

- Reports
- Assessments
- Report Builder

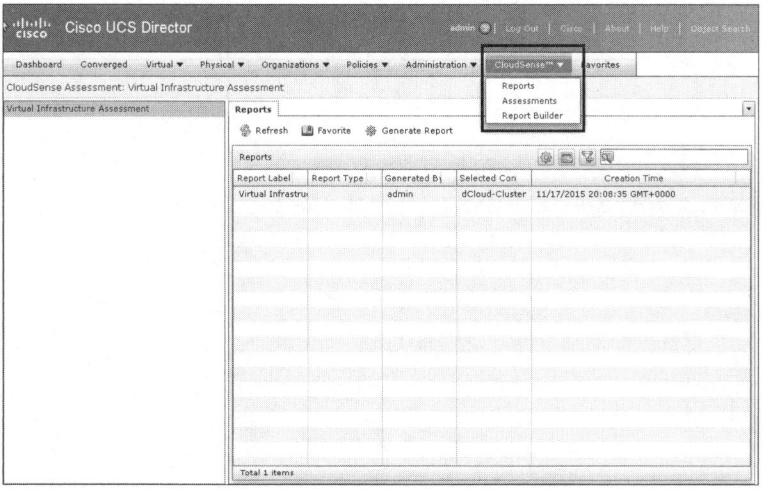

Figure 13-24   *Reporting Areas Within CloudSense*

Let's take a quick look at each in turn.

CloudSense Reports in UCS Director

A vast number of reports are available out of the box, including (in UCS Director 5.3)

- Application Container Report
- Billing Report for a Customer
- Cisco C880M4 Inventory Report
- Group Infrastructure Inventory Report
- Hyper V Cloud Utilization Summary
- EMC, IBM Storwize, and NetApp Storage Inventory Reports
- Reports for Service Request Statistics or SR statistics per Group
- UCS Data Center Inventory Report
- VM Activity Report by Group
- VM Performance Summary
- VMware Cloud Utilization Summary
- VMware Host Performance Summary
- Virtual Infrastructure and Assets Report

These give you, the cloud admin, a vast set of prebuilt reports to instantly understand capacity and utilization of resources within the cloud environment. Figure 13-25 shows the output of the VMware VM Performance Report. The report shows trends over time for CPU, memory, disk, and network usage.

13

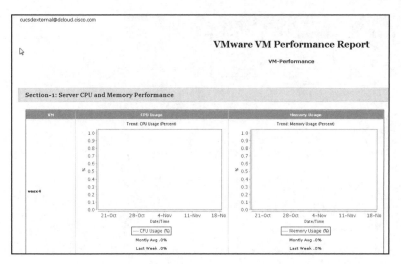

Figure 13-25   *UCS Director VMware VM Performance Report*

CloudSense Assessments in UCS Director

Within Assessments in UCS Director, you will see the Virtual Infrastructure Assessment. Generating this report provides information such as Fault Counts by Severity, Fault Counts by Rule, Hardware Compatibility Information, and information about all clocks registered with UCS Director. As you will see in the configuring serviceability options section toward the end of this chapter, having all system time sources synchronized to a common NTP target can be very helpful when troubleshooting an issue across the multiple components of a Cisco cloud solution. Figure 13-26 shows output from the Virtual Infrastructure Assessment report.

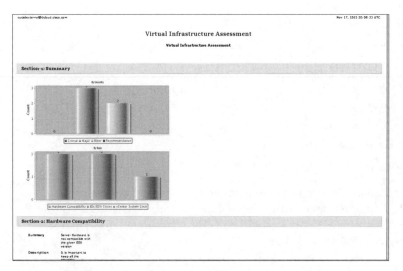

Figure 13-26   *Virtual Infrastructure Assessment Report*

CloudSense Report Builder in UCS Director

Within Report Builder in UCS Director, you get an extremely powerful engine for building custom reports to understand both capacity and utilization of various cloud resources.

Step 1.   Within Report Builder, you must first add a template by clicking the **Add Template** icon. Doing so brings up the Add Template dialog box shown in Figure 13-27.

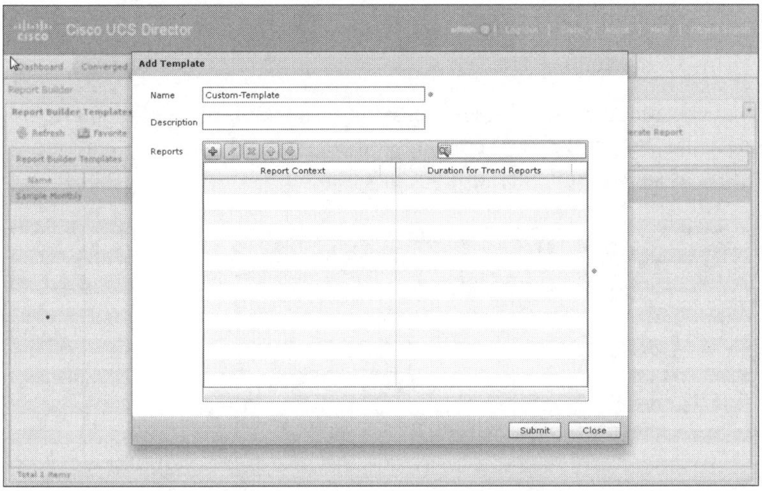

Figure 13-27   *Report Builder Add Template Dialog Box*

Step 2.   Click the green **+** icon to open the Add Entry dialog box (see Figure 13-28). In this form, you have the option to select the reporting context for the report. Options in the Report Context drop-down list include

- VDC (virtual data center)

- Cloud (for example, the VMware hypervisor)

- Physical Account

- Multi Domain Manager (for example, UCS Central)

- Global

- Global Admin

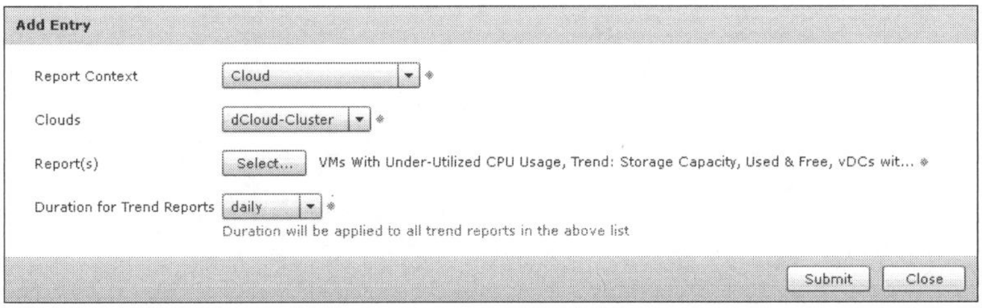

Figure 13-28   *UCS Director Report Builder Add Entry Dialog Box*

Step 3. To view a sample report, select **Cloud** as the Report Context, choose the cloud names in the Clouds drop-down list box, and select a few options by clicking the Report(s) **Select** button. For the report shown in Figure 13-28, we'll select the following reports and set the Duration for Trend Reports field to **Daily**:

■ VMs with Under-Utilized CPU Usage

■ Trend: Storage Capacity, Used & Free

■ vDCs with the Most CPU Usage

■ VMs with Most Memory Usage

Step 4. Once you have added these entries successfully, click **Submit**, and then **OK**. Now, select the Report Builder Template you created and click the **Generate Report** icon, as shown in Figure 13-29. Click **Submit**.

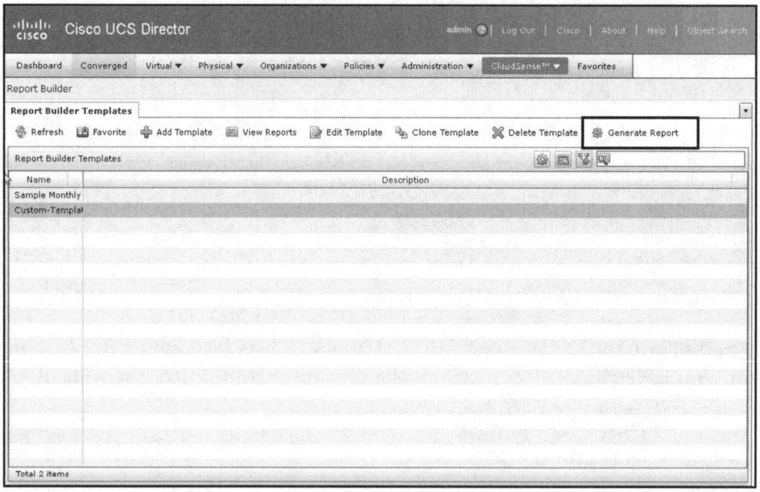

Figure 13-29 *UCS Director Generate Report Icon*

Step 5. Give the report a Report Title and then click the **Generate** button.

Step 6.   Click the **View Reports** icon, as shown in Figure 13-30.

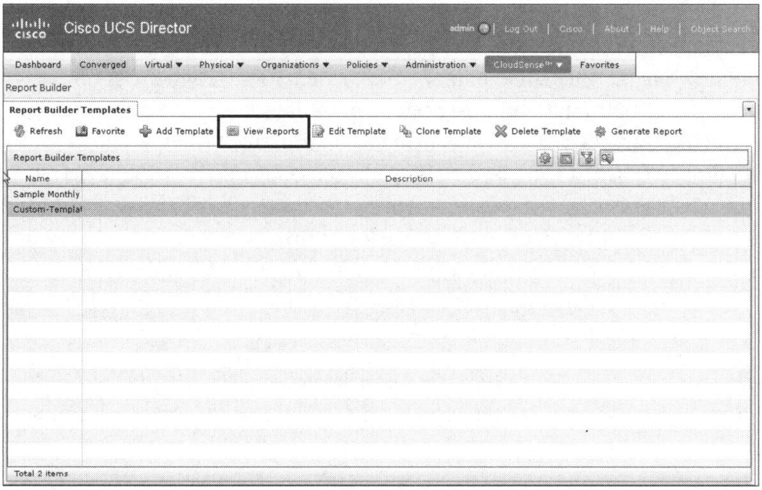

Figure 13-30   *UCS Director View Reports Icon*

Step 7.   Select the report you just created and click **View Report**. Choose the output format as **HTML** to view the report as shown in Figure 13-31.

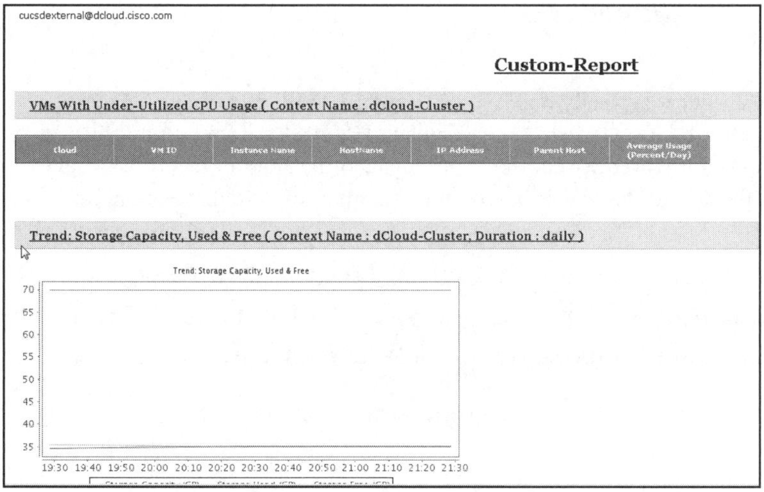

Figure 13-31   *UCS Director Custom-Report*

As you can see, there is a very rich set of reporting resources available within UCS Director for understanding cloud capacity and consumption. Next, we'll look at the features that exist in UCS Performance Manager.

13

Performance Management in UCS Performance Manager

UCS Performance Manager is a product that was designed to address the question that too often arises when multiple performance management suites are used in an organization. For example, the storage team may be using one tool to assess performance of the storage infrastructure, while the network team is using a separate tool to view the network. The compute team uses a third tool, and perhaps hypervisor information is being monitored via a fourth tool. As is often the case, when performance issues arise, you are stuck trying to use your "decoder ring" across a variety of tools and vendors to try to assess performance impact. Further complicating matters, often if an application is impacted, it can be very hard to ascertain what infrastructure may be contributing (or not contributing) to the application issue.

UCS Performance Manager was designed to help answer just such questions, giving you the ability to see into multiple aspects of the system and get a picture quickly of what is going on in the environment.

Cisco currently offers two versions of UCS Performance Manager. You should assess your needs to decide which version is right for you:

- **UCS Performance Manager Express:** Covers only the physical and virtual compute platform and the operating system
- **UCS Performance Manager:** Covers physical and virtual compute, Fabric Interconnects, Ethernet and Fibre Channel switches, and supported storage arrays from EMC and NetApp

UCS Performance Manager is typically deployed as a virtual appliance using a VMware OVA package. It can also be installed via a self-installing ISO package for systems like Microsoft Hyper-V. Data is stored within the appliance, and the amount of vCPUs, memory, and storage you allocate to the VM is based on the number of systems being monitored, as summarized here:

- **Small UCS domain/site (1–50 servers):** 4 vCPUs, 32 GB RAM, 50 GB storage
- **Medium UCS domain/site (51–100 servers):** 8 vCPUs, 64 GB RAM, 100 GB storage
- **Large UCS domain/site (101–500 servers):** 12 vCPUs, 96 GB RAM, 150 GB storage

Now let's look at some of the features of UCS Performance Manager.

Dashboard

When you first log in to UCS Performance Manager 1.x, use port 8080, which is the default port for login. Note that in USC Performance Manager 2.x, the port defaults to HTTP/HTTPS standard port numbers of 80/443.

Upon logging in, you'll be presented with the Dashboard pane. The GUI is made up of HTML5 portlets, and you have a variety of options available at first login, as shown in the upper right of Figure 13-32:

- **Reset Portlets:** Return to the default view of UCS Performance Manager

- **Configure layout:** Change the order of what is displayed on the Dashboard summary view

- **Add portlet:** Add new portlets from the UCS PM database to the Dashboard summary view

- **Stop Refresh:** Manually disable refreshing of portlets (which happen on a 30-second interval by default)

Also note in Figure 13-32 the navigation options at the top level from the home screen. You can navigate into Dashboard, Event, Infrastructure, Reports, and Advanced.

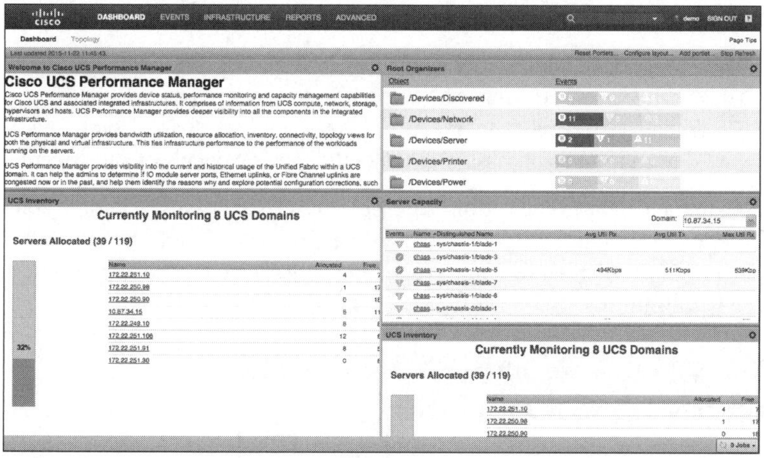

Figure 13-32   *The Dashboard Summary View in UCS Performance Manager*

Dashboard Topology

On the main Dashboard screen, click **Topology** (to the right of Dashboard) to see an overview of all the connected UCS domains in the navigation pane and two quick charts per domain (see Figure 13-33):

- Overall Ethernet Bandwidth Utilization
- Connected Ethernet Ports Bandwidth Utilization

13

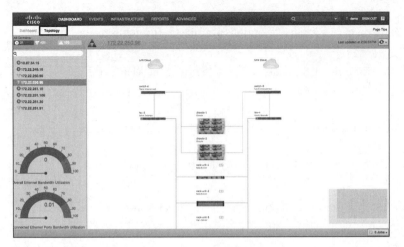

Figure 13-33 *Dashboard Topology View*

Clicking different domain names or IP addresses will navigate you quickly through all the UCS domains being managed by UCS Performance Manager. In the action pane, you will see a view of the entire UCS domain as well as connections to LAN Cloud and SAN Cloud. This action pane can be zoomed in and out as necessary to drill into specific details of the system.

From this view, clicking any element in the action pane (such as a UCS chassis) will drill you into details on that particular element. In Figure 13-34, you are presented with the view of chassis-2 from domain 172.22.251.91. Here you can see blades, associated service profiles, and transmit and receive utilization.

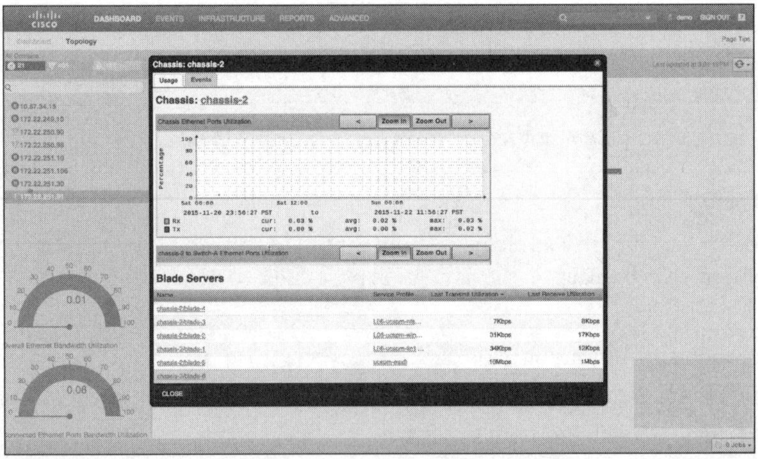

Figure 13-34 *Topology View Chassis Drill Down*

Monitoring Infrastructure

Within UCS Performance Manager from the home screen, clicking the **Infrastructure** top-level choice will take you into a list of all the devices in the system. Devices are classified by object type, such as Cisco UCS, Storage, Network, and Hypervisor. See Figure 13-35.

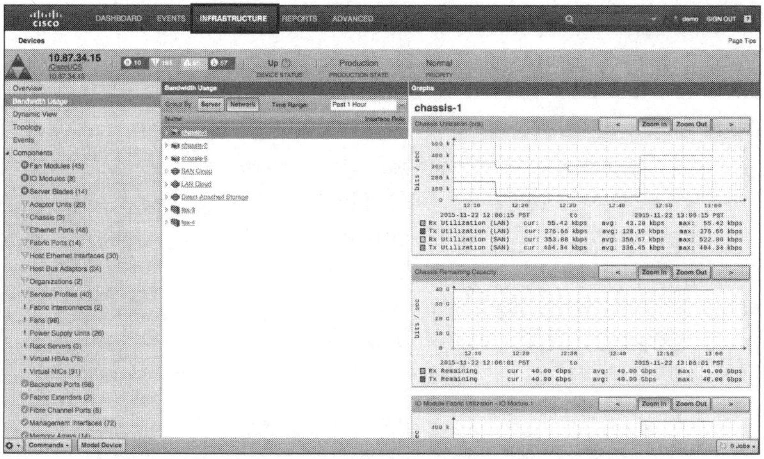

Figure 13-35 *UCS Performance Manager Infrastructure View*

Clicking any object will drill down into that object. In this example, we have clicked the first object in the view, /CiscoUCS system 10.87.34.15. From this next view, shown in Figure 13-36, you will see very detailed information about the UCS system. In the navigation pane there is overview information of the system as well as some useful additional views:

- **Bandwidth Usage:** Shows very detailed bandwidth information for chassis, SAN uplinks, LAN uplinks, direct-attached storage, as well as any Fabric Extenders (FEXs) attached to the UCS chassis. Reporting time frames are configurable to show statistics ranging anywhere from the last hour to the last day. In the example shown in Figure 13-36, we have clicked chassis-1.

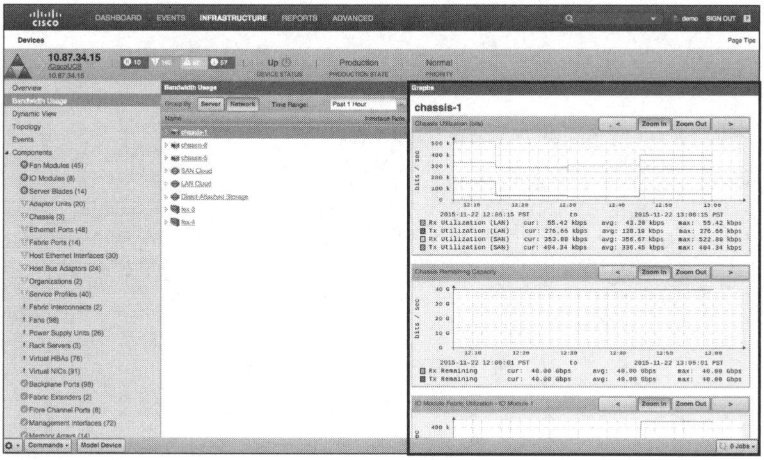

Figure 13-36 *Bandwidth Usage View for chassis-1*

13

- **Dynamic View:** Generates a real-time view of all the components in the entire system being monitored by UCS Performance Manager. For example, if you are looking at a top-level object type of /CiscoUCS and you click Dynamic View, you will see all Service Profiles, Fabric Extenders, Fabric Interconnects, UCS Chassis, UCS Blades, UCS IO Cards, UCS Racks, and UCS Fabric Ports for the entire domain.

- **Topology:** Takes you back to the same view you see in the Dashboard/Topology view for the particular element you have drilled into (shown previously in Figure 13-33).

- **Events:** Shows all faults by severity level. This view can be queried, sorted, exported, and filtered in a variety of views.

- **Components:** Lists all the components that make up the top-level object. In our case, having clicked /CiscoUCS, we see all fans, blades, adapters, and all aspects of the entire UCS domain in the Components list.

This is a very quick overview of the information available in the Infrastructure view. For CCNA study, drill down on the available performance and capacity metrics within Infrastructure view and discover just how powerful and complete UCS Performance Manager is.

Application Groups

Often, understanding what infrastructure an application resides on in large organizations can be a daunting challenge. As an application becomes performance impacted, it often takes minutes, hours, or days to fully understand what storage array the application resides on, which Ethernet and Fibre Channel switches pass the application's traffic, which UCS blade/domain the application resides in, etc. Application Groups within UCS Performance Manager can assist in the task of understanding all infrastructure comprising an application and, therefore, if any impacts or faults in the infrastructure could be the cause of an application performance issue.

Take the following steps to view an existing Application Group within UCS Performance Manager:

Step 1.   From the top-level menu, click **Infrastructure**.

Step 2.   In the navigation pane, expand **Application Groups**.

Step 3.   Click an already defined Application Group. As you can see in Figure 13-37, clicking the AppGrp1 Application Group shows an application composed of five Windows Servers.

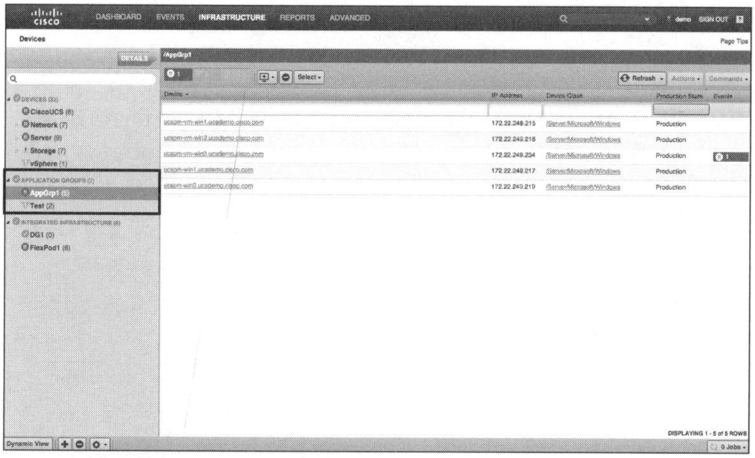

Figure 13-37 *Application Groups*

Here we can see that ucspm-vm-win3.ucsdemo.cisco.com has an event. Double-clicking the object shows that the VM is down (see Figure 13-38).

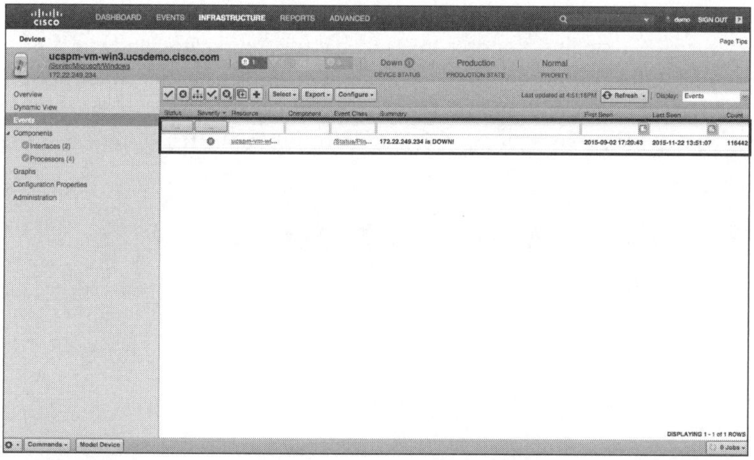

Figure 13-38 *UCS Performance Manager Application Group VM Down*

Application Groups give you a very powerful means to group pieces of infrastructure together in meaningful ways to understand the impact of traffic paths through devices as well as systems that support particular applications. Understanding all the components that make up a particular application can increase the awareness of the infrastructure supporting those applications (such as switches in the application path, storage, etc.), decrease time required to troubleshoot issues, and assist with capacity and performance monitoring.

13

Available Reports in UCS Performance Manager

Finally, let's look at reports available in UCS Performance Manager. The system comes with a variety of reports that you can view out of the box after you've added the infrastructure you want to manage. These reports can provide valuable information to determine utilization of bandwidth, discover memory expansion opportunities for your UCS systems, compile a hardware inventory report, determine CPU and memory utilization for your systems, and much more.

From the top-level menu, click **Reports** to see a list of reports available out of the box. Reports are grouped into four key areas:

- Cisco UCS Capacity Reports
- Cisco UCS Reports
- Enterprise Reports
- Performance Reports

Each reporting area is briefly discussed next in turn.

Cisco UCS Capacity Reports

Capacity Reports in UCS Performance Manager focus mostly on areas of bandwidth consumption within your UCS domains. Reports are available for Aggregate Bandwidth Utilization, Aggregate Port Pool Utilization, Bandwidth Utilization vs. Capacity, Interface Volume, Interface Utilization, and overall Port Utilization. Figure 13-39 shows a Bandwidth Utilization vs. Capacity report for a UCS Domain. It shows, for example, the system average for sys_switch-A Tx is 2.95 percent.

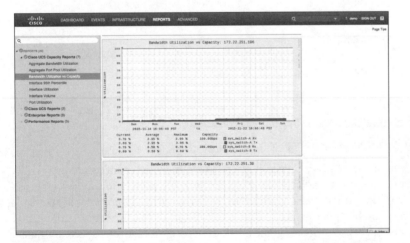

Figure 13-39 *Bandwidth Utilization vs. Capacity Report*

Cisco UCS Reports

The Cisco UCS Reports section of UCS Performance Manager shows free memory slots as well as hardware inventory per managed UCS domain. Figure 13-40 shows Free Memory Slots Report by UCS domain. Note that you can export these results to a CSV file.

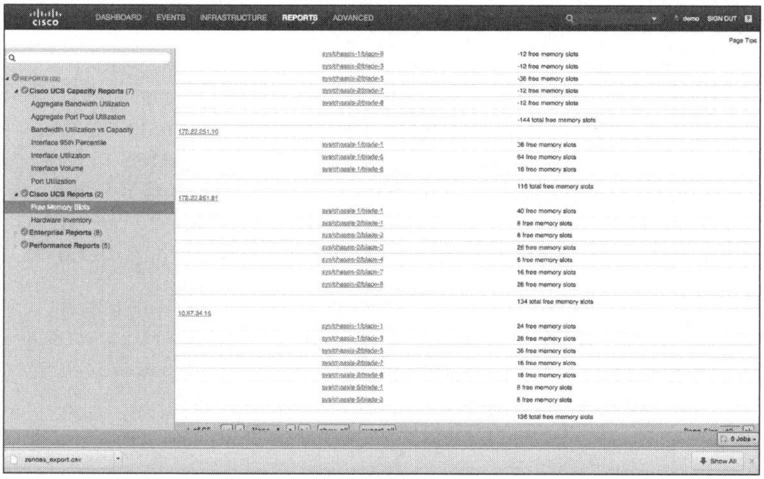

Figure 13-40 *Free Memory Slots Report*

Enterprise Reports

Configuration parameters such as how many datapoints have been collected, how many devices are being managed, and what thresholds have been defined are all options in the navigation pane under the Enterprise Reports action pane in UCS Performance Manager.

Performance Reports

Performance Reports in UCS Performance Manager include Availability Report, which reports on overall availability of the system, CPU Utilization, Interface Utilization, and Memory Utilization, and Threshold Summary, which provides a summary view of all thresholds set in the system. Figure 13-41 shows a CPU Utilization report organized by /Devices/ Server spanning a one-week reporting period.

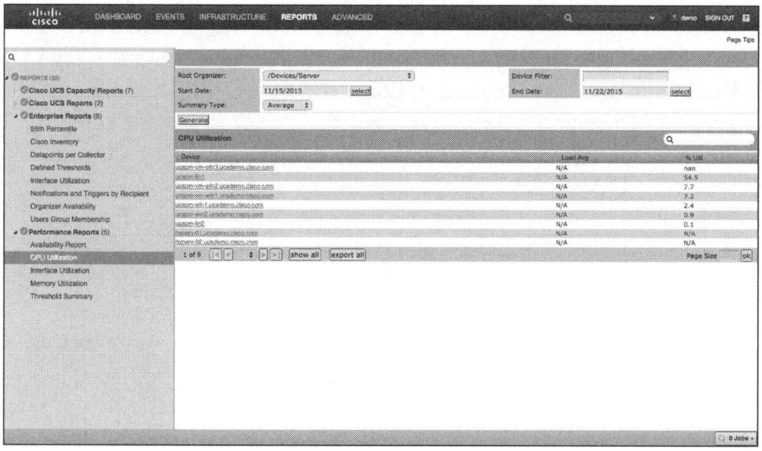

Figure 13-41 *CPU Utilization*

Configuring Serviceability Options

There is much more to providing an effective cloud than just installing the software that provides automation, management, and user portals. The goal is to build an easy-to-use cloud, but that doesn't mean the cloud itself is a simple system that doesn't require active monitoring, maintenance, and troubleshooting of problems. *Serviceability* refers to how the cloud operators go about these and other day-to-day tasks. Note that these are features that the end users of your cloud offering will likely never see, but they impact your ability as the operator of the cloud to provide the highest levels of SLAs for the cloud offering.

There are many tools, services, and network protocols that you will configure as part of your cloud setup that will aid in keeping it running well and serving clients. In this section we review some of the most common of these that you should become familiar with as you prepare for the CCNA Cloud exam.

Syslog

Syslog has long been a standard for message and event logging by applications and network devices and is described in RFC 5424. The messages logged in syslog range from normal details about the operational status and processing of an application, to critical alarms indicating failure conditions. Although most systems generate and store syslog messages locally by default, a highly recommended practice is to leverage a centralized logging server for combining logs from multiple systems in your organization. When deployed in the client/server mode with a centralized syslog server, the syslog messages are typically sent over UDP port 514 or TCP port 6514.

Leveraging a central syslog server provides two main benefits. First, it is much easier to search for patterns and correlate logs across systems when you view and report on them from a single interface. And second, one of the important times to access the syslog messages is when troubleshooting during a failure scenario. Often you may find it difficult or impossible to access the local syslog service in these states, and looking at the messages on a remote syslog server will provide details leading up to the error.

Syslog messages are made up of several component parts used to provide detailed information on the event being logged. Figure 13-42 provides an example message with the key parts identified. The Timestamp provides the date and time the message was created and is very important for correlating events across systems. The Facility describes the category and source of a message and an integer between 0 and 23 mapped to a value by the sending system. RFC 5424 includes a recommended mapping of Facility numbers to uses, but it will not be uniform across all systems. The Severity is a numerical value ranging from 0 to 7 that indicates the level of importance of the message; Table 13-2 lists the different Severity codes and their meanings. Note that in Figure 13-42, an actual syslog entry shows the severity code of "info" for an Integer value of 6, Informational error. The details of the event being logged are contained in the Message component.

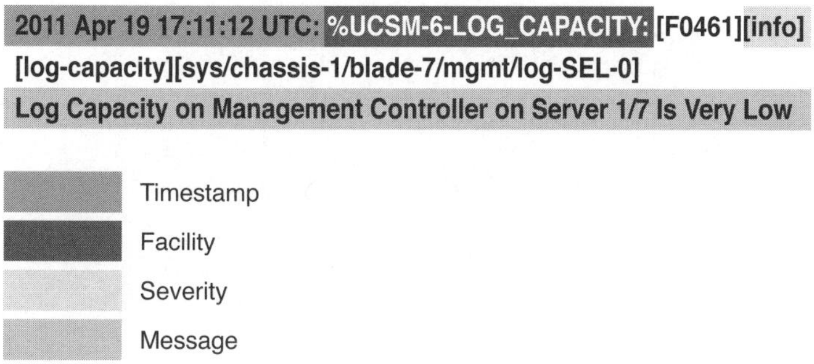

2011 Apr 19 17:11:12 UTC: %UCSM-6-LOG_CAPACITY: [F0461][info]
[log-capacity][sys/chassis-1/blade-7/mgmt/log-SEL-0]
Log Capacity on Management Controller on Server 1/7 Is Very Low

Timestamp

Facility

Severity

Message

Figure 13-42 *Example Syslog Message*

Table 13-2 Syslog Severity Levels

Integer	Severity	Description
0	Emergency	System is unusable.
1	Alert	Immediate action is needed.
2	Critical	A condition that should be corrected immediately has occurred.
3	Error	Non-urgent failure.
4	Warning	An error will occur if no action is taken.
5	Notice	An unusual but non-error condition.
6	Informational	Normal operating behavior.
7	Debug	Used for debugging an application, but not typically tracked.

To configure UCS Director to forward syslog messages to a central server, navigate to **Administration -> Integration**. Click the **Syslogs** tab and check the box to **Enable Syslog Forward**. And, as shown in Figure 13-43, configure the details for what level of severity to send. UCS Director will forward the selected severity messages as well as all messages of higher severity (represented by lower integer values). UCS Director can forward to one or two different servers for redundancy and will send either plaintext or XML-based messages.

13

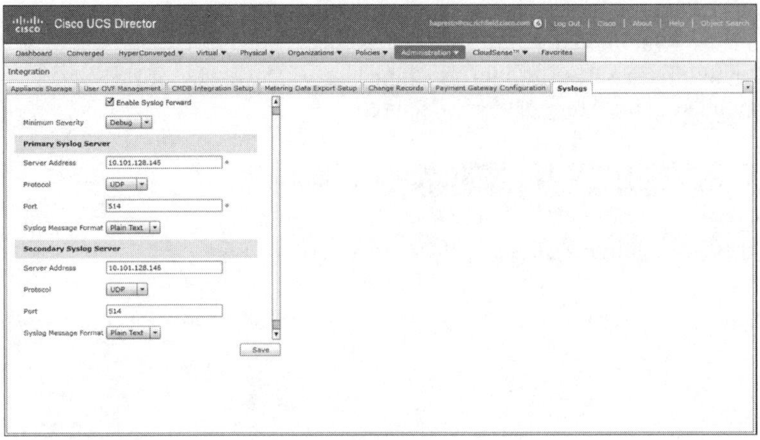

Figure 13-43 *UCS Director Syslog Forwarding Configuration*

Network Time Protocol

In the previous section on syslog we discussed how the timestamp is included in every message to allow operators to correlate events across multiple systems, as well as find events that may have occurred around a particular point in time. In order for this to be effective, it is critical that every system have accurate and configured time. Network Time Protocol (NTP) is deployed and leveraged to ensure a consistent reference time for all network devices, servers, and applications.

NTP is a hierarchical service where different NTP server levels, called stratum levels, are used to allow consistent time across an entire environment but allow for scaling the client server traffic across multiple systems. The most preferred stratum level is 0 and would represent the master time server for a network. Each level of client would move to the next higher stratum level. For example, a network core switch can be configured to be a client of the master NTP server (stratum 0), and then act as the NTP server for all other switches in the network as a stratum 1 server. NTP communications occur over UDP port 123.

UCS Director can be configured to synchronize to an NTP server either from the Shell Menu or as part of the Guided Setup Wizard within the administrator portal. Figure 13-44 shows the process to set an NTP server from the Shell Menu. After choosing option **9** in the menu, you'll be provided an option to first sync time with the underlying hardware time of the virtual appliance. This time is typically pulled from the hypervisor layer where UCS Director is running. Next you will be given the chance to sync with NTP. Type **Y** and enter your NTP server address.

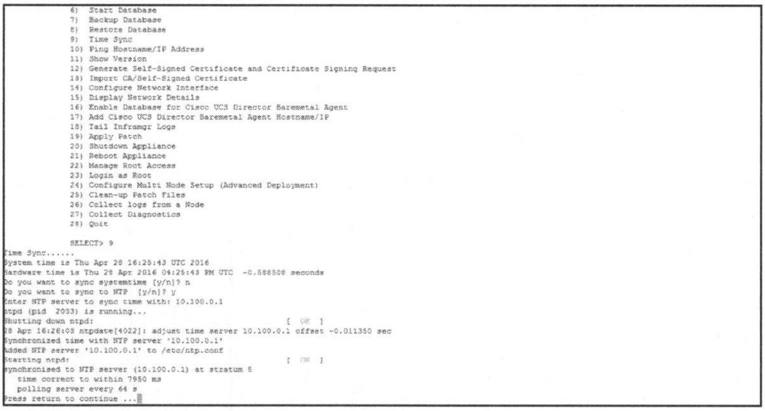
6) Start Database
7) Backup Database
8) Restore Database
9) Time Sync
10) Ping Hostname/IP Address
11) Show Version
12) Generate Self-Signed Certificate and Certificate Signing Request
13) Import CA/Self-Signed Certificate
14) Configure Network Interface
15) Display Network Details
16) Enable Database for Cisco UCS Director Baremetal Agent
17) Add Cisco UCS Director Baremetal Agent Hostname/IP
18) Tail Inframgr Logs
19) Apply Patch
20) Shutdown Appliance
21) Reboot Appliance
22) Manage Root Access
23) Login as Root
24) Configure Multi Node Setup (Advanced Deployment)
25) Clean-up Patch Files
26) Collect logs from a Node
27) Collect Diagnostics
28) Quit
SELECT> 9
Time Sync......
System time is Thu Apr 28 16:25:43 UTC 2016
Hardware time is Thu 28 Apr 2016 04:25:43 PM UTC -0.588508 seconds
Do you want to sync systemtime [y/n]? n
Do you want to sync to NTP [y/n]? y
Enter NTP server to sync time with: 10.100.0.1
ntpd (pid 2033) is running...
Shutting down ntpd: [OK]
28 Apr 16:26:08 ntpdate[4022]: adjust time server 10.100.0.1 offset -0.011350 sec
Synchronized time with NTP server '10.100.0.1'
Added NTP server '10.100.0.1' to /etc/ntp.conf
Starting ntpd: [OK]
synchronised to NTP server (10.100.0.1) at stratum 5
time correct to within 7950 ms
polling server every 64 s
Press return to continue ...

Figure 13-44 *UCS Director CLI NTP Server Configuration*

Figures 13-45 through 13-47 walk through the process of configuring NTP as part of the Guided Setup. First choose **Administration > Guided Setup**, and then click **Launch Guided Setup.** NTP configuration is part of the Initial System Configuration Wizard, so check that box (see Figure 13-45) and click **Submit.** This wizard allows you to identify which parameters to set; for NTP you can simply check **Initial System Configuration** for that task only, as shown in Figure 13-46. Click **Submit** again and the wizard will display the currently configured NTP servers and provide an option to modify the list of servers, as shown in Figure 13-47.

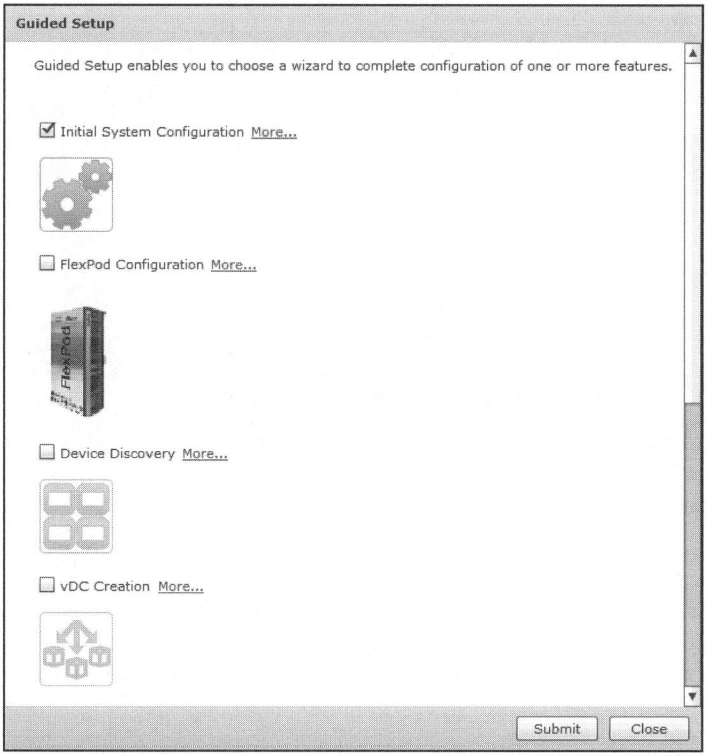
Guided Setup
Guided Setup enables you to choose a wizard to complete configuration of one or more features.
Initial System Configuration More...
FlexPod Configuration More...
FlexPod
Device Discovery More...
vDC Creation More...
Submit
Close

Figure 13-45 *UCS Director Guided Setup Wizard Options*

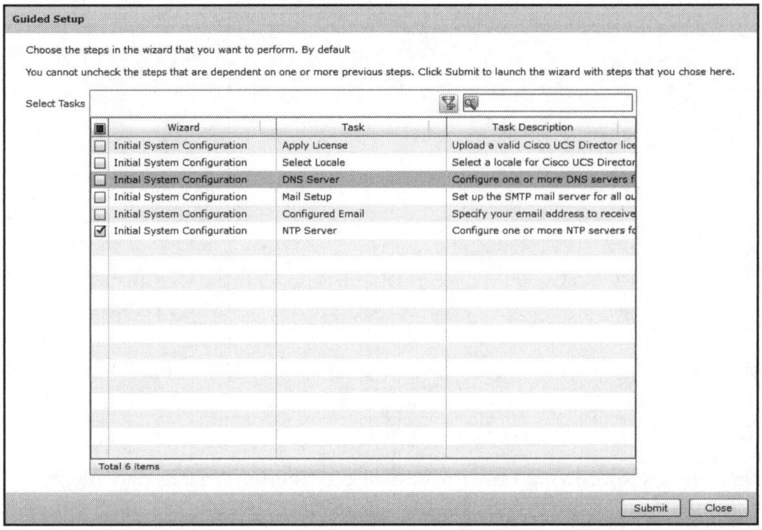

Figure 13-46 *UCS Director Guided Setup Wizard Task Selection*

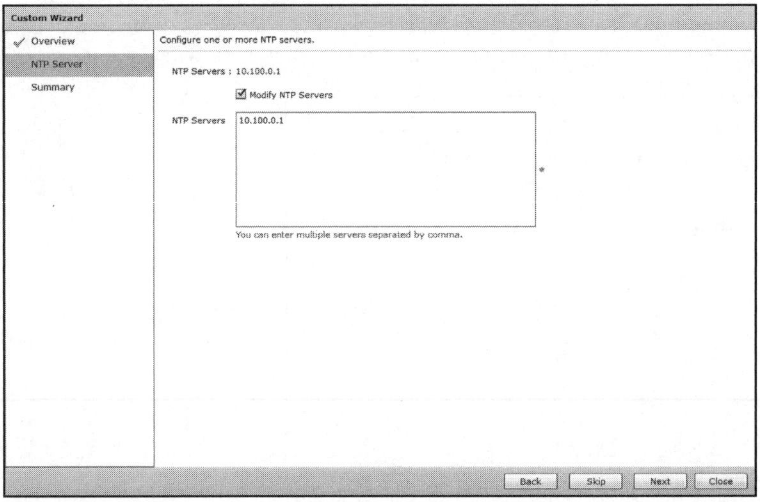

Figure 13-47 *UCS Director Custom Wizard NTP Server Configuration*

Domain Name Service

Applications, devices, and services are all accessed over the network at their IP address; however, IP addresses on their own aren't very intuitive and can be difficult to remember. The Domain Name System (DNS) is a network protocol that allows the mapping of a human-readable name to an IP address to make locating and connecting to services easier for the end user. DNS servers provide this translation service to client devices over UDP or TCP port 53.

When a user or system makes a request for an Internet service, such as browsing to a website such as http://www.cisco.com, the first step to deliver the web page for the end device is to perform a DNS lookup of the hostname www.cisco.com at the configured DNS servers. The DNS servers will resolve this name to one or more IP addresses and return the result to the client. Then the browser will make the HTTP request to the IP address provided.

UCS Director can leverage DNS servers to allow administrators and users to provide details such as the address for physical and virtual accounts, NTP servers, SMTP servers, etc., by using hostnames rather than IP addresses. In addition to the usability advantages, this also means that should the IP address for a device change, as long as the name remains the same, UCS Director will not need to be updated with the new IP address.

Like NTP server configuration, DNS servers can be configured from the Shell Menu or via Guided Setup in the Initial System Configuration Wizard.

To configure DNS servers through the Shell menu (shown previously in Figure 13-44), enter option **14**, Configure Network Interface, and then specify the IP address(es) of the DNS server(s) you wish to add, then press **Enter** to save those changes.

To configure DNS servers from the administrator portal, launch the Initial System Configuration Wizard as instructed for NTP, check the **Initial System Configuration** check box for the DNS Server task only, and click **Submit**. Figure 13-48 shows the page in the Initial Configuration Wizard where DNS servers can be configured.

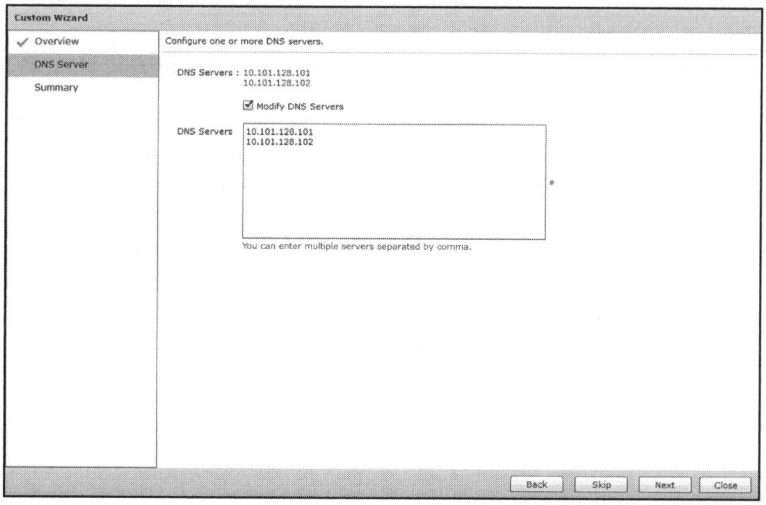

Figure 13-48 *UCS Director Guided Wizard DNS Server Configuration*

Dynamic Host Configuration Protocol

Anything that will communicate over the network requires an IP address. Within the context of your Cisco Powered cloud, the primary use case for DHCP is for PXE builds from the UCS Director Baremetal Agent (BMA) appliance. Other use cases of DHCP on other networks within the enterprise (other than the PXE deploy/build networks specified during your cloud setup) are out of scope for this discussion and the exam.

Devices can leverage a static IP address that is manually configured on the device, or they can use a dynamic IP address that is learned through DHCP. DHCP servers listen on UDP port 67 for requests from clients on UDP port 68. The communication between clients and servers follows a four-step process.

1. A DHCP client sends a DISCOVER message as a broadcast looking for any DHCP servers available on the network.

2. A DHCP server sends an OFFER back to the DHCP client with an IP address and additional configured options.

3. The DHCP client sends a REQUEST for the offered IP address back to the DHCP server.

4. The DHCP server sends an ACKNOWLEDGE to the DHCP client to complete the process.

As mentioned in Step 3 in the process, a DHCP server can provide configuration details other than the IP address to the client. Nearly every DHCP server provides at least the router or gateway address, DNS server addresses, and the local domain name. These are provided as DHCP Options in the OFFER message. The UCS Director Baremetal Agent acts as a DHCP server as part of a deployment where PXE services are used to configure bare-metal or virtual servers through network boot. To accomplish this, the DHCP OFFER includes these additional options:

■ **DHCP Option 67 – filename:** The name of the file to request over TFTP from the server identified in the next-server option

■ **DHCP Option 66 – next-server:** The IP address of the Baremetal Agent that is also running the TFTP service hosting the PXE configurations

To configure the DHCP server on the Baremetal Agent in UCS Director, choose **Administration > Physical Accounts**, click the **Baremetal Agents** tab, select the BMA instance, and then click **Configure DHCP**. Figure 13-49 shows the DHCP Configuration dialog box where you provide the DHCP subnet, network mask, starting IP address, and ending IP address to use in the address pool. If the servers will need to communicate with resources on other IP networks during the PXE loading phase, be sure to provide the optional Router IP Address for the default gateway on the network.

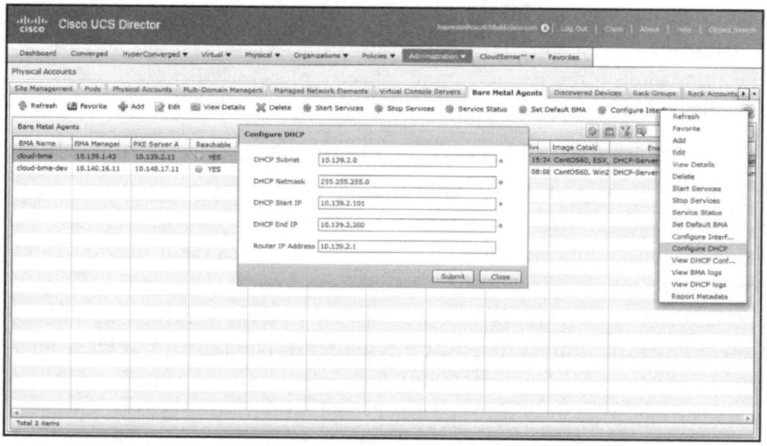

Figure 13-49   *Configuring Baremetal Agent DHCP Server*

Once configured, you can view the configuration of the dhcpd service running on the BMA by clicking **View DHCP Configuration** from the interface. An example configuration is shown in Figure 13-50. Note at the bottom the "next-server" and "filename" settings that were added by UCS Director automatically.

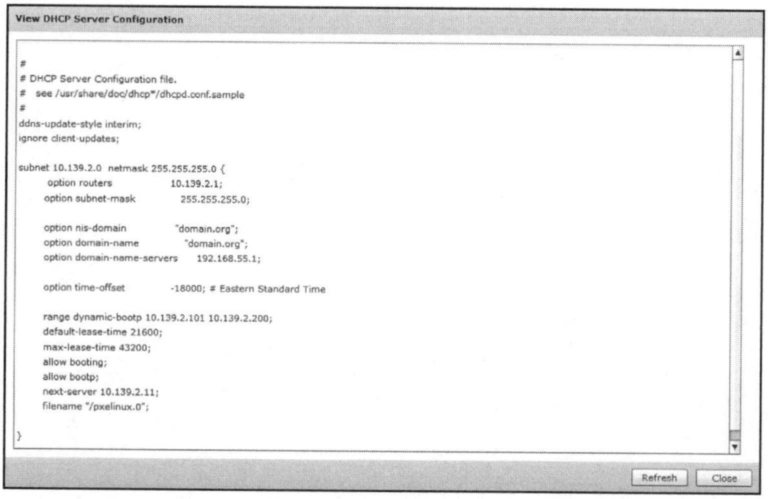

Figure 13-50   *Viewing Baremetal Agent DHCP Configuration*

Simple Mail Transfer Protocol

One of the most common methods of communication today remains through email messages. Simple Mail Transport Protocol (SMTP) is the protocol over which email messages are delivered to email servers. Related protocols like Post-Office Protocol (POP) and Internet Message Access Protocol (IMAP) are used by mail clients to retrieve messages from email servers for reading and viewing. SMTP has long used TCP port 25, but ports 587 and 465 are also used by some servers, often when implementing secure SMTP services.

13

UCS Director can send email messages to users and administrators as part of typical management and operations of the private cloud. Administrators can be notified through email of alert conditions. End users will often receive details about ordered services through email. And Approval notifications are sent to users and administrators through email messages. Configuring email integration should be considered a key part of UCS Director setup.

You can configure SMTP servers as part of the Initial System Configuration Wizard in the same manner as previously discussed for configuring NTP and DNS servers (by checking the Initial System Configuration check box for the Mail Setup task; refer to Figure 13-46), but you can also configure SMTP servers by choosing **Administration > System** and clicking the **Mail Setup** tab. As shown in Figure 13-51, you need to provide the address and port for the email server as well as an email address to use as the sender of all messages. If the email server requires authentication to send messages, include the username and password in the configuration. To verify settings are successful, and the connection to the email server is working as expected, check the **Send Test Email** check box before clicking the Save button.

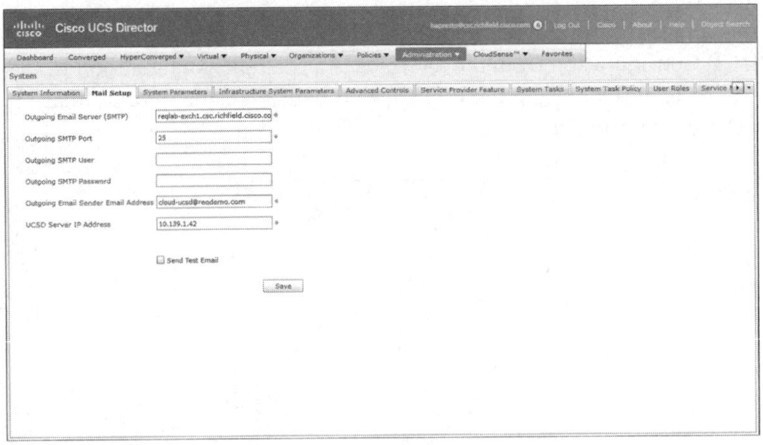

Figure 13-51 *UCS Director Mail Setup*

Exam Preparation Tasks

Review All Key Topics

Review the most important topics in this chapter, noted with the Key Topics icon in the outer margin of the page. Table 13-3 lists a reference of these key topics and the page number on which each is found.

Table 13-3   Key Topics for Chapter 13

Key Topic Element	Description	Page Number
Figure 13-8	Port channel statistics	394
Steps	Creating reports in UCS Central	402
Figure 13-23	Dashboard in UCS Director	404
Section	CloudSense reports in UCS Director	405
Section	UCS Performance Manager Dashboard	410
Section	Available reports in UCS Performance Manager	416
Section	Syslog configuration	418
Table 13-2	Syslog severity levels	419
Section	Network Time Protocol	420
Section	Dynamic Host Configuration Protocol	423
Section	Simple Mail Transfer Protocol	425

Define Key Terms

Define the following key terms from this chapter and check your answers in the glossary:

UCS Performance Manager, IO Module (IOM), Fabric Interconnects, UCS domain, UCS Central, port channel, UCS Director Dashboard, CloudSense, Report Builder, Application Group

13

This chapter covers the following exam topics:

4.0   Cloud Systems Management and Monitoring

4.5   Perform cloud monitoring using Cisco Prime Service Catalog, Cisco UCS Director, Cisco Prime Infrastructure

   4.5.a   Describe fault monitoring

   4.5.b   Describe performance monitoring

   4.5.c   Describe monitoring of provisioning outcomes

4.6   Create monitoring dashboards

   4.6.a   Configure custom dashboards

5.0   Cloud Remediation

5.2   Interpret Logs for root cause analysis

   5.2.a   Analyze fault logs

   5.2.b   Analyze admin logs

   5.2.c   Analyze application logs

5.3   Configure backups

   5.3.a   Configure database backup

   5.3.b   Configure database restore

CHAPTER 14

Monitoring and Maintaining the Health of Your Cloud

Once you and your users become accustomed to the advantages of self-service ordering, management, and data center automation, maintaining a healthy environment will become a critical part of day-to-day administration. Tracking current usage statistics across the infrastructure supporting the cloud, monitoring faults and events, reviewing system logs, and managing backups will become routine activities. In this chapter we will explore the most common and important mechanisms for monitoring and maintaining the health of your cloud.

"Do I Know This Already?" Quiz

The "Do I Know This Already?" quiz allows you to assess whether you should read this entire chapter thoroughly or jump to the "Exam Preparation Tasks" section. If you are in doubt about your answers to these questions or your own assessment of your knowledge of the topics, read the entire chapter. Table 14-1 lists the major headings in this chapter and their corresponding "Do I Know This Already?" quiz questions. You can find the answers in Appendix A, "Answers to the 'Do I Know This Already?' Quizzes."

Table 14-1 "Do I Know This Already?" Section-to-Question Mapping

Foundation Topics Section	Questions
UCS Director Dashboards	1–3
Fault Severities and States	4
Cloud Monitoring	5–7
Visibility and Troubleshooting Through Logs	8, 9
Backing Up the Cloud	10

CAUTION The goal of self-assessment is to gauge your mastery of the topics in this chapter. If you do not know the answer to a question or are only partially sure of the answer, you should mark that question as wrong for purposes of the self-assessment. Giving yourself credit for an answer you correctly guess skews your self-assessment results and might provide you with a false sense of security.

1. What actions are available from an individual widget's action menu in UCS Director?

   a. Export Report

   b. Expand View

   c. Close View

   d. Clone View

   e. Add to Dashboard

2. Where would you find a view showing summary statistics comparing the consumption of resources across all virtual accounts in UCS Director?

   a. CloudSense > Reports > Cloud Summary

   b. Administration > Virtual Accounts > Dashboard

   c. Virtual > Compute > All Clouds > Summary Tab

   d. This information is not available within UCS Director

3. True or False. Dashboard views are only available in UCS Director on the administrator portal.

   a. True

   b. False

4. Which fault severity indicates a service-affecting condition that is causing severe degradation of services?

   a. Critical

   b. Major

   c. Minor

   d. Warning

5. Within UCS Director, where is the best place to look for the reason behind a service profile association failure?

   a. Organizations > Service Requests > Service Request Details > Log

   b. Organizations > Faults > UCS Manager Account > Service Profile

   c. Physical > Compute > UCS Manager Account > Faults

   d. Physical > Compute > UCS Manager Account > Service Profiles > Faults

6. Within UCS Director, where would be a good place to identify the most utilized vSphere hosts in your cloud?

   a. System Dashboard

   b. Virtual Account Hosts Report

   c. CloudSense VMware Host Performance Summary

   d. Virtual Account Top 5 Reports

7. Your manager wants to know the percentage of virtual machine deployments that have completed successfully since UCS Director has been in use. How could you quickly provide this information?

   a. Review the Archived Service Requests report in UCS Director, filter for Virtual Machine Deployments, and calculate the success percentage.

   b. Interview the users of the system and gather anecdotal data to give a report on general impression to your manager.

   c. Export the data from the Service Requests Statistics report to Excel and use it to calculate the success ratio and build graphs to represent the overall data across all types of deployments.

   d. There is no way to provide this answer to your manager.

8. Which UCS Director log would be useful in determining the cause of errors related to gathering the inventory of a storage array?

   a. Authenticator Log

   b. Patch Log

   c. Infra Manager

   d. Tomcat Log

9. Where could you go to gain access to the Orchestration Log for Prime Service Catalog? (Choose two.)

   a. Log in to web as **administrator** and choose **Service Designer > Logs**

   b. Log in to web as **administrator** and choose **Administrator > Utilities > Logs and Properties > psc-c.orchestration.log**

   c. Log in to the **Shell Menu** and choose **View Logs > View Orchestration Log**

   d. Contact Cisco TAC and open a case

10. True or False. Database backups for both UCS Director and Prime Service Catalog must be taken from the command-line interfaces, because there is no way to generate a database backup from their administration portals.

   a. True

   b. False

Foundation Topics

UCS Director Dashboards

Whether in an automobile or software system, a dashboard provides the user with immediate access to the most important pieces of information about the status of the underlying system. UCS Director leverages dashboards and summary views in many places to provide you, the cloud administrator, with the information needed to understand which areas may require further investigation. The dashboards, and widgets viewed on the dashboards, are in addition to the reports that were covered in Chapter 12, "Chargeback, Billing, and Reporting."

Dashboard Widgets

UCS Director dashboards are made up of one or more available widgets that bring together key data points for some element of the cloud. UCS Director has hundreds of available widgets that display details related to physical or virtual infrastructure, virtual data centers, groups, and more. Figure 14-1 shows four widgets that provide details related to a UCS Manager account from UCS Director. Each widget is designed to provide the administrator with the most important details in the easiest-to-consume fashion. In this case, details related to the equipment from the compute domain are presented in bar and pie charts. When viewing a dashboard with many widgets on the screen all at once, you may want to investigate a single widget closer. The Expand View action shown in the figure will take a single widget and zoom it out to full screen size temporarily. You can also use the Export Report option to pull the raw data that is feeding the widget into another system for more processing. Exports can be taken in PDF, CSV, or XLS format.

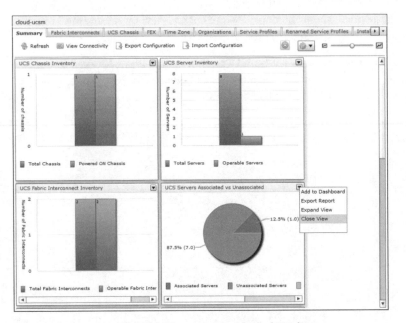

Figure 14-1 *Sample UCS Manager Dashboard Widgets*

Key Topic

When viewing a dashboard and reviewing the data within the widgets, you have control over the order and size of the widget display on the screen. While viewing a dashboard, you can click and drag widgets around the screen as shown in Figure 14-2, allowing you to customize the layout of the dashboard. And to adjust the default size of the widgets, use the slider highlighted in the same figure in the upper-right corner of the dashboard. By making the widgets smaller, you will fit more widgets on the screen at once, providing more information in a single glance; however, as widgets get smaller, you may find the data difficult to comprehend.

Figure 14-2 *Manipulating Widget Location and Size*

Infrastructure Summary Dashboards

Widgets are mostly found throughout UCS Director on the Summary tab when viewing an element of infrastructure. Nearly all physical and virtual infrastructure types that can be added to UCS Director will have a Summary tab with at least one widget listed. Also, as you drill into the details of a component, you may find additional Summary tabs available at lower levels.

For example, Figure 14-1 displayed the Summary tab from a UCS Manager account, while in Figure 14-3, the details of an individual Fabric Interconnect from the same domain are being investigated and the Summary tab is displayed. The widgets available at the account level provide details across the domain, and the widgets available within an individual Fabric Interconnect are focused on just its characteristics. In Figure 14-3 we can see graphs related to data transmitted and received through the device, as well as CPU and memory utilization trends. For dashboards like this one where widgets provide trending details over time, the user is provided a drop-down list box to indicate the time range over which he would like to see the data. Finally, note in the figure that the Customize button has been clicked to display the drawer of available widgets. From this drawer you can drag currently closed widgets back onto the dashboard.

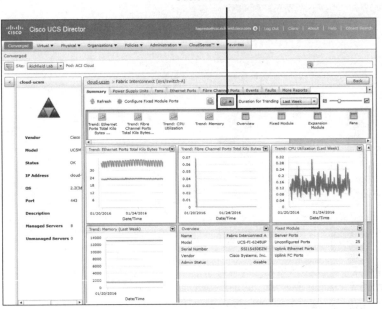

Figure 14-3 *UCS Fabric Interconnect Summary Dashboard*

Dashboards are often used to get details at a very macro level before drilling down into details. For example, look at the Summary dashboard in Figure 14-4 displaying details across all clouds configured in this UCS Director deployment. As the administrator of this system, you should quickly be able to identify that there is one cloud account with a consumption level more than twice that of the others. Though this fact may or may not indicate an actual problem, the value of the dashboard is in the ability to quickly deduce trends and characteristics across the environment.

Summary dashboards are available not only in the administrator portal for UCS Director, but also in the end-user portal, which provides Summary tabs in several areas for individual users to understand the health of their group's provisioned resources. Figure 14-5, for example, shows the Virtual Resources Summary tab of the end-user portal. In this dashboard, end users can view the amount of resources being consumed in the cloud. Particularly once your organization begins implementing chargeback or showback, users will find it very important to be able to get a quick glimpse of their cloud consumption.

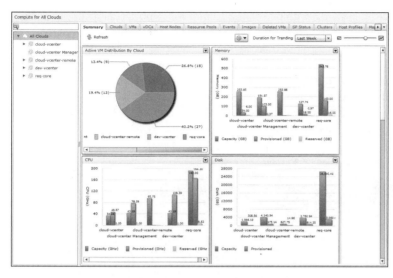

Figure 14-4 *All Clouds Summary Dashboard*

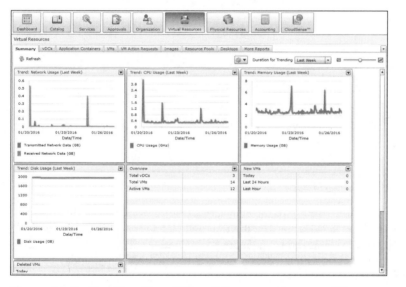

Figure 14-5 *End-User Portal Virtual Resources Summary View*

System Dashboard

Each of the infrastructure Summary view dashboards available within UCS Director is loaded with widgets focused on the particular context being viewed at one time. These can be very helpful as you are investigating one part of the cloud or another, but what about when you want to get an overall view of the key details across the deployment? UCS Director offers a top-level, system-wide dashboard that can be enabled and populated with widgets from any individual dashboard.

The System Dashboard is available within both the administrator portal and end-user portal and is enabled and customized per user login. To enable the Dashboard, access the user information dialog box by clicking your username in the web page header, highlighted in Figure 14-6, and clicking the Dashboard tab in the dialog shown. Simply check the **Enable Dashboard** check box and click **Apply**. This will add the Dashboard link at the very beginning of the main navigation bar within the portal. If you immediately navigate to the Dashboard, you will likely find it completely empty, as each user needs to identify which widgets they'd like to see on their Dashboard.

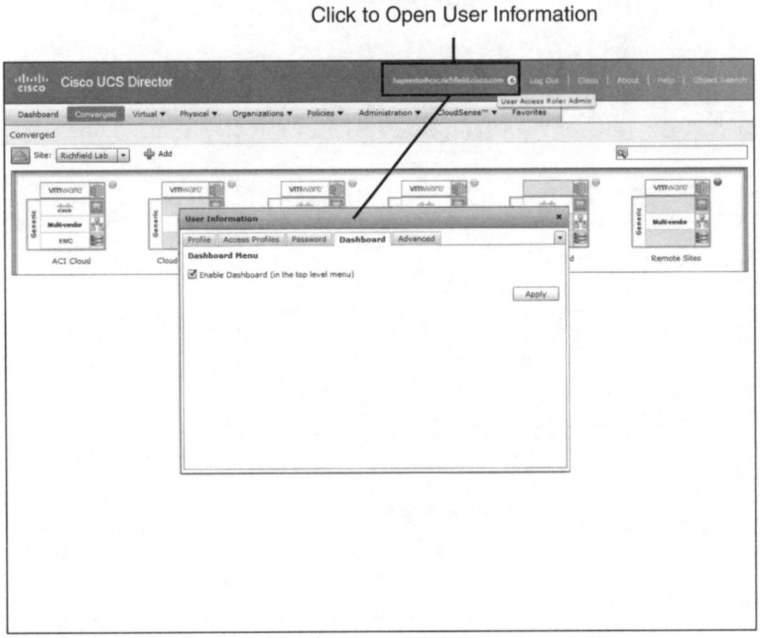

Figure 14-6   *Enable System Dashboard*

Once the Dashboard is enabled, return to the Summary dashboards containing the widgets you'd like to place on the System Dashboard. In the action menu for each widget, there is an option to Add to Dashboard, as shown in Figure 14-7. Continue adding whatever mixture of widgets will provide you with the details that will be interesting in your day-to-day administration of the cloud.

Once you've finished, navigate to the System Dashboard and you will see a nice cross-system Dashboard like the one shown in Figure 14-8. You can customize the display of the Dashboard by arranging the widgets in the desired order, adjust their size, and manipulate the time range over which any trending widgets are displayed. There is also an option to turn on auto-refresh of the Dashboard if you wish to leave it up in a browser tab throughout the day to make it easy to check the current status and health of your cloud.

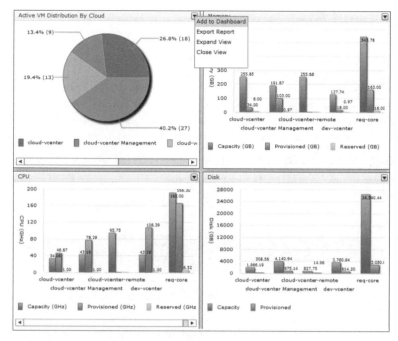

Figure 14-7 *Add Widget to Dashboard*

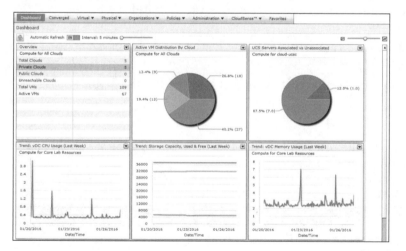

Figure 14-8 *System Dashboard*

Fault Severities and States

Part of the day-to-day administration of the cloud will be reviewing entries related to system events, faults, and debug logs. It will be important to be able to quickly understand the relative importance of each entry and identify those that are purely informational, and those that indicate a system state that requires remediation and action. Within the infrastructure and cloud management solutions leveraged in the cloud, there is a framework for classifying entries into monitoring systems to indicate their severity and state. Having a solid understanding of these classifications will be very important.

Table 14-2 breaks down the severity levels you will see related to events and faults within the UCS Director management reports, as well as within some of the available troubleshooting logs.

Key Topic

Table 14-2 Severity Levels

Severity Level	Description
Critical	A service-affecting condition that requires immediate action to resolve. This severity indicates that some element is completely out of functional service.
Major	A service-affecting condition that requires urgent action to resolve. This severity indicates that there is severe degradation in capabilities of the affected element.
Minor	A nonservice-affecting condition that needs to be resolved. This severity indicates a noted alarm condition, but no service degradation is being experienced.
Warning	An indication of a potential service-affecting condition that should be investigated and resolved to prevent future problems.
Condition	An informational detail about a current condition within the system.
Info	A basic notification or informational message.

Table 14-3 identifies the different states that a fault condition could be in at a given point in time. Fault states are expected to change over time.

Table 14-3 Fault States

State	Description
Active	The fault condition was experienced and is currently still active.
Cleared	A fault condition occurred but has ended. Also, after clearing, it didn't reoccur within the flapping interval.
Flapping	A fault occurred, ended, and reoccurred within a short time interval, known as the flapping interval.
Soaking	A fault occurred and ended in a short amount of time, known as the flapping interval. The short time between start and end could indicate a flapping condition, and this condition is temporary while awaiting another occurrence of the fault within the flapping interval.

Cloud Monitoring

As the console for managing your private cloud, and the infrastructure it is constructed from, UCS Director provides several methods for monitoring the status and health of your cloud. In fact, we have covered many of them in previous chapters of this book, in addition to the coverage in the previous "UCS Director Dashboards" section. In this section we discuss three specific types of cloud monitoring that you should understand and leverage daily in your operations:

- Infrastructure event and fault monitoring

- Performance monitoring

- Service request monitoring

Infrastructure Event and Fault Monitoring

It has been said that there is no cloud, just someone else's computer. Though typically meant as a joke, there is definitely a kernel of truth within the statement. To be effective, every cloud relies on physical and virtual infrastructure operating efficiently and without error. A large portion of administering a cloud involves maintaining the storage, compute, network, and virtualization infrastructure in use. UCS Director isn't meant to be a replacement for dedicated monitoring, alerting, and centralized logging tools you may be leveraging in your enterprise, but it does provide its administrators ways to check the status of infrastructure elements within the portal.

The Cisco Unified Computing System (UCS) is the leading computer platform for cloud builders, and one reason is the way it centralizes the monitoring within UCS Manager and exposes it through the open API. In addition to the policies, pools, equipment, and service profiles that are made available for management and automation within UCS Director, so are the faults, called *events* in UCS Director, at both the system and component levels. In Figure 14-9 you can see the Events report from a UCS Manager account within UCS Director. Even a stable, well-performing UCS domain will have lots of events at any point in time, so be sure to leverage the available filtering capabilities within UCS Director to narrow the scope of what is displayed.

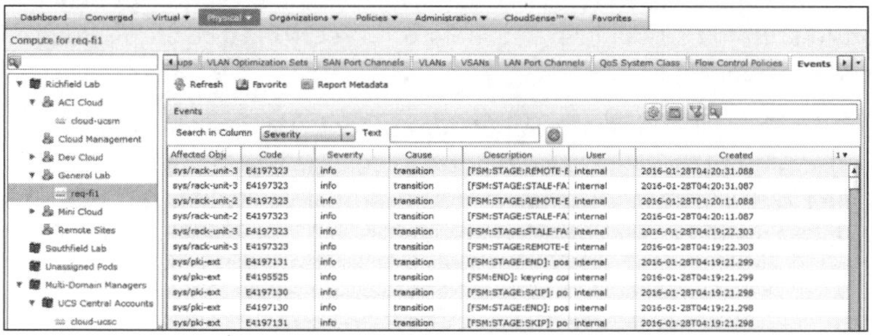

Figure 14-9 *UCS Manager Events and Faults*

Another way to limit the displayed information is to look at the reports from within a particular component's details. For example, in Figure 14-10 the Events page for an individual server blade is displayed.

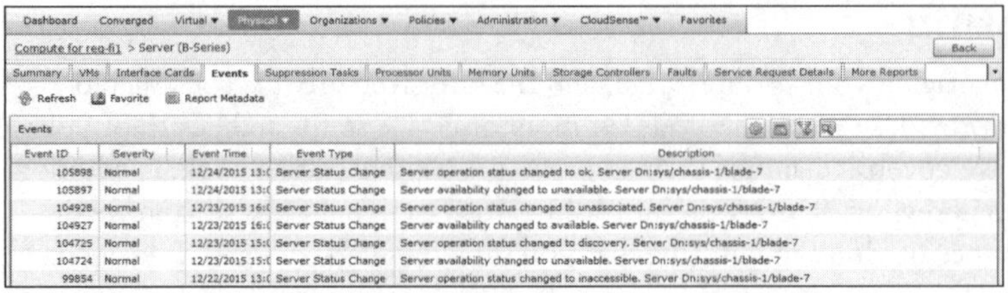

Figure 14-10 *UCS Blade Events*

VMware vCenter provides similar centralized management and reporting for the virtual compute environment as UCS Manager does for the physical compute, and UCS Director likewise exposes events from the virtual accounts within its administrator portal. As key components of the cloud, having this information easily available, as shown in Figure 14-11, within UCS Director can make checking the current status and health a routine part of the cloud operator's day. In cases where an event is identified as needing deeper investigation, the administrator will often decide to move from using the reporting and management capabilities of UCS Director to using individual element managers.

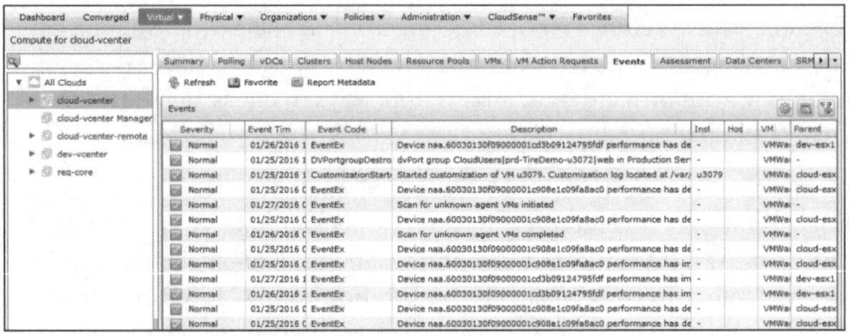

Figure 14-11 *VMware vCenter Event Report*

Performance Monitoring

Maintaining a well-performing cloud requires a way to understand and track cloud usage and reporting. Chapter 12 covered reporting options available within UCS Director in detail, and two of the reports discussed that can help you monitor the performance of the cloud are the Top 5 Reports and Trending Reports.

Top 5 Reports provide administrators with several options to look for elements of the environment that are overutilized, or simply find the largest consumers of cloud resources. Figure 14-12 shows the Hosts With Most Memory Usage report along with the drop-down list of other available host-focused reports. With these reports you can make determinations about when adding additional cloud capacity in the form of new hypervisor hosts may be necessary.

Figure 14-12 *Top 5 Report: Hosts With Most Memory Usage*

Most reports in UCS Director provide current details that are accurate as of the most recent inventory checks across the infrastructure. The one class of report that provides some historical details about the environment is Trending Reports. Trending Reports can show how a metric has changed over time, and allow the administrator to look for common patterns, or extrapolate what will likely occur based on past behavior. Figure 14-13 shows an example Trending Report for the Number of VMs over the Last Month. Other Trending Reports will show CPU, disk, or memory performance as well.

Figure 14-13 *Trending Report: Number of VMs in Last Month*

Service Request Monitoring

A successful cloud is a cloud that is being used, and that means you will spend a lot of time monitoring the status of service requests being executed by UCS Director. In the Chapter 9 section on service requests, you learned about how service requests provide the audit trail for all automation actions executed by UCS Director, as well as detailed information about each step of the workflow execution, and any objects created or modified. We'll review some of the key elements related to monitoring cloud consumption in this section.

Navigating to **Organizations > Service Requests** from the administrator portal will show you all unarchived service requests in a display like that shown in Figure 14-14. In the figure, you can see in the rightmost column that there are several service requests that are Complete, three In Progress, and one that Failed. If you were to open one of the In Progress requests, you'd be able to track the automation as it progresses in real time through the Status and Log tabs in the display. This view will automatically update on a regular basis, but you can click the **Refresh** button to get the latest information at any time. That can be very interesting, but you will be far more likely to investigate Failed requests to identify and resolve the cause of the failure.

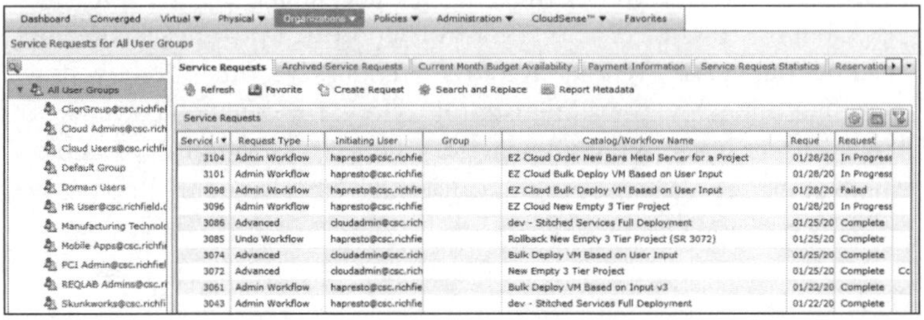

Figure 14-14   *Service Request Report*

The Service Request Status view shown in Figure 14-15 will identify the step in the workflow that failed, but the real information is available in the Log tab shown in Figure 14-16. When you review the error messages and warnings (shown in red and orange in the log) and details in the log, the cause for the failure should be easily identified. In this example the problem, framed in the figure, is that UCS Director "Failed to allocate resources." The service request was to deploy a new virtual machine, so this error indicates a problem identifying a compute, storage, and network to provision the new virtual machine into based on the vDC policies. This is often caused by a cloud that has run out of available capacity.

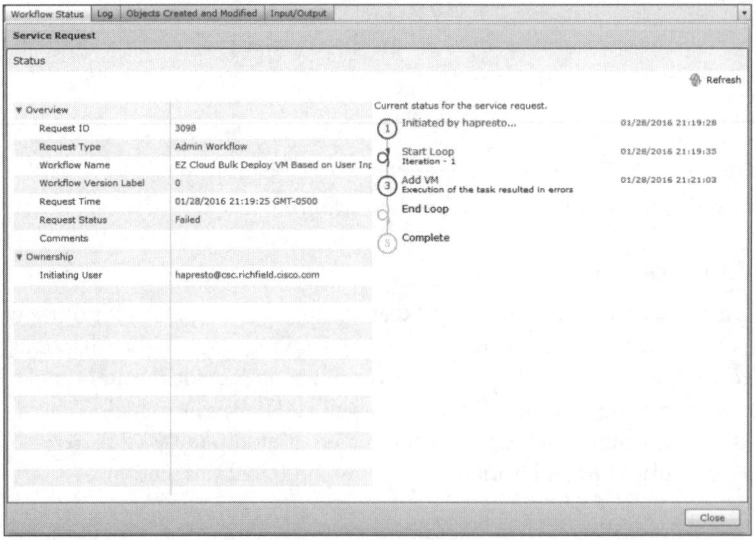

Figure 14-15   *Failed Service Request Status*

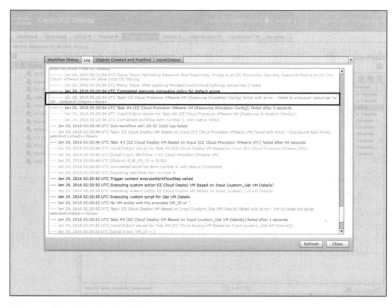

Figure 14-16 *Failed Service Request Log*

UCS Director also provides a CloudSense report for service requests that provides statistics about all the service requests that have been executed by the system. You can find the information available on the Service Request Statistics tab, shown in Figure 14-17, as an instant report, or from the CloudSense tab, where you can generate a point-in-time report to save for later analysis. The report provides details about the total number of service requests, including child service requests, that have been executed, the workflows they were running, and details on the numbers that were successful, failed, or are currently in progress.

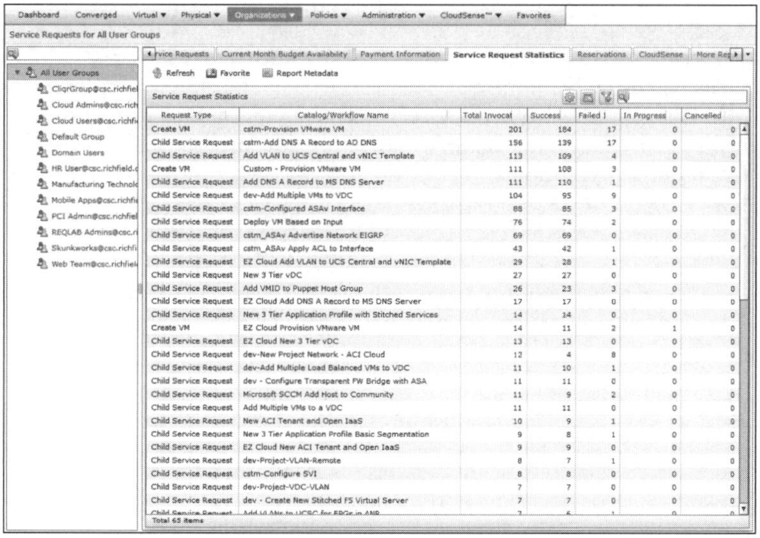

Figure 14-17 *Service Request Statistics*

Visibility and Troubleshooting Through Logs

Much of the day-to-day monitoring of cloud activities will involve leveraging the dashboards and reports that are readily available within the application portals. However, in some cases you may find yourself troubleshooting a system failure, installation problem, or some more challenging problem that requires you to look into the debug logs that are maintained by the appliances, but typically hidden from view. Often this will be at the request of Cisco TAC, but as you become more experienced with the components of the solution, you may find yourself consulting the logs on your own.

UCS Director Logs

Under the Administration menu, navigate to the Support Information section of the portal. From this page you can generate one of several reports providing a deep look at the operational status of the UCS Director appliance as well as key logs from the appliance. The logs can either be displayed immediately or be downloaded for offline analysis. Figure 14-18 shows the list of different logs that can be generated, and Table 14-4 provides some details about what information each provides.

Figure 14-18 *Support Information Logs*

Key Topic

Table 14-4 UCS Director Logs

Log	Description
Infra Manager	Provides details on the infrastructure management and automation services of UCS Director. This log captures very detailed information related to regular system tasks that inventory underlying infrastructure as well as service requests execution.
Web Context Cloud Manager	Provides details on all web resources accessed by web and API users.
Tomcat Log	Provides details on the status and health of the Tomcat Server that executes the underlying Java programs that provide access to the administrator and end-user portals.
Authenticator Log	Provides details regarding both local and LDAP authentications from UCS Director as part of both web and API access.
Mail Delivery Log	Provides details related to sending of emails from UCS Director as part of alerts, approvals, or workflow notifications.
Patch Log	Provides detailed information about any updates and patches applied to the system.

Along with the logs listed in Table 14-4, the System Information (both Basic and Advanced) report, generated from the **Administrator > Support Information** interface, is very helpful when seeking details related to the UCS Director appliance operation. A portion of the Basic report can be seen in Figure 14-19, but the full report provides information on the following:

- UCS Director Version
- System Clock and Uptime
- Service Status
- Licensing Information
- System Resource Usage (CPU/RAM)
- Physical and Virtual Account Status
- Catalogs Published
- Processes running
- And much more

```
Cisco UCS Director[5.3.2.0] System Information

***********************************************************
                System Clock and Uptime
***********************************************************
Software Clock
Fri Jan 29 03:14:20 UTC 2016

Hardware Clock
Fri 29 Jan 2016 03:14:21 AM UTC  -0.728335 seconds

Uptime
 03:14:20 up 45 days, 22:00,  0 users,  load average: 0.36, 0.37, 0.43

***********************************************************
                Services Status
***********************************************************
Service              Status        PID
----------           ----------    -----
broker               RUNNING       12344
controller           RUNNING       12468
eventmgr             RUNNING       12502
client               RUNNING       12560
idaccessmgr          RUNNING       12603
inframgr             RUNNING       12661
TOMCAT               RUNNING       12718
websock              RUNNING        12744


----------------------------------------------------------
Database Service Status
Invalid node
----------------------------------------------------------




***********************************************************
                System License Status
***********************************************************

[
License:Production Base,
Remarks:,
Licensed_Limit:1,
Available:-1,
Used:1,
Status:Licensed,
],
```

Figure 14-19 *System Information (Basic)*

In the case of a major system failure, the administrator portal may be inoperable. In that case, you can access the same details by connecting to the appliance through Secure Shell (SSH) and accessing the command-line interface (CLI). From the main Shell Menu, shown in Figure 14-20, there is an option to view the Inframgr Log (option 18), but all the other information is available by gaining root access to the appliance (option 23).

```
           Cisco UCS Director Shell Menu

                  Standalone Node

      Select a number from the menu below

          1)  Change ShellAdmin Password
          2)  Display Services Status
          3)  Stop Services
          4)  Start Services
          5)  Stop Database
          6)  Start Database
          7)  Backup Database
          8)  Restore Database
          9)  Time Sync
         10)  Ping Hostname/IP Address
         11)  Show Version
         12)  Generate Self-Signed Certificate and Certificate Signing Request
         13)  Import CA/Self-Signed Certificate
         14)  Configure Network Interface
         15)  Display Network Details
         16)  Enable Database for Cisco UCS Director Baremetal Agent
         17)  Add Cisco UCS Director Baremetal Agent Hostname/IP
         18)  Tail Inframgr Logs
         19)  Apply Patch
         20)  Shutdown Appliance
         21)  Reboot Appliance
         22)  Manage Root Access
         23)  Login as Root
         24)  Configure Multi Node Setup (Advanced Deployment)
         25)  Clean-up Patch Files
         26)  Collect logs from a Node
         27)  Collect Diagnostics
         28)  Quit

      SELECT> ▌
```

Figure 14-20 *UCS Director Shell Menu*

Prime Service Catalog Logs

Similar to UCS Director, Prime Service Catalog provides access to logs through both the web interface and the Shell Menu. Figure 14-21 shows the Shell Menu for Prime Service Catalog with option 10 selected to reveal the View Logs menu, which provides quick access to key troubleshooting logs, descriptions for which are presented in Table 14-5. For deeper troubleshooting, the menu also provides the ability to log in as root (option 13), but doing so is recommended only under the advice and direction of Cisco TAC.

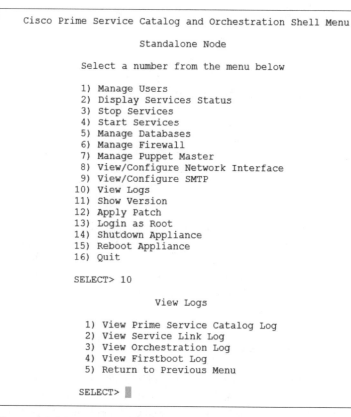

```
Cisco Prime Service Catalog and Orchestration Shell Menu

                      Standalone Node

      Select a number from the menu below

      1) Manage Users
      2) Display Services Status
      3) Stop Services
      4) Start Services
      5) Manage Databases
      6) Manage Firewall
      7) Manage Puppet Master
      8) View/Configure Network Interface
      9) View/Configure SMTP
      10) View Logs
      11) Show Version
      12) Apply Patch
      13) Login as Root
      14) Shutdown Appliance
      15) Reboot Appliance
      16) Quit

      SELECT> 10

                      View Logs

      1) View Prime Service Catalog Log
      2) View Service Link Log
      3) View Orchestration Log
      4) View Firstboot Log
      5) Return to Previous Menu

      SELECT>
```

Figure 14-21 *Prime Service Catalog Shell Menu*

Table 14-5   Prime Service Catalog Logs

Log	Description
Prime Service Catalog Log	Provides details on the web portal and catalog interface for end users and administrators.
Service Link Log	Provides details on the integration between Prime Service Catalog and external systems such as UCS Director accomplished through Control Agents and messaging services.
Orchestration Log	Provides details on end-user orders and the execution of service plans.
Firstboot Log	Provides details from the first boot of the appliance after installation, when the initial configuration, database, and application setup was executed.

From the Administration module of the web interface, you can find access to the logs as well as other tools from the Utilities view. Figure 14-22 shows the Logs and Properties tab. Within the page you have access to view both the current and previous instances of the logs that have been compressed for archiving.

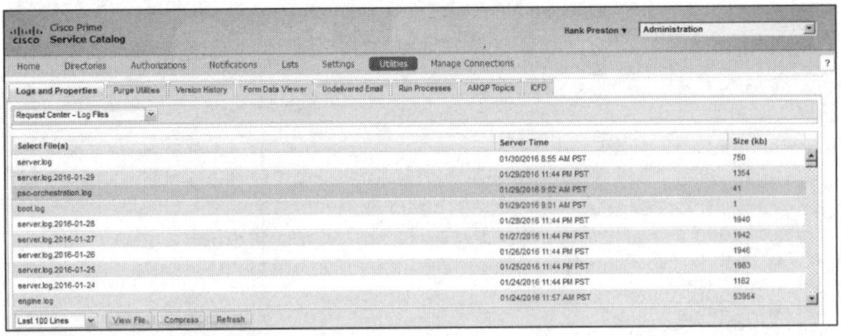

Figure 14-22 *Prime Service Catalog Administration Utilities*

Backing Up the Cloud

There are numerous reasons in every IT field for making regular system backups and testing the ability to effectively restore from backups as part of standard procedures, and a cloud solution is no different. Whether the reason for backing up is to be prepared for a disaster condition, to fulfill a demand to have a second setup to test upgrades or new features, or to be able to roll back from some unintended mistake, you can be assured that during your role as a cloud administrator you will be called upon to back up, and perhaps restore your systems many times.

Before looking at how to get database backups from UCS Director and Prime Service Catalog, it is worth discussing one of the many benefits that compute virtualization provides and how to best leverage it as part of your backup strategy. All virtualization technologies today include the ability to take a snapshot of the current state of a virtual machine and roll back to that saved state in the future. This powerful capability makes some elements of backup and recovery much simpler than full system recovery from source and database backups; however, it does have some limitations and caveats. Snapshotting captures the current state of the running virtual server, and typically all storage disks, but it saves that information in the same location as the virtual server itself. This means that it does not protect against the underlying infrastructure failure. Also, the nature of snapshots means that over time the performance of the virtual machine will begin to decline as the hypervisor platform is maintaining the difference between the snapshot and the currently running virtual machine. Typical recommendations are to keep snapshots for no more than 72 hours, with many recommending no longer than 24 hours. This makes snapshots a great short-term backup and recovery option, but definitely not a long-term solution.

The ease of creating snapshots and restoring to them, plus their limited shelf life, make them ideal for use when implementing a major change to the system such as a patch or upgrade. Before executing the change, take a snapshot. Then, after you have completed the change and verified it was successful, you can delete the snapshot. However, should something go wrong in the change, you can easily roll back and return to a known good state. Many virtualization solutions allow for live snapshots—that is, while the virtual machine is running—but for UCS Director and Prime Service Catalog, it is recommended to shut down the virtual appliances before taking the snapshot. This is to be sure there is no problem due to active transactions in the database or open files.

Backups in UCS Director

UCS Director database backup and recovery is done from the Shell Menu (previously shown in Figure 14-20), and not from the web administration portal. Again, this is due to the need to shut down all services prior to taking the database backup to ensure that it is complete and accurate. You will also need to have an FTP server available and an account with write permissions because the backup task includes transferring the backup to an external server. Choose option 7, Backup Database, from the Shell Menu to begin the following set of steps, an example of which is shown in Figure 14-23. If you are deployed in a multinode configuration of UCS Director, backups require some additional steps, but that procedure is outside the scope of the CLDADM exam and this book.

Step 1.   Stop the services.

Step 2.   Provide FTP server address, login, and password.

Step 3.   Wait while UCS Director backs up the database, compresses the backup, and copies it to the remote server.

Step 4.   After the backup is complete, press Enter and then manually restart the services using option 4, Start Services, in the Shell Menu.

```
             SELECT> 7
Services will be stopped before Database Backup. Do you want to continue [y/n]? y
Stopping services.........
Backup will Upload file to an FTP server. Provide the necessary access credentials

   FTP Server IP Address: 10.100.1.8
   FTP Server Login: hapresto
   FTP Server Password:
Backing up database please wait....
Warning: Using a password on the command line interface can be insecure.
Warning: Using a password on the command line interface can be insecure.
confmgr_production.sql
db_private_admin.sql
Database backedup.....
Verbose mode on.
Connected to 10.100.1.8 (10.100.1.8).
220 (vsFTPd 3.0.2)
331 Please specify the password.
230 Login successful.
200 Switching to Binary mode.
local: /tmp/database_backup.tar.gz remote: cuic_backup_01-29-2016-15-58-03.tar.gz
227 Entering Passive Mode (10,100,1,8,156,69).
150 Ok to send data.
226 Transfer complete.
39490939 bytes sent in 0.537 secs (7.2e+04 Kbytes/sec)
221 Goodbye.
Press return to continue ...
```

Figure 14-23   *UCS Director Database Backup*

Restoring the database from backup follows a very similar process using option 7, Restore Database, from the Shell Menu. The steps are as follows and can be seen in Figure 14-24:

Step 1.   Stop the services.

Step 2.   Provide the FTP server address, login, and password.

Step 3.   Provide the path and filename to the database backup file.

Step 4.   After the restore completes, manually restart the services using option 4, Start Services, in the Shell Menu.

```
          SELECT> 8
Services will be stopped before Database Restore. Do you want to continue [y/n]? y
Stopping services..........
Restore will recover file from an FTP server. Provide the necessary access credentials

  FTP Server IP Address: 10.100.1.8
  FTP Server Login: hapresto
  FTP Server Password:
  Remote Backup File (Absolute Path to File): cuic_backup_01-29-2016-15-58-06.tar.gz
```

Figure 14-24 *UCS Director Database Restore*

Using the Shell Menu to capture a backup is easy, but it is a one-time activity. Because UCS Director is based on a CentOS appliance, you can easily leverage the included **cron** utility to schedule regular backups. You can find an example of how to set this up in the Cisco Community at https://communities.cisco.com/docs/DOC-56973.

Backups in Prime Service Catalog

Similar to UCS Director, database maintenance for Prime Service Catalog is accomplished from the Shell Menu (shown previously in Figure 14-21), with backups and restores accessible within the top-level menu option Manage Databases, option 5. In the Manage System Databases menu, shown in Figure 14-25, you will find backup and restore options for the Prime Service Catalog Database and the Orchestration Database. To capture a full backup of the appliance, both databases are needed.

```
              Manage System Databases

        1) Backup Prime Service Catalog Database
        2) Restore Prime Service Catalog Database
           --------------------
        3) Backup Orchestration Database
        4) Restore Orchestration Database
           --------------------
        5) Return to Previous Menu

        SELECT>
```

Figure 14-25 *Prime Service Catalog Manage System Databases Menu*

Whereas the backup option in UCS Director automatically copies the file to a remote FTP server, Prime Service Catalog saves the backup locally at the path /opt/cisco/.backups/ with subdirectories for each database. Each database backup or restore will require the services on the appliance to be stopped, just as with UCS Director. One extra piece of required information to execute the backups is the database password configured during initial installation, so be sure to have that readily available. Figure 14-26 shows an example of taking a backup of the Prime Service Catalog Database. Some of the informational output has been removed from the figure to focus on the key steps in the process.

```
        SELECT> 1
This will create a backup of the Cisco Prime Service Catalog database.

All Prime Service Catalog processes will be automatically stopped if you
proceed with creating the backup.

Please ensure all users of Prime Service Catalog are logged out, or any
active work may be lost.

Do you want to proceed? (y/n): y

Please enter the Prime Service Catalog Database Administrator password:
Testing database connection...Success.
Stopping servicelink.service...Done.
Stopping servicecatalog.service...Done.
Stopping psc-orchestration.service...Done.
Disconnecting database sessions...Done.
Performing backup...

Export: Release 12.1.0.2.0 - Production on Fri Jan 29 08:58:46 2016

Copyright (c) 1982, 2014, Oracle and/or its affiliates.  All rights reserved.

Connected to: Oracle Database 12c Enterprise Edition Release 12.1.0.2.0 - 64bit Production
With the Partitioning, OLAP, Advanced Analytics and Real Application Testing options
Starting "SYSTEM"."SYS_EXPORT_SCHEMA_01":  system/********@orcl schemas=CPSCUSER directory=CPSC_BACKUPS
       dumpfile=CPSCUSER_backup_2016-01-29_085846.dmp logfile=CPSCUSER_backup_2016-01-29_085846.log
       exclude=statistics

**** Messages Removed ****

Dump file set for SYSTEM.SYS_EXPORT_SCHEMA_01 is:
  /opt/cisco/.backups/oracle/cpscuser/CPSCUSER_backup_2016-01-29_085846.dmp
Job "SYSTEM"."SYS_EXPORT_SCHEMA_01" successfully completed at Fri Jan 29 09:01:18 2016 elapsed 0 00:02:32

Backup performed successfully.

Do you want to start all Prime Service Catalog services and Orchestration service? (y/n): y
Starting servicecatalog.service...Done.
Starting servicelink.service...Done.
Starting psc-orchestration.service...Done.

Press [Enter] to continue:
```

Figure 14-26 *Prime Service Catalog Database Backup*

After using the menu commands to create the database, you will need to copy it from the appliance to a remote server manually. You can do so using any number of commonly supported transfer protocols such as FTP, SFTP, or SCP. Another typical practice is to leverage **cron** on the underlying appliance to schedule automatic regular backups and remote copies, instead of relying on manual backups.

Foundation Topics

Exam Preparation Tasks

As mentioned in the section "How to Use This Book" in the Introduction, you have a couple of choices for exam preparation: the exercises here, Chapter 15, "Final Preparation," and the exam simulation questions on the Pearson IT Certification Practice Test.

Review All Key Topics

Review the most important topics in this chapter, noted with the Key Topics icon in the outer margin of the page. Table 14-6 lists a reference of these key topics and the page number on which each is found.

Key Topic

Table 14-6   Key Topics for Chapter 14

Key Topic Element	Description	Page Number
Paragraph	Understand how to manipulate the size and position of dashboard widgets.	433
Section	Describe how to enable and customize the System Dashboard.	435
Table 14-2	Differentiate between severity levels.	438
Section	Describe infrastructure event and fault monitoring features.	439
Section	Describe how to leverage service requests to monitor the provisioning of resources.	441
Table 14-4	Describe the available UCS Director logs and the details they contain.	444
Table 14-5	Describe the available Prime Service Catalog logs and the details they contain.	447
List	Describe the steps required to take a backup and restore UCS Director.	449

Complete Tables and Lists from Memory

Print a copy of Appendix B, "Memory Tables" (found online), or at least the section for this chapter, and complete the tables and lists from memory. Appendix C, "Memory Tables Answer Key," also online, includes completed tables and lists to check your work.

Define Key Terms

Define the following key terms from this chapter and check your answers in the glossary:

widget, dashboard, fault, event, snapshot, cron, flapping interval

CHAPTER 15

Final Preparation

The first 14 chapters of this book cover the technologies, protocols, design concepts, and considerations required to be prepared to pass the CCNA Cloud CLDADM 210-455 exam. While these chapters supply the detailed information, most people need more preparation than a cover-to-cover reading can provide. This chapter details a set of tools and a study plan to help you complete your preparation for the exams.

This short chapter has two main sections. The first section lists the exam preparation tools useful at this point in the study process. The second section lists a suggested study plan now that you have completed all the earlier chapters in this book.

NOTE   Appendixes B and C, "Memory Tables" and "Memory Tables Answer Key" respectively, also exist as soft-copy appendixes on the companion website. See the instructions in the Introduction to this book on how to access this site.

Tools for Final Preparation

This section provides some information about the available tools and how to access the tools.

Pearson Cert Practice Test Engine and Questions

The companion website includes the Pearson Cert Practice Test engine—software that displays and grades a set of exam-realistic multiple-choice questions. Using the Pearson Cert Practice Test engine, you can either study by going through the questions in study mode, or take a simulated (timed) CCNA Cloud CLDADM 210-455 exam.

The installation process requires two major steps: installing the software and then activating the exam. The companion website has a recent copy of the Pearson IT Certification Practice Test engine. The practice exam (the database of exam questions) is not on this site.

NOTE   The cardboard sleeve in the back of this book includes a piece of paper. The paper lists the activation key for the practice exam associated with this book. Do not lose the activation key. On the opposite side of the paper from the activation code is a unique, one-time-use coupon code for the purchase of the *CCNA Cloud CLDADM 210-455 Official Cert Guide, Premium Edition*.

Install the Software

The Pearson IT Certification Practice Test is a Windows-only desktop application. You can run it on a Mac using a Windows virtual machine, but it was built specifically for the PC platform. The minimum system requirements are as follows:

- Windows 10, Windows 8.1, or Windows 7
- Microsoft .NET Framework 4.0 Client
- Pentium-class 1-GHz processor (or equivalent)
- 512 MB RAM
- 650 MB disk space plus 50 MB for each downloaded practice exam
- Access to the Internet to register and download exam databases

The software installation process is routine as compared with other software installation processes. If you have already installed the Pearson IT Certification Practice Test software from another Pearson product, there is no need for you to reinstall the software. Simply launch the software on your desktop and proceed to activate the practice exam from this book by using the activation code included in the access code card sleeve in the back of the book.

The following steps outline the installation process:

Step 1. Download the exam practice test engine from the companion site.

Step 2. Respond to Windows prompts as with any typical software installation process.

The installation process will give you the option to activate your exam with the activation code supplied on the paper in the cardboard sleeve. This process requires that you establish a Pearson website login. You need this login to activate the exam, so please do register when prompted. If you already have a Pearson website login, there is no need to register again. Just use your existing login.

Activate and Download the Practice Exam

Once the exam engine is installed, you should then activate the exam associated with this book (if you did not do so during the installation process) as follows:

Step 1. Start the Pearson IT Certification Practice Test software from the Windows Start menu or from your desktop shortcut icon.

Step 2. To activate and download the exam associated with this book, from the **My Products** or **Tools** tab, click the **Activate Exam** button.

Step 3. At the next screen, enter the activation key from the paper inside the cardboard sleeve in the back of the book. Once entered, click the **Activate** button.

Step 4. The activation process will download the practice exam. Click **Next**, and then click **Finish**.

When the activation process completes, the **My Products** tab should list your new exam. If you do not see the exam, make sure that you have selected the **My Products** tab on the menu. At this point, the software and practice exam are ready to use. Simply select the exam and click the **Open Exam** button.

To update a particular exam you have already activated and downloaded, display the **Tools** tab and click the **Update Products** button. Updating your exams will ensure that you have the latest changes and updates to the exam data.

If you want to check for updates to the Pearson IT Certification Practice Test engine software, display the **Tools** tab and click the **Update Application** button. You can then ensure that you are running the latest version of the software engine.

Activating Other Exams

The exam software installation process, and the registration process, has to happen only once. Then, for each new exam, only a few steps are required. For instance, if you buy another Pearson IT Certification Cert Guide, extract the activation code from the cardboard sleeve in the back of that book; you do not even need the exam engine at this point. From there, all you have to do is start the exam engine (if not still up and running) and perform Steps 2 through 4 from the previous list.

Premium Edition

In addition to the free practice exam, you can purchase additional exams with expanded functionality directly from Pearson IT Certification. The Premium Edition of this title contains an additional two full practice exams as well as an eBook (in both PDF and ePub format). In addition, the Premium Edition title also has remediation for each question to the specific part of the eBook that relates to that question.

Because you have purchased the print version of this title, you can purchase the Premium Edition at a deep discount. There is a coupon code in the cardboard sleeve that contains a one-time-use code as well as instructions for where you can purchase the Premium Edition.

To view the Premium Edition product page, go to http://www.ciscopress.com/title/9780134305561.

The Cisco Learning Network

Cisco provides a wide variety of CCNA Cloud CLDADM preparation tools at a Cisco Systems website called the Cisco Learning Network. This site includes a large variety of exam preparation tools, including sample questions, forums on each Cisco exam, learning video games, and information about each exam.

To reach the Cisco Learning Network, go to https://learningnetwork.cisco.com, or just search for "Cisco Learning Network." You will need to use the login you created at www.cisco.com. If you don't have such a login, you can register for free. To register, simply go to www.cisco.com, click **Register** at the top of the page, and supply the requested information.

Memory Tables

Like most Official Cert Guides from Cisco Press, this book purposefully organizes information into tables and lists for easier study and review. Rereading these tables can be very useful before the exam. However, it is easy to skim over the tables without paying attention to every detail, especially when you remember having seen the table's contents when reading the chapter.

Instead of simply reading the tables in the various chapters, this book's Appendixes B and C give you another review tool. Appendix B lists partially completed versions of many of the tables from the book. You can open Appendix B (available on the companion website) and print the appendix. For review, you can attempt to complete the tables. This exercise can help you focus on the review. It also exercises the memory connectors in your brain; plus it makes you think about the information without as much information, which forces a little more contemplation about the facts.

Appendix C, also a PDF located on the companion website, lists the completed tables to check yourself. You can also just refer to the tables as printed in the book.

Chapter-Ending Review Tools

Chapters 2–14 each have several features in the "Exam Preparation Tasks" section at the end of the chapter. You might have already worked through these in each chapter. It can also be useful to use these tools again as you make your final preparations for the exam.

Suggested Plan for Final Review/Study

This section lists a suggested study plan from the point at which you finish reading through Chapter 14, until you take the CCNA Cloud CLDADM 210-455 exam. Certainly, you can ignore this plan, use it as is, or just take suggestions from it.

The plan uses four steps:

Step 1.   **Review Key Topics and DIKTA Questions:** You can use the table that lists the key topics in each chapter, or just flip the pages looking for key topics as indicated by a Key Topic icon in the margin. Also, reviewing the "Do I Know This Already?" (DIKTA) questions from the beginning of the chapter can be helpful for review.

Step 2.   **Complete Memory Tables:** Open Appendix B and print the entire appendix, or print the tables by major part. Then complete the tables.

Step 3.   **Define Key Terms:** Try to define the terms listed at the end of each chapter to identify areas in which you need more study.

Step 4.   **Use the Pearson IT Certification Practice Test Engine to Practice:** The Pearson IT Certification Practice Test engine can be used to study using a bank of unique exam-realistic questions available only with this book.

If you have decided to use Appendix D, "Study Planner," to support your learning during the reading of all chapters, you can still benefit from it in your final review. In this case, you can use the "Second Date Completed" column to control the pace of each chapter review and dedicate special attention to the chapters whose "Goal Date" you have missed in your first reading (as signaled by the "First Date Completed" column).

Using the Exam Engine

The Pearson IT Certification Practice Test engine includes a database of questions created specifically for this book. The Pearson IT Certification Practice Test engine can be used either in study mode or practice exam mode, as follows:

■ **Study mode:** Study mode is most useful when you want to use the questions for learning and practicing. In study mode, you can select options like randomizing the order of the questions and answers, automatically viewing answers to the questions as you go, testing on specific topics, and many other options.

■ **Practice exam mode:** This mode presents questions in a timed environment, providing you with a more exam-realistic experience. It also restricts your ability to see your score as you progress through the exam and view answers to questions as you are taking the exam. These timed exams not only allow you to study for the actual CCNA Cloud CLDADM 210-455 exam, they help you simulate the time pressure that can occur on the actual exam.

When doing your final preparation, you can use study mode, practice exam mode, or both. However, after you have seen each question a couple of times, you will likely start to remember the questions, and the usefulness of the exam database may go down. So, consider the following options when using the exam engine:

■ Use this question database for review. Use study mode to study the questions by chapter, just as with the other final review steps listed in this chapter. Plan on getting another exam (possibly from the Premium Edition) if you want to take additional simulated exams.

■ Save the question database, not using it for review during your review of each book part. Save it until the end, so you will not have seen the questions before. Then, use practice exam mode to simulate the exam.

Picking the correct mode from the exam engine's user interface is pretty obvious. The following steps show how to move to the screen from which to select study or practice exam mode:

Step 1.   Click the **My Products** tab if you are not already in that screen.

Step 2.   Select the exam you wish to use from the list of available exams.

Step 3.   Click the **Use** button.

When you complete these actions, the engine should display a window from which you can choose **Study Mode** or **Practice Exam Mode.** When in study mode, you can further choose the book chapters, limiting the questions to those explained in the specified chapters of the book.

Summary

The tools and suggestions listed in this chapter have been designed with one goal in mind: to help you develop the skills required to pass the CCNA Cloud CLDADM 210-455 exam. This book has been developed from the beginning to not just tell you the facts but also help you learn how to apply the facts. No matter what your experience level is leading up to taking the exam, it is our hope that the broad range of preparation tools, and even the structure of the book, will help you pass the exam with ease. We truly hope you do well on the exam.

Glossary

A

ACI context   A tenant network. Also called a private network in the APIC GUI.

ACI contract   A set of rules between endpoint groups (EPGs) that defines communications.

ACI endpoint group (EPG)   A managed object that is a named logical entity that contains a collection of endpoints in ACI.

ACI tenant   In ACI, a logical container for application policies that enables an administrator to exercise domain-based access control.

Advanced Catalog   An end-user orderable item within UCS Director that enables end users to execute workflows.

Amazon Web Services (AWS)   Amazon's public cloud offering.

AMQP   Advanced Message Queuing Protocol, a standards-based method for constructing, routing, queuing, and publishing communications between distributed software applications.

Application Centric Infrastructure (ACI)   The Cisco software-defined networking offering for data center and cloud networks.

application container   An application group within UCS Director designed to enable end users to rapidly deploy and manage a group of virtual machines deployed into one or more network segments as a single entity.

Application Group   The capability in UCS Performance Monitor to group multiple virtual machines (VMs) and/or physical hosts together to see all potential infrastructure faults in the path of that group of systems.

Application Policy Infrastructure Controller (APIC)   The unifying point of management and automation for Nexus 9000 switches using Application Centric Infrastructure (ACI) mode in a Cisco fabric.

Application Virtual Switch (AVS)   Programmed by the APIC, the virtual switching components in a Nexus 9000 SDN architecture.

automation task   A task that completes in a predictable and repeatable fashion without user input.

B

Baremetal Appliance (BMA)   A virtual appliance that ships as part of UCS Director that allows for PXE booting and installation of operating systems on both physical and virtual machines.

base DN   Base distinguished name, the point from which a server will start its search for users.

bind DN   Bind distinguished name, an object in LDAP that you bind to that gives you permission to perform a certain operation.

Budget Watch   A feature of UCS Director used to enforce a per-group governance policy related to the amount of cloud consumption available tracked by Cost Models.

BYOD   Bring your own device is an IT service many companies offer to allow their employees to use personally owned tablets and smartphones on the corporate network. This service can be provisioned through Prime Service Catalog.

C

Catalyst   A popular Cisco Ethernet switch.

change management database (CMDB)   A database used in organizations to track changes to infrastructure so that projects and changes can be referenced centrally over time in a single location.

chargeback   The ability to set up parameters within UCS Director or Prime Service Catalog to allow departmental billing for infrastructure within your private cloud.

Cisco Adaptive Security Virtual Appliance (ASAv)   A virtualized version of the popular Cisco ASA firewall product.

Cisco PowerShell Agent (PSA)   A system that UCS Director can point to that will run PowerShell commands against remote systems.

CloudSense   UCS Director reporting engine.

CloudSense Analytics   A reporting module within UCS Director that uses out-of-the-box or custom templates to create reports based on data from multiple infrastructure reports and saves the data to be retrieved in the future.

Cloupia Script   Based on JavaScript, the language used for creating custom tasks and scripts needed to extend functionality of UCS Director.

compound workflow   A type of workflow that is designed to be used within other workflows.

Computing Policy   Determine on which hypervisor host system to deploy the VM.

container gateway   The boundary between the inside and outside of an application container that provides security and network controls for traffic traversing the boundary.

container template   A grouping of policies and configurations from which individual application containers can be instantiated.

Cost Model   A UCS Director policy used to create a monetary rate card for infrastructure consumption that is applied to virtual data centers.

cron   A Linux utility used for scheduling automatic execution of some action over some time period.

D–E

dashboard   A view that provides the user with immediate access to the most important pieces of information about the status of the underlying system.

End User Self-Service Policy   Provide access to out-of-the-box VM lifecycle action tasks to end users.

event   A record of a change in state of a system or component of a system. Does not necessarily indicate a problem.

F

Fabric Extender (FEX)   Similar to a remote linecard, a fabric extender enables Ethernet ports to be decentralized from a central switch and located closer to hosts in the data center, usually at the top of rack.

Fabric Interconnects   Within a UCS system, aggregate management and I/O for up to 20 chassis, 160 servers. They're deployed in redundant pairs.

fault   An occurrence of a condition that deviates from the normal and expected state of a system or component of a system.

Fibre Channel over Ethernet (FCoE)   A technology that encapsulates Fibre Channel frames within Ethernet frames for delivery over a single Ethernet fabric. It enables Fibre Channel to use 10 Gigabit or faster Ethernet networks for the delivery of storage/Fibre Channel traffic.

flapping interval   The short interval over which repeated changes in failure state of a component indicates a Flapping state.

fully qualified domain name (FQDN)   The LDAP syntax to refer to an object. For example, if user1 is in the acme.com domain, the FQDN for this object would be user1.acme.com.

G–H–I

guest   Another name for a virtual machine.

Heat Orchestration   An orchestration engine that is part of OpenStack.

in-service software upgrade (ISSU)   The ability to upgrade a product or component without interrupting data-plane traffic.

Infrastructure as a Service (IaaS)   Delivering infrastructure resources such as storage, network, compute, and virtualization "as a service" by providing self-service capabilities, easy service catalog ordering, etc.

Intercloud Fabric   A Cisco product that allows you to securely extend your on-premises Layer 2 networks out into public cloud providers such as AWS or Azure or Cisco Powered cloud providers.

IO Module (IOM)   Exists in the back of a UCS Blade Series 5108 chassis and is responsible for delivering Ethernet, Fibre Channel (using FCoE), and management traffic to servers/blades in that chassis.

J-K-L

Juniper Virtual Gateway (vGW)   A hypervisor-based firewall and intrusion detection system.

Keystone   Identify management component of OpenStack.

LDAP search base   A way to limit where in an LDAP tree a search should start.

lifecycle management   The process for managing an IT service from inception to decommissioning.

Lightweight Directory Access Protocol (LDAP)   A client/server protocol used to access and manage directory information over TCP/IP networks.

M

Map Report   A type of infrastructure report available for cloud accounts in UCS Director that displays a color-coded heatmap view indicating relative usage of infrastructure like CPU, memory, and storage.

Microsoft Azure   Microsoft's public cloud offering.

Microsoft System Center Configuration Manager (SCCM)   A Microsoft product used to administer and manage Windows systems, Macs, and UNIX/Linux servers along with cloud-based mobile devices.

Multilayer Director Switch (MDS)   A Cisco product used for Fibre Channel switching.

My Stuff   An interactive list of provisioned resources (service items) where users can view and manage items such as virtual machines.

N

Network Policy   Determine the number and type of network connectivity needed for the VM.

Nexus   A series of Cisco data center networking switches that support Ethernet, Fibre Channel, and Fibre Channel over Ethernet (FCoE).

Nexus 1000V (N1KV)   The Cisco Nexus 1000V virtual switch is a software-only switch that installs on top of popular hypervisors and allows centralized configuration of virtual Ethernet switches in virtualized environments.

Notifications menu   Provides users information about approvals and ongoing orders.

O

OpenStack   Open source cloud computing software.

orchestration   Combining multiple automation tasks together, such as the configuration, creation, provisioning, etc., of infrastructure.

P–Q

Platform as a Service (PaaS)   Delivering platforms such as OS and application stack(s) "as a service" by providing self-service capability, easy service catalog ordering, etc.

port channel   The aggregation of multiple Ethernet or Fibre Channel links into a virtual port that is the sum of the individual links' bandwidth.

Portal Designer   A module within Prime Service Catalog responsible for the look, feel, and operations of the end-user portal and ordering system.

PowerShell   A popular scripting language developed by Microsoft, used to script tasks in Microsoft environments.

Prime Service Catalog   A service ordering solution for self-service, on-demand IT service provisioning and lifecycle management.

Puppet   Commonly used by many organizations to deliver PaaS (operating system plus applications). Puppet Labs produces a variety of free and fee-based tools that assist in the automation of many systems, including Linux hosts.

R

RabbitMQ   An open source project that provides message broker software that uses AMQP as its messaging protocol.

Report Builder   A feature within UCS Director's CloudSense module that allows the administrator to build standard and custom reports.

Rollback   An available action for service requests that will create a new Undo service request that will remove the configuration applied in the initial service request.

S

self-service portal   A single place end users can go to order IaaS and PaaS solutions within UCS Director and Prime Service Catalog.

service catalog   Organized and curated collection of IT-related offerings that support business requirements.

Service Designer   A module within Prime Service Catalog responsible for the configuration and management of service offerings.

service item   An individual object that has been ordered by users or assigned to them, including VMs, vDCs, and applications.

service request   A record of workflow execution within UCS Director.

showback   IT governance policy where the consumption of resources is tracked and value applied to create informational reports without actual transfer of money.

Showcase   The front page of the Service Catalog module of Prime Service Catalog.

snapshot   A mechanism of quickly capturing the current state of a running system, after which changes are tracked and kept separate, enabling users to easily revert to the beginning state.

software-defined network (SDN)   A term to describe various methods by which to make configuration of the network as easy and flexible as configuring virtualized servers revolving around centralized management of policy and network changes.

Stack Designer   A tool within Prime Service Catalog that allows administrators to build full suites of application templates that can then be ordered from the service catalog.

Stack View   A graphical representation of a virtual machine showing the physical and virtual hardware involved in providing compute, storage, and network resources to the virtual workload.

Standard Catalog   An end-user orderable item within UCS Director that will provision a new virtual machine into a given vDC.

Storage Policy   Determine on which data store to create the VM disks.

System Policy   Configure guest operating system details like hostname, DNS, and time zone.

T

template   Prebuilt and standardized set of components and configurations that make up an IT service offering.

Trending Report   A type of report in UCS Director that shows the change of a metric over a given time range.

U

UCS Central   A manager of multiple UCS domains that allows administrators to manage multiple UCS domains from a single manager of UCS Managers.

UCS Director   The Cisco product for automation and orchestration of storage, network, compute, and virtualization of data center infrastructure.

UCS Director Dashboard   A view within UCS Director that shows statistics for storage, memory, and CPU usage within a UCS Director pod.

UCS domain   A UCS system composed of a pair of Fabric Interconnects and all-blade chassis and/or rackmounts connected to them.

UCS Network Policy   A UCS Director Physical Infrastructure Policy that determines the number and configuration of vNICs created within a new service profile.

UCS Performance Manager   Cisco's Performance Management for looking at full stack performance across storage, network, compute, virtualization, as well as storage fabrics.

UCS Storage Policy   A UCS Director Physical Infrastructure Policy that determines the number and configuration of vHBAs created within a new service profile.

User Action Policy   Provide custom VM actions to end users by linking to workflows.

user groups   The ability to group a specified set of users into a group by function, such as End Users, Administrators, etc.

user role   A set of privileges assigned to a user type in UCS Director.

V

vDC categories   A way to indicate different types of workloads within a vDC and apply different compute, network, storage, etc., policies based on need.

Virtual Application Cloud Segmentation (VACS)   A rich set of networking services and interactions between different application tiers used in a Nexus 1000V virtual environment.

virtual data center (vDC)   A logical construct into which users deploy virtual machines.

virtual device context (VDC)   The ability to virtualize a Nexus switch to run separate/unique L2/L3 services in each VDC.

Virtual Ethernet Module (VEM)   In virtual switching such as the Nexus 1000V, analogous to a physical linecard in a modular switch.

Virtual Palo Alto Networks appliance (vPAN)   Created by Palo Alto Networks, the vPAN appliance is a hypervisor-based firewall and intrusion detection system.

Virtual Security Gateway (VSG)   A Cisco software product that provides virtual security services along with Cisco Nexus 1000V.

Virtual Supervisor Module (VSM)   In virtual switching such as the Nexus 1000V, analogous to a physical supervisor in a modular switch.

W–X–Y–Z

widget   A dashboard element designed to provide the most important details in the easiest-to-consume fashion.

workflow   An automation routine created within UCS Director, composed of one or more tasks, that when executed creates a service request.

Workflow Designer   A diagramming-like interface within UCS Director where the administrator can make advanced, multiple-step workflows that can be published in the UCS Director service catalog.

YAML   Yet Another Modeling Language, used for the construction of Heat templates.

Answers to the "Do I Know This Already?" Quizzes

Chapter 1

1. A, C
2. C
3. A, D
4. D
5. A
6. B, D
7. A, B, D
8. A, C
9. C
10. A

Chapter 2

1. B
2. D
3. B
4. D
5. C
6. A, B, C
7. A, C
8. A, B
9. A
10. D

Chapter 3

1. A
2. D
3. B
4. D
5. A

6. D
7. B
8. C
9. C
10. A

Chapter 4

1. A, B, D
2. A, C
3. A, B, C
4. B, C
5. C
6. A
7. A
8. C
9. D
10. A

Chapter 5

1. D
2. B
3. B
4. C
5. D
6. C
7. A
8. A
9. A
10. C

Chapter 6

1. A, C, D, E
2. C
3. D
4. A, D
5. D
6. D
7. B, D
8. A, B, C, D
9. A, B, D
10. B

Chapter 7

1. D
2. C, D, E
3. C
4. D
5. F
6. B
7. E
8. C, D
9. B
10. B

Chapter 8

1. A, B, C, D
2. C
3. A
4. A
5. A, B
6. C
7. A, B, C
8. B
9. A
10. D

Chapter 9

1. A
2. C
3. D
4. D
5. A, B, C
6. B
7. B
8. C
9. A
10. B

Chapter 10

1. B
2. B
3. C
4. B
5. A
6. C
7. B, D
8. C
9. A, B, C, D, E
10. B, C

Chapter 11

1. B
2. B, C, D, E, G
3. A, B, C, D
4. A, C, D
5. A, B, D
6. A
7. C
8. B, D
9. A, C, E
10. A

Chapter 12

   1. A, B, C
   2. B
   3. C
   4. A, B, C, D, E
   5. A
   6. B
   7. A, B, C
   8. A
   9. A, B, C, D
   10. A, B, C

Chapter 13

   1. A, B, C, D
   2. C
   3. A
   4. A, C, D
   5. A, D, E
   6. C
   7. A, B, C
   8. A, C, E, F
   9. A, B, C, D
   10. D
   11. C
   12. B
   13. A, B, C, D

Chapter 14

   1. A, B, C, E
   2. C
   3. B
   4. B
   5. D
   6. D
   7. C
   8. C
   9. B, C
   10. A

A

Memory Tables

Chapter 9

Table 9-2 vDC Policies

vDC Policy	Purpose
System Policy	
Computing Policy	
Network Policy	
Storage Policy	
End User Self-Service Policy	
User Action Policy	
Cost Model	

Chapter 10

Table 10-3   Prime Service Catalog Supported VM Lifecycle Actions

Virtual Machine Action	Description
Power On/Off VM	
	Tell the guest operating system to reboot.
Shutdown VM Guest*	
	Add a new virtual network adapter to a VM. User will need to provide details on port-group assignment and IP information.
Clone VM	
	Create a new virtual hard drive and add it to the VM. Does not perform any OS provisioning.
Create VM Snapshot	
	Delete an individual snapshot of a VM.
Delete VNIC	
	Move the VM to an available vDC in a public cloud and maintain the current configuration of the VM.
Reset VM	
	Restore a VM to a previously taken snapshot state.
Standby VM	
	Execute an OS-level suspend task.

* Requires that the VM have the proper VM management tools for the hypervisor installed.

** Only available when Intercloud Fabric is integrated into Prime Service Catalog.

Chapter 11

Table 11-2   UCS Director Application Container Types

Container Type	Description
	The original and most common type of application container. Doesn't require any specific network architecture to use.
	Leverages the Cisco Virtual Security Gateway zone-based firewall solution to provide enhanced security for container virtual machines.

Container Type	Description
	Tightly integrated with a Cisco Application Centric Infrastructure network deployment, leverages tenant and application profiles for creating application containers. Supports bare-metal workloads as well as VMware virtual machine workloads within the container.
	An application container option for customers with a Cisco Dynamic Fabric Automation (DFA) network deployment.
	Virtual Application Cloud Segmentation* (VACS) is a licensable feature set for UCS Director for customers looking for an advanced application container structure designed specifically for highly flexible and easy-to-deploy virtual network designs using Cisco virtual network technologies for routing, switching, and security.

* VACS was previously known as Virtual Application Container Services.

Chapter 13

Table 13-2   Syslog Severity Levels

Integer	Severity	Description
0		
1		
2		
3		
4		
5		
6		
7		

Chapter 14

Table 14-2   Severity Levels

Severity Level	Description
	A service-affecting condition that requires immediate action to resolve. This severity indicates that some element is completely out of functional service.
	A service-affecting condition that requires urgent action to resolve. This severity indicates that there is severe degradation in capabilities of the affected element.

B

Severity Level	Description
	A nonservice-affecting condition that needs to be resolved. This severity indicates a noted alarm condition, but no service degradation is being experienced.
	An indication of a potential service-affecting condition that should be investigated and resolved to prevent future problems.
	An informational detail about a current condition within the system.
	A basic notification or informational message.

Table 14-4 UCS Director Logs

Log	Description
Infra Manager	
Web Context Cloud Manager	
Tomcat Log	
Authenticator Log	
Mail Delivery Log	
Patch Log	

Table 14-5 Prime Service Catalog Logs

Log	Description
Prime Service Catalog Log	
Service Link Log	
Orchestration Log	
Firstboot Log	

Memory Tables Answer Key

Chapter 9

Table 9-2 vDC Policies

vDC Policy	Purpose
System Policy	Configure guest operating system details like hostname, DNS, and time zone
Computing Policy	Determine what hypervisor host system to deploy the VM onto
Network Policy	Determine the number and type of network connectivity needed for the VM
Storage Policy	Determine what data store to create the VM disks on
End User Self-Service Policy	Provide access to out-of-the-box VM lifecycle action tasks to end users
User Action Policy	Provide custom VM actions to end users by linking to workflows
Cost Model	Assign value to different metrics such as number of vCPUs as part of a chargeback model

Chapter 10

Table 10-3   Prime Service Catalog Supported VM Lifecycle Actions

Virtual Machine Action	Description
Power On/Off VM	Change the power state of a virtual machine. Note that Power Off is different from Shutdown VM Guest.
Reboot VM*	Tell the guest operating system to reboot.
Shutdown VM Guest*	Tell the guest operating system to shut down.
Add vNIC	Add a new virtual network adapter to a VM. User will need to provide details on port-group assignment and IP information.
Clone VM	Create a copy of the VM and place into a designated vDC.
Create VM Disk	Create a new virtual hard drive and add it to the VM. Does not perform any OS provisioning.
Create VM Snapshot	Create a new snapshot of the current state of a VM.
Delete VM Snapshot	Delete an individual snapshot of a VM.
Delete VNIC	Remove an individual virtual network adapter from a VM.
Migrate VM to Public Cloud**	Move the VM to an available vDC in a public cloud and maintain the current configuration of the VM.
Reset VM	Execute a power cycle task on the VM. This is different from Shutdown VM Guest.
Revert VM Snapshot	Restore a VM to a previously taken snapshot state.
Standby VM	Place the VM into a hypervisor-level pause state.
Suspend VM*	Execute an OS-level suspend task.

* Requires that the VM have the proper VM management tools for the hypervisor installed.

** Only available when Intercloud Fabric is integrated into Prime Service Catalog.

Chapter 11

Table 11-2   UCS Director Application Container Types

Container Type	Description
Fenced virtual container	The original and most common type of application container. Doesn't require any specific network architecture to use.
Virtual Security Gateway (VSG)	Leverages the Cisco Virtual Security Gateway zone-based firewall solution to provide enhanced security for container virtual machines.

Container Type	Description
APIC container	Tightly integrated with a Cisco Application Centric Infrastructure network deployment, leverages tenant and application profiles for creating application containers. Supports bare-metal workloads as well as VMware virtual machine workloads within the container.
Fabric container	An application container option for customers with a Cisco Dynamic Fabric Automation (DFA) network deployment.
VACS container	Virtual Application Cloud Segmentation* (VACS) is a licensable feature set for UCS Director for customers looking for an advanced application container structure designed specifically for highly flexible and easy-to-deploy virtual network designs using Cisco virtual network technologies for routing, switching, and security.

* VACS was previously known as Virtual Application Container Services.

Chapter 13

Table 13-2 Syslog Severity Levels

Integer	Severity	Description
0	Emergency	System is unusable.
1	Alert	Immediate action is needed.
2	Critical	A condition that should be corrected immediately has occurred.
3	Error	Non-urgent failure.
4	Warning	An error will occur if no action is taken.
5	Notice	An unusual but non-error condition.
6	Informational	Normal operating behavior.
7	Debug	Used for debugging an application, but not typically tracked.

Chapter 14

Table 14-2 Severity Levels

Severity Level	Description
Critical	A service-affecting condition that requires immediate action to resolve. This severity indicates that some element is completely out of functional service.
Major	A service-affecting condition that requires urgent action to resolve. This severity indicates that there is severe degradation in capabilities of the affected element.

Severity Level	Description
Minor	A nonservice-affecting condition that needs to be resolved. This severity indicates a noted alarm condition, but no service degradation is being experienced.
Warning	An indication of a potential service-affecting condition that should be investigated and resolved to prevent future problems.
Condition	An informational detail about a current condition within the system.
Info	A basic notification or informational message.

Table 14-4   UCS Director Logs

Log	Description
Infra Manager	Provides details on the infrastructure management and automation services of UCS Director. This log captures very detailed information related to regular system tasks that inventory underlying infrastructure as well as service requests execution.
Web Context Cloud Manager	Provides details on all web resources accessed by web and API users.
Tomcat Log	Provides details on the status and health of the Tomcat Server that executes the underlying Java programs that provide access to the administrator and end-user portals.
Authenticator Log	Provides details regarding both local and LDAP authentications from UCS Director as part of both web and API access.
Mail Delivery Log	Provides details related to sending of emails from UCS Director as part of alerts, approvals, or workflow notifications.
Patch Log	Provides detailed information about any updates and patches applied to the system.

Table 14-5   Prime Service Catalog Logs

Log	Description
Prime Service Catalog Log	Provides details on the web portal and catalog interface for end users and administrators.
Service Link Log	Provides details on the integration between Prime Service Catalog and external systems such as UCS Director accomplished through Control Agents and messaging services.
Orchestration Log	Provides details on end-user orders and the execution of service plans.
Firstboot Log	Provides details from the first boot of the appliance after installation, when the initial configuration, database, and application setup was executed.

Index

Numbers

A

X - Y - Z

REGISTER YOUR PRODUCT at CiscoPress.com/register
Access Additional Benefits and SAVE 35% on Your Next Purchase

- Download available product updates.
- Access bonus material when applicable.
- Receive exclusive offers on new editions and related products.
  (Just check the box to hear from us when setting up your account.)
- Get a coupon for 35% for your next purchase, valid for 30 days.
  Your code will be available in your Cisco Press cart. (You will also find
  it in the Manage Codes section of your account page.)

Registration benefits vary by product. Benefits will be listed on your account page
under Registered Products.

CiscoPress.com – Learning Solutions for Self-Paced Study, Enterprise, and the Classroom
Cisco Press is the Cisco Systems authorized book publisher of Cisco networking technology,
Cisco certification self-study, and Cisco Networking Academy Program materials.

At **CiscoPress.com** you can
- Shop our books, eBooks, software, and video training.
- Take advantage of our special offers and promotions (ciscopress.com/promotions).
- Sign up for special offers and content newsletters (ciscopress.com/newsletters).
- Read free articles, exam profiles, and blogs by information technology experts.
- Access thousands of free chapters and video lessons.

Connect with Cisco Press – Visit CiscoPress.com/community
Learn about Cisco Press community events and programs.

Cisco Press